# CATS

# The
# Big Book of
# CATS

EDITED BY SUSAN FEUER

ILLUSTRATED BY ANA CIÇA PINTO

Ariel Books

**Andrews McMeel
Publishing**

Kansas City

www.andrewsmcmeel.com

98 99 00 01 02 03 BIN 10 9 8 7 6 5 4 3 2 1

ISBN: 0-8362-6936-5
Library of Congress Catalog Card Number:
98-85182

The writers (and the cats who love them) for The Big Book of Cats are: Karen Liljedahl (Candy and Wally), Paul Lipari (Nicole), Patricia Cronin Marcello (Draco, Pearl, and Zuzy), Catherine Murphy (Bumblebee and Panda), Joan Schweighardt (Sammie and Speedy Clark), Carolyn Short (Butterfinger and Tiger), Mitchell Uscher (Ceil and Flakey), and Daniel R. White (Lucy, Sylvia, and Willie).

# CONTENTS

Introduction • 9

Kitty Quips: Some Cat
  Quotations • 11

Verses on the Cat: A Selection
  of Poetry • 39

What to Name a Cat • 61

Cats in History • 113

Cats in Literature • 163

Celluloid Cats • 199

Little-Known Facts about
  Cats • 255

Funny, Amazing, and True Cat
  Tales • 297

Believe It or Not • 313

Well-Bred Cats • 337

Superlative Kitties: The Best,
   Biggest, Most Popular, and
   More • 403
Care Tips and Helpful
   Hints • 435
The Evolution of
   the Cat • 519
Famous Cat Owners, Past and
   Present • 545
Scared Silly: Cat Superstitions
   from Around
   the World • 587
Surfing the Pet Net: Some Cat
   Web Sites • 607

# INTRODUCTION

You love cats. It's that simple.

More than mere pets, they are companions, friends, and confidants. They are your babies, your children. Your cat—or cats—have you wrapped around their paws. Felines rule your life, which is just fine with you. In fact, you wouldn't want it any other way. This book is written for you and your fellow cat fanciers. From quotations to cat care tips, from the history of the feline to descriptions of breeds, from little-known facts to fun anecdotes, it's in here. And lots more! So curl up on the couch with you-know-who and read on about these wonderful, special creatures.

# KITTY QUIPS: SOME CAT QUOTATIONS

If cats could talk, they wouldn't.

— *Nan Porter*

The problem with cats is that they get the exact same look on their face whether they see a moth or an ax-murderer.

— *Paula Poundstone*

Cats are absolute individuals, with their own ideas about everything, including the people they own.
                            —*John Dingman*

If stretching were wealth, the cat would be rich.
                            —*African proverb*

It is easy to understand why the rabble dislike cats. A cat is beautiful; it suggests ideas of luxury, cleanliness, voluptuous pleasures.
                            —*Charles Baudelaire*

*A* kitten is chiefly remarkable for rushing about like mad at nothing whatever, and generally stopping before it gets there.

—*Agnes Repplier*

*A* dog is a dog, a bird is a bird, and a cat is a person.

—*Mugsy Peabody*

*W*hen a Cat adopts you there is nothing to be done about it except to put up with it and wait until the wind changes.

—*T. S. Eliot*

Living with a cat is like being married to a career woman who can take domesticity or let it alone, so you'd better be nice to her.

—Margaret Cooper Gay

A cat can purr its way out of anything.

—Donna McCrohan

Cats seldom make mistakes, and they never make the same mistake twice.

—Carl Van Vechten

*A*s soon as they're out of your sight, you are out of their mind.
—*Walter de la Mare*

*A*ll animals are equal, but some animals are more equal than others.

—*George Orwell*

We should be careful to get out of an experience only the wisdom that is in it—and stop there; lest we be like the cat that sits on a hot stove lid. She will never sit down on a hot stove lid again—and that is well; but also she will never sit down on a cold one anymore.

—*Mark Twain*

Because his long, white whiskers tickled, I began every day laughing.

—*Janet F. Faure*

I called my cat William because no shorter name fits the dignity of his character. Poor old man, he has fits now, so I call him fitz-William.

—*Josh Billings*

There is no more intrepid explorer than a kitten.

—*Jules Champfleury*

Those who'll play with cats must expect to be scratched.

—*Miguel de Cervantes*

*E*verything that moves serves
to interest and amuse a cat. He
is convinced that nature is
busying herself with his diversion; he can conceive of no
other purpose in the universe.
— *F. A. Paradis de Moncrif*

*C*ats must have three names—
an everyday name, such as
Peter; a more particular, dignified name, such as Quaxo,
Bombalurina, or Jellylorum;
and, thirdly, the name the cat
thinks up for himself, his deep
and inscrutable singular Name.
— *T. S. Eliot*

 We quickly discovered that two kittens were much more fun than one.
—*Allen Lacy*

Old cats mean young mice.
—*Italian proverb*

The way to keep a cat is to try to chase it away.
—*E. W. Howe*

Dogs come when they're called; cats take a message and get back to you.
—*Mary Bly*

I am indebted to the species of the cat for a particular kind of honorable deceit, for a great control over myself, for characteristic aversion to brutal sounds, and for the need to keep silent for long periods of time.

—*Colette*

Cats are only human, they have their faults.

—*Kingsley Amis*

A sleeping cat is ever alert.

—*Fred Schwab*

The cat has too much spirit to have no heart.

—*Ernest Menault*

If a fish is the movement of water embodied, given shape, then a cat is a diagram and pattern of subtle air.

—*Doris Lessing*

It is in their eyes that their magic resides.

—*Arthur Symons*

A mouse in the paws is worth two in the pantry.

—*Louis Wain*

Of all animals, he alone attains the Contemplative Life. He regards the wheel of existence from without, like the Buddha. There is no pretense of sympathy about the cat. He lives alone, aloft, sublime, in a wise passiveness.

—*Andrew Lang*

"It's going to freeze," she would say, "the cat's dancing."

—*Colette*

If animals could speak, the dog would be a blundering, outspoken, honest fellow—but the cat would have the rare grace of never saying a word too much.
—*Philip Gilbert Hamerton*

Even the stupidest cat seems to know more than any dog.
—*Eleanor Clark*

A cat sneezing is a good omen for everyone who hears it.
—*Italian superstition*

Another cat? Perhaps. For love there is also a season; its seeds must be re-sown. But a family cat is not replaceable like a worn-out coat or a set of tires. Each new kitten becomes its own cat, and none is repeated. I am four cats old, measuring out my life in friends that have succeeded but not replaced one another.

—*Irving Townsend*

The cat is utterly sincere.

—*Fernand Méry*

If you want to be a psychological novelist and write about human beings, the best thing you can do is keep a pair of cats.

—*Aldous Huxley*

Cat: A pygmy lion who loves mice, hates dogs, and patronizes human beings.

—*Oliver Herford*

If a dog jumps up into your lap, it is because he is fond of you; but if a cat does the same thing, it is because your lap is warmer.

—*Alfred North Whitehead*

A cat sleeping with all four
paws tucked under means cold
weather ahead.
>—*English superstition*

The cat has always been associated with the Moon. Like the
Moon it comes to life at night,
escaping from humanity and
wandering over housetops with
its eyes beaming out through
the darkness.
>—*Patricia Dale-Green*

Two cats can live as cheaply as
one, and their owner has twice
as much fun.
>—*Lloyd Alexander*

*A* cat is never vulgar.
> —*Carl Van Vechten*

*I*t [the Cheshire Cat] vanished quite slowly, beginning with the end of the tail, and ending with the grin, which remained some time after the rest of it had gone.
> —*Lewis Carroll*

*A* home without a cat—and a well-fed, well-petted, and properly revered cat—may be a perfect home, perhaps, but how can it prove its title?
> —*Mark Twain*

Cats seem to go on the principle that it never does any harm to ask for what you want.
—*Joseph Wood Krutch*

Should ever anything be missed—milk, coals, umbrellas, brandy—the cat's pitched into with a boot or anything that's handy.
—*C. S. Calverley*

Cats mean kittens, plentiful and frequent.
—*Doris Lessing*

Pure herring oil is the port wine of English cats.

—*Honoré de Balzac*

It is impossible for a lover of cats to banish these alert, gentle, and discriminating friends, who give us just enough of their regard and complaisance to make us hunger for more.

—*Agnes Repplier*

Cleanliness in the cat world is usually a virtue put above godliness.

—*Carl Van Vechten*

*U*nlike us, cats never outgrow their delight in cat capacities, nor do they settle finally for limitations. Cats, I think, live out their lives fulfilling their expectations.

—*Irving Townsend*

*C*ats are notoriously sore losers. Coming in second best, especially to someone as poorly coordinated as a human being, grates their sensibility.

—*Stephen Baker*

*N*o one can have experienced
to the fullest the true sense of
achievement and satisfaction
who has never pursued
and successfully caught
his tail.

> —*Rosalind Welcher*

*A*n old cat will not
learn dancing.

> —*Moroccan proverb*

I shall never forget the indulgence with which he treated Hodge, his cat, for whom he used to go out and buy oysters, lest the servants having that trouble should take a dislike to the poor creature. . . . I recol-

lect him one day scrambling up on Dr. Johnson's breast, apparently with much satisfaction, while my friend, smiling and half-whistling, rubbed his back and pulled him by the tail; and when I observed he was a fine cat, saying, "Why, yes, Sir, but I have had cats whom I liked better than this." And then as if perceiving Hodge to be out of countenance, adding, "But he is a very fine cat, a very fine cat indeed."

—*James Boswell*

Her function is to sit and be admired.
　　　　—*Georgina Strickland Gates*

The cat does not offer services. The cat offers itself. Of course he wants care and shelter. You don't buy love for nothing. Like all pure creatures, cats are practical.
　　　　—*William S. Burroughs*

The more you rub a cat on the rump, the higher she sets her tail.
　　　　—*John Ray*

Way down deep, we're all motivated by the same urges. Cats have the courage to live by them.

—*Jim Davis*

If only cats grew into kittens.
—*R. D. Stern*

Cats always know whether people like or dislike them. They do not always care enough to do anything about it.
—*Winifred Carriere*

Cats are smarter than dogs.
You can't get eight cats to pull
a sled through snow.

—*Jeff Valdez*

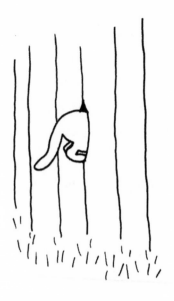

When the cat and mouse
agree, the grocer is ruined.
—*Iranian proverb*

A black cat dropped sound-lessly from a high wall, like a spoonful of dark treacle, and melted under a gate.
—*Elizabeth Lemarchand*

The ideal of calm exists in a sitting cat.
—*Jules Reynard*

They say the test of literary power is whether a man can write an inscription. I say, "Can he name a kitten?"
—*Samuel Butler*

Cats are designated friends.
—*Norman Corwin*

# VERSES ON THE CAT: A SELECTION OF POETRY

Cats are a mysterious kind of
  folk—
there is more passing in their
  minds
than we are aware of.
                —*Sir Walter Scott*

## The Kilkenny Cats

There wanst was two cats of
   Kilkenny.
And aich thought there was
   wan cat too many;
So they quarrelled and fit,
And they scratched and they
   bit,
Till barin' their nails
And the tips of their tails,
Instead of two cats, there
   warn't any.

                    —*Anonymous*

Let take a cat, and foster him
   well with milk
And tender flesh and make his
   couch of silk,
And let him seen a mouse go
   by the wall,
Anon he waveth milk and flesh
   and all,
And every dainty that is in that
   house,
Such appetite he hath to eat a
   mouse.

—Geoffrey Chaucer

She sights a Bird—she
    chuckles—
She flattens—then she
    crawls—
She runs without the look of
    feet—
Her eyes increase to Balls.
                    —*Emily Dickinson*

As I was going to St. Ives,
I met a man with seven wives,
Each wife had seven sacks,
Each sack has seven cats,
Each cat had seven kits:
Kits, cats, sacks, wives,
How many were going to St.
   Ives?

                    —*Nursery rhyme*


*Verses on a Cat*


A cat in distress,
Nothing more, nor less;
Good folks, I must faithfully
   tell ye,
As I am a sinner,
It waits for some dinner

To stuff out its own little belly.

You would not easily guess
All the modes of distress
Which torture the tenants of
   earth;
And the various evils,
Which like so many devils,
Attend the poor souls from
   their birth.

Some a living require,
And others desire
An old fellow out of the way;
And which is the best
I leave to be guessed,
For I cannot pretend to say.

One wants society,
Another variety,
Others a tranquil life;
Some want food.
Others, as good,
Only want a wife.

But this poor little cat
Only wanted a rat,
To stuff out its own little maw;
And it were as good
Some people had such food,
To make them hold their jaw.

—*Percy Bysshe Shelley*

One is tabby with emerald
    eyes,
And a tail that's long and
    slender,
And into a temper she quickly
    flies
If you ever by chance offend
    her.

                        —*Thomas Hood*

Two little kittens, one stormy
  night,
Began to quarrel, and then to
  fight;
One had a mouse, the other
  had none,
And that's the way the quarrel
  begun.

—*Anonymous*

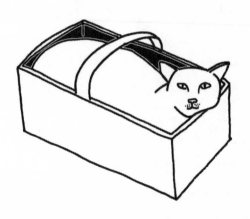

*To a Cat*

Stately, kindly, lordly friend,
Condescend
Here to sit by me, and turn
Glorious eyes that smile and
    burn,
Golden eyes, love's lustrous
    meed,
On the golden page I read.

All your wondrous wealth of
    hair,
Dark and fair,
Silken-shaggy, soft and bright
As the clouds and beams of
    night,
Pays my reverent hand's caress
Back with friendlier gentleness.

Dogs may fawn on all and some
As they come;
You, a friend of loftier mind,
Answer friends alone in kind.
Just your foot upon my hand
Softly bids it understand.
                    —*Algernon Swinburne*

Pussy will rub my knees with
  her head
Pretending she loves me hard;
But the very minute I go to bed
Pussy runs out in the yard . . .
                    —*Rudyard Kipling*


Who's that ringing at my door-
  bell?
A little pussy cat that isn't very
  well.
Rub its little nose with a little
  mutton fat,
That's the best cure for a little
  pussy cat.
                    —*Nursery rhyme*

Dearest cat, honoured guest of
my old house,
Arch your supple, tingling
back,
And curl upon my knee, to let
me
Bathe my fingers in your warm
fur.

—*François Lemaître*

The cat went here and there
And the moon spun round like
  a top,
And the nearest kin of the
  moon,
The creeping cat, looked up.
Black Minnaloushe stared at
  the moon,
For, wander and wail as he
  would,
The pure cold light in the sky
Troubled his animal blood.
Minnaloushe runs in the grass
Lifting his delicate feet.
Do you dance, Minnaloushe,
  do you dance?

          —*William Butler Yeats*

*The Kitten at Play*

See the kitten on the wall,
Sporting with the leaves that
    fall,
Withered leaves, one, two, and
    three
Falling from the elder tree,
Through the calm and frosty
    air
Of the morning bright and fair.

See the kitten, how she starts,
Crouches, stretches, paws, and
  darts;
With a tiger-leap half way
Now she meets her coming
  prey.
Lets it go as fast and then
Has it in her power again.

Now she works with three and
  four,
Like an Indian conjurer;
Quick as he in feats of art,
Gracefully she plays her part;
Yet were gazing thousands
  there,
What would little Tabby care?
                    —*William Wordsworth*

Bathsheba:
To whom none ever said scat,
No worthier cat
Ever sat on a mat
Or caught a rat:
Requies-cat.
                    —*John Greenleaf Whittier*

Pussy cat, pussy cat,
Where have you been?
I've been to London
To look at the Queen.
Pussy cat, pussy cat,
What did you there?
I frightened a little mouse
Under her chair.
                    —*Nursery rhyme*

*Sonnet to Mrs. Reynolds' Cat*

Cat! who hast pass'd thy grand
climacteric,
How many mice and rats hast
in thy days
Destroy'd—How many tid-bits
stolen? Gaze
With those bright languid segments green, and prick
Those velvet ears—but
pr'ythee do not stick
Thy latent talons in me—and
upraise
Thy gentle mew—and tell me
all thy frays
Of fish and mice, and rats and
tender chick.

Nay, look not down, nor lick
  thy dainty wrists—
        For all the wheezy
            asthma—and for all
          Thy tail's tip is
            nick'd off—and
            though the fists
          Of many a maid
          have given thee
  many a maul,
Still is that fur as soft as when
  the lists
In youth thou enter'dst on glass
  bottled wall.
              —*John Keats*

Dame Trot and her cat
Sat down for a chat;
The Dame sat on this side
And puss sat on that.

Puss, says the Dame
Can you catch a rat
Or a mouse in the dark?
Purr, says the cat.

*—Nursery rhyme*

But buds will be roses,
and kittens, cats,
—more's the pity.

*—Louisa May Alcott*

Ding, dong, bell
Pussy's in the well.
Who put her in?
Little Johnny Green.
Who pulled her out?
Little Tommy Stout.
What a naughty boy was that
To try to drown poor pussy cat,
Who never did him any harm,
And killed the mice in his
    father's barn.

—*Nursery rhyme*

Six little mice sat down to spin;
Pussy passed by and she peeped
   in.
What are you doing, my little
   men?
Weaving coats for gentlemen.
Shall I come in and cut off your
   threads?
No, no, Mistress Pussy, you'd
   bite off our heads.
On, no, I'll not; I'll help you to
   spin.
That may be so, but don't you
   come in.

—*Nursery rhyme*

# WHAT TO NAME A CAT

## GENERAL, ALL-PURPOSE, UNDIFFERENTIATED CATS; OR, CATS FOR ALL SEASONS

| | |
|---|---|
| Abby | Blitz |
| Abyssinian | Boise |
| Algernon | Bolo |
| Angora | Boots |
| Arizona | Boro |

| | |
|---|---|
| Bose | France |
| Box | Gateway |
| Budge | Goldilocks |
| Buff | Gypsy |
| Burma | Halifax |
| Bush, Bushy | Heliotrope |
| Calcutta | Herman |
| Captain | Hermione |
| Casca | Holy Smoke |
| Checkers | Hyacinth |
| Chickens | Jellybean |
| Cincy | Jodhpur |
| Courtesan | Lafcadio |
| Crossword | Lafitte |
| Domino | Lobo |
| Egbert | Lord Saville |
| Eliot | Louis |
| Esperanto | Luigi |

Lynx
Magic
Mantelpiece
Marmaduke
Max Factor
Midnight
Muff

Mulligan
Mystery
Pajamas
Peggy
Piggy
Playboy
Playgirl
Pumpkin
Rainbow
Rupert
Sax
Scoop
Scrabble
Seabrook
Silas
Simon
Slick Willie
Smokey

Spinner
Strand
Tabby
Tabitha
Tarantella
Tickee
Tig
Tiger
Tiger Woods
Ultramarine
Valerian
Vesper
Vixen
Webster
Whisper
Willows
Zoney

## ADVENTUROUS AND EXPLORATORY CATS

Amazon
Amerigo
Audubon
Ayesha
Captain Cook
Catlin
Chardin
Clark
Columbus
Coronado
Cortez
Dr. Livingston
Hakluyt

Lewis
Lhasa
Mandeville
Nile
Pathfinder
Quatermain
Rider

Rider Haggard
Sir Richard
   Burton
Stanley
Stargazer
Starman
Tartary
Trailblazer
Vasco
Yucatán

## ARTISTICATS

Bernini
Bosch
Botticelli
Cassatt
Cellini

Chiaroscuro      Modigliani
De Chirico       Monet
Dürer            Munch
El Greco         Phydias
Fragonard        Picasso
Giotto           Picatso
Goya             Piranesi
Hieronymous      Poussin
Hokusai          Raeburn
Kokoschka        Raphael
Laurencin        Rembrandt
                 Renoir

                 Reubens
                 Ririomin
                 Rothko
                 Sargent
Leonardo         Schiele
Michelangelo     Silkscreen

Tintoretto
Titian
Turner
Velásquez
Vermeer
Veronese
Watteau
Whistler
Zurbarán

CINEMATI-
CATS

Al
Antonioni
Astaire
Avenger
Baby

Bergman
Blore
Bogart
Bogey, Bogie
Brando
Buster Keaton
Cary Grant
Casablanca
Chaplin

Christie
Citizen Kane
Coop
De Niro
Diana Rigg
Dino
Dr. No
Dr. Phibes
Eastwood
Fat Man
Federico
Fred
Ginger
Godfrey

Harvey
Hepburn
Hollywood
Holly Wood
Hopkins
Irene
Jack
Joan Fontaine
Judy Garland
Kurosawa
La Brea
Lancaster
Lombard
Maltese Falcon
Mansfield
Max de
    Winter
Merkin Muffley

Michael Caine
Minnelli
Mizoguchi
Mrs. Peel
Nicholson
Olivier
Oscar
Ozu
Pacino
Paradise
Peck
Perry Mason
Powell
Rat Pack
Rebecca
Russell
Sam
Sam Spade

Sean Connery
Sierra Madre
Sinatra
Spielberg
Steed
Sunset
Swing Time
Titanic
Top Hat
Vine
Welles

CLASSICATS
AND
MYTHICATS

Aeschylus
Agamemnon

| | |
|---|---|
| Ajax | Cupid |
| Alcibiades | Cyclops |
| Alexander | Daedalus |
| Alexandria | Diana |
| Anaximander | Emperor |
| Antony | Euripides |
| Apollo | Fury |
| Argo | Hecate |
| Aristotle | Hector |
| Brutus | Helen |
| Caesar | Heraclitus |
| Castor | Hercules |
| Cicero | Hermes |
| Circe | Herodotus |
| Clytemnestra | Homer |
| Colosseo | Horace |
| Cressida | Icarus |
| Croesus | Kato |

Janus  Prometheus
Julius  Psyche
Justinian  Rubicon
Marc Antony  Sallust
Morpheus  Seneca
Narcissus  Socrates
Nero  Sophocles
Octavian  Tacitus
Odysseus  Telemachus
Orestes  Terence
Orpheus  Tiber
Ovid  Tiburon
Pan  Trajan
Pericles  Troilus
Plato  Ulysses
Plutarch  Virgil
Pollux
Praxiteles

## DICKENSICATS

Artful Dodger
Blimber
Boffin
Boythorn
Boz
Bumble
Chuzzle
Chuzzlewit
Copperfield
Cratchit
Cricket
Cuttle
Datchery
Dedlock
Dickens
Dombey
Dorrit
Drood
Estella
Fagin
Fezziwig
Florence
Grip
Guppy
Havisham
Heep
Jaggers
Jarndyce
Jasper
Jellyby
Jingle
Lady Dedlock
Little Nell
Little Dorrit

Magwitch
Marley
Master
  Humphrey
Meagles
Micawber
Miss Flite
Mudfog
Nell
Nipper
Noggs
Oliver
Pecksniff
Peggotty
Phiz
Pickwick
Pip
Quilp

Raven
Sapsea
Skimpole
Squeers
Swiveller
Sikes
Tigg
Tiny Tim
Todgers
Tox, Toxie
Trot
Twist

Varden
Wemmick

DINOCATS

Alamo
Alioram
Allosore
Anato
Anchi
Ankylo
Bactro
Baryo
Brachy
Bronto
Camaro
Campto
Ceratty

Cetiosaur
Compy
Daspy
Deino
Dimetri
Dinocat
Dippy
Dromy
Dryo
Galli
Godzilla
Godzo
Hadro
Iguano
Jurassicat
Kentro
Krito
Lambeo

Longsiquam
Magalo
Maia
Nodo
Notho
Othnie
Ovi
Pachy
Placo
Plateo
Pterry
Quetzal
Rapto
Scutello
Scuto
Siluro
Sordy
Spiny

Stego
T. Rex
Tarbo
Torosaur
Triassicat
Vectio
Velosso

*EDUCATED
PUSSIES*

Barnard
Biblicat
Boss Cat
Boss Tweed
Brown
Bryn Mawr
Columbia

Cornell
Dartmouth
Dr. Seuss
Dr. Katz
Duke
Educat
Harvard
Ivy
Ivy League
Latinicat
Lehigh
Numquam
Numcat
Philosophicat
Princeton
Professor
Quid
Radcliffe

Runecat
Scientificat
Smith
Stanford
Swarthmore
Vassar
Villanova
Wasteland
Wellesley
Yale

FOREIGN CATS

Cattus (Latin)
Chat (French)
Féline
(French)
Feles

Felis (Latin)
Felino (Span
   ish)
Fellini
Gato (Spanish
   and
   Portuguese)
Gatto (Italian)
Katze
   (German)
Kissa
   (Finnish)
Minnaloushe
Minou
Neko
   (Japanese)
Reynard

## FUTURE AND FANTASTICATS

1984
Aldiss
Alien
Andromeda
Ballard
Beetlejuice
Dot Com
Droid
Eldritch
Fritz Lang
Futuro
Gormenghast
H. G.
Huxley
Internet

Lao
Mars
Memison
Mezentian
Mulder
Omni
Orwell
Ouroboros
Pluto
Robo
Rocky Horror
Scully
SF
Sigourney
Timeslip
Toffler
Venus
Viriconium

Wells
Wyndham
X-Cat
X-Tro

HISTORICATS

Aaron Burr
Agricola
Agrippa
Aguirre
Albertus
    Magnus
Alchemy
Alembic
Alexander
    Nevsky
Anastasia

Assyria
Avicenna
Aztec
Bligh
Bonaparte
Borgia
Browne
Burgundy
Burr
Catherine
Charlemagne
Clausewitz
Constantine
Copernicus
Cosimo
Czar Nicholas
Darius
Darnley

Darnton
Darwin
Dastin
Dee
Elizabeth I
Flamel
Fosse
Gregory
Hamilton

Hannibal          Quincy
Inca              Rasputin
Jacobin           Robespierre
Jefferson         Rommel
Justinian         Salamis
Lenin             Savanarola
Lincoln           Spartan
Lucrezia          Trojan
Marathon          Trotsky
Marco Polo        Vlad
Marx
Maya              LITERARY
Medici            CATS, ENGLISH
Napoleon          AND
Newton            AMERICAN
Nicholas
Patton            Aiken
Phoenicia         Alice

Amelia
Arden
Aspern
Austen
Baldwin
Balthazar
Basil
Basil Seal
Beckford
Beerbohm
Ben Bulben
Benson
Beocat
Beowulf
Bertie
Branwell
Brontë
Burgess

Burns
Byron
Byzantium
Carlyle
Carwin
Changeling
Chesterfield
Childe Harold
Clarissa
Clea
Clinker
Colin
Congreve
Conrad
Dahl
Daisy
Darcy
De Quincey

Ethan
Etherege
Fanny Hill
Fata Morgana
Feversham
Fielding
Fitzwilliam
Frome
Gatsby
Gaunt
George Eliot
Gorboduc
Gore
Gulliver
Hawthorne
Heathcliff
Herrick
Ingersoll

Defoe
Dickens
Dido
Dodo
Don Juan
Dorian Grey
Dryden
Duchess
Ecben
Edgeworth
Emma

Jane
Jane Austen
Jane Eyre
Jeeves
Jonathan Wild
Joseph
 Andrews
Jurgen
Justine
Keats
Kipling
Kit
Kotzwinkle
Lewis Carroll
Lizzy Bennet
Lovelace
Lowry
Lucia

Maisie
Malcolm
Malfi
Malmsey
Mapp
Marlowe
Maud Gonne
Maugham
Melville
Millay
Milton
Mountolive
Mrs. Dalloway
Mr. Mulline
Mulliner
Nabokov
Naipaul
Noël Coward

Northanger
Old Possum
Orlando
Ormond
Oscar
Oswald
Otranto
Pale Fire
Pamela
Peacock
Pepys
Peter Quint
Pinfold
Pope
Powell
Poynton
Prufrock
Psmith (the *p*,

of course, is
silent)
Queeg
Quincy
Quint
Radcliffe
Rasselas
Rochester
Rushdie
Sackville
Saki
Santayana
Sapphira
Shamela
Shandy
Shaw
Shelley
Sheridan

Somerset
Sterne
Swift
Theroux
Trilby
Trollope
Truman
Ustinov
Vathek
Verlock
Vernon
Vidal
Villette
Virginia Woolf
Volpone
Walpole
Waugh
Wharton

White Devil
Wieland
Wildfell
Wilkes
Wilkie
Wodehouse
Wooster
Wycherley
Wylder
Wyvern
Xanadu

Yeats
Zelda
Zuleika

LITERARY
CATS,
WORLDWIDE

Ada
Albertine
Anna
  Karenina
Balzac
Baudelaire
Bovary
Broch
Candide
Canute

Cazotte
Céline
Chekhov
D'Annunzio
Decamerone
Dosto
Dostoevsky
Dr. Faustus
Effi Briest
Ferdydurke
Flaubert
Flea
Fléa
Formica
Franz Kafka
Genet
Genji
Gogol

Golem
Gombrowicz
Hamsun
Heimito
Hippocrene
Hoffmann
Jung
Justine
Kleist
Koestler
Krespel
Lady Murasaki
Leopardi
Loki
Lolita
Madeleine
Manzoni
Marrakesh

Maupin
Meyrink
Mirbeau
Munchausen
Murasaki
Musil
Natasha
Odin
Pico
Pierre
Pillow Book
Pirandello
Proust
Pushkin
Quixote
Rabelais
Ragnarok
Sancho Panza

Saragossa
Schnitzler
Sei Shonagon
Senso
Sheherazade
Simplicissimus
Smarra
Smilla
Sposa
Stavrogin
Stendhal
Strindberg
Thor
Tocqueville
Tolstoy
Turgenev
Unamuno
Valéry

Verga
Zhivago

MEDIEVAL
AND
ARTHURIAN
CATS

Aucassin
Bedevere
Blamor
Bleoberis
Bragwaine
Brandegoris
Camelot
Caxton
Chaucer
Clariance

Dagonet
El Cid
Eliazer
Evelake
Galahad, Sir
Gareth
Gawain
Graal
Griflet
Gringamore
Guinevere
Isolde
King Arthur
Lamorak, Sir
Lancelot, Sir
Lanceor
Langland
Lavaine

Lionors
Listinoise
Logris
Lynet
Lyonesse
Malory
Meliagaunt
Meliodas
Merlin
Mondrains
Mordred
Morgan Le
 Fay
Nacien
Ontzlake
Ozana
Palomides
Parzival, Percival

Pearl

Pellam

Pelleas

Pellinor

Piers

Priamus

Roland

Sadok

Sagramore

Sangrail

Tristan


MUSICATS


Allegro

Amadeus

Aria

Aubade

Bach

Ballo

Banjo

Bartók

Beethoven

Berlioz

Bix

Bizet

Camille

Carmen

Cello

Chopin

Clara

Clavier

Cole Porter

Conga

Czardas

Damper

Dancer
Dinu
Dvorak
Elise

Ella
Ellington
Fauré

Foxtrot
Frank
Fugue
Gamba
Gershwin
Grieg
Haydn
Intermezzo
Johann
  Sebastian
Kreutzer
Krumhorn
Legato
Liszt
Ludwig Van
Mancini
Mercer
Moonlight

Motet
Mozart
Narcisco
Nocturne
Offenbach
Operetta
Orfeo
Paderewski
Paganini

Passacaglia
Pink Panther
Pizzicatta
Prokofiev
Puccini
Quintet
Rachmaninoff
Ravel
Rhapsody
Rhumba
Ritornello
Rossini
Saint-Saëns
Salieri
Satch
Scarlatti
Schubert
Schumann

Scriabine
Sibelius
Sinatra
Sinistra
Smetana
Sonata
Sonatina
Stafford
Stave
Strad
Stradivarius
Straus
Stravinski
Symphonetta
Tannhäuser
Tarantella
Telemann
Toccata

Toscanini
Tremolo
Trout
Verdi
Viola
Wagner

MYSTERIOUS
AND
SUPERNATURAL
CATS

Agatha
Algernon
Algiz
Anne Rice
Armadale
Asphyx

Atlantis          Conan
Basil             Conan Doyle
Baskerville       Damballa
Bast              Dash
Bastet            Dashiell
Bathory           Della
Bedlam            Demon
Benito Cereno     Demon Cat
Biggers           Dr. Moriarty
Blackwood         Dragon
Bram              Dragonwyck
Cabal             Dürrenmatt
Cagliostro        Endore
Carmilla          Evileye
Carr              Exorcism
Chan              Father Brown
Chandler          Feer
Charteris         Freya

James Bond
Jera
Judge Dee
Lasher
Le Carré
Lecter
Lemba
Fu Manchu        Lestat
Ghostory         Ligotti
Gideon Wyck      Lovecraft
Gilles de Rais   Lucifer
Goldfinger       Ludlum
Gormenghast      Maigret
Gothic           Manderley
Groan            Marie Celeste
Hammett          Marlowe
Hoffmann         Mayfair
Holmes           Melchior

| | |
|---|---|
| Moloch | Saint |
| Moonfleet | Sandman |
| Moonstone | Sarsfield |
| Moto | Sax Rohmer |
| Mycroft | Sayers |
| Myst | Shadow |
| Nero Wolfe | Sherlock |
| Nevermore | Silver Blaze |
| Ngaio | Stephen King |
| Pertho | Stoker |
| Phantom | Stonehenge |
| Phantasm | Sumaru |
| Philo | Tarot |
| Poirot | Templar |
| Poltergeist | Thriller |
| Red Dragon | Titus |
| Rohmer | Tremors |
| Rune, Runes | Undine |

Vance
Voodoo
Watson
Werecat
Whateley
Wheatley
Whitechapel
Witchcraft
Yeti

Gator
Lassie
Rex
Rover
Smokey the
    Cat
Snoop Doggy
    Dog
Snoopy
Spot
Tweetie Bird

*NAMES THAT
NO CAT
SHOULD EVER
HAVE*

Boxer
Fang
Fido

## ORIENTICATS

Attaturk
Bast
Bastet
Beijing
Bey
Bubastis

Buddha
Butterfly
  Dragon
Byzantium
Chin Ping Mei
Cleocatra
Cleopatra
Confucius
Constanti-
  nople
Dragon
Egg Roll
Genghis
Genji
Hammurabi
Han
Honda
I Ching

| | |
|---|---|
| Inishiro | Osaka |
| Isis | Osiris |
| Istanbul | Ozu |
| Jasmin | Pasha |
| Kaseki | Peking |
| Kobo | Ptolemy |
| Kurosawa | Ramses |
| Kyoto | Ririomin |
| Lao-tze | Rubaiyat |
| Mah Jongg | Saladin |
| Makioka | Scarab |
| Mandala | Scarabus |
| Ming | Sekhmet |
| Mizoguchi | Shiatsu |
| Muhammed | Soong |
| Omar | Soseki |
| Omar | Sultan |
|   Khayyam | Tang |

Tanizaki          Brigand
Tao               Buccaneer
Tojo              Charleston
Torah             Corsair
Tsing             Cove
Waley             Dacoit
Wei               Damsel
Zarathustra       De Soto
Zoroaster         Drake
                  Dubloon
PIRATICATS        Flibuste
                  Freebooter
Armada            Freeboots
Barbary           Galleon
Barrataria        Havana
Benavides         Indies
Blackbeard        Kidd
Booty             Lafayette

Rackam
Raleigh
Shark
Smuggler
Spanish Main
Sumatra

Lascar
Loot
Madagascar
Morgan
One-Eye
Patchy
Picaroon
Pirate
Plank
Poacher
Privateer

*POE CATS*

Amontillado
Annabel Lee
Arnheim
Baltimore
Bells
Berenice
C. Auguste
   Dupin
Camelopard

Charmion
Diddling
Doctor Tarr
Dupin
Edgar
Eiros
Eldorado
Eleonora
Eulalie
Eureka

Fortunato
Helicon
Hop-Frog
Israfel
Lenore
Lespanaye
L'Espanaye
Ligeia
Maelstrom
Marie Rogêt
Masque
Mellonta
   Tauta
Metzenger-
   stein
Minister D.
Monos
Morella

Mr. Poe
Nevermore
Opium
Pendulum
Poe
Professor
  Fether
Pym
Pym, Gordon
Raven
Sleeper
Sphinx
Tamerlane
Telltale
Thingum Bob
Ulalume
Una
Usher

Valdemar
William
  Wilson
Zante

*PUNNY AND
AMUSICATS*

Barbaricat
Calcatta
Captain Cool
Catarrh
Catsor
Cat House
Cat-Ebing
Catamite
Catamount
Catbird

*What to Name a Cat* 103

| | |
|---|---|
| Catkin | Conquisticat |
| Catlin | Crazy Ivan |
| Catnip | Cream |
| Catsalot | Democat |
| Catsanova | Fantasticat |
| Catsup | Felix |
| Catandmouse | Franz Katka |
| Catcall | Halicats |
| Caterwaul | Havlicat |
| Catmouse | Hepcat |
| Catwalk | Heroicat |
| Cheshire Cat | Historicat |
| Citizen Cat | Italicat |
| Cleocatra | Jaws |
| Cool Cat | Jehosecat |
| Cool Kitty | Katmandu |
| Connie | Katsparov |
| Seleccat | Katzenjammer |

Kissy Cat
Kit Carson,
Kitty Carson
Kit Kat
Kitty Cool
Kitty Foyle
Kitty
   O'Rourke
Kitty O'Shea
Lafcatio

Leo
Marquis de
   Cat
Maxicat
Meow
Mercatio
Mexicat
Miss Kitty
Mouse
Mouser
Mouser, Grey
Republicat
Satin Cat
Shadowcat
Sophisticat
Tom Cat
Tom Selleckat
Tweetie

Whiskers
Xcalipurr

SHAKESPEAR-
EAN CATS

Ariel
Banquo
Beatrice
Benedick
Bianca
Bolingbroke
Caliban
Calpurnia
Cordelia
Cymbeline
Dark Lady
Desdemona

Falstaff
Grimalkin
Graymalkin
Guildenstern
Hamlet
Hotspur
Iago
Juliet
Lady Macbeth
Lear
Lysander
Macbeth
Macduff
Malvolio
Mercutio
Miranda
Much Ado
Oberon

Ophelia
Othello
Polonius
Prince Hal
Prospero
Romeo
Rosencrantz
Verona

SOUTHERN
CATS

Alabama
Ashley
Baton Rouge
Beauregard
Biloxi
Calhoun

General Lee
Georgia
Gumtree
Huey
Jackson
Jefferson
  Davis
Johnny Reb
Jubilation T.
  Cornpone
Lester
Lester Mad-
  dox

Louisiana
Magnolia
Memphis
Mississippi
Mobile
Oakey
Orleans
Rhett
Rhett Butler
Savannah
Scarlett
Spanish Moss
St. Augustine
Stonewall
Tarnation
Violet
Virginia

## SPORTING CATS

Ali
Babe Ruth
Big O
Bird
Borg
Boris
Bungee
Champ
Coach K.
Cooze
Daily Double
Hondo
Joltin' Joe
Jordan
Magic

Pippen
Rawlings
Red
Say Hey
Spalding
Sweet Lou
Teddy
  Ballgame
The Greatest
Trifecta
Wilson
Wilt

TASTY CATS

Alfredo
Anise
Anisette

Arabica
Basil
Beanie
Burger
Burgundy
Cajun Rice
Cajun
  Popcorn
Cayenne
Chamomile
Champagne
Chardonnay
Chianti

Chili Pepper
Choco
Chocolate
Chop Suey
Cilantro
Cinnamon
Claret
Cobbler
Coffee
Coffee Bean
Creamette
Curry
Darjeeling
Earl Grey
Espresso
Fennel
Frankincense
Fresca

Fumey
Ginger
Green Tea
Herb
Hot Sauce
Hunan
Incense
Jasmine
Java
King Creole
La Choy
Lanson
Lapsang
Lapsang
    Souchong
Latte
Lichee
Lipton

Macaroni
Marinara
Meaty
Mincemeat
Minty
Mocha
Mocha Java

Moët
Mushroom
Myrrh
Nutmeg
Oolong
Orange Spice
Oregano
Oreo
Oysters
Oysters
  Rockefeller

Patchouli
Peaches
Peachy
Pekoe
Pepper
Pizza Man
Primavera
Riesling
Ronzoni
Rose
Rosé

Rosemary
Sashimi
Souchong
Spearmint
Spice
Spritzer
Sushi
Sweetmeats
Sweets
Szechuan
Tabasco
Tang
Tangy
Tarragon
Tart
Tasty
Tetley
Thyme

Tokay
Violet
Wintergreen

# CATS IN HISTORY

The ancestors of today's cats first evolved about 45 million years ago, during the late Eocene era. By 35 million years ago, ancient cats looked and behaved very much like some members of today's cat family. We're all familiar with the most ferocious ancient cat: the saber-toothed tiger, with its frightening fangs. Though related to the saber-tooth, today's domestic cats descend more directly from another ancestor, an ancient wildcat who was larger than our felines but smaller than lions, tigers, or panthers.

This ancestral wildcat spread slowly around the world, appearing finally in every part of the globe except Australia, Madagascar, Antarctica, the West Indies, and some other islands. By the time the saber-tooth died out about 100,000 years ago, the rest of the cat family had organized itself into the three main groups we still

recognize today. The *Panthera* genus consists of lions, tigers, and other big cats. Cheetahs have a genus all their own, called *Acinonyx,* for cats whose claws do not retract. Small cats make up the genus *Felis,* encompassing pumas, lynxes, and other small wildcats, along with their most familiar descendant, *Felis catus catus,* the domesticated cat with whom we happily share our lives today.

Researchers can track the evolution of cats by their colors. The fur of most ancient cats was probably the shade called "ticked," or *agouti*. Today's wildcats often show this coloration, in which each separate hair is brown or black with a yellow tip. In prehistoric times, a mutation probably caused dark spots to appear in the fur of some cats, giving them a camouflage advantage we still recognize in jungle hunters such as leopards and jaguars. Later, another mutation may have created the stripes we see on today's tabby cats and tigers. White spots appeared last of all. For animals who need the ability to hunt undercover in order to survive, attention-getting patches of white are a major disadvantage. That's why white spots are common today only in domestic cats, who have human help to find food and safety. Cat color offers researchers a way to track the history of domestic cats too. The blotched tabby pattern, for example, first appeared in England. In the United States today, blotched tabby cats are common in areas originally settled by English colonists. But because blotched tabby cats were unusual in sixteenth-century Spain, they're relatively rare now in California, the Southwest, and other areas where the first European settlers were Spanish.

Because cats are loners, they probably found it harder to adjust to domestication than dogs did. Dogs descend from wolves, who are pack animals, used to living as a group and forming strong social bonds. This instinct for close association made it relatively easy for wolves to learn to live with humans, and that's probably why dogs were domesticated thousands of years before cats were. Cats, being cats, they kept to themselves until they found a very good reason to give up their freedom.

The first cats were domesticated 5,000 to 8,000 years ago, in the Nile River Valley in Egypt. Members of the species *Felis sylvestris libyaca,* also known as the African wildcat, were first drawn to domesticity by the human shift from nomadic to agrarian living. Once people learned how to farm, they began to store their harvested crops. Stored food attracted rodents, and the rodents, in turn, attracted wild-cats. As the cats demonstrated their usefulness by controlling the mouse population, grateful farmers fed them to encourage

them to stick around. Liking the food and the freedom from danger, the cats chose to stay. Thus began a long and mutually beneficial re-lationship. The ancient Egyptians named these cats *miu*, a name that tells us that, even in an-cient times, cats spoke the same language that our cats do now!

The first domesticated cats weren't just wildcats who chose to allow themselves to be tamed. They differed from other wild-cats in one crucial respect: They *enjoyed* human contact. African wildcats are instinctively wary of people, and European wildcats are even more difficult to tame. Wildcats don't learn to snuggle in laps and rub affectionately against their owners' ankles, as domestic cats do.

One researcher tamed and bred some of today's African

wildcats to see if their kittens would become domesticated when raised with people from birth. But the wildcats' kittens never lost their fear of humans. Instead, they cowered when people approached them as fearfully as if they'd been born in the wild. And if humans insisted on handling or controlling them, the kittens turned aggressive, spitting, laying back their ears, and even biting. Another researcher made a similar discovery when he crossed European wildcats with domestic kitties.

The hybrid kittens couldn't be trusted not to hunt and kill ducks and poultry, and if they weren't kept in confinement, they promptly disappeared into the woods.

Researchers think that the affectionate, gentle personality of today's domestic cats began thousands of years ago, with a genetic mutation that made some African wildcats more adaptable to human companionship. Through natural selection, these gentler mutant cats gave rise eventually to today's worldwide legions of purring tabbies, curled up snug in the laps of their very own humans.

The ancient Egyptians worshipped cats in the cult of Bastet, which began in about 1000 B.C. and lasted until it was outlawed by Theodosius I in A.D. 390. Bastet was a goddess with the head of a cat and the body of a woman, who represented fertility and health as blessings of the Sun. Domestic cats were sacred to Bastet. At festivals in her honor, attended each year by as many as half a million people, hundreds of thousands of cats were sacrificed, mummified, and buried.

Mummies examined by today's archeologists show that the sacrificed animals were usually kittens or young cats who died of broken necks. Vast cat cemeteries were located in several Egyptian cities. In 1888, a farmer accidentally dug up one of the cat burial grounds in the Egyptian city of Beni Hasan. Hundreds of thousands of mummified cats were exposed. Children played with them or carried them off to sell to travelers on the Nile, scattering mummy cloth and bits of bones everywhere. Most of the dug-up cat mummies were eventually used for fertilizer. Nineteen tons of mummified cat bones were sent to England to be ground into fertilizer for British farm fields. From that massive shipment, just one skull remains, now preserved in the British Museum.

The ancient Egyptians so honored their cats that the punishment for killing a cat was death. One unfortunate Roman soldier who made the mistake of hurting a cat was torn limb from limb by outraged Egyptians. Even when a cat died naturally, everyone in its home had to don full mourning and shave their eyebrows. While people wailed and lamented, the cat's body would be rolled in a linen sheet and embalmed with drugs and spices.

Rich people's cats were encased in colored linen, which was folded and wound in complicated patterns. A cat-faced mask made of papier-mâché, with ears made of the ribs of palm leaves, was placed over the cat's face, and the resulting mummy was placed in a case made of wood or plaited straw, sometimes decorated with gold, crystal, and obsidian. Even kittens were buried in little bronze coffins.

Poor people's cats got simpler treatment, but they were still buried with honor and ceremony. To feed them in the afterlife, mice and shrews were mummified and put into tombs alongside mummified pets.

The most honored cats were those who served in temples.

Their funerals were sometimes so elaborate and expensive that special taxes were levied to pay for them.

Images of cats begin to appear in Egyptian art starting about 2600 B.C., but the first definite evidence of domestication turned up in a tomb dated about 1900 B.C., in which researchers found the bones of seventeen cats buried with little pots of milk. After about 1600 B.C., cats took on a more prominent role in Egyptian art, curled up under their owners' chairs, chewing on bones, playing with one another, and, in what must be the earliest record of human efforts to confine these independent wanderers, tied to the leg of a chair with a red ribbon. One painting shows the mother of Pharaoh Akhnaton at dinner, slipping bits of food to a kitty under her chair. Another depicts a tabby cat eagerly hunting for birds in the company of a human hunting party.

Egyptian artists painted cats by the hundreds on the walls of tombs and on papyrus. They sculpted cats in bronze, gold, stone, and wood, molded them out of faience, and carved them into ivory. Young Egyptian women used cat amulets, called *utchats*, as fertility tokens, praying to have as many children as the number of kittens shown on the amulet. The word *utchat* spread through the world along with cats themselves, eventually becoming the root for the word *cat* in English, French, Italian, Russian, Hindustani, and many other Indo-European languages.

Cats had been domesticated in Egypt for at least a thousand years before they appeared in the rest of the world. Their spread was slowed by the Egyptians themselves, who revered felines so deeply that, for centuries, they prohibited their export. When Egyptian travelers found domesticated cats living in other countries, they purchased or stole them in order to bring them home to Egypt, where they believed they belonged. Seeing a business opportunity in this Egyptian-imposed feline shortage, the trade-savvy Phoenicians smuggled cats out of Egypt when they could, selling them to wealthy animal lovers in other countries. Thus, domestic cats first appeared along established

Phoenician trade routes, spreading later into the rest of the world. Domestic cats arrived in Greece in 500 B.C., in India about 300 B.C., and in China in 200 B.C. It took longer for cats to make it into Europe. The first domestic cats did not appear in Italy and Switzerland until the first few centuries after the birth of Christ.

The domestic cat changed as it

spread through Europe. Inter-breeding with the European wild-cat, *Felis sylvestris sylvestris*, made European domestic cats stockier and broader than the lean, elegant feline that had first emerged in Egypt. We can still see that difference today by comparing the relatively sturdy European or American shorthair, a breed with plenty of European wildcat genes, to the leaner breeds that evolved in Asia or Africa, such as the graceful Abyssinian or the refined Siamese.

When Herodotus, the Greek traveler, visited Egypt in the

fifth century B.C., he was so intrigued by the cats he saw that he wrote cat-sighting reports in his travel journals. Domestic cats must have arrived in Greece soon thereafter. The first representation of a cat in Greek art appears in a bas-relief from about 500 B.C., showing a cat on a leash facing a dog who is also leashed. As cat and dog eye each other, their owners and a few spectators lean forward, waiting eagerly to see how the animals will respond to one another—an explosive outcome that today's cat and dog owners can predict without pause!

The words the ancient Greeks formed for cats still appear in our language today. *Ailouros*, the Greek name for cat, turns up in our words for someone who loves cats—an *ailurophile*—and for someone who detests or fears them—an *ailurophobe*.

Although the 200,000-year-old

bones of a jungle cat have been found near the Thames River in England, no domestic cats lived in Great Britain until Roman soldiers brought them onto the island. Evidence of cats first begins to appear in British ruins dating from about the fourth century A.D. In Silchester, Hampshire, a cat walked across tiles laid out to dry by an ancient kiln, leaving footprints for archeologists to find fifteen centuries later.

Remains of another cat were found in ruins from the same period in Kent, where a fire destroyed an ancient house and trapped a cat in the basement.

Enough of this cat's body remained for researchers to determine that it was larger than our domesticated cats of today, but smaller than its mummified Egyptian forebears, with a skull that showed the beginnings of the foreshortened nose of today's felines.

By the fifth century in Ireland, a cat was included on a list of goods considered essential for a housewife. And in the ninth century A.D., an illustration of a cat was included in the famous Irish illuminated manuscript, *The Book of Kells*.

The first cats in Great Britain

were revered and respected for their mousing abilities. A cat killer would be severely fined by having to give over a lamb or a sheep, a substantial penalty in those days. In Wales in the tenth century, the legal definition of a hamlet consisted of a place with nine buildings, one herdsman, one plow, one kiln, one churn, one bull, one cock, and one cat. Welsh law established the value of cats. Until its eyes opened, a kitten was worth a penny (the value of a lamb, kid, goose, or hen). When its eyes opened, it was worth two pennies, and once it began to kill mice, its value escalated to four pence. When a husband and wife split up, the husband got to keep a valuable piece of property: the household cat. In the tenth century, one Welsh king punished a cat killer by requiring him to pay the penalty of a pile of grain heaped high enough to cover the cat's body, which had been hung up by its tail so that its nose touched the ground. And in twelfth-century Saxony, anyone who killed a cat had to pay its owner sixty bushels of corn.

In Europe in the Middle Ages,

the early reverence for cats began to shift to suspicion, fear, and finally, outright hatred. Pagans worshipped the Norse goddess Freya, who kept cats around her, used cats to pull her wagon, and was worshipped with cat rituals. As the Christian Church grew, it campaigned against witchcraft and barred the worship of pagan gods and goddesses, including Freya. Friday, the day named after Freya, became known as the Witches' Sabbath, and her cat companions were scorned and feared as witch's familiars.

In the fifteenth century, Pope Innocent VIII ordered all cat worshipers in Europe to be burned as witches, making cat-related witchcraft prosecutions common. In seventeenth-century Denmark, a woman was prosecuted as a witch for allegedly giving birth to a baby with the head of a cat. Doctors today would recognize a tragic birth defect, but to the Danes of that time, the baby's strange features were proof that its mother had consorted with the devil. In 1699, more than 300 children were prosecuted as witches for keeping pet cats. For this offense, fifteen of the children were executed, and others were whipped in front of the church every Sunday for a year. As late as the seventeenth century, Edward Topsell wrote, "The familiars of Witches do most ordinarily appeare in the shape of cats, which is an argument that this beast is dangerous in soule and body."

Historians believe that those who persecuted cats in the Middle Ages may also have punished themselves too. The widespread mistreatment of cats caused the feline population to drop by as much as 90 percent from its previous level. This, in turn, allowed rats to overrun human settlements. As rats increased, so did their fleas, which may have contributed to the spread of the dreaded disease that medieval people called the Black Death.

Today, we know this illness as bubonic plague, and we understand that it is caused by *Yersinia pestis*, a bacterium living on fleas. But medieval Europeans believed that the Black Death was caused by witchcraft, Satan, or poisoned wells. In the fourteenth century, bubonic plague swept through Europe and parts of Asia, killing one-fourth to one-half of the population. Ironically, the cats whose mistreatment may have contributed to the plague epidemic may also have helped to bring it to an end.

While the Black Death raged through Europe, people were too distracted by their own suffering to kill and torment cats. In this climate of relative safety, cat numbers increased. The cats brought the rat population under control, which helped to stem the spread of the plague at last. But those who survived the Black Death failed to show proper gratitude to the cats who had helped them. Instead, many people went right back to killing cats again.

While people in Europe were torturing cats, people in the Middle East and Asia were honoring them. Muslims believed that Mohammed was so fond of his cat that he cut off the sleeve of his robe rather than awaken his cat, who was sleeping on it. As long ago as the thirteenth century, a Muslim sultan directed his heirs to use the earnings from his orchards to care for the stray cats in his neighborhood.

The ancient Chinese kept cats as good-luck omens. Many Chinese people still believe that those who are born in the Year of the Cat have admirable catlike qualities, such as refinement, cleverness, discretion, and high virtue.

In Japan, the first cats arrived in the tenth century. For hundreds of years thereafter, only nobles were allowed to own cats, and the lucky felines were cosseted in every way. At that time, the Japanese name for pet cats was *tama*, which means jewel. All cats in Japan were kept on leashes until 1602, when the government ordered them released, perhaps to aid in exterminating rodents who threatened the silkworm industry.

Far from being associated with evil, cats in Japanese folklore often help people or bring good luck. Tourists today can visit a cat cemetery in Tokyo founded centuries ago. The cemetery's temple facade is decorated by a procession of cats raising their right forelegs, as if to bless the felines buried there in honor.

Some of the first domestic cats to emerge in Asia probably developed a genetic mutation that affected their tails. As a result, strange tails have been common in Asian cats throughout history. In 1868, Charles Darwin reported, "Throughout the Malayan Archipelago, Siam, Pegu, and Burmah, all the cats have truncated tails about half the proper length, often with a sort of knot at the end." Ascribing tail problems to all Asian cats may have been an exaggeration. But in 1959, a cat researcher named A. G. Searle confirmed Darwin's observation in part, noting that about one-third of the cats in Hong Kong, and two-thirds of those in Malaysia, had kinks in their tails.

The prevalence of tail oddities in Asian cats led scientists to conclude that the Manx cat, first noticed in England, must have arrived there on ships originating in Asia. Some Manx, called "rumpies," have no tails at all, while "stumpies" have only partial tails.

Siamese cats, who also originated in Asia, often have kinks in their tails. An old legend explains that the purpose of this kink was to allow princesses to keep their rings safe while bathing. The royal ladies were said to hang their jewelry on the tails of their Siamese cats, where the kinks kept the valuables securely in place. A more scientific explanation holds that the kink is an inherited abnormality of the caudal vertebrae, caused by the same genetic mutation that altered the tails of many other Asian cats.

By the seventeenth and eighteenth centuries, European hostility toward cats was beginning to subside. Slowly, cats began to take their places once more as valued pets. In mid-seventeenth-century France,

Cardinal Richelieu kept dozens of them at court, and when he died, he provided for the care of his kitties in his will.

As the eighteenth century began, European princesses and fashionable French court ladies pampered their pet cats, holding salons to discuss their virtues, engraving their images on medals, and burying them in lavish tombs. French artists like Watteau and Fragonard included cats in paintings of pastoral outdoor scenes, as well as in pictures of ladies' boudoirs. One French astronomer, Lalande, even added a new constellation in the shape of a cat, called *Felis*, to eighteenth-century star charts.

In England, too, domesticated cats began to reappear in stories, poems, and pictures of happy family life. The painter Stubbs even celebrated a friendship between a horse and a cat when he included a black stable cat in his portrait of the famous racehorse, Godolphin. By the nineteenth century, Queen Victoria's cat, White Heather, was so popular that she had her own biography. Soon thereafter, the first societies for the prevention of animal cruelty were established, in part to make sure that the cruel treatment meted out to cats and other animals during the Middle Ages would never be socially acceptable again.

As the Industrial Revolution virtually transformed nineteenth-century England, almost everyone went to work in factories, offices, and warehouses—including cats, who controlled rodents for many burgeoning new businesses. In the British Post Office, the rodent-control contributions of cats were so valued that in 1868, a Cat System was inaugurated to provide for the comfort and upkeep of all the Post Office cats.

Muriel Beadle, author of *The Cat: History, Biology and Behavior,* writes that under the system, the secretary of the Post Office financed the purchase of cat food by providing each branch office with six or seven pence per cat. But to make sure the feline employees didn't get so comfortable that they forgot their jobs, the secretary never provided quite enough money. He directed that the cats "must depend on the mice for the remainder of their emoluments." In the tradition of bureaucrats everywhere, branch managers appealed regularly for higher cat budgetary allotments.

In 1873, one postmaster succeeded when he explained that he needed extra money not just for the cost of cat food, but also to make up for "the loss of dignity when carrying the cat's food through the streets in Her Majesty's uniform." The Post Office cats proved to be so helpful in controlling Post Office mice that official cats still prowled British post offices in the 1970s, more than a century after the Cat System first began.

Throughout history, animals have helped people. Cows give milk,

sheep give wool, horses provide transportation—and cats prove their value to humanity by hunting. In the late fifteenth century, Conquistador Diego de Almagro paid 600 pieces of eight for the first domestic cat in South America, imported to control mice. Frederick the Great, king of Prussia in the eighteenth century, ordered every town he conquered to pay a levy of cats, who kept rodents out of his army's stores.

Centuries later, cats came to the rescue one more time as part of the Marshall Plan, executed by the United States to help rebuild Europe after World War II. To feed starving people, Americans shipped hundreds of thousands of tons of grain into Europe. Borrowing a time-honored technique from the ancient Egyptians, they sent 10,000 cats along with the grain to keep it safe from mice. The cats did their part, helping to keep the grain intact so that hungry Europeans could restore their strength and begin the long process of rebuilding the war-shattered continent.

In 1964, an epidemic of Bolivian hemorrhagic fever swept through San Joaquin, a remote settlement in the Andes, caused by wild mice who carried the Machupo virus. After a radio appeal for help, hundreds of donated cats were airlifted to the stricken community, bringing the epidemic to a halt.

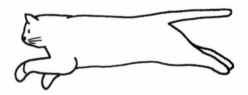

The basic body structure and appearance of the cat has changed surprisingly little through history. People created dog breeds on purpose, selecting traits like size, aggressiveness, or speed that suited dogs for particular tasks. But most cat breeds arose accidentally, as a result of genetic isolation in far-flung parts of the world. People did not begin to notice or value the different cat breeds, with their fascinating variety in color, fur length, and temperament, until Victorian times, when travelers began to bring home some of the odd-looking cats they encountered in exotic spots.

The shorthaired cats are the oldest European breed, descending from the first cats distributed through Europe by the Romans. Manx cats first came from Asia, the Angora from Turkey, the Persian from Asia Minor, the Siamese from the Far East, and the Abyssinian from Ethiopia. As breeds like these acquired names and popularity, cat owners began to want to show them off to one another.

The first cat show was held at

the Crystal Palace in London in 1871. In Europe and North America today, more than 100 different pedigree breeds have been officially established with standards and registries. But for all their remarkable differences, cats from the various breeds are all variations on one theme: the astonishingly beautiful, complex, and well-loved domestic cat.

# CATS IN LITERATURE

It is a little-known fact that James Joyce, the Irish writer best known for his *Dubliners* stories and the epic *Ulysses,* once wrote a fable. What began as a letter to his grandson Stephen in 1936 became the children's story, "The Cat and the Devil." It is the tale of a certain bridge over the River Loire in France that the devil himself promises to build for the people of Beaugency. In exchange for his good deed, he wants for himself the first person who crosses the bridge. The mayor of the town

agrees to the deal, but tricks the devil by sending over a black cat instead of a person. This angers the devil, who from then on calls the townspeople *les chats de Beaugency*, the "cat people." He sympathizes, however, with the poor cat who crossed the bridge and has jumped into his arms. He takes him as his own, and the two (as we know from history) become lifelong companions.

It's not surprising that writer Edgar Allan Poe would pen a spooky short story about a witchy black cat. In his story appropriately titled "The Black Cat," the main character is a man quite fond of animals, including his large black cat, Pluto. As bad luck would have it, the man becomes annoyed with his furry friend, then angry, and finally foul-tempered and abusive, and cuts out the cat's eye. Faithful Pluto forgives him, which upsets the man even more, enough so that he hangs the cat from a tree.

One evening, another cat, black with white markings on his chest (and also missing an eye), follows him home. The two become companions, but in time, the man, in a rage of psychosis, tries to kill the cat with an ax. Luckily for the cat, the man's wife interrupts the scene, only to get the ax buried deep in her head. The man hides her body in a wall, but his hideous act is given away when the cat, who had mistakenly been buried in the wall, too, cries out and is heard by the police. The pattern of the white fur on the black cat's chest now reveals . . . the gallows!

We all know that most cats are good at mousing and taking naps, but they're also pretty good writers. In 1942, Christopher Cat, in collaboration with Countee Cullen, a leading poet of the Negro Renaissance of the 1920s, wrote a book. *My Lives and How I Lost Them* is the cat's account of his nine lives and what fates he met along the way, including drowning and getting caught in a rat trap. It is a humorous, sophisticated piece of writing by one very intelligent cat that was certainly ahead of his time!

What's it like to be a Shakespearean actor and have to learn how to use a litter box? Win-stanley Fortescue, the protagonist in mystery novelist Marian Babson's *Nine Lives to Murder*, can tell you. Babson, who dedicates her book to "all the cats in our lives, and the life in our cats," adds comic fantasy to this story of an actor being pursued by a murderer. Before the evildoer has his chance, Fortescue falls unconscious and lands on the acting company's cat, Montmorency D. Mousa. When Fortescue comes to, his body has been switched with the cat's. What transpires is a tale of feline experiences that make you glad you don't have to eat mice for dinner!

The cat has always been an animal of mystery, so it follows that cats feel right at home in mystery stories. Writer Lilian Jackson Braun features cats as detectives in her mystery novel series that includes *The Cat Who Said Cheese* and *The Cat Who Blew the Whistle*. Journalist Jim Qwilleran and his feline sleuths Koko and Yum Yum wander Pickax City trying to solve mysterious bombings, murders, missing persons, and the like. These books are as tantalizing as catnip and will have readers wishing these cats prowled *their* neighborhoods at night.

Sneaky Pie Brown is yet another cat author who, together with screenwriter and poet Rita Mae Brown, pens the "Mrs. Murphy" mystery series. Sneaky Pie's main characters are Mary Minor Haristeen and her clever cat, Mrs. Murphy. Together, these two solve crimes, sometimes with the help of a Welsh corgi and a fat, gray cat, in novels like *Wish You Were Here*, *Rest in Pieces*, and *Murder at Monticello*. Mrs. Murphy's experiences with her circle of animal friends and insights into human emotions provide the reader with a cat's perspective on life. Still don't believe cats can write? Sneaky Pie Brown's paw-print in the "Author's Note" proves it.

The cat in Rudyard Kipling's "The Cat That Walked by Him-self" is the embodiment of the typically independent nature of the truly curious cat. The story describes a time when animals were wild and Man and Woman lived in caves. Cat is determined not to lose his independence as

Dog, Cow, and Horse did when they became tamed by humans; he declares he will always walk alone and go wherever, whenever, he pleases. He makes the following bargain with Woman: If Cat ever overhears Woman praising him, she will let him into the cave, where he can sit by the fire and drink milk. One day, Cat stops Woman's baby from crying and entertains him by chasing a string. Woman compliments Cat and, thereby, fulfills the bargain. Cat can enter the cave, get warm, and eat at his leisure, but he is still untamed and free to come and go as he wishes. Unfortunately, Dog makes his own bargain with Cat and chases him up a tree whenever he gets the opportunity! Such is the life of a cat.

Tom Quartz, a name later used by Theodore Roosevelt for one of his own kittens, is a miner's feline companion in Mark Twain's short story, "Dick Baker's Cat." Baker tells his fellow mining friends the story of when Tom Quartz, who cared little for hunting rats but had a keen ability to find gold, almost meets his doom in the blasting of a quartz mine. He survives the explosion

with singed whiskers and remains as smug (if not a little intimidating, as cats can be!) as
ever.

Who is not familiar with Dr.
Seuss's fun-loving Cat in the
Hat in his zany striped hat? Perhaps the best-known cat in contemporary children's literature,
the energetic cat who waltzes
into the home of two bored children on a rainy day is known to
inspire young and old to learn
how to read. Quite an under-
taking for such a silly rhyming
puss! Dr. Seuss used only 220
words for this classic, yet it re-

mains a timeless favorite of children and parents all over the globe. If you don't remember what mischievous tricks this cat has under his hat, perhaps you should reacquaint yourself—you'll be glad you did!

Do you remember the three little kittens who lost their mittens? They cried because they could have no pie. They then found their mittens and cried again until their mother gave them the pie. As naughty kittens will do, they soiled their mittens and then had to wash them. What happens at the end of this childhood rhyme? Their mother smells a rat! This somewhat nonsensical poem has pleased generations of kiddies—not to mention *kitties!*

"I've often seen a cat without a grin, but a grin without a cat?" The most famous cat in all of British children's literature is probably the one Alice meets in Lewis Carroll's *Through the Looking Glass.* With a wide, toothy grin, the Cheshire Cat sits in the bough of a tree and looks down at poor Alice, who is lost. When the girl asks him what direction she should take, he, a cat of quick wit, says: "That depends a good deal on where you want to get to." Perhaps more intriguing than his intelligence is the Cheshire Cat's ability to disappear, a little bit at a time, a quality that helps him escape execution by the king.

Did you know that it may have been a mouse who invented the belled cat collar? Aesop writes about mice that fear a cat in his fable, "The Bell and the Cat." The mice are hungry, beginning to starve, in fact, but a cat looms outside their hole, and so they are afraid to go in search of crumbs. A bold mouse makes the suggestion that they tie a bell around the cat's neck so they'll know when the cat is near. Good idea, the mice think, but one elder mouse rises and asks the all-important question: "Who will bell the cat?"

Puss in Boots, the matchmaker cat who wears red boots in the old French children's story, is the type of cat everyone wants: He's clever, charming, and a good hunter. Puss knows his master is poor, so he places himself in favor with the king and devises a way for the man to meet with the beautiful royal daughter. His plan works, and his master becomes rich when he marries the princess. What becomes of Puss? He becomes a lord, of course!

The cat that accompanies an explorer on a 1914 expedition to Antarctica must be one *cool* cat! *Mrs. Chippy's Last Expedition: The Remarkable Journal of Shackleton's Polar-Bound Cat* by Caroline Alexander (with an introduction by Lord Mouser-

Hunt F.R.G.S.), a book you just might mistake for a real-life story, is the heroic tale of Mrs. Chippy, a tiger-striped tabby. He is an optimistic and physically fit male cat (despite the Mrs. in his name) who survives the shipwreck of *Endurance*, a vessel headed into icy waters. The detailed journal of his life on the ship is complemented by black-and-white photography of him and his shipmates.

American horror writer H. P. Lovecraft had a great affection for cats and often included them in his short stories. "Something

About Cats" is an essay on the majestic and highly intelligent qualities of the cat in comparison to the "slavering devotion and obedience" of dogs. According to his wife, Lovecraft, who enjoyed walking the streets of New York City alone in the darkness of night, seemed to speak a language that cats understood. Pet cats doted on him, even when he was not their owner. It seems he was inspired by the mysterious and aloof animal, if not somehow more closely related to them.

William Shakespeare himself

scattered cats through-
out his great works. A
tawny cat sits with
the three witches
at the start of *Macbeth*. One
witch is even named "Graymalkin," an ancient cat name.
As the three hags sit in their
cave preparing evil spells
against the king, their cat friend
gives the signal ("thrice the
brinded cat hath mewed") to
begin their witchy session.

If you think cats and mice can
never put aside their differences
long enough to become friends,
read George Selden's children's

book, *The Cricket in Times Square*. Tucker, a mouse who lives in a New York City subway drainpipe, becomes friends and shares his home with a roving cat named Harry, a fugitive from the East Side. The unusual friendship between cat and mouse is explained by way of the unconventional attitudes characteristic of the Big Apple. "In

New York, we gave up these old habits long ago," says Harry.

A. A. Milne's Tigger may not be domesticated, but he's probably as close as he can get. The beloved, energetic tiger in the Winnie the Pooh stories is clearly not a typical feline. Instead of slinking around with intimidating slyness, Tigger just bounces until he can bounce no more. He is rather optimistic, in contrast to the smug, sometimes sarcastic attitude of many cats in literature. Tigger *is* a cat's cat, however; he likes to do as he pleases, where he pleases . . . and he *doesn't* like honey!

In "How the Cat Became," a story by Ted Hughes, Cat is a lazy animal who just wants to sleep in the sun all day and play his violin at night. The other animals, who think he's strange and unlike any of them, urge him to get a job. Cat likes his life of leisure, but the others' proddings make him get up one day and go ask Man for employment on his farm. Cat becomes the rat and mouse catcher, but makes sure he only catches enough so he won't ever run out of rodents and lose his job. This way, he can lounge in the fields all day and make music at night as soon as he has collected a satisfactory pile of critters for Man.

Edgar Allan Poe wasn't the only person to write a short story called "The Black Cat." William Wintle, a British writer, wrote a story of the same title about Sydney, a wealthy man of leisure who dislikes and fears cats, but at the same time is entranced by the curious creatures. As time passes, he becomes obsessed with the animal, thinking he sees black cats in heaps of dirt and museum antiques. He is visited one night by a large, black cat that has appeared to him in a nightmare, the same cat who begins to follow him like a shadow. Sydney is eventually torn to pieces by the bad kitty, who seems to sense the man's hatred of felines.

"Venus and the Cat," one of Aesop's more famous fables, is about a cat who falls in love with a man. The cat begs the goddess Venus to change her into a woman so that the man might love her back. Venus obliges and the two young lovers marry. One day, Venus decides to see if the young woman has given up her "catty"

instincts and lets a mouse loose in the girl's bedroom. The girl pounces on the mouse to the disgust of Venus, who promptly changes her back into a cat! The moral of the story: One can change one's appearance but not one's nature.

In the Chinese tale "Why the Dog and the Cat Are Enemies,"

there lives a poor couple with a cat and a dog. One day, the dog has the brilliant idea of obtaining a gold ring that will make the couple rich and happy. The cat agrees to help the dog carry out the scheme. The cat is faster than the dog and returns to their masters with the ring, leaving the dog far behind. The cat is praised for being so quick and smart while the dog is beaten for being slow and unhelpful. The cat says nothing, so the angry dog, having been cheated of any reward, chases and bites her. The story explains why cats and dogs don't get along to this day.

Quentin Patrick's 1945 short story "The Fat Cat" once again proves the nine lives theory of tabbies. The fat cat, who remains nameless, has befriended an American corporal in World War II Japan. Knowing the cat will be killed if it follows him into enemy territory, the corporal stops feeding it in hopes it might seek out someone else's company. The cat is devoted, however, and follows the corporal through miles of jungle to a recently deserted enemy camp. There the famished soldier finds a table of food, including a roast chicken, which the cat sees too and starts to eat. The corporal throws a rock at the cat to chase him away but instead hits the chicken, which explodes because it has been booby-trapped. Had the corporal touched the chicken, he would have been killed. So, in an odd and unexpected way, the fat cat—who survives the blast—saves the man's life.

In P. G. Wodehouse's *The Story of Webster*, Lancelot is a free-spirited artist. But once he adopts Webster the cat, he becomes intimidated and insecure whenever his new pet even glances at him.   Lancelot changes his behavior to try to please Webster and hopes that just once he will catch the cat in a weak moment. Of course, he does; he finds Webster lapping up some spilled rum and getting downright intoxicated! The man's self-consciousness disappears and he returns to living his life as he pleases. Webster, after all, is just "one of the boys."

Tom is naughty, and so are his sisters. In Beatrix Potter's "Tom Kitten," part of her *Tales of Peter Rabbit*, Tom, Mittens, and Moppet get dressed up by their mother and are told to wait in the garden for her guest to arrive for afternoon tea. Instead, the bad kittens climb a stone wall, get dirty, and even lose their nice clothes to the puddle-ducks. Needless to say, they are punished when they return home—but that doesn't stop them from climbing the curtains and having still more fun in their bed-room!

Have you ever looked outside at night to see the neighborhood cat staring up into the sky? M. Grant Cormack's story, "Why the Cat Stares at the Moon" offers a perfectly good explanation for pussy's strange behavior. It seems that once upon a time, Dog played a trick on Cat to protect Mouse. Cat was always after Mouse, so Dog told Cat that his tiny, gray prey had gone to visit the Man in the Moon. When Cat sits looking up at the Moon, he is waiting for Mouse

to return on a moonbeam. Silly
old Cat!

Legend has it that a particular
cat used to work grinding coffee
in the king's kitchen. One day,
this cat decides to watch the
king's regal procession into the
city; he swallows the coffee mill
and blames thieves for stealing
it before sneaking out. When he
returns, a low, grinding noise
comes from his throat as the

king pats him. Realizing that the noise comes from the mill in the cat's stomach, the king curses all cats. According to *How Cats Came to Purr*, by John Bennett, when a human strokes a cat, the purring heard is a reminder of the cat's ancestor's guilt and shame. And you thought it was a sign of contentment!

Not all cats are as ungrateful as literature might lead one to believe. Take the white cat in Agnes A. Sandham's story, "The Conscientious Cat." She lives with gold miners in the Sierra Nevadas. As thanks for being adopted and cared for, she takes upon herself the duty of warning the men whenever she feels a wall of the mine beginning to crumble. She earns the reputation of a true feline heroine, while the miners' dog sits in a corner with his tail between his legs, ashamed of his laziness.

# CELLULOID CATS

## PEPPER, THE FELINE SUPERSTAR OF SILENT FILMS

From silent films to the latest box-office blockbuster, cats have captivated viewers on the silver screen.

In fact, the first feline superstar appeared in movies long before "talkies" were invented.

According to the book *Hollywood Cats* by J. C. Suares, Pepper the cat was an audience favorite throughout the silent movie era of the 1920s.

And she became a star without even having to audition!

Legend has it that famed Keystone Cops director Mack Sennett was shooting a movie at his studio in Hollywood when a gray cat snuck in through a broken floorboard. She was included in the scene that was being shot, performed like a natural, and Sennett, who named her Pepper, put her into many of his silent films.

Because of her natural curiosity, Pepper learned fast. For instance, she convincingly played checkers in a scene with comedian Ben Turpin.

However, Pepper's creative career came to an unusual close. The cat had become close buddies with Teddy, a Great Dane who was also in many of Sennett's movies. When Teddy died, Pepper actually went into mourning for her dear, departed partner and retired from movie making.

# ORANGEY, THE FELINE SUPERSTAR OF THE FIFTIES, PART I

One of the most talented cats in the history of the motion pictures was Orangey, a large, ginger tabby who starred in the 1951 film *Rhubarb* as well as many other movies. Orangey's film career lasted from the early 1950s through 1963, and during that time, he won more awards than any other cat in Tinseltown.

A shorthaired, photogenic, fluffy (some would say overweight), fourteen-pound feline, Orangey—for all his movie-star glamour—was short-tempered, hard to work with, and nasty. The cat was disliked even by his trainer, Frank Inn! Orangey's antics were so aggravating that a movie executive actually called him "The World's Meanest Cat," and during one film shoot, guard dogs were even placed at the doors of the movie studio to keep Orangey from running away.

But Orangey could act!

He was considered by many to be one of the best animal actors in the world, and he is the only cat to have won the Patsy Award twice, an honor given for best performance by an animal in a movie.

Orangey won the award for his title role in *Rhubarb*, a movie about a cat who inherits a fortune and then buys the Brooklyn Dodgers baseball team. Based on a novel of the same name by H. Allen Smith, Orangey's costars in this big-screen adventure were Ray Milland, Jan Sterling, Leonard Nimoy, and Gene Lockhart.

During the shooting of this movie, Orangey was kept on a leash so that he wouldn't bolt from the set. Even so, he managed to harass everyone around him—including his four-legged stand-ins!

## ORANGEY, THE FELINE SUPERSTAR OF THE FIFTIES, PART II

Orangey won another Patsy Award for his memorable performance as the appropriately named character Cat in *Breakfast at Tiffany's*, which starred Audrey Hepburn as Holly Golightly, and also featured a first-class cast, including George Peppard, Buddy Ebsen, Mickey Rooney, and Patricia Neal.

In the film, which is based on a Truman Capote novella, Cat is Holly's beloved pet, whom she calls "a poor slob without a name." During his performance,

Orangey had to jump on Hepburn's back while she lay in bed, leap off Peppard's shoulders onto a shelf, and look quite pathetic as he gets drenched in a rainstorm scene. This scene occurs at the end of the movie when Holly throws Cat out onto the streets of New York City to show that she is a free spirit and not attached to anyone—or anything. Minutes later, she has a change of heart and runs through the pouring rain to find Cat, which, happily, she does!

Orangey's other major film roles include an appearance with Jackie Gleason in *Gigot*, and he was also seen on a regular basis on the famed *Our Miss Brooks* television series, starring Eve Arden and Gale Gordon.

Movie critics and animal trainers agree that, in many of his movies, Orangey often stole the show from his famous costars. If there ever was a feline superstar who should have his pawprints in cement, it was this talented, irascible cat!

## THAT DARN CAT, THE ORIGINAL VERSION

When Walt Disney Productions made the movie *That Darn Cat*

in 1965, a Siamese named Syn Cat played the title role of D.C., short for Darn Cat.

In the film, D.C. is a feline that finds a watch belonging to a woman who had been taken hostage during a bank robbery. D.C. brings the watch to her owner, played in the film by a teenage Hayley Mills, and this attracts the attention of an FBI agent. He, of course, finds it difficult to be around cats, yet he follows D.C. through many adventures to crack the case.

"Walt Disney came down to the set when we'd be working with the cat, because he was very interested in how the trainer would get the cat to do certain things," said Dean Jones, who played the FBI agent in the film. "We learned then that cats don't work for love. Cats work for *food*. They're *very* smart."

*That Darn Cat* was a big hit at the box office and won Syn Cat a Patsy Award. The superb Siamese also received raves from critics, including the *New York Times*, calling the cat's performance one of "suavity and grace." The movie was based on the book *Undercover Cat*, written by Gordon and Mildred Gordon, and it featured quite a famous supporting cast, including Roddy McDowall, Elsa Lanchester, Ed Wynn, Frank Gorshin, and Dorothy Provine.

*That Darn Cat* was remade in 1997 as a film that again featured Dean Jones.

## THAT DARN CAT, THE REMAKE

*That Darn Cat* was remade in 1997 by Walt Disney Productions. It starred Christina Ricci as the teenage owner of a cat that finds a clue to a mysterious kidnapping, and Doug E. Doug as the novice FBI agent who follows the cat to solve the case.

As in the original 1965 film, the cat is again named D.C. In this version, however, D.C. is played by a gray-and-white tabby named Elvis, who was found and trained by Larry Madrid.

"I stopped by the North Hollywood animal shelter on my way to the airport for a film assignment and found him there," Madrid said. "I called one of our trainers and said, 'You have to come and get this cat. It's a perfect double for our other cats.' And he ended up being the star of the picture!

"You can tell just by looking at

Elvis. His attitude, his demeanor, the way he carries himself, the looks that he gives you—he acts like a star, and he *is* a star. And he did a great job," the trainer said.

According to the film's production notes, Elvis spends his spare time playing at his scratching post, running around, and hunting. His favorite food is chicken.

"Cats are not the hardest animals to train," Madrid said. "However, people don't expect as much out of them as they do a dog, for example. We teach them to come to a mark and then they are rewarded with food."

The remake of *That Darn Cat* also features a well-known supporting cast, including Academy Award–winner Estelle Parsons, Dyan Cannon, and Dean Jones, who also appeared in the first version of this classic cat comedy.

## CATS IN DRAMATIC FILMS, PART I

Numerous poignant films have been created featuring cats on journeys to find their owners.

*The Incredible Journey*, made in 1963, tells the story of a Siamese cat who joins up with a Labrador retriever and a bull terrier to find the owner they mistakenly believe has left them forever. They embark on a 250-mile trek across Canada's rugged terrain and have many adventures as they search to find their human. This live-action Walt Disney movie was based on Sheila

Burnford's noted book, and it tells the tale from the animal's point of view.

*Homeward Bound: The Incredible Journey* is a 1993 remake by Walt Disney Productions of the original *The Incredible Journey*. However, this time the animals have voices, supplied by stars Sally Field, Michael J. Fox, and Don Ameche.

*The Adventures of Milo & Otis*, made in 1989, tells the delightful story of a trouble-prone kitten named Milo who is carried away by a rushing river, and Otis, a pug-nosed pup who sets out to save his friend. The two have many adventures, which are narrated by Dudley Moore, who also supplies all of the voices for the animals in this live-action movie made by Japanese director Masanori Hata. It was a record-breaking box-office success in his homeland.

## CATS IN DRAMATIC FILMS, PART II

In the memorable 1974 movie *Harry & Tonto*, Art Carney plays an old man who travels across the country with his cat, Tonto. The film was a huge success for Carney, who won an

Academy Award for his role, as well as for Tonto, who won a Patsy Award for his part in the film as a large, aging cat who has his own leash and suitcase, purrs whenever he is scolded, and is a compassionate companion until he sadly passes away.

There is some sadness in the 1963 movie, *The Three Lives of Thomasina*, in which a little girl's pet cat, Thomasina, is diagnosed with tetanus and is put to sleep. However, in this Walt Disney fairy tale, which takes place in Scotland at the turn of the century, a mysterious healer brings the animal back to life and into the arms of the girl who had mourned her.

In the unusual French film, *Le Chat (The Cat)*, Academy Award–winning actress Simone Signoret and Jean Gabin play a long-married couple who fall out of love. The husband then transfers his affections to his pet cat, with upsetting results to the marital relationship. The movie is based on a novel by famous author Georges Simenon.

## CATS IN MYSTERY MOVIES, PART I: THE BLACK CAT

Black cats have been symbols of mystery, mayhem, and even murder in motion pictures.

One of the first famous horror films featuring felines is *The Black Cat*. Made in 1934, it featured a nameless black cat who starred with Bela Lugosi and Boris Karloff in their first movie together. *The Black Cat* was very loosely based on the famous terrifying tale by Edgar Allan Poe about a cat returning from the dead to haunt its master.

This film is still highly regarded. It has become a cult favorite because of its unusual surreal design, its pairing of Karloff and Lugosi, and because it is one of the very few films in which horror star Lugosi actually plays a good guy!

Universal Studios made another version of *The Black Cat* in 1941 that also starred Bela

Lugosi. In this adaptation of the Poe story, the film is about a woman who keeps a creepy crematorium for her adored feline pets. As it turns out, the cats are the villains in this film.

In 1981 another movie version of *The Black Cat* was made as a low-budget exploitation horror flick in Italy. The movie was so graphic, it actually garnered an "R" rating.

### CATS IN MYSTERY MOVIES, PART II: CAT PEOPLE

Perhaps the most famous horror film featuring felines is *Cat*

*People,* made in 1942 and starring Simone Simon and Kent Smith.

The movie is about a timid woman, played by Simon, who believes that she is carrying the curse of the panther with her. In one scene, Simon's character is given a kitten by her boyfriend, and the kitten hisses in terror when it is placed in her arms. In the film, this is the first clue that Simon's character has a troubled relationship with the world of cats.

*Cat People* is a very highly regarded film today, in part because the director, Jacques Tourneur, left much of the horror to the audience's imagination rather than showing it explicitly.

The same cannot be said for the 1982 remake of this scary classic. Also titled *Cat People*, the movie stars Nastassja Kinski and Malcolm McDowell, and it includes profanity, nudity, and over-the-top gore.

## CATS IN MYSTERY MOVIES: PART III

Cats have appeared in many other suspense flicks, mystery movies, and horror films of varying quality over the years. There

is something about the mysteri-
ousness of felines that attracts
the attention of filmmakers—
and audiences—all over the
world.

These feline flicks include the
1946 horror movie, *The Cat
Creeps*, which most critics con-

sidered a true horror. It tells the grisly tale of a cat who possesses a young girl's soul.

In the 1961 shocker *The Shadow of the Cat,* a cat seeks revenge for the murder of its owner.

In the 1969 thriller *Eye of the Cat,* Michael Sarrazin and Eleanor Parker star in the creepy story of a woman living in a house full of very frightening felines.

The 1973 television movie *The Cat Creature* stars Meredith Baxter and Oscar winner Gale Sondergaard in the terrifying tale of a cat goddess who possesses her victims to get a gold amulet.

And *Cat's Eye* is a star-studded 1985 thriller, based on a trio of stories written by best-selling horror author Stephen King. Featuring James Woods, Drew Barrymore, Alan King, and many others, this film stars a silver tabby who, as a stray, wanders through each of the three tales. This cat was trained by Karl Lewis Miller and Teresa Ann Miller, and many critics seemed to feel that the feline outperformed many of his costars.

## CATS IN SCIENCE
## FICTION FILMS

In the 1957 famous science-fiction hit, *The Incredible Shrinking Man*, Grant Williams plays a man who is exposed to a radioactive mist and begins to become smaller—and smaller. As a two-inch-high man, Williams is hunted by a mean-spirited house cat who, of course, is huge in comparison to him. Special effects, including the use of a giant paw, were used to show Williams fighting off the cat in this sci-fi film.

There were felines in outer

space—literally—in the aptly named 1978 Walt Disney movie, *The Cat from Outer Space*. This film tells the story of a cat who comes from beyond the stars and wears a magical collar. The cat needs help from the United States to repair its spaceship and return to its native planet, but gets involved with civilians, spies, and the military before blasting off to a happy ending. The film stars Ken Berry, Sandy Duncan, Harry

Morgan, Roddy McDowall, and Amber the cat, who won a Patsy Award for her performance.

A year later, in 1979's super-successful sci-fi film *Alien*, Sigourney Weaver, who plays Officer Ripley on the spaceship *Nostromo*, is planning her escape from the alien creature who has taken over the spacecraft. However, when she can't find her cat, Jones, Ripley panics and won't leave until she finds him—which she does.

Of course, the character Catwoman, of the hit *Batman* television series and motion pictures, always had many cats surrounding her. Whether Catwoman was played by Julie Newmar, Lee Meriwether, or Eartha Kitt on television, or by Michelle Pfeiffer on the big screen, she was rarely seen in her lair without dozens and dozens of her feline friends surrounding her.

## FELINE MOVIE MUSICALS

Ever since a real-life Gene Kelly danced with the animated Tom and Jerry cat and mouse characters in the 1945 musical *Anchors Aweigh*, felines have been featured in movie musicals.

For instance, in 1962, no less

a composer than the esteemed Harold Arlen of *Wizard of Oz* fame provided the music for the full-length animated musical, *Gay Purr-ee*. The movie featured an all-star cast of voices, including those of Judy Garland, Robert Goulet, Red Buttons, Hermione Gingold, and Mel Blanc.

This feature film told the story of a country cat named Mewsette, who goes to Paris looking for love and adventure. After winding up in the paws of a scoundrel cat named Meowrice, she is rescued by her tomcat boyfriend from home.

In 1997, another full-length animated musical featuring felines titled *Cats Don't Dance* was created. In this major movie, a song-and-dance cat named Danny goes from Kokomo, Indiana, to Hollywood seeking fame and fortune; however, his career dreams get threatened by a ruthless child actress.

Complete with original songs

written by Randy Newman, dance legend Gene Kelly was a consultant on the choreography sequences for this lively film, which features voices provided by Natalie Cole, Scott Bakula, Jasmine Guy, Hal Holbrook, Don Knotts, and George Kennedy.

## FELINE WINNERS OF THE PATSY AWARD, PART I

For almost four decades, the Patsy Awards were given out by the American Humane Association to honor the top performing animal in television and motion pictures. This award also recognized strict compliance with high humane standards in films that featured animals.

Awards were given to animals in four different categories: canine, equine, wild animals, and "special," a category that included cats. The Patsy Awards were established in 1951 and discontinued in 1989, but in those years, cats won numerous honors for their performances in film and on television.

Some of the following Patsy Award winners were actually considered accomplished actors by their peers, and others acted every inch the Hollywood star!

The feline winners of the Patsy
Award include:

1952   Orangey, *Rhubarb*
(Paramount Pictures);
Motion Pictures, First Place

1959   Pyewacket, *Bell, Book,
and Candle* (Columbia
Pictures); Motion Pictures,
First Place. Pyewacket was a
Siamese cat who played a big
part in this film costarring
Kim Novak as a witch who
tries to win James Stewart's
love.

1962   Orangey, *Breakfast at*

*Tiffany's* (Paramount Pictures); Motion Pictures, First Place

1966   Syn Cat, *That Darn Cat* (Walt Disney Productions); Motion Pictures, First Place

1973   Morris, 9-Lives cat food; Special Commercial Award, First Place

1974-Midnight, *Mannix* (Paramount); Television Series, First Place

1975   Tonto, *Harry and Tonto* (Twentieth Century–Fox Studios); Motion Pictures, First Place

1977   Seventeen, *Dr. Shrinker* (Sid and Marty Krofft);

Special Category, First Place
1978   Amber, *The Cat from Outer Space* (Walt Disney Productions); Special Category, First Place
1986   The Cats, *Alfred Hitchcock Presents* (Universal Studios); Special Category, First Place

## CATS IN ANIMATED FILMS AND TELEVISION, PART I: TOM AND JERRY

Many of the most famous cats in movies have been of the animated variety.

For instance, the cat-and-mouse duo of Tom and Jerry has been delighting movie audiences since 1940, when they appeared in the MGM short, *Puss Gets the Boot.* (Tom is the cat, as in "tomcat," of course!) Tom and Jerry have been incredibly popular in movies, on television, and on video.

Created by William Hanna and Joseph Barbera, Tom and Jerry have been so well liked that they have had their own Saturday morning television series in each of the last four decades. Their first show ran from 1965 to 1972. There was another from 1975 to 1978. A third ran from 1980 to 1982, and then there was a *Tom and Jerry Kids Show* that aired from 1990 through 1993.

Tom and Jerry's longevity even resulted in their own feature film musical, made in 1993. *Tom and Jerry: The Movie* had songs created by top motion picture composer Henry Mancini. In this film, the cartoon cat and mouse actually talk and sing, which they had never done before, thanks to the voices of Charlotte Rae, Rip Taylor, Dana Hill, and others. However, most critics agreed that these audible additions were not improvements, preferring the original cartoons instead.

## CATS IN ANIMATED FILMS AND TELEVISION, PART II: GARFIELD AND HEATHCLIFF

In more contemporary times, Garfield has been perhaps the most popular cat in comic-strip pages around the globe, as well as in his well-received television cartoon specials.

This fat and funny feline was created by Jim Davis in 1978, and starred in the first of his prime-time animated shows in 1982. Starting in 1988, Garfield became a staple of the Saturday morning cartoon lineup, where he remained as a regular in *Garfield and Friends* through 1995. On this show, Garfield's voice was supplied by Lorenzo Music, who had also found fame as the voice of Carlton the Doorman on the television series *Rhoda*.

In his specials and television series, Garfield has had many animated adventures, including "Garfield Goes Hollywood," where the wisecracking cat tries out for stardom on a show called

"Pet Search"; "Garfield in Paradise," in which he takes a vacation to a tropical island; and "Garfield: His 9 Lives," where he dreams about his past, present, and future lives.

Heathcliff is another popular comic-strip and cartoon cat. He has appeared on the big screen in *Heathcliff: The Movie,* which was a full-length, animated film actually pieced together from episodes of his cartoon television series, which appeared for many years on Saturday mornings. Heathcliff also appears on video, including various compilations put together from his television series. These videos include "Heathcliff & Cats & Co.," "Heathcliff's Double & Other Tails," and "Heathcliff and Marmaduke," in which the feisty feline teams up with the comic-strip Great Dane, Marmaduke.

## CATS IN ANIMATED FILMS AND TELEVISION, PART III: TOP CAT, FELIX THE CAT, AND THE CAT IN THE HAT

Top Cat, the flinty feline who lived in a Manhattan garbage can, was first seen as the star of a prime-time television cartoon series, *Top*

*Cat*, during the 1961–1962 season. The show then moved to Saturday mornings.

Inspired by the creative antics of comedian Phil Silvers, Top Cat was surrounded by numerous henchcats, including Benny the Ball, Choo-Choo, the Brain, Spook, and Fancy-Fancy. Arnold Stang supplied the voice of Top Cat. There was a revival of *Top Cat* in the eighties, which took the savvy cat from his New York alley to Beverly Hills when he received an unexpected inheritance.

Felix the Cat is another animated feline on the silver screen who has been popular for many decades. Felix has gotten into an amazing number of adventures in hundreds of short subject films that first appeared in movie houses and now continue to pop up on television as well.

Dr. Seuss's famous *Cat in the Hat* has also had numerous cartoon incarnations, including an acclaimed television special in 1972. Numerous cartoon sequels have followed the show business debut of the freeloading feline, and this classic cat continues to be incredibly popular.

## CATS IN ANIMATED FILMS AND TELEVISION, PART IV: WALDO KITTY, CATTANOOGA CATS, AND OTHERS

In the 1970s, there was an animated television series called *The Secret Lives of Waldo Kitty*, which was a Saturday morning takeoff on the famed James Thurber character of Walter Mitty. Waldo Kitty is a daydreaming cat who constantly gets into tussles with a pesky bulldog. In a creative twist, the animals are seen in live-action sequences, while Kitty's dream fantasies are cartoons. Some of these clever adventures have been repackaged under the title of *That's My Hero!* and can be found on video.

In addition to all of the animated felines who have filled the Saturday morning television line-up, there were also the *Cattanooga Cats*. These were actually live cats who, from 1969 through 1971, introduced animal-themed cartoon segments, including the popular Motormouse, who later got his own show.

On the big screen, cats were the villains in the 1986 animated musical film, *An American Tail*, which was produced by Steven

Spielberg. This popular feature tells the story of the cartoon mouse, Fievel, as a young Russian rodent who emigrates to America in the 1880s. He is exploited as cheap labor by his employer cats, but ultimately learns how to survive and triumph in the new land. Featuring voices of Dom DeLuise, Madeline Kahn, and Christopher Plummer, among others, the movie was also highlighted by the top-selling song, "Somewhere Out There."

In 1987 a creative, cat-themed cartoon titled *Cat City* was made in Hungary. In this James Bond spoof, the hero is a mouse who has to defuse a war-like weapon created by a group of evil cats. This animated motion picture has been dubbed into English and is available on videocassette.

## MORRIS, THE CAT KING OF COMMERCIALS, PART I

Perhaps the most famous cat in the history of show business is Morris the Cat, the orange "spokesfeline" who sold millions of cans of 9-Lives cat food.

And Morris's rags-to-riches saga easily could have been a movie of its own!

Morris was a stray discovered in 1968 by noted animal trainer Bob Martwick at the Humane Society animal shelter in Hinsdale, Illinois. Morris was stuck in a tiny cage, scheduled to be put to death. Martwick had been on a talent search for an animal to make a commercial for a mattress manufacturer. He saw the giant, orange tabby, was smitten, and paid $5 for the cat's release.

Morris was actually called Lucky—an appropriate name considering his probable fate— until later that same year when he beat out many other cats to appear in an advertising campaign for 9-Lives. In fact, the producers of the commercial were so impressed with the poised and charismatic cat that they rewrote the ads so that Morris would be the star!

The results turned out to be phenomenal, and Morris became a cultural icon.

### MORRIS, *THE CAT KING OF COMMERCIALS*, PART II

When commercials appeared starring Morris as the finicky cat who would eat nothing but 9-Lives cat food, the former stray became a sensational success!

This ad campaign continued for many years, and Morris won a special Patsy Award in 1973 for his "outstanding performance in a TV commercial." He also had roles in such movies as *Shamus* with Burt Reynolds and Dyan Cannon.

Morris became the toast of the town. He appeared on many television shows, was often seen with Hollywood stars, and even appeared at the White House, where he signed a bill by having his paw dipped in ink and making an impression on the paper.

Morris made an impression in

corporate boardrooms as well. He was named as an honorary director of Star-Kist Foods Inc., which owned 9-Lives, and was even able to give a "paws-down" on new cat food flavors developed by the company if he didn't like them!

Even with all of his success, Morris remained a friendly, cool—and very lucky—cat until he died in 1978.

# LITTLE-KNOWN FACTS ABOUT CATS

Cats may not have supernatural powers, as people once believed, but they do have abilities we don't completely understand— including the power to seemingly predict earthquakes. Some cat owners say that, shortly before quakes, their pets begin to run around in frantic agitation, bolting outside to hide at the first opportunity. In the hours just before a quake, mother cats have been known to move whole litters of kittens outdoors. Scientists think these cats are responding to subtle signs of rising tension around the geological faults where earthquakes occur. Cats may be able to sense early tremors while they're still too faint for humans to pick up. They may be responding to static electricity, which increases sharply just before a quake, or they may sense shifts in the earth's magnetic field. Cats also show some of the same agitated behavior just before volcanic eruptions and severe storms. Researchers are studying this phenomenon in the hope that we may someday be able to use our cats' prescience to protect ourselves from natural disasters.

Can your cat keep you healthy? Don't laugh. Science suggests that if you own a cat, you may live longer. Research has found that cat owners have lower rates of minor health problems like insomnia, colds, flu, backaches, headaches, and fatigue. Cats have been used in psychiatric therapy, where they can help mentally ill people release tension and learn to form healthy relationships. Some progressive nursing homes allow their residents to own cats, finding that elders are healthier when cats give them the pleasure of physical contact and the comfort of affectionate relationships.

How do cats enhance our health? Partly, it's the simple pleasure of touch. Studies have shown that the act of stroking a cat relaxes a person's muscles and calms the whole body. And partly, it's the reassurance that comes from giving and receiving love.

Cats are some of the sleepiest members of the animal kingdom. They doze twice as much as humans do, averaging sixteen hours of catnapping in every twenty-four-hour period. Unlike people, who ordinarily stay awake through the daylight hours and do all their sleeping in one long session at night, cats sleep around the clock in relatively short bursts. This sleep pattern has evolved from the cat's efficiency as a hunter. Unlike other, less ferocious beasts, a cat can hunt for its food so quickly and effectively that it has ample time left over for snoozing. Cats experience three types of sleep. Brief catnaps last only a few minutes. In light sleep, a cat may doze for perhaps half an hour. During its deepest sleep, a cat will drowse for several hours, experiencing cyclical  shifts between light sleep and deeper sleep until it's ready to awaken. During the deeper phases of sleep, cats quiver, twitch, vocalize, and show rapid-eye movements that suggest they are dreaming.

Cats fall asleep more readily than almost any other mammal. But a cat whose diet is short in the amino acid L-tryptophan, found in milk, eggs, and poultry, may lose the ability to drop off naturally. Without this nutrient, a cat will become a jittery feline insomniac!

We've all heard stories about cats who find their way home across improbable distances, turning up at their own back doors weeks after disappearing miles away.

But are these tales true? Science has determined that cats do, indeed, have an innate ability to find their way home. One researcher borrowed pet cats from their owners, shut them in closed boxes, and drove them out of town on a winding, indirect route. He put the cats into an enclosed maze, with many exits located at the points of the compass. In significant numbers, the cats chose the exits that pointed in the compass direction of their homes. When researchers then repeated the tests, they drugged the cats first so that they couldn't possibly remember the twists and turns they'd taken on their journey. These cats, too, unerringly oriented themselves toward home. Scientists have attached powerful magnets to cats in the maze, and the cats lost the ability to find the right way out. Cats, therefore, use Earth's magnetic field as a giant compass, responding to signals from iron particles embedded in their living tissue.

Why do some cats love to play with catnip toys, while others can't be bothered? Some cats have a genetic sensitivity to *hep-etalactone*, the active ingredient in catnip, but others don't. More than 50 percent of adult cats respond to the spicy-smelling herb with a ten-minute frenzy of pleasure. They lick, chew, and claw the catnip, rub their heads and bodies against it and roll in it, while purring, meowing, and even jumping with what looks like sheer delight. The rest of the cat population simply ignores the stuff. Catnip (*Nepata cataria*) apparently affects the brains of sensitive cats by "turning them on," just as some drugs affect people.

The response shows up in lions and other members of the cat family too. But kittens don't care about catnip until they reach the age of two or three months.

Catnip-sensitive cats may show a burst of uninhibited behavior in response to a few other plants, including valerian. But if your cat doesn't play with the catnip mouse you gave her for Christmas, toss it out, or give it to a friend with a more susceptible pet. Cats are either born with catnip sensitivity or they're not. It's in their genes!

The old saying "A cat always lands on its feet" isn't quite true. A cat can be injured or killed in a fall, just like any other living creature. But our feline friends have had to depend for centuries on tree-climbing to hunt for their food. In response, they've evolved a powerful righting reflex that dramatically increases their chances of landing safely in a fall. In a fraction of a second, a falling cat twists automatically through stages that researchers have identified through slow-motion photography. First, the cat's head rotates as the front legs move close below the fragile face to protect it from impact. Next, the spine twists, lining up the cat's front half with its upright head. Last, the hind legs bend up to match the forelegs while the rear half of the body finishes twisting. Just before touching down, all four legs stretch toward the ground, and the cat arches its spine to absorb the shock of impact. Throughout this twisting process, the cat's stiff tail rotates like a rudder, counterbalancing the weight of the body. This righting reflex happens so fast that in most

falls, cats do land safely on their soft, shock-absorbing paws, scampering off unhurt even from terrifying tumbles.

Are cats color-blind? Scientists once believed that cats saw the world in shades of gray. Now, they know that cats do see color—but not very well. Studies have shown that cats can distinguish among many colors, including red, green, gray, blue, and yellow. But felines are so sensitive to color value—that is, the relative darkness or lightness of a color—that they may not be able to tell two different col-

ors apart if both colors have the same level of grayness. That's how scientists were first misled into believing that cats couldn't see color at all.

Cats need sensitivity to relative brightness because their eyes are adapted to seeing in dim light. They're able to perceive movement and shape in much less light than people can. But cats don't need color to see in low-light conditions. That's probably why they don't seem to perceive colors with the intensity and sensitivity of their human companions.

Human eyes don't glow in the dark. So why do your cat's eyes shine like two green lanterns in your backyard at night? Cats' eyes don't glow with their own light, but they do have a special layer at the back of their eyes that is designed specifically to reflect light. It's called the *tapetum lucidum*, which means "bright carpet." This layer works just like a mirror at the back of the cat's eyeball, reflecting every trace of light that enters the cat's eye back toward the retina. With the help of this "bright carpet," cats are able to use all the light that's available to help them see movement and objects. Your cat can't see in absolute darkness any more than you can. To perform its light-enhancing magic trick, the *tapetum lucidum* has to have *some* available light.

Cats seem to be able to see in the dark because, in addition to their wonderfully light-adapted eyes, they use nonvisual signals from their ears, noses, and whiskers to navigate in darkness. Still, because of the structure of their eyes, cats can see shape and movement even in light so dim that their human owners are nearly helpless.

What's in a name? The word *cat* has a similar sound in languages all over the world, from the French *chat* to Italian *gatto* to *quttah* in Arabic. The Maltese say *qattus*, the Icelandic *kottur*. In Greek, a cat is *gata*, in Polish, *kot*, in Welsh, *cath*, and in Czech, *kocka*. Finns say *katti* or *kissa*. The *k* sound in all those words shows up even in countries where languages spring from different roots from the tongues spoken in Europe. In Africa,

Swahili speakers call cats *paka*. Speakers of Hindustani in India say *katas*. A Japanese cat is *neko*, and a Korean kitty is *koyangee*. Even our nicknames for our feline friends have international roots. Tabby cats probably get their name from *attabi*, a type of watered silk from Baghdad marked with wavering bars of color, like a cat's stripes. Our word *puss* may come from the name of an ancient Egyptian goddess, Pasht. Or it might derive from the old Irish-Gaelic *puus*, a word that probably began as an attempt to imitate the sound of a spitting cat.

A cat has about twenty-four movable whiskers, twelve on each side of its nose. Whiskers are more than twice as thick as ordinary hairs, and their roots are set three times deeper than hairs in a cat's tissue. Richly supplied with nerve endings, whiskers give cats extraordinarily detailed information about air movements, air pressure, and anything they touch. The scientific word for whiskers is *vibrissae*, a name that suggests their exquisite sensitivity to vibrations in air currents. As air swirls and eddies around objects, whiskers vibrate too. Cats use messages in these vibrations to sense the presence, size, and shape of obstacles without seeing or touching them. Whiskers are also good hunting tools. A cat whose whiskers have been damaged may bite the wrong part of a mouse it's attacking, indicating that signals from these delicate structures provide cats with vital information about the shape and activity of its prey.

Cats don't have facial expressions. Instead, their whole bodies show their feelings. A cat whose pupils are round may be frightened or excited, while an angry cat will narrow its pupils to threatening slits. A cat's whiskers swing forward when it is curious, threatening, or exploring. But if whiskers point backward, their feline owner is probably feeling defensive or trying to avoid touching something. Ears also signal feeling. The ears of a relaxed cat point slightly outward, but an alert cat's ears swing fully forward to point straight ahead. Upset cats may twitch their ears, and a cat under attack will flatten its ears fully against its head—a protective posture that helps to shield these fragile structures in fights.

Tails tell tales of feelings too. A bristly tail signals a furious or frightened cat. An upset cat may twitch its tail from side to side, indicating that the cat is feeling frustrated and torn between two choices—perhaps deciding whether to run for shelter or to fight back. Attackers will do well to avoid any cat whose ears are rotated backward but not fully flattened. This cat is signaling that it is furiously angry, but not yet scared enough to protect its ears by flattening them. In other words, this cat's ears are shouting a serious warning: "Watch out!"

Your cat will probably live longer than your grandmother's kitty did. A cat's life expectancy today is sixteen to eighteen years, more than twice as long as it was in the 1930s. The oldest cat on record, called Puss, died in 1939. As cat life expectancy grows, Puss may soon lose his spot in the record books. Already, at least one modern-day kitty is pressing hard on his tail. Granpa Rexs Allen, a show cat from Texas, reached the ripe old age of thirty-two in 1997. Granpa is almost bald, but his fur didn't fall out as a result of advanced age. Instead, he's been short on fur all his life because he's half-Sphynx, a breed of cat that's born hairless. His owner says that Granpa's advanced age may result from his unusual dietary preferences. This cat likes to eat broccoli! But don't start paring vegetables in the hope of extending your favorite kitty's life span. A vegetarian diet may be good for people, but it is hazardous to a cat's health. Anyway, most cats aren't nearly as fond of vegetables as long-lived Granpa. Their owners are likely to have trouble convincing them that a few extra years are worth the bother of broccoli.

Have you counted your cat's claws lately? Most cats have four toes on their hind feet and five on the front. But some cats have extra toes—as many as seven or eight on one foot! These cats are called *polydactyl*, from the Greek *polus* (many) and *daktulos* (finger). A polydactyl cat may have extra toes on just one of its feet, or on two, three, or all four of them. The extra toes result from a dominant gene that expresses itself differently in different cats. Most common on the forepaws, extra toes may not develop completely. Cats who have eight extra toes also sometimes have internal problems associated with high mortality. But most polydactyl cats are perfectly healthy. Polydactyl cats first appeared in Boston, spreading from there to Newfoundland,

Nova Scotia, and the rest of New England, where they're still common today. Sailors used to believe that cats with extra toes were good luck. By carrying them on board on their world-wide journeys, ship captains helped to disperse polydactyl cats across the seven seas.

A cat of a different color—green!—appeared in Denmark in 1996. Miss Greeny, a two-month-old kitten, was completely covered with grass-colored fur except for a gray spot on her back. Suspecting that the leafy tint wasn't natural, veterinarians tried to wash the green out of Miss Greeny's fur. But it wouldn't come out! On closer inspection, they discovered that the green color extended into the follicles below Miss Greeny's skin.

A cat's color is normally determined by its genes. The colors orange and black, for instance, are each carried on the X chromosome. Since male cats only have one X chromosome, they

can't ordinarily be calico (a mix of orange and black). A few male calico cats have turned up, though they're very rare. These cats are likely to have an extra X chromosome, and they're also probably sterile.

Miss Greeny's owner, Pia Bischoff, told Danish newspapers that vets thought her kitten's decidedly different shade could be caused by a metabolic disorder. But except for the unusual tint of her fur, Miss Greeny seems to be perfectly healthy and normal.

If you see a white cat with blue eyes, don't bother to call, "Kitty,

kitty, kitty." Chances are, the cat can't hear you. Most white cats with two blue eyes are deaf. If just one of a white cat's eyes are blue, the cat is likely to be deaf in the ear closest to the blue eye. And if the cat's eyes are orange, it probably has normal hearing. A white cat whose eyes have no color at all, causing a pink appearance when light reflects off the blood vessels in the eye, is an albino. In these cats, the pigment melanin, which gives color to skin and fur, is almost completely absent. No matter what color the rest of a cat's body is, if its ears are white, they'll be susceptible to sunburn. Just like fair-skinned people who've soaked in the sun too often, white cat ears are at risk of skin cancer. If you have a white-eared cat, use sunscreen to protect its vulnerable skin, or keep your cat inside, away from the damaging rays of the sun.

Counting cats is a tough job. Researchers estimate that between 57 and 67 million cats live in the United States. There are at least 3 million cats in Canada, 7 million in Great Britain, 35 million in western Europe, and 12 million in Australia. But nobody knows how many cats live in Africa, Asia, and South America. What's more, cat counters can't agree on *how* to count cats. Felines are often counted by keeping track of the amount of cat food purchased in a country over a period of time, rather than by counting the kitties themselves.

In the United States, for instance, cat owners spend $2.15 billion on cat food in an average year, dropping another $250 million to buy cat litter. This method is effective for counting pets, but it leaves out the millions of stray cats all over the

world who support themselves without help from humans. When researchers try to count these cats, they run into another disagreement: When is a stray a stray? Some cat counters include cats who live in cities, eating human garbage, but exclude feral cats who live with no human contact at all. Others count all unowned cats, stray or feral. The reality is that nobody knows for sure how many cats are alive on Earth today. But researchers do agree that cat numbers are increasing. That's why humane societies urge cat owners to neuter their pets, unless they're certain they can find a willing owner for every kitten in a litter.

Cats are popular pets in most countries. But in Australia, they've become Public Enemy Number One. There were no cats at all in Australia until European colonists imported them as they settled the isolated continent more than 200 years ago. With no cats preying on them, the continent's native species evolved without the natural ability to protect themselves from feline ferocity. Now, about 12 million cats call Australia home. These immigrant felines have been so successful at hunting lyrebirds, woylies, boodies, and other native animals that they've driven some species to near-extinction. To save Australia's unique species, many of whom exist nowhere else on Earth, one politician has called for the total eradication of all cats in the country by the year 2000. There's even a new slogan: "Do Australia a favor—kill a cat." Not all Australians agree that cats have to go. Instead, cat lovers are working for reasonable precautions, like neutering, that should allow responsible cat ownership while also protecting Australia's precious native animals. A 1991 law requiring household cats to be kept indoors has already helped the lyrebird population. But so many stray cats still hunt vulnerable Australian wildlife that it remains to be seen whether cats and kangaroos will ever coexist peacefully Down Under.

Scent defines a cat's world much

as vision defines ours. A cat's exquisite sensitivity to scent is one of the reasons you'll often see your cat wash herself thoroughly right after you've petted her. When you stroke your cat, sweat glands in your hands transfer your scent to your cat, covering up her own. Even though your cat may love to be handled, she does not like smelling "wrong." After a petting session, she won't feel fully comfortable until she has fixed matters by making sure she smells like herself again. She may also enjoy tasting you, as she licks your scent carefully off every square inch of her fur.

Cats are territorial creatures who know where they belong. The size of your cat's range depends on where you live, how much you feed your pet, and whether your cat is a male or a female. Male cats cover about ten times as much ground as females do. In the country, a male farm cat may hunt, explore, and lay claim to 150 acres of land, while females limit themselves to a range of fifteen acres on average. Wild cats range farthest of all, covering territories up to 175 acres. But ur-

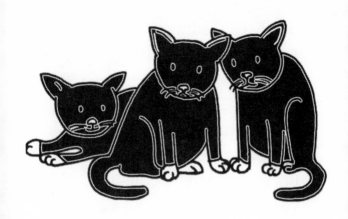

ban cats limit themselves to much smaller territories than their rural counterparts. Cats in crowded cities may never leave an area of about one-fifth of an acre around their homes. An urban pet cat may define its territory by the size of its own backyard. Researchers have established that stray city cats range farther than their pampered pet  cousins, showing that a cat's territory shrinks in direct proportion to how much food is provided by its owner.

Female cats' territories may overlap, with shared neutral areas where cats can meet without conflict. Male cats are less likely to share portions of their territories with other male cats. But a male cat's territory *will* in-

clude the ranges of several females, allowing the male to
check on every member of his
harem as he pads through his
daily rounds.

# FUNNY, AMAZING, AND TRUE CAT TALES

## RESCUE ME!

Who says cats have no compassion toward dogs? The Los Angeles S. P. C. A. gave an award to Thug, a tomcat, for saving the life of a dog. Missy the Labrador was in danger of drowning under a pier when Thug saw her and began to howl. Her cries got the attention of nearby people, who pulled the dog from the water and saved her life.

NOT WHAT HE WANTED
TO HEAR!

A friend of Dorothy Parker's was upset to find out that his cat was terminally ill and would need to be put down. He wondered aloud, "How could I possibly kill my cat?" Parker, a writer well known for her witty remarks, then replied: "Have you tried curiosity?"

## HE CHANGED HIS TUNE

Harrison Weir attended and wrote about the world's first cat show, held at London's Crystal Palace in 1871. En route to the show, he met a friend who, hearing where Weir was off to, spent some time berating felines. Weir somehow convinced the man to accompany him to the cat show.

A few months later, Weir visited his friend, only to find him in the company of two happy, sleeping cats. Apparently, the cat show had impressed the former cat hater!

## CATS 1, BIRDS 0

When Adlai Stevenson was governor of Illinois, he once vetoed a bill to keep cats from wandering out of their owners' yards and, thereby, killing birds. He didn't believe it was possible to legislate a change in cats' behavior, saying,: "[It is the] na-

ture of cats to do a certain amount of unescorted roaming. The problem of cat versus bird is as old as time."

## BOMBS AWAY!

Cat ears can detect sounds with higher frequencies than human ears can. In World War II England, cats would become agitated before bombs landed near their owners' homes. Families learned that once their cat became upset, it meant another attack was on the way, so they knew it was time to slip into the bomb shelter.

## CANARY-GATE?

Timmie the cat belonged to a Washington newspaperman, Bascom Timmons, in the 1920s. Timmons used to take the kitty to the White House for visits with President Coolidge and his

canary, Caruso. Caruso and Timmie got along famously. Caruso
would walk across Timmie's
back, singing as he went, and he
would even rest in the cat's paws.
Eventually, the president gave
Caruso to Timmons.

## BREAKING THE CODE

A Los Angeles Siamese, Missy,
liked to run across her owner's
computer keyboard, perhaps to
chase the mouse. One day, she
pawed a combination of letters
that turned out to be a code
that deleted $50,000 worth of
files from a local business's com-

puter. The company had to repair its entire computer system.

## NEWTON'S FIRST LAW . . .
## OF CATS

Sir Isaac Newton, English physicist and mathematician, cut an
opening in the bottom of a door
in his house so his cat could pass
in and out at will. When the cat
had kittens, Newton made a
smaller hole next to the original
one.

## THAT ENGINE PURRS LIKE A KITTEN

Imagine Jerry Ditzig's surprise when he pulled two mewing kittens out of the engine of his boat. Before the Bud Lite International Outboard Grand Prix in Missouri, he was doing practice laps when he discovered the wet stowaways, who were later named, appropriately, Speed and Racer.

## DO YOU TAKE CREAM IN YOUR CAT?

A White House guest who was

breakfasting with President Calvin Coolidge was surprised to see his host pour some coffee into a saucer, then add milk and sugar. Thinking he ought to follow etiquette, the guest began to pour his own coffee into a saucer. When he looked up, the president had placed the warm drink on the floor for the White House cat.

## TASTES LIKE CHICKEN

Imprisoned by Henry VIII in the tower of London, Sir Henry Wyatt was close to starvation until his cat showed up at his cell with a pigeon for him to dine on.

## A SWEET TRIBUTE

British prime minister Winston Churchill adored his cat Jock, whom he received for his eighty-eighth birthday. Jock lived at Chartwell, Churchill's famous home, for years after his master died. There was a clause in Churchill's will that stipulated that a marmalade cat shall always be kept at Chartwell; he also left a nice sum of money to cover room and board for all the "Jocks" that would live after the original. The house is open to the public, where visitors can see the present Jock look-alike.

## MIGHTY MOUSER

Mickie, a cat employed as a mouser for Shepherd and Son Ltd. in Lancashire, England, is reported to have caught more than 22,000 mice while on patrol for the business from 1945 to 1968.

## THAT'S THE WAY THE COOKIE . . . WANDERS

Dogs usually get all the credit for being able to find their way home after getting lost, or finding their owner's new house during a move. However, in December

1949, Cookie the cat proved that felines have quite good navigational instincts too. Cookie got shipped (accidentally, we hope) from her home in Chicago to Wilber, Nebraska, 550 miles away. Then six months later, she was back on the doorstep in Chicago.

## KITTY IN THE CORNER POCKET

Mark Twain, self-proclaimed cat lover, had a kitten that liked to snuggle itself into a corner pocket of Twain's billiard table. From there, it would watch—and disrupt—the game by batting at the billiard balls.

## THE GREATEST SHOW IN FUR

Englishman Leoni Clarke had a troupe of fifty performing cats. These acrobatic felines walked on tightropes, stepping over arrangements of mice, rats, and canaries. They also jumped through flaming hoops.

## THAT'LL BUY A LOT OF CAT FOOD!

It's not totally unheard-of for cats to inherit estates and large bank accounts when a wealthy owner dies. Take Hellcat and Brownie, for instance. In the 1960s, these two lucky pusses received almost half a million dollars from their owner's estate.

# BELIEVE IT OR NOT

Cats are the most popular pets in America! They surpassed their canine contenders in popularity during the mid-1980s. According to the latest estimates, there are more than 66 million pet cats in the United States as opposed to approximately 58 million dogs. This means that nearly one in three American households has a pampered puss in it.

Americans don't have a term for a mixed-breed cat (in other words, the feline equivalent of a mutt)! But in England they call their nonpedigreed cats "moggies." Perhaps this name will catch on in America?

A whopping 95 percent of cat owners talk to their cats!

Many of the worst dictators in history were also cat haters. Hitler, Mussolini, Napoleon, and

Genghis Khan are all said to have been enemies of felines—and they didn't seem to fare any better with people. Perhaps cat-hating should be considered a sign . . .

A one-year-old cat is considered to be the age equivalent of a sixteen-year-old human. However, this ratio does not stay the same through their life spans. A twelve-year-old cat is approximately the same age as a sixty-four-year-old person, while a twenty-two-year-old cat would be 104 in people years!

Owning a cat can lower your blood pressure, cut your cholesterol level, and possibly even save you from a heart attack. According to a University of Pennsylvania study, doctors found that petting a cat can reduce both a human's heart rate and blood pressure. Researchers have also shown that the survival rate for heart patients with pets is considerably higher than for those who have no animal companionship.

The most popular names for cats today are said to be Tiger and Samantha.

In China, there actually are seismologists with cats who use their
furry friends to save thousands of
lives. For instance, in 1975 in
Haicheng, China, these scientists saw their cats acting in a
strange manner and then alerted
city officials to evacuate the area.
Twenty-four hours
later, a devastat-
ing earthquake
hit and caused
tremendous dam-
age—which would
have been a lot worse
had it not been for
the warning.

Nobody knows for certain what makes a cat purr! Some scientists believe that the sound comes from false vocal cords, which are a bundle of membranes that are located near the cat's actual vocal cords.

Other researchers think purring originates from the vibrations of the hyoid apparatus, a series of small bones that connects the cat's skull to its larynx, and that also helps to support its tongue.

Still others believe that purring

is created by the pressure of a cat's blood as it passes through its chest. There is another group that insists the sound comes from the puss's voice box when its mouth is closed.

Even though the reason is still unknown, a cat's purring is one of the most pleasing sounds a pet lover can hear. However, owners should know that cats don't just purr when they're happy. In fact, cats will purr for many reasons—even when they are hurt or frightened. For instance, by purring, a cat may try to pacify an enemy animal.

Cats that live indoors tend to live twice as long as cats that are allowed to go outside. With all the dangers from traffic, diseases, and other animals, being out and about can end up curtailing a kitty's life.

Chocolate can be fatal to your feline. It may be mouthwatering to you, but your dandy dessert contains oxalic acid and alkaloid theobromine, both of which can be very harmful to your kitty.

The average mass-produced cat meal is equivalent in quantity to five mice! (Yum.)

Most felines dislike orange and lemon rinds. This can be a boon to you if your curious cat likes to dig its paws into your furniture. Rubbing an orange rind on your furniture will often dissuade your puss from using it as a scratching post.

Some male cats will rub up to certain shampoos and hand creams in your medicine chest! This is because they contain an ingredient called methylparaben—which has a scent resembling a female feline in heat.

Cat hairs *do* stick to your clothes more than the hair of almost any other animal! There are a number of reasons for this. One is that a cat's hair is considered to be the most electrostatic. Another is that a cat has three types of hairs. They have primary hairs with microscopic barbs on them that make them more susceptible to sticking to clothes. They also have "awn" hairs that tend to be rough and clingy. Finally, they have secondary hairs that, because they are so thin, easily get caught in the rougher fibers of most human clothing.

The result? Hairy clothes!

It's possible that, unlike humans, most cats are left-pawed! There has not been much research on this subject, but in tests, a majority of cats seem to have a noticeable preference for using one paw more than the other. And of that majority, two-thirds prefer to use their left paw instead of their right to reach for food.

Cats *do* have belly buttons! Even though felines are born from amniotic sacs, they have belly buttons that are, in essence, a scar located next to the rib cage. However, because most cats have so much fur, these are often very hard to see.

All kittens are born deaf, blind— and with blue eyes! Their sense of hearing comes quickly as they grow, while their sight will usually develop completely in about a month and a half. Their eye color will change over the course of their first four months of life. Cats have three eyelids! This third lid is called a nictitating membrane, which helps to keep your kitty's eyes moist.

Cats have such great hearing that they can tell your footsteps are approaching—from hundreds of feet away! Your puss also seems to have perfect pitch and will often leave the room when a singer or musician is performing off-key. (Everybody's a critic!)

You should *never* trim a cat's whiskers. Intrepid felines need them to find their way in the dark or to figure out how they can get into—or out of—tight spots.

You shouldn't give most cats a bath. Some soaps can remove a feline's important natural oils. Water can also chill the cat, leaving it vulnerable to sickness.

Many cats will try to get your attention when you are talking on the telephone because they do not see anyone else in the room and think you are talking to them!

There once was a talking cat! Peter Alupka was known as "The Wonder Cat" when he performed in the 1920s with the Circus Busch in Berlin, Germany. This cat had been taught to cry out names such as "Helen" and "Anna," to sing along with songs, and to cry out "Hurrah!" at the end of his act.

In fact, this conversational cat was so famous that his performance was recorded.

There *have* been flying cats—in a manner of speaking. According to *The Cat Name Companion*, by Mark Bryant, a California cat in the 1920s is said to have jumped on a duck's back and flown in the air until the scared duck landed again. And supposedly in 1939, a cat in Turkey was picked up by an eagle who soared away and then dropped the poor puss from a great height. However, except for a broken leg and a clipped tail, the cat survived and soon recovered from its unexpected flight.

Some cats are said to have wings. Over the course of the century, photographs have been taken of winged cats on both sides of the Atlantic Ocean. One such cat is

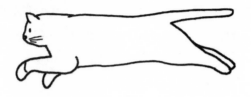

said to have been killed after swooping down on a child in Sweden in 1949. The documentation of such cats, however, is about as reliable as the "proof" of the Loch Ness Monster.

There were once cat-racing tracks in England! In fact, the first official cat racetrack opened in Dorset, in 1936. This track was a 220-yard circuit, and more than fifty felines would chase after an electric mouse. There were other cat racetracks in the country as late as 1949. However, the sport never seemed to catch on like horse or dog racing.

A cat was once elected to the student senate of Southern Illi-

nois University in September 1971. The cat, D. E. Gordon Oltman, won the election on a platform concerning the problem of stray dogs roaming the campus. This political puss was actually entered in the campaign by its owner, Diane Oltman, to prove that students paid little attention to the way they cast their votes.

The expression that someone "let the cat out of the bag" actually has a lot to do with pigs. In medieval times, pigs were often stuffed into burlap bags when they were sold at fairs. Because customers could not see what they were buying, they might—and often did—end up with a cat instead of a pig!

The only way they would know for certain is when they "let it out of the bag."

The expression that it is "raining cats and dogs" comes from a country where there seems to be as much snow as rain!

In Norse legends, animals were supposed to have magic powers. For instance, cats were rumored to be able to create storms. Dogs were symbols of wind. Hence, in Scandinavia, when it was "raining cats and dogs," it meant there was a violent storm full of wind and rain.

The legend that a cat has nine lives is said to have come from the ancient Egyptians, who were amazed at how cats could survive falls from great heights unscathed.

There is a breed of cat that looks like a dog. The Peke-faced Persian has very canine-like characteristics. Many cats through the ages have had doggy propensities: It is said that the ancient Egyptians would use cats when they went hunting, much as dogs are used today. Images of felines retrieving prey have been found on several relics and tombs in Egypt.

The hairless cat is not really hairless! The Sphynx cat seems to have no hair, but actually is covered in a very fine layer of fur.

There is a word in the English language if you suffer from the delusion that you are a cat. It is *galeanthropy*.

According to *The Whole Kitty Catalog* by John Avalon Reed, our feline friends are subject to some pretty strange laws in the United States.

For instance, cats in Idaho are legally prohibited from joining in a fight between two dogs.

In Dallas, any cat running in the street after sundown must wear a headlight.

In Lemonine, Montana, cats must wear three bells to warn birds of their approach.

In Morrisburg, Louisiana, cats may not chase ducks down city streets.

In Natchez, Mississippi, cats are forbidden to drink beer.

# WELL-BRED CATS

## THE SPOTTED EGYPTIAN MAU

In Egyptian, "mau" means "cat." Some trace the Mau's ancestry back to the ancient cats pictured in Egyptian temples and revered as gods. Others claim that the Mau's resemblance is only a result of selective breeding. In either case, the Mau is the only naturally spotted domestic breed.

This medium-size, shorthaired cat has soft, silky fur. Its banded legs and tail, the barred M on its forehead, and gooseberry-green eyes give it a distinctive appearance. But years of inbreeding have created health problems:

heart disease, knee problems, and missing limbs.

Although the Mau is gentle and affectionate with its own family, it may be shy or aloof with strangers. Alert and observant, these cats will often chirp to warn their owners of a stranger's approach.

### THE ACTIVE, AGILE ABYSSINIAN (AB-AH-SIN-EE-AN)

The Abyssinian probably originated near the Indian Ocean or in Southeast Asia, not in Abyssinia (now Ethiopia). When

British soldiers left Abyssinia in 1868, they brought some of these cats home. Soon, the British were importing them from Abyssinia.

The first of this breed arrived in the United States in the early 1900s. Americans fell in love with this graceful-looking cat with long, slender legs and neck. Its soft, silky fur lies close to its body. Each hair has alternating dark and light bands, tipped with the darker color, giving the coat a ticked effect.

This intelligent cat can be trained to do stunts. Abyssinians appear in television commercials and movies. They love company and will follow their owners around the house. Although they make great companions, Abyssinians aren't lap cats—they're explorers. These fearless cats love high places, such as banisters and refrigerators. There's never a dull moment with an Abyssinian in the house.

## SAVED FROM EXTINCTION: THE TURKISH ANGORA

For centuries, Turkish Angoras roamed the region of Angora, now Ankara, the Turkish capital. They first arrived in Europe in the 1600s. Early in the twentieth century, indiscriminate breeding virtually eliminated them as a breed. But in 1962, American servicemen discovered Turkish Angoras in the Ankara Zoo. Back in the forties, zoo officials had started their own breeding program to prevent the extinction of one of their national treasures.

This small- to medium-size longhaired cat has a long, lithe body. Unlike any other breed, the Angora carries its plumelike tail horizontally over its body, with the tail's tip brushing its neck. The very fine hairs of the Angora's single coat shimmer as it walks.

These affectionate, gentle cats often choose one or two special family members to whom they devote much of their attention. They prefer a calm household where someone makes sure the cat's eating area and litter box are spotless.

## TURKISH VAN: THE SWIMMING CAT

This ancient breed probably originated in central and southwest Asia. It's thought that the breed took its name from Lake Van (pronounced "Von") located in southeastern Turkey. In

1955, two British women vacationing in Turkey returned home with two Turkish Van kittens, starting this breed's development in Great Britain. Nearly thirty years later, Vans arrived in the United States.

Turkish Vans are white, semi-longhaired cats with distinctive markings on their head, ears, and bushy tail. This piebald pattern in other breeds is called the Van pattern. Their soft, silky coat is waterproof. These big, broad cats often grow to be three feet long.

Unlike other domestic breeds, Vans love to swim. If a lake or stream isn't available, they'll settle for a sink or tub. At home, they're affectionate and enjoy amusing themselves with toys, playing hide-and-seek, and retrieving.

## THE PLACID PERSIAN

These longhaired cats may have originated in Persia (now called Iran), but hieroglyphic references to similar cats, dating from 1684 B.C., cast some doubt on that assumption. But, whatever their origin, there's no doubt that the Persian is the most popular longhaired breed.

Long-term breeding has changed its original look. Today's modern Persian has a massive head with a round, flat face that looks as if someone pushed in on its short snub nose. The traditional "doll-faced" Persian has a more moderate-looking head with a normal nose. Both have short, squat, stout bodies with thick, woolly coats. Their dense undercoat causes the outer coat—which can grow up to six inches long—to fluff out from the body.

This luxurious coat needs daily maintenance, but these placid cats won't mind sitting still for their grooming. Although some Persians remain playful into adulthood, most prefer to lounge and sleep. Their quiet, gentle manner makes them perfect indoor cats.

### THE GOOD LUCK KORAT

In Thailand, the Korat symbolizes wealth and good luck. This silvery blue cat's Thai name is Si-Sawat (see-sah-what). *Si* means "color" and *sawat* is a wild fruit with a silvery blue seed. When presented with a Si-Sawat, King Rama V of Siam (now Thailand) named it the

Korat after the province from which it came.

The Korat's short, blue fur lies close to its body. Silver tipping on each hair makes the coat shine. This sweet, gentle cat has a heart-shaped face with huge round eyes that change from blue to amber to luminous green as it ages.

When first placed in a home, the Korat forms strong bonds with one or two family members. From them, this cat demands attention. The lap-loving Korat enjoys petting. Strangers, sudden noises, and boisterous pets and children scare them, so the Korat

does best in a quiet, orderly
home.

## THE ROYAL CATS OF SIAM:
### THE SIAMESE

The world first learned about
this cat when the royal family of

Siam (now Thailand) gave pairs as gifts to visiting dignitaries. Although these cats had roamed the royal rooms of Siam for centuries, they may have originated elsewhere. The Siamese people called them "Chinese cats." When these handsome cats arrived in Europe in the late 1800s and in the United States in the early 1900s, people clamored for more.

Heavily built, with round heads and small ears, these early Siamese were called "apple-heads" and are now referred to as "traditional" Siamese. Early breeders bred for length. The resulting "classic" Siamese had a longer head, body, and legs. Breeders didn't stop there. Modern Siamese have extremely slender bodies with long, narrow heads and huge flared ears. These "extreme" Siamese are mainly show cats because their personalities are as extreme as their appearance.

All Siamese are "pointed cats." Their pale-colored bodies have darker colors on their points: face, ears, legs, and tail. The original point colors were seal (dark brown), chocolate (milk chocolate), blue (bluish gray), and lilac (pinkish gray).

Their short, silky coat enhances their long, graceful look. The crowning touch on these beautiful cats is their slanted, almond-shaped eyes that shine a deep, sapphire blue.

Siamese are loudmouths. Experiments reveal that they use eleven consonants and all the vowels in their vocalizations. They're fastidious, fussy cats with strong opinions and an independent will that drives some people crazy and endears them to others. The latter appreciate their affectionate, intelligent personality. Their nimble paws can empty drawers and flush toilets. For people who crave a talkative, cuddly companion, the Siamese is the perfect cat.

## BIRMAN: THE SACRED CAT OF BURMA

In Burma, many believe that the souls of departed priests return to their temples in the form of Birman cats. Natural breeding between shorthaired Siamese and longhaired, free-running cats may explain the origin of these longhaired, pointed cats. In 1919, a pair of Birmans were shipped to France. The male died en route, but the pregnant female survived to start this breed in the Western world.

This large, blue-eyed cat has a light-colored, longhaired coat with a darker color marking its face, legs, and tail—its "points." A silky ruff surrounds its neck. Unlike other pointed cats, the Birman has four distinctively white paws.

Birmans are quiet, dignified cats that don't demand attention. They'll happily play by themselves while their owner is busy. They're active, but not athletic, so they don't tend to get into trouble. These easygoing cats do well in multiple-pet households.

## THE BECKONING BOBTAILS OF JAPAN

Stylized, ceramic statues of Japanese Bobtails with one paw raised in welcome sit in the doorways and windows of many Japanese homes and stores. These "good luck" Japanese cats first arrived from China or Korea more than a thousand years ago.

This small- to medium-size

cat's three-inch tail is as unique to it as a set of fingerprints. Each tail is distinctly kinked, curved, notched,  and/or angled. The tail hairs grow out in all directions, resembling a pom-pom. The Japanese favor Bobtails with brilliant red and black patches on white. This color combination is called *mi-ke* (MEE-kay), Japanese for "three-furred."

These talkative cats respond to human conversation with chirps, hums, clicks, and chants. Their fearless adaptability and sweet tempers make them excellent travelers and children's pets. However, this active, strong-willed cat requires companionship and activity or it may behave destructively.

## SKOGKATT: THE NORWEGIAN FOREST CAT

For centuries, this hardy, long-haired cat stalked the vermin of Scandinavian farms. It's thought that *Skogatt*, as they are known in their native land, might have resulted from interbreeding between shorthaired cats left by the Vikings and longhaired cats brought by the returning Crusaders. On their own in the forests, they developed the characteristics necessary for survival in the harsh northern environment.

The Skogkatt's thick, water-repellent outercoat shields against rain and snow. Its woolly undercoat insulates from the cold. A thick ruff and full bib protect its neck and chest. While waiting for prey, this hunter covers its feet with its thick, bushy tail. Long tufts of hair on its wide paws create miniature snowshoes. Three- to four-inch hairs in the ears protect against frostbite.

Although these large cats love the outdoors, they do well as indoor cats if given adequate room and a climbing tree. They're gentle, friendly, intelligent, and soft-spoken.

## THE ARCHANGEL CAT: RUSSIAN BLUE

Legend holds that Russian czars kept these cats. When the czar exiled former friends, their Russian Blues traveled with them to such faraway places as Arkhangelsk, located on the White Sea, roughly 150 miles south of the Arctic Circle. Six

hundred years ago, ships visiting this far northern seaport picked up these regal cats and brought them to distant shores. That's how they received their name: the Archangel Cat.

How did this shorthaired cat survive the Arctic cold? The Blue's fur stands out from his body in a plush, double coat and has been compared to the coat of the seal and beaver. Tips of silver on each gray-blue hair give the coat a lustrous sheen. This coat plus vivid green eyes make the Russian Blue a handsome cat.

In the days of the czars, Russian Blues were trained to jump through hoops and somersault. Today, these intelligent cats open doors and enjoy playing fetch. And when attention isn't available, the undemanding Blue will entertain itself.

## THE CALM, CONTENTED BRITISH SHORTHAIR

Nearly 2,000 years ago, Roman soldiers brought domestic cats to Britain. Natural breeding among these cats produced several varieties, one of them being the British Shorthair. Through the ages, the British have valued them as rodent exterminators.

*Round* describes this large, stocky cat. The Brit's chubby, round cheeks and curved-up lips inspired the Cheshire cat's smile in *Alice in Wonderland*. Of all cats, the British Shorthair probably has the densest coat. Blue-gray is the most popular color, but Brits come in many colors and patterns.

Although young Brits like to play, adults prefer to lie around and sleep. Nothing bothers the placid British Shorthair, not even large dogs. These peaceful, quiet cats are easy to live with. Because they're a favorite with animal trainers, they've appeared in numerous films and television commercials. This is the perfect cat for the busy family with little time to fuss over the cat.

## THE BLUE CATS OF FRANCE: CHARTREUX (SHAR-TROO)

Roman crusaders returning from Turkey and Iran may have brought the Chartreux's ancestors to France. Whatever their origin, these blue-gray cats have wandered the French countryside for centuries. Commoners prized them for their hunting abilities and pelts.

Their soft, dense, blue-gray coat is woolly and water repellent. Slightly longer than most shorthair coats, it stands out from their body. Silver tipping gives it a sheen. The strong, sturdy Chartreux are large cats, with males weighing up to sixteen pounds. Because of their curved lips, these gentle giants always appear to be smiling.

The Chartreux's tiny voice is seldom heard. One breeder describes this feline as "slightly more talkative than a stuffed cat." That's indicative of their unassuming ways. They enjoy being with people, but not underfoot. These tolerant, gentle cats make good travelers, and they don't mind being left alone for long periods of time.

## THE TAILLESS MANX

Spontaneous mutations resulting in tailless cats have occurred throughout the centuries and around the world. However, when this mutated gene occurred or arrived hundreds of years ago on the small, isolated Isle of Man off the coast of England, it perpetuated itself, creating the famous Manx breed.

Not all of these round-looking, shorthaired cats are tailless. "Rumpies" are the truly tailless cats. "Risers" have a small knob, while "Stumpies" have a movable stump. Fully tailed Manx are essential for healthy breeding since the gene responsible for the taillessness is lethal when doubled. "Rumpies" shouldn't be bred together. Tailed Manx are rarely seen since breeders dock the kittens' tails to avoid a painful arthritic condition in adult cats that often requires the tail's amputation.

Like dogs, Manx retrieve objects, follow their owner, bury their toys, and growl at suspicious noises. If let outdoors, they're dedicated hunters, but these even-tempered cats make perfectly contented indoor pets as well.

## AMERICAN SHORTHAIR: THE "ALL-AMERICAN" WORKING CAT

The ships carrying the first settlers to the New World had cats on board to kill the shipboard rats. When the passengers disembarked, so did the cats. On land, they worked as farm cats. In the late 1800s, Siamese and Persians mated with these cats, producing a mixed breed. Alarmed that this would be the end of the American

Shorthair, some breeders began selective breeding to preserve this uniquely American cat.

Although "mixed-breed" cats often resemble the American Shorthair, differences exist. A litter of mixed-breed cats may contain short- and longhaired kittens having different temperaments. A litter of American Shorthairs contains only short-haired kittens with quiet, sweet dispositions.

Easygoing American Shorthairs adapt to any living situation from the barn to the apartment. Their hard, protective coats come in more than eighty different colors and patterns. Although most don't enjoy cuddling, they'll purr contentedly, curled up beside their owner's feet.

## MAINE'S STATE CAT: THE MAINE COON

America's only naturally occurring longhaired breed probably evolved from the first settlers' domestic shorthaired cats and free-running longhaired cats. The longhairs may have been seafaring cats that jumped ship or cats the Vikings introduced to the New World. Natural selection and Maine's harsh climate created this large, rugged breed.

The Coon's long, shaggy coat

resists water and provides warmth. The large paws act as snowshoes. Thick tufts of hair protect the cat's ears from frostbite. Its resemblance to a raccoon earned this breed its name: Black stripes ring the Maine Coon's tail, and the cat's most common color, brown tabby, resembles the raccoon's coloring.

Like raccoons, Maine Coons are intelligent and agile. They like to jump and climb, and are superior hunters and playful clowns. Even older Coons act like kittens, willingly playing fetch or chasing marbles. These even-tempered cats make great pets for active families with children.

## THE DRAIN CATS OF SINGAPORE: THE SINGAPURA (SIN-GA-POO-RA)

The Singapura roamed Singapore's streets, fending for themselves and taking refuge in the gutters, earning them the name "drain cats." An American working in Singapore brought some back to the United States in the seventies, and breeding efforts began shortly thereafter.

This smallest of the cats weighs six pounds or less. It has

a ticked coat of dark brown against an ivory background. Very large ears and eyes give it an expressive, alert look. Singapuras have an unusual gait; like lions, they move with a sinuous, rolling amble.

The Singapura's compact size and silky coat make it irresistible for hugging. Although this feline is affectionate with its own family and follows them

around the house, it's shy with strangers. The Singapura loves curling up in warm places: on laps, near heating ducts, in spots of sunshine, and under blankets. When it's not cuddling, this inquisitive cat can be found exploring all the home's high places.

## BURMESE: THE SMILING CLOWNS

Wong Mau, a sable-brown cat, arrived in the United States in the 1930s from Burma. Her owner mated her with a Seal Point Siamese. Over time, selective breeding of Wong Mau and her kittens resulted in a new breed, the Burmese.

These medium-size cats carry a lot of weight for their size and have been called "bricks wrapped in silk." *Round* describes their heads, feet, chests, eyes, and even  their ear tips. Their thick whisker pads and tipped-up mouth corners make them appear as if they're always smiling.

These clowns entertain with their acrobatics and mischievous tricks. They drape themselves around necks and perch atop shoulders. These attention-loving cats curl up in laps or snuggle next to their owner in bed. Since the Burmese have few survival instincts, they need to be kept inside. That can be difficult, however, as these escape artists rival Houdini.

## HAVANA BROWNS: THE CONSTANT COMPANIONS

In the 1950s, English breeders set out to develop a brown, Siamese-built cat. They crossed a Siamese with mixed-ancestry, black shorthairs to produce Havana Browns. Some insist this breed was named after a brown rabbit by that name. Others claim that the color they share with the Havana cigar inspired the name.

Their glassy-smooth, short-haired coat looks like polished mahogany and feels like mink. Each hair is brown from its root to its tip. Even this cat's whiskers are brown. Its green eyes, protruding corncob-shaped muzzle, and forward-tilting, large ears give the medium-size Havanas a distinct appearance.

These gentle cats enjoy constant physical contact and will ride around on people's shoulders or worm their way onto laps. When they feel ignored, they'll tap their owner gently with their paw to gain attention. Their quiet friendliness, as well as their front paw, is almost always offered to all.

## THE BOMBAY: A PETITE PANTHER

In 1953, a Kentucky breeder set out to create a pantherlike cat. She crossed a grand champion Burmese with a black American Shorthair. After years of selective breeding, she succeeded in creating the Bombay, so named because of its resemblance to the black leopard of Bombay, India.

The Bombay's black-to-the-roots coat lies close to the body, shimmers like patent leather, and feels like satin. Its large, wide-set, gold to deep copper eyes shine like lights in the night. This muscular, small to medium-size cat is heavier than it looks.

These agile cats have no fear of heights. They enjoy playing with people and purr when held. Like dogs, Bombays fetch objects and can be taught to walk on a leash. These petite panthers will even guard your house!

## EXOTIC SHORTHAIR: THE BUSY PERSON'S PERSIAN

The breeding of Persians with shorthaired cats such as the Burmese, American, and British Shorthairs, and even the Russian Blue resulted in the creation of the Exotic Shorthair. Today, only outcrossings with Persians are allowed to maintain this breed's standards.

Exotic Shorthairs look like shorthaired Persians. They have

the same pushed-in face and short, chunky body. Their dense, plush, double coat stands out from their body and doesn't mat or tangle.

They're the perfect cat for the person who wants a Persian, but doesn't have the time to groom it. Like the Persian, Exotic Short-hairs are quiet, undemanding cats that enjoy sleeping. They're slightly more responsive and playful than Persians and, even as adults, enjoy jumping for a toy on a stick or batting a piece of paper across the floor.

## ORIENTAL SHORTHAIRS: COLORFUL SIAMESE

Old books from Siam describe Siamese cats of other colors than the pointed, but since the Siamese Cat Club of Britain only allowed pointed Siamese in their competitions, breeders stopped breeding anything other than pointed Siamese. The other colors disappeared from the Siamese gene pool. In the 1950s, several breeders crossed Siamese with domestic shorthairs to see if they could bring back some of these other colors and patterns. These colorful Siamese were eventually named Oriental Shorthairs. Today, this breed boasts more than 300 different colors and patterns. All have the familiar Siamese build and personality.

## THE CURLY CAT OF CORNWALL: THE CORNISH REX

In 1950, a spontaneous mutation created a long-limbed,
curly-coated male in a litter of
straight, shorthaired kittens. By
selectively breeding this male,
his owner produced more curly-
coated kittens. She named this
new breed "Cornish Rex" because of the similarity of its coat
to that of the "Rex" rabbit,
whose fur trimmed the royal

robes of King Henry VIII.

Large, flared ears sit atop the Rex's small, narrow head, giving this cat a "space alien" look. His curly coat feels silky soft, but doesn't hold in body heat. In order to stay warm, this cat's metabolism works harder and requires more food.

Muscular legs enable this athletic cat to jump high, start quickly, reverse directions in a flash, and chase at high speeds. This gymnast loves to wriggle into nooks and crannies. One breeder described these active, friendly cats as "slightly less lively than a hurricane."

## THE DELIGHTFUL, DEVOTED DEVON REX

Ten years after the Cornish Rex mutation, a similar mutation occurred in Devonshire, England. A male kitten named Kirlee had a curly, black coat. When he was bred to Cornish Rex females, only straight-haired kittens resulted. Obviously, a different gene mutation had caused Kirlee's curly coat. From then on, each breed developed separately. Kirlee's descendants were named Devon Rex.

The Devon's batlike ears, prominent cheekbones, and

enormous wide-set eyes give it a pixielike appearance. Compared to the Cornish Rex, Devon Rex have a smaller build, and shorter, less wavy coats. Their rippling fur feels velvety soft.

Like the Cornish Rex, this breed requires additional food to stay warm. Not only are Devons enthusiastic eaters, but they adore unusual foods like asparagus and cantaloupe. These lively, intelligent cats want to be included in the family's activities. They enjoy cuddling in laps, snuggling in bed, and riding atop their owners' shoulders.

# THE RAGDOLL: THE HEAVYWEIGHT OF PEDIGREED CATS

The crossing of Persian, Birman, and Burmese cats in the early 1960s resulted in the development of a longhaired, pointed hybrid, the Ragdoll. These cats earned their name because of their tendency to go as limp as ragdolls when held.

Ragdolls are large. Four-year-old males can weigh twenty pounds or more, and females weigh up to fifteen pounds. Their nonmatting, silky coat feels as soft as rabbit's fur.

Ragdoll kittens are all-white at birth. It takes two to three years for their coat markings to develop fully.

Because of the Ragdoll's docile personality, it doesn't require a huge space in which to live. This gentle cat tolerates almost anything. It loves to be stroked and cuddled. Like a puppy, it greets people at the door and follows them around the house. This nonaggressive cat lacks the instincts to defend itself, so it must be kept indoors.

# OCICAT: THE HOMEMADE OCELOT

In the 1960s, a breeder crossed an Abyssinian with a Siamese. When she crossed one of those kittens with another Siamese, she obtained the cats she'd been hoping for, Abyssinian-pointed Siamese, and one surprise—a spotted kitten. Since it resembled an ocelot, her daughter called it an "ocicat." Other breeders liked this cat and simultaneously began breeding ocicats. Later, they were crossbred with American Shorthairs to increase their size and variety of colors.

Like the Abyssinian, contrasting colors band each hair. The hairs in the spots are tipped with the darker color. Its short, satiny coat is usually cinnamon, silver, tawny, or chocolate.

The gentle Ocicat loves to follow its owner around, but is not demanding. These intelligent cats are easily trained to respond to commands and walk on leashes, making them good travelers.

# SOMALI: THE LONGHAIRED ABYSSINIAN

Now and then, a longhaired kitten would be born into a litter of shorthaired Abyssinians. Most breeders would quietly give away these "mistakes." In the 1960s, some breeders campaigned for acceptance of these longhaired siblings as a separate breed. Since "Longhaired Abyssinian" was dull, breeders suggested "Somali," for Somalia, the country bordering Ethiopia, formerly Abyssinia.

Sometimes called the "fox cat," the Somali has medium-length, ticked fur and a full, brush tail.

 Like the fox, it moves swiftly and gracefully. They're slightly larger than the Abyssinian, but otherwise have the same lithe body, long legs, and alert look.

Somalis share the Abyssinian's intelligence, liveliness, and curiosity. Unlike the Abyssinian, they enjoy being on people, riding their shoulders or cuddling in their laps. They have no fear of strangers and see them as people to befriend.

## BANNED IN BRITAIN: THE SCOTTISH FOLD

A Scottish farm cat gave birth in 1961. When the kittens were a few weeks old, a spontaneous mutation caused one of the kitten's ears to fold forward and down. She was the first Scottish Fold. Unfortunately, it was soon discovered that folded-ear cats had a high incidence of ear mites and deafness, among some other health problems, and the registries of Great Britain and Europe refused to register them. Although ethical breeders can avoid these problems, Scottish

Folds are still banned by England's official cat registry. United States registries recognized this new breed in the 1970s.

These medium-size cats have round bodies with round heads and large, round eyes. With folded ears, their wide-eyed expression reminds one of an owl. They can be either long- or shorthaired and have folded or straight ears.

Scottish Folds have many unusual behaviors, such as sleeping on their backs, sitting up on their haunches like prairie dogs, or sitting on their rumps with their back legs pointing forward.

These sweet-natured cats adore companionship and will supervise their owner's household activities.

## THE ENERGETICALLY FRIENDLY TONKINESE

A Canadian breeder developed the Tonkinese in the 1960s and 1970s, by crossing a seal point Siamese with a sable Burmese.

This breed may have been around earlier, but wasn't recognized as a separate breed. It is thought that Wong Mau, the mother of all Burmese, was a Tonkinese.

This pointed cat has an intermediate build, not as stocky as the Burmese nor as slim as the Siamese. It reminds many of the traditional "apple-head" Siamese. Their fur lies close to their body and feels like mink. No other pedigreed breed has the aqua-colored eyes of the Tonkinese.

The gregarious Tonks demand attention from friends and strangers. Its sociability, plus adaptability, make it a great traveler. Famous for their acrobatics, they fearlessly leap from high spot to high spot in the house and tightrope-walk on the curtain rods. Some owners describe their Tonkinese as part puppy and part monkey.

## SPHYNX: THE FURLESS PURR

Although reports of hairless cats go back at least a century, today's Sphynx breed traces its founding to hairless kittens born in Minnesota and Ontario in the mid-1970s. In both cases, a spontaneous mutation caused hairless kittens to be born to domestic shorthaired cats.

Sphynx appear hairless, but most have fine down over much of their body. Their skin feels like warm chamois. Two huge ears sit atop their small head. The Sphynx's muscular body has a pear-shaped appearance and ends with a whiplike tail.

This ultimate lap cat is famous for its neck hugs and face licks. Sphynx get along well with both pets and people. When not cuddling, they investigate cupboards or play fetch. No fur means they need to eat more food to maintain their body temperature. Since they have no coat to absorb their body oils, they require regular baths, or they'll leave oily spots on the furniture.

# SUPERLATIVE KITTIES: THE BEST, BIGGEST, MOST POPULAR, AND MORE

## BIG, FAT KITTY CATS

The heaviest domestic cat on record seems to be a porky puss named Himmy. Owned by Thomas Vyse of Cairns, Australia, Himmy tipped the scales at forty-six pounds, fifteen and a quarter ounces. With a fifteen-inch neck and thirty-three-inch waist, Himmy would have made a trim human, but he was one big cat!

Another feline fatty was a Welsh-born puss named Poppa who weighed in at forty-four and a half pounds. In the United States, the heavyweight champ is thought to be a forty-three-pound ginger-and-white tabby who lived in Connecticut.

On average, most domestic cats weigh somewhere between five

and seven pounds, although some breeds can weigh as much as twenty pounds. Of 330 breeds, the ragdoll is the heaviest, with males weighing in at an average of fifteen to twenty pounds.

## ITSY, BITSY KITTIES

Talk about teeny kitties: a male named Ebony-Eb-Honey Cat weighed in at a mere one pound and twelve ounces in February 1984, when the small Siamese was already nearly two years old. He was owned by Angelina Johnston and lived in Boise, Idaho.

Tinker Toy, a male blue point Himalayan-Persian, was merely two and three quarter inches tall and only seven and a half inches long.

The smallest breed of domestic cats is the Singapura or "Drain Cat" of Singapore. The average adult male weighs a mere six pounds and adult females weigh in at a waifish four pounds.

### WRINKLED PUSSES

Cats may have nine lives but we usually only measure one. The oldest cat on record is Puss. Said to have celebrated his thirty-sixth birthday on November 28, 1939, he then passed away peacefully the next day.

Another feline senior citizen was Ma, who was probably a great-great-great-grandma when she was put to sleep in 1957 at the ripe old age of thirty-four.

In the United States, a Los Angeles feline lived to be thirty-three years and four months before taking his final catnap. And Bobby, an Irish cat, was thirty-two years and three weeks old before he went up to kittycat heaven.

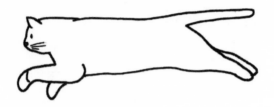

## SPEED DEMONS

Over the distance of sixty yards, a cat was once recorded doing twenty-seven miles per hour. (Perhaps it needed to use the litter box?)

The speediest member of the entire cat family is the cheetah, which has been recorded at speeds of up to seventy miles per hour over a distance of 100 yards.

## TELL ME A TAIL...

The cat with the longest tail is Pinky, who hailed from London. In 1978, his tremendous tail measured a whopping fourteen inches—and probably caused quite a breeze every time he flicked it!

## ONE COOL KITTY

While most pusses want to

warm up to the fireplace, one breed actually *likes* the cold. The Norwegian Forest Cat has adapted to the frigid temperatures of Scandinavia. And even though this brawny breed has lived for thousands of years in the wild, it can also be perfectly content indoors.

## ONE BUSY MAMA

Talk about a lot of litters—a cat named Dusty gave birth to her 420th kitten on June 12, 1952, at the age of seventeen!

Most female felines are able to have kittens until about the age of eleven (the equivalent of the human age of sixty). However, cats usually give birth to fewer kittens as they get older. Male cats as old as sixteen have been known to father litters, which is more than the human age of seventy!

## A LOTTA MOUTHS TO FEED

The largest litter on record

(ouch!) consisted of nineteen kittens, which were delivered on August 7, 1970, to a very fertile feline named Tarawood Antigone, a Burmese cat who was four years old at the time. Unfortunately, four of the kittens were stillborn. Of the surviving fifteen, only one was a female.

## HIGH-ALTITUDE TABBIES

A four-month-old kitten followed a group of climbers to the top of the 14,691-foot Matterhorn Mountain in the Alps on September 6, 1950.

Some other astounding instances of high-altitude tabbies:

In 1928, the members of a mountaineering club in the Swiss Alps were surprised when a cat showed up at the club's hut—which was a whopping 9,000 feet above sea level! The hutkeeper immediately adopted the cat, which made itself at home at the mountain retreat and often followed climbers up the craggy, frozen slopes to a peak that was more than 12,000 feet high.

In 1962, a kitten named Zizou moved in with a mountaineering club at the Albert Premier shelter at Mont Blanc in France, which is almost 9,000 feet high. Zizou liked to zigzag up the slopes with mountaineers to the peak—which is more than 15,000 feet into the clouds.

And in Yorkshire, England, a female cat was driven up the wall by a dog—literally—in 1980. Scared by the pooch, the kitty zoomed up some seventy feet to the roof of a five-story apartment building.

# TABBY TAKES A TUMBLE

Patricia, a one-year-old pregnant puss, truly knows what a comedown is. This kitty seems to hold the world record for surviving a fall from the greatest height.

On March 8, 1981, she was thrown off St. John's Bridge in Portland, Oregon, and fell 205 feet into the whirling Willamette River. Two fishermen rescued injured Patricia and brought her to a vet. She was operated on, and although she lost her kittens, not only did she survive, she was adopted by a loving family that later displayed her proudly in cat shows.

Perhaps Patricia was able to survive her incredible tumble because, by spreading their legs and arching their backs as they fall, cats seem to make a natural parachute of themselves.

### WELL-TRAVELED FELINES

According to *The Cat Name Companion* by Mark Bryant, during the course of sixteen years, a kitty named Princess Truman Tai-Tai logged in more than 1.5 million miles as a crew member of the British ship *Sagamire*.

Doodles, a regular aboard the ocean liner *Cedric*, also traveled more than a million miles in his seafaring career.

Up in the skies, a remarkable kitten took some tremendous flights during World War II. Members of the U.S. Fifth Air Force Division found him climbing aboard a cargo plane in Australia. With a face that looked a little like the German dictator, the kitty was christened Adolf. Adolf logged in almost 100,000 miles during many perilous combat flights. Once the engines started, the cat would appear just minutes before the plane took off—and would spend most flights sleeping peacefully near the plane's radio equipment.

### CURIOSITY ALMOST KILLED THE CAT!

In 1983, an eight-year-old cat named Buttons got stuck under the hood of a car. Unfortunately, she was stuck there for six hours before being rescued at a gas station.

The cat was taken to a vet; when an airline found out about her misadventure, the frazzled feline flew home free of charge to be reunited with her owner— the neighbor of the driver.

## FREQUENT FLYER

A black-and-white cat named Tom got lost in the hold of a British Airways jet and flew more than a half-million miles in two months. Before being rescued at Heathrow Airport by his owner, Tom visited such far-flung places as Australia, Canada, Jamaica, and Kuwait.

## TREMENDOUS TREKS

The record for a feline finding the way to its owner's home is said to be held by Tom, who traveled an amazing 2,500 miles from St. Petersburg, Florida, to San Gabriel, California! This journey took Tom two years and six weeks—and, by the time he arrived in California, he was much the worse for wear. But the courageous cat was happy to be back with his owners again.

There have been other stories of felines finding their families after becoming separated during a move or a vacation.

In Australia, a Persian cat named Howie is said to have traveled 1,000 miles across the continent to find his teenage owner, after she and her family moved. It took the cat a year to traverse the rivers, deserts, and wilderness of the Australian Outback, but somehow he made it back to his owner.

## MORE REUNIONS OF CAT AND OWNER

Other persistent pusses who have made tremendous treks to find their owners include a cat named Clementine who, in 1949, made her way from New York state to Denver, Colorado—a place she had never been—to find the family that had left her behind!

In 1953, a soldier from Indiana had taken his cat with him to his new base in Georgia. Shortly after, the cat disappeared. The disappointed military man searched for her to no avail. He later found out that in three weeks, the cat had made its way back to Indiana and was hanging around its former home.

And in 1955, a woman was

shocked to find that her persistent puss named Ling-Ling, whom she had left behind in the care of her sister, had somehow managed to travel from Sandusky, Ohio, to Orlando, Florida—an area that was completely foreign to him—to join her.

## MARVELOUS MOUSERS

Rodents should have run from a female tortoiseshell cat named Towser, who was owned and employed by the Glenturret Distillery Ltd. of Scotland. By the age of twenty-two, she is credited with killing 28,899

mice, averaging three ravaged
rodents per day.

## WET BEHIND THE PAWS

A black-and-white Persian
would regularly paddle between
the ships in the harbor of St.
Mary's in the Scilly Isles. He was
also known to go swimming in
the sea every evening to catch
his dinner with his bare paws!

In fact, there are some breeds
of cats that like water. These include the auburn-and-white
Turkish Van cat as well as the
Fishing Cat of Malaysia, India,
and Sri Lanka. The latter actu-

ally has slightly webbed feet that help it fish for its supper!

## THEY'RE IN THE MONEY

Mark Bryant, in *The Cat Name Companion*, tells of a number of lucky cats who are in the money because of generous owners who predeceased them and left a bounty of booty in their wills.

In 1992, a seven-year-old feline named Cyrus inherited an $850,000 mansion in Bridgeport, Connecticut, and the litter boxes (one in each of the fifty rooms) that went along with it.

An alley cat named Charlie

Chan was the sole recipient of a $250,000 estate. The will stipulated that the entire estate—which included a three-bedroom house, seven-acre pet cemetery, and collection of valuable antiques—should be auctioned off when Charlie Chan passed on, and the proceeds donated to a number of humane societies.

In 1991, a pair of Burmese named Damon and Pythias were the recipients of a $750,000 Manhattan co-op on Fifth Avenue—with a view, of course. The will required the cats' caretakers to give the friendly felines toys to play with and make sure that they got their hairball medicine.

Cat charities have also benefited from some wonderful wills. Three charities that support stray cats received an astounding $14 million from Ben Rea, an eccentric millionaire and miser. Britain's Royal Society for the Prevention of Cruelty to Animals will receive $5 million in exchange for taking care of a cat named Blackie. And in France, a couple of rich cat lovers donated a spectacular $60 million to charities that look after the country's abandoned felines.

## PRICEY PUSS!

A California Spangled cat was purchased for $24,000 in January 1987 from the Neiman Marcus Christmas catalog. Quite a number of people feel that paying such a price for a cat is the ultimate in conspicuous consumption and is not in the animal's best interest.

## MVP—MOST VALUABLE PUSS

In 1967 an English woman was offered $5,880 for her cat by an American breeder. Coylum Marcus, her copper-eyed white Persian, was an international champion. The woman refused to sell her cat, who kept her company for eleven more years.

## PARTY ANIMAL

Certainly one of the most popular

cats of contemporary times was Tommy Clark, a yellow tomcat who lived in Seneca Falls, New York, during the 1930s.

On Tommy's twenty-third birthday, more than 700 cats attended his birthday party. The next year, more than 1,500 guests (felines and people) were invited—including President Franklin D. Roosevelt, who, alas, had to send his regrets.

## FAN CLUBS

With more than 600 cat clubs throughout the United States, the largest cat organization in

the country is the Cat Fanciers'
Association, Inc.

The largest cat show
ever held in the United
States attracted a record
1,200 feline participants.
Held on November
17 and 18, 1995, at
McCormick Place in
Chicago, the International Cat
Show was the place to be for cat
lovers!

The first cat show in America
took place on March 6, 1881, at
a museum on Broadway in New

York City. According to published reports of the time, the cats in question were not happy about being exhibited—there was much hissing, scratching, and clawing!

## BELOVED PERSIANS

The most popular breed of cat in the United States is the Persian. According to the Cat Fanciers' Association, there are approximately 45,000 registered Persians in the country.

Rounding out the top ten most popular cat breeds in the United States are: Maine Coon, Siamese,

Abyssinian, Exotic, Oriental, Scottish Fold, American Shorthair, Birman, and Ocicat.

However, only a small percentage of house cats in America are pedigreed. Unlike dogs, who are often bred for their performance as working animals, cats are bred only for their good looks and temperaments.

# CARE TIPS AND HELPFUL HINTS

Dry, crunchy food helps keep a cat's teeth healthy, but soft, moist food has the benefit of supplying water, which cats need. (Mice and birds, a staple of cats in the wild, are about 80 percent liquid—like humans.) A shortage of water in the diet is suspected of contributing to feline bladder problems. Therefore, whenever dry food is served, an ample supply of clean water should also be made available.

For cats that have grown up eating dry food, drinking enough water is seldom a problem. They learned as kittens to drink water (or milk) in adequate quantities, and they maintain that pattern throughout their lives. A mature cat that is switched to dry food may not do so well, however. Cats are creatures of habit, and their habits may not include drinking water as a part of their daily routine. A cat that fails to increase its water intake upon being switched to dry food may develop concentrated crystals in its urine, which can cause painful bladder inflammation and infection. Regular monitoring of fluid intake is important under these circumstances.

Although your cat is friendly and cuddly with you and your family, do not assume it will act cordially to the neighbor's cat or to another cat you introduce into its environment. Cats are essentially solitary creatures. They come together in nature for only one reason: sex. Otherwise, they view each other as competitors—for food, sex, or territory. Domesticated cats view humans, on the other hand, not as competitors but as providers of life's necessities. Humans don't mark turf the way cats do, nor do they (normally!) feed on local rodents and birds.

True, some cats—though by no means all—who live in the same human household will become fast friends and cuddle together adorably. This is because the abundance of food provided by their humans (along with neutering and spaying) blunts the normal competitive urge.

Even in these circumstances, however, another cat, especially an unfamiliar one, may well receive an extremely unfriendly reception.

More than a few people are allergic to cats, far more than are allergic to dogs. The problem is not necessarily cat hair itself. The more likely culprit is dead skin, which is sloughed off in the natural course of things, and cat saliva on the hair. One helpful step an allergic person can take is to brush the cat and cut its nails outside, so the skin and nails don't end up covering the floor and furniture. Another is to have a nonallergic person rub the cat frequently— several times daily, if possible— with a damp sponge, the goal

being to remove the saliva with which a cat coats itself in the course of its numerous daily baths.

Although they may eat vegetables and fruits from time to time, cats are true carnivores. In this respect, they differ from humans (and dogs), omnivores whose bodies are capable of converting plant life as well as animals into the nutrients essential to survival. It's fine if you and your family want to be vegetarians, but cats can acquire certain vital fats and amino acids only by consuming the bodies of other

animals that have already manu-
factured them.

Cats have little need for food
other than meat. Note that
when they eat their prey, they
typically eat the entire thing—
skin, bones, and internal or-
gans, as well as muscle. The lesson for humans attempting to
duplicate the cat's natural diet
is that food served should contain 25 to 30 percent protein
and 15 to 40 percent fat.

Cats want and need variety in
their diet. Not only will they get
bored with the same food day
after day, but they can develop
disease as a result of prolonged

feeding on a single type of meat. Note that cats throughout the world have widely varying diets. Cats in America consume lots of chipmunks. European cats thrive on mice and rabbits. Australian cats enjoy ring-tailed possum. Cats on certain islands eat penguins and noddies (a type of tern).

Cats are often willing to try something new, but like humans, they will often turn up their noses at something they don't like, even if eating it would be "good for them."

There is no point in trying to discourage your cat from raising its tail and sticking its rear end in your face—or in the face of your boss, who is visiting for the first time and whom you are desperate to impress! In the presence of those they trust, human or animal, cats carry their tails high and present their posteriors for inspection and sniffing as a means of acknowledging the other's superiority (or at least equality). Odor is very important in the cat world, and when a cat allows you to "capture" its odor, which is produced by two glands in the anal area, you are receiving a compliment not to be sneezed at.

Even the most finicky cat is likely to drink out of the toilet bowl, the sink, or a dripping tap. This is not inherently worrisome. Drinking from a dripping tap or even a running hose is simply more fun than drinking from the same old bowl every day. Tap water may also taste better than water that has been sitting out in a bowl for any length of time. Also, some believe that cats evolved with a preference for moving water because in the wild they found that stagnant ponds and the like were unsafe.

If your cat drinks from alternative sources, the challenge for you is to make sure those sources are safe. Toilet bowls may contain toxic cleaning chemicals, and plant vases may contain poisonous residue of plants.

Note that if you deliberately leave the tap dripping to ensure that your cat has an adequate water supply (some people do this when they go out of town for a day or two), behavior that began out of curiosity may become a habit that is difficult to break.

The normal cat has thirty teeth, the nature of which clearly reflects their development as carnivores. The knifelike canine teeth, in particular, are ideally suited to clasping prey and tearing flesh.

Because of how their teeth are constructed, cats cannot chew food. They are able, however, to perform cutting or slicing. Therefore, any food served to a cat should be chopped up or at least served in lumps small enough that a cat can get its mouth around it for purposes of tearing it into digestible pieces.

While some veterinarians advise against ever serving a cat food with bones, others believe that the only bones to watch out for are fish bones, which have a tendency to get caught in a cat's throat. Vets of the latter opinion point out that cats in the wild are hardly known to leave tidy piles of mouse or bird bones after each meal. (One thing cats do typically avoid, however, is feathers.)

Do not worry if your cat eats grass (unless you have a really big cat and a really small lawn!). This is natural. Cats eat grass mainly to facilitate throwing up furballs and other ingested but indigestible items, but also be-

cause they occasionally enjoy a "salad."

Outdoor cats often prefer one type of grass over another, just as humans prefer one type of vegetable over another. Typically, the preference is for young, succulent grasses, over older, drier forms.

If your cat is eating grass, the most important thing for you to do is make sure that any fertilizer or pesticides you use on your lawn are nontoxic.

Vomiting furballs is a perfectly natural function for cats. It is less than pleasing from an aesthetic viewpoint, however, and the output can stain rugs and furniture. There are a couple of things you can do to reduce the frequency of such incidents.

First, note that a cat's fur lengthens in the winter and

shortens in the summer—which means that the longer winter hair will begin coming out as spring arrives, typically aided by the cat's grooming process. This tendency is much more pronounced in the outdoor cat; the indoor cat engages in hair removal throughout the year. It is also more pronounced in the longhaired cat, which is more likely to develop furballs in its stomach rather than pass the hair through its intestines.

It is good to brush your cat regularly to rid it of excess hair, and this is especially true during the molting season. Also, there are products you can feed your cat that will assist its intestines in passing the hair along with other waste, rather than vomiting it onto your favorite sofa. Consult your veterinarian about the latest options. Finally, if you are really concerned about this, make your next cat a short-haired one.

If you are disappointed in your cat's performance as a mouser, the problem may rest with you. The better you feed your cat, the less likely it is to be a good hunter.

Some level of stalking urge is innate in cats, but generally a kitten must be taught to hunt. Thus, if its mother was not a hunter, or if it was removed from its mother very soon after birth, the kitten will probably never learn to hunt and may be incapable of surviving in the wild.

Interestingly, some cats occupy an intermediate ground. They know how to hunt and seem to enjoy it, but the local humans feed them so well that they don't really need to hunt for food. Hence the notorious

tendency of some cats to vanquish local prey and then do
nothing with it (other than
leave it conspicuously on the
doorstep, apparently as a present for humans).

If your cat constantly seems to

crave food but is notably thin, or if it appears to be eating normally but is losing weight, something is definitely wrong. The problem may involve kidney malfunction, which causes food protein to be lost in urine. It might also signal intestinal problems, which can render a cat unable to digest the nutrients in its food. In this situation, the cat is literally starving, although its food intake appears optimal.

Increased appetite and/or weight loss might even indicate an overactive thyroid gland, which causes the body's metabolic rate to increase, raising the cat's daily energy requirements and also causing it to become jumpy and high-strung.

All of these problems are amenable to treatment, but because the treatments will vary depending on the core problem, immediate consultation with a capable veterinarian is in order.

If your cat ever exhibits a marked increase in thirst, and there is no obvious explanation, such as a change from moist food to dry, you should assume that something is seriously wrong.

Kidney malfunction is the most likely culprit. Kidney problems are often treatable by a measure as simple as putting the cat on a low-protein diet, either through one of the commercially available low-protein foods designed specifically for cats with kidney problems or through dilution of the cat's normal protein source with something like rice.

Diabetes can also manifest itself through heavy water intake. In this situation, insulin injections may be necessary.

Other possible explanations include: fever, anemia, bladder

infection, and the side effects of some medication the cat may be taking. In any event, immediate consultation with a veterinarian is mandatory.

There are various good reasons for your cat to turn up its nose at food, most having nothing to do with the oft-cited feline tendency to be fickle. For one thing, a cat's acute sense of smell enables it to detect chemicals, food deterioration, and other repugnant odors that humans are incapable of discerning. Toxic products used to "clean" the cat's food bowl, for example, may escape your notice but be obvious to your cat. Any impairment of a cat's sense of smell, such as an upper-respiratory infection, may induce it to stop eating altogether, because it cannot smell the food.

A cat's appetite may also be reduced by sores on its mouth or tongue, or by environmental disturbances, such as unfamiliar noises or unusual levels of light.

A cat may also refuse food that is too cold, preferring its  victuals at room temperature.

A number of foods that are acceptable or even highly beneficial for a cat are not acceptable on an exclusive basis. If you feed a cat nothing but liver, its bowels may become upset. If you feed it nothing but lean meat, it may experience calcium and other deficiencies. A diet consisting heavily of raw fish may lead to a vitamin $B_1$ deficiency, due to an enzyme in fish that destroys that vitamin and could also transmit tapeworms. A solution to both fish problems is simply to cook it (and make sure to remove any bones).

Eggs are a bit more complex. Uncooked egg whites destroy certain types of vitamins. Egg whites that are cooked, while safe enough, have no nutritional value. The best approach with eggs is to feed the cat only the yolks, raw or cooked.

Do not feed your cat dog food. There is a difference—beyond the fact that one type of food is labeled "Cat" and the other "Dog." Perhaps most important, cat food has more meat. This is because cats *need* more meat. Also, dog food has ingredients that cats cannot digest. In this respect, among others, dogs more closely resemble pigs than cats do.

When buying cat food, look for compliance with guidelines set by the Association of American Feed Control Officials (A. A. F. C. O.), a nonprofit group made up of federal and state officials. The February 1998 issue of *Consumer Reports* discusses cat (and dog) food at length and analyzes a number of specific, commercially available brands. Some highlights of that issue: (a) Dry food is typically cheaper (per day) than canned food; (b) if your cat has been thriving on a given food for, say, the last six years, there's no need to change to a "senior" food; (c) any food that meets the A. A. F. C. O. nutrition requirements, whether labeled "lite," "low calorie," or something else along those lines, must be capable of maintaining the animal's current weight. Thus, you'll have to feed it smaller quantities.

Under standards set by the Association of American Feed Control Officials, cat food that is labeled, for example, "beef cat food," must contain at least 95 percent beef (minus the water

used in processing), whereas a food that is labeled "*with* beef" need not contain more than 3 percent beef. An in-between label—"beef *dinner*" (or "platter" or "meal") must have at least 25 percent of the indicated food product.

When buying a cat, you're probably going to pay top dollar at a pet shop, and the animal you get may well come from one of the large, commercial breeders who sometimes separate kittens and their mothers too early and pay inadequate attention to socialization. Also, young cats are especially vulnerable to infection and illness, which are more likely to spread in the comparatively crowded conditions at some pet stores.

Your best bet is to go to a reputable breeder who raises the cats at home. You can find breeders at cat shows, or you could check *Cat Fancy* magazine. A purebred cat may cost from $250 to $1,000, depending on factors such as the rarity of the breed.

Alternatively, you could adopt a cat from the local humane society or the Society for Prevention of Cruelty to Animals, where you might pay anything from zero up to $50, which often includes the first round of shots, an initial health checkup, and spaying or neutering.

Feeding a stray kitten milk is a classic gesture of compassion. The problem is that cat's milk is different from cow milk. The former has more protein and fat. Also, some cats can't tolerate cow milk and will develop diarrhea.

When feeding kittens whose mother is for some reason unable to provide milk (the mom may have died, or she may be neglectful or physically impaired), there are several options. One is evaporated milk, prepared at up to twice the normal concentration (one-half the water) as that used for humans. Another is baby-milk formula, also prepared at up to twice the normal strength used for human babies. Also, there are commercially available cat milk substitutes (usually in powder form, requiring the addition of water).

Finally, for cats of any age that are sensitive to milk (or, to be precise, the lactose in milk), one remedy may be simply to dilute the milk with water, carefully monitoring the cat's waste output for negative reactions. And cats that will eat yogurt and similar products should be permitted to do so, because the lactose in these has already been chemically broken down.

There are several good reasons for spaying or neutering a cat not intended for breeding. As for males, the unneutered cat may wander, get into fights (which can lead to disease, not to mention bloody wounds and hostile neighbors), and mark its territory by spraying strong-smelling urine on rugs and furniture. As for females, the unspayed cat is likely not only to turn up with unwanted pregnancies but also to generate strong interest in un-wanted visitors.

When obtaining a cat, check it yourself, look-ing for various things. First, go for one that appears friendly and amenable to human handling. If you're looking at kittens, go for the bolder one, the first one to venture toward your outstretched hand. Whatever the age, its coat should be smooth, unmatted, and free of ticks, fleas, and other crea-tures. Its ears should be dry and wax-free. Its nose should be damp, its mouth pink, its teeth white, and its anal area clean (and otherwise free of signs of diarrhea). Watch it walk around a bit, checking the cat for signs of lameness.

Any new cat, especially one you're planning to allow outside on a regular basis, should be kept inside for at least a few days—better yet, a full week. The goal is to give the cat a sense of your place as its home, the place it should return to from its explorations. You can promote this goal by fussing over it as much as possible in the first week, spoiling it with special tidbits, minimizing environmental irritations (e.g., don't begin home renovations the very next day), and so on.

When you finally let your cat out, be sure it is wearing a tag with your name and phone number. Escort it on its first outings, and make sure to get it back inside before nightfall.

All the guidelines regarding the introduction of a new cat to your home are equally applicable when you and your old cat are moving to a new home. First, keep it inside for at least several days. You don't want it to go out and immediately begin searching for its old home.

Also, retain as many elements of the old and familiar as possible. Keep all its toys, its favorite blanket, its usual brand of food. Don't change its brand of litter or the litter box itself. You would even do well to keep at least a portion of semiused litter in the box. Cats are highly sensitive to smell, and nothing will give it a sense of being "home" more than the aroma of its own urine.

When lifting a grown cat, be sure to support its weight at both ends. Do not utilize the classic approach of small children, which is to grab it under its front legs and leave the rest of it dangling.

As tempting as it is to cradle a cat like a baby, with its tummy facing up, note that some cats do not enjoy this position and will struggle and even bite to get away.

When lifting a kitten, don't pick it up by the scruff of its neck, the way you might have seen its mother doing. A mother cat has the benefit of thousands of years of evolution to make sure she does this correctly. When handling kittens, note that their rib cages are highly delicate and bruise easily.

If you're planning to separate a kitten from its mother, do not—except under special circumstances—do so until the kitten is at least six weeks old. Better yet, wait eight weeks, when it is fully weaned from mother's milk.

It is good to begin picking up kittens, however, around three weeks after birth (some veterinarians say six weeks), to accustom them to handling. Have visitors pick them up, too, to accustom them to a variety of human hands and scents. The latter point is especially important if you are planning either to show your cat or to place it with a new family (rather than keep it). In either case, your cat will benefit from becoming used to handling by unfamiliar people.

Cats are notorious for choosing their own places to sleep. You could set up a custom-made, color-coordinated kitty house with a four-poster bed, complete with mattress, box springs, and heating pad, and your cat might end up spending the night in a cardboard box.

It might also end up spending the night with you. If you like this, or at least don't mind it, there is no problem. If you find that it cramps your style, however, you should establish an alternate routine as soon as possible, ideally from the moment the cat first enters your house.

Begin the routine by putting the cat in its own "room," fully equipped with litter box and food and water (or at least water), just before you go to bed. Make sure the room is warm enough, by using either a radiator (or the like) or an electric blanket or heating pad. Ideally, the room will have space both close to the heat source and further away, so the cat can choose a warmer or a cooler location, depending on its own needs and preferences.

Finally, close the door and brace yourself for some heartrending protests. If you're lucky, the room will be far enough from your bedroom that the crying won't keep you up all night. In any event, it should end in a week or two.

Cats need exercise. The typical outdoor cat gets plenty from its normal routine of hunting, climbing, exploring, and so on. The indoor cat can get enough from climbing on furniture and playing with toys, but you should help it out in this regard as much as possible. You can do this, first, by introducing it to toys (and play) early on, thereby accustoming it to running, jumping, and rolling around inside. You can also help by providing it with climbing and scratching posts, as well as an

ample supply of toys, perhaps ro-
tating the toys that you leave out
from week to week so as to prevent the cat from getting bored
by seeing the same things lying
around all day. Any personal time
you can put in throwing a cloth
ball or wiggling a feather-on-a-
wire toy of course helps.

If you live in a high-rise apartment or for some other reason are planning to keep your cat indoors, you're better off starting with a kitten (or, next best, a cat that has always lived indoors). Cats that are used to hunting, wandering widely, and enjoying the other stimulations of an outdoor life do not adapt as well to indoor life as those that grew up in it.

Similarly, if you're going to get two cats, you're better off getting two kittens, because cats that have not yet reached puberty are more likely to get along than two with all the sexual and territorial drives that puberty triggers.

You don't often see a cat on a leash. There is a reason for this: It is hard, if not impossible, to get a cat to walk on a leash like a dog. If you're to have any chance of success with this method, you are well advised to start early, with a weaned kitten. The sooner you familiarize the kitten with both the collar and the leash, the better your chances. Start off with short walks, preferably around familiar areas, and depending on the results, branch out from there.

Certain breeds, such as the Siamese, appear more amenable to leashes than others, but you may find that your particular cat will never go for it. In no event should you drag your cat on a leash against its will. This won't achieve compliance and only risks hurting him.

A cat that literally never goes outside can get by without a collar, but a cat that goes outside even just occasionally should definitely have a collar and a tag with your address and phone number. This is also a good idea for a cat that lives in a house where people, especially children, go in and out often. Lots of cats lie in wait to make an escape, and an adult loaded down with groceries or a kid rushing off to the playground can accidentally provide the necessary opening. Even if you live in an apartment or condo, a collar and tag may make sense. If your cat escapes into a hallway or stairwell, you want the person who finds it to call you, rather than the building manager.

Note that the collar should always be of the type (now available at pet stores everywhere) that contains at least an element of elastic so that the cat can wiggle out of it if, for example, the collar gets caught on a branch while the cat is climbing a tree, or on a nail while the cat is scaling a fence.

A cat door, which basically consists of a small flap covering an opening in your garage or some inconspicuous area of your house, can be a handy way of giving your cat the opportunity to come and go as it pleases. Available at pet stores and hardware stores everywhere, cat flaps can be of the type that opens either way, allowing the cat to both enter and exit, or the type that allows the cat only to enter. The latter might be useful if, for example, you'd like to permit your cat to return from its evening romp without having to awaken you by howling outside your bedroom, but you'd like to keep it in once it's back.

Note that a lock of some sort is useful in case unwant-ed visitors, feline or otherwise, discover the door.

Some cats take to cat doors instantly. Others require a bit of instruction, usually as little as holding the door open for them and placing a cat treat on the opposite side.

Perhaps the single greatest complaint about cats as pets is their tendency to scratch the furniture. And somehow, to add insult to injury, cats seem to zero in on the most expensive items.

Cats claw things, because (a) it feels good, (b) it keeps their nails in good condition, and (c) it leaves their mark, sort of like a flag posted in the dirt. (A cat's "mark" consists of paw sweat, which other cats can quickly identify, as well as scratches.) If provided with ample, suitably textured scratching posts located in adequately central locations—cats want to leave their mark *prominently*—a cat can often be persuaded to leave the furniture alone. The chances of attaining this sort of behavioral modification are best if coaching of the cat occurs early and often. Specifically, any time you see your cat (better yet, your kitten) scratching the furniture, grab it firmly, plop it down in front of the scratching post, and physically rub its claws along the post to demonstrate the appealing texture.

Note that allowing a cat outdoors, where there are typically many socially acceptable scratching opportunities (trees), also reduces its tendency to scratch furniture.

Some cats seem incapable of giving up scratching the furniture, perhaps because their training commenced too late, perhaps because they're just hardheaded. Whatever the reason, the owner of such a cat is presented with a troubling dilemma: to declaw or not to declaw.

Supporters of declawing (as an option, when all other approaches have failed) contend that this relatively "minor" surgery—only the front two paws are ever declawed—can literally save the cat's life, because many cat owners would otherwise give the cat to the local humane society or the like, where it could end up being destroyed.

Opponents of declawing characterize the operation as "major"—it involves general anesthesia and a stay at the hospital—and as nothing short of mutilation, in the form of severing the cat's last "knuckles." They point out that it removes the cat's primary means of defense, in that a declawed cat can neither fight nor climb. In England, the procedure is illegal except when deemed medically necessary.

As with other debates over medical and moral issues, including many involving humans, the outcome in any given case seems more likely to be a matter of the heart than the head.

Maintaining strong, healthy

teeth is a challenge in cats, especially those that live on soft canned food. Cats in the wild clean their teeth by chomping on the tough skin, gristle, and bones of their prey, but domestic cats have to rely on dry food and regular dental checkups. Tartar accumulation is a particular problem. It can lead to painful inflammation of the gums and worse, ultimately causing loss of teeth. Not every cat will tolerate the otherwise highly beneficial weekly treatment with salt and water (rubbed on with a piece of cotton, or even a child's toothbrush) that can remove tartar, so annual (or more frequent) monitoring and cleaning by a professional is genuinely necessary.

Cats spend a huge amount of time grooming themselves, primarily with their tongues, though their teeth and forepaws also play a role. This is not only natural, but desirable. Such grooming cleans the fur, stimulates blood circulation, and even tones muscle.

There is also a nutritional aspect to grooming. Sunlight enables the fur to produce vitamin D, which the cat ingests in the

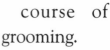

course of grooming. Finally, saliva on the fur performs essentially the same cooling function as sweat on human skin, cooling it via the evaporation process. Hence the increased grooming one can observe in warm weather or following periods of heavy activity.

If your cat should lose its interest in grooming, consider taking it in for a checkup. Physical illness, ranging from a mild bug to a serious disease, may be the explanation. Depression is also a possibility. Few veterinarians doubt that cats grieve the loss of a companion, whether feline or human. A depressed cat may require medication, but gentle, abundant care and nursing will in most instances remedy the problem.

Cats are as capable of developing eye trouble as humans. The greatest danger is not blindness, but foreign objects in the eye. If your cat is keeping one eye closed or pawing at it, or if you observe discharge from the eye, you should act promptly. First, hold the cat so as to prevent it from pawing the eye. Then, holding the cat's body firmly, and raising part of the eyelid, examine the eye. If you observe a superficial scratch or speck of sand or something similar, you may be able to ease the pain and remove the object by flooding the eye with a liquid such as tea. If you observe blood, or if the foreign object is in any way penetrating the surface of the eye, consult a vet immediately.

Cats love cozy, secure places, many of which may strike humans as hideaways. Although cats do enjoy curling up in small boxes, in dark corners of closets, and in similar spots, they aren't really hiding and will typically emerge after several hours for food, to use the litter box, or to enjoy a bit of companionship, feline or human.

On the other hand, a cat that is seriously ill may go into true hiding, not (as the myth goes) because it wishes to die alone, but because it senses when its diminished strength renders it most vulnerable to predators, and its natural self-preservation instinct leads it to seek out places where predators can't find it. The problem, of course, is that hiding may cost it the care of someone who could in fact save it. If your cat appears to be seeking a genuinely remote, unfindable hideaway, examine it closely for signs of illness.

Not many cats live beyond the age of twenty, and one that survives to the age of seventeen is doing well. As with humans, cats change as they grow older. Their hearing and eyesight decline, their bowels may become sluggish, their livers and kidneys may fail, and their eating habits may change.

The general rule in caring for an older cat is to be alert, noting any changes in its appearance or habits, and to respond appropriately. If your cat's hearing or eyesight appears to be failing, for example, you'll need to start keeping it inside. The danger from cars, dogs, or other cats is just too great. And you'll need to make sure its feeding bowls and litter box aren't moved.

Another age-related problem: If your cat shows signs of constipation, you may need to add mineral oil or oily fish to its diet. Try to clean the cat's teeth of

tartar more frequently now (as often as twice a week), and take it in for a checkup two or three times annually, as your vet recommends.

If your cat seems hard of hearing, the first thing to check is the color of your cat's coat and eyes. There is a genetic link between white coats, blue eyes, and deafness, especially among Persian cats, which for years were bred to achieve the bluest possible eyes, with a high incidence of deafness occurring incidentally. Many cats with one blue eye will be deaf (or partially deaf) in the ear on the same side. Hearing is, of course, less important for an indoor cat than an outdoor one, and many deaf cats develop such superb compensating senses that you may never notice the problem.

Still, it's worth getting a vet to look into it, though not urgently. Meanwhile, check for such things as buildup of wax in the ear, discharge or other signs of irritation in the ear, the cat holding its head to one side (which might indicate an infection in the ear), and anything else unusual.

A shorthaired cat that is normal and healthy can and usually will perform all the grooming (which generally means licking) that is necessary for the health and appearance of its fur and skin. Longhaired cats, on the other hand, absolutely require human help. A single day without brushing a longhaired cat can cause the hair to become matted, especially on the cat's stomach and inner legs, and the resulting tangles can generally be removed only by shaving the area.

Pedigreed (purebred) cats have distinctive traits, in terms of personality types and other features. To take just one example, Persian cats are comparatively quiet, and Siamese cats are comparatively noisy (and demanding). The benefit of this is that with a pedigreed cat, you know what you're getting, and you can choose accordingly. The downside is that pedigreed cats tend to have a higher incidence of certain types of diseases—the result of generations of inbreeding. Mixed breeds, in contrast, are relatively healthy and hardy, and they often have more relaxed dispositions. A mongrel kitten may be a bit of an uncertain commodity, but it could well prove to be a happier, healthier pet.

Sometimes a cat will go well beyond normal grooming and lick some area of its body (often its abdomen) entirely bald. There are several possible explanations for such behavior. First, check for fleas or other external parasites. If you find nothing, the problem may have psychological origins. Specifically, some change in the cat's world may have made it anxious or worried, and it may be responding just as humans often do in comparable situations—namely, with compulsive (excessive) levels of a type of conduct from which it is used to deriving comfort and a sense of order in its universe.

Have you just moved? Have you just had a baby? It would be enough if you were simply *preparing* for one of these things. A cat is a highly sensitive creature, and this applies not only to its sense of smell and hearing. Even in the early stages of a human owner's pregnancy, a cat just knows something dramatic is about to happen.

If the prospect of a new baby (or some other change) is genuinely diminishing your level of interest in the cat, the kindest course might be to find it a new home. Alternatively, give it some extra care and cuddling. Over time, your reassurances will likely ease the anxiety, and the cat will cut back on its grooming to normal, healthy levels.

Don't feed your cat aspirin. It's fine for humans and dogs, but it can be toxic, even lethal, for cats, whose bodies aren't equipped to break it down in the same way. If your cat is hobbling or otherwise acting in such a way as to make you suspect arthritis (which is conceivable but statistically far less likely

than in humans or dogs), a tiny amount of aspirin—say, a third of a standard tablet, administered every fourth day—might do some good. But your best bet is to consult a veterinarian.

Contrary to persistent myth, cats do not present a terrible threat to pregnant women. To be sure, a cat or any other animal that has contracted rabies is dangerous, but a rabid creature is a threat to everyone, not just to pregnant women. You can and should protect against that by having your cat vaccinated against rabies.

The one cat-related disease that is an appropriate subject of concern among pregnant women is toxoplasmosis, which can cause birth defects or miscarriage. Note, however, that cats themselves can acquire the internal parasite that causes this disease only by consuming live (or recently deceased) prey, and humans can contract it only by handling cat feces. Thus, if your cat consumes only commercially prepared food, there is no cause for concern, and the same is true if the pregnant woman doesn't clean the kitty litter. If you are in doubt as to what your cat might have consumed, either because you allow it outdoors or because it chases the occasional indoor mouse, reliable tests for toxoplasmosis are available, and the cat that tests positive can be treated. Thus, if someone in your household is pregnant, your cat certainly need not be given away or destroyed out of concern for the fetus.

All cats should be vaccinated against the major infectious diseases. If you're about to acquire a kitten, make sure it has been vaccinated, preferably at least one week before you take it. If you're getting an adult cat, check its records to confirm that it received all appropriate vaccinations as a kitten and regular booster shots thereafter.

The first vaccinations—for *feline influenza* ("cat flu"), *feline enteritis*, and *feline leukemia*—should come at eight or nine weeks after birth. The second vaccinations (for the same diseases) should come three or four weeks later. Annual boosters should be given thereafter.

Vaccinations against rabies also are available, advisable, and often they are required by law.

You may at some point observe your cat engaging in the bizarre and somewhat comical-looking act of "scooting." Starting from a seated position, the cat will drag its rump across the floor (or sofa or bed), almost invariably leaving a visible fecal trail ranging in length from a few inches to a few feet. It is not unreasonable to suspect that your fastidious cat is, in effect, "wiping" his bottom.

Actually, however, your cat is trying to relieve itself of the considerable discomfort that accompanies impacted (or possibly infected) anal glands. These are two small sacs on either side of the anus that discharge a bad-smelling (to humans) fluid each time the cat defecates. For any of various reasons, the cat may find itself unable to discharge this fluid in the normal way. The resulting impaction may lead to infection, parasite infestation, and—almost certainly—pain.

The bad news is that this problem is unlikely to go away on its own. The cat's scooting may relieve the itching for a while, but you're almost certain to see it, with similarly displeasing results, again. The good news is that vets can quickly, easily, and inexpensively empty (or "express") the glands simply by squeezing them with their fingers, and there's no real pain involved for the cat.

Feline first aid is a challenge, to say the least, for the average nonveterinarian. This is why, in the event of an emergency, your best bet is to call a vet right away. (Better yet, have someone else call the vet, while you tend to the cat.) Keep the telephone number of your vet and the local around-the-clock animal hospital in a convenient place near the phone.

Meanwhile:
- If your cat has stopped breathing, open its mouth, check for obstacles to breathing, and use your fingers to remove anything you see. You could even try swinging the cat around by its hind legs.
- If your cat gets burned, apply cold water or ice to the injured area. If chemicals are involved, wash the site thoroughly, using huge amounts of water.

- If your cat is bleeding, try to stop the flow by applying pressure.

- If your cat has suffered a blow and is unconscious or very weak, keep it horizontal. Do not lift its head, lest blood, vomit, or saliva flow back and block its airway.

- If your cat has consumed poison, the proper response depends on the particular type of poison. For example, sometimes you should feed the cat an emetic, and sometimes you shouldn't. In any event, keep a sample of whatever the cat has consumed, so the

vet can determine the precise nature of the poison. If the cat has consumed the poison by licking it off its fur, prevent the cat from further licking, perhaps by wrapping its body in a blanket, with only the cat's head sticking out.

# THE EVOLUTION OF THE CAT

Cats are mammals—which means, among other things, that they produce living offspring (rather than eggs that hatch into offspring), they feed their young with milk from the female mammary glands, their bodies are substantially covered with hair, and their body temperature is self-regulating.

The carnivorous (meat-eating) mammals from which modern-day cats evolved prowled the earth some 40 million to 45 million years ago. Fossils showing a strong resemblance to today's cat date back approximately 12 million years, and animals essentially the same as the creatures we would readily recognize as cats made their first appearance between 3 and 5 million years ago, in the Early Pliocene epoch. While other mammals' ancestors of that era would hardly be recognizable today, cats seem to have changed comparatively little for several million years.

More than a few members of the cat family have passed into extinction over the millennia. At least 13,000 years have passed since the saber-toothed tiger, which once prowled virtually everywhere, ceased walking the earth. Other now-extinct cats include the giant tiger of Asia and the cave lion of Europe, both of which may have vanished even earlier than the saber-toothed tiger. More recent breeds that have met extinction include the Mexican Hairless, which existed only in Mexico in the late 1800s.

One breed that almost died out but has since returned to abundance is the Abyssinian  (which strongly resembles the sacred cats of ancient Egypt but is not believed to be directly related). The Abyssinian found itself on the brink of extinction during World War II, when meat, a critical component of its diet, was in perilously short supply.

Although some disagreement among taxonomists persists, the cat family ("Felidae") is generally considered to include three genuses (in the traditional scheme of zoological classifications: phylum, class, order, family, genus, species, and variety). These genuses are: (1) *Panthera*, which includes the big cats, such as lions, whose bones in the mouth area are configured in such a way that they are able to roar; (2) *Felis*, the smaller cats, whose bone structure does not permit them to roar; and (3) *Acinonyx*, which includes only the cheetah, distinguished by several features, including its relatively small canines, its wide nasal apertures, and the fact that its claws are not fully retractable.

Some forty species of cat exist today. The species with the greatest variety is the domestic house cat, which has thrived and multiplied in diverse forms largely as a result of the aid of humans. Before humans entered the picture, the colors and patterns of cats' coats reflected their environment, evolving primarily so as to camouflage them from both their predators and their prey. Controlled breeding by humans, however, has yielded physical variety unrelated to environmental considerations.

Cats now live on every continent except Antarctica. By a few million years ago, cats had spread throughout most of the globe on their own, but humans introduced them to a number of new places, including Australia.

Human introduction of cats into new environments has sometimes produced troubling consequences. For example, humans introduced felines to the

Galápagos Islands, in the Pacific Ocean off the coast of Ecuador; the result was disastous for a number of indigenous creatures that until then had never required the need for defense against this type of predator.

Today, some 34 percent of the homes in the United States have at least one cat, and Americans own almost 70 million cats over-

all. (There are more dog households in the United States—about 36 percent—but fewer dogs overall: about 58 million.)

The earliest instances of feline domestication are difficult to pinpoint, but it has been authenticated as having occurred at least by 1500 B.C. (and probably took place a good bit earlier than that). The cat was declared sacred during the fifth and sixth Egyptian dynasties (approximately 2500 B.C. to approximately 2100 B.C.), although kitties may not have been actually scratching furniture and eating houseplants quite that early!

Art and literature suggest that cats were prowling human abodes in Greece and China as early as the fifth century B.C., and Sanskrit records speak of cats in India around the first century B.C. On the other hand, Arabia and Japan may have had to wait until A.D. 600 for feline domestication. And in Britain, the earliest records of domestic cats involve a Welsh prince who passed feline protection legislation in the tenth century A.D.

Cats, especially black ones, have

long been associated with religion and the occult. Ancient Egyptians worshipped a cat-headed goddess named Bast, and archeological digs in Egypt have turned up numerous cat mummies. (These digs have also turned up mouse mummies, presumably to serve in the hereafter as food or perhaps entertainment for the cats.)

Cats have played similarly sig-

nificant roles in religions of Scandinavia and Asia. And the history of the English-speaking countries, certainly including the United States, is rife with references to cats as major players in sorcery and witchcraft.

In at least one respect, feline evolution has paralleled that of camels and giraffes more than, for example, dogs. Specifically, cats run not by moving both

 front legs and then both rear legs, the way a dog (or horse) does, but by

moving both the front leg and rear leg on one side, and then the front leg and rear leg on the other side. No other animals except the camel and the giraffe run in this manner.

Scientists speculate that Egyptians first domesticated the cat upon recognizing the feline talent for catching and destroying grain-eating rodents. Necessary precursors of that development, however, were the more fundamental shifts in human existence involving the development of agriculture and the trend toward urbanization, which together generated not only food surpluses, but also food waste—in sufficient quantity to attract and support otherwise feral, solitary, free-roving cats.

These cats were scavengers, and their move into proximity to—and cohabitation with—humans proved a spectacularly successful evolutionary development. The key to evolutionary survival is a capacity for adaptation, and by allowing themselves to be domesticated, cats adapted magnificently to one of the greatest changes imaginable, namely, the spread of human beings across the globe.

Saber-toothed tigers were the first "cats" to propagate and survive in large numbers on this planet. They became established some 34 million years ago (as did various other mammals, largely in response to the cooling of Earth's climate). Their strikingly elongated upper teeth, which surely hindered the basic process of eating, would seem to have made them unlikely candidates for an evolutionary success story, but in fact they survived substantially longer than modern cats have been around (or, for that matter, humans). Their demise coincided with the extinction of the

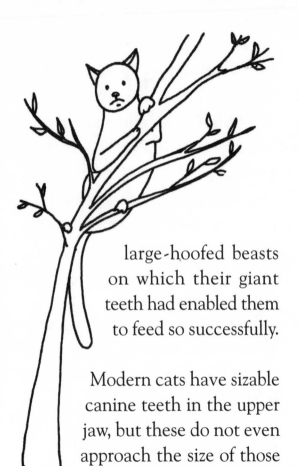

large-hoofed beasts
on which their giant
teeth had enabled them
to feed so successfully.

Modern cats have sizable
canine teeth in the upper
jaw, but these do not even
approach the size of those

of the now extinct saber-toothed cats. On the other hand, modern cats also have sizable (almost as large) canines in the lower jaw. Together, these upper and lower canines approximate the length of the daggers of the upper jaw in their ancestors.

The cheetah, which is the world's fastest land animal (clocked at speeds approaching seventy miles per hour), is at the opposite end of the spectrum from the saber-toothed cats, in that it has proportionally the smallest canine teeth of any cat. On the other hand, it has large nasal openings that permit the rapid air intake necessary for high-speed chase, and it possesses other unique structural and physiological features that contribute to the same end. Thus, while the cheetah may not have evolved with the fierce weaponry of the saber-tooths, evolution has endowed it with other assets such that, in a one-on-one footrace for survival (loser gets eaten), the cheetah usually prevails.

Cats present special challenges for taxonomists, scientists who specialize in the classification of living creatures. For one thing, the cheetah occupies an entire genus all by itself. Also odd is the puma, which by any calculation in inches or centimeters should rank as at least a mid-size cat, but is generally called a "small" cat because of minute features of certain bones in its throat. Then there are the ocelot and margay, which are placed in the subgenus *Leopardus,* because they have only thirty-six chromosomes, rather than thirty-eight, like most cats, including domestic house cats. (Humans have forty-six.) Disagreements regarding various aspects of cat taxonomy persist to this day.

Although a number of cats such as the saber-toothed tiger passed into extinction without "help" from humans, others have been forever lost or are on the verge of being lost as a direct result of human causes. Consider, for example, the different forms of tiger. The Balinese tiger vanished from the earth in 1937. The Javanese tiger followed soon after, as did the Caspian tiger. Guns, poison, and deforestation have reduced the population of tigers in Asia by

95 percent in the space of less than one human life span.

A similar fate has befallen various types of lions. What was believed to be the last southern Cape lion was killed by hunters in 1865, and the Barbary lion passed out of existence in 1922.

Particularly at risk among the

world's remaining cats are those like the tiger and jaguar, which require not only large spaces in which to hunt, but large spaces of a specific type (for example, forests). (This requirement is in contrast to leopards, for example, which are able to survive in somewhat more diverse environments.)

On average, mixed-breed cats live substantially longer than purebred cats. The former are simply genetically hardier. As a result of that fact alone, 90 percent of all domestic cats are mixed breed, notwithstanding the opposite impression one might get at cat shows and the like.

Only in a few geographically isolated areas have purebred cats developed naturally. The Japanese Bobtail in Japan, for example, or the Angora in Anatolia, or the Siamese in Thailand (once Siam)—all developed without dilution by other breeds.

The role of humans in the development and geographic dissemination of diverse breeds is hard to overstate. Among numerous individual examples:

- The Japanese Bobtail, a cat distinguished by its short curled tail (typically four or five inches in the adult), was introduced to the world outside Japan by American soldiers, who carried some home after World War II.

- Siamese cats, now popular throughout the Western Hemisphere, did not reach

England until the late 1800s, as gifts from the king of Siam to the British consul-general in Bangkok.

• The first Himalayan cat was born at Harvard Medical School in 1935, the result of deliberate crossing of several breeds, including the Persian and Siamese.

Evolution, with or without help from man, has yielded notable differences in the personalities and temperaments of various breeds of cats, as well as differences in their color and other physical features. For example:

- The Siamese cat is one of the few that can be trained to walk on a leash like a dog.

- The Turkish Van cat likes to swim.

- The Maine Coon cat habitually sleeps in odd positions in odd places.

# FAMOUS CAT OWNERS, PAST AND PRESENT

## ARTISTIC CATS

*Pierre Auguste Renoir*

Renoir loved his three sons and had a fascination with cats. Both his sons and various cats were portrayed in many of his paintings. In one of them, *Child with Cat (Miss Julie Manet)*, a beautiful, wistful young girl holds a cat that is so perfectly content it appears to be smiling.

## CATS OF THE BIG AND LITTLE SCREENS

### *Christina Applegate*

Christina Applegate is the actress who portrayed Kelly, the ditzy blond daughter of Al and Peg Bundy, on *Married with Children*. Natasha and Jesse are her two black cats.

## Downtown Julie Brown

This former MTV-VJ and current host of E! channel's *The Gossip Show* owns two cats. They were originally named Rum and Coke, but Brown's neighbors gave her funny looks whenever she'd call out the back door "Coke! Coke!". To avoid trouble, she renamed the cats Vodka and Tonic.

## Regis Philbin

The star of *Live! with Regis and Kathie Lee* owns a Persian cat.

## The Simpsons

Even a cartoon family needs pets! The Simpson's first cat, Snowball, never appeared "on-screen." The poor kitty was killed in a car accident and replaced by Snowball 2. Unlike the Simpsons' dog, Santa's Little Helper, Snowball 2 is a minor cartoon character.

## Martha Stewart

Stewart, unlike a cat, is said to need only four hours of sleep a day. She is, however, the proud owner of six cats, two of whom are named Teeny and Weeny.

*Patrick Stewart*

Since leaving *Star Trek: the Next Generation*, Stewart has been taking on some dastardly roles. In a *Today Show* interview, he said of his bad-guy role in the film *Conspiracy Theory*, "I think

I'm going to have to take out ads in the trades when this movie opens. You know, to explain that I have a cat and I'm nice to her."

*Jonathan Taylor Thomas*

This sixteen-year-old actor appears weekly in the popular sitcom *Home Improvement*. He has also played lead roles in the films *Huck and Tom* and *Wild America,* and is a major animal lover who won't eat meat or use products that have been tested on animals. In 1994, he did the voice-over of the young lion destined to be king in *The Lion*

*King.* Is it any wonder that he has a cat named Simba? Samantha, a Himalayan who is Simba's mom, is his other kitty.

*Vanna White*

As hostess of the game show *Wheel of Fortune,* Vanna White has been destined to turn heads and letters. Vanna often speaks lovingly of her two cats on the show.

### LITERARY CATS

*Dr. Samuel Johnson*

The son of a bookseller, Johnson

grew up to become the most famous writer in eighteenth-century England. He had a pet cat named Hodge and fed him extravagant treats like oysters. He didn't ask the servants to run this errand because he feared it would make them dis-like the cat.

*Lewis Carroll*

Cat-lover Carroll created the Cheshire Cat, who would slowly fade away and leave only his smile.

*Charles Dickens*

When Dickens's cat gave birth

to a litter, the author allowed only one to remain in his house with the mother. The kitten was known thereafter as the Master's Cat, and it would snuff out Dickens's reading candle to capture his attention.

## Alexandre Dumas

The author of *The Three Musketeers* and *The Count of Monte Cristo* had an unusual cat named Mysouff. Every day, Mysouff would accompany Dumas to his office and then walk back home. At the end of a long day, the cat would scratch on the door to be let out so he

could meet Dumas at his office and accompany him home. This behavior isn't all that unusual; cats seem to have an internal clock that senses what time it is. They always know when it's time to be fed, don't they? What made Mysouff so unique was his extrasensory perception. When Dumas had to work late, the cat seemed to know it, and he wouldn't ask to be let out at the normal time.

## Ernest Hemingway

This American writer owned about thirty cats, including some six-toed polydactyls. Descendants of these cats still live in Hemingway's old home at Key West, Florida.

## Victor Hugo

Many entries in Hugo's diary refer to his pet cats.

## Edgar Allan Poe

Poe often used cats as sinister figures in his stories, such as "The Black Cat." Yet Poe loved cats, and that particular story had been written with his pet Catarina in mind. Over the years, he had many cats. The winter of 1846–1847 was one of Poe's particularly destitute times; he and his wife, Virginia, had no food, no fuel, and no money. One visitor found Virginia, dying from tuberculosis, with only her husband's overcoat and one large tortoiseshell cat to warm her.

*Sir Walter Scott*

Hinse was the name of Scott's vicious tomcat. He would terrorize Scott's dogs to the point of distraction and often swatted them away to seize their meals. Is it any wonder that he finally met his death at the teeth of a dog?

*Harriet Beecher Stowe*

The author of *Uncle Tom's Cabin* befriended a cat she named Calvin when he showed up on her doorstep one day. A true writer's cat, Calvin would often sit upon Stowe's shoulder as she worked.

## Carl Van Vetchen

Carl Van Vetchen, the American novelist who wrote *Peter Whiffle* and *Spider Boy*, owned a cat named Ariel. Ariel, an orange Persian, had an uncharacteristic love of water. She loved to sit under a running tap or leap into the author's bath with him. Ariel was also a retriever and a hider, and would stash small items under the rug.

## Horace Walpole

Horace Walpole, the English

writer considered to have established the Gothic genre with *The Castle of Otranto*, had a cat named Selima. When Selima

drowned in a goldfish bowl, Walpole's companion, Thomas Gray, wrote a poem entitled "On the Death of a Favorite Cat Drowned in a Tub of Goldfish."

# MUSICAL CATS

## Mark Lindsay

The former lead singer of the 1960s group, Paul Revere and the Raiders, and his wife, Deb, travel between two homes—one in Idaho and one in Maui. Their cat, Sparky, is always with them.

## Ric Ocasek

Singer-songwriter Ocasek, former member of the band the Cars, leaves his television on twenty-four hours a day for his cats because he feels "they like

the voices and the action. They all hang out in the kitchen with the TV."

*Domenico Scarlatti*

The Italian composer owned a cat named Pulcinella, who would often leap onto the keys of his harpsichord. Might she have helped him write his famous "The Cat's Fugue"?

## Albert Schweitzer

Sizi lived with Nobel Prize winner, musician, and medical missionary Schweitzer at his clinic in Africa. It was obvious to visitors that Schweitzer had deep affection for the cat because he was often seen catering to her every need.

### POETIC CATS

## Matthew Arnold

Victorian poet Arnold had a canary named Matthias and a Persian cat, Atossa. When the cat was very old, he would sit in front of the canary's cage for hours, never moving, realizing his bird-catching days were at an end. Arnold captured the scene and the essence of his old cat in one of his poems:

Cruel, but composed and bland,
Dumb, inscrutable and grand,
So Tiberius might have sat,
Had Tiberius been a cat.

*Edward Lear*

Victorian artist and humorist Lear, known for making the limerick famous, wrote:

The Owl and the Pussy-cat went to sea

In a beautiful pea green boat,

They took some honey, and plenty of money,

Wrapped up in a five pound note.

Lear's beloved cat, Foss, wasn't known for his beauty. He had a wide body, a strange expression, and a short tail. His tail was the victim of one of Lear's servants,

who believed that by chopping off the cat's tail, he could prevent the cat from wandering. Although the cat came away tail-impaired, Lear adored him, and when Foss died, he received a full burial in Lear's Italian garden.

*Pierre Loti*

Pierre Loti was the pseudonym of Louis-Marie-Julien Viaud, a French naval officer, travel writer, and novelist. In 1906, the painter Henri Rousseau did a portrait of Loti that may have been in honor of Loti's acceptance into the Academie Française. Loti, a great cat lover who often wrote of his pets, is portrayed wearing a fez and standing behind a tabby.

*Dorothy L. Sayers*

The creator of Lord Peter Wimsey also wrote poems. Two of them, "For Timothy" and "War Cat," were written for her pet cat, Timothy.

*W. B. Yeats*

Yeats was a cat lover and owner. He studied the movements of cats' pupils and likened them to the waxing and waning of the moon in his poem about the black cat Minnaloushe:

Does Minnaloushe know that his pupils

Will pass from change to change,

And that from round to crescent

From crescent to round they range?

## POLITICAL CATS

*Ron Brown*

Alma, the wife of the late secretary of commerce Ron Brown, was once told she could not board a plane with her cat; there wasn't enough room.

Brown canceled their flight—
although he was running late—
and booked a later flight so that
he, his wife, *and* the cat could all
travel together.

*Sir Winston Churchill*

Sir Winston loved his cat so

much that he commissioned a portrait of the orange tabby. In 1953, a stray black kitten showed up at 10 Downing Street and was also adopted by the prime minister. Since Churchill had just delivered a powerful speech at Margate that had been well received, he named the cat Margate.

## Charles de Gaulle

This French general once owned a Chartreux cat, known for its dense, blue-colored fur and its orange eyes.

## The Downing Street Cat

A longhaired black-and-white stray appeared at the door of Number 10 Downing Street one day to be adopted by Margaret Thatcher. "Humphrey" became the official mouser of the prime minister's quarters. He stayed on through the term of Prime Minister John Major and into the term of Prime Minister Tony Blair.

Early in Blair's term, rumors arose that all was not bliss between the new Downing Street family and Humphrey. To assure everyone that everything was just peachy at home, Mrs. Blair—a known feline hater—was forced to sit for a photograph with the cat to prove that there was no enmity between the new residents and the resident cat.

Mysteriously, in late 1997, Humphrey disappeared. The Blairs told the press that the cat was old and infirm, but the public wasn't buying the story. The government released photographs of Humphrey on his sickbed, but some complained that they weren't photos of the same cat.

## The Third Earl of Southampton

During the reign of Elizabeth I, the earl was imprisoned in the Tower of London. His cat, Trixie, traveled across London all by herself and down the chimney to her master's cell. She stayed with him until his release two years later.

## Harold Wilson

Nemo, the pet of Prime Minister Wilson and his wife, would accompany his owners on their annual vacation to the Scilly Islands, a group of small islands off the coast of England. This was as far as the Wilsons would travel; they wanted to avoid quarantining their cat, which would have been necessary had they left England.

## RELIGIOUS CATS

### Mohammed

One day, when Mohammed was called to prayer, he found his cat, Muezza, asleep on the sleeve of his robe. Mohammed cut off the sleeve rather than disturb the feline. When Mohammed returned, the cat awakened and bowed in thanks to his master. Mohammed stroked Muezza three times, and assured him a permanent place in Islamic paradise.

## Pope Leo XII

Micetto was a black-striped, grayish-red cat born in the Vatican. He was frequently seen nestling among the folds of the Pope Leo's robe.

## Cardinal Richelieu

Richelieu served as the chief minister of state to Louis XIII from 1624 to 1642, and he was known for his affection for cats. He was particularly fond of Lucifer, a black Angora.

### SCIENTIFIC CAT

*Sir Isaac Newton*

Sir Isaac had so many cats that he invented the swinging cat door for their—and undoubtedly his own!—convenience.

### WHITE HOUSE CATS

*George Washington*

The Washington cats never

lived in the White House, since it wasn't ready for occupants while George was still in office. However, Martha may have been the first American to have Newton's ingenious cat door installed, at Mount Vernon.

## Abraham Lincoln

Lincoln had a tender heart for cats. Once, when Lincoln was

visiting Ulysses S. Grant's headquarters, he came upon three kittens wandering aimlessly. Lincoln was told that their mother had been killed. He picked them all up, lovingly petted them, then advised a high-ranking member of Grant's staff, "Colonel, I hope you will see that these poor, little, motherless waifs are given plenty of milk and treated kindly."

*Mrs. Rutherford B. Hayes*

Upon coming to the White House, Mrs. Hayes left her cats in her home state of Ohio. She felt they would be happier and better cared for there, but she missed them terribly. Eventually news of her sadness reached the press and was noticed by the U.S. consul in Bangkok, David Sickels. He had been hoping to gain favor for Siam with the new president and thought the gift of a Siamese kitten to Mrs. Hayes would be a good way to get noticed. After all, it would be the first Siamese kitten in America.

The Siamese breed was considered royal in Siam and had not been exported, although sailors had snuck out a few. Sickels got permission from the king to make his gift and chose the female kitten himself. Although Sickels named the kitten Miss Pussy, Lucy Hayes renamed her Siam.

## William McKinley

William McKinley and his wife, Ida, were owners of the first longhaired cat in the White House, an Angora. Known only as "Ida's Cat," she became "Ida's Mamma Cat" after she had a litter of kittens.

## Theodore Roosevelt

Roosevelt owned two cats— Tom Quartz and Slippers, who

moved into the White House in 1901. The president is said to have loved them very much. With Tom Quartz, he played a kind of tag that involved Tom's nipping at the president's trousers. The cat is said to have carried the game a bit too far when he nipped at the trousers of a visiting dignitary and would not let go.

Slippers was a gray tabby with six toes on his front paws. The tips of all his paws were white, which is how he got his name. Once while the cat was sleeping in the White House hallway, Roosevelt led distinguished guests around him, rather than disturb his rest. After seating his guests comfortably in the East Room, Roosevelt went back to scoop up the cat. He returned to the East Room and sat Slippers on his wife's lap, where he could be petted and admired.

### Woodrow Wilson

Wilson owned a white cat with golden eyes.

### Calvin Coolidge

Coolidge was the owner of three felines—Blackie, Tiger, and Bounder. But Coolidge wasn't only a cat owner. He owned an entire menagerie, including a pigmy hippo, a bear, and a bobcat.

### Caroline Kennedy

Tom Kitten, the pet of President John F. Kennedy's daughter Caroline, became a White House cat in 1960. When Tom died in 1962, he was lovingly remembered in a newspaper obituary. But Tom Kitten wasn't the most famous Kennedy pet. It was Caroline's dog, Pushinka, a gift from Nikita Khrushchev. Pushinka was suspected by some of being a Russian spy.

## Susan Ford

Chan, the Siamese cat of President Gerald Ford's daughter, Susan, took up White House residence in 1974. He padded the White House halls for two years, until the next Siamese came along.

## Amy Carter

In 1977, Amy Carter's Siamese, Misty Malarky Ying Yang, replaced Chan and remained in the White House for four years.

## Chelsea Clinton

The present First Cat is a black-and-white, mixed-breed stray that was adopted by the current First Daughter, Chelsea Clinton. Socks, the lucky feline, is named for the white at the end of his four paws. He is the first First Cat to have been reelected in the twentieth century, and the first cat to reside in the White

House since Amy Carter's Misty Malarky Ying Yang left in 1981. Socks's diary, *Socks Goes to Washington,* was published in 1993, and he has his own fan club and a home page on the World Wide Web. At the click of a mouse, you can even hear him "meow."

# SCARED SILLY: CAT SUPERSTITIONS FROM AROUND THE WORLD

## BEST WISHES

Cats with only one eye are known as harbingers of luck. If, after encountering one, you spit on your thumb, jab it into the palm of your hand, and make a wish, no doubt the wish will come true.

## WHITE IS BLACK

In some parts of England, white cats are considered bad luck.

## BREATH ROBBERS

People once believed that cats might creep into nurseries to steal babies' breath. Nursemaids were ordered to stand constant watch over the little ones to protect them from the dreaded cat.

CATCHOO!

Some Italians believed that a cat sneeze meant good fortune for all who heard it. In other parts of the world, a cat sneeze on the morning of a wedding day meant the couple would have a happy marriage. On any other day, however, it signaled rain. If a cat sneezed three times in a row, some were convinced that everyone in the house would come down with a cold.

## CATGUT DOESN'T REALLY COME FROM CATS' GUTS

Around A.D. 1300, saddle makers in Salle, Italy, realized that strands of sheep's intestines they'd been using to sew saddles made sweet musical tones when stretched and vibrated. A man named Erasmo, who later became St. Erasmo, found that these strands could also be used to make the strings for musical instruments.

The people of Salle developed an important industry out of string making, but kept their ingredient a secret to safeguard their corner on the market. So, whenever anyone asked what the strings were made from, they would reply, "catgut." Around that time, the killing of a cat was considered bad luck, and by lying, the string makers were able to protect their indus-

try; few others were willing to take the chance of killing cats.

## CHASING LUCK

Never chase a black cat away or it will take the luck of your home with it. However, it is lucky to own a black cat or to meet one outdoors. Just never let it cross your path or you're in for a stretch of rocky road!

## CURES FOR WHAT AILS YOU

You can cure a sty on the eye by moving a cat's tail downward over the eye and reciting the charm: "I poke thee. I don't poke thee. I poke the queff [the sty] that's under the eye. O qualyway, O qualyway." This procedure is also said to work well for warts and itching.

Applying dried cat skin to the face was thought to cure toothaches, and a whole cat boiled in oil was a seventeenth-century cure for wounds. If you wanted to relieve any other illness or one that wasn't remedied by these methods, it was considered best to throw the ailing person's bathwater onto the cat and to drive the animal from the house. Yet if a cat left home of its own accord, it was considered a portent of death.

In the southern portion of the United States, the broth from a boiled black cat has been said to be a cure for tuberculosis.

## EXORCISM

The liver of a black cat was often included in the tools of exorcism.

## THE WITCHING HOUR

Black cats aren't the only felines associated with witches. People have believed that witches could transfer their spirit into any cat. A witch could only perform this ritual transfer nine times, though, because a cat only had nine lives. And when a witch was killed, the witch's cat was often murdered with her.

## FELINE TIMEPIECES

In New England, cats were once used to tell the time: It was believed that the pupils of their eyes contracted at low tide and dilated at high tide.

## KEEPING YOUR LUCK

Cats were sometimes sealed inside the walls of houses and other buildings during the Middle

Ages to guarantee the structure's good luck. In parts of England, it was standard practice to abandon the family cat after a spell of hard times. To avoid bad luck in school, some English children will spit or turn around in a circle and make the sign of the cross whenever they see a white cat on the way to school.

Through the ages, actors have considered cats lucky, but believe that kicking one would bring misery. In the southern United States, it was believed that kicking a cat would cause rheumatism, but if you drowned it, you would meet up with the devil. In Pennsylvania, however, it was believed that by boiling a black cat, you could keep the devil away.

## KITTY SHIELDS

During the Persian invasions of Egypt in the sixth century B.C., Persian soldiers often captured and tied cats to their shields. It was impossible for the Egyptians, who worshiped cats, to kill or even harm them, thus

giving the Persians the upper hand in the battle.

## CATS AND DEATH

Sick and dying cats were often put out of the house, out of fear that death would be carried through the feline to other members of the household.

Some Irish believed that if a

cat crossed your path in the moonlight, you would die—in an epidemic.

## HOW TO COOK A CAT

On Easter Sunday and on Shrove Tuesday in England, cats were roasted to drive away evil spirits. And on the English holiday of Guy Fawkes Day, sacks of live cats were thrown into bonfires.

On St. John's Eve, a cat or two would be cooked over a fire while other domestic animals were driven through the smoke. The ashes of the poor cats were scooped up and retained as a magical powder.

## SAILING CATS

Seamen believed that it was lucky to have a cat on board a ship. If the vessel needed wind, all the crew had to do was place a cat under a pot on deck. Throwing a cat overboard was to be avoided at all costs, as doing so could cause a storm, especially if the feline was all black. If a cat licked its fur in the wrong direction or scratched the legs of a table, a storm was also expected.

## SECOND SIGHT

In the Scottish Highlands, during Taigheirin (a ritual from the Middle Ages in which cats were sacrificed and offered to the devil), black cats were burned alive in order to obtain the gift of second sight—clairvoyance. This practice continued until close to the end of the eighteenth century.

## SOUL CARRIERS

In parts of West Africa, it is still believed that when people die, their souls pass out of their bodies and into the bodies of cats.

## UNLUCKY MAY

Cats born in May were usually drowned, since they were thought to be poor mousers, capable of hunting only glowworms and snakes. They were also thought to exhibit a melancholy disposition that was quite undesirable in a cat.

## VAMPIRE MAKERS

It was once believed that if a cat encountered a human corpse, it would snatch the soul of the dead person, who would then become a vampire.

Another belief held that it

was bad luck for a cat to leap over a coffin, since it meant ill tidings for the deceased in the afterlife. The unsuspecting cat usually met an untimely death for its innocent behavior.

## VICTIMS OF THE SPANISH INQUISITION

The Spanish Inquisition, which began in 1231, was a terrible time in cat history. Cats were considered representatives of the devil, and anyone known to harbor or aid a cat was punished by death. Cats were tortured and sometimes burned alive because it was believed that no torture was too severe for the devil.

## WEATHER BAROMETERS

If a cat sits with its back to the fire, it can mean there will be frost or a storm. When a cat sleeps with all its paws tucked underneath its body, there will be cold weather.

If a cat scampers about wildly, there will be wind, but if it washes its ears, you'd better get your umbrella—it's definitely going to rain. And when Indonesians want it to rain, they just pour a little water over a cat's back.

# SURFING THE PET NET: SOME CAT WEB SITES

## COMPREHENSIVE SITES

*Acme Pet Marketplace*

http://www.acmepet.com/
feline/market/index.html

A whole page of click-through buttons awaits. Find information on everything from cat insurance to urns for your pets, and where and how to buy such items.

*Cat Lovers Home Page at the Mining Company*

http://catlovers.miningco.com/mbody.htm

"Greatest Cat" contests, clip art, and kitty postcards can be found on this site, along with a list of links, a bulletin board, a cat chatroom, and even a newsletter about cats to which you can subscribe.

## The Cat Fanciers' Association

http://www.cfainc.org/

Learn about cat breeds, cat shows, and the latest cat news, hosted by the world's largest registry of pedigreed cats.

## Waltham

http://www.waltham.com/pets/cats/c.htm

Hosted by the pet-food giant Waltham, this site offers extensive information on cats and cat care. You can learn how to choose a cat, how to train a cat, and even how to play with a cat. And if you like taking pictures of your darling, this site offers tips on cat photography.

## JUST FOR FUN

*Basic Rules for Cats Who Have a House to Run*

http://geog.utoronto.ca/reynolds/pethumor/catrules.html

Cats have to learn how to control their humans, right? This guide provides plenty of

useful information for kitties—
and their owners!—who know
how to read.

*Cat Dictionary*

http://www.maths.qmw.ac.uk/~
lms/cats/catdic.html

Do you know what a "basket
case" is? It's a cat who sleeps in
a basket, of course. Or how
about an "alarm cat," as in "It is
4 A.M. and the alarm cat just
went off"? Wonder no more
about such terms. They're all
defined here at the click of a
mouse.

## Feline Reactions to Bearded Men

http://www.improb.com/airchives/cat.html

This site offers a study that tested the reactions of felines to men with and without beards. The conclusions are astounding and funny!

## Library Cats Map

http://www2.thecia.net/users/ironfrog/catsmap.html

Did you know that there are 257 known library cats—that is, cats who live or have lived in libraries—in the United States, past and present? This interac-

tive map will tell you where to
find them.

*Map to Cat's Brain*

http://www.ee.techpta.ac.za/
cats/catbrain.html

Where is the "licking gland"
in a cat's brain? How about the

"hatred of dogs" area or the "infatuation with people who hate cats" spot? At this hilarious site, these and other mysteries of the cat's brain are given a complete—and comic—evaluation.

## MARKETPLACE

*Cat Faeries Catalog*

http://www.catfaeries.com/catalog1.html

This catalog of fine gifts and accessories sells everything uniquely "cat." Buy a cat-shaped backpack or grow your own indoor grass specially for your cat

pal who lives indoors or is suffering from the winter doldrums.

*Kitty Korner*

http://healthypaws.com/kitty.html

Here you will find lots of things for a cat to "get into." Scratching posts, electronic mice, and even a kitty condo will entice the loving owner of the pampered cat.

## SERIOUS SITES

*Alley Cat Allies: Guidelines to Trap, Neuter, and Release*

http://www.alleycat.org/ffn/tnr.html

If you're an activist and want to help control the feral cat population, this site offers information you will need to begin "managing" a feral cat colony.

*Cats Belong Indoors*

http://www.austinspca.com/catsindoor.html

In case you've been wondering, there are many good reasons why cats should remain indoors. This comprehensive list covers the main points concerning this issue and will help you to make an informed choice.

*The Cat Consultant*

http://www.angelfire.com/ar/aruba1/cat.html

At this site, find answers to common questions like "What should I do when my cat has runny eyes?" or "What if my cat won't eat?" For a fee, you can even consult an expert and have your question answered via e-mail.

## Feline CRF Information Center

http://www.best.com/~lynxpt

Feline Chronic Renal Failure is a problem for many older cats. The answers to many questions relating to feline kidney disease are available at this site.

## A Pet Owner's Guide to Common Small Animal Poisons

http://www.avma.org/pubhlth/poisgde.html

Get tips on how to avoid a cat disaster—here, you'll learn all about plants, drugs, household products, and miscellaneous items that are poisonous to your cat.

## Adoptable Cats

http://www.access.digex.net/ ~rescue/CATS/cats.html

Here you can find many cats available for adoption. Some are months old, others are years old, while some are still newborns. All cats are described in detail and some even have pictures. Learn how to go about adopting the cat of your choice.

## Cat Quilts

http://www.execpc.com/~judy-heim/catqlts.html

If you like to quilt and you like cats, this page presents many possibilities. There are plenty of pictures of cat quilts to view and information on how to obtain cat-quilt software to craft an "electronic quilt."


## Names for Your Cat

http://expage.com/page/names-foryourcat

Anyone looking for the perfect name for a cat will find this categorized page very helpful.

WONDERFUL LINKS

*Individual Cat Pages*

http://pibweb.it.nwu.edu/~pib/
catindiv.htm

This comprehensive list of individual cat pages boggles the mind. You could spend an entire day just trying to wade—or paw—through them.

## CAT-RELATED NEWSGROUPS

Newsgroups are a kind of electronic bulletin board where folks go to discuss a wide range of topics, from child-rearing to Karl Malden's nose. Many groups are silly, while some are infinitely helpful. Usenet, a facet of the Internet, is a collection of newsgroups. To access Usenet, you'll need a "newsreader," incorporated into most browsers. Another way to access newsgroups is to go to http://www/dejanews.com. Here is a list of groups relating to our friend, the cat:

rec.pets.cats
rec.pets.cats.anecdotes
rec.pets.cats.health+behav-
    ior
rec.pets.cats.misc
rec.pets.cats.rescue

This book was designed and
typeset by Diane Hobbing of
Snap-Haus Graphics in
Edgewater, New Jersey.

# GOLDEN BEARS

A Celebration of Cal Football's Triumphs,
Heartbreaks, Last-Second Miracles,
Legendary Blunders and the Extraordinary
People who Made It All Possible

BY RON FIMRITE

# GOLDEN BEARS

A Celebration of Cal Football's Triumphs,
Heartbreaks, Last-Second Miracles,
Legendary Blunders and the Extraordinary
People who Made It All Possible

BY RON FIMRITE

MACADAM CAGE

MacAdam/Cage
155 Sansome Street, Suite 550
San Francisco, CA 94104
www.MacAdamCage.com

Library of Congress Cataloging-in-Publication Data

Fimrite, Ron.
Golden bears : the history of football at UC Berkeley / by Ron Fimrite.
p. cm.
ISBN 978-1-59692-351-5
1. University of California, Berkeley—Football—History. I. Title.
GV958.U518F53 2010
796.332'630979467—dc22
2009027004
Printed in the United States of America.


10 9 8 7 6 5 4 3 2 1


Book design by Dorothy Carico Smith

*To Linda, with love eternal*

# TABLE OF CONTENTS

1882-1926

| | |
|---|---|
| Sons Of California | 5 |
| On The Brink | 19 |
| The Quest | 39 |
| Building Blocks | 49 |
| A Wonder To Behold | 61 |
| The Varsity Drag | 77 |
| Ashes to Ashes | 93 |

1926-1946

| | |
|---|---|
| Going My Way? | 105 |
| Crash | 115 |
| Navy Bill | 125 |
| A Roll of Thunder | 143 |
| Before the Storm | 157 |
| The Storm | 171 |

1947-1957

| | |
|---|---|
| Pappy | 189 |
| Roses Have Thorns | 201 |
| Pappy's Boys | 215 |
| Decline and… | 231 |
| Fall | 245 |

1957-1982

| | |
|---|---|
| A Rose by Any Other Name | 259 |
| "The Fighting Phi Beta Kappa" | 271 |
| Free Speech | 285 |
| Mixed Blessings | 297 |
| Winning Isn't Everything | 307 |
| The Way the Ball Bounces | 317 |
| Star-Spangled | 333 |
| Uninvited | 351 |
| Out, Out, Brief Candle | 361 |
| Philosophical Differences | 371 |
| The Mouse Trap | 381 |

1982-2008
The Play                                397
Kapp's Last Jape                      417
Stranger in a Strange Land       431
The Forest and the Trees         445
Gilby                                     455
The Nadir                              467
The Phoenix                         485
Planning for the Future          499
Epilogue                             515

All-Time Cal Teams by Eras       521
Bibliography                      533

# ACKNOWLEDGMENTS

Thanks first of all to my longtime friend, mentor in worldly affairs and abiding conscience, Lefty Stern, whose energy, goodwill and ingenuity helped this project surmount the usual bureaucratic hurdles and draw support from sometimes unexpected sources. Without his brilliant work behind the scenes, I can honestly say this book could never have been written. Thanks also to his wife, Gay, for forgiving him his many absences from hearth and home in the pursuit of book business.

I am also deeply grateful to the unflagging support of the University of California Alumni Association, most especially to Executive Director R. Tucker "Tuck" Coop, Director of Business Development Bill Reichle and Membership Director Nancy Brigham Blattel. The history project was one they inherited from a previous alumni administration, but they adopted it as their own and provided invaluable service in championing it to the extended university family.

Speaking of family, I am forever indebted to my daughter, Deborah, whose computer skills more than compensated for the technological shortcomings of her troglodytic father. She also proved to be a most perceptive editor. In fact, there is not a word of the text she hasn't read firsthand. Thanks also to her friend, Deborah Rich, who shared some of her chores on my behalf. And to my journalist son, Peter, for his contributions.

I owe more thanks to my good friend, Cal classmate and former football star, Paul "Boomer" Andrew, who provided me with enough research material—scrapbooks, game programs, media guides, magazines, books—to keep me going for years on end. His memorabilia collection was a prime source for this history. So, too, was the "humongous" scrapbook of 1920s and '30s Bay Area football provided by Father Michael Rebato of St. Peter and Paul Church in San Francisco.

I also leaned heavily for material on Johnny Miller, the *San Francisco Chronicle*'s superb Research Librarian. No matter the time of day or the oddness of my requests, Johnny was ever at the ready. And to my amazement and gratitude, the requested information was cheerfully provided in record time.

Herb Benenson, Cal's assistant athletic director for media relations, was important not only for supplying me with football media guides but for bringing the book to the attention of newspapers and local television channels.

Thanks also to former *Chronicle* sportswriter David Bush and veteran Golden Bear followers Adrian "Cib" Cibilich and Dick Melbye for their careful copy reading of the manuscript and for uncovering otherwise overlooked mistakes. Margo Smith Cheml used her years of experience in the Cal Athletic Department to keep the project alive in university inner circles. Thanks also to Dr. Charles Faulhaber, director of the Bancroft Library on campus, and Bancroft archivist David Farrell for their counsel and for opening for perusal their considerable resources. And to Dick Erickson, executive director of Pappy's Boys, for his loyal support. And to Cal alum Adolph Rosekrans for providing memorable art work.

I would also be remiss if I didn't acknowledge MacAdam/Cage publisher David Poindexter and editor in chief Pat Walsh for keeping the faith.

Now, dare I say it…"Go Bears!"

## HEARTFELT THANKS FOR THE GENEROUS SUPPORT
## OF THESE LOYAL FRIENDS OF CAL FOOTBALL:

Adams, F. Lawson
Adams, William H.
Agler, Harry
Amling, Raymond
Amling, Wallace
Andrew, Paul
Atkinson, Gilbert
Ausfahl, Bill
Barker, Dwight L.
Bartlett, Edmund G.
Beale, Pax
Bingham, R.C.
Boeri, Giulio
The Bowen Family
Briggs, Jr., George C.
Briggs, Jr., Robert O.
Brown, Barry
Brunk, Jr., B. Frank
Bush, David
Callender, William C.
Chapman, Samuel
Chrisman, Jr., George
Cibilich, Adrian J.
Coblentz, William
Collins, James
Coop, R. Tucker
Craig, John R.
Dalton, John R.
Dempsay, Linda
Denison, Robert Charles
Dorward, Donald F.
Duncan, Douglas
Dunn, Roger C.
Ellsworth, Robert
Ely, Honorable Dwight
Engs, Stuart R.
Engs, III, Edward
Fisher, Donald
Fry, J. Wesley
Gardner, David P.
Gelardi, Patrick
Gierlich, James
Gilbertson, K.S.
Glynn, Patricia

Goldman, Richard N.
Goodin, Robert
Gordon, Stuart M.
Gray, Robert L.
Haas, Mimi
Haas, Robert D.
Hamilton, Jr., Noble
Hanifan, James
Hering, John
Higson, Jr., John Wayne
Hill, Marcia T.
Hodge, Fred
Holloway, David
Holloway, Jan and Maurice
Hyde, Crosby
Jackson, Robert
Keckley, Jr., Paul C.
Kirby, David
Lee, Douglas
Ley, Peter C.
Loughran, Kenneth
Lovejoy, James
Lowry, Gail
MacDonald, Lloyd S.
Maggetti, James
Marinos, James
McCaw, Donald B.
McKee, W. Stuart
McKnight, Paul
McManigal, Jr., James K.
McVicar, Robert
Melbye, Richard and Anne
Melo, Sheila
Miller, Henry S.
Miller, Paul J.
Murray, Jr., Dr. Dwight
and Jeanne
Nelson, S. Victor
Newell, Minton J.
Newmark, Kent
O'Brien, Jr., Walter
Osborne, David H.
Parrish, Edwin
Pihl, General Donald

Price, P. Anthony
Pyle, Robert W.
Rawlings, Kenneth B.
Rhode, Dr. John
Richardson, Kennedy P.
Rosekrans, Adolph
Rotary Club of Oakland
Rubin, Robert
Ruegg, David
Sarhatt, Timothy
Schacht, Henry
Schmitz, M.D., Thomas
Schwocho, Kenneth
Shippey, David
Smith Chmel, Margot
Spence, Jr., G. Stuart
Stallworth, Darryl
Stathakis, George
Stauffer, Donald J.
Steiner, Bob
Stern, Hans "Lefty"
Stock, John
Stoney, Jr., Carl J.
Thompson, Katharine S.
Tietz, Kenneth
Tozer Scholz, Josefa
Trione, Henry F.
Trutner, Thomas
Tunney, Matthew
Upshaw, Montague
Vallerga, John
Verling, Richard
Vlahos, John J.
Vohs, John
von der Lieth, Robert H.
Warren, Jeffrey
Wilhelm, Robert G.
Winton, Michael
Wong, Dr. Michael
Yaich, Branislav
Zischke, Peter

PART I

1882-1926

# CHAPTER ONE

# SONS OF CALIFORNIA

On a clear summer day in 1866, Frederick Billings, a lawyer, mining entrepreneur and trustee of what was then the College of California, stood gazing across San Francisco Bay from a barren hillside just north of the city of Oakland. Billings envisioned this isolated plot as the site of a grand new campus for his thirteen-year-old college. He was so moved by the majestic panorama before him of the Bay, Golden Gate and vast Pacific beyond that he burst into verse, quoting from a poem by the 18th-century Irish clergyman and philosopher Bishop George Berkeley:

> *There shall be sung another golden age,*
> *The rise of empire and arts,*
> *The good and great inspiring epic rage,*
> *The wisest heads and noblest hearts...*
> *Not such as Europe breeds in her decay;*
> *Such as she bred when fresh and young.*
> *When heavenly flame did animate her clay,*
> *By future poets shall be sung.*
> *Westward the course of empire takes its way...*

It occurred to Billings as he recited these lines that Berkeley, in fact, would be a fine name for the westward-facing city that must inevitably spring forth at the foot of this new campus. And so, as the good Bishop himself might have decreed, it came to pass.

One thing was certain: The college itself had come some distance from its uncertain 1853 beginnings in rented space at a one-time Fandango dance hall at 5th and Broadway in downtown Oakland. Funded by a group of Protestant ministers as a liberal arts college, it was originally called the Contra Costa Academy. Two years later, the school moved farther downtown and was renamed the College of California.

But there were palmier days ahead. In 1862, President Lincoln signed the Morrill Land Grant Act, which offered public land to those states establishing, in the interests of the westward-ho migration, "a college of agriculture and the mechanical arts." And with the Civil War then raging, a further provision of the Act called for such colleges to include military training in the curriculum. In 1866, the California State Legislature voted to establish one of these so-called land grant colleges.

Meanwhile, in Oakland, the ministers were having trouble keeping their fledgling school financially afloat. One of the founders, the Reverend Henry Durant, despaired of convincing San Francisco's rough-hewn nouveaux riches that higher education was worthy of investment and that colleges were not merely sanctuaries for the idle and the improvident, as such tycoons as George Hearst and Collis P. Huntington seemed then to believe. "Individualism," complained Durant, "is carried to an extreme in California. Idealism seems lost from the mass of the people. They are sensualists and materialistic."

Their college all but broke, the ministers made an offer to the state of California it could not refuse: They would transfer their buildings and property, including the Berkeley site, to the state on assurance that the new land grant school should become "a complete university," offering not just courses in agriculture and "the mechanical arts" but in language, art, science and all the other intellectual pursuits common to the better colleges. The legislature readily agreed. In this new public university, Durant and his fellow clerics hoped to have their dreams fulfilled of creating a Harvard of the West.

On March 23, 1868, the legislature passed the act creating the University of California, and Governor Henry Haight signed it into law. The date is annually celebrated as "Charter Day." The university opened for classes in 1869 with a faculty of ten and a student body of 40 men. Women were admitted the next year. The move to Berkeley was made in the Fall of 1873, not quite in time for the commencement ceremonies of the first graduating class, known thereafter as the "Twelve Apostles."

The university's motto, "Fiat Lux" (let there be light), was perhaps best expressed by its president that year, a former science professor from Yale named Daniel Coit Gilman. The school's purpose, he declared, should be to train students "in all the intellectual callings of life" and to direct them toward "a prolonged search for the truth, which is to be found in the rocks, the sea, the soil and air, the sun and the stars...but let us also learn the lessons which are embodied in language and literature, in laws and institutions, in doctrine and opinions, in historical progress."

In 1879, the new State Constitution proclaimed the university "a public trust...independent of all political or sectarian influence." Its growth was astonishing. Within its first decade, schools of law and medicine were established and an impressive new library opened. And with growth and hard work came the need for extracurricular diversion.

On November 6, 1869, in New Brunswick, New Jersey, an exciting new game was introduced when Princeton and Rutgers played something called American football. It combined some of the ingredients of rugby and soccer, in that there was more kicking than ball-carrying, but, with its rules only vaguely defined, it was much rougher and certainly more chaotic than either of the older games. In these formative years, football more closely resembled the riotous freshman vs. sophomore "rushes" first popularized by Yale earlier in the century. These events, involving scores of participants, were essentially just organized brawls. The Civil War had left young Americans with an experience of violence difficult to expunge, and in this new game of football, with its blocking and tackling and barely inhibited mauling, they found a convenient outlet for pent-up hostility. The game soon became popular among students—if not administrators and professors—at supposedly serene Ivy League colleges.

It would take nearly a decade for some variation of the new game to reach the Pacific Coast. Football was first played on these shores November 3, 1877, on the Cal campus between the freshman and sophomore classes. Kickoff was scheduled for 11:05 a.m., with no set time limit for play and with only one harried official. The victory trophy was to be the game ball itself, which was then shaped like a good-sized watermelon. At 1:30 that afternoon, after sophomore Vince Buckley kicked his second field goal—to zero points for the frosh—his teammates hoisted him to their shoulders and marched off the field in an apparent victory celebration. Game over. But not for the freshmen.

As Buckley was being packed off to the post-game party, freshman Jim McGillivray snatched up the ball and sped off with it toward what there was then of downtown Berkeley. The sophs gave mad chase and finally cornered the culprit as he attempted to crawl to safety under a backyard fence a good half-mile from the field of play (surely, the longest run ever by a Bear back). Trapped, McGillivray fumbled away the ball. It was recovered by his most dogged pursuer, sophomore Ora "Iron Duke" Enslow. Then, in a Solomonic gesture of class fellowship, the ball was cut in half, each side receiving its share, the final score be damned.

The interclass rivalry continued in some form or other until in 1882 the university decided to field its own first football team. There being no available collegiate opponent, the first game was played on

December 2, 1882, against the Phoenix Club of San Francisco, a team composed of expatriated British ruggers. A mostly bewildered crowd of 150 watched at the Old Recreation Grounds in the city. The rules were nearly as ill-defined as those that governed the frosh-soph melees. Crossing the goal line, for example, did not necessarily signify a score, since tacklers could either wrest the ball from the runner before he could touch it down or drag him bodily back onto the field of play.

Linemen were permitted to kick the ball backward to running backs. Touchdowns counted for only two points, but conversions were worth 5 and field goals 7. Neither team wore identifiable uniforms, which contributed significantly to fan confusion. There were frequent disputes on the field over rule interpretations, although both sides agreed the game should last seventy minutes with two thirty-five-minute halves and a ten-minute intermission. The Phoenix won, 7–4. A campus publication, the *Berkeleyan*, reported buoyantly that though "our boys" were beaten, "they surprised themselves." No question about that.

In 1884, the team wore uniforms for the first time, sporting blue and gold jerseys and white shorts. Its star that season was Charles A. Ramm, whose athleticism would come into play twenty-two years later when, as a Catholic priest, he saved St. Mary's Cathedral from destruction in the great San Francisco earthquake and fire by scaling the church spire, beating out the flames with a cloth bag while clinging for his life high above the street. Monsignor Ramm later served as a university regent for thirty-two years (1912-44).

On February 14, 1885, the first game was played on the Cal campus, at a field near the current Life Sciences Building, against the Merion Club of San Francisco, another team of British ruggers. In fact, all of the games played in these first seasons were, though something of a mishmash of the two sports, more rugby than football. Meanwhile, in the east, the American game was evolving into something entirely separate from the British one and gaining popularity, much to the dismay of academicians. Among those resisting the game's charms was Cornell president Andrew D. White, who in rejecting a team request to play a road game in Cleveland, commented briskly, "I will not permit thirty men to travel four hundred miles to agitate a bag of wind."

It would take an Ivy Leaguer to develop the game as it should be played in the Bay Area. Home in San Francisco after his 1885 graduation from Harvard, Oscar Shafter Howard was astonished and disheartened to find that the game Cal and the club teams were playing bore little resemblance to football on the east coast. He volunteered to teach the rules to Cal students and to coach their team, if only for the one season of 1886. The university promptly hired him. So, in fact, the first real game of American football, as it then existed, was played between Cal and an all-star team from San Francisco called the Wasps on January 16, 1886. Touchdowns now counted four points, conversions two, field goals five and safeties two.

Under Howard, the Bears ran an offense roughly akin to the modern T-formation, with the quarterback positioned under center and tossing laterals to backs split wide behind him. They easily defeated the Wasps, 20–2. On April 30 of '86, they trotted out new uniforms with blue Jerseys emblazoned with a gold "UC," with knickerbockers and blue sox. Howard's neophytes finished that first season with a record of six wins, two losses and a tie, although three of the wins came as a result of forfeits from teams on the schedule unfamiliar with or reluctant to try the new game. Howard would be Cal's last head coach until 1892, the teams relying instead on elected captains. And, as opposed to the east where traditional rivalries had long been in place, the west coast Bears had no collegiate foes. In 1892, they finally found one. A big one, at that.

Although his own formal education was limited, railroad magnate Leland Stanford had for many years harbored aspirations to become part of California's burgeoning collegiate scene. He was reportedly miffed when he was passed over as a candidate for the U.C. Board of

Regents in 1883. Then tragedy intervened. On a European vacation the next year with his wife Jane and son Leland Jr., the boy contracted typhoid fever and died at a hospital in Florence at the age of fifteen. The Stanfords were devastated by the loss, so much so that Leland suffered from hallucinations while trying to sleep at night. On one such occasion, he told a friend, he was visited by the boy's ghost. The shade urged his father to stop grieving and get busy building a university so that California youth might be afforded the higher education of which his own premature death had deprived him. Stanford said he awakened proclaiming, "The children of California shall be our children."

Thus was born Leland Stanford Jr. University, built on the nine thousand-acre stock farm Leland Sr. owned near Palo Alto on the San Francisco peninsula. The university opened for classes on October 1, 1891 with 539 students and David Starr Jordan, a Cornell graduate and former president of Indiana University, as its first president. Its buildings were designed to look like California missions. Its goal was to equal and eventually to surpass the prestige then enjoyed by its cross-bay neighbor. A natural rivalry seemed ready-made. And with that in mind, Cal football manager Roy Gallagher, after waiting what he considered a decent interval, issued a challenge to the new school to play a football game at a neutral site on Thanksgiving Day of 1891.

The challenge was referred to John Whittemore, a transfer student from Washington University in St. Louis who had actually played college football. Whittemore, then an academic senior in engineering who would soon be elected Stanford's student body president as well as its football captain, replied that he could not possibly assemble a competitive team on such short notice. He suggested the game be played instead the following spring. Gallagher said that would be fine. What both schools then called "The Intercollegiate Football Game" was scheduled for March 19, 1892, at the Haight Street baseball grounds in San Francisco. It would be another ten years before Cal vs. Stanford would be called the Big Game, but this first meeting generated the same sort of excitement and sense of fun as those that followed.

At first glance, Cal appeared to have a decisive advantage over its new rival. This, after all, would be the Bears' tenth season of football. But even Cal's senior players that year were only slightly more experienced than Stanford's freshmen. Their 1889 season had been cancelled because of freakishly persistent torrential rainstorms. In 1890, they played and won four games against a single opponent, a club team called the Posens in honor of their sponsor, an actor. And in 1891, the season consisted of exactly one game, a 36–0 loss to the San Francisco Club.

Stanford, meanwhile, had five men on its roster who had played the game at Boys (later Lowell) High School in San Francisco, and in Captain Whittemore it had both a veteran player and a canny on-field tactician. Still, there were some pre-game jitters down on the farm. "We didn't even know if we had enough players for a team," commented Stanford left tackle Ellsworth R. Rich.

In warm-up games that winter of 1891-92, Stanford scored wins over Hopkins Academy and the Berkeley Gym preparatory school before suffering a 10–6 loss to the Olympic Club. Cal scored consecutive shutout wins over Boys High and easy wins over Hopkins and Boys Gym. Then they, too, lost to the Olympic Club in February by a 6–0 score. All of these games were considered to be merely exhibitions before the big one. And the comparative scores seemed to give neither team an edge. Cal beat Hopkins, 16–4, while Stanford won by 10–6. Cal defeated Berkeley Gym, 30–0, and Stanford won by 22–0.

The pre-game festivities set the pace for more than a century of Big Games to come. The rival school colors (Stanford's would be cardinal and white partly in deference to President Jordan's Cornell background) festooned store windows throughout downtown San Francisco. There were parades, rallies, band concerts and the usual round of collegiate hijinks. The Cal team spent the night before the game at the opulent new Baldwin Hotel on Market Street, Stanford at the elegant Palace a few blocks away. Both teams traveled in style to the ballpark aboard horse-drawn carriages. The five thousand tickets printed for the game were instantly sold. Cashiers thereafter were obliged to nod assent to ticket-takers in order to admit paying customers. The first Big Game attracted an overflow crowd of nearly fifteen thousand.

But when referee Jack Sherrard blew his whistle to begin play, it was discovered that neither team had bothered to bring a ball, a grievous oversight blamed legendarily but unfairly on Stanford football manager Herbert Clark Hoover, a cherubic youth who some years later became the thirty-first President of the United States. And it was not a chastened Hoover, as legend has it, but a spectator, David Goulcher, who volunteered to ride off in search of a proper ball. Goulcher, fortunately, was the proprietor of a sporting goods store, so he raced on horseback to his place of business, even though he was not at all certain he had such a ball in stock. What he finally brought back to the ballpark was an object that looked on the exterior like a regulation football but, thanks to Goulcher's ingenuity, was inflated with a bladder removed from a punching bag. The kickoff of this singularly unresilient ball was delayed an hour-and-a-half.

Stanford dominated the first forty-five-minute half, scoring twice on 45-yard touchdown runs by Paul Downing and Carl Clemens. For years afterward, Clemens was credited with both touchdowns, although, unseen by press box observers, he had reversed the ball to Downing for the first. Whittemore completed the first-half scoring with a 30-yard run and then somehow kicked that leaden ball through the uprights for the conversion. Since touchdowns were then worth four points and conversions two, Stanford led by a score of 14–0. But Cal came back in the second half with two touchdowns by Ray Sherman and a safety. Final score: 14–10 Stanford.

The gross receipts from Big Game 1, as tabulated afterward at the California Hotel by Stanford's Hoover and Cal's Herbert Long, came to $30,000. After subtracting the $250 fee for renting the ballpark, the schools split the remainder evenly. And they agreed their game should be an annual event. Intercollegiate football in California had truly arrived. And in preparation for more to come, the schools hired professional coaches, Stanford's first ever, Cal's first since 1886, and both from Yale.

Stanford signed the bigger name, hiring Walter Camp, a man already recognized as the game's preeminent authority, indeed its father figure. "What George Washington was to his country," said fellow coach John Heisman (he of the trophy), "Camp was to football—the friend, the founder and the father." Born in 1859, Camp entered Yale in 1876, playing varsity football for six years, the last two as a medical student. He was team captain his last three years, and later its highly successful coach. He became a member of football's first rules committee and dominated it almost until his death in 1925. It was he who conceived of the idea of selecting All America teams, and for many years after his first All America team in 1889, his was the only team that counted. He was easily football's biggest booster, and for reasons of bettering the game's west coast standing, he volunteered to coach the Stanford team without pay for the 1892 season.

At the same time, Cal hired a younger Yale man, Thomas "Bum" McClung, a star halfback and teammate of Pudge Heffelfinger and Amos Alonzo Stagg on the famous Bulldog team of 1888 that went undefeated in thirteen games and outscored opponents, 694–0. McClung would become the first of four consecutive Yale men and seven straight Ivy Leaguers to coach football at Cal. Originally from Tennessee, McClung had been a tough and resourceful player, famous for his tackle-resistant scissors stride and devastating straight-arm.

"Football in those days," said the great coach Fielding Yost, "was a man-to-man fight on the field. It was part of football to be rough—to use hands and knees and elbows any way you could…to do about everything except slug with a closed fist, and even that wasn't always penalized."

McClung was tough, but he was also something of a football scholar, a staunch advocate of the punting game as a means of establishing favorable field position. He was disappointed to find that aspect of play sorely lacking in the west, employed only when "absolutely necessary." Under his influence, that would change.

Alas, McClung coached just the one season at Cal, the fall of '92. It was a season constructed entirely around the Big Game. Cal's only other opponent was the Olympic Club, which it played three times, winning two. Stanford prepared itself with a win and a tie against… who else?…the Olympic Club. The Big Game itself ended in a 10–10 deadlock. Ever the analyst, McClung suggested afterward that "in justice to both teams, it may be said that neither played the best game that it was capable of…But a feeling of encouragement should, I think, prevail among our men as regards football prospects for the future, for although some of the best players are to leave this spring, there are many players who have late taken an active interest in football, and who when they come to understand more of the requirements of the game, will be able to take their places; for the knowledge of football never graduates."

Bum took his knowledge elsewhere, eventually becoming Treasurer of the United States. His replacement at Cal for 1893 was his old teammate, William Walter "Pudge" Heffelfinger. Still in his twenties, Pudge was already a football immortal, although he acquired his inapt nickname playing hockey as a Minnesota teenager. At 6-3 and 200 pounds, he was far from pudgy, though a giant at a time when most linemen weighed only about 175 pounds. He made Camp's very first All America team, as well as the next two, and for decades afterward was regularly voted onto All-Time All America teams. As late as 1930, the Touchdown Club of New York named him "the greatest college football player of all time."

He virtually invented football line play, vaulting over or tossing aside blockers on defense and delivering crushing blocks on behalf of McClung and fullback Billy Bull as a pioneer pulling guard. He was considered the first professional player when in 1892 he accepted $500 to play for the Alleghany Athletic Association, the year after his graduation from Yale. He played the game well into his forties and even took part in a charity game when he was sixty-five.

Like McClung, Pudge was a student of the game, an analyst who wrote scores of magazine articles about it and when he wasn't actually playing enjoyed coaching, just as he did at Cal in '93. A restless soul, he, too, stayed just the one season, but it was a longer and more productive one than Bum's. He had five wins and lost just once, to the Reliance Club. But the Big Game, played in the rain, ended again in a tie, this time at 6–6. Cal's tying two-point conversion was booted by a back who would become the school's first bona fide football star.

Arthur Wilfred Ransome was called "Wolf," not because of any lupine characteristics but because his teammate Bob Ludlow botched, much to the amusement of Wolf and the other Bears, the pronunciation of his middle name. Ransome was a spectacular all-round player, the finest punter, place-kicker and drop-kicker of his or many another day. He would have made glad the heart of Bum McClung, Pudge marveled at his skills, sometimes placing a handkerchief on the practice field and asking Wolf to hit it with a punt from 60 yards away. Wolf came close just often enough to give Pudge bragging rights among fellow enthusiasts of the kicking game.

He averaged better than 40 yards for his 21 punts on the wind-raked and rain-soaked turf of the Haight Street Grounds in the '93 Big Game, keeping Stanford at bay and the eighteen thousand soggy fans "mad with excitement," according to the San Francisco *Examiner.* Ransome played every minute of that game. Nothing unusual about that, though, because in his four-year career at Cal, he played every minute of every game his team played, twenty-five in all.

Cal's coach of the year for '94 was yet another Yalie, Charles O. Gill, an ordained minister. Providence, however looked the other way in his one winless three-game season in Berkeley. He did have two ties,

though, the loss coming from Stanford, coached then by Camp, returning after a year's hiatus. Gill's brief tenure was significant only for
his organizing Cal's first freshman and junior varsity teams.

A fourth former Yale star, Frank Butterworth, took over for '95,
and he served twice as long as his three schoolmates. Butterworth
was responsible for what would become a time-honored football cli-
ché when, frustrated by an indifferent 3-1-1 first season, he bellowed,
"Men, it's back to fundamentals." It was during his reign, also, that Cal
cheerleaders introduced a live bear as mascot for the 1895 Big Game.
The unfortunate beast barely survived the kickoff, tormented as he was
by the noise and shenanigans. Snarling menacingly, he was removed
from the field at San Francisco's Central Park, never to return.

Butterworth was something of a bear himself, a slavedriver at practice who regularly incurred the wrath of his players. In the evening he
transformed himself into one of San Francisco's more energetic social
climbers. According to Cal's "eternal sophomore," the newsman-poet
Clinton R. "Brick" Morse, "if Mr. Butterworth had mingled with his
pupils and California alumni as freely as he did in San Francisco society, there might have been a little better spirit in that team of 1896."

Butterworth quit Cal immediately after the 20–0 loss to Stanford
in '96, missing a four-game season-ending sweep of southern California teams on a trip arranged by football manager George Reinhardt.
Counting those Southland wins over the Los Angeles Athletic Club,
two high schools and Whittier College, the Bears would seem to have
enjoyed a respectable 6-2-2 season, despite the Big Game whipping. But
under Butterworth, they were just 2-2-2.

Butterworth's unlamented departure concluded Cal's Yale era, if
not its Ivy League dependency. And in Charles P. Nott, originally from
Brown and an assistant under Butterworth (he also taught botany), the
team hit a new low, finishing a winless '97 season with a 28–0 drubbing by Stanford. In five games, two of them ties, the Bears scored just
eight points.

And yet the game had taken hold on these western slopes. And as the century turned, it would achieve tremendous popularity, only to fall victim to its own excesses.

CHAPTER TWO

# ON THE BRINK

The close of the nineteenth century—the famous *fin de siecle*—would bring revolutionary changes both to the university and its often unsteady football program. These were changes attributable in large part to a pair of dynamic, if seemingly diametrically opposed, personalities, the one a distinguished scholar, the other an inspirational coach. And an oxymoronic "Splendid Little War" provided each with a philosophical underpinning.

In 1899, the university hired as its ninth president, Benjamin Ide Wheeler, a forty-five-year-old professor of classics from Cornell, where, according to Cal's Blue & Gold yearbook, "he was adored by students, known and courted by people of culture and held in the highest honor by the world of letters." The new president saw in this still young campus an opportunity to build in mind, body and spirit a "city of learning" in the tradition of his beloved classical Greece. Wheeler was something of an autocrat, a commanding figure, impressively mustached, who rode his domain, the emerging campus, on horseback. Among his good friends was another man on horseback, Theodore Roosevelt, who returned from the Spanish-American War of 1898 as a national hero. Wheeler shared Roosevelt's expansionist philosophy, seeing in the Pacific, as Roosevelt did, what the ancient Greeks saw in the Aegean—the wave of the future.

At Wheeler's request, the then President Roosevelt delivered the 1903 commencement address at Cal, certainly a prestigious event for the school. But first, the friends had, in Wheeler's words, "a gallop over the magnificent hills which give us our background and overlook the Bay and Gate."

Before Wheeler, Cal presidents on average lasted fewer than four years on the job; Wheeler lasted twenty. In that time, the student body grew from 1,717 to 9,967, the faculty from 105 to 600. Wheeler shepherded an all-star roster of professors that included such widely acknowledged experts in their fields as Bernard Moses (political science), Griffith Evans (mathematics), A.L. Kroeber (anthropology), Henry Morse Stephens (history) and Charles Mills Gayley (English). He skillfully balanced the university's land-granted utilitarian courses with the intellectual and artistic. He began what would become the university's world-renowned research departments. He encouraged women students (by 1900, forty-six percent of the student body was female) and he employed women professors, most notably Jessica Peixotto (sociology, economics) and Lucy Sprague (English, economics). For most of Wheeler's term, a Cal student could not graduate without knowing Latin and Greek.

He believed that the university should serve as a "family." He saw to it that traditions were preserved and that school spirit throve. And though football and its sideshows were perhaps alien to his scholarly nature, he faithfully attended games and rallies. He could be a skilled politician who recognized in San Francisco's social establishment a budding source of philanthropy, all the while proclaiming his conviction that "we must resist the tendency of wealth to tell us what we shall teach."

Wheeler sought to change the very face of the university, an endeavor abetted by two other good friends, William Randolph Hearst, the "Yellow Press" lord who championed and helped start the

Spanish-American War, and his widowed mother, Phoebe Apperson Hearst. The son's San Francisco *Examiner* assured its readers that though the new Cal president was both an easterner and an intellectual, he would soon enough become "a good westerner who wouldn't bag at the knees." Wheeler even adopted as a motto a popular western locution, "Boost, don't knock." This from a man with a doctorate in philology from Heidelberg University.

Phoebe Hearst would prove in the long run a far more valuable ally than her son. A former schoolteacher who in 1862 married George Hearst, a semi-literate self-made man and self-acknowledged anti-intellectual who through his successes in mining gold, silver and copper became one of the nation's richest men. When George died in 1891, leaving the forty-eight-year-old Phoebe with untold riches, she immediately began indulging her lifelong passion for cultural pursuits, particularly in the field of architecture. Inspired by chief architect Daniel Burnham's "Great White City" of Chicago's World's Columbian Exposition of 1893, she planned to transfer some of his "city beautiful" ideas to Berkeley. In 1897, she became the first woman to serve on the university's Board of Regents, a shrewd appointment if ever there was one, since she would shortly become one of Cal's most generous and important benefactors.

With the wise counsel of the brilliant Berkeley architect Bernard Maybeck and the wholehearted support of her Berkeley neighbor, President Wheeler, Phoebe financed an international competition among architects to design a Cal campus that would be a monument to beauty for "centuries to come." "Cost is no object," she wrote her fellow regents. "I have only one wish in this matter—that the plans adopted should be worthy of the great university...that they should harmonize with and even enhance the beauty of the site..."

"Time," said Maybeck of the project, "will give to the whole that earnestness and seriousness that will awaken love in the hearts of men who behold it, and it will be an incarnation of that which prompted

Mrs. Hearst to do as she has done."

The winner was a French architect, Emile Benard, but he soon ran afoul of the regents when he refused to modify his plans as they requested and of Phoebe whom he foolishly disparaged as a mere female. In his stead, the university employed a talented thirty-five-year-old New Yorker and fourth place finisher in the competition, John Galen Howard, who would remain at Cal for more than a quarter-century, the last fourteen of those years as director of the School of Architecture.

Howard significantly altered Benard's original plan, moving the campus axis five degrees south so that, as Billings envisioned it thirty-four years earlier, it looked out directly over the Golden Gate. Howard would eventually design some of the most magnificent buildings on campus, including the Campanile, the Doe Library, the Greek Theater, Wheeler Hall and, finally, Memorial Stadium. With him at the drawing board, Wheeler and Phoebe would have their beautiful city of learning, an "Athens of the West."

A year before Wheeler's arrival, twenty-two-year-old Garrett Cochran, an 1897 All American end at Princeton, became Cal's football and baseball coach at an annual salary of $1500. The embittered former coach, Butterworth, tried to dissuade him from taking the job, his very first in coaching, but Cochran accepted it with great enthusiasm. As events would prove, the times were ripe for an ambitious young man with a passion for violent sport. The war, which resulted in the widely publicized exploits (particularly in Hearst newspapers) of Roosevelt's "Rough Riders" in Cuba and Admiral George Dewey's Pacific fleet, had imbued America with a new faith in men of action. The sinking of an American battleship in Havana harbor—the presumed casus belli—had even given the public a battle cry, "Remember the Maine!"

Fulfilling its military requirement as a land grant college, Cal had in training by 1898 a full regiment of infantry cadets. Even the faculty was in a warlike state. "The war with Spain has revealed us to ourselves as well as to the rest of the world," Professor Moses, founder of the university's political science department, told a delegation of northern California teachers. "It has made us think that in spite of a strong tendency to luxurious living, the nation has not lost its virility. It has shown that in spite of our joy in peace congresses, we are still possessed of a warlike spirit, and that underneath a veneering of cultivation, there remains the uneradicated qualities of the old Viking or ancient Germanic warrior."

What better sport than football to vent that uneradicated warrior spirit. The author Frank Norris (*McTeague*), Cal class of 1894, praised the game at its roughest as being "true to the instincts of the race"— presumably the human race. The bellicose mood of the times could not have been more conducive to what became known on campus as "The Cochran Revolution."

The new coach's eagerness and energy proved contagious. In his first season of 1898, nearly ninty candidates turned out for the opening of football practice, a then record number amply swelled by Cochran's demon recruiting. Cochran believed in fitting the job to the man, not, as with so many of his contemporaries, the reverse. As a result, position switches were plentiful. Former guards became fullbacks, halfbacks became ends. And he gave the fans an exciting, relatively wide-open style of play. Cochran recognized the inherent virtues of the star system, and he coached some of the most colorful players in Cal history. Chief among them was Warren "Locomotive" Smith, a halfback with, as his nickname suggests, a hard-driving running style. Smith was at his best in important games, particularly The Big Game, as witness his three touchdowns in the 1899 classic. His power game was complemented by the flights of fancy of Lawrence "Pete" Kaarsberg, a back with another apt sobriquet—"Kangaroo." When confronted with a tightly bunched defensive line, the agile Kaarsberg simply jumped over it. When greater altitudes were indicated, his teammates took hold of special straps he had sewn into his uniform trousers and hurled his

145-pound frame over the line. It goes without saying that Kangaroo Kaarsberg's antics led to several rules changes.

Cochran's 1898 team went undefeated with two ties in ten games. Cal football was emphatically back. Before the Big Game that year, Cochran delivered a locker room talk that remains to this day a classic of the genre:

*"Boys, this is the opportunity of your lives. A greater opportunity to immortalize your names, stamp them indelibly upon the pages of the history of your university, has never been given you. For eight long years have those lobster backs made you bite the dust. It is your turn now. Make them bite and bite hard. Play, everyone of you, until you drop in your tracks; and when you can't play any longer, we'll put another man in your place. If you are repulsed once, come at them again harder. Just think what it means! Here are twenty thousand people to watch you! Your whole college is here, and they expect you to win. Some of you have mothers and fathers and sisters here today. Yes, boys, some of you have sweethearts here, who are wishing and praying that you may win. Play fellows, play for their sakes! Let your motto be, 'Hit 'em again, harder, harder!'"*

That final plea has, of course, been part of the football lexicon ever since. And Cal did hit 'em harder, winning 22–0, its first Big Game victory after four losses and three ties since the series began. Team captain Percy Hall led all rushers with 183 yards. Smith had 131 and Kaarsberg 61, many of them airborne. Cal outscored opponents that season, 221–5, the five surrendered in a tie with the Olympic Club.

Cal clobbered Stanford 28–0 in 1899, completing a 7-1-1 season. The only loss came in a post-season game with coach Pop Warner's Carlisle Indians when a bad snap from center led to a safety, the only points scored in what was considered football's first coast-to-coast intersectional game, played before fifteen thousand at the Folsom Street Grounds. The narrow defeat stood as a moral victory, since Carlisle was then considered by some experts to be the unacknowledged best team in the country. Warner gave high praise to Cochran's Bears, commenting afterward, "The two best football teams in the country today beyond any doubt are Carlisle and California."

The game had never enjoyed greater popularity in the Bay Area, Coach Cochran and his star players achieving almost legendary status in the community. To immortalize those two triumphant seasons, San Francisco Mayor James Duval Phelan, a cultivated man of means not ordinarily enthralled by sports, commissioned a bronze statue, "The Football Player," to be sculpted by his favorite contemporary artist, Douglas Tilden. Completed in 1899, it depicts a stalwart athlete anomalously clad in rugby wear having an injured leg bandaged by a teammate. At its base the inscription reads, "The Prize of Superiority in football won by the University of California in 1898 and 1899." Elsewhere are etched the names of the players, most notably Smith and Kaarsberg, as well as those of sculptor Tilden and donor Phelan. It stands today in a secluded grove opposite Evans Diamond and Haas Pavilion, the once glorious names on its pedestal unrecognizable to all but a few declining passersby.

Another surviving, if somewhat less aesthetic token of the Cochran Revolution, is the Big Game victory trophy. The origins of the Axe are at best obscure. One version has it that it was unearthed in the 1880s during excavation for a pipeline on the Stanford property. Another claims it was a lumberman's broadaxe rescued from a pile of scrap metal. Either way, in the spring of 1899, it fell somehow into the hands of Stanford yell leader Billy Erb, who, in a further complication, was the uncle of future Cal quarterback Charlie Erb. Billy Erb found ready use for the implement, brandishing it at pep rallies as a symbol of what Stanford would inflict on unwary opponents. The Cardinal would "give 'em the axe...right in the neck!"

In the sixth inning of a Cal-Stanford baseball game in April of 1899 at the Folsom Street Grounds, an axe-wielding Erb jumped in front of the Stanford rooting section and either severed a blue and gold ribbon or beheaded a toy bear clothed in Cal colors. Cal rooters were outraged, vowing vengeance. They got it. Stanford was leading 6–0 at the time, but the Bears soon rallied and behind a bases-loaded triple by Kangaroo Kaarsberg in the ninth won the game, 9–7.

As Stanford fans, including Erb, sat in stunned silence afterward, a band of Cal men, led by football star and future coach Jimmy Hopper wrested the axe from the hapless yell leader and raced off with it.

What followed was a city-wide chase that would have done credit to the then fledgling movie-maker Mack Sennett. At some point in the pursuit, Cal's Billy Drum, a sprinter on the track team, mistakenly handed off the Axe to what he thought were Cal men but were actually Stanfordites. These in turn were overwhelmed a few blocks later by another Hopper-led mob. A delivery wagon was hailed which carried the thieves to a butcher shop where most of the handle was sawed off so that the Axe might better be concealed. Finally, with the truncated Axe tucked into his trousers, Cal's Clint Miller sneaked aboard a ferry boat bound for Oakland, the Berkeley boats being watched more scrupulously by police alerted to the theft.

The Axe was finally deposited in a safety deposit box at a Berkeley bank, to be withdrawn, much to Stanford's frustration, in time for the Big Game. But the Axe, as we will learn, would never be entirely safe.

Cochran, in keeping with an unfortunate tradition at Cal then of short coaching tenures, departed after his second season, leaving behind a memorable 15-1-3 record and the undying respect of his players. In the short time he was on campus, Cochran was dead loyal to the university. In fact, said quarterback and Axe pilferer Hopper, "Garry had more Cal spirit than any of us, and we had plenty." The coach had said, "a man has only one alma mater. Mine is Princeton, but she has a sister and she is California."

In a rare tribute, Hopper, a quarterback with a literary bent, wrote in the *Blue and Gold*, that the departing Cochran had the "personal qualities that made him the idol of football men—an inflexible sense of justice, the kindness and patience of the true gentleman and a father-like solicitude to our needs...Garry was not a vulgar, physical athlete. He had raised the game to a science. The style of play, the formations, the slightest action of each man was based on scientific principle. He was a rare combination of thought and action...He was our Napoleon..."

The task of replacing a man of such imperial stature fell to one Addison Kelly, aptly nicknamed "King," not after any of the Bourbons but for a then popular baseball star, Mike "King" Kelly. Addison Kelly had been Cochran's teammate at Princeton and his loyal assistant at Cal. He was a likeable and effective coach, much respected by both students and players for turning in a respectable 4-2-1 season in 1900 with a team decimated by the graduation of such stars as Kaarsberg, Hall, Hopper and Jimmy Whipple. But Kelly survived just the one season. He was such a popular figure on campus that a large delegation of students accompanied him to the train station to give him a proper sendoff.

Kelly was simply a victim of circumstances, his abrupt dismissal more a result of events shaped at Stanford than at Cal. Kelly's coaching counterpart on the Farm that year was Fielding H. Yost. By 1900, Yost, then only twenty-nine, had already coached at Ohio Wesleyan, Nebraska and Kansas, posting winning records at all three. He was innovative—he invented the Statue of Liberty play—energetic, ambitious and obviously restless. In addition to coaching Stanford in 1900, he also coached Lowell High School of San Francisco in the morning and San Jose Normal (later San Jose State) at night, multi-tasking that did not sit well with the Stanford administration, particularly since the Cardinal played the San Jose football team twice that season. Still, with all of his responsibilities, he coached Stanford to a 7-2-1 record that included two wins over San Jose and a 5–0 shutout of Cal.

Yost left after that one season to accept an attractive offer from the University of Michigan. His 1901 team there finished 11-0 and outscored opponents 550–0. It was the first of his famous "Point-a-Minute teams at Ann Arbor. And in a delicious piece of irony, the Wolverines humiliated Stanford 49–0 in the first Rose Bowl game on New Year's Day behind the 170 rushing yards of halfback Willie Heston who had played in 1900 for…San Jose Normal. Stanford authorities were, to say the least, somewhat peeved.

In fact, Yost's exit after one year represented a pattern Stanford found objectionable, even before the Rose Bowl disaster. Since it began playing the game in 1892, the school had employed seven coaches, including Yost, and had grown weary of watching the revolving door spin round. The Athletic Committee concluded that hiring nomadic professionals like Yost was a losing proposition, no matter what their competence and records might be. Wave more bucks in the face of these transients and they're gone to greener pastures. Cal, too, had had its fill of such men, seven of whom had likewise passed through their doors since '92.

The solution to the problem seemed simple to the Stanford people—hire only alumni. Old grads would put loyalty above money. They'd see success as not so much a personal matter but as a boost to the school's prestige. They'd be good for the long haul, not subject to traipsing from school to school in search of the almighty dollar.

Cal had yet to employ an Old Blue as coach, and happy as it had been with most in its succession of Ivy League mentors, it spotted the logic in the home boy theory. As much as Kelly had wanted to stay and as happy as players and fans had been with him, it was time to put some stability into the program.

Cal's first graduate coach was Dr. Frank Simpson, a tackle on the '96 and '97 teams. Although his 1901 team averaged only 165 pounds per man, it finished with a scintillating 9-0-1 record, which included a 2–0 squeaker over Stanford, coached by Charles Fickert, class of '98. Despite their winning records and as a refutation of the old school ties theory, both coaches left after one year. Meanwhile, at Michigan, Yost completed the first of the forty-one seasons he would enjoy there as coach and, finally, athletic director.

Jimmy Whipple, a tackle on Cochran's great teams of '98 and '99, was the coach of the year for '02, a season marked by the bitterest controversy yet in the Big Game. The Bears had a fine team that finished undefeated in eight games. It was led by Locomotive Smith, back in school after taking a year off to earn some money coaching part-time at the University of Oregon, and Orval "Ovie" Overall, a 200-pound lineman and star kicker who after graduation would become a 20-game winning pitcher and World Series hero (two shutout wins in '08) for the Chicago Cubs.

When Stanford authorities learned of Smith's coaching job, they protested that as a football professional he should be declared ineligible for the Big Game. Cal submitted the case to the Pacific Association of Amateur Athletics and received a favorable ruling. Smith had not played professionally and had coached only part-time. He could play in the Big Game. Stanford insisted, however, that the "intercollegiate agreement" between the two schools, dating to 1898, took precedent. Smith was a pro; he could not play. Both schools agreed to have the matter taken before an impartial jury of fifteen members of the University Club in San Francisco. On November 4, just four days before the Big Game, the verdict was reached—Smith could not play.

Cal was stunned by the loss of its star running back. At a joint meeting of the university Executive Committee and the Associated Students, threats were made to withdraw from the game. But cooler heads prevailed. And at the Axe Rally before the game, a faculty representative stepped bravely before students angrily shouting Spanish-American War style, "Remember Smith!" and urged them to "Hold your tempers, hold your tongues, do nothing to bring disgrace upon us."

Whipple, meanwhile, announced that Bobby Sherman, a small but shifty runner, would replace Smith in the backfield.

The game that year would be played at a new site, a hastily constructed wooden stadium called Richmond Field in San Francisco between California and Lake streets and 7th and 8th avenues. The previous three years the Big Game site had been the Folsom Street Grounds, but that property had been sold in August. So despite neighborhood protests, Richmond Field was cobbled together barely in time for the kickoff. Instead of turf, the playing field was made of clay, sand and loam. It sloped noticeably downhill toward the north goal. And as a further impediment, game day came up cold, windy and damp with a thick fog common to the Richmond District. The wind kicked up miniature sand storms on the field, and there was a threat of rain. And yet a capacity crowd of twenty thousand showed up, while another two thousand or more gathered on rooftops and atop hills at the nearby Presidio, forerunners of the "Tightwad Hill" crowds of a later day. Stanford had a rooting section of five hundred, Cal of seven hundred fifty, most of them chanting the Remember Smith" refrain.

Kickoff was set for 3:00 p.m. Cal's team, even with the "massive" Overall, averaged only 169 pounds per man Stanford's a hefty 171. Sherman was not a powerful runner like the Locomotive he was replacing, but he was fast and elusive in the open field. Already that season he had returned a punt 85 yards to a touchdown and run 65 yards from scrimmage for another. But with Smith out of the game, Stanford foolishly disregarded him.

Neither team gained much on the dusty, lopsided field in the first half, the only points scoring on a 20-yard field goal by Overall, who had missed a 48-yarder by inches earlier. Field goals then counted for five points, the same as for touchdowns, so that was the score at halftime. Stanford held firm in the second half with the wind at its back. Twenty minutes into the half, a Stanford drive stalled on its own 45, and Cardinal Ed Smith went back to punt. Smith got off a wind-blown beauty, which Sherman misjudged and bobbled on his own 10-yard line, the ball bouncing free back to the 5—this on a field then 110 yards long. Sherman finally retrieved the loose ball on the west side of the field and, running laterally, dodged tacklers deftly until he picked up interference on the east side. Then he set off downfield, running full speed against the wind. Punter Smith was the last Cardinal to have a shot at him, but Sherman danced by him and streaked across the goal line to complete an amazing 105-yard return that would stand as a Cal record for sixty-four years. Sherman may not have been a locomotive, but he was certainly the Little Engine that Could.

The epic run demoralized the Cardinal, and Overall's point-after and another field goal ended the scoring. Cal had won, 16–0, and after a post-season win over an Indian team from southern California, the Bears under Whipple completed an unblemished season, Smith or no Smith.

Whipple returned in '03, as did Overall as team captain. This year the Cal line averaged an immense 193 pounds, and the team sported flashy new uniforms—bright blue jerseys with gold stripes on the sleeves. But a 6–6 tie with Stanford and a 2–6 loss to Nevada marred an otherwise successful 6-1-2 season.

Jimmy Hopper, he of the Axe caper, replaced Whipple in 1904. On October 8 of that year, the new California Field on the south side of the campus was dedicated with a 10–0 win over the Olympic Club. A wooden frame structure that seated more than twenty thousand, the new stadium replaced five thousand-seat West Field as the home stadium and made it possible to play big games, including the Big Game, on campus and not in San Francisco. The first Big Game on the grounds of either university was played there on November 12, 1904, before a capacity crowd of 21,500. The event lost much of its luster, though, when the Cardinal, under second-year coach Jim Lanagan, thrashed the Bears, 18–0. It was the only loss in the 6-1-1 season.

That '04 season represented a genuine milestone for football in the Bay Area. Cal played five major college teams that year—Oregon, Pomona, Nevada, Stanford and Washington, all on successive weekends following three early season matchups with club teams. Stanford also faced five intercollegiate foes. It was the first year for either school in which the majority of the schedule was played against respectable college opposition. Traditions were being established; the college spirit was taking hold.

At the same time, a mounting chorus of the game's detractors was being heard across the land. The 1904 Big Game, for all of the campus spirit it engendered, was one of the roughest yet played. According to the Examiner, "Berkeley's men were hurt on nearly every play" as "Stanford bucked the ball down the field almost at will." Presidents Wheeler and Jordan, once ardent rooters but now grimly skeptical observers, took careful and disapproving note of this development. Jordan, the more athletic of the two (he once scaled the Matterhorn), had at one time considered football the perfect expression of youthful vigor and the college spirit. But the increasing brutality on the field, as well as the ever more riotous post-game celebrations—liberally fueled by alcohol—left this abstemious outdoorsman sadly disillusioned. Where once he had festooned himself with Cardinal paraphernalia and led cheers in the rooting section, he now sat grey-faced before the mayhem he saw on the gridiron. And both university presidents were embarrassed by complaints from San Francisco city officials about the sometimes violent antics of intoxicated students roaming the streets after Big Games.

In the east, meanwhile, reports of widespread recruiting violations were emerging. It was reported, for example, that only three players on the 1900 Columbia varsity were actually undergraduates and that one player, Thomas J. Thorp, had played freshman football at Manhattan College before he joined the Columbia freshman team the next season. Cheating on entrance exams by football recruits was common, McClure's magazine reported, and Yale lineman James Hogan not only ate his meals at the exclusive University Club but was rewarded with a ten-day free vacation to Cuba.

Harvard president Charles Eliot, a vociferous opponent of the game, protested that football was changing universities to "places of mere physical sport and not of intellectual training." The Chicago

*Tribune* issued damning statistics showing that the game was growing ever more dangerous. The 1905 season, it reported, accounted for eighteen deaths and 159 serious injuries. Even Amos Alonzo Stagg, a football icon since his days at Yale and now coach of the University of Chicago, joined the chorus, expressing serious concern. That champion of the "strenuous life," President Roosevelt, declared that, "brutality and foul play should receive the same summary punishment given to a man who cheats at cards."

In fact, Roosevelt called together athletic, medical and faculty representatives from football's "Big Three"—Harvard, Yale and Princeton—to a meeting at the White House on October 9, 1905, to discuss ways of curbing the violence. The conferees left the session convinced they had "an honorable obligation to enforce the rules of fair play." The President urged them to draw up a statement of principle to that effect.

As Roosevelt biographer H.W. Brands recalled the meeting, "Roosevelt didn't intend to eliminate the occasional broken nose or fractured arm; without a certain element of physical risk the game would lose its zest and character-building qualities. But the head and neck injuries that were literally killing dozens of players every year were hardly improving the physical or moral health of the nation."

Still, it would take many more meetings under T.R.'s continuing encouragement to face up to the fact that rules changes were needed to repair the game. And a new organization, the Intercollegiate Athletic Association of the United States (the future NCAA) emerged ahead of the Camp-dominated Intercollegiate Rules Committee as the dominant force in these discussions. Harvard's Eliot scoffed at all the fuss: "It is childish to suppose that the athletic authorities which have permitted football to become a brutal, cheating, demoralizing game can be trusted to reform it."

Somehow, though, the job got done. New rules opened up the game and in so doing, saved it over most of the country. But not at Cal and Stanford.

Cal unceremoniously and unilaterally dropped the alumnus coach requirement in 1905, hiring J.W. "Bill" Knibbs from Dartmouth as a successor to Hopper, who like his fellow Old Blue headmen, didn't linger long on the job. Hopper, in fact, would actively pursue the literary career he had begun as an undergraduate. After joining the staff of the San Francisco magazine, "The Wave," he wrote a series of then popular short stories and joined an artists' colony in Carmel that included such already esteemed compatriots as novelist Jack London and poet George Sterling.

Not that anyone, alum or outsider, stayed in Berkeley much longer than to have a cup of coffee. Of the dozen coaches hired thus far, none lasted longer than two years. Through no fault of his own, Knibbs would be included in that itinerant number.

His brief stay was notable, however, on several accounts. Of Cal's seven opponents that year, six were college teams, further evidence that football on the Pacific Coast, as in the east and midwest, was becoming strictly a college sport. And for the second year in a row, the Big Game was played on campus, this time at Stanford. Student rooting sections were growing in size and competitiveness, their antics a reflection of the game's growing popularity. Cal rooters suffered something of a setback early in the '05 season, though, when fans complained about the garbled nature of many Oski-wow-wows and other yells. A Daily Cal investigation found that the root cause of the problem was indiscriminate consumption of peanuts. The ASUC, adopting a firm anti-goober stand, ruled that for the rest of the season peanuts could be sold only before and after games and for the first few minutes of halftime. Clarity was restored to the section's exhortations.

But there was little to cheer about in that year's Big Game. In the first half, a 75-yard run for an apparent touchdown by Cal halfback Ollie Snedigar was called back when officials ruled he had stepped out of bounds en route. Snedigar did score on a 42-yard dash in the second half, but Stanford had scored in each half after long drives and converted after both touchdowns for a 12–5 victory.

This was in many respects, though, a truly historic Big Game. The two officials, referee John Prentiss Poe, Jr., and his brother, umpire Nelson Poe were among Princeton's most celebrated football heroes, and both were descendants of Edgar Allan Poe. And it was John Poe who, as an undergraduate ten years earlier, first uttered what has since become one of sport's time-honored cliches: "A team that won't be beat can't be beat." This was not only the first game of American football to be played on the Stanford campus but also the last for fourteen long years.

Well before the end of the 1905 season, school presidents Wheeler and Jordan had met privately to consider discontinuing a game they both felt was far too injurious to be a part of college life. Rugby, they both agreed, would be an improvement. The old English game was rough enough to satisfy student bloodlust, but not nearly as dangerous because there was no blind-side blocking. And the mass collisions so common to football at the time were relatively few in rugby. Both presidents, each in his own way a cosmopolite, also subscribed to the notion that rugby was a game traditionally played by gentlemen respectful of the rules of fair play. Wheeler, who had studied abroad for years, was the more emphatic of the two. "The game of football," he declared," must be made over or go."

Actually, the game was at least partially being made over by rules changes that would go into effect in 1906, one of which was absolutely revolutionary. Legalizing the forward pass, as Allison Danzig wrote in his history of football, changed play from "the heavy-handed, unimaginative mass attack of brute force and labored progress" to "an open, quick-striking offense."

But that was not enough for Wheeler and Jordan. Weeks before the Big Game, they reached the decision in private that football must go and be replaced by rugby. Students at neither school knew of this decision. But the coaches did. Lanagan, having set a Stanford record by coaching three full seasons, agreed to stay on and coach the English game. Knibbs, strictly a football man, knew he must leave. At a team banquet at the Palace Hotel some two weeks after the Big Game, Cal's only loss that season, the popular coach rose to speak: "Boys, I can't tell you why, but I won't be with you next season." The room fell silent.

Then on December 5, 1905, Dr. Oscar Taylor, who had played for Cal in the 1890s but who had been living in England the past year, was named Knibbs' successor. No one knew it at the time, but the game he was hired to coach would not be football.

And yet the switch to rugby was not yet official, even though the school presidents endorsed it. On March 3, 1906, in fact, the athletic committees of both universities voted to oppose the change, therefore yielding to the sentiments of both players and students. Less than three weeks later, on March 22, the committees, after conferring with Wheeler and Jordan, reversed themselves. The faculties of both schools quickly approved the decision. Rugby would be the game.

American football, at the very moment it was approaching its greatest popularity and, because of the new rules, adding finesse to force, was, at least in the Bay Area, finished. It wouldn't be back at Cal for another ten years.

*PRECIS: A few California colleges, USC among them, and ath-letic clubs also abandoned football in favor of rugby. Elsewhere in the country, football remained the collegiate game of choice. California became the nations's rugby center—the 1920 and '24 Olympic rugby teams were composed almost exclusively of Californians—but it fell well behind the midwest and east in the American game. Under considerable pressure from alumni and students to rectify this discrepancy, Cal returned to the football wars in 1915.*

CHAPTER THREE

# THE QUEST

Cal's decision to return to football in 1915 after nine seasons of rugby was enthusiastically received by students, alumni and diehard fans of the American game. But it certainly created its share of difficulties, some anticipated, some not.

For starters, the transition deprived Cal of its Big Game rival, Stanford having elected to continue playing rugby. Actually, relations off the field between the two Bay Area universities had grown increasingly contentious over the past five years so the split when it finally came had an aura of inevitability. The schools' five-year accord covering athletic rules and eligibility standards expired on January 1, 1915, and they could not agree on an extension. At issue was Stanford's insistence that freshmen be declared eligible for varsity sports. Cal's faculty representatives were strenuously opposed, arguing piously that at such a tender age freshmen were insufficiently prepared both physically and academically for big-time competition.

That, at least, was the public position. Privately, Cal people both deplored and envied Stanford's success in recruiting experienced rugby stars from Australia and New Zealand as first-year players. For its part, Stanford was sorely offended by insinuations from Berkeley that its enrollment procedures were anything other than above board. Its faculty offered the counter argument that separate teams for freshmen would constitute an even bigger distraction from academic pursuits than varsity competition. Not to mention the added expense involved.

Representatives of the two schools met in a series of increasingly volatile meetings at the Palace Hotel in San Francisco in January of 1915. The Palo Alto *Times* concluded in a headline that the universities, like much of the rest of the world then, were "on the verge of war." At the third session, though, on January 22, a tentative agreement seemed within reach, pending student and faculty approval. Then on April 24, the Stanford student body voted to reject any compromise on the freshman issue. Cal students responded by voting to sever athletic relations with Stanford. University authorities agreed, citing "irreconcilable differences."

On June 16, Cal announced its return to football, declaring that the University of Washington would be its replacement arch-rival, an opponent in not one but two "big games," home and away, in the 1915 season.

Stanford promptly accused Cal of using the eligibility dispute as nothing more than a smokescreen to hide its real motive for rupturing relations. "Stanford's belief," said negotiator D.M. Folsom, "is that California engineered the break with Stanford in order to return to the old game." The "old game" being American football, which rugby predated by at least forty years.

So, no Big Game. But what of the other games? Cal, after all, would be playing football with a rugby team. It would be asking players who had never thrown a block or a forward pass (both being against rugby rules) to compete against teams such as Washington that had continued playing football while Cal cavorted on the rugby pitch. It was, to say the least, a dilemma.

And if the players knew little or nothing about the "old game," their affable coach, one James Garfield "Jimmie" Schaeffer, knew scarcely more. Schaeffer, who had been the rugby coach for the past six seasons, agreed to preside over the football transition for the 1915 season only. He had played just one year of football on the Cal freshman team in 1905. When the sport was dropped, he became a starting scrum half on the rugby team in 1906 and '07. In 1908, he became assistant rugby coach under headman Dr. Oscar Taylor while earning a degree in engineering. (Dr. Taylor, paradoxically, had played varsity football as a Cal undergraduate in the 1890s.) When the good doctor resigned to resume his medical practice fulltime, Schaeffer, at his recommendation, replaced him as head coach in 1909.

Though only a few years older than his players and looking younger than many of them, Schaeffer built an imposing 65-11-8 record in his six years on the job. A notoriously stern taskmaster on the practice field, he was a charmer away from it. As S. Dan Brodie wrote in his 1949 history, *66 Years on the California Gridiron*, "there wasn't a man on the entire squad who didn't thoroughly hate Schaeffer after every practice session. And off the field, there wasn't a man on the squad who wouldn't be ready to fight the person who said a word against the head coach."

Schaeffer seemed an exemplar of all the manly virtues. His physical courage was unquestioned. He was honest, forthright and steadfast. He was also a prolific pep-talker, and like another silver-tongued orator of the time, William Jennings Bryan, he championed moral uplift and reverence for a higher power. But he had a lighter touch. After winning his first rugby Big Game as head coach, he rejoiced, "May loyal Californians sing out 'Boola' on the first day of next season as they have on the last day of this one."

Schaeffer was a stickler for detail. Even though he'd been a fine player and capable assistant coach, he embarked for Australia after he was named head coach to study the game as played there. He even brought back to Berkeley an Australian assistant, Bill Howe, nicknamed for reasons best left unexplored, "Mother." Now, in 1915, as coach of a game of which his ignorance was boundless, he persuaded the university to send him on another educational field trip, this time to gridironland. He would seek out experts there and pick their brains. And while he was at it, he'd try to find someone to mercifully succeed him after his year at the helm was up.

He soon realized there was much to learn, since the game had radically changed since he last played it a decade earlier. New rules designed to make football safer and more exciting to watch had legalized the forward pass, shortened playing time from seventy to sixty minutes, reduced the length of the field from 110 to 100 yards, made it necessary to advance the ball ten yards, not five, for a first down and increased the value of a touchdown from five to six points.

So, notebook at the ready, football novice Jimmie Schaeffer set off with the university's blessing on a possibly quixotic mission that summer of 1915. His first stop was at the University of Washington in Seattle, Cal's double foe in the fall. In Washington head coach Gilmour "Gil" Dobie, however, he could not have picked a less likely source of encouragement. Dobie was an expert, all right; he was preparing that summer for what would become his eighth straight undefeated season with the Huskies. But Dobie was not exactly the big-hearted, open-minded coaching colleague Schaeffer had in mind as a confidant.

He was, in fact, a confirmed sourpuss, a cynic and doomsayer. Tall, lean and unsmiling, Dobie most resembled a comics-page staple of the day—the undertaker. His nickname, "Gloomy Gil," was well-earned. Despite his undefeated record at Washington (which would finally reach the astonishing total of 61 games), his pre-game forecasts were invariably dire—"Gildobian," the press called them. Once, before a critical game late in his career, he lined up his starters with their backs to the goal line, explaining that this is where he expected them to spend much of the afternoon. His relations with his players might generously be described as distant. "He was never known to congratulate a player in public and seldom in private," said one former minion.

In fact, he rarely knew a player's name, although there were exceptions. Andy Pierce, who played halfback for Dobie at Cornell, re-called that "Gil always knew my name. He unerringly referred to me as 'Fat Ass Pierce.'" Dobie made no pretense about building character or developing student-athletes: "You can't win games with Phi Beta Kappas." For that matter, he didn't see much of a future in coaching. "A football coach can only wind up two ways," he once said. "Dead or a failure."

Before such a man, a hopeful Jimmie Schaeffer appeared unan-nounced one rainless afternoon on the University of Washington campus. Dobie offered him a chair in his office, assuming this was merely some sort of courtesy visit from a rival coach. Stone-faced, he listened as the young intruder (Schaeffer was not yet thirty) confessed his unfamiliarity with the game and said how he hoped the older coach might fill him in on some of its finer points. When Schaeffer finished, Dobie sat silently behind his desk, blowing smoke rings from the ciga-rette he contemplatively puffed. Finally, after what seemed an eternity to Schaeffer, the great man spoke.

"This is the damndest thing that has ever happened to me," he be-gan. "Here across the table sits the head coach of a team I am supposed to whip soundly on two separate occasions six months from now, and he's asking me, 'How do you play football?'"

Ever resourceful, Schaeffer argued that it was only for the good of the game on the west coast that he was making such inquiries, because if Cal should be humiliated on the field this coming season, chances are the Bears would drop out of the proposed new Pacific Coast Con-ference and return to rugby. Washington would then lose a prime gate attraction and future traditional rival.

Schaeffer reached back into his reserves of persuasiveness and mi-raculously won Gloomy Gil over to his side. Possibly amused by this tyro's plight, the dour coach treated him to what amounted to a three-day seminar on football fundamentals. He further recommended that Schaeffer seek more advice from coaches in the midwest, where some of the best football was then being played.

His brain spinning with Gildobian Xs and Os, Schaeffer took the next train to the gridiron heartland. In Minneapolis, he sought out Dr. H.L. Williams, a Yale man who had been head coach at the University of Minnesota for the past fifteen years. Dr. Williams was polite but unreceptive. He suggested Schaeffer talk to Bob Zuppke, then in his third season at Illinois and soon to become a football legend as coach of the great Red Grange. Zuppke took Schaeffer on a tour of his practice facilities but was of little help otherwise.

By this time, though, Chicago newspapers had gotten wind of the Californian's bizarre quest. Interviewers found in Schaeffer a willing and almost embarrassingly honest subject, and he quickly became something of a midwest celebrity. It mattered little to this self-assured young man that his innocence should be so widely exploited. He needed information at whatever cost to him personally. He wanted entree into the coaching inner sanctum.

Then one day, weary of his wanderings, Schaeffer sought respite in a cozy little bar in Champaign near the University of Illinois campus. The bartender recognized him instantly from his photographs in the Chicago papers. The two struck up a warm conversation, enlivened for Schaeffer by a couple of beers. And in the honorable tradition of bartender-customer consultations, Schaeffer received some sage counsel:

"What you ought to do, Jimmie, is go on down to Purdue and talk to the coach there, Andy Smith. He's doing a great job. Drops in here from time to time when he's playing the Illini. Funny kind of guy, but nice and friendly, particularly after a couple of drinks."

Schaeffer confessed he'd never heard of Andy Smith of Purdue, although he did have a friend who was acquainted with an Andy Smith who was coaching back in California.

"Not the same guy," said the bartender. "This Andy's originally from Pennsylvania. He was an All-American at Penn. Still a young guy in his early thirties."

He sounds like a good source for information, thought Schaeffer. And more to the point, young enough to be a prospective successor. Schaeffer entrained that afternoon for West Lafayette, Indiana.

Andrew Latham Smith, then thirty-three, grew up in Dubois, Pennsylvania, only a few miles from the Penn State campus, where, in fact, he began college in 1901. He was a football whiz who despite a slender build was a fearless hard-driving fullback. He played so brilliantly against rival Penn in a 1902 game in Philadelphia that he was recruited virtually on the spot by the older, more prestigious school. Recruiting regulations, even on hallowed Ivy League campuses, were so lax at the time that Smith even worked out the next week with the Penn scrubs. He finished out the season, though, at State and transferred formally to Penn in '03. He received All America recognition the next year, his senior season, from football's high priest, Walter Camp.

Smith coached Penn's freshman team in '05 and '06 and served as a varsity assistant in '07 and '08. He became the head coach in 1909, and in four seasons compiled a handsome record of thirty wins, ten losses and three ties. He moved west to Purdue in 1913 and would finish 12-6-3 in his three seasons there.

He was an extraordinarily homely man, tall and gangly with a flat-nosed freckled face and narrow eyes that seemed to be in a perpetual squint. The top of his head was so knotted from his days as a helmetless line-plunger that he was obliged to wear his cap canted to one side, giving him a rakish look his ordinarily reserved demeanor scarcely merited. He was, like Schaeffer, an authoritarian figure on the field but a sociable sort off it, particularly, as Schaeffer's bartender friend advised, after a few drinks. Smith was no stranger to bartenders and, later, bootleggers, for he enjoyed his drink. But as players and fellow coaches agreed, his off-hours imbibing never interfered with his coaching duties.

Despite his basically conservative approach to the game, Smith was fond of the occasional trick play. Unlike Dobie and other coaches schooled in football before the advent of the forward pass, Smith liked throwing the ball deep downfield, as the most famous play of his coaching career would dramatically demonstrate.

Schaeffer called Smith as soon as he reached town, and the two met that evening in the Cal coach's hotel room. They hit it off immediately. Smith shared Schaeffer's obsession with discipline and conditioning. He, too, preached moral fiber. They talked through the night, and as the sun climbed in the morning sky, Schaeffer rather precipitously offered Smith the Cal coaching job for 1916, the season after their respective contracts expired.

Smith said he'd always wanted to coach in California and he was intrigued by the prospect of teaching the game to inexperienced and therefore presumably unspoiled players. He conditionally accepted the offer.

But Schaeffer's work was hardly done. Now, he had to convince his superiors, including university president Benjamin Ide Wheeler, that Smith was their man. He also had a season of coaching football ahead of him, armed only with what little knowledge he had absorbed on his trip.

He succeeded first with the Smith project. The university could not officially offer Smith the job until his contract with Purdue ran its course on New Year's Day, but a contract was ready a month later calling for him to receive a salary of $4500, about $1500 above what Schaeffer's 1915 contract called for. Smith's anticipated arrival was much heralded in the Bay Area press. With a true football man in charge, the American game was now back for good. "At Purdue," the *Chronicle* breathlessly reported, "Smith was held in high regard." Local fans soon learned that in their future coach they had a football evangelist. "As a character builder, the American game has no superior," he proclaimed. And upon his arrival in Berkeley, he wrote, "Outlawed as it has been in the past, the American game has finally gained its own here once again."

In the meantime, to help him survive his 1915 ordeal, Schaeffer hired as his chief assistant another Smith, Dr. Andrew W., a former player and assistant coach at Michigan under the famous Fielding H. "Hurry Up" Yost and his "point-a-minute" teams. Needless to say, Dr. Smith enjoyed unusual authority for an assistant, though he must have been mystified by a Schaeffer offense that had the ball pitched backward more often than forward.

It was, in every respect, an unusual season. The Bears played three winning games with the San Francisco Olympic Club, which also returned to football from rugby that year. They played three more games against club teams, split two with St. Mary's College and were soundly thrashed by USC, 28–10, the newly nicknamed Trojans having returned to football a year earlier. But in a rematch a month later, the Bears, gaining experience as the season progressed, avenged that loss with a 23–21 win.

Cal played Dobie's powerful Huskies in back-to-back games the first two weeks of November. In the first, played before seventeen thousand five hundred in Berkeley on November 6, Dobie showed his true colors, administering to his summertime pupil a horrendous 72–0 whipping, the worst defeat up to then in Cal history. That should show the whippersnapper what football is about, Dobie may have gloated. But he had made a costly miscalculation in running up the score, since, according to the agreement between the universities, the home team pocketed the gate. So at the rematch in Seattle a week later, only two thousand fans turned out for what was expected to be another grim slaughter.

And yet, with Schaeffer's silver tongue and Dr. Smith's tactical prowess—he found a way to turn Dobie's mass blocking sweeps inside—the Bears nearly pulled off the upset of the young century. Dobie's players were overconfident, even to the point of finding their coach's warnings of imminent disaster more amusing than usual. How, indeed, could they take seriously a team they had so mercilessly whomped only a week earlier? Imagine their astonishment then at being held scoreless until the fourth quarter and to find themselves needing a last-minute drive to win, 13–7, after Cal had scored on, of all things, a pass thrown forward from Roy Sharp to Rudy Gianelli, only minutes before. Let that be a lesson to teacher Dobie.

Schaeffer finished his only season as head football coach at Cal with a winning (8-5) record. Engineering was his game, thereafter, and he would be one of the chief designers in 1928 of UCLA's new campus at Westwood.

The man he recruited as his replacement would become quite simply one of the great coaches of his era, setting winning records never surpassed at Cal. He would raise west coast football to national prominence and become one of the leading lights of the "Golden Age of Sports." And at the university he grew to love, he would become a towering and enduring legend, the very symbol of triumph and tragedy.

CHAPTER FOUR

# BUILDING BLOCKS

The new coach arrived in February of 1916, barely in time to set up shop and prepare for spring practice. It was an eventful time to be in the Bay Area. The magnificent Panama Pacific International Exposition, celebrating both the opening of the Panama Canal and San Francisco's rise from the ashes of the 1906 earthquake and fire, had closed two months earlier after an eleven-month run on the city's marina that attracted more than eighteen million visitors.

A construction boom, meanwhile, was underway on the Cal campus that would within the next year add five new buildings, including the massive Benjamin Ide Wheeler Hall with its sixty-two classrooms, forty-seven faculty offices and thousand-seat auditorium.

Andy Smith came to Berkeley with few illusions about his team's immediate prospects. Despite the relatively smooth transition the players had made from rugby to football under Schaeffer, they remained in the eyes of their experienced coach gridiron neophytes. Smith wryly expressed that view to the press when on the first day of spring practice he welcomed "one hundred twenty-five of the finest specimens of humanity that I have ever laid eyes upon. However, under a hasty investigation, I discovered that about all they knew about football was that the ball was spherical and that the game was played on a field one hundred yards long and fifty yards wide. As far as knowledge of the game was concerned, I might as well have gone to Russia…Experience has taught me that successful teams cannot be built overnight."

Smith also recognized that a good part of his new job would be selling the game itself to a still dubious university administration, as well as his team to the paying public. Among the remaining skeptics was Cal's president. Despite the enthusiasm football's return had generated on campus the sixty-two-year-old Wheeler still harbored reservations about the direction the game was taking, not the least among these the necessity of hiring expensive professional coaches whose allegiances, he was convinced, lay not with the institution but with the pursuit of the almighty dollar, wherever it might be found. The purist in him deplored the game's evolution from campus recreation to public spectacle. He foresaw a time not long ahead when football would become so big that American colleges and universities might soon owe their identity not to academic excellence but to the prowess of their teams, the athletic tail wagging the academic dog. He also feared that even with the rules changes supposedly opening up play, football was still a dangerous game.

Wheeler also regretted the split with Stanford that Cal's return to football apparently brought about. Finally, for all of his onetime Rooseveltian aggressiveness in foreign affairs, the Cal president was increasingly troubled, for distinctly personal reasons, by football's martial airs—the marching bands, the uniforms, the cheering, the warlike terminology. As Gay Brechin would write in "Imperial San Francisco," "Not coincidentally, collegiate military training and college football developed in tandem, for football was and remains a vital metaphor for the warrior virtues."

In 1916, America's entry into the war then raging in Europe seemed imminent, despite campaign promises to the contrary by President Woodrow Wilson. This time, the enemy would be Germany, a country for which Wheeler had developed great affection during his student days at Heidelberg. War with Germany was unthinkable for this increasingly conflicted educator.

So who should appear on his campus but a football militant championing Cal's return to "the good old sturdy game developed by red-blooded Americans back in the early '70s of the last century." To Andy Smith, "the 11 men who go out on the gridiron represent the cooperative will of the entire student body. As the years passed, Smith would temper his jingoistic rhetoric, but in 1916, facing a daunting challenge, football for him *was* war.

Ironic then, that he should lose one of his most trusted aides to the Army before the season even began. Pete Vaughn, who had been with Smith at Purdue, was called to duty that spring as a National Guard officer to help General Pershing track down the Mexican renegade Pancho Villa. But plenty of talent remained on Smith's first Cal staff. As line coach he hired a former 1904 teammate from Penn, A.B. "Gus" Ziegler, known in his playing days but certainly not in 1916 as "the German Oak." His backfield coach was one of the most celebrated stars of the era, Eddie Mahan, Harvard's triple-threat All American halfback in 1915. Smith urged Mahan to teach Cal's novice backs his famous technique of giving defenders "the foot, left or right, then taking it back."

Eighty-five football aspirants turned out for practice in the fall. They were exposed to a training regimen of unprecedented rigor. "Never before in the history of football at California," the *Blue and Gold* reported, "has a squad been worked so hard." Smith's practices at California Field routinely lasted from four in the afternoon to seven at night. Incandescent lamps illuminated the field and footballs painted white were put into play after sundown. Smith believed that his style of play, which emphasized defense over offense, demanded hard work and extensive instruction.

"It takes about two minutes to tell a man the proper form to use in tackling and interfering (blocking)," he said, "but it often takes two years to get him to do it instinctively and well...Defensive methods are much more difficult to acquire than offensive methods. And while it is easier to teach offense than defense, it is my opinion that there never was an offense in any one exclusive style of play that could not be stopped by the defense...If there is time enough to drill it into the man."

For Smith the game was never just a test of physical ability. It required from his players "aggressiveness, obedience, concentration and determination...Add to this harmonious cooperation and you have the making of a real team."

The coach would have to wait a few more years for that "real team" to show up, but even in the incubation stage, he had some players endowed with the sterling attributes he most cherished. Notable among these early stars was an interior lineman named Walter Arthur Gordon, who played as a sophomore in 1916 at 174 pounds. Gordon would add some weight before he left school, become the university's heavyweight boxing champion and as a senior be named a third-team All American by Walter Camp, the first Cal player to receive such national recognition. Gordon would attend law school, work at least part-time as an assistant coach for several head coaches, enjoy a distinguished legal career, become chief of the State of California's Parole Board, be appointed a district court judge and be selected by President Eisenhower to serve as governor of the Virgin Islands. Gordon was that rare figure on a college team of his time—an African American. In fact, when Gordon entered Cal in 1915 there were only two thousand black college students in the entire country and no more than fifty in schools not specifically meant for black students. But two of them, Fritz Pollard of Brown and Paul Robeson of Rutgers, made Camp's All America football team during those years. Robeson, of course, achieved far greater fame as a singer, actor and civil rights activist.

Andy Smith's first season was also the first for the Pacific Coast Intercollegiate Athletic Conference, organized on December 2, 1915, at the Oregon Hotel in Portland with Cal, Washington, Oregon and the Oregon Aggies (Oregon State) as charter members. Alas, the coach's debut was hardly legendary. After holding athletic club opponents scoreless in the first four games —three wins and a tie with the Olympic Club—the Bears had a close call before beating Whittier, 23–17, and then suffered consecutive losses to Oregon (39–14) and Occidental (14–13). After wins over USC and St. Mary's, they lost the final two games, home and away, to Washington. The final 6-4-1 record was respectable considering the relative inexperience of the players, but scarcely indicative of things to come. Smith did, however, see promise not only in the sturdy Gordon but also in halfbacks LeRoy "Roy" Sharp and Carlton "Dummy" Wells. He eagerly looked forward to the 1917 season.

Then, on April 6, what had long seemed inevitable came to pass: the United States declared war on Germany with the avowed purpose, as articulated by President Wilson, of "making the world safe for democracy."

Football quickly became secondary to the military presence on campus, as represented by the Student Army Training Corps and a Naval Unit. The football training table was eliminated and players not involved in Army or Navy programs were subject to the military draft. Travel restrictions forced cancellation of the annual trip to Seattle for the second Washington game. The schedule was also reconfigured to include games with service teams whose ranks were suddenly swelled by the induction of former college stars. The potent Mare Island Marines, which became in this manner an early day equivalent of a professional team, twice demolished the Bears by nearly identical scores of 27–0 and 26–0. Cal fared better against foes of its own caliber, beating Occidental, 20–0, splitting a pair of games with the Olympic Club and scoring the first win yet over a team, the Oregon Aggies, that had played football while the Bears were playing rugby. Cal shut out a draft-depleted Washington team, 27–0, but closed out the season with losses to St. Mary's and Oregon and a scoreless tie with USC. The 5-5-1 finish was not exactly what Smith had in mind for his second year on the job, but it was not the embarrassment it might have been under the strained circumstances.

The 1918 season was even more war-torn, even though the 7-2 record was an improvement. Five of the nine games, including the first three, were with military teams. For that matter, the Cal varsity that year was itself composed primarily of military trainees subject to call-up for active duty at a moment's notice. Among those lost for at least a portion of the season were team captain Wells, the 1919 captain-elect, center George "Fat" Latham, and star running back Albert "Pesky" Sprott. The devastating influenza pandemic, which killed twenty million worldwide and five hundred thousand in the U.S., struck the campus in mid-season, causing cancellation of two games and postponement of another.

But out of the chaos there emerged some promising newcomers, including three from San Diego High School: Sprott and linemen Olin "Cort" Majors and Stan Barnes. Their high school coach, Clarence "Nibs" Price, a Cal graduate, class of 1914, and former rugger, stopped by the campus to visit with his proteges that December following his discharge from the Army Air Corps. When he suggested that there might well be other similarly gifted young players willing to come north from San Diego, Smith hired him on the spot as freshman coach for 1919.

The 1918 season was significant as well for the return, in a manner of speaking, of the Big Game. When Stanford acquired its own Student Army Training Corps unit, the military brass there encouraged trainees to form a football team as a means of improving their physical fitness. This, of course, became little more than a pickup team of mostly inexperienced players. Nevertheless, a sort of little Big Game was proposed that season to be participated in only by military recruits on the two campuses, proceeds from ticket sales to benefit the United States War Fund Drive. Limiting participation to military trainees may have seemed on the surface a way of balancing the odds, but this did not take into account that fully fifty members of the Cal varsity were in the service at the time.

After the Armistice was signed on November 11, ending the war, the promoters from both schools agreed that the game should be played as scheduled on November 30, but open this time to all students, not just trainees. A mismatch of monstrous proportions was assured. With this in mind, at Stanford's reasonable insistence, the game was to be "unofficial," the results and any statistics accumulated to be excluded from the record books.

Stanford did have a coach of sorts in Lieutenant Arthur Badenoch, a former player at the University of Chicago and a coach at the University of New Mexico. Cal had Andy Smith.

In "warmup" games for the big one, Badenoch's sandlotters lost 80–0 to the still talent-laden Mare Island Marines, 70–0 to Mather Field and, showing rapid improvement, 25–8 to USC. And yet the not-so-big-game, played at California Field, revived some of the old excitement. There were the usual pranks, parties and parades, and a pre-game rally at the Greek Theater on the Cal campus drew a capacity crowd on a rainy night.

The game program understandably deemphasized the competitive imbalance, hailing instead the revival of "the greatest event in the collegiate world on the Pacific Coast" while cautioning that "the score of today's game is of little consequence." Stanford, the program said, would be represented by "a team of clean-playing fighting men, not as heavy, as experienced or as well-trained as California's varsity...Their team is not coming with the expectation of winning, but of putting up a losing fight, and in doing so, doing their part toward bringing back to the Pacific Coast its great Football Classic, the California-Stanford Big Game."

As forecast, the game was a rout, Cal winning 67–0. Sprott scored what would ordinarily have been a record seven touchdowns. But as agreed, there is no mention of this feat in official statistics. Stanford's media guides thereafter have listed the entire season, such as it was, as "unofficial." Cal's guides still print the Big Game score without so much as an asterisk disclaimer. Still, this non-game did restore an honored tradition, as well as football relations between the two schools.

The university presidents who had engineered the abandonment of football after the '05 season were no longer a factor. The war, more accurately the mere prospect of war, had effectively removed both from the scene. Jordan, a fervent pacifist appalled by pre-war saber-rattling, traveled extensively on speaking tours in support of the World Peace Federation. By 1911, his work for peace consumed so much of his time that he began gradually to withdraw from his duties as president of the very university he labored so nobly to build. And in 1913, he formally resigned, accepting at the insistence of Stanford trustee Herbert Hoover, the essentially honorary position of university chancellor. Though the United States' entry into the conflict saddened him, he continued to lecture, write books, entertain students at his home near the campus and, yes, go to football games until his death at eighty in 1931.

Wheeler, too, was an emotional casualty of the Great War. During the 1909-10 academic year, he had taken temporary leave of the Cal presidency to teach at the University of Berlin, where he was welcomed by Kaiser Wilhelm II as a distinguished visiting scholar. His time there served only to reenforce his "longstanding admiration for German culture and institutions," historian Henry F. May of Cal wrote in his monograph on the Wheeler era in Berkeley. Years later, when U.S. participation in the war had become a topic of intense national debate, Wheeler defended the Kaiser as a benevolent monarch, whereas in much of the western world he was denounced as a bloodthirsty dictator. It was an unpopular position, needless to say, and Wheeler suffered for it. "Up to the last moment," wrote May, the Cal president "blamed Russia and England for the crisis."

But once war was declared, Wheeler worked through his disillusionment to ensure Cal's active participation in military training and research. And yet, because of his pre-war posture, he remained suspect among super-patriots in the university hierarchy. A committee of deans was appointed to keep him in line and assume many of the powers he had once enjoyed. In 1918, Wheeler announced his retirement, effective at the end of the college year in 1919 when he would be sixty-five.

Despite the wartime turmoil, Wheeler remained popular with Cal students, and in May of 1919, only weeks before his retirement, some five hundred of them held an impromptu rally outside his Berkeley home, expressing, according to the *Blue and Gold*, their affection for a "stirring executive." Wheeler thanked the students for their support and told them he hoped "we shall become closer friends now than ever before."

"He received full (university) honors," wrote May, "and lived until 1927 the happy and active life of an elder statesman, commenting freely on university issues…and never missing a football game."

Wheeler was succeeded by David Prescott Barrows, a political science professor who had served in the war as a cavalry officer and eventually retired from the National Guard as a major general. He was, in nearly every respect, his predecessor's philosophical opposite. If Wheeler had become in retirement a converted football fan, General Barrows was a committed one, a fierce advocate of the game's hardy virtues and a campaigner for bigger and better athletic facilities. Under Barrows, the university would build a $1.5 million, eighty thousand-seat football stadium designed by architect John Galen Howard in the image of the Roman Colosseum.

Ray Lyman Wilbur, who became Stanford's president in 1916 (following John Casper Banner, who succeeded Jordan), was also a fan, even though he had loyally backed Jordan's ban ten years earlier. So now, with all the obstacles removed, the Big Game was not only back but Bigger than ever.

And yet, even with new and returning talent, the removal of wartime restrictions and the official blessing of a new university administration, Smith's 1919 season was hardly free of strife. He had the players, though. Wells and Sprott were available without military interruptions and the line, anchored by Barnes and Majors, was solid and, averaging about 185 pounds per man, plenty big for the time. The Bears held three of their first four opponents scoreless, a 6–6 tie with the Olympic Club marring the shutout streak. Then, following a crushing 61–0 win over Occidental, Smith made a move that very nearly ruined the rest of the season and, as a consequence, his own career at Cal.

Convinced that his players were becoming smug and overconfident after their early success, he decided to shake them out of their lethargy with a practice session the Wednesday before their fifth game that he called, menacingly enough, "Elimination Day." From this prolonged ordeal, he promised to "separate the men from the boys." What Elimination Day led to instead was a near revolt by players, both present and future, against a coach to whom they had previously been devoted.

In his 1949 history, S. Dan Brodie describes this brutal session:

"Promptly at 3:30 p.m. on Wednesday, October 28th, the scrimmage started. It went on, without time out for anything, until nearly seven that night. Plays were run off as fast as the ball could be placed down. Many players begged to be taken out—but the pleas landed on deaf ears. Andy wanted only MEN! Exhausted players who tried to catch a moment's rest between plays were called to their feet and soundly cussed. If a player was injured, he was merely picked up and tossed aside like a sack of potatoes, until at last, about 6:30 p.m., Andy started sending the players into the showers one by one."

The marathon scrimmage didn't so much separate the men from the boys as leave the survivors badly battered in body and spirit. So much so, in fact, that they lost, 14–0, that Saturday to Washington State. Beyond that, Elimination Day had potentially disastrous long-term consequences.

Cal's 1919 freshman team was easily the best yet in school history. Among its stars were a doughty little quarterback named Charlie

Erb and a remarkable all-round athlete named Harold Muller, called "Brick," both for his red hair and a physique solid as a wall. Though he weighed more than 190 pounds, Muller was a world-class high jumper, a silver medalist in the 1920 Olympic Games. And he could throw the fat football then in use more than 50 yards in the air, as well as catch passes unerringly from his end position with his huge but flexible hands.

But after witnessing the horrors of Elimination Day, many of these able freshmen were tempted to take their talent elsewhere, a threat some conveyed to coach Price. Nibs quickly informed Smith that if there were to be any more Elimination Days, the head coach might lose the nucleus of what seemed to be a fine 1920 team. The two coaches even took a trip to Erb's home in Bakersfield that summer to work out the problem. On the way home to Berkeley, Smith assured Price that Elimination Day was a thing of the past.

And the 1919 team did recover from the ordeal. They scored close wins over the Oregon Aggies (21–14) and USC (14–13) before meeting Stanford on November 22 for the first "official" Big Game since 1905. There was no confusion this time over who should play or if the game should really count. By joining the Pacific Coast Conference before the season, Stanford had agreed to the freshman-ineligible rule, which was reinstated following the Armistice, and had assembled from the remains of its rugby squad and 1918's ragtag footballers a respectable team. And in "Fighting Bob" Evans it had a professional coach. As his nickname suggests, Fighting Bob took guff from no one. He once rudely ejected several influential members of the Stanford Board of Trustees from his practice field, and on another occasion, took a swing at a sportswriter he decided had been overly critical.

Stanford had won four games and lost only one, to the Olympic Club, before hosting Cal in this renewal of the classic. This time the game was close. It was also notable for the first touchdown pass yet thrown in a Big Game. Unsurprisingly, the play had its origins in rugby, Stanford's Jack Patrick lateraling to halfback Preston Holt, who then threw 25 yards downfield to end Fred Adams for the historic fourth-quarter score. Earlier in the game, Stanford rugby and track star Robert "Dink" Templeton had kicked a field goal. But Dummy Wells scored twice for the Bears and Jim Cline kicked both points-after for a 14–10 Cal win. The score was identical to the first of these games twenty-seven years earlier, only this time the Bears had won.

In his first season with a team undiminished by inexperience, war or influenza, Andy Smith finished with a 6-2-1 record. Not bad. But nothing compared with what would soon follow.

Stanford's Big Game touchdown pass had also clicked something in the fertile brain of Cal's defense-minded coach. Not long after the game, he drew up an even trickier pass play, this one involving an end sneaking into the backfield. During a dinner with his good friend Jimmy Phelan, then coaching at Missouri, Smith diagrammed the play on a table cloth. Instead of taking a short lateral, the end would drop back deep enough to receive a long backward pass. Then, from perhaps 15 to 20 yards behind the line of scrimmage, he would throw the ball maybe 50 yards or more to the end zone.

Phelan regarded the diagram skeptically. Finally, chuckling in disbelief, he said, "Well, Andy, it might work if you've got a man with a shotgun for an arm."

Andy smiled. "I've got one."

## CHAPTER FIVE

# A WONDER TO BEHOLD

Andy Smith's football philosophy—kick and wait for the breaks—was as deceptively simple as Descartes' "I think, therefore I am." But his, like the famous Frenchman's, was a pretty complex proposition. And so was the coach who conceived it.

Smith could be gregarious, even on occasion the life of the party. He was an accomplished storyteller, a rough-cob humorist in the western manner he so readily affected. And yet, according to those who knew him best, he could be withdrawn, surprisingly vulnerable to criticism and subject to occasional bouts of depression. He was, wrote Ed R. Hughes in the *Chronicle*, "a man of peculiar temperament, and he was really known to but a few. He had the frame of a giant, the fighting heart of a lion, yet he was as sentimental as a woman. I have seen him cry for joy when his boys were winning."

That he drank, often to excess, was no secret, except maybe to his younger players. "I never knew how much he drank," Barnes told the Chronicle's David Bush many years later, "That is, I didn't until after I graduated and became an assistant coach for a year. He drank quite a bit."

After practice and games, it was Smith's custom to down a few with equally bibulous pals at the Berkeley Elks Club, where he found safe haven from the pressures of a life lived all too publicly for his taste. Under no circumstances could Andy Smith be described as a devoted family man.

In 1919, he had married one "Bobbie Hollingshead," a young woman who, according to the *Chronicle*, was "prominent socially in Illinois." Brought west by her new husband, she also became "popular in Berkeley circles." Alas, only briefly. Her husband, splitting his time between the campus and his club, pretty much left her bereft of even the remotest marital companionship. She endured only a few months of these prolonged absences before returning to the social whirl of her home state. There she quietly obtained a divorce, citing cruelty.

Smith's real family was his football team. And though he could be a martinet on the practice field, he was "idolized," Brick Muller said, by his surrogate sons. Smith imposed few training rules on his players beyond their staying in shape, a condition his long and strenuous practices adequately enforced. He forbade gambling of any sort. He also, quaintly enough, prohibited the consumption of popcorn, a dietary stricture never fully comprehended and regularly violated, most particularly in movie theaters.

Smith was what would be known today as a "hands-on" coach. Barnes recalls feeling so frustrated at missing an open field tackle in practice one day that he lay on the turf pounding his fist and shouting, "I'm no good. I'm going to quit." Suddenly he was jerked to his feet by the powerful hands of his head coach. "Quit?" Andy snarled at him. "Quit!' No, you're not going to quit. What you're going to do is get up and fight. Fight harder!" Barnes did.

Barnes recalled another practice session when a new and otherwise promising halfback insisted upon turning his back to tacklers just as he hit the line. Smith watched this procedure with mounting irritation. "Why," he finally inquired in a voice heard by all, "are you hitting the line with your ass? You've got to dive in there head first." When the runner ignored this advice and continued to plunge full stern ahead, Smith could tolerate it no more. He physically yanked the player out of the scrimmage, ordered him off the field and, for emphasis, chased him back to the gym, trying all the while to kick him squarely on the offending derriere.

Interestingly enough, for a man so dedicated to winning, Smith preached that defeat, if ever it should come, must be accepted with dignity and grace. In his first few up-and-down seasons and in the routinely victorious ones that followed, he religiously sought out the opposing coach for congratulations or condolences. It was a courtesy not always reciprocated. And when one of Smith's players, caught up in a wave of pre-game fervor, cried out that he'd gladly "die for California," Andy cautioned him in words that survive as his epitaph: "We do not want men who will lie down bravely to die but men who will fight valiantly to live. Winning is not everything, and it is far better to play the game squarely and lose than to win at the sacrifice of an ideal."

But Smith's teams were not about losing. And in 1920, the coach was convinced he had the players he needed to win consistently. Muller and another near 190-pounder, Bob Berkey, were his starters at end; Barnes, though weighing only 183 pounds, and Dan McMillan, just three pounds heavier, were the tackles; Majors and Lee Cramner were at guard and Fat Latham at center. Erb was the quarterback, Sprott and Irving "Crip" Toomey the halfbacks, while Morrison and the almost equally talented Archie Nisbet shared time at fullback. In reserve, Smith had a speedy pass-catcher at end, fresh off the "goof squad," named Howard "Brodie" Stephens.

Together, these stalwarts ran roughshod over eight regular season opponents, outscoring them, 482–14. Only Nevada, beaten 70–7, and the Oregon Aggies scored touchdowns against them. The Aggies, defeated 17–7 in a rainstorm at Corvallis, were the only team to hold the Bears under twenty points that season. In fact, they and a veteran Olympic Club team with six former All Americans in the lineup were the only foes to hold them under 25 points. The proto-pro Olympians fell, 21–0. The other five regular season shutouts were lopsided to the point of absurdity. Despite Smith's best efforts to hold the scoring down, St. Mary's was clobbered 127–0, a defeat so devastating the school cancelled the rest of its 1920 schedule. The once powerful Mare Island Marines lost by 88–0, Utah by 63–0, Washington State by 49–0 and Stanford by 38–0.

After the Utah drubbing in Berkeley on October 23, "Old Blue" Brick Morse, writing for the San Francisco *Call*, dubbed Smith's apparently unbeatable Bears "the Wonder Team." Far from being flattered, Andy was furious. He telephoned Morse, complaining that no team, certainly not his, merited such hyperbole. Besides, a nickname so boastful can only inspire opponents and possibly even jinx his own players. But the name caught on and, following one overwhelming victory after another, became something of an understatement.

The Big Game attracted a then record crowd of twenty-seven thousand seven hundred to California Field, a wooden structure that seemed more than ever both outdated and undersized. Stanford, coached then by Walter Powell, was a capable opponent with a 4-2 record and a defense that had allowed only 27 points. But the Bears scored 21 in the fourth quarter alone on the way to another easy win. Sprott ran for 3 touchdowns and Morrison for two. Toomey chipped in with a field goal. The Bears rushed for 294 yards to the Cardinal's 16 and passed for 88 to Stanford's 10—382 total yards to 26, 18 first downs to 0. It was a rout nearly as complete as the "unofficial" one of two years before.

By now, the Tournament of Roses post-season football game in Pasadena had become a newly popular holiday event. The first of these games, in 1902, when Michigan crushed Stanford, 49–0, represented a cruel setback for west coast football aspirations, effectively discouraging any followup East vs. West games. The Rose Bowl became just a one-year phenomenon. And with the switch to rugby by California schools, its demise seemed assured. Bravely, though, the tournament committee revived the idea in 1916 after Cal's return to the gridiron. Then, after a rough period during and immediately after the Great War, it came up with a sterling and deliciously even matchup on January 1, 1920, Harvard squeezing past Oregon, 7–6.

The Wonder Team gave the organizers their first major west coast attraction, its exploits well publicized, if provincially dismissed, in the East. So even though local favorite USC had also gone undefeated, Cal received the invitation. The Bears and Trojans had not met during the season, but SC coach Elmer "Gloomy Gus" Henderson issued an unqualified endorsement of his northern rival. "I consider California to be the greatest team I have seen since the University of Washington team of 1913," he told the press. "Being a Pacific Coast coach, I am very anxious that the West be represented by a team that will be a credit to this section of the country."

Cal's opponent would be Ohio State, champions of the Western Conference (the Big Ten). Its acceptance was momentarily delayed when officials of that conference announced their opposition to member participation in post-season play. They relented, however, when Ohio State's athletic director L.W. St. John and faculty representative Thomas E. Lynch made it clear that the Buckeyes were so eager to play the so-called Wonder Team that they'd head west with or without official blessing.

Ohio State, also undefeated and playing a supposedly more difficult schedule in a tougher league, was immediately made an 8-to-5 favorite. This pairing of an established midwestern power and an upstart team from the comparatively backward Pacific slope was easily the most attractive so far in the history of the event. Requests for tickets exceeded one hundred thousand, bringing forth hordes of rapacious scalpers to previously puritanical Pasadena. Ten thousand seats were added to Tournament Park's existing thirty-one thousand five hundred to handle the expected overflow. Still, on game day, some twenty thousand fans gathered outside the stadium in hopes of buying some of the twenty-five hundred remaining tickets placed on public sale or, failing that, paying the escalating prices offered by scalpers for tickets that might well be counterfeit.

It was as apparent now to Rose Bowl organizers as it had been to Bay Area football followers that ever larger stadiums were needed to meet the demands of the game's surging popularity. The 1920s would usher in a stadium-building boom unprecedented up to then in sports history. By the end of this extraordinary decade, gigantic concrete saucers and horseshoes would appear on the campuses of Stanford, Cal, Michigan, Illinois, Ohio State, Minnesota and Pittsburgh. Soldier Field in Chicago, the Coliseum in Los Angeles and Yankee Stadium in New York—a baseball park that would also be the site of memorable football games—were all built in the Roaring Twenties. And Pasadena would have a Rose Bowl of its own by late 1922.

Cal and Ohio State would play in a park smaller by more than twenty thousand seats. But a then record crowd of forty-two thousand, including hundreds of standees, watched in…yes…wonder as Smith's Bears overpowered the favored midwesterners. Defeat came early for the Buckeyes. In the first quarter, their All American halfback Pete Stichcomb fumbled and Latham recovered for Cal on the Ohio State 28. Sprott then passed to Muller for 13 yards and ran for 10 more before scoring two line plunges later from the one. Toomey converted.

The Buckeyes retaliated with their only valid threat of the day, advancing after the kickoff to the Cal 8-yard line before fumbling once more, Muller recovering on the six. Nisbet got his team out of further trouble by punting on first down from his own end zone for a soaring 62 yards.

At the start of the second quarter, Cal moved to the Ohio State 39, setting up the very play Smith had diagrammed for pal Phelan before the season. It would soon become the stuff of legend.

After gaining two yards to the 37, Nisbet feigned injury, sprawling on the turf in apparent agony as his teammates gathered sympathetically around him in what appeared to be no particular order. In fact, they were lining up in a bizarre formation that put center Latham at Muller's right end position, a miraculously healed Nisbet at center, Sprott six yards deep in the backfield and Muller a full ten yards behind him. The fleet Brodie Stephens, enjoying a rare start at left end because of an injury to Berkey, lined up wide near the sidelines. Suddenly, Nisbet snapped the ball to Sprott in hopes of catching the defenders unawares, but the Buckeyes had been cautioned against Smithian skullduggery and were ready for anything. At least, they thought they were.

Sprott ran laterally to his right as if skirting the end. Then he stopped, set himself and passed backward ten yards to Muller, who still stood 16 yards behind the original line of scrimmage. Stephens, meanwhile, streaked past a thoroughly befuddled Stinchcomb toward the goal line. "Just where do you think you're going?" the Buckeye bellowed as Stephens passed by, seemingly headed completely out of the play. Muller let fly with a perfectly timed low line drive of a pass that Stephens pulled in just as he stepped into the end zone. Muller's throw had traveled fifty-three yards in the air, an undreamed of distance at a time when footballs were nearly as plump and grip-resistant as rugby balls. Asked after the game why he made so little effort to cover Stephens, Stinchcomb replied, "Frankly, I didn't think anybody could throw the ball that far."

Officially, of course, the pass covered 37 yards from the line of scrimmage. And its distance from the spot of origin was correctly calculated as 53 yards. But for decades afterward, supposedly eyewitness reports persisted that Muller had hurled a 70-yarder, a Herculean feat that, despite Brick's embarrassed denials, stuck with him to the grave. What is missing from most accounts though, is that even without that monumental heave, Brick played a remarkable game that day. His two long-gainers on end-around plays, the first on a statue-of-liberty, set up Cal's third touchdown, scored by Sprott from the five. He also recovered three fumbles and disrupted Ohio State's vaunted end sweeps with his interference-busting hard charges. He caught three passes for 33 yards and completed two more of his own for a perfect three-for-three day. He even connected with Lowell "Shrimp" Hall on an even longer throw from scrimmage than the legendary one—50 yards—that was called back by a penalty. After the game, an awestruck "Gloomy Gus" called Muller, then merely a sophomore, "the best man I ever saw in a football suit. If Walter Camp had seen this game, he'd have picked Muller for *both* ends on his All America team."

Cal finished the scoring in the final quarter with reserve halfback Karl Deeds driving in for the TD from the five. The 28–0 upset of the midwest's best startled football savants across the land. Stung by the loss, the Big Ten would not send another team to the Rose Bowl for twenty-six years. The win elevated the west coast game to a prominence it had never previously enjoyed and boosted Andy Smith to a top rank in the coaching fraternity. Camp, who had overlooked Muller in 1920, made him a first-team All American the next two years, the first Cal and west coast player so anointed.

After a frustrating four years in Berkeley, Smith had finally lived up to his elusive promise. Criticized so starkly in some quarters in 1919 that rumors of his dismissal had unfairly circulated, he was now celebrated as a revolutionary genius. Coaches everywhere now sought to duplicate his practice of combining ultra-conservative tactics with the downright radical. Sure, Smith's teams might just kick and wait for the breaks, but at some critical juncture in a game they might come up with a wing-dinger like Sprott-to-Muller-to-Stephens. Smith was unpredictable and therefore hard to beat. As a matter of fact, for five straight seasons, he wouldn't be beaten at all.

The 1920 season was admittedly a hard act to follow. Sprott and team captain Majors had graduated, replaced at their positions by Don Nichols and Webster Clark, but the heart of the Wonder Team was intact—Muller, Erb, Toomey, Nisbet, Stephens and Morrison. With the notable exception of Muller, Morrison was the most talented of this wondrous crew. Sharing time with Nisbet at fullback in 1920, the Duke rushed for 17 touchdowns and had two conversion kicks for a season points total of 104, edging Sprott and Toomey, both of whom had 90, for honors as the Wonder Team's top point-maker. Morrison had not been on that powerhouse 1919 freshman team, preferring instead to play with much older players and against tougher teams for the Olympic Club. Twice that season he had played against the Cal varsity. His coach that season with the club had been Dr. Boles Rosenthal, who would join him at Cal in 1920 as an assistant to Smith.

In yet another touch of coincidence, the Wonder Team's 1920 opener was against the Olympic Club, a game in which Morrison scored two of Cal's three touchdowns and kept his former teammates in unfavorable field position all day by averaging 41 yards on his eighteen punts. In his three seasons on the Cal varsity, Duke Morrison would score 42 touchdowns and kick 22 points-after and a field goal—all this in just twenty-eight games, in some of which he played only sparingly because of injury, time shared with Nisbet, or runaway scores. His 277 career points would remain a Cal record for seventy-one years.

His noble nickname would also be borrowed by scores of young men fortunate enough then to be named Morrison, notable among them an aspiring lineman at USC with the first name Marion. Some sources claim that this particular Duke lifted the rest of his stage name from another Cal football player of the time, reserve quarterback John Wayne Higson. But, John "Duke" Wayne gained most of his fame away from football.

Cal's 1921 wunderkinder didn't quite rack up the outrageous scores of the previous season, but they did well enough. Washington was trounced 72–3 (Morrison scoring five TDs), Nevada 51–6, Oregon 39–0, Sanford 42–7 and USC 38–7. All told, the Bears scored a comparatively modest 312 points to 33 in winning all nine regular season games. The closest was a 21–10 win over an all-star Pacific Fleet team whose player-coach was a former Naval Academy All American fullback named Bill Ingram. Ten years later, that same "Navy Bill" would become a familiar name on the Berkeley campus.

The Big Game of '21, though resulting in another easy victory for the Bears, represented a triumph of sorts for the Cardinal since it was played in the impressive new Stanford Stadium before 62,740 fans, a crowd that exceeded the new stadium's then capacity of sixty thousand and was the largest yet to attend an athletic event in the state. The athletic departments at both schools had been campaigning hard for bigger stadiums, since it was obvious now that college football, on the cusp of the decade's "Golden Age of Sports," was outgrowing its humble origins. Indeed, by the 1920s, the game had become a national obsession, rivaling baseball and boxing for the sports dollar.

Football's warlike nature, its built-in capacity for melodrama, and the old school loyalties it inspired made it ideal material for the "purple prose" of that generation's expansive sportswriters. The game became the subject of movies and song—"You gotta be a football hero to get all the beautiful girls." And network radio broadcasts transformed it from a regional to a national phenomenon.

Paul Gallico, then a prominent sportswriter, later a successful novelist, described college football at the time as "one vast fall pageant, played in crisp, zippy air that held the smell of burning leaves, a pageant of pretty girls and fur-coated, well-dressed men, of military bands in scarlet capes, of yellow footballs in the air, running and diving figures, gold in the fields and on the trees and in the till." Rugby, gone but a half-dozen years, now seemed as foreign to Bay Area sports fans as quoits. "You know," said old rugger Jimmy Schaeffer to sportswriter Jack James at a Cal football game then, "it was the best thing that ever happened to amateur sport, this switch (from rugby) to American football."

But it was Stanford, not Cal, that won the Bay Area stadium-building game. The horseshoe-shaped Stanford Stadium (later expanded to a seating capacity of nearly ninety thousand) was built in just four-and-a-half months for a reported $211,000, construction costs underwritten by alumni subscriptions and from the gate receipts of the first event held there, the November 19, 1921 Big Game. The massive earth-colored building was properly inaugurated when the Stanford team scored the first touchdown there, a fourth-down desperation plunge by Jack Patrick that was set up by the recovery of a Toomey fumble of the opening kickoff on the 15 that Patrick himself returned to the two.

After that, the deluge. Cal held its hosts to just 53 net yards while scoring at will. Morrison scored only once, but Nisbet had two TDs and Nichols, Toomey and Dick Dunn one apiece. Erb converted after each for the final of 42–7.

Cal, meanwhile, had launched plans for its own modern stadium, a month before Stanford's opened. And though it would be reverently dedicated as a memorial to the American dead of World War I, it still encountered opposition, first from Berkeley neighbors at the Strawberry Canyon site fearing game-day disruptions and then, predictably, from faculty appalled by the very idea of erecting a costly cathedral to a sport already falsely worshiped. Not to mention fears expressed by those both within and without the university family that the stadium would be erected squarely atop the Hayward earthquake fault line.

"How much," inquired psychology professor G. M. Stratton, "will this proposed million-dollar expenditure add to the real welfare of the student body?" In other words, how about the kids who came to Cal to learn something beyond the scores of football games?

Smith countered with his favorite "collective will of the student body" argument. But Cal graduate manager Luther Nichols offered a somewhat more compelling and certainly more practical answer: "The one tremendous force which binds the student body and the alumni together is intercollegiate athletics…the alumni do not come back to California to roam through the library—they come to see the game." And so, two years later, Cal would have its own big playpen.

In the meantime, a second straight undefeated season earned the Bears a repeat invitation from the Tournament of Roses committee, this time to meet an opponent, Washington and Jefferson College of Washington, Pennsylvania, that was hastily derided by press, public and, most vexingly, by Cal itself as being unworthy of the honor. The small school—a co-educational student body of barely 450—was, in fact, a desperation choice after the Big Ten flatly rejected a return trip to Pasadena and such candidates as Cornell, Notre Dame, Centre College (upset winners that season over Harvard) and Pennsylvania State were declared, for various reasons, unavailable.

Although Washington and Jefferson had completed an undefeated ten game season, with victories over such prestigious opponents as Carnegie Tech, Syracuse, Pittsburgh and West Virginia, almost no one on the west coast had ever heard of the place. "All I know about Washington and Jefferson," Jack James wrote, "is that they're both dead."

But these "Presidents," as the school's teams were aptly called, were very much alive and kicking. Their coach was the engaging Earle "Greasy" Neale, better known then as a big league outfielder with the Cincinnati Reds. But he had also been a pioneer professional football player and that in the end would be his game. Decades later, in 1948 and '49, Neale would coach the Philadelphia Eagles to consecutive National Football League championships. In 1921, though, Greasy had yet to make his mark. He did, however, endear himself to the press before the Rose Bowl game by acknowledging that his recruiting methods were not entirely above board. Asked how he managed to compete successfully against far larger schools, Greasy responded, "That's easy. We just went out and got the players. We brought 'em in. Didn't make much difference how many people were in the rest of the school."

Cal's faculty representatives did not respond kindly to such refreshing candor, grumbling that the university had no business consorting with such undesirables. Even Smith deplored W&J's academic standing. And after whipping the powerhouse likes of Ohio State, matching his Wonder Team against such a nondescript foe struck him as demeaning. Cal was ready to pull out of the game. But when tournament officials pleaded that without the Wonder Team, the gate would not be substantial enough to help finance the construction of the new Rose Bowl stadium, the Bears generously agreed to come south once more.

They were quickly installed as a 14-point favorite, much to the delight of the underdog players, many of whom, unbeknownst to coach Neale, bet on themselves to beat the odds. "Not that we were cocky," recalled Presidents' right guard Ralph Vince in an interview a half-century later, "but we felt pretty good about ourselves. We felt we could handle most any situation."

Cal guard Cramner admitted that the Bears were probably too cocky. The 1920 team, he recalled, was out to prove something to the football world. "In 1921, we *knew* we were good, and pretty darn good— so good we sometimes felt we knew everything there was to know about football."

Neale called the pre-game odds, "hogwash. California couldn't score on us if we played all day." And when a deluge of Biblical ferocity descended on southern California the night before the game, Smith agreed with him, telling friends he didn't see how under these weather conditions either team could score. And neither team did.

The field was a hundred yards of mud, a surface so treacherous it negated all but the most elementary straight-ahead plays. The Presidents did, however, have a 36-yard touchdown run by their Wayne Brenckert called back because of an offsides penalty and they surprisingly outplayed the Bears from start to finish. Smith's mighty offense was held to just 49 net yards compared with 137 for the despised Presidents. Only Archie Nisbet's prodigious punting with a rain-heavy ball held the enemy in check. Nisbet punted thirteen times for a 39.7-yard average, a figure reduced by a pair of 27-yard "coffin corner" kicks in the first quarter. He averaged a daunting 44 yards in the critical last quarter.

The Bears were further harassed by a nasty tactic Neale had brought to college football from baseball—bench-jockeying or, in modern usage, trash-talking. The Presidents' star tackle and team captain Russell Stein was particularly adept at hurling invective across the line, infuriating the diminutive Erb early in the going by accusing him of escaping mayhem by crouching behind the few remaining blades of grass on the field.

Halfback Nichols, the only sophomore in the Bears' starting lineup, admitted that Stein's constant patter about his supposedly having a lookalike relative in Pittsburgh so distracted him at one point that he had to ask for a time out. Muller, recovering from a leg infection, missed most of the first quarter, so when he finally trotted onto the field in a spotless uniform, he was heckled mercilessly by the muddy Presidents, some of whom gleefully placed filthy hands on his clean jersey. The normally mild-mannered Bear was so angered he had to be restrained from throwing punches. When he finally calmed down, Brick played his customary brilliant game on defense.

Still, after eighteen straight victories, many of them by ridiculously lopsided scores, the Wonder Team suffered its first setback, in the form of a scoreless tie.

The recovery was swift. The 1922 team, missing Latham, Barnes, Stephens, McMillen and Toomey, still cruised to another undefeated season, shutting out six of nine opponents and adding to their accumulating lore. In a 61–0 rout of Washington State, for example the versatile Nisbet kicked an ultimately superfluous but then record 54-yard field goal. But this would be finis for the original Wonder Teamers who began as sophomores in 1920, their swan song a 28–0 win over Stanford. And though they rejected a third invitation to play in Pasadena on New Years Day, they did, in fact, play the first game ever in the new Rose Bowl, a 12–0 win over USC on October 28, 1922. It was the Trojans' only loss of the season and the Wonder Team's closest game. The Bears needed a classic four-down goal line stand in the second quarter to hold S.C. scoreless. Morrison...who else?...scored the only touchdown, the remaining points coming on a safety and Nisbet's point-after and field goal. The Trojans accepted the Pasadena bid and defeated Penn State, 14–3, in the first Rose Bowl game actually played in the Rose Bowl.

And so, it was generally believed, an era had ended in Berkeley.

In three years, the Wonder Team had won twenty-seven games, eighteen of them in succession, seventeen by shutout. The Bears in that time had outscored opponents 1220–81. The Rose Bowl mud wrestle was the only tie at a time when ties were not at all uncommon. Muller had won his All America honors. And in his last season, Duke Morrison scored 131 points—18 touchdowns, 20 points-after and a field goal. There would be many touchdown-happy running backs after him, the seasons would grow longer by three and four games and beginning in the second half of the century high-scoring soccer-style placekicking specialists would emerge, but as of this writing, Morrison's point total in 1922 is still Cal's single season record. It is surely one of the most durable in all of college football.

By 1922, Andy Smith had become a hot coaching commodity, this in an era of legendary coaches—Rockne, Zupke, Warner, Stagg, Yost, Dobie, Jones, Heisman. In December of that year, Ed R. Hughes of the *Chronicle* reported anxiously that "a definite proposition has been made to Andy Smith by one of the biggest universities in the East to sign him for five years at a bigger salary than California pays him... Andy is no moneygrubber...but like every other man, he feels that his services are worth what they will bring in the open market, so this offer...has caused him to do some thinking on the subject." In a sidebar story, Hughes named coaches who were better paid than Smith, a number that included not only the biggest names but also the relatively unsung service academy mentors, Bob Folwell at Navy and Charles Daly at Army.

Smith's contract at Cal had a year to go, but goaded by the prospect of losing him, the university promptly signed him for four more years, a term limited by a policy binding all new contracts to the duration of a college generation. Actually, Cal's fears of losing the great coach were probably unwarranted. Andy Smith just plain liked it in Berkeley.

His turbulent soul found peace in the campus's rolling landscape, its groves of oak and eucalyptus. He enjoyed strolling the banks of a rain-swollen Strawberry Creek in the quiet of an off-season winter. He'd made good friends among the faculty, for he thought of himself, first and foremost, as a teacher. He was proud that his best players were also outstanding students—Morrison in engineering, Barnes in law, Muller and Stephens in medicine. He took pride also in knowing that his teams, more than any other, had raised West Coast college football out of obscurity. And if there were times when the black hole of depression yawned before him, he always had his pals downtown at the Elks Club.

He supposed it was true, as he was told so often, that he was married to his team and the university. If so, he sometimes joked, he hoped it was a marriage that would last until death did them part.

## CHAPTER SIX

# THE VARSITY DRAG

By 1923, with an enrollment of better than ten thousand and a reputation for academic excellence, the Berkeley campus had become one of the nation's liveliest—and among its most crowded. "Almost never is our beautiful campus free from the disturbance of new construction or alterations," wrote President Barrows, not quite in sorrow. But Barrows did deplore the inadequacy of student housing on or near the campus, a condition sorely exacerbated by the "Great Berkeley Fire" in September that year. Originating in the dry grass of the Berkeley hills, the flames swept into the northeastern part of the city, destroying some 584 buildings, including many private homes and apartment buildings. With its center only a few blocks north of the campus, the conflagration left at least a thousand students without a place to live.

Finding space for the newly homeless, as well as for an ever-larger student body should be the highest priority, said Barrows before leaving office in '23. "Grown as we are, to huge proportions, we cannot find acquaintanceship and solidarity as a student body in the absence of college living accommodations…" In a somewhat harsher tone on future growth, Barrow's successor, William Wallace Campbell, an astronomer, warned starry-eyed students applying for admission that

"The State of California owes no one a higher education. It simply provides, through the university, the opportunity for higher education to any son or daughter who desires it and can qualify for it."

In fact, steps had already been taken to expand the university beyond the Berkeley campus. A so-called "Southern Branch" had been opened in downtown Los Angeles as early as 1919. Initially, a two-year teachers college with a student body predominantly of women, it had become by 1924 a full-fledged four-year school with an enrollment of 4418 and its own football team. By the end of the decade, it would move from Vermont Street to a sparkling new campus in the city's Westwood section. It would also shed the demeaning "Southern Branch" designation and become the University of California at Los Angeles—or, as it is more popularly known, UCLA.

There was also talk as early as the 1920s of converting property in Davis near Sacramento—known as the "University Farm" since it was acquired in 1908 —into a future campus for students of agriculture. Cal was taking the first positive steps toward becoming a rarity of the time, a "multi-campus" institution.

Meanwhile, in Berkeley, students, like those apparently everywhere in the Roaring '20s, were having the time of their lives. It was a decade that fostered a youth movement unlike any other yet in the nation's history, one that not only cast aside the restrictive mores of the previous generation but created its own distinctive culture. Twenties' prosperity, tenuous though it may have been, coupled with the rapid development of relatively inexpensive state universities and colleges, opened the campus gates to young men and especially young women who might otherwise never have considered passing through. Higher education was no longer the province of male scions of the wealthy. And these new collegians eagerly freed themselves of the remaining strands of Victorian convention, most conspicuously perhaps in the matter of women's apparel. Skirts were shorter, stockings were rolled at the knee, and the foundation garments— corsets, girdles and the like—were rejected as ridiculous impediments to sports, dancing and, yes, petting.

"Collegiate…collegiate…yes, we are collegiate," assertively went the lyrics to one of the peppier new tunes. Twenties' youths had their own music—jazz—their own dances—the Charleston, the Black Bottom—and what amounted to their own musical instrument—the omnipresent ukulele. They spoke their own language—slang. They drank illegal "hooch" from hip flasks. They "necked" and "petted."

*She doesn't drink,*
*She doesn't pet*
*She hasn't been*
*to college yet*

Even popular entertainers were turning to the campuses for material. The most collegiate of this bunch was Rudy Vallee, a onetime Yalie who crooned stein songs and sentimental ballads through a yell leader's megaphone.

These were banner years for the so-called "Greek" system of fraternities and sororities, where partying, pranksterism, hazing and boozing flourished virtually unchecked. In 1923, for example, the Berkeley campus had forty-four social fraternities and twenty-five sororities.

College men of the time may have affected an air of cynicism and worldliness, but their disenchantment did not exclude having one helluva good time. Why not? The war had demonstrated that the world had the capacity to blow itself to smithereens. So pity those who took themselves too seriously. In 1923, Daily Cal editor Francis W. Bartlett saw ominous signs of solemnity in the campus literary publication, *The Occident*, and in that year's *Blue and Gold* took its editors to task for their "long affliction of self-conscious high-browism."

Football in this escapist milieu was king, its players the big men on campus. A '20s football-star need not be, as so often before, a latter day knight-errant. Frank Merriwell was nothing more than a story-book character. And flesh and blood Merriwells like Princeton's Hobey Baker, whom F. Scott Fitzgerald once described as "an ideal worthy of everything in my enthusiastic imagination," might as well have been fictional. Red Grange, football's ultra-hero of the '20s, was a much more down-to-earth figure, a blue-collar guy who worked during the summer as an iceman. In this era of "wonderful nonsense" a sports star could even be a rogue and a rake. Babe Ruth, after all, was no Boy Scout. But he had the grand manner so favored then.

With the new monster stadiums, fan and athlete were separated by even greater distances, so organized rooting took on added impor-tance. Bands got bigger, cheers got louder and card stunts, which began in Berkeley as early as 1910, got more creative. And as the 1923 season began in Berkeley, workmen labored furiously in Strawberry Canyon to finish the new stadium in time at least for the Big Game. It would be the supreme stage for the big show college football had become.

On the actual field of play, though, Andy Smith faced what was gen-erally seen as a crisis. Seven of his ten starters from 1922 were gone, and in the view of many, they were irreplaceable. Andy had other ideas. He saw new talent filling his vacancies. Besides, there were still some hold-overs on the premises. Don Nichols and Dick Dunn, a pair of elusive 165-pound halfbacks were returning, and though both were overshad-owed by such now departed fixtures as Toomey, Nisbet and Morrison, they had had their moments in '22. In Cal's 45–7 defeat of Washing-ton, Nichols had reeled off six runs of more than 17 yards, including a 48-yarder and a 62-yard touchdown scamper. And in the 61–13 pum-meling of Nevada, Dunn, in reserve of Toomey, scored 6 TDs.

There were important newcomers, too, the most promising a 5-7½, 158-pound scatback memorably named Talma "Tut" Imlay, a dropkicker extraordinaire in Bill Blewett and a triple-threater in the classic mold, Jimmy Dixon. Edwin "Babe" Horrell replaced Latham at center so ably he would become, in 1924, Cal's second first-string

All American. The unenviable job of replacing Erb at quarterback fell to Howard "Hoggy" Evans, until then a career bench-warmer. And Charles "Snooky" Mell inherited the even more intimidating responsibility of filling in at right end for Brick Muller.

Snooky, Hoggy, Babe? Well, it was the '20s, a time when an athlete without a nickname was practically anonymous. Even Coach Smith was called "the Big Swede," despite his protests that he lacked even a trace of Scandinavian heritage. But certainly the most imaginative of all these handles, was Talma Imlay's "Tut." While its onomastic origins may well date to Imlay's childhood, one prefers to believe the nickname was inspired by the discovery by British archaeologists in 1922 (Imlay's freshman year) of the thirty-two-hundred-year-old tomb near Luxor of the mummified remains of the Egyptian king Tutankhamen. "King Tut," as he was affectionately known thereafter, became all the rage in the Jazz Age, launching a wave of Ancient Egypt faddism and a plethora of riches-to-rags mummy jokes, songs and movies. On the gridiron, though, Cal's Tut was no mummy's boy.

The season began, routinely enough, with six straight Smithian shutouts, all featuring the running and passing of single-wing tailback Nichols, the broken field darts of the latter-day Tut and Blewett's accurate kicking. In a 16–0 win over the Olympic Club on October 13, Blewett booted three field goals, a feat which a month later set the stage for more Smith chicanery. Playing before seventy-two thousand in the first Pacific Coast Conference game at the new L.A. Coliseum, the Bears had a long drive stalled on the Trojan six-yard line. On fourth down, Smith sent in Blewett, presumably to try a field goal, a short one at that since the goal posts were then on the goal line. Awaiting the snap from center, Blewett took three practice swipes on the coliseum turf. And when the ball was centered, he faked dropping the ball for the kick, then faded to pass and connected with Nichols for an easy touchdown. It proved to be the winning margin in a 13–7 game. The S.C. touchdown, made in the last few seconds of play was the only one scored against this first post-Wonder team in yet another undefeated season.

Ah, but there was a tie, an embarrassing one. To spare Nevada a shellacking comparable to the one in '22, Smith decided to use only his reserves and, with the permission of game officials, to play ten-minute quarters. Andy didn't even stay around for the game, electing to use his time scouting Stanford. Such munificence only served to enrage Nevada's players, who fought hard and valiantly, holding Cal's subs to a scoreless tie, the sole blemish in an otherwise perfect 9-0-1 season.

In the final game ever at California Field, played before a full house of twenty-seven thousand five hundred, the Bears whitewashed a resurgent Washington team, 9–0, Blewett kicking his seventh field goal of the season and Dunn scoring the only touchdown.

Preparations were now complete for the grand opening of the giant bowl in Strawberry Canyon. Financed through subscriptions that assured investors of choice seats, the stadium was finished at a cost of $1,437,982 and built in sections with expansion joints, the better to absorb the shock of—heaven forfend —an earthquake. It was situated amidst the serene splendor of the Berkeley hills and surrounded by groves of pine and oak. The views from the upper rows of seats were spectacular—the Bay and the great city across it to the west, the forested hills and graceful homes built upon them to the east. It was the same vantage point that held trustee Billings in its thrall sixty-seven years before. The stadium itself, designed by chief architect Howard to resemble the Roman Colosseum, was breathtakingly beautiful, and with no running track or other obstruction to spectator viewing, a near perfect place to watch a football game. And to watch one free of charge for those willing to climb "Tightwad Hill" above the bowl's northeastern rim.

A capacity crowd of 72,609 turned out for the opening on November 24, 1923, the largest yet to watch a football game in the West. The forecast was for a close game since Stanford in its second season under coach Andy Kerr seemed to be a formidable opponent. The Cardinal's only loss in eight games was to USC by 14–7, and in sophomore fullback Ernie Nevers, it had a player already touted as among the nation's best. After years of mostly humiliating losses to Smith's teams, the Cardinal appeared ready to meet the challenge.

But the game was a stinker, a punt-punctuated defensive stalemate with neither team gaining even a hundred yards in total offense or collectively reaching double digits in first downs. Deadeye Blewett missed all five of his field goal tries, although two of those misses led to the game's only scores.

Early in the second quarter, Blewett was so wide of the mark that the ball bounced out of bounds on the Stanford four, an unintentional coffin corner kick. Nevers tried to punt his team out of trouble from there, but his kick was blocked by Horrell, who fell on the ball in the end zone for the first touchdown ever scored in the new stadium. Cal got positive results out of another faulty field goal try in the fourth quarter. This time Blewett at least reached the end zone, but well wide of the uprights. The ball was fielded there by Stanford captain John "Scotchy" Campbell who foolishly tried to run it back. Instead, Scotchy was dropped in his tracks by a host of Bears for a safety. In this 9–0 win, all of Cal's points were scored on defense, proof positive, it would seem, of their coach's postulate about what constitutes a good offense.

The dreary loss was particularly painful for Stanford supporters. Their team had not won a Big Game in football since 1905 and, discounting the unofficial blowout of '18, three of the five post-rugby losses had been humiliating: 38–0 in 1920, 42–7 in '21 and 28–0 in '22. Nine-to-nothing may have been an improvement, but hardly cause for celebration. Something had to be done. What the school clearly needed was a coach with a track record approaching that of the apparently unbeatable one in Berkeley.

In fact, the Stanford Board of Athletic Control—established in 1917 by university president Wilbur—was already on the case. In 1921,

Board members settled on their man—Glenn Scobey "Pop" Warner. Warner was not merely a "name" coach; he was already by then one of the game's legendary figures, an innovator variously credited with introducing the three-point stance, the screen pass, the spiral punt, the wingback formations, the shifting line, the rolling body block, the blocking dummy, thigh and shoulder pads and the numbering of players' jerseys.

"Most of us coaches are imitators," said Kerr, Warner's friend and longtime colleague. "Pop is an inventor, the game's greatest creative genius."

Warner had been a star lineman at Cornell, captain of the 1894 team. As a graduate student in law, he was slightly older than his teammates, so they gave him, when he was just twenty-two, his paternal nickname. After law school, he coached at Georgia and at his alma mater for two years each and then, in 1899, accepted the head coaching job at the Carlisle Indian Industrial School in south central Pennsylvania. Established in 1870 to educate children of Indian tribal families relocated by the U.S. Army, Carlisle already had by the time of Warner's arrival a distinctive football reputation. The Indians—as they were, of course, called— played all of their games on the road, unlike their warrior forebears who were, by heritage, the home team. But they were still the perennial underdogs in these gridiron recreations of the cavalry vs. redskin wars.

Sportswriters of the time had a field day covering them, dredging forth such dime novel locutions as "warpath," "scalping," "tomahawk," "Big Chief" and "ambush" for their game stories. The New York *World* described Carlisle's 1896 team as having been "drawn from the uncivilized sections of the Far West and trained in the ways of the white men." The players were routinely depicted in sports page illustrations as fierce savages, wily in the ways of warcraft. In fact, Carlisle's teams, unlike so many of their paleface foes, practiced exemplary sportsmanship in the vain hope of dispelling such slanderous effusions. And under Warner, they became a finely tuned football force, capable of competing on an equal basis with such established powers as Harvard, Yale, Princeton and Pennsylvania—as well as, in one historic 1899 encounter, California.

Pop coached the Indians through 1903, then after another interlude at Cornell, returned for the pivotal years of 1907 through 1913, a period during which he coached all-time All American Jim Thorpe. Carlisle then had the game's greatest player and certainly one of its greatest coaches. The Indians were no longer an exotic curiosity.

Pop Warner was in his seventh year at Pitt in 1921, a winner there over one stretch of thirty-three straight games, when he was first approached by Leland Cutler of the Stanford athletic board. Would the great man be interested in coming west? He would, he said, but there was a hitch: his contract at Pitt had two more years to run and he had every intention of honoring it. Cutler, who would later head San Francisco's World's Fair of 1939, was undisuaded. "No more glib, eloquent or persuasive tongue ever blessed the mouth of any man I have ever known," wrote Stanford publicist Don Liebendorfer of Cutler in his memoir, *The Color of Life is Red*. And Warner, in his own memoir, described Cutler as "the greatest salesman in the world."

Cutler saw a way out of Warner's contractual dilemma: Pop should sign a Stanford contract now that would not take effect until 1924 when his obligations to Pitt were fulfilled—a deal not unlike the one Jimmy Schaeffer worked out with Smith six years earlier. Now the twist: in the interim, while he was finishing up at Pitt, Pop should dispatch a few loyal assistants to Palo Alto to install the Warner single and double wingback system with all of its complicated spinners and reverses. That way, when he finally did arrive, he would find his players prepared to do his bidding.

"I was stunned," Warner recalled. "Undoubtedly, it was one of the strangest proposals that I had ever heard."

But he agreed to it, sending his chief assistant, Kerr, to Stanford as the interim head coach and another Pitt assistant and onetime star lineman, Claude "Tiny" Thornhill, as the line coach. Both stayed on at Stanford when Warner finally took over in '24. In his two years as Cardinal headman, Kerr had a respectable 11-7 record and, with help from another persuasive Stanford alum, W. Finlaw Geary, lured the great Nevers, then living in Santa Rosa, away from other recruiters, including Cal's. Actually, it was Warner in absentia who closed the deal, for as Nevers recalled years later, "I knew Pop was coming, and that sold me."

But Nevers, a 205-pound bruising runner and brilliant all-round athlete (he also lettered in baseball and basketball at Stanford) missed virtually all of Warner's debut season on the Farm, breaking his left ankle in a scrimmage before the first game and his right attempting a late-season comeback. But even without its star, Pop's team entered the epochal 1924 Big Game undefeated and untied in seven games. Smith, too, was undefeated, the only imperfection a 7–7 tie with Washington and its sensational tailback, George Wilson, in Seattle. This was the only game the Bears played away from their new Memorial Stadium the entire season, a home-field advantage if ever there was one.

Cal's schedule was not the only peculiarity of the '24 season. Only hours before the game with USC on November 1, Cal graduate manager Nichols informed his S.C. counterpart, Gwynn Wilson, that because of coach Henderson's overly aggressive recruiting practices, Cal was severing football relations with the Trojans in 1925. And, he added, so was Stanford. Despite Wilson's indignant response, the game was played, anyway, the Bears winning, 7–0, on a Dixon touchdown in the second quarter. Still smouldering over what they deemed petty jealousy by the northern schools over the Trojans' rather sudden emergence as a rival football power, S.C. authorities promptly cancelled their scheduled game with Stanford the next Saturday.

That left Warner with a large hole in his schedule he sought frantically to fill. The University of Utah was available, but Stanford Stadium was not, since the Cal and Stanford freshman teams were already booked to play that day. The only Bay Area stadium that was, in fact, available, and available for the first and only time that season, what with the home team in Seattle, was the new one in Berkeley. And so, in a once-in-a-lifetime event, Stanford would play at home in Cal's home. The ordinarily hostile environment didn't faze Pop and his boys as they clobbered Utah, 30–0.

The rift between the northern schools and USC was, fortunately for all, short-lived; Stanford resumed play with the Trojans in '25 and Cal in '26. But the recruiting accusations cost Gloomy Gus Henderson his job as head coach, despite an outstanding five-year won-lost record of 45-7. Henderson himself freely admitted to persuading athletes from southern California to reject northern advances and stay closer to home at S.C. But as graduate manager Wilson said in his defense, "There were no rules in those days. It was an open season situation. We weren't any worse or any better in that regard than anyone else."

Maybe so, but in hastening Gloomy Gus's departure with their complaints, Cal and Stanford made a horrendous miscalculation, for the coach their southern rival picked as his replacement was the redoubtable Howard Jones, and his "Thundering Herds" would soon begin stampeding them both.

But not yet. Cal and Stanford were still dominant in 1924, and their Big Game that November 22 was *the* sports event of the year on the Pacific Coast. But it, too, would not be free of controversy. A week before the game, Cal protested that Stanford's star halfback, Norm Cleaveland, a senior, should be declared ineligible because he'd actually played two minutes of a game against Nevada in 1921. He was, therefore, a four-year player when conference rules limited varsity eligibility to three years. This was sort of a belated tit-for-tat for the Locomotive Smith debacle of twenty-two years earlier. And it worked. Stanford apologetically removed Cleaveland from the lineup—almost but not quite over Pop Warner's dead body—and even volunteered to forfeit all of its conference wins, an offer graciously declined.

Cleaveland's banishment, coupled with Nevers' injuries, deprived an angry Warner of his two best backs for the most important game of his new career. The Bears were promptly made 2-1 favorites. This was another superior Smith team, stingy as ever on defense—only thirty-one points allowed in eight games—and newly potent on offense with a Dixon-to-Imlay passing game supplementing the traditionally tough running attack. Bert Griffin was another dangerous back. And the impenetrable line was anchored by All American Horrell and, as he was once described in a game program, the "gigantic" Dana Carey at left guard. Carey in 1924 weighed all of 194 pounds.

This was a year when Smith showed no mercy. Angered by the Nevada debacle of the previous season, his Bears trounced the Wolfpack, 27–0, even though the Nevada team was coached by old friend Charlie Erb.

Though the biggest guns in his arsenal may have been missing, Warner was not without his weapons. At ends, he had Jim Lawson, the first Stanford player to make All American, and young Ted Shipkey, who would become another one before he graduated. And in Murray Cuddeback, Pop had the sort of all-round player he most admired. Cliff Hey, Nevers' sub, was also a strong runner and passer.

The pre-game coverage in the Bay Area press was predictably lavish. "Gladiators On Edge/ And Rarin' to Go," headlined the *Chronicle*. "This is the day we have been waiting for all season," wrote Ed R. Hughes. "The football games played earlier in the season were merely warm-ups for the Big Game." The *Chronicle* assigned six writers to the game, including a women's page reporter, Florence Muir, to capture the feminine angle, and, most imaginatively, the game's referee, George Varnell, for the whistle-blower's point of view. Varnell's day job, as it develops, was as a sportswriter in Spokane, Washington.

Stanford had a slight edge in weight: 187 pounds in the line to 184 and 177 to 168 for the backs.

Rarely does such a game live up to its hype—Smith vs. Warner, the conference championship and a Rose Bowl bid at stake, the most evenly matched Big Game between the two best teams in the West. But this one, on November 22, 1924, did. Extra seats were installed in Memorial Stadium, enlarging its capacity to seventy-seven thousand, and such was the demand for tickets that a pair sold for $100, a princely sum at a time when even $5 for a ticket seemed exorbitant. Counting the parsimonious adventurers atop Tightwad Hill, the *Chronicle* estimated the crowd for this game at ninety thousand. No Big Game had ever been bigger.

The two teams sparred warily through a scoreless first quarter. Then in the second, the Cardinal—largely on the strength of a 17-yard Lawson end-around and a Hey-to-Shipkey pass for 25 yards—drove to the Cal 7. There, the Bears held fast, and on fourth down Cuddeback kicked a field goal from the 18. Another Cuddeback field goal, this one a boomer from the Bear 43, gave Stanford a 6–0 lead at the half.

But Smith roused his team for the second half. Early in the third quarter, the Bears uncorked an 81-yard drive, highlighted by a 52-yard pass play from Dixon to Imlay and finished off with a five-yard run by Griffin. Glen "Scoop" Carlson dropkicked the extra point for a 7-6 Cal advantage. Near the end of the quarter, Cal again drove deep, a Dixon-to-Gordon Huber pass moving the ball to the Stanford 22. A couple of running plays advanced it to the 16 as the quarter ended. As the fourth began, Dixon fired a flat pass to Imlay who dodged his way through the Stanford secondary for the score. With Carlson's conversion, the Bears improved their lead to 14–6 and seemed clearly in command.

They moved in for the apparent kill minutes later when tackle John Sargent recovered Cardinal Howard "Mugs" Mitchell's muff of a punt on the Stanford 29. Three runs by Dixon moved the ball to the 17, and from there Griffin found a hole at right guard and weaved into the end zone. Barely ten minutes were left to play. Carlson unaccountably missed the extra point. Or did he? The kicker rushed over to referee Varnell afterward complaining that he had made his negative call too soon, that the ball, though appearing at first to be headed wide, had actually hooked over the crossbar.

Carlson years later grimly recalled the ref-writer's response: "You may be right, but you're so far ahead now, what do you have to worry about?"

In fact, that missed point gave the Bears a great deal to worry about. With six minutes remaining and his team now ahead, 20–6, Smith replaced his battle-warn backfield stars, Dixon and Imlay, with the relatively inexperienced Johnny Clymer and Myron Brown. According to the rules of the time, players removed in one quarter could not return until the next, so Dixon and Imlay were through for the day, replaced by players who might prove a liability, particularly on defense.

A few minutes earlier, Warner made a substitution of his own, summoning from the bench one Edgar Walker to go in at right halfback. Walker was a stocky (5-10, 181 pounds), slow-talking, slow-moving, prematurely balding sophomore originally from Wyatt, Louisiana. He seemed an odd choice to come in at such a critical time. "Pop knew better than anyone that Ed was not a great back," wrote Liebendorfer. In fact, Warner would shift him to end the next season. But the coach also knew that Walker was an accurate passer and that his disposition was of such implacable placidity that the tension generated by the huge and largely unsympathetic crowd and the precariousness of his team's situation would have no greater effect on him than might the buzzing of a housefly. Ed Walker may have been slow, but he was cool.

With the ball in Stanford's possession just past midfield, Walker connected with a pass to another sub, Quarterback Fred Solomon, for 26 yards to the Cal 20. And from there, he passed to Shipkey for a touchdown. Cuddeback converted for 20–13. But there were only a few more minutes remaining, and when Cal ran some more time off the clock and backed the Cardinal up to its own 19, the game seemed a lost cause. There were no technically refined two-minute drills in 1924, no deadly passers and deft receivers to work the clock with sideline plays. As a matter of fact, there were no hash marks then. Instead the ball was placed only a few feet from where it went out of bounds. But Stanford managed. First, Cuddeback, not known as a passer, surprised Cal with a 43-yard strike to Shipkey. Then Walker calmly faded and passed to an open Cuddeback on the 18, and the Cardinal star dashed down the sidelines for the touchdown. It was 20–19. Amid a tremendous howling from both sides of the field—and from the thousands on Tightwad Hill—Cuddeback kicked the tying point. The game ended two plays later.

Cuddeback had scored 14 of his team's 20 points, the first player in Big Game history to kick a field goal (actually, two), score a touchdown and kick a point-after (two). Along with six Cardinal linemen, he played the entire sixty minutes, even though he'd been knocked cold earlier in the final quarter when he collided on the sidelines with a movie camera filming the game. His co-star, Walker, played just 10½ minutes. But they were timely ones.

Games without a winner or a loser are not ordinarily considered "classics," but this noble deadlock has been heralded over the many years since as one of the greatest of all Big Games. Bay Area newspapers gave it banner front page headlines the next day, the San Francisco *Examiner* correctly reporting that the huge crowd was held "Spellbound." There were sidebars aplenty, including one about a spectator so overcome with emotion he dropped dead in his seat. The headline most difficult to fathom was the one in the *Chronicle* asserting that "Andy Smith Drank Two Full/Gallons of Water While/Stanford Men Tied Score." Water was hardly the coach's beverage of choice. Varnell wrote that the game gave him "the greatest of all thrills." And Walter Camp, who favored the event with his august presence, told the *Chronicle* that "for sustained suspense, I have never seen a football game like this."

High praise from football's father, particularly since it was well known that Camp was no fan of the passing game. In fact, he had opposed legalizing the forward pass during the rules turmoil of 1906. And in this '24 thriller, both teams threw the ball with relative abandon. Stanford's two touchdowns came through the air. Cal's first was set up by a long pass play and its second was scored on a pass. At a time when teams ran off fewer plays overall (the clock didn't stop as often and teams often punted before fourth down), Stanford completed 9 of 17 passes for 169 yards and Cal 9 of 15 for 116 yards. Stanford had 76 yards more passing than running.

Both coaches were naturally disappointed in the outcome. Warner dearly wanted to beat the Wonder Team's wonder coach in his first Big Game. And Smith, the water drinker, wanted to keep his winning streak alive against the despised Cardinal. To think it all came down to a missed (maybe) point after.

This was indeed a memorable Big Game, though perhaps not quite as memorable as Brodie described it in his book twenty-five years later: "When generations thousands of years from now come prowling through the scene of the Bay Area civilization it is a certain bet that, no matter what else is found, they will find plenty about the California-Stanford game of November 22, 1924."

Actually, this wasn't even the last game of the season for either team. Stanford went on to the Rose Bowl where it lost to Notre Dame and the Four Horseman 27–10, despite the heroics of Nevers, who played sixty minutes and gained 114 yards on his two busted ankles. The Bears played their coach"s alma mater, Penn, on New Year's Day (at Memorial Stadium, of course), closing out Smith's fifth straight undefeated season with a 14–0 win. In that time, his teams had built a 44-0-4 record and scored 1564 points to just 146 for the hapless opposition.

Would the wonders never cease?

CHAPTER SEVEN

# ASHES TO ASHES

The 1925 season began routinely with two decisive victories, shut-outs over Santa Clara (28–0) and Nevada (54–0). Against the rugged Broncos, Dixon again established himself as one of the most versatile tailbacks on the coast, scoring on a 62-yard run and passing 40 yards to team captain Imlay for another touchdown. In the Nevada rout, fullback Earl Jabs, a 185-pound power runner from Anaheim who somehow escaped to Berkeley from the clutches of Howard Jones and USC, scored five TDs, four in the second half.

These Bears were somewhat bigger than their forebears, averaging 190 pounds in the line and, even with tiny Tut, 173, in the backfield. And they had depth, Dixon was backed by two subs, Griffin and Paul Perrin, who could easily have been starters elsewhere. And Jabs shared his position with another strong runner, John Young. But this would be a season like no other for Andy and his boys.

Cal's third game was with the Olympic Club, a team expertly pieced together by coach Orin "Babe" Hollingberry from former college stars and the best available club and high school talent. With an age range from the teens to the thirties and comparable gaps in size and experience, the Olympians presented an odd yet formidable challenge for the Bears. It was a challenge further complicated by the appearance in the lineup of former Stanford players Jack Patrick (1919-21), Scotchy Campbell (1921-23), Harry Shipkey (1922-24), and Norm Cleaveland (1922-24), none of whom as collegians had ever played in a winning game against Smith's Bears. All sought sweet vengeance for past humiliations. Cleaveland was especially motivated since it was at Cal's insistence that he was declared ineligible for the last Big Game of his college career. Now, coincidentally, he and his fellow Cardinals were wearing red and white once more, only this time under the ensign of the Winged O. In yet another oddity, the club roster also included two future Cal stars, quarterback Lee Eisan, fresh out of Lowell High School in San Francisco, and end Russ Avery, who at twenty-one was already a veteran of club football.

The Olympians had shut out Stanford and Ernie Nevers, 9–0, in the season's opener, convincing evidence of their newfound luster. Andy Smith knew that despite the handicaps endemic to club football—limited practice time, day jobs, improper conditioning, family responsibilities—the Bears were meeting, save for the paychecks, the equivalent of a good professional team. The '20s, in fact, would represent the final football fling for athletic clubs in the country, what with the founding of the National Football League and its pocketbook appeal to former collegians. When campus heroes like Red Grange and, eventually, Nevers turned pro, it became clear there was little future in the game for amateur clubs. Most gave it up before the end of the decade, although the Olympic Club hung on with decreasing success until 1934.

But the Olympians were far from finished in '25, and they came to Memorial Stadium that October 10 loaded for Bear. They even brought along a marching band and a rooting section liberally estimated at several thousand. A crowd of forty-five thousand turned out for this battle between Smith's still unbeaten legions and what was in all probability the finest club team ever fielded on the west coast.

After a scoreless first quarter, the Bears found themselves backed up to their own goal line early in the second by a long coffin corner kick by Cleaveland. Dixon tried to punt his team out of danger, but the kick was blocked by tackle Shipkey and retrieved on the three-yard line by the other club tackle, John Daly, who the day before had celebrated his thirty-fourth birthday. Daly jogged untouched into the end zone. Former Santa Clara star halfback Jimmy Needles, later an outstanding basketball coach at USF and Loyola, missed the extra point.

Then in the third quarter, the club's offensive defense struck again. With the ball on the Cal 20, Dixon, attempting to pass, was smothered by Shipkey and end Bob Brown for a 15-yard loss. In defiance of the era's prevailing orthodoxy Dixon tried another pass from his end zone. It was intercepted by club lineman Percy Locey and run in for another score. Patrick converted for 13–0.

In the Sunday *Chronicle*, Hughes would lecture the improvident Dixon and, subliminally, his coach: "Football men have labored hard and long to pound into their charges the dangers of trying forward passing deep in their own territory. And there was never a better illustration of the danger than was shown yesterday."

Finally, in the last quarter, Cal halfback Charles Willi fumbled a Patrick punt near his goal line when he, of course, should have let it go. The ball bounced off his hands into the end zone where Cal center Ross Baze, fearful of an Olympian getting there first for another touchdown, fell on it for a safety. Every point in the club's 15-0 win was scored by linemen, the last two by one of Cal's.

"If there was ever a game when one team made the other beat itself, that was yesterday," wrote Hughes. "It is not often that a team coached by Andy Smith makes so many mistakes in one game."

Smith's Bears had not been beaten since the final game of the 1919 season when Washington won, 7–0. The fifty-game streak was over, but Andy hid his disappointment and hurried across the field to congratulate Hollingberry and his players. There was no disgrace in this loss; the Winged O would finish the season undefeated and send seven players to the inaugural East-West All Star game in San Francisco. But friends knew, as Hughes wrote, that the defeat "hurt Andy more than he would admit." Still, he bore it with the same grace and dignity he demanded of his players.

Smith rallied his team to shutout wins over St. Mary's (6–0), Oregon (28–0) and Pomona (27–0) and a 35–7 shellacking of Washington State. Seven games into the decade's sixth season, the Bears had yet to lose to a college team. But that streak, too, would come to an end when, a week before the Big Game, Washington, the last school to beat them, did it again, and by the same score of 7–0.

Cal and Stanford entered the Big Game with identical 6-2 records, and both had lost to the same two teams, the Olympic Club and Rose Bowl-bound Washington. Obviously, they were evenly matched for this second meeting of their super coaches, and a record crowd of seventy-four thousand two hundred showed up at Stanford Stadium on November 21. But this matchup was a mismatch. Much to Cal's grief, Nevers was healthy this time, and he dominated play on both sides of the ball, gaining 111 yards rushing, scoring twice and recovering a fumble that set up another score. "Ernie Nevers 27, Cal 14," read the *Examiner* headline.

The Bears labored in vain to overcome a 20–0 halftime deficit, with Griffin, playing in place of the injured Dixon, scoring twice. In retrospect, Griffin played nearly as well as Nevers, rushing for 99 yards and matching him for touchdowns. But to no avail. As they walked off the field together Warner turned to his star halfback, Dick Hyland, and said, "It will be a long time before California wins another Big Game."

The win was Stanford's first over Cal in American football since 1905 and the Bears' third loss of the season, the most since the wartime year of 1917. But it was also Smith's eighth straight winning season and the ninth of his ten years in Berkeley (he finished 5-5 in 1917). His record in that time was 74-16-7 the best winning percentage of any Cal coach lasting longer than two years on the job. His team's "reign as undefeated champions of the coast" may have come to an abrupt end, but Andy's place among college football's coaching elite was firmly entrenched.

And so, only weeks after the Big Game loss, the ASUC offered him a four-year contract extension worth $50,000, to take effect January 1, 1927. The coach, traveling in the East to watch some late-season football, wired his acceptance. Andy Smith presumably would be head football coach at the University of California until at least 1931. He had, in effect, become a Berkeley Institution.

"The campus reflected a spirit of jubilance with the announcement of Smith's acceptance," the *Chronicle* reported. "Supporters of the Golden Bear intend to forget this year of comparative famine and look forward to many years of plenty under Andrew L. Smith's tutorship."

Smith had gone east after the Stanford game to watch the Penn-Cornell game on Thanksgiving Day. Though nursing a cold, he stayed on to catch the Army-Navy game that Saturday at the Polo Grounds in New York. Watching two football games in different cities the same week in typically frigid East Coast weather could hardly be considered an antidote for the common cold. His illness might have been worsened further by his own propensity for partying into the wee hours. A rumor circulated, in fact, that after one such frolic in Philadelphia he fell asleep in a porch chair outdoors on an evening when temperatures dipped below freezing.

Whatever the cause, Andy Smith was admitted to University Hospital in Philadelphia on December 19, 1925 with bronchial pneumonia and pulmonary ulcers. He never recovered, dying in the hospital on January 8, 1926 with two former Penn teammates, William H. "Big Bill" Hollenback and Dr. Robert S. Torrey, at his bedside. Andy Smith was just forty-three years old.

News of his death sent shock waves across the country. Most Cal fans were either unaware of his illness or not informed of its severity.

The university community was jolted. "This is a terrific personal shock to me," said ASUC general manager Luther A. Nichols, who had tendered the new contract to Smith a little more than a month earlier. Pop Warner was equally aghast: "I am so overcome that it is impossible for me to comment on the death of my friend."

Smith's loyal assistant Nibs Price was also taken by surprise: "I can't believe it is true. I don't know how we are going to get along without him. There simply can never be anyone to fill the place his going has left vacant." Actually, at Smith's earlier suggestion, Nibs himself would fill that place.

Tut Imlay, Smith's last team captain, spoke for the team: "We loved him. He made men. Andy is gone and we can't understand why."

Brick Muller affirmed the loyalty of former players: "We idolized him, and he was intensely loyal to us. It was one big family with Andy coaching."

Others, including university President Campbell praised him for his concern for his players' academic standing. "Football on the coast has lost a man who stood for high scholarship standards," said Bill Spaulding, coach of the emerging football team at UCLA. And Edward "Slip" Madigan, St. Mary's College's colorful coach, said, "His characteristics were reflected in his players after they left the gridiron." "He was a man who could honestly be called a perfect sportsman," said Washington All American George Wilson.

Though he had scores of friends and thousands of admirers, Smith died virtually bereft of close family ties. His father died when he was an infant, his mother in 1924. He was divorced and childless. His only surviving family member, a brother, Richard, lived in Kansas City, rarely saw Andy and recognized that he "centered all of his affections on the University of California and the boys he coached."

Smith's estate was estimated at $30,000 and, according to his will, drawn up by San Francisco attorney and U.C. regent Milton F. Farmer, he left $10,000 to the university to support two football scholarships and $2000 to his beloved Berkeley Elks Club. The remainder, after funeral expenses, was to be divided between the Skull & Keys Society at Cal and the Berkeley chapter of his college fraternity, Sigma Alpha Epsilon. His body was to be cremated with funeral services at the Elks Club. And then, in the will's most revealing entry, he declared that his ashes were to be "scattered to the winds" over Memorial Stadium.

Services were held on Friday, January 15, 1926, exalted ruler James Dunlap of the Berkeley Elks presiding. Andy drew, as always, a capacity crowd with four hundred more standing outside the packed club in a drizzling rain. The audience indoors included coaches and players, former players, faculty members and university administrators, opposing coaches, fraternity brothers and any number of old pals.

The next day, thousands of mourners marched in solemn procession to the north gate of the stadium for one final farewell. Brick Morse led the Cal Glee Club in the singing of his own composition, "Hail to California." In his eulogy, president Campbell said of his friend: "Even in death a successful man may be a valued and influential teacher of the living. Through five years of victory, coach Smith's prestige as a teacher of football grew and grew, but his exemplary conduct in defeat last October and November did more to establish him in the affections of the general public than did all his victories combined."

As the massed thousands joined in the singing of the university hymn, the droning of an approaching airplane could be heard in the distance. The pilot, Army Lieutenant J.R. Glasscock of Crissy Field in San Francisco, had been another of Smith's close friends. "As the plane shot down into the stadium," wrote Eddie Boyden in the *Chronicle*, "Lieutenant Glasscock cast Andy's ashes to the breeze which bore them to the green sod of the stadium, over which his boys fought so many a famous gridiron fight..."

On December 31, 1927, before the Bears' game with Andy's alma mater, Penn, a players bench of granite, built with funds raised by Smith's former team captains and "friends of the university," was installed and dedicated on the Cal (east) side of the field. Inscribed on it was Andy's now famous counsel to his players: "We do not want men who will lie down bravely to die but men who will fight valiantly to live—Winning is not everything, and it is far better to play the game squarely and lose than to win at the sacrifice of an ideal."

In 1951, Andy Smith and his first great star, Muller, were elected to the college football Hall of Fame. In 1960, the Helms Athletic Foundation in Los Angeles selected Smith's 1920 team as "the greatest college football team of all time."

And for years after his death, efforts were made to keep Andy's legend alive on the Cal campus. The Andy Smith Award is given annually to the Cal player with the most minutes of action. Tributes to him were given periodically at the Big Game Bonfire Rally at the Greek Theater. Then, in 1948, an affable speech professor named Garff Wilson (he was later the chief of protocol on the Berkeley campus) was asked to write a proper eulogy for him to be delivered at the Rally. Liberally borrowing from and distinctly improving upon old newspaper accounts of Smith's two-day funeral, Wilson prepared what became for years an essential part of Big Game ritual.

The eulogy was read that first year and the next by a student, George "Bud" Hobbs. But Wilson himself took the stage after that and for the next twenty-four years he gave the Andy Smith Eulogy the full measure of his considerable talent as a reader of melodramatic prose. Standing alone on the Greek Theater's massive stage, illuminated by the bonfire below and by candles held by eighty-five hundred suddenly silent rooters, Wilson delivered in hushed tones his panegyric to the departed coach as in the background the Glee Club hummed Cal tunes. On a hill above the amphitheater a bugler stood poised to play taps as Wilson reached his closing lines:

"The multitudes stood silent while an airplane circled overhead; then it dipped low; and as it passed over the locked and silent stadium, it scattered the ashes of Andy Smith—as he had wished—over the field where he had worked and fought his battles, there to remain forever."

It was great theater, and somehow the Eulogy touched a deep reserve of sentiment in its young listeners, many of whom may not have had the foggiest idea who Andy Smith had been. But nothing is forever. The "green sod" where the great coach had "fought his battles" and had his ashes cast is now composed of a synthetic material called "Momentum Turf." The Smith bench remains in place, but it is rarely sat upon since, with the multiple substitutions employed in the modern game, players now stand for the length of the game, unless they are injured. And when Wilson died at eighty-nine in 1998, so, for all purposes, did the Eulogy.

The coach whose death sent the university, the Bay Area and the world of college football into mourning is now but a misty figure from an increasingly distant past.

PART II

1926-1946

CHAPTER EIGHT

# GOING MY WAY?

Months before he died, Andy Smith had confided to Brick Morse that if anything should happen to him he wanted Nibs Price to succeed him as the Cal Football coach. Price was, in fact, the logical successor. He'd been with Smith almost from the beginning of his reign in Berkeley and was at the time of Andy's death his top assistant. He'd also had two years of head coaching experience, albeit in another sport—basketball. And yet, perhaps because of his small stature and a diffident manner, Nibs was perceived as somewhat of a perennial underdog. When he replaced Earl Wight as basketball coach for the 1924-25 season, critics deplored his comparative lack of experience in the game. But over that season and the next, Nibs' teams strung together a twenty-nine-game winning streak. For that matter, he would remain Cal's basketball coach for thirty years and win six Pacific Coast Conference and twelve conference southern division championships.

Now, in March of 1926, the "little giant," as he was affectionately if unimaginatively known, was asked to follow a true giant of coaching. If anyone merited the underdog label, it was he. "Poor Nibs" was heard about as often on campus as "Go Bears." The *Blue and Gold* sympathetically dedicated its 1926-27 edition to the new coach, after first observing that "California's football season was carried on in spite of the death of Andy Smith."

"Carried on," yes, but not with the usual results, since Smith had left the talent cupboard nearly bare. Gone were offensive stars Dixon and Imlay, as well as muscular linemen like Carey who had cleared paths for them. Griffin, however, remained, and he was elected team captain.

Price's Bears opened promisingly enough with wins over Santa Clara (13–6) and a talent-depleted Olympic Club (32–0), but were clobbered by Madigan's St. Mary's Galloping Gaels, 26–7. It was the first of four straight defeats, all at home. The most telling of these was to Howard Jones's USC herd by 27–0, a score, though bad enough, that didn't begin to spell the difference between the two teams, the Trojans gaining 587 yards to Cal's 46 and racking up twenty-six first downs to just one. And in the Big Game, Pop's prophecy of the year before seemed more valid than ever, the undefeated Cardinal scoring a re-sounding 41–6 victory before moving on to the Rose Bowl and a 7–7 tie with Alabama.

The Bears finished with three wins against six losses, not exactly a stellar debut for Poor Nibs. It was Cal's first losing season in American football since 1897. And yet the team set an attendance record of three hundred seventy-seven thousand for the eight home games, crowds of better than seventy thousand showing up for the lopsided losses to USC and Stanford and sixty-one thousand for St. Mary's.

The Bears returned to their winning ways in '27, a team led by All Coast linemen Irv Phillips and Fritz Coltrin and featuring some able sophomores in backs Benny Lom and Lee Eisan and a slim cen-ter named Roy Riegels, who, despite an unimposing 6-foot, 175-pound physique was an indomitable force both offensively and defensively. It was a season when the goal posts were moved from the goal line to the back of the end zone, a rule change that took some of the scoring zing out of the kicking game and therefore dictated more aggressive offensive tactics.

Price's squad won its first five games, four by shutout, before losing again to USC, this time by just 13–0 before eighty-two thousand fans in Los Angeles. An easy 33–13 win over Montana was then followed by losses to Washington (6–0) at home and Stanford (13–6) before eighty-eight thousand in an enlarged Stanford Stadium. The Cardinal's winning touchdown was scored on a play reminiscent of the skullduggery Pop Warner regularly practiced during his experimental days at Carlisle. With the ball on Cal's four-yard line, star fullback Clifford "Biff" Hoffman, who gained 142 yards that day, took the snap and after some double-wing spinner-play legerdemain circled end with the ball concealed on his hip, almost, in fact, behind his back. The play was called, in tribute to the purveyors of illegal spirits during these Prohibition years, the "bootleg." Hoffman ran virtually undetected across the goal line. As Morse wrote somewhat later, "Benny Lom suspected something fishy, but wasn't sure what it was. He ran up to Biff to examine him, but got a poke under the chin while Mr. Hoffman ran on over the line."

Cal finished off this 7–3 season with a 27–13 win over Penn in the Smith Bench dedication game on New Year's Eve. Nibs had cast off the "poor" part of his name....at least for awhile.

Captained by All American end Phillips, the 1928 team completed the regular season with just one loss, that to a rejuvenated Olympic Club team by 12–0. The Winged O, sparked by Mort Kaer, the flashy former Trojan tailback, would finish the season undefeated in what was essentially the club's swan song in big-time football. The only other blemishes on the Bears' record were ties with USC (0–0) and Stanford (13–13). Nibs had a virtually impenetrable defense that surrendered only fifteen points in the eight games preceding the big one. Phillips and former Olympian Avery, now a twenty-four-year-old sophomore, were outstanding defenders at end and tackles Steve Bancroft and Frank Fritz and guards Bert Schwartz and Harry Gill—the first of five brothers to play for Cal—anchored the interior line. Riegels was a "roving center" on defense, the equivalent in modern play of a middle linebacker.

But despite the triple-threat talents of All Coast tailback Lom, Price's single-wing offense was hardly the steamroller of Wonder Team vintage. Toss out the 60 points scored against outclassed Nevada, and the Bears averaged little more than a touchdown per game before playing a Stanford team that had thrice that season scored more than 40 points. The Bears entertained the hope, nevertheless, that the high-scoring Cards might be distracted by the election earlier that month of their former football manager, Herbert Hoover, as the 31st President of the United States.

Before a crowd of 82,070 at an also enlarged Memorial Stadium, the Bears moved smartly out to a 13-0 lead at halftime, the touchdowns split equally between offense and defense, Bancroft scoring on a 76-yard interception return and Lom passing 38 yards to Avery. But Stanford revived in the second half, largely on the passing and running of reserve backs Bill Simkins and Lud Frentrup. Simkins scored at the conclusion of a long third-quarter drive and then with less than a minute to play passed 24 yards to Frentrup for the tying touchdown. Fritz blocked the conversion kick. Had it been good it would have given Stanford the win and deprived the Bears of a third trip to the Rose Bowl. And had the Bears not gone to Pasadena that January, their history and the history of the Rose Bowl would be lacking a moment of unsurpassed bizarrerie.

Cal's opponent in the Rose Bowl on January 1, 1929, was Georgia Tech, undefeated and untied in nine games and considered in polls to be either the best or second best team in the nation. Among the Engineers' victims were Notre Dame (13–0), Alabama (33–13) and archrival Georgia (20–6). The Tech offense, which averaged 24 points per game, included a series of plays run out of a most unusual variation of the T-Formation, the quarterback situated rump-to-rump with the center and accepting the ball between his legs before dispensing it to the remaining backs. Sports announcer Bill Monday called it, possibly with scatological insinuation, the "Crapshoot Formation."

The Crapshoot set the tone for what would become one of the most peculiar football games ever played. At one point in the third quarter, the ball unaccountably deflated as Lom punted it, fizzling to the turf only a few feet away from the astonished kicker. Referee Herb Dana ruled, incredibly, that since a Tech defender had touched the ball in its whistling descent Lom's puntless punt had been blocked. He awarded the ball, such as it was, to Tech at the point of its final expiration. Earlier, in the second quarter, Lom—who, as we shall see, had a busy afternoon—picked off a Tech fumble and ran 68 yards to an apparent Cal touchdown. But Dana, also busy, ruled that the play had been blown dead before Lom caught the ball. On yet another occasion, Tech halfback John "Stumpy" Thomason shot a straight arm directly into the open mouth of Cal's Bancroft. Capitalizing on this unusual opportunity, Bancroft bit down hard on the intrusive fingers, causing a howling Stumpy (he was 5-7, 190) to warn his teammates that the opponents might well be bears in more than name only.

But these oddities were merely preliminaries and postscripts to a play that would distinguish this game from all others, in or out of the Rose Bowl. It came about on the Engineers' second possession of the second quarter, with the ball on their own 24-yard line and the game still scoreless. On first down, Thomason plowed off tackle for six yards before he was hit hard by Phillips and Lom. On impact, the ball squirted out of Stumpy's grip and bounced forward to the 34, where Riegels, the Rover, fielded it cleanly on the hop. It was…. so far…a big play for the Bears.

But Riegels kept running, headed for the near sidelines. He was hemmed in there by four defenders. Swerving to avoid them, he spotted what looked like a clear path to the goal line. So, gaining speed, he ran resolutely in that direction, picking up, in the beginning at least, a few blocks. Unfortunately—and memorably—the goal line he was running toward under a full head of steam was his own.

"Boy, am I glad I didn't pick up that fumble," Bancroft called out to Schwartz at the original line of scrimmage, "because I'd have run the other way." His was an accurate reflection of the prevailing level of confusion while Riegels pursued his wayward course. Upstairs in the broadcast booth, Graham McNamee, a legendary announcer not necessarily celebrated for the accuracy of his play-by-play accounts, betrayed his befuddlement to a national radio audience. "What's the matter with me," he bellowed into the microphone. "Am I going crazy here?" Even field judge Bill Striet admitted later that he thought Riegels' mad dash was merely the start of some kind of "daring play Cal had cooked up."

Lom, however, recognized that something was dangerously amiss. He gave chase, tearfully shouting what would become this singular event's mantra: "Roy, you're running the wrong way!" His admonition was lost in the deafening roar of a crowd of 66,404.

Lom caught up with Riegels near the Cal 20, but instead of tackling him there, he called for the ball, hoping against hope to salvage something positive from the disaster. Riegels was a lineman, though, and he knew how few chances to score there were for his kind. "Get away from me," he called out to his teammate, "this is *my* touchdown."

Finally, on the one-yard line, Lom was able to grab Riegels by one arm and prevent him from crossing his own goal line. But before he could explain to him the error of his ways, a host of Tech tacklers, led by end Fred Waddey, catapulted both Bears into the end zone. Referee Dana properly placed the ball back on the one, where Cal, pressed in these hashmark-free days against the sidelines, took over.

Foolishly, the Bears did not call a timeout to reconnoiter the situation, and on first down, Riegels centered the ball to Lom (his call for the ball finally answered), who was positioned at the very rear of the end zone. Lom tried from there to punt his team out of trouble. The air didn't go out of the ball this time, but it did go out of the Bears. The kick was blocked by Tech tackle Vance Maree, the ball rolling out of the end zone for a safety. Price then finally pulled Riegels from the game, fearing that a blow to the head he'd received earlier may have cost him his sense of direction. But Roy was not physically hurt. And the 2–0 score held at the half.

Such a slight lead hardly seemed insurmountable, so the mood at halftime in the Bear lockeroom was almost jocular. His teammates fully intended to kid Riegels out of his embarrassment, but before they could get started, Roy retreated to the bathroom where he had a solitary cry. He was finally retrieved by fullback Jim Cockburn in time to be subjected to some well-meaning but heavy-handed jokes. "What's the idea of running sixty-five yards on such a hot day," went one, "when you only had to go thirty-five in the other direction." Riegels smiled politely but was unamused.

He returned to the lineup for the second half and played with such ferocity that his opposing center, the All American Peter Pund, remarked after the game, "He's the best center I've played against all year...some boys might have folded under the situation, but Riegels didn't, and I admire him for it."

Riegels was given one golden opportunity to compensate for his boo-boo when he blocked a punt in the second half in Tech territory and seemed ready to score as the ball bounced goalward. But it trickled out of bounds before he could get his hands on it.

In the third quarter, Thomason scored on a 15-yard run, missed the point-after, but increased the lead to a more imposing 8–0. Cal finally crossed the right goal line with just 1:15 to play when Lom completed a ten-yard pass to Phillips, a play set up by a Lom 42-yard completion to Phillips and a 16-yarder to Eisan. Stan Barr kicked the PAT out of Phillips' hold. But an attempted onside kick failed and the game ended with the appropriately odd score of 8–7. It might well have been a 7–6 Cal victory but for one play, a circumstance scarcely overlooked in the next day's newspaper coverage. The sad odyssey of "Wrong Way Riegels" was the subject of some forty-five hundred feature articles across the country and an estimated two hundred fifty thousand column inches on January 2, 1929, alone. It was also seen by millions on movie newsreels.

Many stories welcomed Riegels into the exclusive brotherhood of top rank "boner" perpetrators. He was most often compared with baseball's Fred Merkle, whose infamous failure to touch second base in a game against the Chicago Cubs cost the New York Giants the 1908 National League pennant. Only twenty years or so separated these two classic miscues, after all, and to be coupled with Merkle, whom author Douglass Wallop once described as an "eternal goat" destined to be "maligned for posterity," was indeed a rare if unenviable distinction. In this vein, Stub Nelson of the Los Angeles *Record* put Riegels alongside Merkle on his "All-Bonehead Team." The Cleveland *Plain Dealer* accurately forecast that the "tragedy" of Riegels' wrong turn was that, like Merkle's absent-mindedness, it would "likely stick with him through life."

A gallant few rose to Roy's defense. Georgia Tech coach Bill Alexander said that "things happened so fast" after Riegels scooped up the fumble that "even my men had difficulty getting their bearings." And he recalled that in the first steps of the ill-fated journey, Riegels actually benefitted from some crisp blocking. Lom admitted he should have tackled his confused teammate when he had the chance instead of asking for the ball. But an inconsolable Riegels would have none of these excuses. "It was a terrible boner," he said afterward. "I'm sick about it, especially since it cost us the game."

But like Merkle, who played another fifteen years in the major leagues after his boner, Riegels persevered. He was elected captain of Cal's 1929 team and president of the Big C lettermen's society. He played so well in his senior season that he made the all-conference team and was named a first-string All American by the Associated Press. He was graduated with a degree in agriculture and after coaching high school football joined the Army Air Corps during World War II and rose to the rank of major. After the war he worked for a Sacramento canning company before founding his own firm manufacturing agricultural chemicals in the northern California town of Woodland. He became a pillar of the community, active in civic and service club affairs. He became a director of the Cal Alumni Association and president of the Woodland Rotary Club. He fathered four children and doted over ten grandchildren and two great-grandchildren. He was elected to both the Cal and Rose Bowl Halls of Fame.

But he could never quite shake the "Wrong Way Riegels" stigma. Although there were times when it appeared to slip mercifully back in time, something would inevitably occur to restore it to popularity. When in 1938, aviator Douglas Corrigan landed in Ireland after saying he was flying to California, a whole new spate of "Wrong Way" gags appeared, most of them naturally recalling Riegels. People never seemed to forget. Campaigning for the Presidency in 1971, Senator George McGovern said of the incumbent, "Wrong Way Riegels must be directing President Nixon's economic policies."

At the same time, Riegels found the time to commiserate with other boner victims. He wrote an encouraging chin-up letter to Alabama player Tommy Lewis, who leaped off his team's bench to tackle Rice's touchdown-bound Dickie Moegle in the 1954 Cotton Bowl. But he suffered in relative silence when Minnesota Vikings star lineman Jim Marshall ran 60 yards the wrong way to a safety in a NFL game against the 49ers in 1964. Once again, Riegels became the subject of commentary on the air and in print. Marshall's boner, dismissed as merely a sequel to the original, was soon forgotten over his long and distinguished professional career. Besides, it hadn't happened in college football's biggest showcase at a time when the collegiate game was the only one that counted.

In the fall of 1990, I drove to Woodland to interview Riegels for a magazine piece I was writing. He was eighty-two then and enduring with remarkable fortitude and good cheer the early stages of Parkinson's disease. I stopped at the local Chamber of Commerce to check on the directions to Riegels' house. A functionary there confirmed that I was on the right track, and then, with a wink and a knowing chuckle, cautioned me against "going…. the wrong way."

I didn't, meeting up with a cordial man of medium build—"I never did weigh more than 175, sometimes five pounds less"—who seemed surprisingly open to talking about the long-ago. Though he still took no pleasure in his mistake of nearly sixty-one years earlier, he had learned to live with it and to regard it with a compensating sense of the absurd.

Together, we thumbed through seemingly acres of scrapbooks, most of them devoted almost entirely to his signature play. He'd thought about it over the years, of course, but confessed, "for the life of me, I still don't know how or why I did what I did." He laughed and closed, with a bang, one hefty volume of newspaper clippings and photographs. "Now, I ask you," he said slowly, "isn't this a hell of a way to become famous."

Roy Riegels died on March 26, 1993, at the age of eighty-four in his Woodland home. The lead sentence of his obituary in the San Francisco *Chronicle* began, "Roy M. Riegels, the University of California football star whose 64-yard wrong-way scamper during the 1929 Rose Bowl created one of sport's most memorable moments, died yesterday…"

# CHAPTER NINE

# CRASH

In the fall of 1929, it was the national economy that went the wrong way. Price's Bears were three games into a season seemingly of great promise—they had held Slip Madigan's high-scoring St. Mary's Gaels to a scoreless tie and beaten Santa Clara and Washington State—when they traveled east of the Rockies for the first time yet in their football history to play Penn at Franklin Field in Philadelphia. On the way, they stopped off in Washington D.C. to be received by Stanford grad Herbert Hoover, then only months into his so-far-so-good but ultimately grievous term in the White House.

The Penn game, a 12–7 win for Cal, was played before a crowd of seventy-one thousand on October 19. Five days later, on what has since been remembered grimly as "Black Thursday," the stock market crashed—or as the theatrical publication *Vanity Fair* headlined the event, "Wall Street Lays an Egg." The New York Stock Exchange lost $4 billion that day in the worst trading session in its history and within a week the nation was plunged into an economic depression which led within the next three years to eighty-six thousand business failures. By 1932, one of every five Americans was unemployed, and for those with jobs, weekly wages had dropped to an average of $16.21. Financially prudent Americans saw their life's savings disappear with widespread bank closings. The Roaring Twenties, when anything seemed possible, had ended with a bang felt around the world. As Cabell Phillips wrote in his history of the era, *From the Crash to the Blitz:*

"The great stock market boom, a real-life fantasy that for four years had bewitched scholars and statesmen as well as knaves and fools into a common illusion of easy riches, had incontestably collapsed. In its place stood the gaunt specter of the Great Depression."

But the effects of this catastrophe did not immediately register with most Americans, who preferred believing, as President Hoover erroneously predicted, that "prosperity is just around the corner." The 1920s' "Golden Age of Sports" may have ended with the Depression, but ballparks and stadiums still provided a ready escape from the country's escalating woes. And Cal was then enjoying one of its better post-Smith seasons, the highlight of which had been a 15–7 upset of Rose-Bowl-bound Southern California at the L.A. Coliseum on November 2. The game introduced a new star in Ralston "Rusty" Gill, a 198-pound fullback and third of five Gill brothers to play for the Bears. Red-haired Rusty played with a demonic abandon and supreme arrogance best characterized in modern sports vernacular as an "attitude." Though his manic nature would eventually be his undoing, it was seen on the gridiron as a distinct asset.

Gill scored the Bears" first touchdown against S.C. on a short plunge and his crushing block on Trojan end Garret Arbelbide set Lom free on an 85-yard TD scamper on a fake punt play in the second quarter. Later in the quarter, Riegels blocked a punt by future S.C. All American Erny Pinckert for a safety. The Thundering Herd didn't cross Cal's goal line until late in the third quarter.

The Bears confidently approached the Big Game undefeated in eight games, the tie with St. Mary's scarcely a blemish since the Gaels, undefeated that season, had given up exactly one touchdown all year and that on a desperation pass in the last quarter of their last game, a 31–6 win over Oregon. Stanford had won seven games before the Big Game, but had lost to USC (7–0) and Santa Clara (13–7), teams the Bears had beaten by a combined score of 42–13. Cal was installed as a solid 2-1 favorite.

The Cardinal trotted onto the Stanford Stadium turf in trendy new uniforms—white jerseys with red numbers front and back and red stripes on the sleeves and red pants with a wide white stripe down the back. The Bears were more conventionally attired in blue jerseys with gold stripes on the sleeves and canvas-colored breeches. The host players clearly won the fashion competition. They also won the game, 21–6, outgaining Cal 268 yards to 146. The Bears' only score came on an eight-yard pass from Lom to end Ellis Thornton. Ted Beckett's conversion attempt was blocked by the hero of the game, Stanford's captain and right end Don "Mush" Muller. "Mush" also blocked a Lom punt from the Cal 25 and returned it for a touchdown.

Four Bears—Lom, Riegels, guard Bert Schwarz and end Bob Norton—were first-team All Conference that season, and Riegels and Schwartz made several first-string All America teams. But the Stanford loss, Price's third against one tie, in four Big Games left the football program in a state of lingering malaise. The very decisiveness of this defeat, coupled perhaps with the embarrassment of the previous New Year's Day, caused university President Campbell to withdraw the Bears from any consideration for a Rose Bowl invitation, even though they had finished 7-1-1 and in a three-way tie with Stanford and USC for the conference title. The Trojans, who had lost to Cal but beaten Stanford, received the bid and clobbered Pittsburgh, 47–14, in Pasadena.

A Cal season that had begun so favorably had reached a melancholy denouement. Then, to make matters worse, Stanford, through means most diabolical, got the Axe back.

It had become a Cal tradition to commemorate the theft of that now symbolic implement in April of 1899 with an "Axe Rally" held every year that month in the Greek Theater. Stanfordites were particularly offended by these observances because the Axe, after all, was originally theirs and so was the "Give 'Em the Axe" yell (composed in 1896 by undergrad Will Irwin) that led to its first appearance. But their many attempts to recover it had met with dismal failure —until the fateful day of April 3, 1930.

The exquisite planning that preceded this caper would have done credit to another famous miscreant of the time, Al Capone. Stanford's mastermind was a pint-sized pre-law student named Don Kropp. From among his dormmates at Sequoia Hall on campus, Kropp assembled an enthusiastic and coolly efficient gang, all twenty-one members of which would have a role to play in the daring robbery. Here was the setup:

Immediately after its appearance at the Rally, the Axe was returned each year by armored car to a vault at the American Trust Company in downtown Berkeley. Along with some Cal rooters and other bystanders, Kropp's gang was there waiting for it that April 3, a few of them posing as newspaper reporters and photographers. The moment the Axe's official custodian, Bear baseball pitcher Norm Horner, stepped from the armored car outside the bank, camera flashbulbs popped in unison, temporarily blinding him and his guard. As Horner stumbled in confusion, the Axe was wrested from his loosened grip by gangmember Howard Avery. Avery then tossed it to colleague Bob Loofbourow, the son, shamefully enough, of a Berkeley minister. At this juncture, what Axe historians have variously identified as either a smoke or tear gas bomb was detonated, shrouding the scene in a cloak of impenetrable and cough-inducing fog. Under cover of these fumes, Loofbourow reached undetected the getaway car driven by Jim Trimingham. Trimingham swiftly drove off for Palo Alto.

Others among the twenty-one fled in at least three more phony getaway cars, while those who remained behind feigned pursuit, offering up contradictory directions to befuddled Cal fans and Berkeley police.

A  William Walter "Pudge" Heffelfinger (left) and Thomas "Bum" McClung, stars on Yale's mighty teams of the 1880s, both coached at Cal in the 1890s.

B  Nineteenth-century star Kangaroo Kaarsberg was more celebrated for his jumping than his punting.

MONTY PUNTING    VARSITY-ORIGINALS, 7 - 0    CALIFORNIA FIELD, OCTOBER 9

*"The signals rattle, a pigskin thud — they're down"*——

# American Football's Back!

*"It's Root, Hog, or Die"*

## All Classes Celebrate

### 1866 - 1915

*On the eve of the Big Game—California versus Washington*

# Joint Football Banquet

*An Old - Time Good Time*
Save the Date

## Friday Night, November 5

 *A Great Mob*
*A Square Meal*
*Lots of Song and Jubilation*
*A Battery of Twenty One-minute Speeches*

**Commercial Club, San Francisco**
*Top Floor, Merchants Exchange*                    **Two Dollars a Plate**

*Under the auspices of the Association of Alumni Classes*

C

**C** An invitation to a banquet at San Francisco's
Commercial Club celebrating the return of American
football to Cal in 1915 after nine seasons of rugby.

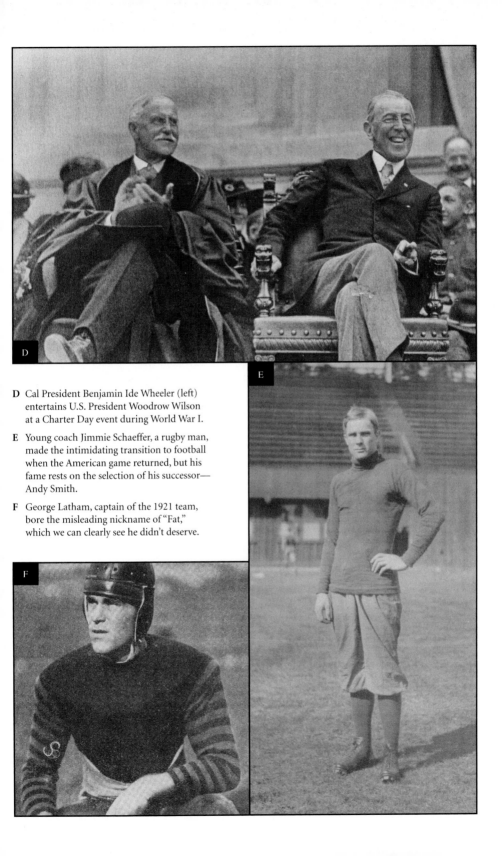

**D** Cal President Benjamin Ide Wheeler (left) entertains U.S. President Woodrow Wilson at a Charter Day event during World War I.

**E** Young coach Jimmie Schaeffer, a rugby man, made the intimidating transition to football when the American game returned, but his fame rests on the selection of his successor—Andy Smith.

**F** George Latham, captain of the 1921 team, bore the misleading nickname of "Fat," which we can clearly see he didn't deserve.

**G** Walt Gordon, a pioneer African-American in college football, was the first Cal player to receive All America mention.

**H** Coach Andy Smith enjoys a light-hearted moment with his players. Brick Muller is kneeling, lower left, and Charley Erb is standing in the middle.

I

I Snappily dressed fans make their way into the new Memorial Stadium
for its grand opening at the 1923 Big Game.

**J** The first Wonder Teamers celebrate their fortieth anniversary during the 1960 Big Game.

**K** Center Babe Horrell, captain of the 1924 team and an All American, (left), performs the pre-game handshaking ritual with Ed McGinley of Penn.

**L** Roy Riegels' infamous Wrong Way Run. In panel three, he cuts away from tacklers, then, regrettably, continues in the direction of his cut. Teammate Benny Lom gives chase, but catches him too late.

# SENIORS
## AND ALL-AMERICANS

M

M Each of six seniors on Cal's 1937 team had the distinction of making one or more All America teams. Here they are, as pictured in the Rose Bowl program.

Upper left, Perry Schwartz, right end (No. 99); lower left, John Meek, quarterback (no. 49); center, Sam Chapman, right half-back; upper right, Bob Herwig, center; right center, Claude Evans, left guard; lower right, Vard Stockton, right guard.

N Cal's first Nobel Prize winner, Ernest O. Lawrence.

O Tailback Vic Bottari was the engine that kept Stub Allison's Thunder Team rolling.

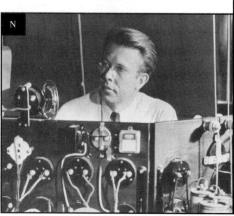

N

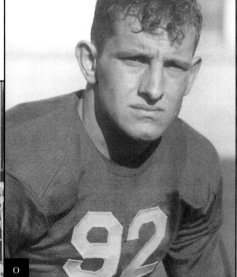

O

The Axe arrived safely on the Stanford campus, where it was housed overnight in a safe at the offices of the Board of Athletic Control. Enraged Cal invaders searched in vain for the missing Axe, vandalizing dorms and shattering a few windows at the Encina gymnasium before being sent on their way.

Cries of "we've got the axe" echoed throughout the night on the Stanford campus. Kropp's gang of thieves was hailed as "The Immortal Twenty-One" and awarded block letters for their achievement. The Axe episode became for many years an essential chapter in Stanford lore. As university historian Edith R. Mirrielees wrote, it was an episode worth "remembering, retelling…a day and an adventure set aside from ordinary college days."

To curtail further incidents of this felonious nature, though, the student body presidents of both universities agreed in 1933 that from then on the Axe should be reconstituted as the Big Game trophy and awarded each year to the winning school. But this act of diplomacy scarcely discouraged future adventurers from seeking the sort of kudos heaped on "The Immortal Twenty-One." The Axe, in fact, has been stolen at least eight times since the agreement and many more attempts on it have been either thwarted or botched.

An event of somewhat greater significance occurred at Cal in the summer of 1930 when, on July 1, Robert Gordon Sproul became the new university president, replacing Campbell who, at sixty-eight, retired after seven years on the job. Sproul, then thirty-nine, became not only Cal's youngest president but the first native Californian and the first alumnus to take office. And over the next twenty-eight years, he would also become the university's longest-serving president.

A 1913 graduate in civil engineering, Sproul first joined the campus administration in 1920 as the replacement in the cashier's office for an employee who had absconded with University funds. From this humble start, he rose rapidly through the system, at one time, while still in his early thirties, holding down four influential positions simultaneously–vice president, comptroller, secretary of the Board of Regents and University land agent.

He was a convivial presence among faculty and students alike, easily identifiable on campus by a reverberating voice of such sonority it was said he could crack crockery miles away. One oft-told story has it that a visitor to his outer office was surprised to discover he could distinctly hear every word Sproul bellowed in a conversation behind closed doors in the next room.

"Who's he talking to?" the visitor asked Sproul's secretary.

"Oh," she replied, "he's calling Sacramento."

"Next time," said the visitor, "tell him to use the telephone."

The thunderous voice was a source of both wonder and amusement on campus. At the same time, Sproul was a formidable administrator and a dedicated academic committed to building a university second to none. It was under his guidance that the multi-campus concept achieved its greatest advances and, like Wheeler before him, he both sought and retained a top faculty. It was Sproul who persuaded physicist Ernest O. Lawrence to resist eastern offers and remain in Berkeley to continue his research on atomic energy, and in 1939 Lawrence became Cal's first Nobel Prize winner. Sproul's powers of persuasion were particularly valuable in his fund-raising forays into the chambers of the State legislature. As Vern Stadtman wrote of him in his history of the University, "his quick recall of facts and statistics made him virtually unchallengeable in debate. His knowledge, love and mastery of the sounds of spoken English made him one of the nations's finest orators. These talents alone would have made him awesome, perhaps even unapproachable, had he not also been blessed with a cordial nature and easy humor that revealed his appreciation of the hopes and anxieties of common men."

Early in his term, Sproul wrote of what he expected of Cal undergraduates: "The first duty of a university student is not to learn but to think, not to accept but to question and solve, not to take the word of a book or a professor for anything except as a basis for his own investigations."

The new president was also a sports fan, though one with firm views on the role of sports, particularly football, in the university community. While admitting that he could "work myself into a fit of sophomoric enthusiasm" in Memorial Stadium, he said, "I am assuming that the teams engaged in the contest are in truth representative of the institutions from which they come, not a group of professional athletes hired by well-meaning but misguided alumni and 'friends'...In other words, I want the teams for which I cheer—win, lose or draw— to be a natural outgrowth of the university which I love, and not a group of gladiators who have gathered where the pay is best...At California we want students playing at athletics, not athletes playing at being students."

Sproul's notions about upholding the purity of college sports did not, however, reflect the reality then, according to a 347-page report issued in October of 1929 by the Carnegie Foundation for the Advancement of Teaching. Based on a three-and-a-half-year investigation involving one hundred thirty colleges and universities, the report found that abuses in the recruiting and subsidizing of football players were fully as widespread then as when the first scandals were exposed a quarter-century earlier. Under-the-table payments, fixed entrance exams, altered transcripts were still common practices, if a shade more sophisticated than in the bad old days. The report's broad-based indictment once again fingered most of the Ivy League schools, excusing only Yale and Cornell.

Carnegie's findings cast an unfavorable light on the college game as a whole, exposing it as well to ridicule in print, on the radio and on the screen in the new "talkie" motion pictures. In fact, the careers of several comedic actors, most notably Jack Oakie and Cal alum Stuart Erwin, were considerably enhanced by playing chuckleheaded college football stars.

Under these less than propitious circumstances, Cal began a 1930 season that would become Nibs Price's worst and last as head football coach. The overall record that year of four wins and five losses seemed at least superficially respectable, but four of those losses were by shutout and, discounting a 46–0 win over weak Montana, the Bears scored only 41 points all year while giving up more than four times as many. This anemic offensive performance might not have in itself been cause enough for despair, but there were two losses among the five, inflicted by Cal's biggest rivals, that were so horrendous as to impel even the most pervervid of Old Blues to call for "Poor Nibs's" head in a basket.

The first of these horrors, committed before nearly eighty thousand in the Los Angeles Coliseum, came against USC on November 8. Until then, the Bears had scored wins over Santa Clara (19–7), St. Mary's (7–6) and Montana and been beaten by Washington State (16–0), the Olympic Club (13–7) and Washington (13–0). But that day they met a Trojan team, led by star backs Orv Mohler, Gus Shaver and Pinckert, that was primed to avenge the unlikely loss of the year before. And Howard Jones had no intention of corralling his Thundering Herd.

Starting with a safety on a blocked punt in the first quarter, the Herd rode mercilessly over the Bears, scoring in double digits in three of the four quarters, including 13 points in a fourth shortened five minutes supposedly because of darkness but probably out of Christian charity. The 74–0 loss, achieved through 734 Trojan yards rushing and passing, remains to this day the worst in the history of Cal football.

Afterward, in his room at the Huntington Hotel, a crestfallen Nibs met in lamentation with Wonder Teamers Stan Barnes and Muggs Van Sant and Frank Storment of Cal's class of 1923. What Cal needed to protect itself from the Trojan hordes, the visitors concluded, was a southern California alumni group that could extol the virtues of Berkeley to high school stars otherwise destined to join Jones's team at S.C. Hadn't Nibs himself been responsible for luring to Cal so many fine players from San Diego in the Wonder Team era? A few days later, in a meeting at the prestigious Jonathon Club in downtown Los Angeles, just such a group was organized with Barnes as its first president. At first the alums thought of calling themselves the "Southern Cs," but they changed that finally to the more exotic and less obvious "Southern Seas."

It was in so many respects exactly the sort of "well-meaning but misguided" alumni bunch that Sproul had warned against and that the Carnegie Foundation had condemned.

Nibs's troubles were hardly over. Only three thousand fans showed up at Memorial Stadium to watch his team's rain-soaked 8–0 win over little Nevada. And then came Stanford, a team he had yet to beat as a head coach. Once again, the results were gruesome.

Emboldened perhaps by the return of the Axe, this was a Stanford team that had lost only once that season, to USC, and been tied by Minnesota in Minneapolis. Its star was a slender (5-11, 156 pounds) halfback, Phil Moffat, who was dangerous as a runner (a 5.9 yards per carry average for his three years), receiver, punt returner (10-yard average on a career 72 returns) and pass intercepter (9 in 1930 and 20 career). He was selected a first-team All American in '30 by the United Press. But in this Big Game, he was overshadowed by yet another great Stanford athlete; fullback Harlow Rothert, the reigning world record-holder in the shot put (52 feet, one and 5/8 inches), a future Olympic medalist and three-year letterman in football, basketball and track.

Rothert did not play in the first half, giving way to former Big Game hero Simkins, and Stanford was held to a 6–0 lead. But within 19½ minutes of the second half, Rothert scored three touchdowns and passed 63 yards to Moffat for another. In his short stint, he was the game's leading rusher with 88 yards on 19 carries. Stanford's 41–0 win was the worst beating ever administered to the Bears in Big Game history.

On the Monday after the game, Nibs Price resigned as head football coach, quelling a mounting chorus of discontent in the press and on campus. But he stayed on at Cal for another twenty-four years as basketball coach and as a loyal assistant to a succession of four football headmen.

On Tuesday, Stanford's student body executive committee voted to change the nickname of school athletic teams from the amorphous "Cardinal" to "Indians," a pre-politically-correct cognomen that, in the committeemen's view, better reflected the "give-'em-the-Axe" tradition and the take-no-prisoners hostility so vividly expressed in the Big Game massacre. Then, too, archaeologists were always digging up Indian artifacts on and around the campus. And hadn't coach Warner first achieve national renown teaching football to real-life Indians?

The now Stanford Indians had one more game to play a week after the 1930 Big Game—against the Dartmouth....Indians. The Indians won, 14–7.

CHAPTER TEN

# NAVY BILL

The Depression scarcely slowed the Berkeley campus's continuing growth. By 1931, the student population had reached 11,222, and from the end of the '20s to 1933, eight important new buildings were erected on campus—the Henry Morse Stephens Student Union, named for the late and much revered history professor; Giannini Hall, a classroom building named for its donors, the San Francisco banking family; the International House for foreign students, financed by a grant from the Rockefeller Foundation; Eshleman Hall, the new center for all major student publications dedicated to John Morton Eshleman, Class of 1902; the Ernest V. Cowell Hospital; the new Harmon Gym., a sixty-five hundred-seat arena named as was its much smaller predecessor for Oakland philanthropist and sports enthusiast Albion Keith Paris Harmon and built for $485,000 from funds provided by the State Legislature, the Cowell estate and athletic ticket revenues; and, finally, the twenty-five thoudsand-seat track stadium and adjoining baseball park, both named for Harmon's son-in-law, Colonel George Cunningham Edwards, who in forty-five years at Cal as first a student and then a professor of mathematics, founded the first ROTC unit on campus and was fondly called "the father of Cal athletics."

In 1931, the university also hired a new head football coach. After a nationwide search reminiscent of but certainly better organized than Jimmy Schaeffer's of sixteen years earlier, ASUC general manager W.W. "Bill" Monahan settled on a surprising but highly qualified candidate in William A. "Navy Bill" Ingram. The new coach came by his nautical nickname predictably enough. He had starred at the Naval Academy in 1916 as a tailback who scored that season a mind-boggling 162 points. It probably didn't hurt his ball-carrying opportunities that his older brother, Jonas, was head coach at Annapolis that year. In truth, Jonas was much more of a Navy man than "Navy Bill." He had himself been a star back at the Academy in 1906, and had distinguished himself afterward as a much decorated officer. He achieved the Medal of Honor for his service in the Mexican conflict of 1914-15 and the Navy Cross for heroism in World War I. In the second World War, he commanded the Navy's Atlantic Fleet. But "Navy Jonas" just didn't have much of a ring to it.

Navy Bill also saw active duty in the Great War and afterward. And he was the player-coach of the Pacific Fleet team that gave the 1921 Wonder Team its closest regular season game before losing 21–10. After active duty, Ingram coached at Indiana University for three years before returning to the Naval Academy as head coach in 1926. Perhaps coincidentally, Jonas was athletic director there at the time. Navy Bill's first Navy team finished undefeated and was ranked number one in the country by two national polls. His last team, in 1930, finished 6-3, and his overall record for five years at Annapolis was an impressive 29-11-4.

Ingram had taken a fancy to the Bay Area during his tour of duty there a decade before, and was more than ready to make the move west. He brought to Berkeley what Monahan considered a necessary virtue—toughness. Indeed, Navy Bill was a taskmaster steeped in service discipline. Concerned on one occasion that his Navy players were not quite ready for a game that day, he had them practice in a Chicago public park on their way by bus to Soldier Field. While Monahan didn't necessarily advocate measures quite this stringent, he felt that a touch of Ingram's iron resolve would shake the Bears out of the blues inflicted by the disagreeable finish to the 1930 season. And Navy Bill brought with him to Berkeley a pair of stern assistants in Frank Wickhorst, who had been an All America tackle for him at Navy in '26, and Leonard B. "Stub" Allison, a former line coach at Wisconsin whose service in World War I had earned him a second nickname, "Top Sarge," which he disliked.

Ingram's toughest immediate challenge in reviving the Bears was to find some way to harness the considerable talent and rein in the wayward behavior of star fullback Rusty Gill, now in his senior season. Rusty drove Nibs to near distraction. Only days after his breakthrough game as a sophomore against USC, Rusty was in court for his part in an off-campus brawl and for resisting arrest. It was neither the first nor the last time, he would find himself in trouble with the law. As the *Examiner* observed, his "extra-curricular activities kept the local police forces ready." His off-field problems, mainly fighting, had prevented him from fulfilling his potential as a dominant player.

The cold fact was that Rusty Gill was a deeply troubled young man. But Ingram was so determined to "handle" him that he had himself declared the player's legal guardian for the 1931 season. And for that brief period, Rusty seemed to respond to Navy Bill discipline. In fact, he would enjoy his best season, even making first-team All America in two national polls.

Gill was not the new coach's only problem, though. In Hank Schaldach, a 165-pound junior from San Francisco, he had what appeared to be a tailback of infinite promise, a speedy and shifty runner, accurate passer and terrific punter and dropkicker. But Schaldach's nickname pretty much summed up his college career. He was called "Hard Luck Hank."

In the '31 season opener against Santa Clara, Schaldach effectively won the game for California, connecting with end Louis DiResta on a fourth quarter pass to the Bronco's two-yard line and scoring from there on the next play for the 6–2 win. That, however, was the last fans would see of him for awhile. Schaldach had survived injury the year before until the season's third game, which he also won almost single-handedly by scoring Cal's only touchdown against St. Mary's and kicking the extra point for a 7–6 win. He didn't make it through the fourth quarter of this first game, dispatched to the infirmary with a broken wrist. He wouldn't return until more than a month later.

Without their hard luck star, the Bears' offense virtually disappeared. They were shut out by St. Mary's, 14–0, in their second game, managing only one pass completion in 12 attempts and gaining a measly 24 yards rushing. The score might have been even more lopsided had it not been for the stout play of the interior linemen, all five of whom lasted the full sixty minutes. Among that durable quintet was John Ransome, a rangy 195-pound tackle who was the son of the legendary Wolf.

Ingram's team squeezed past the Olympic Club, 6–0, and went on a scoring rampage, so to speak, in beating Washington State, 13–7. Then came the Thundering Herd. Again, the Bears were held scoreless, but this time the Trojans were limited to just a single touchdown, sans conversion. This represented a 68-point improvement over the previous season. And Cal came within a foot of at least tying the score when Gill was stopped that close to the S.C. goal line on the third of his desperate plunges into the line from the five. This, mind you, was a Trojan team just embarking on a 27-game winning streak. Neither team completed a pass in the game, and the Herd was held to fewer than 200 yards on the ground. Ingram's toughness had paid off with a superior defense.

Schaldach returned in time for the Washington game on November 7, and he led the Bears to a decisive 13–0 win, scoring one touchdown, dropkicking the extra point and consistently placing the Huskies in poor field position with his quick kicks. Gill scored the other touchdown on a 37-yard return of a pass interception.

Cal entered the Big Game with a 6-2 record to Stanford's 6-1-2. Both had lost to USC, the Indians by 19–0. A crowd of eighty-seven thousand five hundred at Stanford Stadium watched the Bears win their first Big Game in eight long years. Schaldach scored the game's only TD from a yard away, concluding a drive that began on the Stanford 35 after a short punt. Hank's 13-yard pass to quarterback Joe Smith set up the lonely score.

But this wouldn't be the Bears' final game, since the schedule called for a holiday rematch with Georgia Tech in Atlanta on December 26. The Bears entrained for the deep south a week ahead of time, the better to prepare for their Rose Bowl conquerors of two years before. Taking his cue from Slip Madigan, who had made a grand tour out of his St. Mary's team's trip to New York to play Fordham the year before, Navy Bill was in no rush to come home either. He did not book side trips to Canada or Cuba as Madigan eventually would, but he wanted to reward his team with a proper transcontinental tour, while never losing sight of the need to avenge the Wrong Way Riegel's game. Ingram hosted a Christmas Eve party in Atlanta with coach Wickhorst playing a burly but reasonably jovial Santa. The game itself may have intruded on the social doings, but the final score of 19–6 for Cal made it part of the fun. Schaldach and Gill scored for the Bears on short runs and end Ralph Stone recovered the punt he himself blocked in the end zone for the final TD. The win gave Ingram a fine if unspectacular 8-2 debut season.

"After the game," it was written in the *Blue and Gold*, "the excursion assumed a more interesting character." Indeed. On the leisurely trip home, the players were received once more by President Hoover, who at that point in his beleaguered term undoubtedly welcomed the diversion. Then it was on to New York for sightseeing and then a New Year's party in Chicago. His players were delighted to discover that Navy Bill was not all spit and polish.

Borrowing this time from Pop, not Slip, the coach scheduled a double-header for opening day of the '32 season, an innovation Pop Warner had brought to Stanford six years earlier. The idea was to play two inferior teams early and in this quasi-scrimmage format give game experience to players previously lost in the shuffle. There also remained the faint hope that from this flock of unknowns a future star might spring forth. Sure enough, one did in the first game of the twin bill, in the form of a then fourth-string tailback named Arleigh Williams. Williams scored one of Cal's three touchdowns in the opener against the Cal Aggies and impressed his coaches with his punting, passing, and defensive play. First-stringer Schaldach passed to quarterback Gus Castro for 40 yards and ran 50 himself to account for the other scores. The Bears also won the second game, against the West Coast Army, by 13–0.

This season introduced the fifth and final Gill to Cal football, end Carol, nicknamed improbably "Pill." He teamed with older brother Sam, a guard, in '32 and then played two more years before closing out the dynasty. In a rare family reunion, all five Gill brothers were in Memorial Stadium on October 1 for Cal's 22–6 win over the Olympic Club. Frank was then playing for the club and Sam for Cal. Carol was on the Cal bench with an injury, Harry was in the stands as a spectator and Rusty sat in the press box trying his hand at sportswriting. But Rusty never did find his true calling. He tried selling stocks and bonds, hardly a promising career during the Depression. He had bit parts in two motion pictures, both involving…what else?…fight scenes. He worked briefly in an automobile factory. He tried professional boxing, a seemingly apt career choice for a prolific street fighter, but after he was knocked out in his third bout, he quit the ring. He said he would next take up wrestling, an immensely popular sport in the '30s, but he never did.

And his rap sheet grew longer, with arrests for speeding, battery and vandalism. He was married and soon after divorced in 1934. And in October of that year, he was admitted to the Alameda County

Hospital with rheumatic arthritis. After his release, he was arrested again for fighting and for pulling a public telephone off the wall of an Oakland service station. In December of '34, he was committed by his father, Frank, Sr., to the Agnew State Hospital, after suffering a "nervous breakdown." He was confined to the psychiatric ward, prompting this alarming headline in the *Examiner*: "Rusty Gill Sent to Insane Ward." He was released in 1936, but readmitted three years later. He died in the hospital on April 13, 1939, of a heart attack. Rusty Gill was all of twenty-nine years old.

Navy Bill's second season at Cal was meanwhile jolted by several unsettling defeats. For the first time ever in a rivalry dating to 1922, Santa Clara beat the Bears. On the second Saturday of the season, the Broncos, led by their "pogo passer," Frank Sobrero, shut out Ingram's team, 12–0. Schaldach, naturally enough, was injured in that game and missed the next two, a 22–6 win over the Olympic Club and a 12–12 tie with St. Mary's, during which Cal safetyman Gus Castro averted defeat by returning a punt 76 yards for a touchdown. The Bears were beaten by Washington State, 7–2, and clobbered by USC, 27–7. Schaldach was again injured in a 21–6 victory over Idaho after scoring early on an eight-yard run. Williams replaced him and ran for 153 yards on 27 carries.

Both teams had 6-3 records entering the Big Game, Stanford having lost to USC for the fifth year in a row and, surprisingly, to an emergent UCLA by 13–6. The Indians' third loss was to Washington (18–13), a team Cal had slipped past, 7–6. The teams were obviously evenly matched, and both were afflicted with influenza the week of the game, enfeebling offenses that were none too robust to begin with. The end result was the only scoreless tie in Big Game history. Cal failed to complete a pass in eight attempts and Stanford averaged barely more than 2 yards on 5 completions. Cal punted eighteen times for a 41.4-yard average, Stanford 17 for 36.6. But the ailing Schaldach, coming off the bench to replace Williams late in the fourth quarter, nearly pulled this desultory game out of the dumpster. Gaining 55 yards on 7 carries, he had propelled the Bears to the Stanford 6 when the gun sounded. A less-than-capacity crowd of 68,646 in Memorial Stadium gave evidence that the economic crisis was inhibiting even diehard Big Game fans from spending money. As further evidence, thousands watched for free from Tightwad Hill.

This Big Game's only real significance was that it was Pop Warner's last one. Following a season-ending 7–0 loss to Pittsburgh, the great man resigned, deciding to accept the challenge of rebuilding the football program at Temple in Philadelphia. He left behind a 71-17-8 record at Stanford which included three trips to the Rose Bowl, where his teams won, lost and tied, and a 5-1-3 success against Cal. But he fared not nearly as well against USC, losing the last five games after winning the first two and tying the third. There was considerable speculation that his inability to corral Howard Jones's Herds hastened his departure from the Farm. And his last season there, with its four losses, was his worst.

But the Trojan jinx which so bedeviled Pop did have a positive side effect. On the Monday following the varsity's loss in '32, Stanford's freshman players, undefeated, untied and unscored upon up to that point, met in the locker room before practice. Quarterback Frank Alustiza, called "Owl Eyes" because of his resolute gaze, called out, "They'll never do that to us. We will never lose to USC." Halfback Robert "Bones" Hamilton seconded the motion "Let's make that a vow," he suggested. And so they famously did.

There were sixty applications for Stanford's head coaching vacancy, but the honor of replacing Pop fell to his longtime assistant, Claude "Tiny" Thornhill. It would be his great good fortune to inherit as sophomores the "Vow Boys."

Cal, too, had one more game to play in '32, a 27–6 win over Georgia Tech in Berkeley on December 17. This would be "Hard Luck Hank" Schaldach's last game for the Bears but not his last game. On January 2, in the annual East-West Shrine All Star game in San Francisco, Hank scored all of the West team's points in a 21–13 win, setting up two of his scores with punt returns of 35 and 38 yards and backing up the opposing All-Stars with his own long punts, one of which bounced out-of-bounds on the East two-yard line. For good measure, he finished the game with all body parts intact.

Cal's home attendance of 191,908 for nine 1932 dates was easily the lowest since Memorial Stadium opened, a further reflection of Depression woes. But in the dramatic figure of the new President, Franklin Delano Roosevelt, there seemed hope for recovery. In his inaugural address of March 4, 1933, Roosevelt boldly proclaimed, "Let me assert my firm belief that the only thing we have to fear is fear itself." National morale got another boost later in the year when Prohibition, the scourge of the '20s, was repealed by the 21st Amendment. Speakeasies and bootleggers were out of business, and a thirsty soul could order a good stiff drink without first whispering through a crack in the door, "Joe sent me."

Cal opened the '33 season with another shutout loss to Santa Clara and then scored two of its own, by a combined score of 73–0, in a double header sweep of the Cal Aggies and Nevada. The Bears played the last game ever with the Olympic Club on October 14, ending a series that began in 1892. The 23–0 win would also be the last game played against any athletic club, marking the end of a tradition that dated back fifty-one years.

The most exciting game of the season was with St. Mary's. The Gaels had scored two touchdowns within the first five minutes and seemed well on their way to a rout when a new Cal star, Floyd Blower, led a comeback. With only minutes left to play and St. Mary's still leading, 13–7, Blower scored on a 12-yard run and then, with the crowd of fifty-five thousand silent with anticipation, kicked the winning point-after. "Pandemonium ruled," Brodie wrote, possibly in an excess of enthusiasm. "Wild California partisans had never given vent to their enthusiasm as they did at that moment. Who knows how many women were kissed by men they had never seen before?"

The annual loss to USC, while certainly less emphatic than customary, was even more painful. With just 8 ½ minutes left to play, the Bears were actually leading, on the strength of a 28-yard Williams field goal in the first quarter and a defense that had held the Trojans scoreless. Williams' kick was all the more amazing since it was made from a difficult angle and in a Memorial Stadium fog so dense, he could barely see the goal posts. From the stands, especially the upper rows of seats, the players far below looked to be phantoms frolicking in the mist. One such ghostly figure, much to the Bears' frustration, was one Irvine "Cotton" Warburton, a tiny (145 pounds) tailback who happened to be one of the finest broken field runners of the time. And so, with the clock running down, Cotton slid off tackle, cut back to his right and behind a block by Trojan All America tackle Aaron Rosenberg, sped down the sidelines past Cal linebackers Howard Christie and Jim Keefer for 59 yards and the game's only touchdown.

A week later, in Los Angeles, the Bears took on for the first time a member of their own household. No longer the inconsequential "Southern Branch," UCLA was now actively seeking its own place, academically and athletically, in the California sun. It had joined the Pacific Coast Conference in 1928 and even before that had played both Stanford and USC. But both Sproul and UCLA provost Ernest C. Moore had discouraged any sense of rivalry with the mother campus in Berkeley. Sproul had insisted on central control of university campuses from his office, denouncing "local prides and prejudices." And Moore was properly acquiescent. In an essay he wrote for the Cal yearbook in 1932, he declared that UCLA "is as much a part of the University of California as though it were on the grounds at Berkeley." The multi-campus system, he added, is "one which we believe is infinitely to be preferred to the development of separate state universities engaged in the game of cutting each other's throats in an inescapable competition which would fate them not merely to public contention but to perpetual mediocrity."

But competition, particularly on the gridiron, was inevitable. By 1932, at its attractive campus in Westwood, UCLA had a student body in excess of 6000. And it was ready for big-time football. Through most of the 1920s, USC had ignored its upstart neighbor, dismissing the Sourthern Branch as merely a "twig" in the Cal family tree. At first, in keeping with the ursine theme, UCLA teams were called "Cubs," This was changed in 1924 to the more menacing "Grizzlies." Then it was learned that the University of Montana had claim to that nickname. So, in 1926, the name was changed to "Bruins." There was some growling about this in Berkeley, since Golden Bear teams were often called Bruins by synonym-seeking sportswriters, but the UCLA Bruins held their ground.

The former Southern Branch's first attempts at stepping up in football class were markedly unsuccessful, though. The team filled in a hole in the Stanford schedule in 1925 and was beaten 82-0, prompting new coach Bill Spaulding to admit that UCLA was not yet ready for such stiff competition. They, now Bruins, tried Stanford again four years later and showed marked improvement, losing by the far more respectable score of 57–0. That same year, 1929, USC finally agreed to meet its increasingly impudent neighbor. Jones's first Herd trampled the Bruins 76–0.

Obviously, Spaulding, who'd had eighteen years of coaching experience before coming to UCLA, was a patient man. He was convinced, despite these embarrassing setbacks, that in time the victories would come. The breakthrough year was 1931, when the Bruins beat a St. Mary's team by 12–0 that had wins that year over both Cal and USC. The Bruins and Trojans wouldn't meet that year, but UCLA took enormous pleasure in defeating a team that had defeated USC. That St. Mary's game, said Bruin fullback Norman Duncan, "was the making of UCLA."

So now, on November 4, 1933, the Bears and Bruins would, despite some lingering misgivings in Berkeley, launch a long and profitable football series. And true to the united-we-stand philosophy espoused by President Sproul and Provost Moore, the final score was 0–0.

Exhausted perhaps by the gallant yet losing effort against USC and the emotional stress of the new sibling rivalry, the Bears stumbled badly against lowly Idaho before winning, 6–0, a week before the Big Game.

The vengeful Indians, meanwhile, had made good their vow, ending USC's 27-game winning streak with a 13–7 victory in Los Angeles. The win was accomplished despite a seven-hour train delay caused by washed-out tracks that kept them awake most of the night. The sleepless Vow Boys didn't arrive at the Coliseum until barely an hour before game time. And they overcame a dazzling first-quarter 43-yard touchdown dash by the irrepressible Warburton to hold the Trojans in check the rest of the way. Star fullback Bobby Grayson scored Stanford's touchdown and All America guard Bill Corbus, affectionately called "the baby-faced assassin," kicked two field goals.

By then, the Vow Boys were all the rage, their pledge of the year before extravagantly publicized, particularly by San Francisco sportswriters Harry Borba and Bud Spencer, both Stanford alums. Even without their stars' signature oath, this was a team with personality. As Spencer, a former track great at his alma mater, wrote in the San Francisco News, the Vow Boys "flaunted their sass and vinegar…Every day was a waltz…"

"I don't think there ever was a team that had more fun playing football than we did," recalled star end James "Monk" Moscrip years later.

There was, however, nothing terpsichorean or amusing about the way they played the game. They considered forward passing "sissy stuff," preferring to simply ram the ball downfield while holding opponents in check with hard-hitting line play. And they were astonishingly durable, even for a time when players were expected to play both offense and defense. In his one season with the Vow Boys, senior guard Corbus played a total of five hundred fifty minutes in eleven games, counting the Rose Bowl. Tackle Claude Callaway, nicknamed "Cab" after the popular bandleader, played 545 minutes and Alustiza 543. Tackle Bob "Horse" Reynolds, a near unanimous All America selection in '34, set a record in his career that, it is safe to say, will never be broken. He played all sixty minutes in each of the Vow Boys's three Rose Bowl games.

In the days just before the 1933 Big Game, reporters persuaded the players, for purposes of pre-game hype, to extend their vow to include Cal. The always accommodating Boys thought that was a fine idea. But they almost violated this expanded vow on Saturday before eighty-eight thousand in Stanford Stadium. The Bears scored in the second quarter on a 25-yard field goal by Williams and, though giving up many yards between the 30-yard lines, held on to that precarious advantage until, with just five minutes remaining in the game, Alustiza hit end Al Norgard with a sissy-stuff 57-yard touchdown pass. The Bears threatened in the last few minutes, reaching the Stanford eight-yard line. But Hamilton intercepted Blower's pass in the end zone and returned it to the Bear 40 as time ran out.

The Bears finished the season with a 6-3-2 record. The Vow Boys moved on to the Rose Bowl where they were upset, 7–0, on a muddy field by underdog Columbia. The only score came on a naked reverse from quarterback Cliff Montgomery to halfback Al Barabas, a play thereafter enshrined in Rose Bowl annals as KF-79.

Cal's near upset in the Big Game gave promise of a far more rewarding 1934 season. But the rewards were few. Following the usual double-header win on the opening Saturday, this time by a combined score of 87–0 over the Aggies and Nevada, the Bears were beaten, 7–0, by St. Mary's. The lone touchdown was scored on what was either a lucky break for the Gaels or a typical bit of knavery by their scheming coach. In the first quarter with the ball on the Cal 11, St. Mary's fullback Lou Kellogg plowed off tackle where, after a short gain, he was tackled by 210-pound Bear linebacker Al Thorell. The ball unaccountably popped out of Kellogg's hands and bounced forward into the end zone where the Gaels's Herb Schreiber was conveniently waiting for it. Since Madigan's team had scored by way of a similar coincidence against Fordham the year before, skeptics in the press box were convinced the "fumble play" was part of Slip's game plan. But there was no proof and no more scoring in the game, even though the Gaels fumbled five more times.

The next week, Navy Bill faced a coaching icon. If Walter Camp was football's George Washington, Amos Alonzo Stagg was surely its Thomas Jefferson. Born in 1862, Stagg starred at end for the great Yale teams of the late 1880s. He had coached at the University of Chicago for forty-one years, during which time he compiled a record of 214-111-27 and led the Maroon to a national championship in 1905, shutting out eight of nine opponents. He has been variously credited with creating the huddle, the lateral pass, the reverse, the man-in-motion, the end around, padded goal posts, the charging sled and lighted practice fields. When asked by Chicago to retire from coaching at age seventy and accept an administrative sinecure, Stagg responded, "I will not accept a job without work. I am fit, able and willing, and I refuse to be idle and a nuisance." Instead he accepted the head coaching job at College (now University) of Pacific in Stockton, California.

On October 13, 1934, he took his COP team to Memorial Stadium, for the first meeting between the two schools. The Bears learned soon enough that the "Grand Old Man of Football" didn't coach like an old man. The circumference of the football had been narrowed that season from 22½ inches to 21½ inches, the difference favoring the passing game and discouraging dropkicking, soon to become a lost art. Although the pass hadn't even been legalized until after he'd been coaching fourteen years, Stagg was a great believer in putting the ball in the air. Against Cal, besides confusing the defense with a dazzling series of reverses, COP passed 23 times, completing eight. The Bears were lucky to pull out a 7–6 win, the result of a successful conversion kick by Charles "Chili" Bertoli following Monty Reed's short touchdown run.

After three-and-a-half quarters of scoreless football, the Bears and Bruins, playing for the first time in Memorial Stadium, appeared on route to another dreary family outing. Then in the fourth quarter, Bear captain Arleigh Williams connected on an 18-yard field goal. And that was the game. In eight quarters of play, neither team had managed to score a touchdown, scarcely a portent of the offensive fireworks that would characterize future encounters between the two.

The Bears lost their next two games, to Washington (13–7) and Santa Clara (20–0) before scoring a signal victory that would have ramifications beyond the immediate. Cal was 4-3 in the '34 season going into the November 10 game with USC in Los Angeles, but two of those wins and most of the scoring had come in the opening double header against lowly foes. In the five games since, including the single-point win over hardly formidable COP, the Bears had scored only 17 points. This feeble production had not set at all well with influential alums, many of whom believed it might be time for Navy Bill to weigh anchor.

As a matter of fact, Ingram was not even on the sidelines for the Trojan game, having traveled east to be with his ailing mother. Stub Allison coached the team in his stead. And the Bears opened with a bang under his guidance. Starting after the opening kickoff from their own 33, they drove to the S.C. 30. From there, Williams ripped through the Trojan line and down the sidelines for a nifty 30-yard touchdown run. The Bears held S.C. scoreless until, finally in the fourth quarter, an errant Cal pass from center sailed out of the end zone for a safety. The 7–2 win was Cal's first over USC in five years. But this Trojan team was not one of the Thundering Herds of legend. The Vow Boys handled them, again as pledged, (by 16–0) and five other teams took their measure. The 4-6-1 season was an acute embarrassment for coach Howard Jones.

The anti-Ingram demonstrators were not particularly assuaged by this victory. In fact, since Navy Bill had absented himself from the bench that day, they were inclined to credit the win to Stub. Ingram returned from the maternal bedside in time for the Big Game. It was bad timing since the Vow Boys were then undefeated. Their lineup included four players who would receive All America honors—Grayson, Moscrip, Reynolds and Hamilton. Moscrip would miss the Cal game with a leg injury, but one of his several replacements, fourth-stringer Carl Schott, played the game of his life. He blocked a punt to set up Stanford's first score, a 22-yard run off a double reverse by Hamilton, and he kicked a 22-yard field goal. Cal finally scored with three minutes left in the game when Williams, an All America selection himself that year, passed 33 yards to end Jack Brittingham. Williams kicked the point-after for a final score of 9–7 that made the game seem closer than it actually was.

The Vow Boys, significantly, missed on all six of their pass attempts, which was for them positive support for their conviction that football games were won on the ground, not in the air. Then, in the Rose Bowl, they were walloped, 29–13, by University of Alabama players who considered passing a way of life, quite possibly because they had in their lineup an end named Don Hutson, who would later become as a professional among the greatest of all receivers. Alabama also had a pretty fair passer in tailback Millard "Dixie" Howell. All told, the Crimson Tide gained 214 yards through the air, Hutson accounting for 110 of them on five receptions for two touchdowns.

Ingram resigned immediately after the Big Game, passing up a two-game vacation excursion to Hawaii in December. Allison, immediately hired as Navy Bill's replacement, coached the Bears to two losses on the pleasure trip, but no one at Cal took that seriously. And few then took Stub all that seriously. Even his most ardent supporters didn't envision this stolid, unimaginative advocate of smash-mouth football as the coach who would restore the Bears to the glory that had eluded them since the death of Andy Smith nearly a decade before.

But he would.

## CHAPTER ELEVEN

# A ROLL OF THUNDER

Stub Allison had been coaching football since his graduation in 1920 from tiny Carleton College in Minnesota, where he had played tackle with considerable distinction. Before coming to Cal he had had coaching stopovers at Washington, North Dakota State and Wisconsin. There was nothing at all "stubby" about him —he was nearly six feet tall—except for his stubbornness in refusing to acknowledge that there was any play in the game, certainly including the forward pass, worth calling other than the off-tackle smash. Football for him was a simple matter of blocking and tackling. When these were found wanting, he would declare in a voice verging on despair that it was time to "go back to fundamentals."

Broad-shouldered and with a head shaped like an artillery shell, he affected the irascible temperament of the First Sergeant he'd been in World War I. "He would say you're not hurt until the bone is sticking out," recalled one of his former players from the 1930s, Milt Pollack, in a 2004 interview with the *Chronicle*. He was adamantly opposed to the star system, preaching instead the virtues of team-work and team unity. Once when still a line coach under Ingram, he instructed All American tailback Arleigh Williams to explain to the squad how blocks by his teammates had paved the way for one of his well-publicized long gains. "All I did," Williams modestly averred, "was run with the ball."

On at least one occasion, Stub had his first-stringers, not the subs, wheel the blocking sleds and other workout paraphernalia onto the practice field. Stub even outfitted his players in uniforms of uncompromising blandness. Ingram's teams, in comparison, were almost gaudily clad in dark jerseys with gold-striped sleeves, gold pants and gold-striped sox; his players looked if anything more like tigers than Bears. In fact, the football fashion trend across the country in the late 1930s was toward flashier garb. Madigan's players at St. Mary's wore fetching ensembles of silk and satin, complete with epaulets and colored breeches. As one observer remarked, they could have passed for high ranking French military officers in the Franco-Prussian War. Even stolid Howard Jones had his USC bruisers in silk pants on occasion. But Stub's teams took the field in plain blue jerseys, brown leather helmets with blue stripes and the sort of canvas pants worn decades earlier before color and stylish fabric were introduced to trouserwear. Chic they were not.

But hard-nosed Stub was, at the same time, readily accessible to fans and the press. And in a tradition he started, he'd appear after home games on the stadium balcony outside the locker room to talk about what happened and introduce worthy players. All this in response to rooters' chants of "We want Stub!" Like Smith before him, he freely mixed with professors, periodically checking on his players' academic progress. He wanted them all to graduate.

In the grand tradition of curmudgeons, dating to Ebenezer Scrooge and portrayed in movies of the time by either Lionel Barrymore or Clarence Kolb, Stub Allison had a softer side. One of his reserves, Ray Rosso, recalled that though Stub was "the prototype of the tough coach of that era—like Pop Warner, Bernie Bierman—he was very considerate of players at the bottom (of his roster)…He encouraged me to stay with it even though I was a marginal player in every way."

And under Stub, those players at the bottom didn't spend all their time seated forlornly on the Andy Smith Bench. Unlike his contemporaries, notably Jones and Thornhill, Allison was not a fan of the sixty-minute man. Whereas Thornhill might use fifteen players in a game, Stub would routinely play twenty-five or thirty, replacing his starters with bench warmers as soon as he sensed the game was well in hand. His version of free substitution served the dual purpose of keeping his regulars fresh and, he hoped, free of injury and of providing game experience for those who might otherwise sit and wait. With Stub, everyone got into the act. In 1935, for example, he alternated five players—Don Fowler, Floyd Blower, Bill Archer, George Cornell and Morris "Mushy" Pollack—at left halfback, the prime tailback position in the coach's single wing and short punt formations. The next year, he used six.

But there was little envy among that tailback throng, recalled Archer in an interview for this book in 2006 when the so-called "Wild Bill" was all of ninety-four. "We were friends. We rooted for each other. The others called me 'Wild Bill' for reasons I never really understood. There was nothing at all wild about me. I might have been a little goofy, though."

Navy Bill bequeathed Stub a young team with as yet unfulfilled potential. On the 1935 roster, there were twenty sophomores with experience only in freshman ball, seven players with just one year of varsity play and a comparatively grizzled nine seniors. But the '34 freshman team, captained by center Bob Herwig, had been undefeated in six games. The emerging sophomores reflected the gathering influence of the industrious Southern Seas, since not only Herwig but future stars Johnny Meek, Vard Stockton, Claude Evans, Ken Cotton and both Milt and Mushy Pollock were all southern Californians. They would represent in large part the nucleus of what in two years time would become Stub's *chef d'oeuvre*.

The '35 season itself seemed to portend a return to what President Roosevelt, speaking certainly in broader terms, called "happy days." The Bears began with five straight shutout wins, although two of them, came in the opening doubleheader against lesser foes Whittier and Cal Aggies. At the same time, they beat favored St. Mary's, 10–0, on the second Saturday and traditionally tough Santa Clara, 6–0, in the fifth game. Then, back-to-back, they defeated USC, 21–7, at home and UCLA, 14–2, before seventy-five thousand at the L. A. Coliseum. Both games held significance beyond the final scores. The S.C. win was Cal's first over the Trojans in five years, and in beating their little brother Bruins, they prevailed over a team that would hand the Vow Boys their only defeat that year, if only by 7–6.

Blower, putative chairman of the five-man tailback committee, tossed touchdown passes of 10 yards to Meek and 29 to end Hank Sparks in a 14–0 win over Washington and committeeman Cornell scored three touchdowns in a 39–0 win over Pacific.

The Bears were undefeated in nine games before confronting the last of the Vow Boy teams. Up to that point, Stub's debut team had allowed only one touchdown, and that on a blocked kick by USC. The UCLA safety had raised the points scored against the Bears to a niggling nine. They had, meanwhile, scored 163. Their celebrated Big Game opponents had fulfilled their original vow, edging S.C. 3–0, while surrendering touchdowns only to UCLA and Santa Clara in winning six of seven games. This was obviously going to be another really big Big Game, with the winner dispatched to the Rose Bowl. A Stanford Stadium crowd of better than eighty thousand was there to catch the excitement.

But there was none, at least for the Bears. The Vow Boys were simply not to be denied a third straight trip to Pasadena, and behind touchdown runs by Jimmy Coffis and All American Grayson, they handed the '35 Bears their only defeat. Both scores came in the first quarter, Grayson's after a 12-play, 80-yard drive against a Cal defense that until then had not given up three first downs in a row all season. The Vow Boys closed out their melodramatic career with a 7–0 win over Southern Methodist in the Rose Bowl, their first there after losses to Columbia and Alabama.

Cal's 9–1 season under the new coach reinvigorated previously dispirited supporters. And there were honors all round. Team captain Larry Lutz at tackle received All America mention and joined Herwig, Blower and Jack Brittingham on the All-Conference team.

The world outside was meanwhile going to hell in a handbasket. Adolf Hitler, the self-appointed "fuehrer," was busy rebuilding Germany's military power in violation of the Versailles Treaty while at the same time preparing to host the 1936 Olympic Games, the supposed symbol of international amity. Italy under fascist leader Benito Mussolini had invaded Ethiopia. Japan was all set to invade China. The Spanish Civil War, which would serve as a showcase for both German and Italian air power, would begin in 1936. Edward VIII would inherit the English throne that year upon the death of his father, George V, then abdicate soon after to marry an American divorcee, thereby creating a *scandale d'amour* the likes of which hadn't afflicted the international community since the marital adventures of King Henry VIII four hundred years earlier.

In a bleak assessment of world conditions in the late 1930s, the British economist Sir Arthur Salter declared at a Cal Charter Day celebration that "the tragic reality is that almost half the world's governments are now totalitarian." Isolated by its protective oceans, the United States, said Sir Arthur, was now "responsible for the preservation of democracy."

In anticipation of the forthcoming Berlin Olympics, Cal's 1935 *Blue and Gold* observed an international theme that in its naive execution would have decidedly embarrassing consequences. The publication's Athletic section, for example, was preceded by a collage featuring a large black swastika near which apparently joyful laborers are delivering the Nazi salute. "The blazing defiant swastika stands out in bold relief," read the explanatory text, heralding "Germany's rebirth since the war and its glory in the 1936 Olympic Games. Workers united under the Nazi government are shown on the right in characteristic posture." The Italian collage preceding the "University Life" section showed a fascist figure expressing "the intense national spirit of the country." And for Japan, the yearbook featured "the rising sun of Asiatic domination,' eerily reminding readers that this was "the only nation in the world with both a first class army and navy."

Contrarily, Cal was at this time under persistent fire from the Hearst newspapers for acting as a safe harbor for the "Red Menace," a campaign inspired perhaps by a proposal from student groups to make ROTC optional not compulsory. The campus was obviously not immune from the world's maladies, both right and left, nor would it ever be.

Nevertheless, optimism prevailed in football quarters. Experts had the Bears picked as Rose Bowl material. But Allison's 1936 team proved to be little more than a work in progress. Among its five losses in eleven games was the first ever to UCLA, a 17–6 upset at Memorial Stadium during which President Sproul diplomatically changed sides at halftime. As a matter of fact, Sproul and family spent that entire school year headquartered on the Los Angeles campus, further acknowledgment of the still-youthful offspring's continuing advancement.

St. Mary's reversed the 1935 Cal score, winning this time by 10–0. Washington, then ranked eighth in the country, scored a 13–0 shutout in Seattle and Washington State sneaked by the Bears, 14–13, its winning touchdown the result of a questionable pass interference call against Sam Chapman following an end zone collision in the waning minutes. The Bears did beat USC in Los Angeles, a game best remembered for the belated appearance of a sophomore tailback who would render obsolete the committee system at his position. Cal scored first when committeeman Mushy Pollock passed in the flat to end Will Dolman who lateraled to the ubiquitous Herwig who ran 23 yards more for the touchdown. But Southern Cal countered with a 33-yard touchdown run by Davie Davis and after making good the PAT led 7–6 at the half.

But Chapman, enjoying a fine junior season, returned the second half kickoff 50 yards to the Trojan 45. It was then that Allison, thumbing through his voluminous tailback directory, called on one Victor Bottari of Vallejo. "Vallejo Vic" passed first to Meek for 14 yards and then, from the 31, to Chapman for the winning touchdown. Against Oregon the following week, he passed 42 yards to Hank Sparks for one touchdown and scored another in a 28–0 win.

These late season dramatics caused Stub to reevaluate the overcrowded situation at this key position. Until Bottari's emergence, the job had been almost equally shared among six candidates with surprisingly similar results. Cornell had rushed 56 times for 175 yards, Pollock 50 for 171, Archer 48 for 189, Bottari 43 for 145, Blower 40 for 194 and Eddie Vallejo 12 for 71.

Pollock, the smallest at 145 pounds and fastest (9.6 for the 100-yard dash) started the Big Game, but Vallejo Vic—not Eddie Vallejo—entered late in the first quarter. And from that moment on, what would become Allison's famous "Thunder Team" came into being. Bottari quickly passed 35 yards to Sparks, who made a spectacular falling-down catch in the end zone of a ball partially deflected. Allison played only his seniors in the third quarter, with Archer at tailback. Wild Bill first caught a pass from Chapman for 29 yards to the Stanford 6, then scored on third down from the 1.

Bottari returned for the final quarter. And following a long drive, rammed into the Stanford line from the two, then unexpectedly whirled and tossed a basketball pass lateral to Chapman, who scored. Final score: 20–0, Cal. It was the Bears' first Big Game win since '31 and the first at home since 1923. It was also a humiliating defeat for the Vow-deprived Indians. They completed just four of their 26 pass attempts and had nine intercepted, while gaining only 69 yards running the ball.

This, however, was not the Bears' final game. They left Berkeley on December 20 for Atlanta, where the day after Christmas they lost to Georgia Tech, 13–7. They took the long way home via Mexico City and Guadalajara and didn't return until January 6. It had been a wonderful Christmas vacation, except, of course, for the loss. But no worry there. They wouldn't lose another game for almost two years.

There was nothing physically imposing about Allison's 1937 team. In sharp contrast to today's game when linemen routinely outweigh defensive backs, receivers and some running backs by more than one hundred pounds, these Bears were all roughly the same cruiserweight size. Stub's line averaged 188 pounds per man and so did the backs. The smallest lineman, guard Claude Evans, weighed 178, the biggest, center Herwig, weighed 203. Bottari, at 175 pounds, was the lightest back, Meek at 206 the heaviest. The two tackles, Dave DeVarona and Bill Stoll, both weighed 188, light even then for the game's heaviest position. Stockton, the other guard, was 185. Perry Schwartz, 190, and Dolman, 184, were the ends. Chapman at the right half or wingback position was 184 and fullback Dave Anderson played at 187.

They weren't particularly fast either. Neither Bottari nor Chapman could have been considered a breakaway speedster on the order of, say, USC's Cotton Warburton or Stanford's Phil Moffatt. But both had their strengths. Bottari, only 5-9, ran close to the ground and, as Archer remembered, "kept his feet well" after being hit. He was also very efficient at following his blockers. "He'd go where Stub told him to," said Archer. "He'd get behind Anderson and Meek and just dig hard." He was also an excellent passer, capable of whistling the ball 50 yards or more downfield, though rarely called upon to do so. At Vallejo High, where the football throw replaced the more dangerous javelin in track, Bottari once hurled a 70-yarder. Under a more pass-oriented coach— and there were few of them then outside the South—there is no telling what Vallejo Vic might have accomplished. "But I don't think Stub had a real understanding of the passing game," said Archer. Even with the narrower, more passable ball, Allison's Bears rarely threw as many as ten passes in a game.

Chapman, who would be named to six All America teams in '37, was "just a great athlete," Archer recalled. "He was not real speedy, but he was fast enough and like Bottari he could keep his feet under him. He could catch and throw and kick and he almost never made a mistake." Chapman was a two-sport star, an outfielder and third baseman on the Cal baseball team who went directly from the Berkeley campus to Connie Mack's Philadelphia Athletics after his college eligibility expired.

Anderson and quarterback Meek were the blockers, though both had other talents, Anderson was a tough inside runner, capable on occasion of tearing off a long gain. Meek was a fine pass receiver coming out of the backfield and a ferocious linebacker. Aside from Herwig, he was the hardest hitter on the team, offensively and defensively. Called "Jellybelly" because of his comparative girth, there was nothing gelatinous about the way he played. "When he hit someone," Archer said, "you could hear them groan…unhhhh…as the breath ran out of them." Single-wing quarterbacks of the '30s were blocking backs, but most of them, including Meek, called the plays, and Jellybelly was good at that, too.

And all of these Bears played tough defense, as witness the paltry five touchdowns scored against them in 11 games. "There were 11 hats on the ball all the time," guard Perry Connor recalled in the 2004 interview with the *Chronicle*.

As opposed to the '36 season, when the Bears were expected to win and didn't, forecasters were more circumspect regarding the '37 team. When in the September 25 opener, Stub's stalwarts walloped St. Mary's 30–7, experts were quick to say that this did not appear to be one of Madigan's better teams. And they were right. The Gaels finished the season with an un-Slip-like 4-3-2 record, the worst in ten years. After piling up a 17–0 halftime lead over them, Stub typically went the rest of the way with his reserves, but there were intimations of glory to come in those first thirty minutes. Bottari connected with Schwartz on a 39-yard touchdown pass, Anderson ran 49 for another and Chapman booted a 19-yard field goal.

Bottari scored twice on short runs and Chapman once on a 22-yarder as the Bears beat Oregon State, 24–6. Bottari scored twice more and passed 31 yards to Chapman for another touchdown in a 27–0 rout of Washington State. In the annual doubleheader, Allison played only his reserves in a 14–0 win over the Cal Aggies in the opener, the highlight of which was a record 102-yard kickoff return by sub fullback Ed Solinsky. In the second game, the varsity beat Pacific, 20–0, Bottari scoring yet another TD.

A capacity crowd turned out for the October 23 showdown with USC at Memorial Stadium. The Trojans were then campaigning to regain past eminence with a fine team led by talented backs Ambrose Schindler and Grenville "Granny" Landsdell. The Bears had by then awakened the experts and were ranked first in the country; USC was eleventh. But the game was another Cal runaway. Bottari scored twice and Anderson once after long power-play drives in the convincing 20–6 victory. The Trojans' lone touchdown came late in the last quarter against Stub's busy reserves. In his account of the game, the *Chronicle*'s Bill Leiser wrote, "Along with the seventy-five thousand who watched, the Trojans themselves are wondering where, if anywhere in the land, is a team which can stop the roll of California's Thunder Team."

The nickname seemed apt—Thunder after Wonder—and it had been used earlier, often in poetic jest. But Leiser, then and for many years the Bay Area's most respected and certainly most prolific writer about football, gave it authenticity. This was the Thunder Team forever after.

A week after trouncing the Trojans, the Bears rolled over UCLA, 27–14, sweet revenge for the '36 embarrassment. Bottari scored twice, once on a 25-yard ramble, then after Anderson scored from the one,

Stub's subs took over. UCLA's last touchdown came on a spectacular 50-yard run against them by a sophomore tailback named Kenny Washington, who would soon become the scourge of the conference with his brilliant all-round play. Washington and end Woody Strode had broken into the Bruin lineup as part of a pioneering group of African-American stars who brought honor and new prestige to a school once known as the Southern Branch. They would soon be joined by another black player who, though a football sensation, would achieve somewhat greater fame in another sport. His name was Jackie Robinson.

Bottari suffered a minor injury against UCLA that kept him out of the Washington game on November 6 until the third quarter. He arrived too late and too infirm to prevent the only setback of the season, a scoreless tie that dropped the Bears off the top of the national rankings. The subs played most of the way in a 26–0 win over Oregon in Portland's habitually moist Multnomah Stadium. Bottari played just enough of the first half to connect on three consecutive passes, two to Meek, the last to Sparks for the Bears' third score.

Pelting rain did not intimidate the eighty-eight thousand who attended the Big Game at Stanford Stadium. Cal's first string played only the first half against the then 4-2-1 Indians. Bottari scored from the four at the conclusion of a 77-yard drive with no passes and Chapman from the eight after a 65-yard march that featured a 38-yard Bottari-to-Chapman pass. Only the indomitable Herwig among the Bear starters played the full sixty minutes, mainly because he wanted it that way in his last Big Game. Though they played barely half as long, Chapman gained 70 yards on 16 carries, Bottari 55, also on 16, and Anderson 50 on 12. For the regular season, Bottari scored ten touchdowns and passed for three more; Chapman scored 39 points on four touchdowns, a field goal and 12 conversions.

Five Thunder Team seniors—Chapman, Herwig, Meek, Schwartz, Stockton—received All America mention. Bottari, inexplicably ignored by the All America voters, joined his teammates on the All

Pacific Coast Conference team.

The Bears would now return to the Rose Bowl after a much de-plored absence of eight years. Their opponent would be the undefeated and untied Alabama Crimson Tide, long a fan favorite in Pasadena. The Tide, in fact, had not only played in more Rose Bowl games than Cal—four to three—but had never lost. Cal's record in Pasadena was a middling 1-1-1, the only win coming over Ohio State back in January of '21. There followed the mudbath scoreless tie with Washington and Jefferson and the wrong way loss to Georgia Tech in '29.

This would be an attractive matchup of undefeated conference champions, and the ticket prices of $3.30, $4.40 and $5.50 would be the highest yet in Rose Bowl history. Not that there were any tickets available, save through the smarmy hands of scalpers. In fact, for the first time ever, there would be no public sale of tickets. The scarcity was largely attributable to Cal's eleven thousand alumni, many of whom jumped at the chance to purchase the maximum of six tickets to which by conference tradition they were entitled. Cal's ASUC general man-ager Ken Priestley stoutly defended the alums' rights against protests that no previous conference representative had accommodated such a large number of ticket-hungry grads. Among those expressing out-rage was one C. W. Koiner, whose application for choice seats had been summarily rejected, his check returned. Koiner just happened to be Pasadena's City Manager.

Allison didn't resume practice until after Christmas, arousing concern among Cal supporters that the month's layoff might have a deleterious effect on a team so dependent on timing and fundamen-tals. When the Bears arrived in Pasadena, two prominent sportswriters, syndicated columnist Grantland Rice and Henry McLemore of the United Press, asked Stub if they might have a personal look at a prac-tice session to assess the team's readiness.

Allison, ever accommodating but reluctant to expose his game plan to journalistic scrutiny, agreed, but he scheduled the practice at dusk when visibility was limited. The two writers complained afterward that they couldn't see much in the fading light, but as Stub recalled, "they sure as hell could hear the rockin' and sockin. I could, too, only to me it was sweet music."

The Bears were ready in body and spirit, their vaunted homogeneity intact. In his history of the Rose Bowl, Rube Samuelson described Allison's players as "the closest-knit ensemble ever to play in the New Year's Day Classic." And though outwardly stern and demanding, the head coach was in the final analysis just one of the boys. After rejecting a lucrative, for the time, offer to appear on a popular radio show, Stub told his team, "I could make a small fortune off what you boys have done this season. But that wouldn't be right. If you'll promise to keep on the way you have, I'll do the same and skip the extras."

The game itself, witnessed by a crowd of 89,650, scarcely lived up to its advance billing, Cal administering a sound thrashing to the southerners. In the second quarter, the Bears drove 61 yards on 13 power running plays with Bottari scoring from the four. In the third quarter, they muscled straight ahead 47 yards, Bottari again scoring from the four. And that was the ballgame, a 13–0 Bear win, their school-record tenth of the season.

It was vintage Stub football. The Bears passed only nine times, completing just two for 16 yards. But they gained 192 on the ground, mostly on Bottari off-tackle slants. Vallejo Vic carried the ball for what was then a Rose Bowl record thirty-four times, gained 137 yards and scored the game's only touchdowns. The Bears throttled the Tide offense all day, intercepting five passes, two more than were completed. Herwig was the defensive hero, intercepting a pass, recovering a fumble and stunning 'Bama backs all afternoon with his teeth-rattling tackles. Tide coach Frank Thomas said afterward that Cal was the hardest-hitting team he'd yet faced and the best all-round since the Vow Boys in the '35 Rose Bowl. Faint praise, perhaps, since Thomas's Tide had beaten the Vow Boys in that game, 29–13.

After their shutout victory over a previously undefeated team, many thought the Bears should be considered the number one team in college football. But since the dominant Associated Press poll was released before the Bowl games, Pittsburgh, with a 9-0-1 record, was accorded that honor, with Cal, also 9-0-1 after the regular season, ranked second. But Pitt had rejected all Bowl invitations. So the Bears knew in their hearts they were the best. And so did the Cal record five hundred eighteen thousand fans who watched them home and away that triumphant season.

There was one revealing aftermath to the Rose Bowl victory. In a departure from his usual policy, Stub played only fifteen men against Alabama, the better to expose the nation to the Thunder Team starters' extraordinary cohesiveness. But this rare decision hardly affected the sense of unity the coach had instilled. When the Rose Bowl committee proposed giving commemorative gold watches to the fifteen who had played, they said no thanks. Unless the bench-sitters were also included, the committee could keep its watches. This, after all, was a Team.

CHAPTER TWELVE

# BEFORE THE STORM

Civilization may have been teetering on the brink of war's abyss, but, paradoxically, the years immediately preceding the bloodshed happened to be a grand time to be young, American and a college student. There was certainly no shortage of entertainment. Hollywood was at its peak with such classics as "Gone With the Wind," and a vast array of screwball comedies in the manner of "Bringing Up Baby" and "Nothing Sacred." Marvelous comedians like Jack Benny, Fred Allen and Bob Hope enlivened radio listening.

But above all, there was the music, the great swelling sounds of the Big Bands playing "swing." Never before in the history of popular music—and certainly not since—has such pure artistry enriched a mass audience. Swing's throbbing rhythms sounded the heartbeat of a generation. The "Top 40" then was occupied by such superb musicians as Benny Goodman, Artie Shaw, Count Basie and Duke Ellington. There were soloists such as Bunny Berigan and Harry James on trumpet, Teddy Wilson and Jess Stacy at the piano, drummers like Chick Webb and Gene Krupa. They were all available on records and from the ubiquitous juke boxes. You could find them in hotels, ballrooms, public auditoriums, theaters and dancehalls. And you danced, always you danced, jitterbugging to Goodman, cheek-to-cheek to the slower beat of Glenn Miller or the Dorsey brothers.

There were dance parties on the Cal campus then for every conceivable occasion. And at the Claremont Hotel on Berkeley's south border or across the newly-bridged Bay at the Mark Hopkins, the Fairmont or the St. Francis dance bands led by the likes of Anson Weeks, Joe Reichmen, Skinnay Ennis, Freddy Martin or Ray Noble held sway. And in the middle of the Bay, on man-made Treasure Island, there was more music at San Francisco's magnificent "World's Fair," the Golden Gate International Exposition.

While it was true that the new Bay Bridge offered swifter access to the Fair and the city, there were those, like the anonymous writer in the Cal yearbook, who deplored the passing of ferry boat voyages. The ferry, he wrote, "allowed time to scan the myriad lights of the city or watch the antics of seagulls...In the final analysis, it is another instance of sacrifice of a romantic student tradition to progress."

Ferries or no, these were romantic times on campus, rendered all the more so by the imminent threat of U.S. involvement in the war already raging overseas. There was the sense that time was swiftly running out, particularly with the passage in September 1940 of the Selective Service Act imposing the nation's first peacetime military draft. Speakers from abroad and at home warned Cal students of the danger awaiting them. Prominent visitors included the Danish atomic physicist Niels Bohr, the British poet and essayist Alfred Noyes, Harvard's president James Bryant Conant, President Roosevelt's Secretary of the Interior Harold Ickes and actor, singer and civil rights activist Paul Robeson. Then, too, "circumstances" overseas had made it impossible for Cal's Nobel winner, Dr. Ernest Orlando Lawrence, to accept his prize in Sweden. The presentation was made instead on campus with Swedish consul-general in San Francisco Carl E. Wallerstedt doing the honors.

The campus itself was not without a distinguished group of undergraduates. A 1937 Phi Beta Kappa named Robert Strange McNamara, depicted in the *Blue and Gold* looking earnest in typical student garb of cords, sweater and sport shirt, was chairman then of the Men's Judicial Committee. He would become better known years later as the Secretary of Defense under presidents Kennedy and Johnson. In 1939, a pretty co-ed named Marguerite Higgins was elected vice president of the junior class. She would make her mark outside as a famous war correspondent. Pauline Kael, later the country's most influential film critic, was a star on the varsity debate team. And Eldred Peck, a rangy member of the varsity crew who dabbled in dramatics, played the male lead in Cal's Little Theater production of Eugene O'Neill's "Anna Christie." A *Blue and Gold* reviewer wrote that he handled well the role of "the big, noisy, eloquent Irish stoker who was determined to marry Anna." Peck made some movies later using his middle name, Gregory, in place of Eldred. And Gregory Peck enjoyed a pretty fair career.

Although Stub Allison lost much of the thunder from his championship team—Chapman, Meek, Herwig, Schwartz and Stockton—he still had Bottari for the '38 season. And Vic added to his already impressive repertoire a talent for dropkicking. Also returning were fullback Anderson, end Dolman and starting tackles DeVarona and Stoll. Louis Smith, a 6-3, 197-pounder, was the new right half and 191-pound Bill Elmore the quarterback. And the team took off pretty much from where the Thunderers left off, winning its first seven games, four within the conference. By the time these Bears met USC on November 5 before ninety-five thousand in the L.A. Coliseum, they were ranked third in the country and being compared favorably with their revered predecessors.

But they came a-cropper against the rejuvenated Trojans. After a scoreless first half, Granny Lansdell scored at the finish of a 70-yard third quarter drive. And in the final quarter Jack Banta topped off another drive with a short run. Cal didn't make it past its own 30 until late in the fourth quarter when Bottari launched a pass attack from the 33, connecting with Angelo Reginato for three in a row and then a

26-yard scoring toss to Morley Mathewson. Vic dropkicked the extra point. But it was too late. The 13–7 loss ended Cal's undefeated streak at seventeen games.

The Bears recovered nicely the next week against Oregon. Smith scored twice, on a 30-yard pass from Bottari and a 12-yard run. Anderson got the final TD on a four-yard run, completing a 20–0 rout.

Bottari's brilliant all-round game was never on better display than in the 1938 Big Game where he was the defensive as well as the offensive star. In a third-quarter goal-line stand, he made four straight game-saving tackles, twice stopping Stanford's Bill Paulson and then holding off halfback Pete Fay and finally, one of the game's most powerful runners, Norm Standlee. And in that same quarter, he passed 28 yards to Reginato for the game's only score.

Once again, the Bears played Georgia Tech in a post-season game, this time, on December 26, in Berkeley. It was a relatively easy win, so with only a few minutes left to play, sentimental Stub pulled his senior stars—Anderson, Dolman, DeVarona, Stoll—one-by-one from the game, saving the best, Bottari, for last. And with time running out, the first-string All American trotted to the sidelines for the last time amid booming cheers of gratitude.

And though the Bears were conference co-champions with USC, the Trojans went to the Rose Bowl on the strength of their November win. There they played one of the most thrilling of all Bowl games, defeating previously undefeated, untied and unscored-upon Duke, 7–3, behind a fourth-string tailback, Doyle Nave, who completed four passes in succession to end "Antelope Al" Krueger, the last for the winning touchdown just forty-one seconds before the final gun.

The methodical "Stubber," as he was now being called with a mixture of affection and sarcasm, had seemed in his first four seasons a soberer reincarnation of Andy Smith. His teams had won thirty-five games and lost only seven, with one tie. In those four years, he had won outright or shared the conference championship three times. He had yet to endure a losing season. He had won ten games in both '37 and '38 and nine in his first year on the job. And he'd won a Rose Bowl game. In fact, his first four seasons were even more successful than the sainted Smith's. Andy didn't win a conference title until his fifth year. But after that, he just kept on winning until providence cruelly intervened.

The Stubber's career path would head in another direction. After his sprinter's start, he fell back into the pack. Oh, he would have his moments in the six years remaining to him at Cal, but he would never again enjoy a winning season. The decline began in 1939, and in of all the unlikely circumstances, at the season's opening doubleheader on September 30.

In the first game of that fateful twin bill, the Bear subs were having such a rough time with the Cal Aggies, who led 14–6 at the half, that Stub was obliged to send the varsity in to the rescue. The first-stringers played much of the third quarter, insuring the final 32–14 victory, but they were also obliged to play the second game against the College of the Pacific. They simply pooped out, and Stagg's Pacific team won the game, 6–0. It was Cal's first ever loss to COP.

The Bears then lost to Slip Madigan's last and possibly worst (3-4-1) team at St. Mary's by 7–3. That was followed by a 6–0 loss to Oregon. They defeated Washington State, 13–7, then lost four straight conference games, including back-to-back thrashings by USC, 26–0, and UCLA, 20–7.

There was nothing at all Big about that year's game with Stanford. Cal's record of two wins and seven losses actually looked Notre-Dame-ish alongside Stanford's 0-6-1, although the Indians' 14–14 tie with UCLA was cause for concern. Still, this "Big" Game had the makings of an even, if possibly scoreless, matchup. Both teams had been shut out four times, but Cal, with 61 points in nine games, was a veritable offensive juggernaut compared with Stanford's 26 in seven. The Bears were averaging a touchdown per game, the Indians a field goal, and a

6–3 final score either way seemed probable.

But no. Behind the running and passing of a new tailback, Orville Hatcher, the Bears won handily, 32–14, before an abnormally modest crowd of fifty-eight thousand in Stanford Stadium. Hatcher ran for 99 yards on 23 carries, scored on a six-yard run and passed 22 yards to Smith for another touchdown. Stanford didn't cross the goal line—Cal's, that is—until the fourth quarter when a 165-pound, left-handed halfback named Frankie Albert passed 30 yards to Fred Meyer. Standlee got the Indians' last TD on a one-yard plunge.

Coach Tiny Thornhill didn't know it at the time, but he had among that wretched bunch the very ingredients of Stanford's greatest team, one that in just a year's time would make football history. But Tiny had these future heroes operating out of the wrong system—his. And he wouldn't be around for their astonishing comeback. After the Indians won their only game of 1939, 14–3, over highly embarrassed Dartmouth before a sparse December crowd at New York's Polo Grounds, Tiny got the axe.

All that can be said about the Bears' 1940 season is that they played supporting roles to one of college football's greatest players at the start of the season and to the game's most influential team at the end of it. After the 1939 misstep, Stub dropped the early season doubleheader idea he'd inherited from Navy Bill. Instead, the Bears scheduled Michigan for their 1940 opener. That was a mistake, for the Wolverines had a top team led by tailback Tommy Harmon— "Old 98"—who was then considered not only the game's finest all-round back but a broken field runner so swift and adroit he merited comparison with the deified Red Grange. The Michigan team made headlines even before the game by arriving for it, with stops in Des Moines, Denver and Salt Lake City, by chartered airline, thus becoming the first college team ever to fly cross-country to a game.

As it happened, that September 28 was Old 98's twenty-first birthday, and the Bears threw him a big party. Harmon returned the opening kickoff 94 yards for a touchdown, then, still in the first quarter, returned a punt 72 yards for another. In the second quarter, once again leaving would-be tacklers grasping air, he tore off an 86-yard scoring run from scrimmage, a dazzler made even more memorable by the appearance on field of a twelfth man. As Harmon approached the end zone he was confronted by one Bud Brennan, a balding, pot-bellied real estate salesman who, fortified by flasked brandy, had popped out of his end zone seat vowing to bring Old 98 to earth. He had informed his seatmates after Harmon's punt return that "if Hatcher misses that so-and-so again, I'm going after him myself." A much amused Harmon easily avoided his newest pursuer, casting him aside with a gentle straight-arm.

Harmon scored once more in the second half on a comparatively uneventful eight-yard run and then passed five yards to right half David Nelson for another score. The Bears never crossed midfield in the 41–0 loss, gaining only 56 yards from scrimmage all day to Michigan's 407. It was a helluva way to start a season.

Meanwhile across the Bay that same day at San Francisco's Kezar Stadium, history of a different sort was being made as Stanford opened against the University of San Francisco. Thornhill's improbable successor as coach of the Indians was Clark Shaughnessy, who as coach the previous season at the University of Chicago had suffered even more humiliation than Tiny, absorbing losses by the galactic scores of 85–0 to Michigan, 61–0 to both Ohio State and Harvard and 47–0 to Virginia. And yet he was considered one of the game's most innovative theorists, an Einstein of the gridiron who had worked with George Halas of the Chicago Bears in developing a souped up version of the old T-formation.

Shaughnessy was convinced the T, as alien to college football in 1940 as the flying wedge, would work at Stanford. He recognized that in Albert, a so-so double-wing halfback, he had an ideal T quarterback with the quick hands, keen mind and passing ability needed to make the system work. At the halfbacks, he had Pete Kmetovic, a shifty runner ill-equipped for the multiple tasks of a double wing back, and Hugh Gallarneau, a strong runner who could make the T's quick openers work. And at fullback, he had the powerful Standlee. For his new system, he shifted blocking backs, like Chuck Taylor, to guard and promoted other linemen on the basis of their quickness getting off the ball, not necessarily a high priority in the wingback system. And he outfitted his teams in sparkling new uniforms—white helmets, red jerseys, white pants (unusual then) and red socks. They looked like pros, and that, to the grief of their opponents, was the way they played. The USF Dons, completely baffled by Albert's fakery, were the first to fall, by 27–0.

Cal, stunned by Michigan, lumbered on with the single wing, Allison being certain that in sophomore Jim Jurkovich he had his tailback of the future. At a muscular 185 pounds, Jurkovich was heavier than Bottari and, a 9.8 100-yard sprinter and near 25-foot broad (now long) jumper, faster and more agile. He was also, as it developed, much more fragile. But Joltin' Jim got off to a fast start. In a 14–6 win over Oregon, he reeled off a 30-yard touchdown run in which he went from one sideline to another, eluding tacklers virtually on his own. And in a 20–7 victory over USC, he first caught a short pass from Hatcher and ran 42 yards for one touchdown, then intercepted a pass on his own goal line and returned it the length of the field, mercilessly taunting his hapless pursuers as he sped past them. But he would never play a full season for the Bears.

The '40 season was also in many ways a series of mathematical oddities. After the Michigan debacle, the Bears played three straight games in which the final score was either 9–6 or 9–7, prompting one reporter to suggest that while he could not predict the outcome of the coming game with Washington, he was dead certain of the final score. Actually, Cal lost to Washington, 7–6. The only real positive in that game was that the Bears discovered in big tackle Bob Reinhard (6-3, 215) a superlative punter. It was unusual then to have anyone but a back, generally the tailback, do the kicking, but Reinhard consistently outdistanced all the Bear backs in practice, and against Washington he averaged an impressive 47.7 yards on 12 punts.

Because of Shaughnessy, Albert and the T, the 1940 Big Game attracted national attention. Just as Cal had rhymed its Wonder and Thunder teams, Stanford was now calling its '40 team "Wow Boys" after the earlier 'Vow Boys." The name was apt, for this team had wowed football experts everywhere. The Wow Boys were undefeated in eight games coming into the Big Game, their only really close call a 7–6 win over Buck Shaw's nationally ranked Santa Clara Broncos. Their turnaround from the '39 disaster, coupled with the revolutionary formation, had made them the darlings of the national press. Albert was virtually a unanimous choice for All America and Shaughnessy would be named Coach of the Year.

When a reporter credited Shughnessy with "inventing" the T, the normally dour coach replied, "I appreciate the compliment, but must admit that I played the T under Doc Williams at Minnesota in 1911. I've just added a few extras."

Still, the Bears put forth a heroic effort against a superior team running out of an offense they had never before opposed. Allison's strategy was to nail the quarterback before he could begin his legerdemain. It worked in a scoreless first quarter, but the Wow Boys scored twice in the second, on short runs by Kmetovic and Gallarneau after impressive drives, the first featuring a 20-yard dash by Kmetovic. The Bears were playing without Reinhard, who was in Cowell Hospital with the flu, and Jurkovich, who was injured five minutes into the game and did not return. They finally scored in the fourth quarter when fullback Jack McQuary went in from the ten, a touchdown set up by Hatcher's fine 34-yard run. The 13–7 loss might have rated as a moral victory had it not been in a Big Game.

In the Rose Bowl, Shaughnessy's team completed its undefeated, untied season with a 21–13 win over Nebraska. Three weeks earlier, another T-team, the Chicago Bears, crushed the Washington Redskins, 73–0, in the National Football League championship game. It was clear that this reinvented old formation represented football's future, and within the decade nearly 75 percent of college teams had dropped their old ways and joined what was now being called the "T-party."

Allison's Bears were not among that number. They had lost their final game of 1940 to Georgia Tech, 13–0, but looked forward to the new season, confident that the speedy Jurkovich was the player who would lead them out of the football wilderness. Besides, these Bears gave new meaning to the age-old practice of likening a sports team to a family, as in "we're like brothers out there" or "we're a real family." Well, the 1941 Bears were in large part an actual family. Bob Reinhard's younger brother, Billy, played left half; George and Jack Herrero were star linemen and so were the twins, Stan and Stu Cox. And assistant coach and Cal legend Walt Gordon had a son, Walt, Jr, playing halfback. In their opener, the Bear family downed St. Mary's, now coached by Norman "Red" Strader, by the encouraging score of 31–0. Jurkovich got one of the touchdowns on a 28-yard scamper. But in a 13–6 loss to Washington State the following week, "Joltin' Jim" was K.O.'d with a head injury so severe he was advised by doctors to give up the game. His replacement as game-breaker was a dimpled, myopic 165-pounder, Al Derian, who had been a star at San Francisco's Polytechnic High but had seen relatively little action on the Cal varsity.

The Bears promptly lost their next two games, to Santa Clara, 13–0, and Oregon, 17–9. But they beat USC, 14–0, on touchdown runs by Derian and another tailback, Hank Zacharias, and UCLA, 27–7. It was against the Bruins in the Coliseum that Derian emerged as a legitimate star. UCLA was among the first teams to make the shift to the T, although coach Babe Horell, the former Cal All American, had his own version of it, the "QT" which used a wingback rather than Shaughnessy's man-in-motion, And in quarterback Bob Waterfield, Horrell had his Frankie Albert, though one with a stronger arm. But this was a transitional season for Babe and the Bruins, and they were vulnerable, particularly, as it turns out, to Derian. The small, not especially fast Bear halfback scored three touchdowns that day, one on a 51-yard return of an intercepted Waterfield pass. In defeat, future NFL Hall of Famer Waterfield completed 13 of 28 passes for 240 yards and his team's only touchdown. Four years later, he would lead the then Cleveland Rams to the NFL championship.

The Bears lost their next two games to Washington and Oregon State and were a sorry 3-5 entering the Big Game. Stanford, minus the graduated Gallarneau and Standlee and with Kmetovic playing hurt much of the season, were 6-2, following unexpected losses to Oregon State, 10–0, and Washington State, 14–13. Still, if Oregon could upset Oregon State that day, the Indians had a shot at a second straight Rose Bowl appearance. Albert, now a two-time All American, was still running the deceptive offense with consummate skill and decisiveness. Stub once again focused his defense on getting to the quarterback quickly. On offense, he hoped Derian might gain yards behind the crisp blocking of Reinhard and a bigger (200-pound average) line.

The opening kickoff by Cal center Brunel Christensen reached the end zone, so Stanford started on its own 20. When the first two running plays gained only two yards, Albert decided to punt on third down. But the ball slithered off the side of his foot after a heavy rush and bounced out of bounds on his own 46. Derian took the snap on Cal's first play from scrimmage near the east sidelines and started as if to circle his own left end. Then, behind McQuary, he cut back sharply and with blocks by Christensen, tackle Stan Cox and Reinhard, reached the sidelines virtually untouched. From there, he raced straight forward to the goal line. Only Stanford halfback Eric Armstrong had an unimpeded chance to stop him. He dived headlong at the fleeing Bear, getting a hand on one foot and tipping him off balance. But Derian tumbled into the end zone for a Cal touchdown, barely a minute-and-a-half into the game. With Joe Merlo's conversion, the Bears led 7–0.

They played a wicked and productive defense thereafter, tossing Albert for 62 yards in losses and applying such maddening pressure that he completed only four of 16 passes for 45 yards. The defense also accounted for the rest of the scoring, all in the fourth quarter. Cal guard Jean Witter first blocked an Albert punt out of the end zone for a safety, and then fellow guard Jack Herrero blocked sub quarterback Al Cole's punt, the ball popping straight into the arms of Reinhard in the Stanford end zone. It was the All American's second touchdown of the year, he having scored earlier against Washington on a tackle-eligible pass play. Altogether, the Bears blocked three punts and induced four fumbles—in the 16–0 win. A distraught Albert apologized afterward to his teammates for his play in this, his final college game.

For the Bears and their coach this was a grand victory, one of the biggest upsets in Big Game history. And in Berkeley there were parties, impromptu parades and illegal bonfires. The celebration lasted through the night. But this was a year darkened by a lengthening shadow. At its start, Pulitzer Prize winning author John Steinbeck wrote to a friend wondering "if any year had less of a chance of being happy."

And on December 7, 1941, just eight days after the Big Game, Japanese aircraft bombed the U.S. Naval Base at Pearl Harbor in Hawaii. President Roosevelt called it "a date which will live in infamy." World War II had come to America.

CHAPTER THIRTEEN

# THE STORM

The war changed just about everything on the Berkeley campus, even, if only fleetingly, Stub Allison's Rosetta Stone of a playbook.

Male students—a declining number in the war years—were either called to military duty or assigned to training units on campus, the most significant of which was the Navy V-12 officers program. Most fraternity houses, Bowles Hall (the largest men's residence building) and even the International House were occupied by military and naval personnel. And with the men in training, campus activities, including student government and ASUC publications, were almost run entirely by women. In 1943, Natalie Burdick became the first woman ever elected president of the ASUC. She presided over an Executive Committee consisting of thirteen women and three men. Both the Daily Californian newspaper and the *Blue and Gold* yearbook were edited by women. "The campus," the yearbook observed, had become "a women's world...They step in and fill the shoes of departing men and they reveal a wealth of undiscovered ability."

An accelerated three-semester, six-days-a-week academic schedule was introduced in 1942 which allowed students to graduate inside three years instead of four. At commencement exercises it was not at all unusual for a male student to receive his diploma and his military commission at the same time. In addition to students, many prominent faculty members and administrators were called to duty, including Dean of Undergraduates Hurford E. Stone, head track coach Brutus Hamilton and football assistant coach Frank Wickhorst.

The war effectively curtailed the social life that flourished on campus in the rollicking years immediately preceding the attack on Pearl Harbor. Only twelve of thirty-two fraternities remained open, and students in military and naval training programs scarcely had the leisure for the sort of around-the-clock revelry that prevailed at the peak of the Swing Era.

Classroom attendance was compulsory for trainees, many of whom carried as many as twenty academic units, five or six more than the peacetime norm, in the speeded-up semesters. Blackouts eliminated many of the traditional dances and parties on campus and gas rationing discouraged weekend excursions, Saturday night drives across the Bay and even romantic spins up Grizzly Peak boulevard. "It wasn't a particularly good time for women students," recalled Harry Agler, an end on Stub's football team awaiting, as were the majority of his teammates, the inevitable call to active duty.

And yet, in all likelihood, there probably wouldn't have been football at Cal, or at many other colleges and universities, had it not been for the Navy's sports-oriented training programs. This was especially true of the V-12, which at one time enrolled nearly two thousand men at Berkeley and was run from Naval headquarters in Washington by Captain Tom Hamilton, another former Navy All American who would later become executive director of the Pacific-8 Conference, and Cal's own Wickhorst. Many schools lacking such units, notably Stanford and Santa Clara on the west coast, were forced to abandon the sport for the duration of the war. Cal soldiered on, its wartime teams populated almost exclusively with Navy trainees, among them paradoxically, seven future lettermen at Stanford.

The best football played then, though, was by teams representing the various service bases around the country. The Bay Area was particularly favored with an abundance of these, their rosters stocked with former college and professional stars. With the shortage of available collegiate competition and with wartime travel restrictions, it was Cal's good fortune—or cruel fate—to play what were essentially all-star squads from such now forgotten bases as the pre-flight schools at St. Mary's College and Del Monte, the debarkation site at the so-called Fleet City in southern Alameda county and the Coast Guard station in Alameda.

Cal's 1942 team, which finished a comparatively successful 5-5, was its wartime best. Jurkovich was medically cleared to play his senior season, although for much of the time he was obliged to wear an exaggerated chin guard to protect him from the knockout blows he'd suffered too often in the past. The press joshingly referred to him as "The man in the Iron Mask," taking inspiration from the Dumas character portrayed in a movie of the time by the dashing British actor, Louis Hayward. Jurkovich was in good company on the screen as well as on the gridiron since the Heisman Trophy winner that season, Georgia's Frankie Sinkwich, had sported a similar protective apparatus.

"Joltin' Jim"—or, more properly, "Jolted Jim"—was joined in Stub's backfield by another trackman, Grover Klemmer, then the world record holder in both the 400 meters (46 flat) and the 440-yard dash (46.4). Klemmer, who had also lettered in basketball, saw limited action in his only year of varsity football, but he sent a shudder through defenders every time he touched the ball. Oddly enough, in his best game, an upset win over St. Mary's Pre-Flight, it was his passing, not his running that sparkled. His 17-yard touchdown heave to halfback Billy Reinhard was the winning score in a 12–6 victory over a service team that featured Bay Area football legends Bobby Grayson, Vic Bottari and Frankie Albert.

The Bears, deep then at most positions, were helped immeasurably by wartime rules that allowed free substitution and made freshmen eligible. But it was Jurkovich's team, and his consistent play kept the Bears from enduring a fourth straight losing season. He scored the only touchdown in the team's opener with St. Mary's, the deciding score against Oregon and both TDs in a surprisingly close 13–0 win over Montana. But losses to Oregon State, Santa Clara (in its last season until war's end), both UCLA and USC and finally to Stanford, reduced this once promising season to another exercise in mediocrity.

The lopsided 26–7 Big Game loss was particularly painful. Shaughnessy, the T-genius, had resigned after the '41 season, believing correctly that Stanford was about to discontinue football for the duration. But the school decided to play one more season and hired Shaughnessy assistant and former Notre Dame All American halfback Marchie Schwartz to replace his boss. Schwartz's Indians were led that year by All American guard Chuck Taylor, quarterback Ray "Duke" Hammett, fullback Randall "Buck" Fawcett and speedy halfback Don Zappetini. But they were only 4-4 before meeting Cal, losing their first three games before righting themselves in mid-season with a 14-6 upset over USC at a neutral site, San Francisco's Kezar Stadium. And they effectively demolished the Bears, piling up a 26–0 lead before the home team scored late in the final quarter on a three-yard plunge by halfback Gene Pickett, whose two pass completions in a row got the ball that far.

And that was it for football at Stanford for the war years. Cal had been humiliated by a team giving up the game. Significantly, only fifty-five thousand showed up at Memorial Stadium for this farewell Big Game. The Bears also lost their most faithful supporter that year when Clinton R. "Brick" Morse, the "eternal sophomore," died. Morse, who delighted in depicting himself as "the red-headed kid who crashed the gate to watch Cal games in the early 1880s," had played halfback in the first Big Game in 1892, had written a history of Cal football in 1924 (updated in '37), had been director of the university's Glee Club for thirty-three years and composed two of the school's most rousing songs, "Sons of California" and "Hail to California."

By now, there were rumblings of discontent among Bear alums not as immutably steadfast as the departed Brick. Stub hadn't had a winning season since 1938 and had been under continuing fire for his stubborn allegiance to a formation, the single wing, that, though dominant only a few years before, was by 1942 considered, with the advent of the T, about as au courant as the Bowler hat. His Bears, save for a few isolated outbursts, were not much fun to watch, win or lose.

Fans depended on opposition stars for the glamorous long-gainers, and in the 1943 opening game against St. Mary's, a team composed of under-draft-age freshmen and military rejects, they were amply rewarded. The Bears actually won the game, 27–12, but that was not the story; a spectacular Gael freshman was. Indeed, the star of that day— and for many days thereafter—was an astonishingly versatile tailback from Hawaii with the seemingly incongruous name for a Polynesian of Herman Wedemeyer (his paternal forebears were German seamen).

In the second quarter, "Squirmin" Herman" stood on his own 30 waiting to receive a Cal punt. Surprisingly, he allowed the ball to drop untouched. It rolled to the Gael 24, Wedemeyer jogging casually in its wake. Then, as Cal defenders prepared to touch the ball dead, Wedemeyer snatched it from them and sped back upfield toward the Cal goal, leaving discombobulated pursuers sprawling on the turf. Finally, he appeared to be trapped on the sidelines at the Cal 25, but with what seemed to be a single gesture, he lateraled to teammate John Ryan and took out Cal's Art Honegger with a perfect block, leaving the way clear for Ryan to score.

Even the most partisan Cal fans cheered that amazing play. But there was more. Just before the half, Wedey, as he was now being called, made a sensational one-handed interception of a Bill Joslyn pass on the Bear 45 and once again sped goalward. This time, hemmed in on the 30, he faked a lateral and slipped past his befuddled foes to the 16. And from there he tossed a touchdown pass to teammate Tom Pearson.

The next day's papers were so full of the "Hawaiian Hurricane"—"he won the hearts of every man, woman and child present"…"Not since Tom Harmon has Memorial Stadium seen anything like young Wedemeyer…"—that the winning team rated scarcely a mention.

The Bears broke even in their first four games, then faced the first of the region's great service teams, St. Mary's Pre-Flight, on October 23. It was a predictable mismatch. With the 1941 Heisman Trophy winner, Bruce Smith of Minnesota, scoring three times, the Navy team clobbered them, 39–0. Actually, by this time, Cal itself was a service team, since thirty of the forty-three players on the varsity were either Navy or Marine trainees. And shortly after the Pre-Flight game, four of them, including tailback Joslyn, were called to duty elsewhere.

The Bears played two more top service teams in '43, losing to the Alameda Coast Guard by a respectable 7–0 and then by an excusable 47–8 to a Del Monte Pre-Flight team powered by former Missouri All America quarterback Paul Christman and future San Francisco 49ers Len Eshmont and Parker Hall. Del Monte linemen outweighed Cal's by nearly 20 pounds per man and its roster contained both former college stars and players, like Hall, with professional football experience. So there was no disgrace in losing to such foes. Of the Bears' six losses that season, half, in fact, were to service teams. In intercollegiate play, Southern Cal beat them twice in a home-and-away series prompted by travel restrictions and the College of the Pacific, another school benefitting from Navy trainees, edged past them, 12–6. This was a year when the now eighty-one-year-old COP coach, Amos Alonzo Stagg, was named college football's Coach of the Year. The '43 Bears did beat UCLA twice and, in the first game ever between the two schools, the University of San Francisco.

When it is taken into account that, because of military transfers, Stub scarcely knew who was available to play from week-to-week, he did a fine job of coaching that unsettled season. But this was his fifth straight year without a winner, and fans and alums, war or no, were growing restless. Then in 1944, Old Sarge did the unthinkable: he experimented with that new-fangled T-Formation. For a coach so beholden to off-tackle power plays, this represented an ideological shift comparable at the time to Norman Thomas running for president on the Republican ticket.

Stub's grudging concession to the twentieth century did little, however, to change the end result: another losing season, and, at 3-6-1, one worse than the last. Again, three of those losses were to service teams. In other games, the Bears split with UCLA, tied USC in Los Angeles, then lost at home to the despised Trojans by 32–0. They lost to Washington, 33–7, but beat both Pacific and St. Mary's, the Gaels playing without Wedemeyer that season while he was serving in the Merchant Marine.

If there was a high to this otherwise down year, it was in the sometimes spectacular play of halfback Joe Stuart, another in the Bears' long line of bantam scatbacks dating to Kangaroo Kaarsberg and Bobby Sherman and including Tut Imlay, Hank Schaldach and Al Derian. "Little Joe"—he was 5-8, 160 pounds— had touchdown runs of 37 yards against Pacific and an 87-yarder against the Coast Guard that then ranked as the longest from scrimmage by a Cal player since Heine Heitmuller went 90 on a tackle-back play against the Perris Indians in 1902. And in the season's finale, against St. Mary's Pre-Flight, Stuart returned an interception 45 yards for Cal's only score in a 33–6 defeat.

But Little Joe's gallant play could not compensate for the losses, six of them in a row from mid-season to the end. By this time, Stub's post-game balcony addresses were about as well-received as Benito Mussolini's. And so, after that final game loss, he, too, was deposed. Stub had been a full ten years on the job, equaling Andy Smith's record for longevity, and finishing a winner overall at 58-42-2. But he was a mere 23-35-1 in those dreary final six years. It can be said on his behalf, though, that in this last season, he lost sixteen players from his roster to military callups or V-12 transfers. Coaching college football in wartime was a thankless job. But Cal wanted somebody to try it who had closer ties to modern methodology.

The selection of Stub's successor was as inspired as it was unconventional. Lawrence T. "Buck" Shaw had played tackle for Knute Rockne at Notre Dame and had afterward become a highly original and successful coach. Called "the Silver Fox" as much for his tactical cunning as for his prematurely gray hair, he had taken Santa Clara to Sugar Bowl championships in 1937 and '38 and in seven years there had built an impressive 47-10-4 record. But the Broncos, like Stanford, had dropped football after the 1942 season, and Shaw, like Shaughnessy, had resigned. In the interim, he had signed a contract, effective at war's end, to coach a new team, the 49ers, in a new professional league, the All America Football Conference.

The war ended less than a month before the start of the 1945 season, and the new league scheduled its grand opening for '46. Shaw was available until then and anxious to try out some new schemes—the T-formation among them— he planned to use as a pro. The ASUC, grateful for the chance, signed him to a one-year contract, to expire as soon as his new job opened. It was hoped that in this admittedly brief period, the Silver Fox could at the very least get Cal football moving in the right direction. The press, in response to this possibly screwy one-season deal, called Shaw the "lend-lease coach," drawing inspiration from the contract FDR and Churchill negotiated in 1941 for the loan of U.S. warships to Britain.

Shaw would become the first Notre Dame graduate and Rockne disciple to coach a Cal football team. And his task was even more complicated than Stub's had been because, with men still being called to duty and others returning from the war, he literally had players coming and going. Quarterback Billy Agnew, like Stuart a onetime Piedmont High star, showed up, for example, in time for the Bears' third game of the season, against Washington. As an Army Air Corps pilot, Agnew had been shot down over Europe and locked up in a German Prisoner of War camp. After experiences such as these, playing football again was a day at the beach, and in his very first game, Agnew connected with Stuart on a 37-yard touchdown pass. Stuart, enjoying another fine season, also reeled off a 61-yard TD run that day as the Bears swept past the Huskies, 27–4.

Shaw did get the most out of his peripatetic players, and in casting aside Allison's drab uniforms, he had them looking particularly snappy in pro-style dark blue jerseys and socks and bright gold pants and helmets. But the Bay Area's favorite team in '45 was at St. Mary's, which, with Wedemeyer back and supported by the pass-and-lateral-happy "Whiz Kids," knocked off both Cal and USC and made it all the way to the Sugar Bowl.

Though the war was over, this was not really a peacetime season. The troops were coming home, but slowly; rationing had ended, but goods were still scarce and veterans and civilians alike were uncertain what lay ahead in an as yet mysterious new world. At the time of V.J. (Victory in Japan) Day, the U.S. had 12 million men and women in military service, seven million of them in foreign countries or at sea. Demobilizing such a mighty force would be as challenging as assembling it had been. And many veterans would return not entirely whole in body and spirit. Cal's provost Monroe E. Deutsch took pains to remind younger students that some of these vets reentering or just entering school with aid from the G.I. Bill of Rights would bear "incapacitating wounds."

Some 2.3 million vets eventually enrolled in the nation's colleges and universities under the G.I. Bill between 1945 and '50, swelling campus enrollment to the breaking point and creating unprecedented access to higher education for many who might otherwise not have considered advancing past high school. In 1939-40, for example, U.S. colleges and universities graduated 216,521 men and women; in 1949-50 that figure rose to 496,661. The Berkeley campus certainly reflected these dramatic fluctuations. From a pre-war high of 16,904 undergraduate and graduate students in the 1938-39 academic year, enrollment declined during the war to a low of 9,928 in 1944-45. But by 1946-47, the student population had more than doubled, reaching a then record high of 22,130. And 10,985 of those students were returning veterans.

Football returnees would bring maturity, experience and increased size to their teams. And though 1945 was essentially a wartime season played in peacetime, excitement-starved fans flocked to the games. Cal's attendance increased from a home-game average of thirty-one thousand per game in '44 to nearly forty thousand in '45. The real post-war attendance boom, though, was still a year or two distant. But, Shaw's Bears were fun to watch. Although they finished only 4-5-1, they were in the running in most every game and closed out the season with a pair of shutout wins over UCLA and a peace-weakened St. Mary's Pre-Flight.

The UCLA game on November 24, 1945, played before twenty-five thousand rain-soaked Memorial Stadium partisans, merits special notice since it helped perpetuate Cal's richly deserved reputation for oddball football. The weird play in this game may not have had the lasting impact of Roy Riegels' Wrong Way Run, but unlike that classic of the genre, it did win the game for the Bears. It went this way, sort of:

In the middle of the third quarter of an as yet scoreless battle, Cal's Jack Lerond, a splendid multi-sport athlete and Navy trainee, went back to punt from his own 34-yard line. Rain had transformed the verdant gridiron into a murky sea. Lerond momentarily bobbled the snap from center, a forgivable transgression on such a day, and barely got his kick away. In fact, according to some accounts, hard charging Bruin tackle Don Malmberg got a muddy hand on the ball. Blocked or botched, the punt dribbled off to one side and a few yards backward.

Cal quarterback Ed Welch, who had been blocking for Lerond, retrieved the loose ball on or about the Cal 30 and headed upfield through the surf, abetted by several key blocks, one of them by Lerond. Welch was finally trapped on the Bruin 40. Then, taking a page from the Whiz Kid playbook, he tossed a lateral to a trailing teammate...who just happened to be Jack Lerond. And Lerond completed the 70-plus-yard play by slogging the final 40 for the game's only score. This may have been the only occasion in football history when a punter scored the game-winning touchdown on a kick he either missed or had partially blocked. Actually, it was just football as usual at Cal.

It was time again, though, to look for a new coach, Shaw having moved happily across the Bay. The deliberations continued for two full months even though the final choice had been on campus for nearly a dozen years. Frank Wickhorst had come to Berkeley in 1931 as Bill Ingram's line coach. When Navy Bill departed after the '34 season, Wickhorst stayed on as an assistant to Allison until he was called to active duty as a Navy reserve officer in April of 1941. Even so, he remained at Cal as an instructor in the campus NROTC unit. He continued to coach Stub's line that year. Then, in January of 1942, he was reassigned to Navy headquarters in Washington D.C. where he and Captain Tom Hamilton were placed in charge of training at pre-flight schools across the country. In December of 1944, his request for combat duty was granted and he was assigned to the aircraft carrier USS Siboney. Holding the rank of Commander, he was aboard the ship in Tokyo harbor when in November of 1945 his discharge orders were issued.

Wickhorst had never been a head coach, but his credentials for the job seemed substantial. He had played freshman football at Illinois with Red Grange before his appointment to the Naval Academy. In 1926, with Ingram as his coach, he earned All America recognition as a tackle for the Midshipmen. An eye injury he suffered playing football exempted him from active duty, so he went into coaching, first at Iowa in 1927 and then four years later at Cal.

Under both Navy Bill and Stub, he'd done a commendable job, coaching such All America Cal linemen as Larry Lutz, Bob Herwig, Vard Stockton, Perry Schwartz and Bob Reinhard. After signing a three-year contract to replace Shaw, Wickhorst hired as his assistants some more well-known Cal football figures, including Irv Uteritz, the Bear backfield coach since 1935; Lutz, Vic Bottari, Nibs Price and former V-12 instructor Zeb Chaney.

With his fifteen years of coaching experience and wartime duty as a high-ranking Naval officer, Wickhorst, the ASUC assumed, would command the respect of a team composed principally of returning vets. Sadly for him, precisely the opposite was true. Rather than knuckle under to yet another authority figure, the veterans resented Wickhorst's military demeanor, a character trait—or defect—they'd had quite enough of during the war. These, after all, were older players not easily intimidated by harsh discipline. Thirty of the forty-five players on the 1946 varsity were over twenty-one, five were over twenty-five and center Jack Suseof was a twenty-eight-year-old junior. And Commander Wickhorst was not much good at reaching out to those beneath him. "He didn't meet people easily back then," recalled quarterback Dick Erickson. "He was not at all what you might call gregarious."

Contrary to what might ordinarily be expected of a Navy Commander, Wickhorst was hardly the organizational mastermind required to bring order out of the chaos brought on by a massive fall football turnout of two hundred thirty bodies. And he was sometimes painfully slow in recognizing unexplored talent. In fact, this was a team fairly brimming with future stars. A freshman guard (freshmen were still eligible that season under wartime rules) named Rod Franz would become Cal's only three-time All American. Tackle Jim Turner, who had played under Stagg at Pacific, would also become an All American. Power runner Jack Swaner and guard Jon Baker would soon be All Coast, and Baker would subsequently have a fine career with the NFL New York Giants.

There was one other player on that roster whose skills were so transcendent that not even Wickhorst and his less than observant assistants could lose in the shuffle. In fact, the very first time Jackie Jensen touched the ball in a Cal uniform, he returned a Wisconsin punt for a 56-yard touchdown in the season's opening game. And this was no ordinary run. At least five Wisconsin tacklers had a clear shot at him before falling by the wayside as Jensen whirled and danced gracefully upfield. Since at that point, Cal players on the overpopulated bench scarcely had had time to get acquainted, Jensen's spectacular dash surprised them almost as much as it had the visiting Badgers. As Jensen's teammate and boyhood friend, Charles "Boots" Erb (son of Wonder Team Charlie) recalled, "The rest of us just stood there on the sidelines with our mouths open. Jack was all over the field, dodging and leaping over guys. Finally, somebody on the sidelines yelled, 'Who the hell is that guy?'"

Jensen's mad scramble was the Bears' only score in a 28–7 opening day defeat, a game during which Wickhorst used forty-six players in a largely futile attempt to find out who was who. Against Oregon the next week, Jensen, playing left half in Wickhorst's version of the T, jump-passed 47 yards to Herb Poddig in the end zone in a 14–13 loss. Against UCLA, in a 13–6 defeat, he tossed a 15-yard touchdown pass to John Cunningham. Against Washington, he took a flat pass at the line of scrimmage from Erickson and scampered 58 yards for a TD; the Bears lost 20–6. Against Washington State, he ran 56 yards to a touchdown in a rare 47–14 Bear win.

Jensen had even more deceptive moves than Cal's legendary scatbacks—he was a master of the head and shoulder fake as well as the sharp cut at full-speed. But he was much more than a breakaway runner. As a robust 190-pounder he was capable of running through those tacklers he could not elude. A classic single-wing tailback from nearby Oakland High School, he was in Cal's T, the long passer (his rushing stats would always be skewed by sacks), the punter and punt returner as well as a top defensive back. He'd come to Cal after one year in the Navy, and at nineteen was one of only five teenagers on the '46 team. And with three touchdown runs of better than 55 yards and two

TD passes, he was clearly its star. But this was, for him, merely the beginning.

The Bears won only two games that year—over St. Mary's and Washington State—and lost seven. It was the worst record in modern Cal football history. By the time of the Big Game renewal, Wickhorst had lost all control of his players, many of whom were in open revolt against him. Stanford, of course, hadn't even played football in three years, and the feeling was that if the Bears couldn't beat these game-rusty Indians, they'd sunk to a new low. And they couldn't beat them. The Indians, again coached by Marchie Schwartz, scored seemingly at will, racking up a 19–0 halftime lead and then tacking on another score in the final quarter on a 17-yard run by a halfback, Bob Anderson, whose real sport was swimming. The Bears didn't score until the game's final minutes when Swaner, after carrying nine times in a 60-yard drive, plunged in from the three.

Like the players, Cal's post-war student rooters were also on average older than their pre-war counterparts. In the white-shirted all-male central rooting section at the stadium, returning vets set the mood. And with all the losses, it was a querulous mood at best. Fueled by what eventually became known as "Jackie Jensen Orange Juice"— vodka and orange crush—these rooters often punctuated their cheers with language not ordinarily associated with rah-rahism. If an official penalized the Bears, the rooters might count out the yards as he marched them off and then bellow en masse, "You Bastard!" And the balloons seen soaring above their section were more often than not inflated birth control devices.

Rooters such as these were not likely to accept with equanimity a Big Game loss as humiliating as that of '46, and as alums looked on in shock, they began dismantling the seats in their section after the game and passing them down to the field, there to serve, at least metaphorically, as planks for Commander Wickhorst to walk.

Still, the coach's most relentless detractors were his own players.

A petition drawn up by Welch and star halfback Ted Kenfield calling for Wickhorst's dismissal was signed by forty-two of forty-four varsity players. Welch at the time was student body president, a position of unusual authority since the ASUC governed all extra-curricular activities on campus, including athletics. The ASUC, founded in 1887, had been granted such extraordinary authority by President Wheeler as early as 1904. The student governing body did have on staff graduate managers to render counsel and a graduate "general manager" to watch over finances and make recommendations on coaching hires, but final decisions were rendered by the ASUC's "Executive Committee." At no other major university then could undergraduates fire a football coach.

But Cal's finally did just that. In the past, condemned coaches Price, Ingram and Allison all resigned before the axe could fall. But Wickhorst was convinced that with only one year of admittedly inferior football under his belt, he'd not been given a proper chance to set matters straight. Complaints from his players, however, were devastating. As halfback Bob Dal Porto, a Marine veteran and himself an elected ASUC Representative at Large, testified at a meeting of the Executive Committee just four days after the Big Game fiasco:

"The past season has served to bring the athletic situation at the university to a head. The men on the football team lack confidence in the coach. By being pushed around by the coaches, the team lost confidence in themselves, and the whole situation caused disruption and disunity all season."

The players, said Dal Porto, want the coaching staff and "the entire athletic management staff removed from office." A petition calling for Wickhorst's ousting was also submitted to the committee. Circulated by the Big C (lettermen) Society, it was signed by twenty-six hundred students. Clearly, Coach "Wick" was not the most popular man on campus. But the Ex-Com tabled a motion for his dismissal at both that November 27 meeting and again on December 6. Then on December 11, 1946, the motion passed by a vote of 7–1, the lone dissenter being a graduate manager just returned from the war, Dean of Students Hurford E. Stone. Gone with Wickhorst were his two top aides, Uteritz and Lutz. Spared were Price and Chaney, who also coached basketball. According to a settlement, the ASUC would buy out the remaining two years of Wickhorst's contract and pay him wages due. But the coach was hardly assuaged. In a prepared statement, he contended that "this was all instigated by a very few people and in some cases by ex-football players and certain Cal factions. Instead of looking to help the situation, they looked around for someone to blame—not themselves…I have not lost confidence in my coaching ability and feel that I can hold my own with the next man—all things being equal." Wickhorst would subsequently enjoy a long, uncontroversial and apparently enjoyable career with Kaiser Industries in Oakland. But the Cal business still stuck in his craw.

And it had repercussions within and well beyond the campus. The national press took pleasure in describing Cal as a place where the inmates ran the asylum. What reasonably sane football coach, columnists asked, would consider working at the pleasure of a bunch of kids? Cal had proved itself to be a "coaches' graveyard." In retrospect, even Executive Committee participants in Wickhorst's cashiering expressed embarrassment. "There's no question I felt uncomfortable about the whole thing," recalled Jane Baker Lotter more than sixty years later. "Here we were, a bunch of students meeting to fire a grown man… someone like my own father."

President Sproul was noticeably displeased at the time. He'd known early in the season that trouble was brewing on the football team. His athletic adviser, Robert "Skinny" Johnson, had reported to him that the players were questioning the coaching staff's ability "to teach them the T-Formation." Sproul was also determined that firing a "grown man" would never again be left to the students. He assigned Brutus Hamilton, the dean of men and head track coach newly returned from duty as an Army Air Corps intelligence officer, to find a new coach. And after Hamilton did just that, the president presided over a restructuring of the ASUC into divisions of "general activities" and "intercollegiate athletics." And in May of 1947, Hamilton was appointed the first ever Cal administrator to hold the title of Athletic Director and given the authority to hire and fire coaches.

Hamilton was the perfect man for the job—or, for that matter, any job. As much a philosopher as a coach or administrator, he was blessed with a keen understanding of his fellow man and a droll sense of humor. Deploring the new technology in coaching, he said, "One can't slide rule anything so complicated as a human being." Serving in North Africa during the war, he wrote home, "I must tell you about a brave little songbird we have here. He sings gloriously just at daybreak and for the thirty minutes that follow. Then he finds a cool spot and is heard no more until the next morning. Maybe he figures he's done his day's work pulling the sun up from India. Or maybe he's seen too much of what man has done to man on these battlefields and hides his face the rest of the day."

A native midwesterner and a graduate of the University of Missouri, Hamilton had been at Cal, save for his military service, since 1932 when he was first hired as the track coach. He had won a Silver Medal himself in the decathlon at the 1920 Olympic Games in Antwerp.

Hamilton first offered the Cal football job to his friend Fritz Crisler, then at Michigan. Crisler quickly rejected it, citing Cal's recent history of losing, its bickering alumni and mutinous players. Then at a meeting in January of 1947 of the American Football Coaches Association in New York, he encountered another old friend from their days together on the athletic staff at the University of Kansas. In the years since then, Lynn O. "Pappy" Waldorf had done wonders coaching football since 1935 at Northwestern, a university like Cal, imposing lofty academic standards while participating in a tough football conference.

In the course of their reminiscing together, Hamilton asked

Waldorf if he might, by any chance, be interested in the Cal job. Somewhat to his surprise, Waldorf said that, yes, he would. He had grown fond of the Bay Area while assisting at the East-West Shrine Games in San Francisco and he had long held the theory that ten years was long enough on one job for any football coach. Waldorf also understood the problems at Cal, theorizing that since returning veterans "have been through a lot of stress and regimentation," coaches needed to exercise greater tolerance and understanding of their needs. And above all, he regarded Hamilton, his future boss, as "one of the finest gentlemen who ever lived."

On February 14, 1947, Waldorf accepted a contract calling for an annual salary of $13,500 and giving him the authority to hire his own assistants. He arrived by train later that month, having been excused from the two years remaining on his Northwestern contract. He was met at the Oakland station by Hamilton, ASUC sports publicity director Norrie West, star player Rod Franz and an assortment of local sportswriters.

That night at a meeting with the press in the Claremont Hotel, the new coach confidently asserted that he had come west "to awaken a sleeping giant."

PART III

1947-1957

## CHAPTER FOURTEEN

# PAPPY

Waldorf's hiring was received by the local press with a skepticism born of eight long seasons of futility and the gathering sense that football at Cal might just be a hopeless proposition. Prescott Sullivan, the *Examiner*'s waggish sports columnist, expressed it best:

"Big, meaty Lynn O. "Pappy" Waldorf is the new coach at the University of California. We realize there is nothing particularly distinctive about that. California's always getting a new football coach. Waldorf is the fourth the school has had in as many years. We hope Waldorf is a man of independent means. The job over there in Berkeley ain't too steady."

But among the new coach's myriad attributes was a talent for charming reporters. Unlike the aloof Wickhorst and the grumpy Stub, Waldorf enjoyed their company. He hosted cocktail parties for beat writers in his hotel room on road trips and even invited them to his home. He was a gifted storyteller with a self-deprecating wit. An avid collector of limericks, both naughty and nice, he would gleefully recite them by the hour while puffing a cigar and sipping a hearty glass of fine bourbon whiskey. The most erudite of all Cal Football coaches to date, he was as conversant with the works of Plato and Shakespeare as with those of Stagg and Yost. A lifelong reader of history, he was such an expert on the American Civil War that at Northwestern he was sought out by Carl Sandburg for consultation on the concluding chapters of the Chicago poet's epic biography of Abraham Lincoln.

As Paul Christopulos, then an aide to Hamilton in the athletic department, recalled: "I had majored in history at Cal and taken an M.A. in International Business at the School of Advanced International Studies at Johns Hopkins. And yet I learned more history from Pappy than in all those courses put together."

Columnist Sullivan soon dropped the "big and meaty" references, though Waldorf was well over 250 pounds, and began calling him somewhat more congenially, the "Wise Walrus."

Waldorf turned forty-five his first season at Cal, but because of his considerable girth and prematurely graying hair, he looked older. The son of a Methodist minister, he was born in Clifton Springs, New York, but grew up in Cleveland and was graduated from East High School there. He entered Syracuse University in 1920 and tried out for both football and crew, but he soon grew too ponderous to fit comfortably in a shell, so he gave up rowing. He excelled, however, on the gridiron, twice making Walter Camp's All America team as a tackle.

He majored in philosophy at Syracuse with a minor in sociology, and by his own admission entertained no ambition to become a football coach. But in August of 1925, he'd married Louise Jane McKay, whom he'd met on campus, and he needed a job. He found one through his father's church connections at a small Methodist school, Oklahoma City University, that needed a football coach. "I didn't know what I was getting into," he recalled years later. "I became a head coach because I had to."

His team was called the "Goldbugs," and at his first practice a grand total of fourteen candidates turned out. His line averaged 158 pounds, his backs 163. But he finished that 1925 season with a 4-6 record, the best in Goldbug history. Two years later, he won the conference championship. In 1928, he left Oklahoma City to become an assistant at the University of Kansas, the only season in his career when he was not a head coach. In 1929, he became the head man at Oklahoma A&M (now Oklahoma State) and in five seasons there won four Missouri Valley Conference championships.

In 1934, he moved to Kansas State, where he employed Wes "Plowboy" Fry, a onetime All America halfback at Iowa, as his chief assistant. In his only season there, Waldorf coached his team to its first ever Big Six Conference title.

Then in 1935, he became head coach at Northwestern, which was not so coincidentally yet another Methodist school with ties to his father, then a trustee there and a church bishop. The young coach knew he faced a severe challenge at a university with demanding academic standards belonging to a league, the Big Ten, that regarded football with a fervor bordering on the evangelical. Along his career path, though, Waldorf had received some valuable counsel from two coaching legends. Stagg had told him, "Your players are your pupils, with more interest in your subject than any of their other classes. For that reason, you should be the best teacher in school." And Bob Zupke advised him that when stuck with just a fair team, as Northwestern's seemed to be, look for somebody big to beat. Upsets, he said, can build a reputation.

Waldorf in '35 picked one of the best as his target: the then unbeaten Fighting Irish of Notre Dame, coached by one of the school's famous Four Horsemen of the 1920s, Elmer Layden. Notre Dame's star that season was a halfback with an even more famous name—William Shakespeare, called, as perhaps his forebear was, "Bill." Waldorf's roster contained no one with quite that literary pedigree, but he did have an end with bad hands named Henry Wadsworth Longfellow. And on a rainy November 9, 1935 game at Notre Dame Stadium, Longfellow somehow caught a touchdown pass and recovered a key fumble, thereby getting the better of Shakespeare in Northwestern's 14–7 win. Copy desk literati in newspapers across the land had a field day writing headlines heralding the triumph of "Hiawatha" over "Hamlet."

In 1936, his team scored another major upset by ending the Minnesota Golden Gophers' unbeaten streak at twenty-eight games and depriving them of their customary Big Ten title with a 6–0 win. The victory gave Northwestern the conference championship, but a season-ending 16–6 loss to the vengeful Fighting Irish dropped them to seventh place in the final Associated Press rankings. Despite its upset defeat, Minnesota finished number one.

In 1939, Fry joined the Northwestern staff after a stint as head coach at Kansas State. As what would now be called the offensive coordinator, he was no fan of the forward pass, preferring power football. But when in 1941, a sophomore tailback named Otto Graham joined the varsity, both he and Pappy swiftly adjusted their thinking, devising for this supremely talented player a pass-run option play from the single wing which, since Graham was also a fine runner, tended to immobilize defensive backs fearful of overcommitment. Against Michigan on October 17, 1942, Graham completed 20 of 29 passes for 295 yards and two touchdowns, 16 of those completions coming off the option.

During the war, Pappy and Fry regularly attended Chicago Bear games, studying the pro team's pioneering T-formation. In 1945, they developed their own variation of it, preserving the option play in the form of a pitchout to the fullback, presuming, of course, they could find one sufficiently talented to make it work. At Cal they did.

Pappy's T was still essentially a power formation retaining the crisp shoulder blocking of the single wing. And in 1946, he brought to Northwestern a superb teacher of line play in Bob Tessier, a former star player at Tulane, a decorated Navy officer and, like Fry, a law school graduate. Both Fry and Tessier joined Pappy at Cal, as did end coach Ed "Eggs" Manske, another Navy veteran, a former Chicago Bear receiver and an assistant to T-genius Shaughnessy at Maryland. Movie-star handsome, personable, opinionated, Manske drove with Fry from Chicago to Berkeley, arguing with mutual vigor the pros (Manske) and cons (Fry) of the pass attack. It was a debate that would continue unabated for six years.

At Cal, Pappy retained both Price and Chaney on his staff and hired Hal Grant, a longtime high school and small college coach and administrator. Grant would coach the freshman team, since in '47 frosh were no longer eligible for varsity play.

On the first day of spring practice that year, some 255 aspirants turned out for football, a horde that might well have overwhelmed a less organized staff. But Pappy and his assistants, their number augmented by seven graduate assistants, were well prepared. Players were given detailed practice schedules and steno pads for taking notes. Practices were conducted under tight time frames. There were no lulls in the daily routine, and even the lowliest candidates were kept active every minute on the field.

There was also ample opportunity for advancement, since the wartime free substitution rule was held over, allowing players with limited or specialized skills to seek their niches on offense or defense. And under the fiercely competitive thirty-one-year-old Chaney, the Ramblers were no longer disregarded as rejects on the "goof squad" but considered on-the-job trainees. Pappy also simplified the uniform numbering systems so that, pro-style, ends wore numbers in the 80s, tackles in the 70s, guards in the 60s, centers in the 50s and backs from one through the 40s.

Like the '46 team, only more so, Pappy's debut team was composed of decidedly older, larger and more experienced players than the comparatively callow youths of pre-war Cal squads. Forty-three '47 Bears were twenty-one or older, ten were over twenty-four and five had passed their twenty-fifth birthday. Fullback Johnny Graves, twenty-five; tackle Gene Frassetto, twenty-five; end Harry Agler, twenty-four, and center Harry Pieper, twenty-five, had all lettered at Cal as early as 1942. Graves, in fact, had played on the Stub Allison team that upset Stanford in 1941. Most of the older players had service football experience and at least four had lettered as military trainees at other colleges during the war—Jim Turner (COP), Dick Erickson (Michigan), Dal Porto (Colorado) and Paul Keckley (William Jewell College and Iowa State).

Seventeen players on the '47 team weighed more than 200 pounds and three—end John Cunningham and tackles Turner and John Najarian—came in at 230 or more. Only a few years before, when 198-pound college players were called "giants," behemoths such as these would have been considered freaks of nature. In the twenty-first century, of course, 230-pounders would be playing in the backfield.

Actually, Waldorf's starting offensive line for much of that season averaged a relatively modest 207 pounds, the backs 185. The average age was twenty-three.

The Cal press guide for the '47 season was as circumspect in its forecast as the press itself. Waldorf's team, the guide suggested, "expects to lose a game or two—possibly three or four—but they won't be trouncings."

In the opener against Santa Clara, the Bears did the trouncing, stunning an inquisitive crowd of forty-five thousand, with a 33–7 win. The tone was set on the first play from scrimmage when halfback George Fong ran 39 yards for a touchdown. Then after the Broncos countered with a score of their own, Cal's "new" quarterback sensation, Bob Celeri (he'd actually lettered as a seventeen-year-old in '44) passed 30 yards to end Dave Hirschler to put the Bears ahead to stay.

An all-time-high Memorial Stadium crowd of eighty-three thousand showed up for the next Saturday's intersectional game with Navy. It was the Midshipmen's first appearance on the West Coast since they'd played a 14–14 tie with Washington in the 1924 Rose Bowl, and they made a week-long celebration of it with parades, parties and ceremonies. Despite the Bears' impressive opener, Navy was favored, mainly on the basis of its heroic stand against an Army team led by the iconic Mr. Inside (Doc Blanchard) and Mr. Outside (Glenn Davis) in the final game of 1946. The Cadets finally won, 21–18, but the game ended with Navy on the Army three-yard-line. Navy was coached by Captain Tom Hamilton, Wickhorst's wartime boss, and its star was the All America center-linebacker Dick Scott.

But the Bears scored first, in the second quarter, when Celeri scrambled 22 yards on a busted pass play. The game evolved into a defensive struggle thereafter, neither team threatening until early in the fourth quarter. Cal had the ball then on its own 36-yard-line. It was third down after two Celeri incompletions. Jensen was in the game at fullback, a position equivalent then in the Waldorf-T to the single-wing tailback. At least it was when Jensen was in the game, for the blond sophomore from Oakland had all the tools to run the Waldorf option—a strong passing arm coupled with his extraordinary running ability. But he shared the position that year with the veteran Graves, who was no threat to pass. With Jensen in and Graves out, Navy logically looked for the option with Cal in a third-and-long situation.

Instead, Jensen shot through a hole in the middle of the line, feinted the great Scott into helpless immobility and sped 64 yards for what proved to be the winning touchdown. The midshipmen came back with a score later in the quarter and were threatening again after recovering an onside kick when Jensen on defense intercepted a pass from quarterback Reaves Baysinger, preserving the 14–7 victory. It was one of Jack's seven interceptions that season, tying the then Cal record.

Could these new Bears, many of them old Bears from the season before, be this good? Well, they walloped St. Mary's, 45–6, the next week, Celeri tossing 20-yard touchdown passes to Swaner and Kenfield and Graves scoring on runs of 19 and 66 yards. Then they beat Wisconsin in Madison, 48–7, with Jensen scoring one TD on a 22-yard run and passing 23 yards to Cunningham for another. Back home again, they beat Washington State, 21–6, the highlight of which was Cunningham's 82-yard touchdown return of a Cougar fumble.

The astonishing turnaround from '46 was by now attracting national regard. The Associated Press had the Bears ranked fourth in the

country, their highest since Thunder Team days. And now, they were
to play 11th-ranked USC for an assured trip to the Rose Bowl. The Trojans were also undefeated, a 7–7 tie with Rice, the only scratch on their
escutcheon. Coached by Jeff Cravath, they had convincingly beaten
Washington State (21–0), Ohio State (32–0) and Oregon State (48–6).

The game between these two contenders would be broadcast nationwide with the popular Red Barber in the radio booth. The Bears
got off to a grand start when Swaner swept end for 65 yards on the first
play from scrimmage. It was a play decided upon by vote of the players
themselves in the locker room before the start of the game. Cal scored
again in the second quarter after an 88-yard drive, Jensen dashing in
from the five.

From that point on, though, it was all USC, the most telling blow
a 95-yard return by Don Doll of the second half kickoff. Final score:
USC 39, Cal 14.

Pappy had kept alive the tradition of post-game balcony speeches,
and with his natural eloquence and a basso profundo voice that carried nearly as far as President Sproul's, he was better at it than any of
his predecessors. Until that Saturday, most of his addresses had been,
though humble in tone, of an inspirational nature. But after the USC
game, he apologized. "I failed you," he told the faithful below. "No!"
the crowd shouted in response. "Just look at last year!"

The next day on the radio show he co-hosted with Ed Schoenfeld
of the Oakland *Tribune* (in what must have been a smoke-filled room
since both were serious cigar fanciers), Pappy reflected on the consequences of this untimely loss. These things happen, he mused before
the broadcast, and life goes on. "You know, Ed, as I drove by the campus to come to the station," he said on the air, "I noticed the Campanile
was still standing."

True enough, the campus landmark was intact and so were the
Bears, most of them anyway. They next beat UCLA, 6–0, in Los Angeles before another eighty thousand-plus crowd, but in doing so lost

both halfback Swaner and All Coast guard Jon Baker to season-ending injuries. Then on touchdown passes from Celeri to Bud Van Deren and Kenfield, they beat Washington, 13–7, at home. In this game, Celeri set a new Cal single-game record with eight pass completions, a modest achievement indicative of, if nothing else, the low regard in which the aerial game was held over the years in Berkeley. The Bears next demolished outmanned Montana, 60–14, in a tuneup for the following week's Big Game.

"We're sorry the score went so high today," said guest speaker Jensen on Pappy's balcony. He paused for effect, then bellowed, "But we don't care how high it goes next week!" And though the fans below lustily cheered these words promising vengeance over the despised Indians, Jensen should never have uttered them. Even worse teams than Stanford's—and in 1947 Stanford's was about as bad as one could get—have been goaded into implausible deeds by such displays of casual arrogance.

It's true that Stanford wasn't given much chance against Waldorf's steamroller. The Indians had lost eight straight before this, the fiftieth (counting rugby years, subtracting war years) Big Game. Among the losses were the first ever to little Idaho and horrific ones to Michigan (49–13), UCLA (39–6) and Washington (25–0). They had somehow held USC to just 14 points (to their none), but they lost the next week to Oregon by 21–6. Not even the school's infamous 1939 team had lost so many in a row. By all accounts, this 1947 team had earned the dubious honor of being the worst ever to represent the university.

Cal was favored by 28 points with odds at 10-1, the longest so far in Big Game history. But what happened that November 22 gave credence to the fanciful notion that when it comes to this game, you throw the odds out the window. They appeared entirely justified, though, when the Bears marched resolutely upfield following the opening kickoff, Kenfield niftily running in for the score from the Stanford 29. Jim Cullom converted for 7–0.

But the maligned Indians came right back with a 65-yard drive of their own, 1946 Cal nemesis Ainslie Bell tossing 11 yards to halfback Wayne Erickson for the touchdown. George Quist, who had lettered at Cal during the war, missed the conversion attempt. Then, with three minutes left in the half, Cal drove 85 yards, largely on the strength of a 43-yard pass from Celeri to Van Deren. Fong plunged in for the score from the one. Cal led by a mere 14–6 at the half, something of an upset in itself.

Strange things happened after the intermission. Stanford's Erickson finished off another substantial drive by scoring from the two. Again, the point-after was missed, but the Indians were behind by only 14–12. The eighty-eight thousand who had come to Stanford Stadium that overcast day were being treated to an unexpected thriller.

The Indians were not finished. Midway through the fourth quarter, they scored again, on an 11-yard pass from Don Campbell to the aquatic halfback Bob Anderson. The conversion attempt was again botched, but with an 18–14 lead and time running out, the biggest upset in Big Game history seemed in the works. The huge stadium reflected the unfolding drama, constant cheering on the Stanford side, grumbling dismay on Cal's. Matters got even worse for the Bears when in these dying minutes, Stanford launched yet another penetration into Cal territory, this one finally stalling on the 20.

The Bears took over from there with just three minutes left to play and the Stanford goal line 80 yards away. On the sidelines, meanwhile, Cal halfback Paul Keckley, benched for the game with a shoulder pointer, was imploring Pappy to let him play, using dialogue reminiscent of dozens of Hollywood gridiron potboilers: "Send me in, coach. I can play." A reluctant Waldorf finally agreed that, just in case, his supplicant should at least put on his helmet and "be ready."

Nearly fifty years later, Keckley recalled what happened next: "When Pappy looked in my direction, I took it as a nod for me to go into the game (later there was a question about that)…When I went in,

I told Dick Erickson, the quarterback, I had a good play in mind, and he said he had a better one, 'Pass 31-X,' which surprised me as that play involved me."

The play was a Jensen option. Erickson lateraled to the fullback, already Cal's leading rusher in the game, and Jensen ran to his right as if to circle the end. Then he wheeled, jumped and threw to the opposite side of the field to a wide-open Keckley on the 35. The injured halfback picked up blocks, including a critical one downfield by guard Bobby Dodds, and began a tortuous passage through the Stanford secondary. As Pete Schabarum, then a star on the freshman team remembers, "Paul ran for what seemed an eternity in every direction but the goal line" until he finally found the opening he needed and ran for a touchdown." Cullom's third point-after made the final score, 21–18.

Thus ended a Big Game ranked then with the famous 1924 tie as the most exciting of all. Pop Warner, Stanford's coach in the earlier thriller, even thought this one was better since it at least had a resolution. Stars on both sides were plentiful. Former Bear Quist led his team with 54 yards rushing on 11 carries and playing the lone linebacker in a peculiar but effective seven-diamond defense, intercepted two passes and made tackles all over the field. Jensen had 54 yards on 10 carries and in addition to the 80-yard completion to Keckley—still the longest pass play in Big Game history—connected on another pass for 21 yards, bringing his total offense for the day to 155 yards. Cullom's three conversions ultimately won the game. But it was Keckley's plea to his doubtful coach and his subsequent vindication that remain this amazing game's signature event.

Despite this scare and the USC loss, Pappy's first season exceeded even the most optimistic expectations. He had taken a 2-7 loser and transformed it into a 9-1 winner. It was certainly one of the most dramatic turnarounds in collegiate football history. The '47 Bears also set an attendance record, soon broken, by drawing 606,266 fans home and away. They filled Memorial Stadium to capacity three times and averaged 56,857 for seven home games.

Most of the premier players, including Jensen, Swaner, Celeri, Cullom, Baker, Turner and Franz, would be back for a "run for the Roses" in '48. And their ranks would be supplemented by future stars Schabarum and Jim Monachino from the freshman team and Forrest Klein and Herb Schmalenberger from the Ramblers. Waldorf had so much talent at his command that newsmen began likening his roster to a "deep freeze," from which fresh goods could be withdrawn as required.

Above all, there was the feeling that genuinely good times lay ahead. For the moment at least there was peace on earth. America was moving again. And in Berkeley, King Football, as represented in the substantial form and jolly demeanor of Pappy Waldorf, was back in business.

CHAPTER FIFTEEN

# ROSES HAVE THORNS

The first few years immediately following World War II evolved not so surprisingly into a second coming of the Jazz Age on the Berkeley campus. There was seemingly a revival of everything 1920s in the late 1940s. There was, of course, common ground between the two generations. Both, after all, were celebrating the end of a terrible war and both were determined to banish the old ways that led to those wars. Besides, if you're determined to go back to a happier time, you certainly wouldn't pick the Depression 1930s. And to college students of the post-war '40s, the '20s looked even merrier than they actually might have been.

So the novels of such '20s literary icons as Fitzgerald, Hemingway and Dos Passos enjoyed renewed popularity. The silent movies of Chaplin, Keaton and Lloyd became feature attractions at the so-called art movie houses that suddenly sprouted up near the campus. Even vaudeville, believed to have been mercifully extinguished by radio, found fresh new audiences in theaters on both sides of the Bay and, paradoxically, on the newest medium of all—television. Popular music took its cue from the '20s. There was, particularly in the Bay Area, a major revival of traditional New Orleans and Chicago jazz. The "in" dance on campus was the Charleston, and students flocked to a cavernous saloon called Hambone Kelly's in nearby El Cerrito to listen and dance to the trad jazz of Lu Watters' rollicking Yerba Buena Jazz Band. With trumpeters (and cornetists) Watters and Bob Scobey fronting the band, the Yerba Buena took inspiration from the old King Oliver band of the '20s, which featured the mighty horns of Louis Armstrong and the King himself.

As with the earlier decade, there was in these post-war years an exhilarating sense of personal freedom, a rejection of conformity that, while tepid in comparison with the wholesale rebellion of fifteen years ahead, was no less widespread. College kids had the feeling they could do pretty much what they wanted to do. More of them than ever were of drinking age in these years and they had no need to defy the 18th Amendment to down a beer or two, as their bibulous forebears had to do; they simply hung out at such nearby watering holes as the White Horse, Marvin's or the Varsity Lounge—all of them just past the one-mile-from-campus-no-bar zone imposed by university authorities and enforced, if not always stringently, by the State Board of Equalization. It goes without saying that fraternities, freed at last of military occupation, held parties so lively they rivaled those of the good old days. All that seemed to be missing from this new Jazz Age were flappers, racoon coats and hip flasks. Well, maybe not the hip flasks.

And then there was the all-male rooting section at Memorial Stadium. Who better to exemplify the general defiance of conformity? These rooters wore the requisite uniform—white shirts, khaki pants—and dutifully obeyed the spell yells. But they were roused to far greater frenzy by the "ee-yah, ee-yah, drop dead" entreaties of the puckish cheerleader Ed Austin. And, as mentioned earlier, profanity was not beneath them. So when a photographer from the immensely popular Life Magazine snapped them for the October 25, 1948 issue, he caught them in a—typical pose—hands raised on high in rooterish exuberance but with middle fingers prominently extended. The Life photo department had a long day brushing this gesture out of the frame.

Like the '20s, the late '40s ushered in a Golden Age of Sports. Most of the pre-war stars of baseball and boxing were back in action, and attendance records were routinely shattered. In the fall, college football reigned supreme, the pro game still a decade or more removed from becoming a national obsession. And, as before, there was no more glamorous a figure in all of sports than the college football hero. Gone in the late '40s were Grange and Harmon, Albie Booth and Cotton Warburton, but in their stead came Doak Walker and Charlie "Choo Choo" Justice, Johnny Lujack and, for one final season, Mr. Inside (Doc Blanchard) and Mr. Outside (Glenn Davis).

Cal was lucky enough to have an exemplar of that noble breed. Jackie Jensen had all the necessary ingredients—blond good looks, unshakable self-confidence tempered with genuine humility, an uncanny ability to come through at the critical moment and absolutely astonishing athleticism. There was no game Jensen could not play and play better than most. At Oakland High School, he had been All-City in three sports, even though he played only a half-season of basketball his senior year. It was said of him that he was perhaps the only golf beginner to have progressed directly from scores in the 100s to the low 80s, bypassing the 90s altogether. As an All American pitcher-outfielder, he led the 1947 Cal baseball team to the very first College World Series Championship.

Both Wickhorst and Waldorf had brought him along almost too carefully as a running back, exploiting instead his remarkable versatility by using him as a defensive back and the team's punter, long passer and kick returner. In 1947, he had shared playing time with Graves at fullback, the key position in the Waldorf-T. Still, he averaged better than five yards per carry, completed 50 percent of his 22 passes for an average of 25 yards per completion and had punted 43 times for a 37.4 yard average, a figure that might have gone much higher had Pappy not placed a premium on hang-time, not distance. Jensen was fully capable of booming punts 60 yards when needed.

Now, in 1948, Waldorf was ready to turn his "Golden Boy" loose, to make him the prime ball-carrier, to let him run, as he'd so often shown he could, absolutely wild. Pappy was to say of his star's darting, weaving style that "he eludes the hand he cannot see."

Jensen was deceptive in other ways. From the stands, he appeared cocky, even flamboyant. He was one of only a few Cal Players in '48 to wear the new plastic helmet instead of the tried-and-true leather model. An expert swimmer, he generally showed up for fall practice with a deep tan after summers spent lifeguarding. He was engaged then to pretty Zoe Ann Olsen, a silver diving medalist in the '48 Olympic Games in London. And he did have a natural swagger. But he was not at all the cocky guy he seemed. He had experienced a fatherless, impoverished childhood that only sports had alleviated. He was naturally friendly but painfully shy at times. Those who found him aloof mistook reserve for conceit. And as his brilliant but sadly truncated major league baseball career revealed, he suffered from a debilitating phobia, a fear of flying.

But none of his problems became a factor in a football season that would showcase his amazing talent. When asked who in his opinion was the greatest of all the backs who had played at Cal, Bill Archer, who as a player, coach and fan had seen most all of them in his then ninety-four years, replied without hesitation, "Jackie Jensen."

In the '48 opener, a 41–19 win over tough Santa Clara, Jensen reeled off three dazzling runs of more than 60 yards, two of them for touchdowns. He and his Mr. Inside, Swaner, gained just a yard short of 300 in the game. The second game would be played against Navy in Baltimore, and for the first time ever, the team would fly to a road game. Jensen's phobia was in the developing stage; Waldorf's was well past that, arising from a hazardous adventure in a bi-plane twenty-five years earlier. Friends tried unsuccessfully to kid him out of his fear. "When your number's up, Pappy," joked one pal, "your number's up."

"I suppose that's true," Pappy grimly replied, "but what if the pilot's number is up?"

The coach made it to Baltimore safely enough, squirming miserably all the way in an aisle seat so he wouldn't be tempted to glance out a window.

The Bears beat Navy, 21–7, and then St. Mary's, 20–0, a game in which Jensen played only a few downs after spending the night before hospitalized with a bad cold. At home against Wisconsin before sixty-six thousand, Jensen and Swaner led the Bears on an opening 71-yard drive, but the real star of the game was two-way back Billy Montagne, who intercepted two passes, one for a touchdown, and caught one from sub fullback Pete Schabarum for another score in an easy 40–14 victory.

In a 42–0 whitewashing of Oregon State, Jensen tossed a 47-yard touchdown pass to George Souza in the end zone, the ball traveling from the point of delivery 53 yards in the air, the exact distance of Brick Muller's famous Rose Bowl heave twenty-seven years earlier. Muller, then a team doctor, lavishly congratulated Jensen when he returned to the bench. "Now, at long last," he confided in the younger man, "I won't have to answer so many questions about that old pass of mine."

After a 21–0 win over Washington, in which Swaner scored all three TDs. the Bears traveled to Los Angeles for a critical matchup with USC. Both teams needed a win to preserve their Rose Bowl aspirations. It was the ideal stage setting for some Jensen heroics. And Jackie didn't disappoint, gaining 132 yards on 27 carries and scoring both touchdowns in a nail-biting 13–7 win. It was Cal's first victory over the Trojans in seven years and, because of the wartime double headers, nine games.

UCLA was then drubbed, 28–13, with Swaner and the defense sharing the scoring. Linebacker Will Lotter returned a fumble recovery 85 yards for one score and Cullom fell on a blocked punt in the end zone for another. In what was little more than a warmup for the Big Game, Washington State was finished off, 44–14. The Bears, undefeated so far in nine games, were ranked fourth in the nation. But because of the 1947 peril, they were hardly overconfident entering the Big Game.

Stanford in '48 was not the unvictorious team it had been the year before. The Indians were an unflashy 4-5, but had convincing wins over UCLA (34–14) and Washington (20–0) and a narrow 7–6 loss to Southern Cal. But they had lost their star fullback, Emery Mitchell, to a knee injury before the Big Game and their line, averaging only 197 pounds, was outweighed by Cal's by nearly 20 pounds per man. The oddsmakers, undeterred by the near upset of '47, made Cal a 21-point favorite.

The game got off to a frightening start when Stanford's Don "Rock" Campbell was knocked cold on the opening kickoff. Play was delayed for 15 anxious minutes as Campbell lay prostrate on the turf with a concussion. When he recovered and play resumed, Jensen and Swaner led an opening drive of 59 yards on 12 plays, each blocking flawlessly for the other. Swaner's touchdown from the two was set up by a Jensen 11-yard run after he faked a pass. Cullom converted another decisive kick, as it developed, since Stanford came back with a touchdown drive of its own in the third quarter, Tom Shaw passing the final 11 yards to Ken Rose. Cullom took it upon himself to block Aubrey Devine's conversion attempt, so Cal maintained its precarious 7–6 advantage. But from then on, this Big Game became a taut defensive struggle. It also became another Jack Jensen highlight reel.

At one point, from deep in his own territory, Jensen boomed a 67-yard punt, all in the air, to keep Cal out of danger. Then, in the fourth quarter, he pulled off a play that Waldorf called "the greatest individual performance I've ever witnessed on a football field." A series of misplays and penalties had left Cal with fourth down and 31 yards to go, perilously deep in its own territory. Jensen went back in punt formation, but this time his blocking broke down and Indian linemen, led by linebacker Jim Castagnoli, churned down upon him. Certain that his kick would be blocked, Jensen tucked the ball under his arm and headed straight up the middle of the field. His would-be blockers were by now mostly downfield, so he could expect little help. Somehow, though, he threaded his way through the Stanford defense and gained 32 yards and a first down. For the day, Jensen gained 170 yards on 19 carries. He also had a 35-yard run called back because of a holding penalty.

Cal had finished its first undefeated and untied season since 1922. Jensen became the Bears' first 1,000-yard runner and a near unanimous All American. Franz and Turner also received All America mention, Franz for the second year in a row. The Bears were now looking forward to their first Rose Bowl appearance in ten years, although the invitation was hardly a sure thing. Oregon was also undefeated in conference play and, in fact had seven PCC wins to Cal' s six. The Ducks had lost only one game all season, that by 14–0 to the nation's number-one team, Michigan. And, with quarterback Norm Van Brocklin, a future NFL Hall of Famer, they were not lacking in star power. The vote among conference members was, as expected, close, but the Bears finally won out, 6–4. As consolation, the PCC bent one of its own rules and allowed the Ducks to play in the Cotton Bowl, where they lost, 21–13, to Southern Methodist.

There was some uncertainty as well about Cal's Rose Bowl opponent. After years of negotiation, the PCC and what was then, with the University of Chicago's withdrawal, the Big Nine had agreed to play each other annually in the Rose Bowl, beginning on New Year's Day of 1947. The deal was originally set for five years; it would last for fifty-four. The Rose Bowl pact represented a major departure from a previous no-bowl policy in the midwest conference. Its schools had routinely rejected all invitations since Cal thrashed Ohio State in the '21 Pasadena game. But after discussions among representatives of both conferences during the war years, it was agreed that they shared compatible academic standards and recruiting policies and should therefore agree on a "closed shop." Much to the irritation of schools elsewhere, particularly in the South, the Rose Bowl authorities approved the deal.

Big Nine commissioner Kenneth L. "Tug" Wilson's pious pronouncement that "We must set up a policy whereby a boy will choose a school for its educational value rather than the school choosing a boy for his athletic ability" inspired teeth-gnashing resentment in football factories across the land.

So what about the rest of us? inquired schools elsewhere. The PCC-Big Nine deal had left them out of Pasadena entirely. Alabama, which had played in five Rose Bowls, was particularly miffed by the snub. Johnnie Mack Brown, who had starred for the Crimson Tide in the '26 game before embarking on a career in the movies, protested, "Every football player all over America dreams of playing in the Rose Bowl. How can they limit such a thing to one section? The Rose Bowl has cut out its heart. It's a crying shame."

Another controversy of sorts arose when the Big Nine announced it would not send its champion, undefeated Michigan, to play Cal on New Year's Day of '49. According to a policy the conference established at the time of the agreement, no Big Nine team would be allowed to play in the Rose Bowl more than once every three years. It was a share-the-wealth scheme soon enough abandoned, but it was firmly in place for the '49 game. And since Michigan had played in the Bowl the year before, it would be bypassed in favor of second place Northwestern, the very school Cal's coach had left barely two years earlier.

At the time, though, sending an also-ran seemed like an act of charity from the Big Nine, since in the first two games of the joint agreement, Illinois had humiliated UCLA, 45–14, and Michigan had drubbed USC, 49–0, a score identical to that of the first Rose Bowl game in 1902 when Stanford was the Wolverine victim. Northwestern was by all accounts a fine team, "the best so-called second best team the conference has had in many a year," according to Warren Brown of the Chicago Herald-American. The Wildcats were 7-2 on the season, losing only to Michigan (28–0) and Notre Dame (12–7), the numbers one and two teams in the country. They had, meanwhile scored shutout victories over UCLA (19–0), Purdue (21–0) and Syracuse (48–0).

The Waldorf factor gave the game added appeal. Northwestern coach Bob Voigts, only thirty-one, had played tackle for Pappy in the late 1930s, and he got the job on Pappy's recommendation. Eight Northwestern starters, for that matter, had played for Waldorf. Despite Cal's presumed inside dope and the fact that Northwestern quarterback, Don Burson had a muscle inflammation in his throwing arm, the Wildcats were made a 2–1 pre-game favorite, a differential founded almost entirely on the previously demonstrated superiority of Big Nine football over the coast brand.

It rained that New Year's Eve and though it was merely overcast on game-day, the field was treacherously damp and slippery. Both teams started hot, though. Five minutes into the game, Northwestern's Frank Aschenbrenner ran wide and behind a key block by left end Joe Zuravleff sped 73 yards to a touchdown, then the longest run from scrimmage in Rose Bowl history. Cal returned the ensuing kickoff to its own 33. On first down, Jensen faked a run off tackle, then bounced outside and behind an initial block by Cunningham, ran 67 yards for the tying touchdown. Within the space of a few minutes, both teams had scored on very long runs. This promised to be an offensive show like no other in Pasadena.

As it happened, two much shorter runs would shape the outcome of this thriller. In the second quarter, behind the bullish charges of fullback Art Murakowski, Northwestern had moved the ball to the Cal one-yard-line. On first down, Murakowski again carried, but this time he fumbled, the ball bouncing into the end zone where Lotter fell on it for an apparent touchback. But field judge Jay Berwanger (who had been the first winner of the Heisman Trophy) signaled touchdown. So did referee Jimmy Cain. The Bears were astonished by the call. Cal end Norm Pressley had tackled Murakowski from behind, pinning his arms and forcing the fumble. Pressley and his teammates were convinced the ball had come free before Murakowski had crossed the goal line. Newspaper photos the next day seemed to confirm that view. One clearly showed the ball carrier with a foot in the end zone but with the ball in the air. Another showed Burson holding his head as if the play had failed and head linesman Jimmy Hole, a former Cal assistant coach, indicating Bear ball. But Berwanger, who, a-straddle the goal line, was certainly in position to make the call, insisted that the ball had broken the plane before it came out. Waldorf would have none of the controversy, commenting, "Yes, we've seen the pictures, and it's still official. That's all there is to it."

Trailing 13–7 at the half, Cal suffered seemingly irreparable damage at the very start of the second half from a run even more abbreviated than Murakowski's. On the second play of the third quarter, Jensen swept wide to his right on an apparent option play and then, still behind the line of scrimmage but with an open field ahead of him, collapsed untouched by human hand. He had aggravated an old thigh muscle pull on the slippery turf and had to be helped off the field, not to return to the gridiron that day – nor, it would turn out, on any other. An audible groan escaped from the Cal side of the stadium.

Pappy at first considered replacing his injured star with the sophomore flash Schabarum, but decided instead on the backup to the backup, Frank Brunk, Jensen's close friend and sometime golf instructor. Brunk had played all of 8½ minutes the entire season, and his bio in that year's Big Game program consisted of just two sentences, the second of which read, pessimistically, "Will be back for another try next season." As Brunk ran onto the field to replace the fallen hero, Cullom joked in the huddle, "Here comes Brunk. Now we'll have to block." But both Cullom and Pappy knew that the little-used fullback was a fierce competitor who compensated for marginal talent with hard play.

And so, with Brunk sparking them with consecutive runs of 14 and 13 yards, the Bears marched 50 yards to a touchdown, scored by Swaner from the two. With Cullom's conversion, Cal led 14–13 entering the final quarter. The lead might well have been increased had it not been for another debatable call by referee Cain, a onetime star back for Washington. Midway into the quarter, Northwestern halfback Ed Tunnicliff was upended by a ferocious tackle that caused the ball to fly free of his grasp. Cal's Souza recovered it on the Wildcat 12. But Cain said he had whistled the play dead while Tunnicliff was still airborne, if only to spare him further harm on his way down. Once again, news photos, showing Tunnicliff in flight, and Cain's whistle not yet to his lips, seemed to prove the ref wrong. But the call stood and Northwestern kept the ball.

As it happened, Tunnicliff himself would score the game-winning touchdown, and on a trick play. With three minutes left to play and with darkness descending on the big bowl, the Wildcats lined up on the Cal 43-yard line. But instead of taking the ball from under center, quarterback Burson stepped nimbly aside at the last second, allowing the snap to go directly to Tunnicliff. Burson, in a convincing bit of playacting, pretended to hand off to Murakowski while Tunnicliff, who actually had the ball, fled in the opposite direction. The Bears took the fake, and Tunnicliff raced virtually untouched to the end zone. The final score of 20–14 might have been different except for two controversial calls by game officials and an injury that diminished Cal's firepower. Still, the Bears established beyond question that a PCC team could compete evenly with the Big Nine.

And despite the disappointment in Pasadena, the season had been a record-shattering success. Jensen finished with 1,080 yards rushing on 148 carries, an almost implausible average of 7.3 yards per carry. He had easily surpassed Bottari's old record of 770 yards set in 1937. Jensen's record would last 27 years. With his 784 yards rushing, Swaner also surpassed Bottari, and he led the conference in scoring with 12 touchdowns. As a team, Cal led the PCC in both total offense and total defense. And it set a new school attendance record, home and away of six hundred seventy-six thousand.

But the prospects for 1949 were not encouraging. Baker and team captain Frassetto would be gone from the powerful line of '48 and so would ace punt returner Keckley, All Coast end Frank "Bud" Van Deren and the cool quarterback Erickson. Though Erickson and Celeri shared the position in '48, there was no quarterback controversy under Waldorf, because each had his own set of responsibilities. Erickson was the starter, and he was an efficient play-caller who got the offense operating smoothly. Then Celeri, the "Mad Engineer," would come in to ignite it with his passing, scrambling and bootlegging. In '49, the erratic Celeri would assume both duties.

And in 1949, there would be no Golden Boy to light the way. Jensen chose to pass up his senior season and sign a baseball contract with the Oakland Oaks of the Pacific Coast League. After just one season in the minors, he was sold to the World Champion New York Yankees, there to play alongside his boyhood idol, Joe DiMaggio. He would finally become the only athlete to have played in a World Series, baseball's All Star Game, the Rose Bowl, the college baseball World Series and, as a mere freshman, the East West Shrine All Star football game.

In 1954, playing for the Boston Red Sox, he hit 25 homers and led the American League with 22 stolen bases, a rare melding of power and speed for the time. He would drive in more than 100 runs five times in an 11-year career, thrice leading the league. In 1958, when he hit 35 homers and drove in a league-leading 122 runs, he was voted the American League's Most Valuable Player. But major league expansion westward made it necessary for teams to fly to road games, and flying was something, try as he might, Jack Jensen could not do. What had been a scintillating career was brought to a sad and untimely end.

Jensen drifted, for a time, divorcing Zoe Ann, remarrying her and divorcing again. He had some success as a broadcaster. He coached Cal baseball, but found himself incompatible with a new breed of college student. He finally found peace as a gentleman farmer in Virginia with his second wife, Katharine. He'd even overcome his phobia. He died at only fifty-five of a heart attack on July 14, 1982. As his widow wrote in "Pappy's Boys," "He was a rare sort of man. We may all be created equal, but some grow closer to heaven."

## CHAPTER SIXTEEN

# PAPPY'S BOYS

No one, possibly not even their coach, knew what to expect of the 1949 Bears. The loss of Jensen was bad enough. As Truck Cullom said, "Last year, it was just a matter of getting Jensen beyond the line of defense. This season, we figure we've got to escort the ball carriers all the way to the goal line, so we'll be putting out a lot more."

Losses to graduation had depleted the experienced line of '48. To make matters even worse, there were other unanticipated losses before the season began and not long afterward. Billy Main, a fine all-round back who had averaged five yards for his 57 carries in '48, and end John Cunningham, the team's leading receiver with 14 catches for 222 yards, were both declared ineligible for their fourth season of varsity play due to a "revised interpretation" of the conference's wartime eligibility rules. Then during a pre-season practice, Swaner, Jensen's productive running mate, suffered a leg injury that sidelined him for the first seven games. End Norm Pressley, he of the Murakowski fumble debacle, missed the first six games because of another practice injury. And Doug Duncan, the '48 team's starting center, passed up his fourth season to begin training in Naval Intelligence. Finally, the brilliant scatback, Charley Sarver, suffered a career-ending knee injury in the new season's fourth game. Until then, he was averaging a mere 9.9 yards per carry, had caught six passes for an average of 29 yards per reception and had scored six touchdowns.

So the Bears were, by any measure, star-crossed. The pre-season soothsayers picked them no higher than third in the conference. And a possibly sincere Pappy told reporters he didn't expect this team to be playing in Pasadena in January. Pappy also knew there was help on the way. Although among them they had carried the ball a sum total of thirty times in '48, the coach had supreme confidences in his returning running backs, Brunk, Monachino and Schabarum. Celeri had abundant talent as a passing and running threat and, alone at last at the helm, was expected to temper his sometimes exasperating eccentricities. Franz, Cullom and Turner were still there to stabilize a line that would soon enough be anchored by a powerful sophomore equally adept at offense and defense named Les Richter. Three other fine defensive players were also in the mix—safety Carl Van Heuit, halfback Billy Montagne and sophomore end Ed Bartlett. All things considered, the Bears didn't look so bad, after all.

They rolled impressively over their first three '49 foes, beating Santa Clara, 21–7; St. Mary's, 29–7, and Oregon State, 41–0. They lost Sarver but still beat Wisconsin, 35–20, in Madison. Ranked ninth in the country by now, the Bears next met 12th-ranked USC in a game, though played only in mid-season, the experts agreed would determine the PCC's Rose Bowl representative. A capacity-plus crowd of 81,499 that included California governor and Cal grad Earl Warren turned out at Memorial Stadium.

The Bears scored first on a seven-yard Celeri to Bob Minahen pass, a play set up by successive Celeri scrambles of 17 and 21 yards. It was the only score of the first half. The unexpected defensive standoff continued through a scoreless third quarter in which the Bears accumulated just one first down. Then, on the first play of the fourth quarter, the Trojans tied the game after a rare offensive push finished off by Bill Martin's one-yard plunge. Minutes later, future star Frank Gifford, then merely a sophomore defensive back and backup quarterback, kicked a 23-yard field goal that gave S.C. a 10–7 lead. Slight though it may have been, that lead seemed, with nine minutes left to play, almost insurmountable considering Cal's demonstrated inability to move the ball in the second half. Then came a play that surely ranks among the most dramatic at a school already famous for such things.

Waldorf had decided only the day before the game to change tactics on Cal's kickoff returns. Earlier, he'd had his return men head for the sidelines, sometimes after reverses. Then he noticed that on reverses, the official nearest the play invariably followed the man with the ball, thereby tipping off' the opposition. Even without the reverses, though, the sideline returns had not given the team particularly advantageous field position. So the coach on Friday installed a new blocking scheme calling for returns directly up the middle of the field. The deep men on kickoffs, Monachino and Brunk, wore themselves to a frazzle practicing the new play that day, running on every kick from goal line to goal line.

But against USC, the new system didn't seem at first to be working any better than the old. Indeed, on the opening kickoff, Brunk was, as he so graphically put it, "creamed" only a few yards from his own goal line. The Trojan kicker, Bob McGee, had propelled the ball so high and so deep that the Bears were unable to sustain their blocks long enough to give the return man a decent head of steam.

So now, with the game on the line and time running down, Monachino and Brunk awaited McGee's kick following the Gifford field goal. Cal rooters in the huge crowd were hopeful of at least a respectable runback, most likely from Monachino, the speedier and trickier of the two. And yet, Brunk had been the Bears' offensive leader that day with 76 yards rushing and a 43-yard pass reception. But he reminded no one of Jackie Jensen. Bill Leiser of the *Chronicle* disparaged him as a ball-carrier who "has no sidestep, who doesn't dodge, who has no whirl...

And he has only 177 pounds to help him. In fact, Brunk can't run."

McGee's kick was again high and deep. At first, the ball seemed headed for Monachino. "I was all set to yell, 'You take it,'" Brunk recalled, "when it started to curve back to me. So I took it." From two yards deep in his end zone, he ran, as instructed, straight into the heart of the Trojan defense. This time, the blocks held. Brunk counted nine of them, generously crediting everyone but Oski, the costumed mascot, with clearing a path for him. "I was just the lucky guy who got to carry the ball."

"Suddenly," wrote a presumably repentant Leiser, "he emerged in the clear, free and alone save for the screeching and screaming of eighty-one thousand five hundred voices which at that moment must have shaken the foundations of the hillside homes in Strawberry Canyon."

In fact, he still had one man to beat, Gifford, who was poised to make a game-saving tackle at the USC 37. But the runner without a sidestep executed a beauty at that critical juncture, leaving the future NFL Hall of Famer grasping air as he plunged face-first onto the turf. Brunk ran the rest of the way into the end zone, hopelessly trailed by Trojan Johnny Williams.

"This was no normal circumstance in the life of Frank Brunk," concluded Leiser. His 102-yard runback was cause for massive celebration that day and became the subject of breathless reminiscing for more than a half-century afterward. There was such pandemonium in the stands and on the sidelines as Brunk threaded a path through the Trojan defenders that not everyone saw the great man actually cross the goal line. Many in the men's rooting section, for example, were toppled over rows of seats in the crush of excitement, and though they were certainly there that day they can't honestly say they saw the finish of Brunk's historic dash. Unable himself to gain a decent view, Pappy Waldorf watched Brunk's final steps on a television monitor conveniently situated at the end of the Andy Smith Bench.

The Bears would add a final two points before the final gun when

Bartlett tackled a desperate Trojan quarterback, Wilbur Robertson, in the end zone for a safety, making the final score, 16–10. But this game will be forever remembered as "The Battle of Brunk's Run."

After such a thriller, a letdown might have been expected for the following week's game against Washington. But Celeri had a 49-yard touchdown run and Van Heuit had three interceptions. and a fumble recovery in a 21–7 win. UCLA fell 35–21, Monachino scoring twice and Celeri completing 12 of 17 passes for 214 yards. His was the first 200-yard passing game in Cal history. The quarterback passed for 99 yards and two more touchdowns–51 yards to Monachino and 41 to end Dan Begovich–in a 33–14 victory over Washington State. In a 41–14 defeat of Oregon the next week, Monachino scored on runs of 18 and 16 yards and backup halfback, Paul Baldwin returned a punt 68 yards for another touchdown.

Celeri, metamorphosed into a dropback passer by a foot injury, tossed 54 yards to Monachino to give Cal an early 6–0 lead in the Big Game. But Stanford came back with a 16-yard scoring run by Bob White that with star quarterback Gary Kerkorian' s point-after gave the Indians a 7–6 lead at the half. This was a solid Stanford team with a 6-2-1 record entering the Big Game. And in Kerkorian and All America end Bill McColl it had players of national stature. But Cal took control in the third quarter and won, 33–14. The backbreaker for the Indians was an 84-yard run by Monachino from his own 12 to the Stanford 4. In fact, Monachino enjoyed a career game, breaking Jensen's Big Game rushing record by gaining 189 yards on 20 carries. He scored twice. Swaner, finally fit enough for sustained action, gained 100 yards on 15 carries and plunged for three touchdowns.

Seven times in ten winning games, the Bears had come from behind, displaying, said Pappy, "a spirit so thick you can cut it." Considered in the pre-season no better than third in their conference, they had finished the regular season ranked third in the nation. Now, they would get a chance to avenge the Rose Bowl defeat of a year past.

"There they are in Pasadena again," wrote Berkeley Gazette sports editor Jim Scott, "unbeaten, untied and unexpected."

Ah, but there would be another team seeking vengeance in this particular Rose Bowl. The Ohio State Buckeyes were still smarting over Cal's embarrassingly easy 28–0 win in Pasadena twenty-nine years before. And not even its recent successes in the big bowl could completely erase the Big Nine's shame over that long ago thrashing. It remained for coach Wes Fesler's '49 Buckeyes to set matters straight.

They had won a second chance against Cal on a lucky and, sadly enough, prophetic break in the deciding game against Michigan. They had come from behind to score in the last few seconds, only to have their kicker, end Jim Hague, miss the point-after kick. Michigan would be a 7–6 winner, and Minnesota, the only team to beat the Buckeyes, would be the conference's Rose Bowl representative. But the game wasn't over. The Wolverines were offside on Hague's kick, so he and his team were reprieved. Hague didn't miss his second try, and the Buckeyes were on their way to Pasadena, co-champions because of the tie with Michigan, which, according to the silly conference three-year rule, was still not eligible for post-season play.

Although the Buckeyes were both tough and, with a multiple single-wing and T offense, deceptive, Cal was made a six-point favorite. And the Bears scored first on a seven-yard run by Monachino in the second quarter. The Buckeyes tied the game shortly after the half when fullback Fred "Curly" Morrison plunged in from the one. The touchdown was set up by a 35-yard interception return of a Celeri pass by future Heisman Trophy winner Vic Janowicz. A minute-and-a-half later, Ohio State's Jack Lininger blocked Celeri's punt on the Cal 16 and returned it to the 6. Jerry Krall scored the go-ahead touchdown on fourth down.

But Cal tied the score on a trick play, Monachino taking a lateral from Celeri and racing 44 yards behind a perfect block by Schabarum. It was the Bear halfback's 15th touchdown of the season.

The score was still tied with time running out in the last quarter. The Bears were backed up to their own 16 with fourth down and 14 to go for a first down. Celeri dropped back to punt, but the snap from center Charles "Ozzie" Harris was low and Celeri juggled it as Buckeyes bore down upon him. He eluded the first wave and raced to the sidelines to attempt a running Rugby-style kick. Unfortunately, the right-footed Celeri was running to his left and therefore obliged to kick with his left foot. The ball soared a full 11 yards before slicing out of bounds on the Cal 13. From there, Krall gained three, Morrison two and Krall two more to the 6. The Buckeye players campaigned to go for at least a first down, but Fesler decided to try a field goal. An intentional delay-of-game penalty moved the ball back to the 11 and a more favorable angle for Hague and his holder, Dick Widdoes. There were less than three minutes left to play.

Bear fans were not without hope, though. Hadn't Hague missed an easy PAT in the Michigan game before he was reprieved? And reports were that in practice the Buckeye kicker had missed four of five from about the same distance he now needed. For that matter, field goal kicking in 1950 was hardly the art form it has since become.

But Hague didn't miss this time, and when Cal next got the ball there were less than two minutes to play. The Buckeyes held for the 17–14 win. For the second year in a row, the Bears had lost within the last three minutes of play, prompting Pappy to suggest that Rose Bowl officials "shorten playing time by three minutes in the future." And since Ohio State's scoring "drives" had gone all of 30, 6, and 13 yards, he might also have proposed that touchdown drives of less than 35 yards should not count. Alas, neither proposal was accepted. In fact, the Bears could only blame this loss on their own turnovers.

Cal not only lost the game but the halftime show. Before a record Rose Bowl crowd of 100,963 (ten thousand new seats had been added) and a television audience, Ohio State's one hundred twenty-piece marching band strutted its stuff, entertaining with dazzling formations and rousing tunes. The Cal band, attired in laughable new uniforms with mustard-colored pants that made them, by the musicians own admission, look like bellhops, was no match. It was as if the New York Philharmonic had engaged in a cutting session with Spike Jones and his City Slickers. "If the game's outcome depended on the bands," wrote one sportswriter, "the score would have been 60–0." The persistent Pasadena hex could not, however, detract from another productive Cal season. Celeri became the Bears' first thousand-yard passer, connecting on 48 of 117 throws for 1081 yards and a record nine touchdowns. Monachino gained 781 yards on 138 rushes for a 5.66 yard average. Brunk and Schabarum had nearly identical statistics, Pete carrying 94 times for 420 yards, Frank 91 for 400. Celeri, Turner, guard Forrest Klein and, for the third straight year, Franz all made All America teams. Cullom joined them on the All-PCC team.

But the Bears—and, for that matter, the world at large—would have a different look for 1950. The team would lose twenty-five lettermen, including Celeri, Brunk, Turner, Franz and Cullom. They, like most of the other World War II veterans who peopled college squads in the late '40s, were moving on. In fact, the 1950 season would really be the first since before the war to have college teams represented by college-age players. On Cal's team that year, fifteen players were teenagers and only five were twenty-three or older. Star backs Monachino and Schabarum were 21, the customary age for college seniors. Richter, who would make five All America first teams in '50, and All Conference tackle Bob Karpe were both ninteen at the start of the season.

These comparatively beardless youths were joined by a spectacular fullback just up from the freshman team named John Olszewski, or, as he was more commonly known, "Johnny O." Although he would wear the same jersey number 36 and he was a consistent long distance threat, Johnny O could not have been a more different type of runner than his illustrious predecessor, Jensen. Whereas the Golden Boy was a classic broken-field runner always in search of a clear path, Olszewski enjoyed clearing his own path. If, as Pappy had memorably said of Jensen that he eluded the hand he could not see, Olszewski sought out that hand so he could stomp on it.

"If there's no place else to go," backfield coach Fry remarked on the Johnny O method, "he'll take on the other guy, and he usually doesn't come off second best. When he puts his shoulder into a tackler, he seems to take off, as if some hidden spring uncoils to give him power."

"He seems to be made of wrought iron and have a negative pain threshold," said quarterback Bill Mais, who came to Cal with Olszewski as part of a package deal, orchestrated in no small part by the Southern Seas, that included the entire 1948 starting backfield of St. Anthony high school in Long Beach. Mais was a competent enough passer, a two-year starter, and fellow "Saints" Dean O'Hare and John Peterson were good players (and, as it developed, excellent students), but Johnny O was the prize in that package. A muscular 195-pounder, he played much bigger. And he had an ominous mien with deep-set shaded eyes from which emanated a baleful and unnerving glare. Johnny O looked like a man who meant business.

With him at fullback and Monachino and Schabarum returning as halfbacks, the 1950 Bears had in all probability the best trio of running backs in the entire college football world. All they needed was a quarterback. Struggling initially with the inexperienced Brent Ogden and Dick Lee, they essentially won their first three games without one. The Bears beat Santa Clara, 27–9; and Oregon, 28–7, and Penn, 14–7, on the strength of their terrific running game. In his varsity debut against Santa Clara, Olszewski picked up 111 yards on just eight carries, scoring on a 55-yard run. But against Penn, the quarterbacks completed just one of 11 passes and were intercepted twice. Something had to be done.

The players themselves made the final determination, as it turned out. Just before the Southern Cal game in Los Angeles, they met as usual to vote on a game captain. With defensive players Dick LemMon and John Ralston campaigning hard for him, Jim Marinos, heretofore a career Rambler, won the election handily. It was as if Ralph Nader had won the 2000 presidential vote. The coaches were properly flummoxed. Since they had opted for youth at the position, Marinos, a senior, had not figured in their calculations. But as Pappy told him when informed of the election results, "The players have spoken." And, recalled Marinos, "when the coaches were revived and brought back to their senses, they actually let me start the USC game."

"Rescued from oblivion," Marinos played a fine game against the Trojans, quarterbacking Cal to a typically close 13–7 win. Lemmon, his staunch advocate, saved the victory when with time expiring and the ball on the Cal one, he sacked S.C. quarterback Ed Demirjian for a nine-yard loss on fourth down. Marinos would be the starting quarterback for the rest of the season. He would throw the occasional diversionary pass, but his prime responsibility was to make certain the ball got safely into the hands of his three all-star running backs. That he did with cool efficiency.

After subsequent wins over Oregon State (27–0) and St. Mary's (40–25), the Bears played two key conference games in succession, against Washington in Seattle and UCLA at home. Coached by former Yale headman, Howie Odell, the Huskies featured one of the great running backs in conference history in Hugh McElhenny, a future NFL Hall of Famer. They also had a second threat in Don Heinrich, an accurate passer and himself a future professional star. They were made a 3½ point favorite.

And they scored first, but Cal came back with a 63-yard drive finished off by Schabarum's six yard TD run. The score remained tied at halftime. Then, in the third quarter, Marinos passed to Schabarum for 26 yards and what proved to be the winning touchdown. The Huskies threatened in the last few minutes when their Ernie Stein recovered Monachino's fumble on the Cal nine. But Heinrich returned the favor, fumbling after a hard tackle by Bartlett into the hands of Bob Minahen to end the threat and give the Bears a hard-earned 14–7 win.

Rarely does a football team play what may be considered a perfect game. But in crushing UCLA, 35–0, the next week before another full house at Memorial Stadium, Cal came awfully close. Led by Johnny O, who had 144 yards on 18 carries and three touchdowns, one for 73 yards, the Bears outgained the Bruins 321 yards to 39 rushing and 389 total to 112. Schabarum had 11 carries for 57 yards and Monachino 13 for 51. Marinos completed five of his six pass attempts, one for a touchdown to end Bob Fitzgerald.

But it was on defense where the Bears came nearest to perfection, throttling Bruin coach Red Sanders' single-wing attack with the dynamic play of defensive ends Bartlett and Paul "Boomer" Andrew. With these two closing in on him, the 162-pound Bruin tailback Ted Narleski, was tossed about as if he were, in fact, a Teddy Bear. Andrew, another fugitive from the Ramblers, became as a result of his superior play in this game an instant hit with the press. Reporters and columnists were fascinated to learn that until he came to Cal he had no experience of organized football. He had failed to make the team as a freshman at Lowell High School in San Francisco and had then transferred to the private Cate School near Santa Barbara which had no football team. But Andrew was a fine athlete who had played soccer and baseball at Cate. Still, when he turned out for freshman football at Cal, he was embarrassed to confess his inexperience. The then assistant frosh coach Bud Van Deren greeted this revelation with enthusiasm. "Good," he told Andrew, "that means you don't have any bad habits."

Among the *Chronicle* writers who heaped praise on the neophyte for his play against UCLA was Pierre Salinger, who a decade later would serve as Press Secretary to President John F. Kennedy. Salinger quoted Pappy as saying, "That boy didn't play a minute of high school ball, and now he's one of our best." Prescott Sullivan, remarking on Andrew's inexperience, wrote in the *Examiner*, "The Bruins didn't know the difference. They must have thought Andrew an old pro."

The Bears' win that day was, in the opinion of *Examiner* sports editor Curley Grieve, "a football masterpiece, a classic of gridiron artistry." Even Pappy concurred, telling Salinger, "This is one of those days you get once in a blue moon when everything breaks nicely." Later, he admitted, "It's the first time in my career I couldn't find anything to gripe about."

But perfection was still out of reach. After a rain-soaked 13–7 win over a USF team only a year away from its greatest season, the Bears met a grimly determined Stanford team that, while twice coming close, had yet to win a game against Pappy's Boys. The Indians came even closer this time, settling grumpily for a 7–7 tie. Both scores came in the second half and both were the result of fumble recoveries. Cal struck first, in the third quarter, when Don Robison's recovery deep in Stanford territory preceded Schabarum's 31-yard touchdown dash. The Indians scored on the first play of the fourth quarter after end Johnny Bonetti scooped up a loose ball. Kerkorian, who completed 17 of 30 in the game, then passed nine yards to Boyd Benson for the tying TD.

There were some heroic performances that day, though. Olszewski carried 18 times for 118 yards and Richter powered a stubborn defense, saving the day himself with an interception on the Cal two. Stanford's Bill McColl, of course, played brilliantly on both offense and defense, and his Brick Mullerish 65-yard pass attempt in the closing seconds barely missed breaking the tie. But Cal was the PCC champ and for the third year in a row would be its representative in the Rose Bowl.

Only three days after the Big Game, the team suffered a grievous emotional blow when line coach Bob Tessier died of a heart attack. Only forty, Tessier had been an extremely popular and valuable member of Waldorf's staff. "He was a warm and friendly man," said Pappy, "a coach who brought out the best in his players and those around him. He won a place in the hearts of Californians...We are all a little happier because he stopped here."

The opponent this time would finally be Michigan. But these were hardly the all but invincible Wolverines of recent vintage. In mid-season they were just 2-3-1 and seemingly out of contention. Then they rallied to win their last five games, including the bizarre championship decider against Ohio State in a raging blizzard. Michigan's 9–3 win that day came on two blocked kicks, one for a touchdown, the other for a safety. Overall, the Wolverines punted 24 times, accumulated 27 total yards, completed zero passes and finished with no first downs. But that was enough to send them packing to Pasadena. There they would have much to live up to, since in Michigan's two previous Rose Bowl appearances, against Stanford in 1902 and USC in '48, it had won by identical scores of 49–0.

No one expected a rout of such dimension this time around. The Bears, after all, were 9-0-1 coming in and had scored 218 points to their opponents' 76. And the Wolverines' predominantly single-wing attack would be no mystery since Pappy's team that season had already played three teams—Penn, Oregon State and UCLA—employing that supposedly antiquated formation and had allowed just one touchdown among them. Perusing these statistics, Michigan athletic director Fritz Crisler slyly commented, "I hope California goes easy on our fuzz-faced, spindly-legged kids." Pappy responded, "We simply can't afford to lose this time."

Before many of the 98,939 fans there that day had settled into their seats, Schabarum scooted 73 yards on the third play of the game for what appeared to be a touchdown. But the play was called back on a backfield-in-motion penalty, an official spying an infinitesimal movement of the arm by Schabarum before the snap. The Bears' run of Rose Bowl bad luck was obviously still in play. Both teams had early long drives, Cal to the Michigan 17, Michigan to the Cal 19, without scoring.

In the second quarter, Bear linebacker Ray Solari intercepted a pass thrown by Michigan's fine tailback, Chuck Ortmann, on the Wolverines' 46 and returned it to the 39. From there, Marinos passed to end

Bob Cummings, who made a leaping catch over Michigan All American Don Dufek in the end zone. Richter, kicking without his regular holder, Lee, because of an injury, missed the point-after. The Bears lost another scoring opportunity before the half when on third-and-two from the Michigan three, Monachino slipped with a clear path to the goal ahead of him and fell to the turf for a yard loss. On fourth down, Schabarum was stopped two yards short of the end zone. But Cal had dominated the first half, gaining 192 yards to Michigan's 65 and racking up 10 first downs to two. And yet the lead was merely 6-0.

The second half was quite another story. After a scoreless third quarter, Michigan finally pieced together an 80-yard scoring drive with barely five minutes left to play. Dufek plunged one yard for the TD on fourth down and Harry Allis's successful conversion kick gave the Wolverines a 7–6 lead. Then with little time remaining, a Marinos fourth down pass from his own 13 was batted down. Dufek carried four straight times from there for the clinching score. Allis's conversion made the final score, 14–6. Cal had lost again in the last few minutes of play.

"We played good ball for a half," said a disconsolate Pappy afterward, "and fair ball in the third quarter. Then came the fourth quarter. We just got the tar beat out of us in the fourth quarter."

Of the four games Pappy's teams had lost in his four years and forty-three games as coach, three had come in the Rose Bowl. But when the PCC and Big Ten renewed their contract in February of 1951, it seemed certain that the great coach would get other chances against his midwest nemeses.

In 1951, he'd lose Schabarum, who scored 12 touchdowns in '50 and gained 647 yards, and Monachino, who scored six and gained 754. And on defense, he'd miss the doughty little safety, Carl Van Heuit, of whom Pappy said, "He's too short and too slow, but he has a heart that stretches him to the size of the biggest lineman." But Johnny O, who became the second 1,000-yard runner (1,008) in Cal history, would be back. And so would the All America Richter on defense. The future looked almost as promising as the past had been successful, discounting, of course, the Rose Bowl.

But there were decidedly different and far more difficult times dead ahead.

CHAPTER SEVENTEEN

# DECLINE AND...

By 1951, the brief stretch of post-war euphoria had seriously eroded. When the Soviet Union successfully tested an atomic bomb in July of 1949, a new sort of conflict was initiated. The famous journalist Herbert Bayard Swope was the first to define it as the "Cold War." And with it came a new wave of suspicion and fear of communist infiltration into our institutions that proved even more virulent than the "Red Scare" that followed the First World War. Demagogues like Senator Joe McCarthy of Wisconsin ignited the fires of mistrust and hysteria, leveling accusations of treason at the highest levels of government, including, to his ultimate undoing in 1954, the United States Army.

American colleges and universities were hardly immune from suspicion, and at President Sproul's request the U.C. Board of Regents adopted in June of 1949 a so-called "loyalty oath" that required faculty members to deny in writing any past or present affiliation with the Communist Party. The oath was immediately denounced by professors throughout the university system as a violation of academic freedom. And it resulted in an ongoing controversy that Cal Nobel Prize winner Glenn T. Seaborg said "tore at the bonds of collegiality among our faculty."

Thirty-one faculty members lost their jobs because they refused to sign the oath. Significantly among them was David Saxon, a young assistant professor of physics at UCLA with nary a trace of leftist leanings but with an abiding distaste for Red Scare tactics. When the California Supreme Court finally overturned the Loyalty Oath in 1952, Saxon got his teaching job back. And in 1975 he became the fourteenth President of the University of California, a position he held for eight years.

Then in June of 1950, troops from Communist North Korea invaded South Korea, and President Truman ordered U.S. forces there as part of a United Nations effort to repel the advance. The Cold War was heated up considerably when China intervened on the North's behalf. Truman called the fighting there a "police action," but America's military recognized it as the Korean War. And it didn't end until 1953 when an armistice was agreed upon and the borders restored at the 38th Parallel.

Once more, during those years, a player's draft classification or reserve military status became the subject of documentation in football programs. The game itself, meanwhile, had been placed under renewed scrutiny from critics within academe and in the nation's press. The deluge of G.I. Bill-supported military veterans who populated rosters in the immediate post-war years had subsided by the early 1950s. The new players were arriving directly from high school or junior college, many from families unable to meet the ever-rising costs of a college education. The intense competition for these young players led to recruiting and subsidy abuses reminiscent of those in the 1920s that inspired the famously opprobrious Carnegie Report.

In a series of six articles in the New York *Times*, investigative reporter Charles Grutzner wrote that college football recruiting practices had grown even more corrupt by 1951 than those revealed by the Carnegie snoops. And on the floor of the Senate, the scholarly Senator J. William Fullbright of Arkansas declared that "colleges hire players who are not bona fide students and thus make a mockery, a farce, of the whole concept of amateur sport. They corrupt not only hired players but also the entire student body who learn from their elders the cynical, immoral doctrine that one must win at all costs."

Even former USC coach Jeff Cravath, writing in *Colliers* magazine, agreed that "the system reduces the boys to perjurers, scalpers and football gigolos."

There were scandals enough to support such criticism. Sports fans were first shocked to learn of the 1951 point-shaving and game-fixing revelations in east coast college basketball. These were followed in August of 1951 by the "cribbing scandal" at, of all the supposedly sacrosanct institutions, the Military Academy at West Point. Some 90 cadets, including many football players, were expelled for cheating on exams, among them the son of Army's revered coach, Earl "Red" Blaik. A cribbing-depleted Army team that season lost its first opening game since 1893 and won only two of nine games. Included among the defeats was a 42–7 horror to Navy. It was Blaik's only losing season of his 18 at West Point.

Again at Sproul's urging, the Pacific Coast Conference in 1952 appointed a committee of faculty representatives to investigate rules violations and recommend punishment for the offenders. The U.C. president's reformist zeal was seen by at least one conference coach as naive and counterproductive. According to UCLA's Red Sanders, Sproul would better serve the community by routing the "communists on his campus" than interfering with football recruiting.

Seaborg, the Nobel Prize winner for chemistry in 1951, was appointed Cal's faculty representative by Clark Kerr, the first "chancellor of the Berkeley campus." Sproul, who, as his aide Skinny Johnson once said, "not only relished the exercise of power" but feared his loss of it would lead to "the disintegration of the university," had been convinced by 1952 that the job was too big for one man. So he relinquished much of his previously absolute authority to chancellors Kerr at Berkeley and Raymond Allen at UCLA. As president, he was still the final voice on policy matters, but under the new system he left the everyday details in the hands of these campus "chief executives."

There was little question at the time that college football needed looking into. As with most endeavors, money was at the root of its evil. Unable to keep pace with the big spenders, thirty-three schools nationwide abandoned the sport in the early 1950s. Among the casualties were the storied programs at St. Mary's, USF and Santa Clara in the Bay Area, the Gaels and the Broncos having been traditional adversaries of the Bears. These Catholic schools had fallen victim not only to football's prohibitive expenses but to competition for the fan dollar from the increasingly popular professional 49ers.

Cal by then had not been connected with any punishable gridiron wrongdoing, but as watchdog Johnson told Sproul, "there is an inherent danger in organizations like the Grid Club and the Southern Seas Society which collect dues and maintain treasuries…Under the present conditions, the only real assurance of legitimate conduct lies in the character of Waldorf and Hamilton."

Character had risen as another concern in a game that purportedly built it. Were tramp athletes the sort of undergraduates good schools wanted to represent them before the public? In 1951, USC's team had been consistently accused of unnecessarily rough play, of even targeting other teams' star players for violence. Washington was the first to issue such complaints. But these accusations came to a head in Cal' s game with the Trojans on October 20, 1951, at Memorial Stadium. Olszewski had until then been enjoying a superb season. In the four previous games, he had gained a total of 549 yards, 269 alone in a record performance against Washington State a week before the S.C. game. Jensen's season record of 1,080 yards rushing seemed well within his reach.

But on his first carry against the Trojans, only Cal's second play from scrimmage, he was wrestled to the turf by 205-pound linebacker Pat Cannamela after a two-yard gain. As Johnny O lay on his back, Cannamela, in plain view of the Cal rooting section, appeared to deliberately give his right leg an extra twist. No penalty was assessed for what appeared to be a foul most blatant, but the rooters were up in arms. As Olszewski was helped off the field with a badly injured right knee, the male rooters, in a display no less unsportsmanlike than Cannamela's, began shouting, "Get 42 (the linebacker's number)."

The game was in danger of becoming a brawl, both on the field and in the stands. Fortunately, there were cooler heads in both places, and when Johnny O returned to the field in the third quarter, the crisis seemed averted. But his stay was brief. After gaining 26 yards on a trap play, he again limped back to the bench. Without their star offensive player, the Bears were no match for the foe. Frank Gifford, now a tailback in coach Jess Hill's single wing, ran 69 yards for one touchdown and passed six yards for another to lead USC to a 21–14 win. But it was a tainted victory.

As Prescott Sullivan wrote afterward in the *Examiner*, "Whether or not the disablement of Johnny Olszewski was part of USC's master plan will be fodder for argument for weeks to come."

Actually, the argument lasted much longer than that. Hamilton protested to the conference almost immediately of foul play. And when Seaborg assumed his duties in '52 as faculty representative, he too appealed for punitive action against the Trojans. As he wrote in his book *Roses from the Ashes* almost fifty years later, "I had used still photos and medical evidence to show that USC's Pat Cannamela had deliberately twisted Johnny Olszewski's knee after Olszewski had been tackled with the ball and the play had ended. The only satisfaction I got was an evasive nonapology written by USC Coach Jess Hill."

Without mentioning what Seaborg described as Cannamela's "savagery," that "nonapology," written not to Seaborg but to S.C. President Fred D. Fagg, merely reiterated Hill's bromidic assurance that he did not condone "unfair, illegal or unsportsmanlike playing" and that he resented allegations that he had advised his charges "to go out and get certain players."

Asked after that infamous game if he felt he'd been deliberately injured, Olszewski responded, "Well, when I was a little boy, my father told me that if I had nothing good to say, don't say anything at all… But I *do* want to say this: We met a better club. They outplayed us, outfought us."

Johnny O missed the next two games, a win over Oregon State and a loss to UCLA. He returned to play against Washington, reeling off a 51-yard run before hobbling to the sidelines once more. He did not play against Oregon and played only briefly and inconsequentially in Cal's 20-7 win in the Big Game, gaining four yards on five carries. All told, he carried the ball only 12 times after the USC loss for just 63 yards. He was diagnosed with torn ligaments in the knee.

Olszewski would return supposedly recovered for the 1952 season, gaining an impressive 845 yards, and he would thereafter have a 10-year career in the NFL, but he was never again the dynamic ball carrier he had been in his first year-and-a-half at Cal. The injury had clearly cost him speed and cutting ability. Only his extraordinary power carried him through. In truth, Pappy's Bears were never quite the same after that Trojan loss, a condition the coach half-jokingly referred to in a talk before an alumni group the following week: "I have sipped of a dark bitter medicine known as defeat. This medicine enables me to distinguish real friends from bandwagon riders, and we have found few in the latter category. This medicine also increases the appetite for victory. It brings discernment to the taste."

It was an appetite not so easily satisfied after 1951. Cal lost fifteen lettermen for the '52 season, including Richter, a two-time All American linebacker destined for a long and rewarding career in the professional game. Also gone were such first-rate athletes as Bartlett and LemMon on defense and running backs Don Robison and Johnny Pappa.

But the Bears won their first five games, which included intersectional wins over Missouri by 28–14 and Minnesota by 49–13. In routing the Golden Gophers in Minneapolis, they demonstrated some of their old vaunted power on the ground, Don Johnson leading the way with 157 yards on 14 carries for four touchdowns. Paul Larson scored twice and gained 79 yards on just six carries. Olszewski was 12 for 72 yards.

When they whipped Oregon, 41–7, the next week (Olszewski had 172 yards on 17 carries) and Santa Clara, 27–7, they were ranked fourth in the nation. Then came USC, then ranked seventh. The Trojans once again sent a promising season into precipitous decline, winning by 10–0 over a team that had been scoring better than 35 points per game. In the next two weeks, the Bears lost to UCLA, 28–7, and Washington, 22–7. They rallied to defeat Washington State, 28–13, but they were just 6-3 on the season after that 5-0 start before facing the 5-4 Indians in the Big Game.

Ray Willsey, primarily a defensive back until then, had a memorable game playing quarterback against Stanford in place of the injured Mais. In the Bears' 26–0 win, he passed 38 yards to end Bob Beal for one touchdown, scored himself on a sneak from the one and set up a third TD with a 55-yard scramble. Larson ran for a touchdown and linebacker Lloyd Torchio returned an interception 37 yards for another. Olszewski closed out his collegiate career by gaining 122 yards on 25 carries, thereby breaking by five yards McElhenney's existing conference career rushing record–2,504 yards to 2,499.

But 1952 would be Waldorf's last winning season at Cal, a development that seemed as improbable at the time as Ike's losing a presidential race. In six seasons as Bear coach, his teams had won 53 games while losing only nine and tying one. Three of those losses had come in the Rose Bowl and three to USC. But as had happened to Andy Smith and Stub Allison before him, the string was running out.

There were two factors working against him in '53: he had lost twenty-nine lettermen and, the NCAA, in its infinite wisdom, had decided it was time to abandon two-platoon football and return to pre-war substitution rules, thus depriving Pappy of the advantages he had enjoyed with superior manpower. The sixty-minute man, a relic of the past, was back, offensive and defensive specialists gone—at least for the time being. The rule change was motivated in part by the recruiting mess. With fewer players needed, there might be less proselytizing. Besides, playing both ways was the manly thing to do. Why should a pass-happy quarterback be immune from making tackles?

In truth, Pappy had always given his stars the opportunity to play on both sides of the ball. Richter was the classic linebacker, big, strong, fast, but he had also played center and guard on offense. Jensen had played defense, tying the school record of the time with seven interceptions in 1947. Robison had played defense before becoming a top running back. Willsey had proved in the '52 Big Game that he could play both safety and quarterback. And Cal's next great player was in all likelihood the most versatile of them all.

As a tailback in the Notre Dame box and short punt formations at Turlock high school, Paul Larson had been a triple-threater. He also had the small town virtues of humility and congeniality. In his first season at Cal, in 1951, he recalled that "whenever the coaches asked if someone could punt, placekick return kicks or whatever, I'd raise my hand. I just wanted to make the team. I wanted to play." The fact is, he could do almost anything on a football field. With freshmen again eligible for play in '51, he led the team in punt and kickoff returns, played safety and as a halfback gained 103 yards on 15 carries. Against Minnesota that year, he ripped off a 72-yard dash from scrimmage that in terms of zigging and zagging would have done credit to Jensen. In 1952, he again played both offense and defense, leading the team once more in punt returns—24 for a 10.9-yard average—and tying for the lead in interceptions with three for 61 yards. On offense, he rushed for 359 yards on 50 carries for a team-leading average of 7.18 yards per rush.

In those two seasons, Larson had thrown just two passes from his halfback position, completing none. But Waldorf knew from his high school years and from watching him in practice that he was an accurate passer. And so did the canny new assistant coach Jim Sutherland, who as head Coach at Santa Monica High School for nine years, had developed highly sophisticated passing offenses. Eggs Manske, in his six years as Cal's end coach, had consistently urged Pappy to pep up the Bears' passing game, but backs coach Wes Fry staunchly held out for the ground game, and as an old pal of Waldorf, his influence was the stronger. And up to then, who could argue against a running attack annually among the nation's best? Even with quarterbacks as adventurous as Celeri, the pass was employed merely as a distraction. In 1952, for example, the Bears had gained 2,812 yards rushing and only 907 passing.

But Pappy knew that in 1953 he had little chance of overpowering the opposition. So as he had when things got tough at Northwestern, he turned to an overhead approach. The arrival of pass-master Sutherland represented a dramatic tactical departure from the cloud-of-dust norm. Regrettably, Eggs wasn't around to witness his belated triumph. He resigned after the '52 season, frustrated from what he felt was a losing battle with Fry. "He and Wes just didn't see eye-to-eye," recalled star Manske pupil Ed Bartlett.

Disillusioned with his coaching career, Manske first went into the automobile business, but soon found that not to his liking. He then accepted a faculty job at Berkeley High School and remained there until his retirement at age sixty-five in 1978. Bartlett hosted a retirement party attended exclusively by Eggs's former ends. "We thought of him as a god," said Harry Agler.

Manske's abrupt departure signaled other changes in a Waldorf staff that once seemed as tenured as the Supreme Court. Herm Meister, a former assistant at Santa Clara and Pittsburgh, replaced the late Bob Tessier as line coach in 1951, Rambler coach Chaney succeeded Manske as end coach and Sutherland was called in to fix the aerial game.

With Mais graduated, the quarterback job for '53 belonged to Sammy Williams, another fine all-round player who had played mostly defense the previous two seasons. In part-time QB duty in '52, he had completed just four of 14 passes for 60 yards. His lone touchdown pass was a 27-yarder to Larson in the Minnesota game. As the projected starter, Williams was likely to create a media stir, since he would become the first African-American ever to quarterback the Bears. But in the closing days of spring practice, he dislocated his throwing shoulder and, facing months of rehabilitation, was declared out for the season. It was then that Pappy called halfback Larson into his office. And as Larson recalled the meeting many years later:

"Pappy told me about a change he hoped to make, but before he told me what it was, he said the decision was entirely up to me. 'If you say yes or no, that's the way we go,' he said. 'But I'd like you to change positions.' I joked later on that if he wanted me to play guard, I'd probably do it and get killed trying. But he asked me if I'd play quarterback. Well, I'd already played so many positions, including both halfbacks, that I knew most of the assignments. Naturally, I said yes."

Sutherland took Larson aside later on to explain his passing philosophy. "It's simple," he told the new QB. Then, paraphrasing baseball's Willie Keeler, he said, "We go where they ain't."

Playing where he'd never played before, all Larson did in 1953 was lead the nation in total offense with 1,572 yards. He completed 85 of 171 passes for 1,431 yards—both, needless to say, Cal records. He passed for six touchdowns, scored five himself and kicked 20 points-after-touchdown. Even with 256 yards lost on sacks, he gained 141 yards rushing and led the team with six interceptions he returned for 102 yards. His favorite receiver, Jim Hanifan, set a new Cal record with 19 catches. Never before had a Cal team thrown the ball with such frequency and for so many yards. But the Bears finished with a mediocre 4-4-2 record, the worst of Pappy's seven seasons.

There were high and low spots in this middle-of-the-road season. The wins included shutouts over Oregon State (26–0) and Pennsylvania (40–0) a game which included a 91-yard touchdown dash by sub fullback Jerry Drew. The Bears also held Oregon scoreless but failed to score themselves in a rain-soaked deadlock —this after scoring 53 points the week before against Washington. There were big losses to Baylor (25–0), Ohio State (33–19), USC (32–20) and UCLA (20–7).

The Big Game became a shootout between the two QBs, Larson and Stanford's Bobby Garrett, who led the nation in passing that year. Larson completed 13 of 22 passes for 179 yards, Garrett 12 of 27 for 131. Each intercepted two of the other's throws, Garrett returning one for 56 yards and a touchdown, Larson one deep in Cal territory to save a touchdown. Larson also scored on an 18-yard run. Each kicked three points-after to preserve the 21–21 tie, the Bears' second in a row.

This Big Game was not, by any definition, an artistic triumph. Altogether, there were ten turnovers, three alone in one peculiar fourth quarter sequence. Cal's All America center-linebacker Matt Hazeltine first intercepted a Garrett pass on the Cal 41, then, after a five-yard return, fumbled the ball away to Stanford. On the next play, the Indians' Bill Rogers fumbled and Hazeltine—who else?—recovered. Cal then marched 54 yards for the tying touchdown, Al Talley scoring from the three. Cal had one more opportunity to score in the final seconds, but Larson missed his field goal attempt from the 16.

The fledgling quarterback had a remarkable season, though. Playing both ways he won the Andy Smith Trophy for minutes played with 463, nearly a hundred minutes more than the '52 free substitution winner, Willsey, and the most since Bob Lossie clocked 477 in 1945. Larson also won the team's Most Valuable Player award. He'd be even better in 1954. That year, he led the nation in passing, completing 125 of 195 for a 64.1 percentage at a time when a 50 percent completion rate was considered exceptional in college football. Only Don Heinrich of Washington with his 60.6 had exceeded 60 percent among the nation's passing leaders up to that time. In fact, Larson's .641 (in football math) would not be surpassed until ten years later, when the passing game had grown far more refined. Few quarterbacks of any era, however, could match the crazy-quilt statistics Larson amassed in '54. He led the team with a 28.5-yard average on ten kickoff returns, intercepted three passes and did the punting and placekicking. He and roommate Hazeltine made All America

Hanifan, meanwhile, led the nation with 44 pass receptions, scored 7 touchdowns and led the team with 482 minutes played. Scatback Johnny Wilson had a 96-yard touchdown run in the 45–0 win over San Jose State, the second longest in Cal history to Bill Powell's 98-yarder three years earlier.

And yet the Bears muddled through another .500 season, 5-5 this time. Four of those losses, however, came to nationally ranked teams, three of which finished in one-two-three order. Ohio State and UCLA finished one-two in some polls and tied for the top in others and Oklahoma was but one tick behind them. All three were undefeated. The fourth-ranked team was, of course, USC. The 17th-ranked Trojans won their fourth straight from Cal, but lost to Ohio State in the Rose Bowl, UCLA had clobbered S.C. 34–0 in the regular season, but the PCC, in its new contract with the Big Ten (the addition of Michigan State made the conference ten again) had imposed a no-repeat rule, and the Bruins had played in Pasadena the year before. The rule was designed in part to frustrate any repetition of Cal's three straight Rose Bowl appearances and also to give the presumably less advantaged schools from the Pacific Northwest a better chance of making it there. It was as silly a restriction as the Big Ten's and would soon disappear.

In all of its losses to the ranking teams, save for the 27–6 pummeling by UCLA, the Bears were competitive. They held Ohio State to a 21–13 final score, two of the three Buckeye touchdowns coming on runs of 29 and 26 yards by All America halfback Howard "Hopalong" Cassady, who would win the Heisman Trophy the next season. After the game, Ohio State's legendary coach Woody Hayes took Larson aside to tell him, "You're a great quarterback." This from a man who dispensed compliments about as freely as Joe Stalin.

The Trojans barely won, 29–27, and Oklahoma, in the second year of what would become a 47-game winning streak, beat the Bears, 27–13, in the season's opener. Cal fared somewhat better against the mighty Bruins that year than Stanford, which absorbed a 72–0 humiliation in Los Angeles. Larson played the full sixty minutes in the UCLA loss, completing 25 of 38 passes for 250 yards. The fifth loss came against Oregon, a team scarcely in the same league with the other conquerors. After this 33–27 embarrassment, Pappy was asked by a reporter what he might have done differently if he'd had the chance. "Stay home," he replied.

Cal's four wins before the Big Game had mostly been by lopsided scores: 45–0 against San Jose State, 46–7 over Oregon State, 27–6 over Washington and 17–7 over Washington State. In the Oregon State win, Jerry Drew broke Olszewski's single game Cal rushing record, achieved three years earlier, by running for 283 yards on just 11 carries. He scored on runs of 67, 59, and 55 yards. Drew's record would survive for fifty-four years. The fullback had an unusual career at Cal, showing flashes of brilliance, as in this game and with his 91-yard TD against Penn in '53, but seemingly unable to sustain them over the long haul. The yards gained against the Beavers represented 40 percent of his output for '54 and enabled him to be Cal's leading rusher that year with 715. But injuries would deprive him of true stardom.

Though most of his best performances had come against inferior foes, Drew did have a fine game against Stanford. His 33-yard run set up Cal's first score, a Larson quarterback sneak. And he scored himself on a 27-yard run, a play set up by Sammy Williams's 60-yard return of an intercepted pass thrown by the Indians' sophomore quarterback John Brodie. Williams, back from injury and playing halfback, had scored the Bears' other first half touchdown. The 21–0 lead at the half seemed insurmountable. And the start of the third quarter only added to Stanford's misery, Larson passing eight yards to Hanifan to cap off a 72-yard drive.

Behind now, 28 to zip, the Indians made a gallant comeback,

scoring twice before the end of the third quarter on a 34-yard run by halfback Gordy Young and a two-yard sneak by Brodie made possible by his 39-yard screen pass to Bill Tarr. Then, in the last quarter, Tarr intercepted a short Larson pass thrown from his own eight and returned it to the five. Two plays later, halfback Ernie Dorn carried the ball in to bring the final score of what had all the appearances of a Cal runaway to 28–20. The win gave Cal its first lead in the series, 24-23-10, since it began sixty-two years earlier.

Pappy would lose stars Larson, Hanifan and Hazeltine for '55, as well as Drew to injury. And he had already been deprived of a player, by then infamous, who might have been the biggest star of them all.

## CHAPTER EIGHTEEN

# FALL

Of all the tawdry escapades that so tarnished college football in the 1950s, none could approach for sheer audacity the odyssey of Ronnie Knox. After a 1952 season in which he threw 27 touchdown passes for Santa Monica High School, Knox was considered the nations's top quarterback prospect. Frank Leahy, Norte Dame's astute coach, called him the best high school quarterback he'd ever seen. And Leahy knew his quarterbacks, having coached Heisman Trophy winners Angelo Bertelli and Johnny Lujack.

Needless to say, Knox was much in demand among college recruiters, even though, as was commonly known, he came with considerable baggage, that being his, shall we say, overly protective stepfather, Harvey Knox. A dapper gent with pompadoured silver hair and a Douglas Fairbanks mustache, Harvey had at one time or another been a store detective, a private eye, a Las Vegas casino functionary, an encyclopedia salesman, a service station attendant, and the proprietor of a failed haberdashery on Rodeo Drive in Beverly Hills. But his real job was promoting the athletic career of his gifted stepson and, to a lesser extent, the acting and modeling aspirations of Ronnie's older sister Patricia. In effect, with Ronnie as his sole client, Harvey Knox was the sports world's first player agent. And try as they might, his rapacious successors could not match him for hubris or personal offensiveness.

Though his knowledge of the game was no better than that of the average fan, Harvey exercised unusual care in seeing to it that Ronnie's coaches fully appreciated the lad's talent. In the process, Ronnie matriculated at two high schools, Beverly Hills and Inglewood, before Harvey finally settled on Santa Monica and its pass-happy coach.... who just happened to be Jim Sutherland. After Ronnie's banner senior season there, Harvey fielded nearly thirty submissions from college recruiters across the country, informing the most promising to, "just put your real offer on the line, and we'll tell you how it matches with the others." Ronnie became, as Cal's Seaborg described him, "the poster boy for the onrushing athletic scandals."

And yet, after sifting through the numberless solicitations, Harvey chose Cal as Ronnie's first collegiate way station. Ronnie told the *San Francisco Chronicle* that his reasons for heading north were wholly academic: he wanted to learn how to write beautiful prose and poetry with an eye to becoming a latter day Walt Whitman.

Harvey had a somewhat different take. To begin with, the Southern Seas hired him as a football talent scout for $400 a month. Ronnie's literary ambitions would be furthered by a promise from the Seas' chief recruiter, Frank Storment, to get him a job writing sports for the *Berkeley Gazette*. Sutherland, the only coach Harvey deemed suitably appreciative, was hired as a Cal assistant. Ronnie would even be a Sutherland family house guest until he could find his own lodgings. And finally, after he'd made the Cal varsity, Ronnie claimed he was promised "pocket money" of $500 annually for the sale of football tickets in a deal engineered by the San Francisco Grid Club.

Ronnie was subsequently shocked to discover that many of these supposed inducements were not acceptable to the university. The administration would not allow him to be a professional sportswriter, particularly while playing a sport he might actually write about. If

**A** Pappy Waldorf's 1948 coaching staff. Standing, from left to right: Hal Grant, Nibs Price, Pappy, Wes Fry. Kneeling: Ed Manske, Zeb Chaney, Bob Tessier.

**B** Athletic Director Brutus Hamilton provided a philosophical and ethical underpinning to the championship years.

C

**C** Jackie Jensen danced away from defenders with balletic moves all his own.

**D** U.C. President Robert Gordon Sproul, (center) pays his respects to coach Pappy Waldorf and 1948 stars Rod Franz, far left, Gene Frassetto and Jackie Jensen.

D

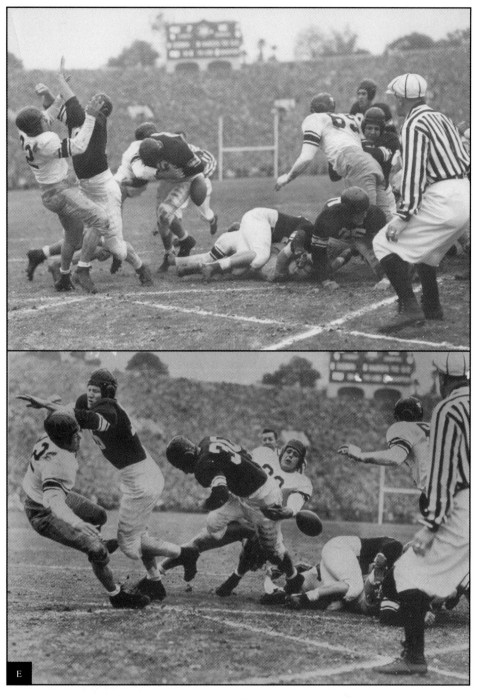

**E**  The question yet lingers: Did Northwestern's Art Murakowski fumble the ball before he crossed the Cal goal line or after, as officials ruled, in the 1949 Rose Bowl game. News photos argued persuasively for before.

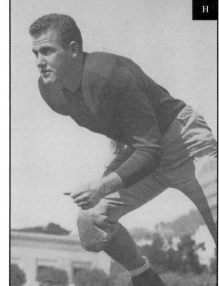

**F** The undefeated (until the Rose Bowl) Cal team of 1948.

**G** Pete Schabarum, (left) and Jim Monachino were twin backfield threats in the Waldorf glory years.

**H** Star 1940s lineman and future pro standout Jon Baker.

I   John Olszewski's baleful glare was an essential part of his game-face mystique.

J   Les Richter was an All American as an offensive guard and a linebacker on defense for Pappy Waldorf's teams of the early 1950s.

K   Pappy Waldorf was lost in contemplation as he strode the turf before games.

L

M

N

L  Handed the unenviable job of following Pappy
Waldorf as coach, Pete Elliott enjoyed a Rose
Bowl season of his own.

M  Joe Kapp was nearly as great a threat running
the ball as throwing it.

N  Center-linebacker
Matt Hazeltine and
quarterback Paul Larson
excelled in Pappy
Waldorf's middle
seasons.

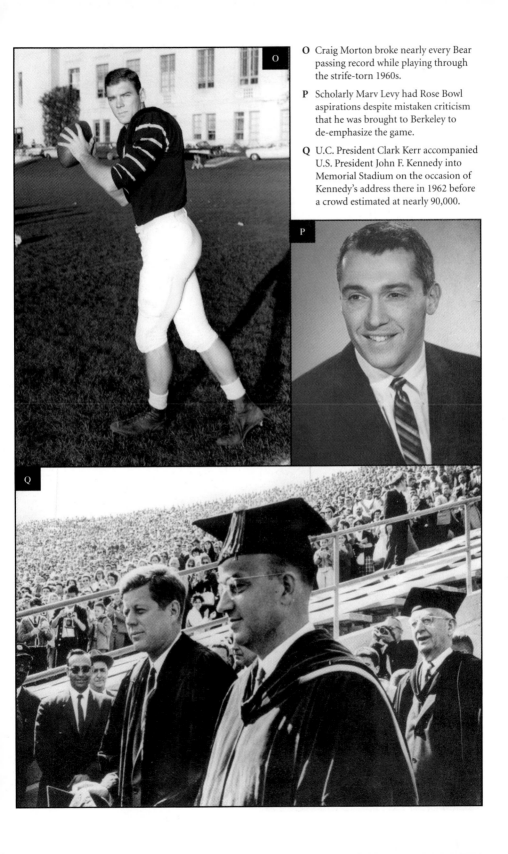

**O** Craig Morton broke nearly every Bear passing record while playing through the strife-torn 1960s.

**P** Scholarly Marv Levy had Rose Bowl aspirations despite mistaken criticism that he was brought to Berkeley to de-emphasize the game.

**Q** U.C. President Clark Kerr accompanied U.S. President John F. Kennedy into Memorial Stadium on the occasion of Kennedy's address there in 1962 before a crowd estimated at nearly 90,000.

R  Coach Ray Willsey gets a Big Game victory ride with the Axe happily in view.

S  Free Speech Movement firebrand Mario Savio rouses his forces for another 1960s campus demonstration.

nothing else, Ronnie Knox writing about the spectacular play of Ronnie Knox was also bad journalism. And he never did receive his proposed salary from the Grid Club because Ronnie never played a minute of varsity football at Cal. When the PCC learned of Harvey's deal with the Southern Seas, it both reprimanded the booster club and ordered Cal to sever all relations with it until it conformed to conference rules and got out of the business of hiring paid recruiters, particularly those who had stepsons on the football team. Sutherland stayed at Cal about as long as Ronnie did before becoming a successful head coach at Washington State.

Ronnie did play one season of freshman football at Cal in 1953, and played exceedingly well. But when Harvey discovered in spring practice of 1954 that his boy was playing second string to Larson, he fairly exploded, complaining bitterly that Waldorf was unwilling to heed either his or Sutherland's counsel on Ronnie's superior qualities. Harvey told Pappy, "We're used to winning, and we've joined a loser." This to a man whose teams had won twenty-two straight conference games only a few years earlier.

That June, Ronnie transferred to UCLA. Waldorf did not seem especially grieved by the loss. Acknowledging the boys' great talent, he remarked, "Perhaps we're better off in the long run." As a transfer, Ronnie was ineligible for the '54 season, even though, in yet another violation of conference rules, he practiced with the Bruin varsity. Under coach Red Sanders, Ronnie would be playing as a single-wing tailback, not as he had in high school and with the Cal frosh as a T-quarterback. Superior athlete that he was, he adapted to the position switch and was enjoying a productive season until he injured a leg the week before the USC game. Still hurting, he played only sparingly in the fourth quarter of UCLA's 17–14 loss to Michigan State in the Rose Bowl.

Unsurprisingly enough, Harvey did not get along well with the equally obdurate Sanders, remarking at one point in their stormy relationship that if the coach didn't "shape up, Ronnie and I are going to be forced to make a serious decision of our own." In fact, faced with only a half-season's eligibility because of conference penalties, Ronnie quit school in 1956 to play for the Hamilton Tiger Cats of the Canadian Football League. After three years at two universities, the nation's hottest high school prospect had played not even one complete varsity season. He lasted three years with four different teams in Canada and part of a season with the Chicago Bears, a brief NFL interlude punctuated by Harvey's challenging the coaching acumen of the legendary George Halas. Then, at age twenty-four in 1959, Ronnie "retired." A game that had once promised him a bright future and certainly a different sort of celebrity than the one he now had was, he concluded, "strictly for animals, and I like to think I'm above that." He would repair to a garret somewhere, he intimated, and write poetry.

Ronnie and Harvey's lasting contribution to the game was to set in motion, through their own improprieties, a series of investigations into West Coast college football that would penalize its most dominant powers and lead finally to the dissolution of the once-prestigious Pacific Coast Conference.

The conference, long tolerant of the increasingly influential booster clubs, decided in 1955 to get tough with them and, as Seaborg put it, their "flouting of the rules" governing recruiting and subsidizing athletes. That year alone, PCC Commissioner Victor O. Schmidt and his staff examined eighty-one allegations of wrongdoing and found thirty-six clear violations. After a number of meetings involving the governing faculty representatives and college presidents, harsh penalties were imposed on the miscreants, most notably UCLA, USC and Washington, but also, to a lesser degree, Cal.

When the dust finally cleared, UCLA was placed on three years probation, meaning that its teams would not only be ineligible to play in the Rose Bowl but also unable to share in the bounty the game ordinarily distributed to all conference schools. Bruin home games were forbidden to be shown on national television during the probation

period. And a fine of $15,000 was levied against the school for at-
tempts made by its administration and coaching staff to stonewall the
investigation. Added together, financial losses from these penalties approached $100,000, a staggering cost in the 1950s. Furthermore, the
school's senior players would be eligible for only half of the 1956 season, those five games to be played consecutively.

Red Sanders, whose behind-the-scenes machinations had in large
part brought about the punishment, was not in the least intimidated
by their severity. "I don't feel a bit wicked," he told the San Francisco
*Chronicle*. "Declaring these boys ineligible was all wrong. We have
been dealt the death penalty without committing a capital offense."
But Sanders' respect for rules was famously lacking. When Pappy once
accused him of ignoring a gentleman's agreement among conference
coaches concerning the use of bootlegged game films, Red replied, "Aw
hell, Pappy, if I'd known I was breaking a gentleman's agreement, I
wouldn't have done it. I just thought I was breaking a conference rule."

For their part, Washington and USC were both placed on probation for two years, with the same restrictions that applied to UCLA,
including the half-season eligibility rule for seniors. This last penalty proved especially vexing for the Trojans, who had in Jon Arnett
a breakaway runner of Heisman potential. Arnett decided to play the
first five games since they seemed more challenging than the last half
of the schedule, and he gained 674 yards on 99 carries for an average
per rush of 6.8 yards, Heisman statistics for sure if carried over for a
full season. He later became a star back for the NFL Los Angeles Rams.
Another outstanding Trojan runner, C.R. Roberts, quit school before
his senior season and, like Knox, headed for Canada. He later played
for the 49ers.

If the restrictions imposed on her three rivals were harsher, Cal's
embarrassment at being penalized at all was considerably greater. After all, it was Sproul who originally championed strict observance of
the rules, and in Athletic Director Hamilton and coach Waldorf, the

school had in place two generally acknowledged pillars of integrity. And though neither knowingly violated the trust invested in them, they suffered the consequences of the investigation. Hamilton, in fact, resigned as A.D. on September 27, 1955, but not, as he wrote, because of "pressure from any student, faculty or alumni groups." He said he simply wished to devote his time to coaching track, which he did at Cal for another ten years. He was replaced as athletic director in March of 1956 by Greg Engelhard, a Cal basketball player of the 1930s and a veteran administrator at the university.

Pappy's situation was more complicated. He had approved a fund, financed by the San Francisco Grid Club to provide loans for players facing financial emergencies. And though such "grants-in-aid" were within conference rules and common elsewhere, at Cal they required Sproul's approval, which was not sought, and most likely would not have been given. As a result, Cal was placed on a year's probation and fined $25,000 (to be paid over three years) "for the part played by the head football coach in the illegal aid given to student athletes." The conference also specified that no Cal player would lose eligibility if his loan was repaid before or by September 1, 1957. Meanwhile, the ban against the Southern Seas had been lifted in 1956 since that organization had revised its rules to conform to the conference's. Now, Cal was instructed to sever relations with the Grid Club, until it too fell in line, which it did rather quickly.

Though both Kerr and Seaborg had great regard for Waldorf, they reluctantly decided that to clear the air and prompt other penalized schools to do the same–they should publicly reprimand their coach. And so, on July 7, 1956, Kerr wrote to Pappy:

> "I must hold you personally and individually responsible for your participation, directly or indirectly, in any activity involving the offer of illegal subsidization of athletes. Your participation in and responsibility for

*the program of illegal aid to athletes, which had recently been disclosed during our investigation of the athletic program of the University of California at Berkeley, is a clear violation of the above stated objective...This constitutes an official reprimand and also official notice that such conduct by you in violation of the rules of the conference will not be tolerated if it should again occur, which I trust it will not. I regret the necessity of sending this reprimand and notice to you for I appreciate your truthfulness in admitting to violations, your stated willingness to comply with conference rules and their intent, your ready correction of the apparent violations in the past when called to your attention, and your position in competition with certain other conference schools with practices clearly in defiance of conference rules..."*

In reply, Pappy wrote:

*"I deeply regret the circumstances which made such a letter necessary. It has always been my purpose and intent to comply with all rules of the Pacific Coast Conference and of the University of California. I am sorry that any actions or mistakes of mine have caused embarrassment to yourself and to the University. I shall not defend myself or make excuses. For the record I want to assure you that the violations in question were individual cases of genuine need which I established after personal investigation. No promise of tuition help was ever made to an athlete as an inducement to enter California nor was such aid ever given as a reward for athletic achievement. In the great majority of cases the individuals involved were not eligible for aid from University loan funds nor did they have anyone else to turn to."*

Any assumptions Kerr and Seaborg may have made about other conference schools coming forth with similar public reprimands were ill-founded. "We were wrong," Seaborg admitted, "and our misjudgement would forever be painful. No other coach in the Pacific Coast Conference was publicly disciplined. At UCLA Chancellor Allen mildly chastised the entire coaching staff; no official criticism was directed specifically toward Red Sanders."

The well publicized scolding of one of the college game's most beloved figures provoked an angry reaction from Cal alums, Bear fans and newspapers in the Bay Area and in, of all places, southern California. In the July 13, 1956, editions of the Los Angeles *Examiner*, sports columnist Mel Durslag wrote:

> "Pappy Waldorf is a fine gentleman who is both personally and intellectually the equal of any member of Cal's faculty. He is giving his school exactly the level of football that the alumni, the Board of Regents and Chancellor Kerr's own administration expect. For Kerr suddenly to get lofty and embarrass Waldorf in public is the most pretentious act yet to come out of the recent scandals."

Sproul's indefatigable aide, Skinny Johnson, also rode to Pappy's defense, writing in one of his voluminous memos to the boss that the coach "as best he may, has attempted to comply with the orders of the president and his conference. If the coach who replaces him makes a better record it will be largely, if not solely, because he lacks Waldorf's scruples."

Kerr's remonstrations had only served to increase the university's discomfort without noticeably reducing Pappy's stature in the football community. And yet, the coach was under fire, not for any moral lapse but because his teams simply weren't winning as they once did. The

1955 season was easily his worst at Cal. The Bears finished a miserable 2-7-1, suffering humiliating losses to Sanders' implacable Bruins, 47–0; USC, 33–6; Oregon, 21–0; Pitt, 27–7, and, worst of all, to Stanford, 19–0. It was Stanford's first and only win over a Waldorf-coached team. Johnny Wilson led the Bears in scoring with just five touchdowns and quarterback Hugh Maguire was the leading passer, completing 38 or 80 for 564 yards and three touchdowns against eight interceptions. Compared with the juggernauts earlier in the decade, these Bears were powerless. In the opener against Pitt, they were held to 85 yards in total offense, and for the season they scored only 107 points, an output surpassed in just the first three games of the '51 season.

Pappy turned fifty-four early in the '56 season, and he told friends in private that, win or lose, this would be his last year at Cal. Certainly, he'd been hurt by Kerr's reprimand, and he was frustrated by three straight non-winning seasons, but the real reason for his decision, he confided, was that after thirty-two years on the job, he had had his fill of coaching football. He would give the game one last good old college try and then look for something else to do. He'd wait until later to make his retirement public.

In fact, he had confidence that his last season would be a good one. He had some promising sophomores on his roster in backs Joe Kapp and Jack Hart and some large linemen like 245-pound Frank Mattarocci to open holes for them. He'd added to his coaching staff former players and good friends Rod Franz, Carl Van Heuit and John Ralston. Things were looking up. But the Cal Media Guide added a cautionary note in its forecast: "Waldorf can't be expected to work miracles."

And he couldn't. The '56 season began, as the '55 had, with two straight losses, to Baylor, 7–6, and to Illinois 32–20, after blowing a 20–0 lead at halftime. The Baylor defeat was Pappy's first at Cal by one point, but to show which way his luck was going, he'd lose another, by 14–13 to Washington State, later in the season. The new players did furnish some isolated highlights. Hart scored twice in a 21–13 loss to

Oregon State, and quarterback Kapp tossed a 27-yard touchdown pass to Norm Becker in the 23–20 loss to UCLA and returned a fumble he picked off in the air 56 yards for a touchdown in a 15–7 win over Washington.

The Bears were just 2-7 entering the Big Game. Stanford at 4-5 wasn't all that much better, but the Indians did have in quarterback John Brodie, the PCC's new all-time leading passer and another All American in tackle Paul Wiggin. Pappy made public his decision to retire from coaching at a team meeting the Tuesday before the Stanford game. He might have waited until just before the game and delivered a tearful Gipperish locker room oration, but that wasn't Pappy's style. "I wanted to end all speculation," he told the *Examiner*, "and above all I didn't want the boys to feel they were playing this one for me."

But of course that's exactly how they did feel. As Mattarocci said after listening to the coach say goodbye, "We're all boiling and we're going out there Saturday and tear Stanford apart."

Pappy was going out in style. The Cal band serenaded him the night of his announcement, the coach greeting the musicians in his pajamas outside his home on Grizzly Peak Boulevard. Tributes flowed freely all week, including one from Kerr that had an almost apologetic tone to it. "Lynn," he said, eschewing the familiar nickname, "has represented the Berkeley campus with great personal dignity and outstanding success for ten seasons now…But more important is the fine example of good sportsmanship, calm composure under stress, and careful consideration for the feelings and interests of his fellow man that he has set for the men who have played under him and for our students generally."

And in storybook fashion, his Bears won his last Big Game before a capacity crowd of eighty-one thousand five hundred at Memorial Stadium. They didn't exactly "tear Stanford apart," as Mattarocci had promised, but the narrow, 20–18, win was no less satisfying. The Bears marched 67 yards with the opening kickoff, fullback Herb Jackson scoring from the three to complete the 10-play drive. Still in the first quarter, Darrell Roberts plunged one-yard for a 14-0 Cal lead. Stanford revived before the half, Jery McMillen scoring from the 14 and Brodie passing five yards to Ben Robinson for what would have been a tie score if Stanford hadn't missed both point-after attempts. Hart scored Cal's third touchdown from the one after a plodding 59-yard, 17-play march for a 20-12 halftime lead.

Early in the last quarter of what had become a defensive struggle, the Indians' Lou Valli, who gained a then Big Game record 209 yards that day, scored from the 14. Cal guard Don Piestrup blocked the attempted point-after, and the Bears held on for the victory. At the final gun, the players, none of whom outweighed him, carried Waldorf off the field to riotous cheers.

Despite his protestations to the contrary, Pappy had indeed inspired the victory. He also crafted it by changing his line's blocking assignments to create openings for the hard-running Kapp. He had guards Piestrup and team co-captain Don Gilkey pull out of the line in opposite directions on quarterback running plays. Stanford's linebackers, who keyed on the guards, followed them dutifully to protect against sweeps, ignoring the fact that with the rules limiting possible ball carriers to one, something was amiss. With the middle left vacant and Mattarocci more than capable of blocking the man opposite him, Kapp had a field day, gaining 106 yards on 18 carries. As in Pappy's heyday, the Bears rushed for 281 yards while passing only six times with two completions for 15 yards.

When the coach stepped onto the locker room balcony for his final post-game address, he was cheered by a crowd estimated at an amazing 18,000. He was visibly moved. Pappy smiled down upon them, and recalling the rooters' questionable behavior in the past, he bellowed in that cavernous voice, "Sometimes they say you're pretty rough. Sometimes they say you're vulgar. Sometimes they say you're even barbaric. I don't care. I love you and I always will."

Waldorf's 67-32-4 record at Cal was second then only to Smith's 74-16-7, both compiled over ten years. He had an even better record than Andy in the Big Game—7-1-2 to 5-2-1. And he didn't stay unemployed too long, joining the 49ers in 1958 as personnel director and head of college scouting, a job he held for another 14 years before retiring for good in 1972. Pappy Waldorf died of a heart attack on August 15, 1981, while taking his nightly walk on Grizzly Peak Boulevard.

But he remains a part of the campus he graced with his portly presence. In 1986, his former players joined in creating an organization, "Pappy's Boys," dedicated to preserving his memory and supporting Cal football. Its annual banquets are attended by as many as 300 or more members and guests. And in 1994, under the leadership of former star back Pete Schabarum, Pappy's Boys unveiled at the west end of Faculty Glade a lifesize bronze statue of the great man by sculptor Doug Van Howd.

There he is, kneeling typically and holding a clipboard on which, we may presume, are etched some devilishly clever plays designed to confound arch foe Stanford.

PART IV

1957-1982

## CHAPTER NINETEEN

# A ROSE BY ANY OTHER NAME

It now fell to Athletic Director Engelhard, Seaborg and ASUC Executive Director Paul "Bud" Hastings to find a replacement for a living legend. They first approached Bud Wilkinson, something of a legend himself as the coach of national championship teams at Oklahoma in 1950, '55 and '56 and who was then in the process of finishing off a 47-game winning streak, the longest in college football history. But after Oklahoma substantially increased his salary to counter Cal's offer, Wilkinson decided to stay put. In his stead, he persuasively endorsed one of his former assistants, Pete Elliott, who was then head coach at Nebraska. Elliott's candidacy was also championed by his former college coach at Michigan, Fritz Crisler, the athletic director there in '57.

Chancellor Kerr was traveling in New Zealand at the time, so he authorized Seaborg to do the necessary interviewing of prospective Waldorf successors. After meeting with Elliott, Seaborg wrote, "I was so favorably impressed that I authorized Engelhard and Hastings to offer him the position, subject to formal approval by Kerr and the ASUC." Elliott immediately accepted, and in January of 1957 was hired as the new football coach at the University of California. "Cal had such a wonderful reputation," he said more than fifty years later. "And such great tradition. I was thrilled."

The new coach cut a handsome figure on campus. He was only thirty, tall, blond and robust. He had not only been an All American quarterback on Michigan's 1948 national championship team but a four-year letterman as well in basketball and golf, the only winner of twelve varsity letters in the history of the university. His brother and onetime Wolverine teammate, Chalmers "Bump" Elliott, was also an All America back and later a successful coach at his alma mater. After coaching ends at Oregon State in 1949 and '50, Pete joined Wilkinson's staff at Oklahoma, where he first learned and then helped refine the Sooners' devastating split-T offense. After five years in Norman, he moved on to Nebraska, where, in his only season before Cal as a head coach, his team finished with a 4-7 record against stiff competition.

Cal's youngest head coach since Jimmy Shaeffer in 1915, Elliott assembled a similarly youthful and energetic staff, ranging in age from twenty-five-year-old Bill Taylor to thirty-six-year-old elder statesman Gene Stauber. All except Waldorf holdovers Rod Franz, thirty-two, and John Ralston, twenty-nine, had experience in the Wilkinson split-T. Buck McPhail, twenty-seven, had been a 1000-yard rusher at Oklahoma in 1952; Dee Andros, thirty-three, had played guard there from 1946 to '49 and had been an assistant with Wilkinson and then with Elliott at Nebraska; and Taylor had been an assistant line coach at Nebraska.

The '57 Bears would not only have a new coach but an entirely new offensive system to learn. And yet, recalled star halfback Jack Hart, the transition was relatively trouble-free. To start with, Elliott had been good friends—as who hadn't been?—with Pappy before he accepted the job, and the former coach was among the new one's more fervent boosters.

"They were two great people,' said Hart. "If anything, Pete was even more outgoing than Pappy. The big difference in the two coaching staffs was the age factor. All the new coaches were younger guys, some of whom, like McPhail, we remembered vividly as players. With a young staff, there was a dramatic change in tempo and style. With Pappy it was all precision. With Pete there was more emotion. It was hustle, hustle, hustle in the Wilkinson style. Bud's influence was definitely there."

The move to the split-T did present some problems though. With the backs moving behind the quarterback as he scuttled along the line, some of the bigger linemen had difficulty adjusting to Elliott's emphasis on speed and agility over brawn. And whereas under Pappy, quarterback Kapp had been given ample opportunity to both run and pass, he was now more often lateraling to trailing backs than running himself, as he had so successfully in the '56 Big Game. And the split-T was definitely not a passing offense.

Elliott's first season was hardly promising. The Bears of '57 won just one game of ten, that lonesome victory coming halfway into the schedule by 12–0 over a USC team that also finished 1-9, thanks to the absence of eight lettermen due to conference penalties. It was, needless to say, the worst season in Trojan history. An injured Kapp missed the S.C. game with an injury and the one before it, against Navy, a 21–6 loss. But he returned to gain 59 yards passing and 55 rushing in a 24–6 loss to Oregon in Eugene. And he had two touchdown passes in a close loss to Oregon State (21–19) and one each in similar squeakers against Washington (35–27) and Stanford (14–12). He finished the season 38 of 77 passing for 580 yards and 197 rushing, also on 77 attempts. Hart led the team in rushing with 396 yards on 101 carries, receiving with 13 catches for 276 yards and in scoring with six touchdowns.

In spring practice before the 1958 season, the young coach added a few pass-run option plays and rollout pass plays to the repertoire of his industrious quarterback. Players not plays, it is said, win games, but there was little question after the miserable record of the year before that Elliott needed to get the ball more often in Kapp's capable hands. "Joe," said Hart, "was the best we had." And behind his inspirational play, the Bears executed in 1958 a comeback at least the equal of Pappy's in 1947. It was achieved at a time of unusual turmoil in west coast football and within the university administration.

As gloomily forecast, the scandals of 1955 and '56 led finally to the breakup of the Pacific Coast Conference, the rift unbreached between the supposedly pure northern schools and the heavily penalized southern California entries. It was the not entirely paranoid view of UCLA and USC supporters that the others, unable to beat them on the field, were out to get them anyway they could. The 1958 season, in fact, would be the PCC's last, its termination after forty-four years scheduled for July 1, 1959. A new conference, the Athletic Association of Western Universities, composed of Cal, UCLA, USC, Washington and, after an initial holdout, Stanford, would replace it. Within the next 10 years, the AAWU would admit the originally excluded northern schools and become the Pac-8 and then, ten years after that, add Arizona and Arizona State, and morph into the modern Pac-10.

On June 30, 1958, Robert Gordon Sproul retired after twenty-eight eventful and certainly productive years as president of the University of California. Statewide, the university had grown from four campuses to nine during his stewardship. Berkeley, meanwhile, had become one of the acknowledged great universities in the world. Kerr was appointed Sproul's successor by the Regents and Seaborg Kerr's as chancellor. Seaborg was at first reluctant to expand his already time-consuming administrative duties, preferring to dedicate himself entirely to science. But Kerr was persuasive, arguing that his experience was sorely needed during this historic transition. And Seaborg was an unstinting admirer of his boss. Kerr, said he, possessed "a logical mind of unsurpassed brilliance."

Kerr, meanwhile, kidded Seaborg that his most challenging problems as chancellor would be "sex for the students, football for the alumni and parking for the faculty."

Then on August 14, 1958, the roguish and unrepentant UCLA

coach Henry "Red" Sanders died at fifty-three of a heart attack in a downtown Los Angeles hotel room. With him at the time was an attractive blonde woman who described herself variously as a clothes model and dress designer who had, she said, no interest in or knowledge of UCLA football. Sanders had just signed a new ten-year contract with the Bruins after rejecting an offer from Texas A&M. Less than a year earlier, he'd been honored at a "Red Sanders Day" on the Westwood campus during which players, coaches and even a few school administrators lavishly sang his praises. Said UCLA Dean of Students Milton Hahn, half-accurately: "Sanders can not only build character but he wins while doing it."

On August 27, 1958, Seaborg's close friend and fellow Nobel laureate, Cal nuclear physicist Ernest O. Lawrence, died at fifty-seven after a bout with ulcerative colitis. "It would be hard to imagine a world without him," said the grieving chancellor.

In these perplexing circumstances the 1958 football season began—and, for Elliott and the Bears, not well. They lost the opener, 24–20, to the College of the Pacific and its sensational running back Dick Bass, who alone gained 215 yards, a 78-yard touchdown dash among them. A rejuvenated Kapp had 216 yards rushing and passing. Against Michigan State at East Lansing, the Bears fell behind, 20–0, at half, but held the Spartans even after the intermission in what was for Elliott an encouraging 32–12 defeat. "We came off the canvas swinging," the coach enthused. And they kept swinging.

In their third game, the Bears beat by the convincing score of 34–14 a Washington State team that would finish second that season in the lame duck PCC. His players "wanted to win so bad," said Elliott, "that every one of them played up to his potential." It was just Pete's second win at Cal. "Football is all heart and fight," he said. "And they (his players) showed it." Utah and star quarterback Lee Grosscup (later and for many years a Cal broadcaster) were next routed, 36–21, in a game the Bears led at the half 22–0.

If the scores in '58 seem odd—22? 15? 8?—it is with good reason, for beginning that year the NCAA allowed teams the option of either kicking for the traditional one-point conversion or running or passing into the end zone for two points after a touchdown. Elliott's Bears used the two-point try after every TD that season except one. Wayne Crow kicked a PAT in the 23–6 win over Oregon, a game in which Kapp ran for a 92-yard touchdown. Otherwise, it was pretty much a hit or miss operation, Cal scoring 13 two-pointers in 27 tries. Save for punts and kickoffs, they had effectively taken the foot out of football.

The two-point option figured prominently, however, in two important victories. Against USC in Los Angeles, the Bears scored touchdowns on two line plunges by Bill Patton in the first half. A Hart run for two points was stopped short after the first TD, but Patton himself was successful running for two after the second, giving him all the Bears' 14 points for the day. The Trojans also went for two after their two touchdowns and missed both, one on a fake kick, the other when Kapp intercepted a pass attempt.

After winning six of seven games after their shaky start, the Bears needed a win in the Big Game to become the Pacific Coast Conference's last champion and Rose Bowl representative. Washington State, USC and Oregon State, each with two losses in conference play to Cal's one (14–8 to Oregon State) were technically still in the race.

A hopeful crowd of 81,490 filled Memorial Stadium for what appeared to be a mismatch with the 2-7 Indians. But as history informs us, there are no mismatches in the Big Game. The Bears drove 62 yards in eight plays on its first series, Kapp passing 12 yards to Hart for the touchdown and Grover Garvin slicing inside his right end for the two-pointer. But Stanford came right back, the key play a 39-yard halfback pass to the Cal two from John Bond to end Irv Nikolai after a double reverse. Skip Face scored from there, but quarterback Dick Norman's two-point pass attempt bounced off star end Chris Burford's hands, and though Nikolai fielded the carom, back judge Bill Simas ruled that he was out of bounds. Face's 19-yard field goal just before the halftime break gave Stanford one of those baseball-score 9–8 leads attributable to the new conversion rule.

Late in the third quarter, Hart scored from the one to close out a 79-yard drive that required the impressive total of 16 plays. Kapp's pass to Crow for the two returned the lead to Cal, 16–9. But with time running out, Stanford launched a 78-yard march in eight plays. Norman finished it off with a 21-yard pass to Joel Fries in the corner of the end zone. Coach Jack Curtice now faced one of those dilemmas the new rule had created. The score was 16–15. A point-after by Face, an accurate kicker, would have given the Indians an easy tie. But the two-point option was there to discourage ties. Curtice decided to go for the win. So instead of kicking, kicker Face took the handoff and steamed ahead toward the end zone. He was first hit by Patton at the line, but somehow shook free before he was finally swarmed under short of the goal line by, among other defenders, linebacker Andy Segale, guard Jim Green and the ubiquitous Hart. The Bears had won, and were headed for Pasadena for the first time in eight years.

Many experts had trouble reckoning how they got that far. These Bears were cub-sized. Their starting lineup included a tackle Pat Newell, generously listed at 185 pounds, and a guard, 180-pound Don Piestrup, better rigged for play in the nineteenth century than the mid-twentieth when linemen were just beginning to approach the mastodon dimensions they have since achieved. And the backs were not exactly speedsters. "We had no Jensens, Olszewskis, Schabarums or Monachinos to get us those long gainers. Instead we had guys like Hart," said Hart fifty years later. "But we did have the ability, with our long possessions, to keep the ball out of the other team's hands. "We'd just frustrate them four yards or so at a time."

"That team had a wonderful attitude," recalled Elliott. "And great leadership with Joe Kapp and Jack Hart." But was that enough to transform a 1-9 team into a champion in the space of a year? The coach was asked. "You know, I really didn't change things very much between seasons. The players just got better. They had the talent and they executed more efficiently. They had the tenacity."

Alas, tenacity couldn't keep them in Rose Bowl competition with Big Ten champion Iowa, the national leader in total offense and ranked by the Associated Press second only to undefeated Louisiana State. The Hawkeyes were led by All America quarterback Randy Duncan and two cat-quick halfbacks, Bob Jeter and Willie Fleming, who both averaged better than six yards per carry that season. And their linemen were forerunners of the mastodon era. Playing opposite the slender Newell at tackle, for example, was Mac Lewis, who, at a listed 6-6 and 305 pounds, outweighed his adversary by 120 pounds.

Iowa led 20–0 at the half, Duncan sneaking in for one touchdown and passing seven yards to Jeff Langston for another. Fullback Don Horn scored the third from the four after a 65-yard march. Despite the big lead, team leader Kapp never lost heart. He engineered a typically prolonged 74-yard drive in the third quarter finished finally by Hart's yard-long plunge. A Kapp to Hart pass for the two misfired. Offended by this impudence, Iowa scored two quick touchdowns on runs of 37 yards by Fleming and a Rose Bowl record 81 by Jeter. Fleming scored the last Hawkeye TD from the nine after a 92-yard, nine-play drive in the final quarter.

Years later, Fleming recalled with a chuckle Kapp's diehard approach to the game. "I'm in the end zone after scoring and I see this madman running straight at me. It's Kapp all right. He grabs me by the jersey and says, 'We're gonna kick your ass.' I tell him, 'Hey, there's five minutes left and we're way ahead.'" But he said that with such conviction, he had me believing we were in deep trouble."

Kapp did, in fact, lead the Bears to the game's final score, a 17-yard pass to Hart after an 88-yard drive highlighted by a Kapp-Hart completion of 47 yards.

The final score of 38–12 accurately reflected the difference between the two teams and, since this was the Big Ten's 12th win in 13 Rose Bowl games against the PCC, the difference then between the two conferences. Iowa set Rose Bowl records with 429 yards rushing and 516 in total offense. Jeter finished with 194 yards on just nine carries; Hart led the Bears with 103 yards on 23 carries. Duncan passed only 14 times, completing nine for 87 yards; Kapp was eight for 17 for 126 yards and added 34 yards rushing on 10 carries. Duncan, Cal assistant Dee Andros said, " was a good quarterback on a great team. Joe Kapp was a great quarterback on an average team."

In his final season at Cal, Kapp led the conference in rushing with 616 yards on 152 carries. He was 64 for 114 passing for another 775 yards and he led his team in minutes played with 442. Hart had 487 yards rushing and another 395 on a team-leading 32 pass receptions. For the third straight season he led the Bears in scoring with 58 points, accumulated, atypically, on eight touchdowns and five two-point conversions.

Neither star would return for 1959, a 2-8 season fully as miserable as Elliott's first in Berkeley but lacking the promise '57 held of brighter days on the horizon. The Bears opened promisingly enough, though, with a 20–6 win over Sutherland's Washington State Cougars in Spokane. Then they lost eight in a row, including, on September 26th, their second thrashing, 42–12, from Iowa that year. There were lopsided losses as well to Texas, 33–0; Notre Dame, 28–6, and Washington, 20 –0. The Huskies would win the first two AAWU championships and, with the no-repeat rule discarded, the first consecutive West Coast wins against the Big Ten in the Rose Bowl. So no great embarrassment for the Bears there.

Wayne Crow, a halfback in '58, was Elliott's new "triple threat" split-T quarterback, but, fine athlete though he assuredly was, his statistics were unimpressive. He completed just 26 of 67 passes, a .388 percentage, for 379 yards. He had thrice as many interceptions (nine) as touchdown passes and he gained a modest 223 yards rushing. For the entire season, Cal gained only 564 total yards passing while suffering 18 interceptions. In a tight 24–20 loss to Oregon State, the Bears gained exactly zero yards through the air, while piling up 365 on the ground. In another painfully close loss, 20–18 to Oregon, the Bears were one for eight passing for 25 yards, a big improvement. They were 2 for 11 against Washington.

The most disappointing and certainly controversial loss was by 14 –7 to USC on October 31. It was a game that revived age-old accusations against the Trojans of dirty play. The most blatant foul was committed in the second quarter when Cal halfback Steve Bates, who had averaged more than six yards per carry so far that season, was knocked out of bounds near the Trojan bench after a short gain. Bates was flat on his back when S.C. linebacker Mike McKeever, like his twin brother Marlin an All American, piled onto him with forearm extended. McKeever had been ejected for excessively rough play the week before against Stanford, but this was worse. Bates' cheekbone was crushed from eye socket to lips, his nose was broken and several teeth were loosened. Helmet bars were just beginning to gain some favor that year, but they offered only minimal protection, and Bates' face was fully exposed.

Seaborg, recalling the Cannamela-Olszewski "savagery" of eight years before, was outraged anew. As chancellor, he authorized Elliott to make a public complaint to USC President Norman Topping, and he and Kerr threatened to break off athletic relations with the Trojans unless prohibitive measures were taken. This time a formal apology was forthcoming. "All necessary actions are being taken to assure avoidance of similar occurrences," Topping wrote Kerr and Seaborg. In fact, though his team finished 8-2 in '59, Trojan head coach Don Clark resigned at the end of the season to enter his family's business. His cunning thirty-year-old assistant, Al Davis, earlier accused of dubious recruiting activities, also left to enter professional football, where in the near future he would make something of a name for himself.

Elliott also resigned after the season to accept the head coaching job at Illinois. But like Pappy before him, he would triumph in his last game, the Big One. And by a nearly identical score.

In keeping with a tradition dating to Frankie Albert, the Indians had a deadly passer at quarterback in the person of junior Dick Norman. And though his team was just 3-6 entering the game to Cal's 1-8, Norman's passing, particularly to All America end Chris Burford, seemed to give Stanford a decisive advantage. Norman had already that season completed 118 of 229 attempts for 1562 yards and ten touchdowns. Cal's pass "attack," as noted earlier, was laughable. The Bears by then had almost as many interceptions (17) as completions (29).

And yet, this Big Game would be primarily fought in the air. The previously ineffective Crow completed his first eight attempts, including touchdown throws of 48 yards to end Gael Barsotti and 12 to fullback Patton, both in the second quarter. Ditching his two-point policy of the year before, Elliott had Patton kick both points-after. The Bears led by 14–0 at the half.

Then, behind a truly startling performance by Norman, the Indians rallied. A Norman 46-yarder to Ben Robinson put the ball on the Cal three, and Face both scored from there and kicked the conversion. Still in the third quarter, Norman connected with Burford for an 11-yard touchdown that concluded a drive during which the quarterback hit five in a row. Face's kick tied the score.

In the final quarter, Stanford took the lead, 17–14, on Face's 41-yard field goal. With less than four minutes to play, the Bears drove 67 yards to regain the lead on Jerry Scattini's plunge from the two. This time, Patton tried running for the two, but was stopped.

The score stood at 20–17 when Norman launched another overhead attack that carried to the Cal nine. With under thirty seconds left to play, Norman again dropped back to throw, but found his receivers covered. He tried desperately to run out of bounds and stop the clock. He didn't make it. Bears Newell, Garvin and Jerry Lundgren downed him inbounds on the Cal five. The Indians were unable to get off another play before the final gun.

It was yet another thriller, and a record-breaking one at that. Norman completed an NCAA record 34 of 39 passes for 401 yards. He finished the season as the nation's leading passer. Burford's 12 receptions set another record, and he led the nation that year with 61 for 757 yards. Even more remarkable was Barsotti's Big Game breakthrough. He caught five passes for 99 yards after snagging only one for 12 in the previous nine games. With six receptions for the season, he was the Bears' leading receiver. Crow finished with nine for 13 for 158 yards. His two Big Game touchdown throws gave him his three for the season. The Bears set another Big Game record with 11 penalties for 110 yards. But, dammit, they won.

Now all Engelhard, Seaborg and company had to do was find yet another new coach.

CHAPTER TWENTY

# "THE FIGHTING PHI BETA KAPPA"

The skein of losing seasons, interrupted only by the anomaly of 1958, had given rise, both in the press and among fans, to the notion that Cal's new administration was plotting to de-emphasize football. Rumors persisted of Cal and Stanford downgrading their programs to Ivy League status and of joining some sort of national association of like-minded scholastic institutions. Cal's stringent entrance requirements—all applicants must have maintained at least a B-average in academic courses in high school—were enough to intimidate many star players from even considering Berkeley as their next stop. The increasing popularity and profitability of the professional game had made of college football in the eyes of such prospects merely a training ground for honing their skills before advancing to the next level. "Students" of this persuasion were seldom seduced by Berkeley's lofty standing in the academic community or by the opportunity it gave to broaden their cultural horizons.

There were, however, some notable exceptions. The now graduated Kapp, a future star in the NFL, was definitely one. Years later, Kapp recalled his experiences at Cal:

"Nobody in my family had been to college before. It was the best thing that ever happened to me. I got to meet a man like Glenn Seaborg. I'd go down to Robbie's for coffee and someone would point out to me that there was a communist sitting over there. I'd go over and talk to the guy. Hell, I'd never met a communist before. They're all here—communists, liberals, conservatives, you name it. I'd get hammered at the stadium on Saturday, then get up aching on Sunday and go lie out on the Berkeley pier watching the sailboats pass, knowing that Jack London sailed on that Bay, went to classes right here. Hey, life here is rich."

But were there enough open-minded Kapps out there to fill a football roster? Doubts were rising, particularly after a promising young coach like Elliott defected to the Big Ten after just three seasons in Berkeley. After Elliott's disheartening last season, Prescott Sullivan wrote in the *Examiner*, "You can go down the list and see for yourself. Team after team has beaten Cal this year with superior players who couldn't qualify academically for the big school across the Bay. We don't say that it should be otherwise. All we're saying is that the conditions of competition under which Cal has had to play have not been equal."

Will Connolly of the *Chronicle* made what for loyal Cal followers was a bleak forecast: "Cal is going Ivy League, and it's going to get tough for a footballer under A-minus to make the grade. A decade from now, Berkeley will be no more a football power than the University of Chicago."

Kerr and Dick Erickson, a former player, then executive manager of the Alumni Association, tried none too convincingly to tamp down such negative assertions. Writing in the *California Monthly* alumni magazine, Erickson first cited the school's "competitive limitations," then insisted there was "no indication of the slightest de-emphasis." Kerr, in another piece for the magazine, issued a significantly more circumspect denial that only fed the rumors: "I cannot predict the future of intercollegiate athletics; I doubt that anyone can. Too many factors, including educational trends, the rise of television and the increasing popularity of professional athletics enter the picture. I *can* say that the university has every intention of continuing a full intercollegiate and intramural athletic program."

Meanwhile, the search for a new coach progressed apace. While he had no particular candidate in mind, Seaborg wrote with tongue-in-cheek, "I certainly had no lack of help and advice. In fact, I have never been subjected to such a barrage of suggestions, tips, requests, demands, even veiled threats and what looked like a possible bribe—an offer of $1 million for Cal athletics if we hired coach Ray Nagel of Utah."

Other candidates put forward included John Ralston, then coaching at Utah State; Elliott assistant Dee Andros, Len Casanova of Oregon and Bob Devaney of Wyoming. But the overwhelming favorite was former Navy coach and longtime Bay Area favorite Eddie Erdelatz. Eddie had starred at end for Slip Madigan at St. Mary's in the mid-1930s and later had been an assistant there, as well as with USF and the 49ers. "In calls, visits, letters, telegrams, whispered conversations, in meetings and in newspaper columns and letters-to-the editor," wrote Seaborg, "I was implored to believe that Erdelatz was the best man and perhaps the only man to restore Cal football to glory."

In a personal letter to the chancellor, *Chronicle* sports editor Bill Leiser wrote that in addition to his proven coaching acumen, Erdelatz would dispel rumors that Cal was de-emphasizing the game. Not hiring him, wrote Leiser, "would add up to the greatest injustice I have known in forty years of college sports."

Erdelatz had coached Navy for nine years in the 1950s, restoring that proud program to the status it had enjoyed as a wartime power. In that time, he had beaten Army five times, including three in a row beginning with a celebrated 14–2 upset in 1950, Erdelatz's first season. His 1954 Midshipmen, called in paraphrase of the Tennessee Williams drama, the "Team Named Desire," finished with an 8-2 record and was ranked fifth in the nation. In fact, Erdelatz coached Top twenty teams for four straight seasons, and in 1957, he took the 9-1-1 Midshipmen to the Cotton Bowl, where they defeated Rice, 20–7. He was an innovative coach who employed a variety of offensive and defensive alignments, depending on the circumstances. He seemed in every way, except one, the perfect man for the job.

But for Seaborg, the exception mattered most. When Erdelatz left Navy after the 1958 season, it was not without ill-feeling. In his history of the Army-Navy Game, Jack Clary wrote that "There was little sadness within the higher echelons at Annapolis because for several years he had flaunted the rules, regulations and traditions of the Academy to build and maintain a winning team." Considering the misdemeanors of the past decade involving Pacific Coast schools, that just wouldn't do. And though Engelhard and Hastings were prepared to offer Erdelatz a contract, Seaborg flatly rejected him. Instead, he appointed a search committee of "men I knew I could trust:" Law professor Adrian Kragen, Dean of Men and 1930s All American Arleigh Williams, Nello Pace of the faculty's Athletic Advisory Committee and O. Cort Majors, the old Wonder Teamer and alumni activist.

It was then that serendipity, as it will, played a role. At the annual NCAA Coaches Convention in January of 1960 Engelhard encountered at a social gathering the young head coach of the University of New Mexico, Marv Levy. In the course of their conversation, Levy inquired about the coaching vacancy at Cal. Engelhard told him the administration already had somebody, presumably Erdelatz, in mind. Levy thought no more of it. A month or so later, Levy's name resurfaced in an entirely different venue. In the course of his scientific research, Seaborg was chatting with John Suttle, then the personnel officer at Cal's Lawrence Radiation Laboratory. Straying from the business at hand, Suttle told the chancellor that he had heard very positive reports from friends at the Los Alamos atomic research laboratory in New Mexico about the head coach at the university. The man was, he had been told, a fine coach and a gentleman and scholar, to boot.

Levy, in his first two years as head coach, had led the Lobos to consecutive 7-3 seasons and had been named in his first season, the Skyline Conference's "Coach of the Year." He had a Phi Beta Kappa key from Coe College in Cedar Rapids, Iowa, where he'd been a star player, and he'd earned a master's degree from Harvard in English history. To Seaborg he seemed the perfect fit for Cal—a young coach, just thirty-four, who had both a winning record and the academic credentials to assuage the purists among the faculty and administration.

Levy was considerably surprised to receive a phone call from Engelhard asking him to come to Berkeley for an interview. As it developed, he was the sole remaining candidate for the job. Seaborg had dinged Erdelatz, who by then had become the first head coach of the Oakland Raiders in the new American Football League, and Devaney had declined Cal's offer in the belief—later characterized by Levy as "clairvoyant"—that under existing entrance requirements the Bears' chances of winning were remote.

After making what Seaborg described as "a strongly favorable impression" with the chancellor and his committee, Levy was offered the job. He gleefully accepted. "We were going to conquer the world," the new coach wrote in his memoir *Where Else Would You Rather Be?* "Win the championship in this league, and you were in the Rose Bowl... What difference did it make if all the alumni, fans and media in the Bay Area were all sniffing smelling salts that the proud Golden Bears had selected as their coach some chap they had never heard of from the cactus country? Give us two weeks with these little Teddy Bears, and we'd make them into ferocious grizzlies once again."

Levy may have been overly optimistic about the Teddy-Grizzly transformation, but he did accurately forecast the media reception to his hiring. "Marv Levy (Who?) is Cal's New Coach," headlined the *Chronicle*. The *Examiner*, meanwhile, hit upon a theme that would plague Levy throughout his stay in Berkeley: "Cal Hires Egghead Coach."

Not long before Levy arrived, the *Chronicle* had promoted a veteran reporter and exceedingly graceful and acerbic writer named Charles McCabe to opinion-page columnist. The paper's editor then was Scott Newhall, whose creative—some would say, lunatic—methods would eventually make the *Chronicle* the Bay Area's circulation leader. Newhall wanted the scholarly McCabe to write about sports in a column entitled "The Fearless Spectator." Not for him the fawning locker room interview or statistical recitation; Newhall didn't care if McCabe ever attended a game. He wanted him to assume an Olympian perspective on the so-called sports world, looking down on it with the air of an amused patrician. He could not have made a better choice than Mc-Cabe. Charlie knew next to nothing about sports, save for what little he recalled of baseball from his Manhattan boyhood. He fancied himself an essayist in the manner of Montaigne and Pascal, his role models. Newhall had him depicted above the column wearing a derby hat.

Levy proved to be a perfect foil for the new columnist. All of the ingredients for merriment at the coach's expense were at hand—the Phi Beta Kappa key, Harvard, de-emphasis, and even Los Alamos with its history of developing the atomic bomb or, as McCabe called it, "the big firecracker." Without ever discussing the matter with Levy, whom he chose to portray as a naive intellectual, or the university administration, McCabe quickly concluded that the new coach was hired to kill football at Cal.

Shortly after Levy's arrival, McCabe wrote, "That implacable enemy of college football, education, is coming through loud and clear these days at the University of California." A month later, he decided that Levy got the job because he was "probably the first university football coach who has used the word 'whom' as though it were not a conversational excrescence." Levy became for him the "fighting Phi Beta Kappa" who expounds "pother about 'Playing the Game' while his superiors are quietly scuttling football in favor of various forms of culture."

With the 1960 season underway, McCabe complimented Levy for

losing his first three games. "Football de-emphasis at Cal is going along according to plan...old Marv had done his job well. He was brought to Cal to murder professional college football, and he's doing it...For Marv is an undertaker, make no mistake about it. Whether or not he knew it, he was called in by an anti-football administration to see to it that football is reduced to a campus status roughly comparable to Poli Sci 3. The Cal administration was at no time enjoined from hiring a football coach, but they preferred to hire Marv."

McCabe had great sport connecting Levy to "big firecracker" research in New Mexico. "The University of New Mexico is in Albuquerque. Albuquerque is infested with physicists. A physicist is a man who makes bombs because he loves humanity...And Dr. Glenn Theodore Seaborg is chancellor at Cal. He is a chemist. He won the Nobel Prize, which was founded by a Swedish chap who made bombs, and had a guilty conscience, too."

It made little difference that McCabe was wrong in just about every particular; his column grew increasingly popular. Neither Seaborg nor even Kerr had plans to junk football, as should have been evident from the ever more difficult schedules they approved. And Levy was a tough and dedicated football coach, not a fussy academic. He'd grown up in a working-class neighborhood on Chicago's south side and after service in World War II as an Air Force enlisted man, he became a three-sport—football, basketball and track—athlete at Coe. He'd intended to study law at Harvard but transferred to the liberal arts side in hopes of getting a teaching and coaching job afterward. His first coaching assignment was as an assistant for a high school junior-varsity team. He later worked as an assistant at both Coe and New Mexico before becoming the Lobos's head coach.

He had come to Cal hoping to reinvigorate the football program, and he assembled a top staff that included future Cal head coach Mike White and an imaginative former high school coach named Bill Walsh (Yes, that Bill Walsh.) And as his career after Cal demonstrated —two

Grey Cup championships in Canada, a record four straight Super
Bowl appearances with the Buffalo Bills—Marv Levy was a pretty fair
coach. In 2001, for that matter, he was inducted into the Pro Football
Hall of Fame.

But his experiences at Cal were hardly indicative of future success. In fact, while there he never could rid himself of the de-emphasis
shibboleth that McCabe and others so insistently trumpeted. "To supporters of Cal football," Levy wrote, "I was viewed as the instrument
by which these perceived administrative objectives were to be achieved.
I came thinking I was going to take them to the Rose Bowl, and they
thought I had come to take them to the Toilet Bowl."

If that was indeed their destination, the Bears were at least snappily dressed for the journey. Levy restored the striped sleeves and dark
blue jerseys of the Ingram era. The players wore silky gold pants and
pro-style Navy blue sox. But they failed to play up to their snappy at-
tire. Levy scrapped the Split-T in favor of his own Winged-T formation,
which featured single-wing type blocking in the line. And though his
running backs were slow and had, as he put it, "the reactions of lava,"
he hoped that his quarterback Randy Gold could compensate with
some reasonably accurate passing. Gold finished the season with an
admirable .556 percentage on 65 for 117 and 696 yards, but he threw
only two touchdown passes against seven interceptions. Bates, fully recovered from the McKeever mauling, was the leading rusher with 384
yards on 82 carries.

But the Bears dropped their first three games—to Tulane, 7–3;
Notre Dame, 21–7, and Army, 28–10—en route to a 2-7-1 season all
too typical of recent years. A 21–21 tie with Washington State gave
Levy some relief, but that game came perilously close to becoming another defeat. On the very last play, the Cougars's fine receiver, Hugh
Campbell, made a lunging finger-tip catch on the Cal 15 and staggered
forward trying to regain his balance. As he stumbled on toward the end
zone, Levy on the sidelines, "twitched through more coaxing gyrations

than a bowler trying to pick up a spare on a 7-10 split." Campbell finally toppled over a yard short of the winning touchdown.

Actually, the Bears played well enough in almost every game. They beat Oregon State, 14–6, in Corvallis and were beaten badly only by UCLA, 28–0, a team sparked by future pro stars Bill Kilmer, Jim Johnson and Kermit Alexander, and then by sixth-ranked Washington, 27 –7. With a 1-7-1 record entering the Big Game, they were odds-on favorites over a Stanford team that, at 0-9, was even worse.

In this littlest of all Big Games, Levy devised a pass-free controlled attack that would keep the ball out of the hands of the Indians' lone threat, quarterback Norman. Gold tossed just one pass all day and completed it for a four-yard touchdown to Bates, concluding a 74-yard, 15-play drive with the opening kickoff that consumed seven minutes and twenty-eight seconds. The Bears held the ball for much of the second quarter, plodding 97 yards in 17 plays, all of them runs by Bates, Scattini and fullback George Pierovich. Scattini finally plunged in from the one. Levy was heartened by "thunderous noise in old California Memorial Stadium…with each first down we eked out." Stanford got a touchdown and a field goal from the redoubtable Face to close the gap to 14–10. But the Bears drove 61 yards to ice the game late in the fourth quarter on Gold's quarterback sneak. Levy had at least won his first Big Game.

Earlier in the year, Engelhard had been replaced as Athletic Director by Pete Newell, who in 1959 had coached Cal's basketball team to its first and, as of this writing, only NCAA basketball championship. Newell was accustomed to winning—ten years earlier he coached USF to the then prestigious NIT title—and de-emphasis was not in his vocabulary. In the meantime, the athletic department had been removed from ASUC control. Newell was now responsible only to the university administration, and funds were tight. He needed the revenue from a heavily populated stadium on football Saturdays. Levy's Bears weren't helping much. In fact, they were even worse in his second season than the first, finishing 1-8-1, the lone win coming in the fourth game against defending Rose Bowl champion Washington by 21–14. The first two losses were to top ten teams Texas (28–3) and Iowa (28–7). The worst was to Kansas, 53–7, a week before the Big Game. And this time they lost to Stanford, 20–7, on a muddy field.

But for all of his travails, Levy remained hopeful. For starters, he'd found a quarterback so skilled in virtually every facet of the game that, with a little help, he might turn Cal's sinking fortunes around.

As a star at Campbell High School in San Jose, Craig Morton was among the nation's most coveted prospects. "We recruited him very hard," Levy recalled years later. But first he had to make certain the prize recruit could get into Cal. Morton had been a good student in high school, but his grades were just short of Cal's stiff requirements. There was, however, a small window of opportunity in that admission directors on all Cal campuses had the option of admitting up to two percent of non-qualified applicants if they possessed "redeeming qualifications." At UCLA, those most frequently represented athletic talent, whereas at Cal that was almost never so. Levy decided Morton should be the exception to the rule. "My plea to the director of admissions," he recalled, "was a model of abject self-degradation." And it worked.

Still, Morton was not yet a sure thing for Cal. Levy would need help from another coach, a dead one, to close the deal. "Growing up in the Bay Area, I'd been a fan of both Stanford and Cal," Morton recalled in an interview for this book. "I knew it would be one or the other. Actually, I was so impressed with coach Jack Curtice at Stanford that I'd decided to go there. Then Joe Kapp started hanging around the house, and you know how persuasive Joe can be. I also had an uncle who was a friend of Paul Christopulos at Cal. So I finally agreed to go to a dinner for recruits on the Cal campus. I talked to coach Levy and Mike White there, and was impressed by both of them. But I was still headed for Stanford. Then professor Garff Wilson stood up after dinner to read the 'Andy Smith Eulogy.' That did it! I was deeply moved. In fact, so moved that I got up out of my seat and announced right then that I was going to Cal and that I hoped all the others in the room would do the same. And I think most of them did. From then on, I realized that you're either a Cal man or a Stanford man and that eventually you'll find out which you are. After listening to the eulogy, I knew I was a Cal man and would always be one."

Morton enrolled at Cal in the fall of 1961 and immediately led the freshman team to an undefeated six-game season. He was, according to the media guide, "a poised passer, tough runner and devastating defender." In truth, he was much more than a "poised passer"; he had an extraordinarily powerful and accurate throwing arm. And at this early stage of his career, he was, at nearly 6-4 and 210 pounds, a swift enough runner to return punts. To top it all off, he was, Levy rejoiced, "a fine young gentleman."

So things were looking up in '62. At quarterback, he had Morton and two effective backups, both former starters, in Gold and Larry Balliett. It was then that the coach's run of stupendously rotten luck betrayed him once more. On the first day of fall practice, Morton suffered a knee injury so severe that team doctors said he might well miss the entire season. Then in the third game, a 26–24 loss to Pittsburgh, Gold suffered a season-ending injury. And in game five, a 32–6 loss to USC in Los Angeles, Balliett went down in the third quarter, and since third-stringer Jerry Walter was already hurt, fourth-stringer Dave Thompson finished the game against the nation's number-one-ranked team. Next up for the 1-4, apparently quarterbackless Bears was Penn State, which would finish the season ranked ninth and play in the Gator Bowl.

Morton, meanwhile, had worked furiously to get back into playing condition. "In all my years of coaching," wrote Levy, "I have never seen a player work with as much resolve and with as much confidence on his rehabilitation as Craig did." He didn't start the Penn State game but, Keckley-style, he begged the doctors and his coach to let him play.

In the second quarter, with the Bears trailing 7–0, they did. He would make his debut as a varsity player against a nationally ranked team while playing on a still gimpy knee and with almost no meaningful practice time beforehand.

So what did he do? He passed 35 yards to Tom Blanchfield, 27 to Mike Gridley and nine more to Blanchfield before connecting with Jim Blakeny for a touchdown from the four. After a rest, the doctors agreed he could play a little more. He passed 24 to Gridley, 13 to Bill Krum, 10 to Gridley and six to Alan Nelson for another score. In the fourth quarter, with Cal behind 23–14, Morton came in for one last drive. He passed 32 yards to Bill Turner, 16 to Ron Vaughn, 12 to Turner, 17 to Blanchfield, three to Dale Rubin and eight to Tom Lutes for the touchdown.

Playing little more than two quarters, Morton in his first college game had thrown three touchdown passes and had set Cal records with 274 yards passing and 285 in total offense. His team had lost the game, 23–21, but the new quarterback had been so sensational that, despite another losing record, Cal fans had reason to cheer again.

The next week, against UCLA, Morton completed 18 of 32 passes for 236 yards, but Bruin star Kermit Alexander scored four touchdowns, and the Bears lost, 26–16. Washington pitched a 27–0 shutout in the rain at Seattle and Kansas won, 33–21, despite three more Morton touchdown passes. Against Stanford, Morton threw touchdown passes of 31 yards to Turner and three to Nelson to give Cal a 13–3 halftime lead, but Stanford rallied behind backup quarterback Clark Weaver to score 27 unanswered points and win, 30–13, before a Memorial Stadium crowd of seventy-two thousand seven hundred.

To illustrate how student life would change over the next decade, the Stanford Band, only a half-dozen years away from the anarchic phase it would so tediously sustain for another forty or more years, paid tribute at halftime of this 1962 Big Game to "March King" John Phillip Sousa. Then, playing "Sons of Stanford Red," the band high-stepped into the "traditional Axe formation from which 'Prince Lightfoot' performed his "authentic Indian dance to the music of 'Redskin.'" The musicians concluded their performance with the "famous Queen Anne Salute, a double row of perfectly timed bows." March music? Traditional? Formations? Redskin? Perfectly timed?

Levy, meanwhile, had now lost two straight Big Games and the 1-9 season had lowered his three-year record at Cal to a hangdog 4-24-2. Still, if Morton could stay healthy, all was not lost. In just half-a-season, the quarterback completed 69 of 126 passes for 905 yards and nine touchdowns. And the Bears did get better. With a fit Morton, they finished 4-5-1 in 1963 and walloped UCLA, 25–0. On the year, Morton completed 101 of 207 for 1475 yards and 14 touchdowns.

Off the field, though, 1963 was by no measure a good year. On November 22, the day before the scheduled Big Game, President John F. Kennedy was assassinated in Dallas. Only the year before, the president had addressed a Memorial Stadium crowd estimated at upwards of ninety thousand at the Charter Day ceremonies. All college games were postponed for one week after his death. And when the Big Game was played before a markedly subdued and below capacity crowd at Stanford Stadium, the Indians won their third in a row, this time by 28–17.

Despite better prospects for '64, Levy knew he was in trouble. He had developed a close attachment to the university, its traditions and physical beauty. He even learned the words to Cal's many fight songs, a feat unprecedented among coaches. "I enjoyed my time there tremendously despite the obstacles," he said many years later. "I would gladly have become the West Coast's Joe Paterno."

But the people who had hired him were gone. In January of 1961, Seaborg resigned as chancellor to become chairman of the Atomic Energy Commission. He was replaced by Edward W. Strong, a dour professor of philosophy. Newell, with increased responsibilities, was the athletic director. And the years directly ahead would not be hospitable for university administrators at any level. Nor would they be for football coaches.

As Seaborg observed before he departed, "The silent generation of the 1950s was fading, and we were entering a period of rising student activism and political controversy." As Patricia A. Pelfrey wrote in her *Brief History* of the university, "In the turbulent years from 1964 through the early 1970s, demonstrations and protests became a routine part of academic life."

Marv Levy wouldn't be around to experience them. He resigned under pressure two weeks after the 1963 Big Game.

CHAPTER TWENTY-ONE

# FREE SPEECH

In the fall of 1964, the most newsworthy figure on the Cal campus was not the tall, handsome All American quarterback but a lanky, frizzy-haired philosophy major with a stutter.

The football team under new head coach Ray Willsey was in its final preparations for the season opener with Missouri at Memorial Stadium when on Monday, September 14, a seemingly innocuous edict was issued by Dean of Students Katherine A. Towle banning political activity on a twenty-six-foot-long strip of brick walkway outside Sather Gate at the dead end of Telegraph Avenue at Bancroft Way. Since for decades there had been commercial activity on that block, the strip was erroneously considered to be part of the city of Berkeley and not of the campus. Its status, though, was at that time something of a mystery, even to ranking university administrators, among them Dean of Men and former Cal football star Arleigh Williams, and, in all probability, Dean Towle herself.

Actually, no one in charge had given the matter much thought until Carl Irving, then a reporter for the Oakland *Tribune*, first called it to the attention of University public affairs officer Dick Hafner in July of '64. A private citizen had called the *Tribune* city desk earlier complaining of the politicking there and wondered who was in charge—the city or the university? City Editor Roy Grimm sent Irving to find out. The *Tribune* was then owned and edited by former U.S. Senator William Knowland, an arch conservative who suspected that opponents of Barry Goldwater's candidacy for the Republican nomination for president had been recruited on the strip. Goldwater was nominated that very month at the Republican National Convention in San Francisco's Cow Palace, and Knowland became his west coast campaign manager. Beyond that, Knowland had long regarded the Berkeley campus as a breeding ground for Communist infiltration. For him, Cal was "the little red schoolhouse."

So if the strip was actually Cal property, Hafner was asked, how is it the rules imposed by President Sproul in the 1930s prohibiting political fund-raising, speechmaking and membership recruiting on campus were not enforced there? Good question, thought Hafner, who sought out Vice Chancellor (for student affairs) Alex Sherriffs for counsel.

University President Kerr was then on an economic mission to Asia and Strong was in Hawaii. So Sherriffs raised the issue at an administrative meeting on July 29 that was originally called to discuss bicycle traffic on campus. Sherriffs, himself a staunch conservative, decided that since the strip was in fact on university property, the Sproul rules should apply and the political activists given the boot. Towle and Williams disagreed. The political tables set up there were "harmless," argued Towle, a former Marine Corps colonel, and the speeches delivered at or even on top of them were valuable as "an escape valve." Unconvinced, Sherriffs instructed Towle to prepare a letter to campus political groups, for delivery at the beginning of the fall semester, declaring the strip out of bounds.

When Williams asked Sherriffs under what authority he was acting, the vice chancellor pointed to the ceiling and said, "God's." Williams said both he and Towle assumed he meant Kerr. They were wrong. The president complained later that he only learned of Sher-riffs's decision when he returned to Berkeley in September and that he considered it "one of the worst administrative blunders in the history of the University."

In their defense, both Sherriffs and Strong, who rigidly backed the ban, had some reason to expect Kerr's support, since the president had long endorsed Sproul's rules against political advocacy. But they missed the point of it. As an economist and industrial relations expert, Kerr was, at heart, a negotiator. And in his efforts to liberalize, not limit, political activity on campus, the Sproul rules were his negotiat-ing tool, his hole card in dealing with the mostly conservative Board of Regents. On his watch, the thirty-year-old debate on mandatory ROTC had been resolved in 1962 in favor of making the course volun-tary and in '63 he had persuaded the Regents to lift the twelve-year ban on Communists speaking at University functions. In each case, the Regents were reassured by Kerr's promises to keep political advocacy out of campus life and to make certain the University functioned as "an educational institution, not a political party." Off campus, the stu-dents were free to pursue whatever political causes caught their fancy; on campus, they were to hit the books.

But Kerr was acutely aware that, as the Bob Dylan lyric proclaimed, "the times, they are a-changin'," and that the civil rights movement had politicized an entire generation of young Americans. The strip itself had been a prime recruiting center for that noble enterprise. So when Kerr returned, he wrote that he was "deeply depressed" by the decree shutting it down. And angry, mainly at Strong, for letting it happen.

The chancellor, he wrote, "did not inform me of what was hap-pening on campus and tell me of his proposed actions, as Seaborg had always done...Was he declaring his autonomy? Or was he just insen-sitive with no idea of the repercussions of his action?...Was he really so alarmed by what turned out to be a nonexistent local Communist menace?...I was astounded."

Kerr's request that the order be rescinded forthwith was, to his further consternation, flatly rejected by the chancellor. "To Strong," wrote Kerr," the request was a slap in the face, a challenge to his authority over student affairs." And Kerr was reluctant to override him since it was he who had advocated giving University chancellors greater control of campus affairs, greater control than he had ever experienced under Sproul. "I was not the 'omnipotent' president my predecessor had been." That he had not exercised his authority and done away with the ban was, he decided in retrospect, yet "another administrative blunder."

There was, in the beginning at least, no real awareness away from the campus of the far-reaching consequences of the administration's blundering. The *Chronicle* treated Towle's edict with the wry humor characteristic of that newspaper in the 1960s. In a five-paragraph story on page two that Friday, it reported that "In the past the area has seen crowds of several hundred persons listening to speakers extolling the virtues of such things as marijuana, conservatism, socialism and Black Muslimism." Towle was quoted as saying that clearing out the political tables would ease the flow of foot traffic into the campus. There were clearly more important issues to cover—like the football game Cal would play the next day.

Coach Willsey's return to his alma mater had aroused new hope among disenchanted fans and alums. A star defensive back and part-time quarterback in his playing days under Waldorf, he became the first alumnus to coach the team since Nibs Price in 1930. In the dozen years since he last wore a Cal jersey, Willsey had played professionally for two seasons in Canada, been a player-coach there, and had served as an assistant to the famous Darrell Royal at Washington and Texas and had coached for three years in the NFL with the Cardinals and Redskins. Among his seven assistant coaches that first season were three more of Pappy's boys—Jim Cullom, Bill Dutton and Bud Van Deren.

Willsey's easy-going manner belied both his intensity and dedication to his craft. The players quickly took to him. One was quoted anonymously in the *Blue and Gold* as suggesting, "If Ray Willsey can't bring winning football to California, no one can." A coach lacking Willsey's ironic nature and sense of history might have been flattered by such a remark. Willsey was merely amused. He might have spotted an omen, though, when just before the kickoff of his first game as Cal head man, a St. Bernard dog named "Brutus" rumbled onto the field and made off with the ball.

Still, his Bears beat Missouri, 21–14, displaying a strong running game out of the coach's flanker-T formation to complement Morton's passing. They also showcased an opportunistic defense highlighted by Jim Hunt's two game-saving interceptions in the second half. Tom Relles, an undersized 183-pound fullback gained 89 of Cal's 226 rushing yards on a day when temperatures approached ninety degrees. With the improved running game featuring Relles and the versatile Tom Blanchfield and with Morton throwing to 6-foot-6 end Jack Schraub and speedy flankers Jerry Mosher and Jerry Bradley, the '64 Bears were picked for the middle, not the bottom, of the newly constituted (the Oregon schools were added that year) Pacific-8 conference. Willsey's debut win was the first for a new Cal coach since Pappy defeated Santa Clara seventeen years earlier.

A 20–14 loss to third-ranked Illinois, coached by Pete Elliott, in the second game was seen as a forgivable bump on the road to what was now being forecast as Cal's first winning season since Elliott himself led the Bears in 1958. And Morton nearly concocted an upset. In the last two minutes of the game, he passed nine yards to Bradley for one touchdown and then, after a successful onside kick, hit the flanker again for a 32-yarder in the end zone. But game officials ruled that Bradley had been out of bounds when he caught it.

The football team was not the story that week, though, nor would it be in the weeks ahead. On the Monday following the Illinois game, student activists protesting the no-politics policy disrupted a University meeting with an angry demonstration. Two days later, in violation of the newly invoked rule, they set up a political table on the disputed strip and then, under the fiery leadership of a twenty-one-year-old junior in philosophy named Mario Savio, invaded Sproul Hall, the University's administration building, for a "sit-in." Chancellor Strong was all for calling the cops, but Kerr, fearing widespread violence, cautioned against it and, after a meeting with Savio and his subordinates in what was now being called, "The Free Speech Movement," achieved a temporary truce.

In Savio, the FSM had a most compelling and yet unlikely leader. Born in Queens, New York, to an Italian-American Catholic working-class family, he had aspired to the priesthood as a youth, a predictable enough career choice in a family that already had two nuns. But after a year at the Christian Brothers' Manhattan College, he somehow lost his faith, substituting in its absence a passionate belief in civil rights and social justice. "In the Civil Rights Movement there were all those ministers," he said in an interview years later. "And so to me this was an example of God working in the world...I couldn't bring myself to believe the religion I was born into on a factual basis. But the spirit of 'do good' and 'resist evil' was an important part of my religious upbringing. I saw that in the Civil Rights Movement—and I wanted to ally myself with that."

Savio transferred to Queens College, where he majored in physics. Then after a summer spent on a Newman Club aid mission to Mexico, he entered Cal in the fall of 1963, where he switched his major to philosophy. "I was not a careerist," he said. "I was someone who took good and evil exceptionally seriously." In Berkeley, he became involved, as had so many of the FSMers, in civil rights protests against job discrimination in San Francisco. In March of 1964, he was arrested with more than five hundred others, one hundred of them Cal students, at a sit-in in the Sheraton-Palace Hotel, an event for which he was recruited on the Bancroft-Telegraph strip. He then joined the Mississippi Summer Project aimed at registering southern blacks to vote. It was an experience, wrote his friend, author-lawyer Jo Freeman, that changed him from "a cautious, inquisitive do-gooder" into "an inspired leader who galvanized others into action by speaking what was in their hearts."

After listening to Salvio "galvanize" his legions at the strip by denouncing the University as a "factory" manufacturing students who enter as "adolescents" and come out the same way, incapable of "taking a strong position as free men," a *Chronicle* reporter described him as "silver tongued." In fact, Savio had struggled for much of his life to conquer a seemingly incurable stammer. Somehow, though, when he had a microphone in his hand and stood before audiences in the hundreds and eventually the thousands, his speech resonated with unimpaired clarity.

On Wednesday, September 30, three days before the football team's game with Minnesota, the FSM leadership, outraged by Strong's decision to expel eight of its members, including Savio, again challenged the no-politics rule. A table was set up on the strip that morning by CORE—the Congress of Racial Equality—and manned by a twenty-four-year-old graduate-school dropout named Jack Weinberg. A 1963 Cal grad, Weinberg would secure a place for himself in anthologies of famous remarks by declaring, as a result of this episode, "We don't trust anybody over thirty."

This time, Strong did call the cops, and a police car arrived to collect Weinberg. It wouldn't depart the premises for thirty-two hours as irate students, not all of them FSM insurgents, surrounded it. The event generated a banner headline in the next day's *Chronicle* (THE BIG UC REVOLT) and a front page story:

"The mustachioed Weinberg, not a student but a catalyst for yesterday's demonstrations, was incarcerated at noon, but three thousand cheering, chanting students wouldn't let the police car move. He sat throughout the night, munching sandwiches handed in the window by students, napping and smiling, apparently pleased by all the attention."

A later report revealed that the captive had "answered nature's call" through the discreet use of empty soft drink bottles.

The Movement had added a new celebrity, one who defined with his remark the then-famous "Generation Gap". But Savio was still its voice, and he used the roof of the stalled police car as his rostrum, again urging demonstrators to occupy "factory" headquarters at Sproul Hall and there to "put your bodies upon gears and upon wheels, upon the levers, upon all the apparatus and make it stop."

Strong again summoned campus and Berkeley police to haul out the intruders, but, grossly outnumbered, the officers were stymied. One Berkeley cop was even passed hand-over-hand down the steps, as if he'd been caught sporting red apparel in the rooting section. SPROUL HALL BATTLE, banner-headlined the *Chronicle*, POLICE IN RETREAT. Once more, Kerr intervened, by now at the insistence of an alarmed Governor Edmund G. "Pat" Brown, and he managed to broker a deal with Savio and other members of the FSM high command. The building was emptied of invaders by 8 p.m. Friday. The police car and its martyr-passenger sped off to jail, where Weinberg was booked for trespassing and released on his own recognizance.

The battle would not truly end until December when, after yet another, even bigger and far more violent sit-in confrontation with police, the University finally relented, at the urging of a faculty committee and the Academic Senate. On-campus political speech would from then on be limited only by the appropriate amendments to the U.S. Constitution. But Cal had come frighteningly close to a full-blown revolution.

"It was an all-consuming event," recalled David Bush, then a sophomore sportswriter for the *Daily Californian*. "It was all anybody talked about. I'm sure that at USC they were talking about football, but not at Cal. For me, personally, it was an awakening. I was brought up to respect adult authority. It never occurred to me until then that adults could be so dead wrong."

The breach between hardliner Strong and mediator Kerr was permanent. "Mutual trust and friendship were destroyed," Kerr wrote years later, "and never restored." The insurgency had also caused, wrote Kerr, "a huge cry of anger from Regents, legislators, alumni, police officials and many others at this attack on law and order." Over the long haul, it and future demonstrations discouraged fund-raising and brought about, at least in part, the election as governor of Ronald Reagan, who referred disparagingly to the "mess in Berkeley."

Kerr himself became a target of FSM vitriol, labeled to his frustration a "proto-fascist ideologue" when in reality, he tried to explain, "I was actually a New Deal liberal and a Keynesian as an economist…I was too combative with superior authority—not too supine…And it was I, in the end, who also paid one of the highest personal prices."

Strong was fired by the Regents on January 2, 1965, Sherriffs on August 20. Dean Towle retired that year, to be succeeded by Williams. Kerr lasted another fretful two-and-a-half years.

The new football coach was amazed by the scope of the campus disruptions. Willsey had come to coach at Cal on the recommendation of his old boss, Royal, and with the firm support of Newell, who, in fact, threatened to resign if Willsey were not hired by the administration. Willsey admits to no second thoughts about taking the job, even after that tumultuous first autumn. He even listened with interest to Savio and the other FSM orators.

"In the beginning," he said, "it was fascinating to hear all those arguments. But no one then could see how far and how deep that thing was going to go." And it occurred to him with gathering dread that the demonstrations, widely covered in the press and on nightly newscasts, might well have long-term effects on his recruiting. Parents, he reasoned, might be reluctant to send their football star offspring to a school so rife with possibly communist-induced rebellion. "I told our recruiters," he joked years later, "that when they call on a prospect make certain the family television set is not tuned to the news."

Against these certainly unexpected impediments, he persevered, though. After a promising 3-2 start, all games against intersectional opponents—Missouri, Illinois, Minnesota, Miami and Navy—his team finished with five straight losses, four of them within the Pac-8. The one constant was Morton's superior play. In the Bears' 27–13 win over Navy, the quarterback convincingly stole the show from the injured 1963 Heisman Trophy winner, Roger Staubach, connecting on two touchdown passes in the second half to break the game open. Alas, it would be Cal's last win of the season.

Morton passed for two touchdowns and ran for another against USC, completing 18 of 28. But Trojan QB Craig Fertig had a career day, throwing for 371 yards and four touchdowns, including the winning one in the waning minutes. The Bears lost, 26–21. Against UCLA, Morton hit Bradley on the Bruin seven with barely a minute left to play, but an incompletion and a sack ended the threat. The Bears lost, 25–21. There followed equally disheartening losses to Washington, 21–16, and Utah, 14–0, a game that ended Morton's streak of at least one touchdown pass in fifteen straight games.

By the time of the Big Game, Morton was hailed as "the best quarterback in Cal history." But he could end neither that season's losing streak nor the ongoing one with Stanford. The Bears dominated the first half, outgaining the Indians in total yards, 137 to 30 and allowing them to pass midfield only once. But their lead was merely, 3–0, the result of Blanchfield's 29-yard field goal. In the second half, the Indians, behind their "real Indian" quarterback, Dave Lewis, scored 21 unanswered points to win their fourth consecutive Big Game.

Morton now held Cal records for single season (14) and career (36) touchdown passes and for season (2121) and career (4501) passing yardage, the last two also conference records. In 1964, his final season, he completed 158 of 308 pass attempts for a .601 percentage. He made five post-season All America teams and was drafted in the first round, sixth overall, by the Dallas Cowboys of the NFL.

But he left Cal without ever winning a Big Game. Savio, who also left school in 1965, probably never saw one. He boasted much later that the FSM "had the moral cachet of the campus. Absolutely." The demonstrations, he said, "had won out over football games, no question about it."

Morton played eighteen years in the NFL, appearing in three Super Bowls, with the Cowboys in 1971 and '72 and Denver in '78. He eventually returned to the University as an athletic department fund-raiser for the Memorial Stadium renovation project.

At age sixty-five, Morton reflected pensively on his undergraduate years. "I think what really caused us to lose our innocence then was the assassination of President Kennedy. I remember how stunned I was to hear about it. I'd just walked out of an English class at Dwinelle Hall...we all remember where we were that day, don't we? Before his death, it had been such a great time to be an American. I'd listened to him speak at the stadium just the year before. Everything seemed to change after he was gone. I have to admit I knew very little about civil rights in those days. I felt that the Free Speech Movement had nothing to do with free speech, that it was just pure radicalism. But what that guy, Savio, created was amazing. You had to give him that. Then when I went to Texas to play for the Cowboys I saw the inequities of life there. I guarantee you free speech and civil rights hadn't made it there yet. It was an awakening for me. And then the war in Vietnam—horrible! You wonder if we'll ever learn."

Savio transferred to San Francisco State where he resumed his studies in physics and earned a masters degree. He later taught mathematics, logic and interdisciplinary studies at Sonoma State University. Savio had long suffered from a heart ailment, but even at bucolic Sonoma State, he refused to lighten his pace. "I have only two speeds," he told a friend, "zero and one hundred." And in the fall of 1996, he embraced a new cause with customary zeal, opposing a proposed $300 increase in student fees which he felt discriminated against poor, mostly black, students.

On November 2, the day following a bitter public debate with school administrators, he collapsed while writing a position paper on the fee hike. He died four days later at age fifty-three.

On December 3, 1997, the Cal administration approved naming the steps at the entrance to Sproul Hall, "Mario Savio Steps." At the dedication ceremony, history professor Leon Litwack expressed the hope that "each generation of Berkeley students will produce its share of dissidents, rebels and disturbers of the peace, that they will continue to provoke, that they will try the university's patience and tolerance... The very health of this university, the very sanity and survival of our nation, depends upon it."

CHAPTER TWENTY-TWO

# MIXED BLESSINGS

The resolution of the FSM conflict did not bring an end, as Kerr &
Co. had faintly hoped it would, to student demonstrations on campus.
There were, as it turned out, causes aplenty to arouse the dissidents, not
the least of them, in March of 1965, a demand to expand free speech
to include profanity—the "Filthy Speech Movement." At its center was
the university's refusal to allow the sale and distribution on campus of
a magazine published by FSM veterans called "Spider," which, as the
Daily Cal observed, printed a "dirty word in almost all the articles."

Although the magazine was originally called "Spider" because it
had as many editors as the arachnid has legs, its founders proclaimed
that it also represented an acronym for "Sex, Politics, International
Communism, Drugs, Extremism and Rock 'n Roll." Demonstrations
in its defense showed some early foot, attracting the usual hundreds of
protesters to Sproul steps, but the movement eventually lost momentum, leaving its salty supporters cursing in frustration. In retrospect,
the issue was merely premature since foul language would soon enough
become a routine part of the national discourse.

Causes of significantly greater heft arose that school year, among
them the continuing struggle for civil rights, the Women's Liberation

Movement, the sexual revolution and, most powerfully, opposition to the war in Vietnam, which gained greater urgency with the dispatch in March 1965 of the first U.S. ground troops to that ravaged land. Anti-war demonstrations would occur with increasing frequency and ferocity on college campuses across the country for the better part of a decade. Draft-eligible youths would flee to Canada to escape induction, draft cards would be publicly burned or mutilated, and politicians, university administrators and even the president of the United States would be subject to incessant taunting and ridicule. Berkeley students, of course were in the front ranks of the ever more warlike Peace Movement. The rebellious, often riotous collegiate world of the 1960s would stand in stark contrast to that of barely a dozen years earlier when "coolness" was all and the nearest approach to mass insurrection was a panty raid on fraternity-sorority row.

Ray Willsey was of that earlier time, but he made the adjustment to changed attitudes and somehow managed in all the turmoil to field representative Cal teams and to recruit quality players. Football, too, was then in a period of change. Ongoing liberalization of the substitution rules restored the two-platoon system and created new specialists. In 1965, for the first time at Cal, "placekicker" became a full-time position, recognized as such in game programs. That year, again for the first time, the team's leading scorer was strictly a kicker, Don Sinclair, who scored no touchdowns but connected on 14 of 16 points-after and 5 of 7 field goals for a modest 29 points. In the years to come, kickers would dominate the scoring, superseding the touchdown-makers of yore. During one stretch in the 1970s and '80s, kickers led the team in points for eleven straight seasons.

Another, and welcome, change was in the steady increase in black players. Not since lineman Walter Gordon in the post-World War I era had Cal had an African-American star. In fact, between then and the Willsey years there had been only a handful of black players, the rare exceptions being Gordon's son, Walt, Jr., in the early 1940s and Staten

Webster, Len Jones, Sammy Williams and Jerry Drew in the Waldorf years. By his count, Marv Levy coached only six black players in his four years as coach, the best being halfback-kick returner Jim Blakeney. Save for the elder Gordon, none of these could be considered a prominent player.

That all changed with Willsey. By the end of his tenure, he had coached an All America tackle in Sherman White and an All-Coast defensive back, Ray Youngblood, the two serving as co-captains of the 1971 team. For the first time in Cal History, he started two blacks in the same backfield—fullback John McGaffie and running back Paul Williams. In 1967, Williams led the team in rushing and in kickoff and punt returns. Two years later, Bob Darby was the kickoff-return leader, and Irby Augustine, though ostensibly playing end in Willsey's flexible defensive scheme, tied for the team lead in interceptions. Also in 1969, the coach recruited one of the nation's hottest prospects in running back Isaac Curtis. And in John Erby, a wounded Vietnam war veteran and earlier, an offensive guard under Levy, Willsey hired Cal's first black assistant coach since Gordon pere last worked for Stub Allison in 1943.

The influx of players was made possible by Cal finally exercising its options under the Special Students Program which allowed state universities and colleges to accept up to two percent of applicants who, though they did not meet the academic standards for admission, showed "exceptional promise" because of special talent. At Berkeley, three hundred fifty students, most of them black, were admitted under that provision in the spring of 1968. By the fall, when the percentage of academic exceptions was raised to four, some six hundred students had registered. And many of those had as their special quality a talent for athletics.

In 1965, Willsey's team broke even in ten games. Three of those losses were by horrific scores: 48–6 in the opener to Notre Dame, 56–3 to Rose Bowl-bound UCLA and its star quarterback, Gary Beban, and

35–0 to USC and its Heisman-winning tailback, Mike Garrett. But the Bears, missing Morton, Blanchfield, Blakeney and Schraub from the offense, held their own in the remaining games, winning three in a row—over Kansas, 17–0, Air Force, 24–7, and Washington 16–12. Excluding the three big whoppings, they held their other six foes to just 46 points before the Big Game, edging strong Penn State, 21–17, on Jerry Bradley's last-second "miracle catch" of Jim Hunt's 46-yard desperation pass.

It rained heavily the day before the Big Game, leaving the Stanford Stadium turf a soggy mess. But it was merely overcast on game day. The game, though, was a defensive slog. After a scoreless first half, Stanford took a 3–0 lead in the third quarter on a 12-yard field goal by their kicker, Terry DeSylvia. The Bears opened the fourth quarter with a six-play drive of 62 yards, 37 of them coming on three Hunt pass completions. Relles scored from the four to give Cal the lead. Stanford then countered with a 70-yard march in 11 plays, halfback Ray Handley scoring from the 11. DeSylvia missed the point-after, but the Indians held on for a 9–7 win.

There was some speculation afterward that a Willsey gamble in the third quarter might have cost Cal its first winning season since 1958. With fourth down on the Stanford 22, the coach called for a fake field goal instead of allowing the consistently accurate Sinclair to go for what would have been the winning three-pointer. But Hunt's pass fell incomplete and the Bears came away without a score. The Indians celebrated their first winning season (6-3-1) since 1957. The Bears would have to wait a few more years for theirs, much to the disgruntlement of impatient alums.

Willsey still had his supporters, though, including, most reassuringly, the new chancellor, Roger Heyns, who formally took over for interim appointee Martin Meyerson the day of the Notre Dame opener, September 18, 1965. Heyns, unlike his immediate predecessors, was a football fan. He came to Cal from the University of Michigan, where during the previous twenty-five years, he had been a graduate student, a professor of psychology, dean of the College of Literature, Science and the Arts and vice president for Academic Affairs. In accepting the Cal job, he remarked that "despite recent conflict, I found deep commitment to it (the university) among faculty, alumni and public... Berkeley is a great university, recognized as such across the nation, and beyond."

He attended both the Notre Dame and Michigan games, discreetly suppressing any expression of lingering fidelity to the Wolverines and pledging his faith thereafter to the Golden Bear.

The Bears started the '66 season with reduced weaponry. The backs would be appreciably quicker, which was important since Willsey's offensive line, from tackle to tackle, had graduated. In rail-thin 154-pound Jerry Bradley, the coach had an effective receiver—22 catches for 360 yards and 3 TDs in '65—and kick returner. John Beasley, a 220-pound tight end, had NFL potential. And Barry Bronk, up from the freshman team, appeared to be a better passer than either Hunt or Dan Berry, who shared the quarterbacking in '65 and between them completed just 54 passes in 136 attempts (.397 percentage) for 6 touchdowns and ten interceptions. In fact, Hunt was a far better defensive back than quarterback and Berry was better suited as a running back.

Workhorse Relles, who in three seasons had gained 1370 yards on 329 carries, would be gone. Only Arleigh Williams (526), John Olszewski (416) and Vic Bottari (388) had had more carries up to then, and Relles' yardage gained ranked him seventh on Cal's all-time list, behind such distinguished forebears as Johnny O., Jack Jensen, Jim Monachino, Bottari, Williams and Jack Swaner. But Relles lacked the panache of those earlier backs. In his most productive season, he gained 519 yards and his career per-carry average was 3.95, a good two yards short of both Jensen and Olszewski. Still, he would be missed.

The Bears demonstrated their newfound speed in a quite

remarkable 21–6 win over Washington State in Spokane. Offensively, they scored no points, gained zero yards passing on three attempts and picked up just 142 yards rushing. But they scored almost every other way possible, and from great distances. In the second quarter, their six-foot, seven-inch safety, Wayne Stewart intercepted a pass and returned it 71 yards for a touchdown. In the third quarter, Don Guest, another defensive back, returned a missed Cougar field goal attempt 108 yards, topping Bobby Sherman for the longest run in Cal football history. And in the final quarter, Bradley returned a punt 73 yards for the last of these extended touchdown jaunts.

Bradley scored Cal's only touchdown on a leaping 12-yard catch of a Bronk pass in a 17–7 loss to one of Michigan's lesser (6-4) teams. Heyns did not openly rejoice after his old school's victory, bemoaning instead Cal's loss with new friend Willsey. Bradley and Stewart were in another long-gain mode against Pitt, the skinny one returning a punt 76 yards, the tall one running back an interception 47 yards. But theirs were Cal's only touchdowns in a 30–15 loss. The team hit a new low the next week, losing for the first time ever to San Jose State, and by the humiliating score of 24–0. The Spartans held the Bears to just 140 offensive yards, 70 each running and passing, while gaining 276 on the pinpoint passing of their quarterback, Danny Holman. Worse yet, the win over Cal was just one of three for San Jose that season against seven losses.

After upsetting Washington, 24–20, mainly on the strength of two Bronk-to-Bradley touchdowns, the Bears then lost their final five games. Despite two fourth-quarter TD passes by Bronk to Bradley and Beasley, they fell, 28–15, to a UCLA team powered by the passing of Beban and the running of Mel Farr. Rose Bowl-bound USC clobbered Cal, 35–9, behind the passing of Troy Winslow. In the ninth game of the season, the Bears lost, 6–3, to a good Army team, their only score coming on a 44-yard field goal by Ron Miller, the longest by a Cal kicker since Archie Nisbet booted that 54-yarder against Washington

State back in 1922. The game at Memorial Stadium drew a less than enthusiastic crowd of 26,547.

Even Stanford wasn't much of a draw that retrograde season, only 63,499 showing up on a rainy November 19, the smallest crowd to watch a Big Game since the wartime season of 1942. All of the scoring was in the first half. Stanford opened a 13–0 lead in the first quarter on touchdown runs of three yards by John Root and 17 by Greg Boughton. Guest scored Cal's only TD on a 58-yard punt return. The 13-7 loss was not only the Bears' fifth straight in '66 but the sixth in a row to Stanford.

"Sure I'm disappointed," Willsey told the *Examiner* after the 3-7 season, "but not entirely so. My first year we were just a pass and a prayer, and the second year we didn't have much of anything. Last year, I thought we started to pick up some of the things that win football games, blocking and tackling...this year, Penn State was the only one that pushed us around physically."

And the season did produce some intriguing statistics. Bradley supplanted the kicking specialists as the team's leading scorer with seven touchdowns, five on pass receptions and two on punt returns. He caught 32 passes for 473 yards, an average of 14.8 per catch, and he returned 23 punts for an average of 12.9 yard per. Guest's two touchdown returns averaged an astronomical 83 yards. Stewart intercepted six passes and returned them for an average of 24.3 yards and two scores. Bronk had a useful season, completing 84 of 183 passes for seven touchdowns and 11 interceptions. He missed by just 35 yards of becoming Cal's fourth 1000-yard season passer, a feat previously accomplished only by Celeri, Larson and Morton. But the Bears had no ground game to speak of. The leading rusher with 319 yards and a 3.32 average was sophomore Rick Bennett, who, shades of Morton, had originally signed a letter of intent to attend Stanford before prudently changing his mind. No Cal back averaged even four yards per carry, and the longest run from scrimmage was 30 yards by Berry.

The football team's troubles were again obscured by events on campus. In January of 1967, Clark Kerr's tortured term as U.C. president was terminated by the Regents. He had further aggravated the university's governing body when, in the aftermath of the "Filthy Speech Movement," he refused to expel the perpetrators. In fact, both he and Meyerson offered their resignations after that 1965 episode. They were persuaded to withdraw them by the Academic Senate. But Meyerson didn't last the year, and though Kerr hung on, he was bombarded with criticism from every conceivable source—students, Regents, legislators and, most damagingly, the newly-elected Governor of California, Ronald Reagan.

Kerr's successor—following the interim presidency of Kerr aide Harry Wellman—was Charles J. Hitch, an economist and onetime Oxford don. Hitch had founded the economic division of the RAND Corporation and worked under presidents Kennedy and Johnson as a planning and budgeting expert in the U.S. Department of Defense. Kerr had persuaded him to come to Cal in 1965 to serve as vice president for Finance and as University Comptroller. Above all, he would find his experience in the Defense Department particularly beneficial in fighting the interminable battles of Berkeley.

On the gridiron, though, things were looking up, mainly because that was the only view available. The coach decided to do some tinkering with his personnel. His wisest and yet most daring move before the '67 season was to move Stewart, an All-Conference defensive back, to wide receiver. With his height, Willsey reasoned, Stewart would enjoy a huge advantage over pass defenders, and his interceptions and touchdown returns had established that he could both catch the ball and run with it afterward. Though he carried only 190 pounds or so on that angular frame, Stewart had a reputation for toughness and durability, as witness the rebound record he'd set as a freshman basketball star. At his new position, Stewart would be a key player in the Bears' return to respectability. And the position was not entirely new to him, since he'd played some end in high school, along with safety and even quarter-back. The 1967 season opened with a 21–13 win over Oregon, the Bears limiting the Ducks to a mere 121 yards of total offense. There followed another whipping by Notre Dame, this time by 41–18. But the Irish had a formidable team that year, led by quarterback Terry Hanratty and running back Rocky Bleir on offense and Kevin Hardy on defense, all future pro standouts. The Bears came back to squeeze past Michigan, 10–9, on the strength of a missed Wolverine point-after and another 44-yard field goal by Miller. The Bear touchdown came on a pass from sophomore quarterback Randy Humphries to McGaffie that covered 77 yards with just two minutes left to play. Stewart caught eight passes for 110 yards in another close win, 14–12, over Air Force. That gave the Bears their first 3-1 start in fifteen years. Then they lost four in a row.

With Heisman winner Beban throwing two touchdown passes, UCLA, gave them another drubbing, by 37–14. Syracuse, behind future NFL Hall of Famer Larry Csonka's three touchdowns and 204 yards rushing, beat them, 20–14, in Syracuse. Paul Williams set up both Cal scores, the first on a 63-yard run to the Syracuse two, the second on a spectacular catch of a Bronk pass on the one. Gary Fowler scored both touchdowns. Washington won in Berkeley, 20–6, despite eight recep-tions for 78 yards by Stewart. USC, the national championship team that year, beat the Bears for the eighth straight time, even without star running back O.J. Simpson, who was injured and did not play.

Then, miraculously, the team came to life, avenging the 1966 embarrassment by beating San Jose, 30–6, and sacking their former tormentor, quarterback Holman, eight times for 73 yards lost. Miller kicked field goals of 37, 38 and 40 yards and backfield mates McGaffie and Williams gained, respectively, 54 and 52 yards running.The Bears evened their '67 record with a resounding 26–3 win over Stanford that put a merciful end to the Indians' six-game Big Game winning streak. They trailed at the half by a pitchers' duel score of 3–2, pulled ahead, 5–3, in the third quarter on a 24-yard Miller field goal, then put the game out of reach with a 21-point final quarter. Humphries, who had replaced Bronk as the starter after seven games, led the way, passing ten yards to Stewart, who made a spectacular catch in the end zone, and 21 to tight end Jim Calkins, then scoring himself on a sneak from the two.

The win presaged better days dead ahead. Stewart rewarded Willsey's daring by leading the team with 45 receptions for 503 yards and two touchdowns. Williams, who missed the Big Game with an injury, led all ball carriers with 432 yards on 116 carries. And Humphries, sharing quarterback duties, completed 47 of 97 passes for 468 yards and five scores. They would all be back in '68, in hopes of giving Cal its first winning season in ten years.

Unfortunately, 1968 wouldn't turn out to be such a good year for the rest of the world.

## CHAPTER TWENTY-THREE

# WINNING ISN'T EVERYTHING

By the time Cal opened its 1968 football season on September 21, the nation already had been shaken by a succession of terrible events.

On January 30, the communist Viet Cong launched its Tet Offensive against American forces—now numbering five hundred twenty-five thousand—in Vietnam. On March 16, U.S. soldiers killed three hundred Vietnamese villagers at My Lai, a massacre that deepened opposition to the war both here and abroad. On April 4, civil rights icon and Nobel Peace Prize winner Dr. Martin Luther King was assassinated by a white ex-convict in Memphis. King's murder led to race riots in major cities across the country. On June 5, Senator Robert F. Kennedy, the murdered J.F.K.'s brother, was himself shot and killed after delivering his California presidential primary victory speech at the Hotel Ambassador in Los Angeles. His death left a nation wondering, as the Senator himself had after King's killing, "Oh God, when is the violence going to stop?" Sadly enough, the non-violent protests King insisted upon had turned increasingly violent. A new generation of rights advocates was now calling for "Black Power"—armed resistance against "oppressors." And in August at the Democratic National Convention, thousands of anti-war demonstrators clashed on

the streets with Chicago police in a prolonged battle that would have
appalled both King and Kennedy.

On the Cal campus at a May 17 anti-war protest, a crowd estimated
at eight thousand watched 773 draft-age students take a public oath
declaring that as long as the U.S. continued its "immoral and unjust"
Vietnamese adventure they would "not serve in the Armed Forces."
Three hundred Cal faculty members pledged their support of the
students in direct defiance of the Regents and the Governor. The participants called this ceremony a "Vietnam Commencement."

The new dissidents, whether anti-war or pro-civil-rights, confronted
their adversaries far more truculently than had their predecessors in
the cause and with a doctrinaire approach so resistant to compromise
that it smacked of the far right dogma they so strenuously detested.
Once sympathetic liberals of the "old left" were now depicted as re-
actionaries virtually indistinguishable from arch conservatives. Even
former FSM icon Jack Weinberg, now approaching his untrustworthy
30s, spotted trouble ahead for the intransigent newcomers, who, he
said, "turned to radical politics as an end in itself and not just as a
means." And in doing so, they aroused a formidable antagonist—the
so-called "Silent Majority" of Americans who elected Richard Nixon
president of the United States in 1968.

Radicalism in its Black Power mode touched the Cal football team
in spring practice that year. A threatened season-long boycott by African-American players was narrowly averted, thanks to wiser heads
among the coaching staff and the protesters and in large part because
of the intervention of black journalist Sam Skinner. At issue was the
coaches' supposed insensitivity to the needs and ambitions of black
athletes, as manifested in position changes that aroused suspicions of
racism and what was interpreted generally as favoritism toward white
players. A specific complaint involved the decision to switch quarterback candidate Bernie Keeles to defensive back. The move struck
Keeles's fellow black teammates as an egregious example of the racist

thinking all too prevalent then among coaches that blacks somehow lacked the leadership ability and mental acuity to play quarterback and that their "natural athleticism" made them better suited to wide receiver or cornerback.

In this instance, though, the coaches' decision seemed entirely justified. Keeles had transferred to Cal from Benedict College in South Carolina after that small school discontinued its football program. He came west with no experience at the major college level, and in returning letterman Humphries and sophomore flash Dave Penhall, the Bears were relatively deep at his position. Keeles was also not quite 5-10 and weighed only 176 pounds, a veritable Lilliputian at a position then, and now, dominated by big men able to spot receivers over the heads of onrushing linemen. At quarterback, Keeles probably wouldn't have played a down in '68, a circumstance that even his most avid supporters eventually acknowledged. And when Skinner, a confidant to many black players, told Cal Sports Information director Bob Steiner that the purported "non-negotiable" demands of the boycotters were in fact negotiable, a rapprochement was quietly achieved. But the incident did create a new awareness of the problem among both coaches and players.

"There certainly was bias in sports back then," recalled star defensive back Ken Wiedemann many years later. "Black coaches weren't being hired, either in college or the pros. And yes, black quarterbacks were not allowed to play their position. Actually, we happened to be on the cutting edge of a major social movement. Still, I too came to Cal as a quarterback (Wiedemann is white), and Ray (Willsey) took one look at me and put me on defense. In the end, all Ray asked you to do was, as he put it, 'put on a helmet and play.'"

"Ray was a hard man," Wayne Stewart remembered. "But he was always fair. He wanted you to give everything you had, and you did. I recall him telling the boycotting players that football was not like an all-night movie theater where you could come in and go out as you pleased. But when it was all over, there was no hangover from the trouble. We all got along beautifully. And we had a great year."

The complaints had to be taken seriously, though. Basketball coach Rene Herrerias, a protege of Athletic Director Newell, had resigned under similar circumstances at the conclusion of his season that year, accused by some players of being "unwilling or unable to relate to the black athlete." His departure that April was followed by Newell's who, after enduring with amazing equanimity eight storm-tossed years on the job, resigned to become general manager of the new San Diego franchise in the National Basketball Association. His replacement as athletic director was Paul Brechler, who had been A.D. at Iowa for thirteen years and then the first commissioner of the Western Athletic Conference. Willsey was given the added duties of Assistant Athletic Director.

Now in his fifth season as Cal coach, Willsey finally had assembled the sort of team he knew could win. These Bears were especially strong defensively, with a line powered by 250-pound nose guard Ed White, a player just then approaching his enormous potential. Other stout defenders included the bookend ends, Augustine and Mike McCaffrey, linebacker Dennis Pitta and safety Wiedemann, who had intercepted six passes in '67 and returned one for a touchdown. Collectively, the defense became known, pun-fully, as "the Bear Minimum."

Offensively, Humphries would return at quarterback and Gary Fowler would become the starting tailback, Willsey having moved Paul Williams to flanker where his speed and catching skills would give the team a worthy deep threat to complement Stewart's possession game. McGaffie, a fine blocker and powerful inside runner would be back at fullback. He was one of five black players from Laney College in Oakland, the 1966 National Junior College champions.

"You don't see color on the playing field," said Wiedemann. "You see only talent and leadership. And to John McGaffie and Irby Augustine, you saw plenty of both. They were true leaders, men who commanded respect."

The Bears opened with a 21–7 upset of Michigan in Ann Arbor. They beat the Big Ten power at its own game, rushing for 240 yards while limiting the Wolverines to just 48. Fowler scored all three Cal touchdowns in a victory made all the more impressive because it was achieved in the "Big House," where the home team seldom lost, and because the Wolverines would go on to win their next eight games in a row before losing the season finale to National Champion Ohio State.

The "Bear Minimum" shut out Colorado, 10–0, next in Berkeley, the touchdown coming on a 38-yard run off the flanker reverse by Williams. Miller kicked a 32-yard field goal and Stewart caught 12 passes for 144 yards. After this second convincing win, the Bears cracked the Top 20 national rankings for the first time in ten years. They advanced a couple of more spots to 16th after humbling San Jose State, 46–0. Sophomore tailback Bob Darby scored twice and gained 96 yards for the day. Humphries completed nine of 16 for 140 yards, including an 11-yard touchdown heave to Stewart. Miller kicked a 39-yard field goal and a record 25th consecutive extra point.

The Bears were 3-0 at the start of a season for the first time since 1952. Then, alas, they ran afoul of an alert Army team which intercepted Humphries four times en route to a 10–7 win. McGaffie got Cal's only score on a yard-long plunge.

But the quarterback and his team rebounded impressively in a 39–15 win over UCLA. Humphries completed 14 of 23 passes for 175 yards and two touchdowns, one of them a 39-yarder to Willaims, who made a diving, finger-tip catch in the end zone. It was Willsey's first win over the Bruins and, as he needlessly exclaimed afterwards, "a helluva positive step in the right direction."

His team took another step that way with a resounding 43–0 shutout of Syracuse, handing that school's proud football program its worst loss in sixteen years. Again, it was a "Bear Minimum" game. The Cal defense forced nine turnovers, six of them interceptions with one returned for a 45-yard score by Keeles. Fowler had a 47-yard punt return for another TD and Miller kicked a 50-yard field goal, the second longest then to Nisbet's 54-yarder 46 years earlier.

The Bears were now 5-1 for the season and ranked eighth in the country. They had scored 166 points while holding opponents to a paltry 32. It was the best start by a Cal team in sixteen years. Not since Pappy's last winning season had the Bears won so many games and been ranked so high that early. In other ways, it had been a typical week in October on the Berkeley campus. Professor Luis W. Alvarez had been awarded the Nobel Prize in Physics, in recognition of his study of subatomic particles, and Sproul Plaza played host to yet another massive demonstration. The confluence of events impelled Dean of Men and former crew coach Jim Lemmon to remark, "Not many places can hold a student strike, have a football team in the Top Ten and have a Nobel Prize winner, all in one week."

The student demonstration, which lasted the better part of the week, had as its source, of all the unlikely things, a classroom issue. An experimental course, Social Analysis 139X, had make its debut that fall. Its fundamental purpose was to examine racial discrimination in the country, a noble endeavor beyond doubt. But the syllabus included a series of ten lectures by the notorious Stokely Carmichael, co-founder of and "Minister of Information" for the fiercely militant Black Panthers. After three such lectures, the Regents decided the course was "improperly structured" and that no academic credit should therefore be awarded for taking it. Guest lecturers outside the immediate academic community were thenceforward to be confined to two classroom appearances. Upon completing his lecture on Tuesday, October 22, Carmichael advised his students to "do your own thing."

Which they did. Later that day, one hundred twenty of them invaded Sproul Hall for yet another sit-in. They were routinely arrested in what had been an unusually peaceful demonstration. On the streets outside, though, rioters in the thousands broke store windows and battled with police from Berkeley and neighboring communities. Many of these combatants were not students but eternally restless "street people" who congregated on Telegraph Avenue spoiling for trouble. Then, on Thursday, protesters attempted to occupy, among other buildings on campus, Dwinelle, Campbell and Moses Halls. The invasions were mostly repelled, although seventy-five students succeeded in barricading themselves inside Moses, seat of the College of Letters and Science, by heaping desks and chairs against the doors.

"It just seemed part of the general deal," said football star Stewart. "You woke up in the morning to the sound of National Guard helicopters whirling overhead."

But by Friday, the eve of the Syracuse game, the energy for this particular insurrection was pretty much sapped, so much so that the Daily Cal described a last-ditch failed classroom boycott as nothing more than "a tragic farce."

New U.C. president Hitch, though, complained wistfully that "I sometimes feel as if I'm surrounded only by angry people."

Meanwhile, the football team's stay among the Top Ten was short. On November 2, in Seattle, the Bears were held to a 7–7 tie by Washington, the Huskies' touchdown scored on Al Worley's 32-yard return of an intercepted Humphries pass. The Bears tied the game in the third quarter on a 10-play, 63-yard drive finished off by sophomore tailback Bob Darby's 2-yard dive. Darby had carried five straight times from the Washington 27 to get that far; he gained a team-leading 83 yards for the day. Actually, the Bears could have won the game late in the final quarter and retained their standing among college football's elite had it not been for a disheartening miscue only a yard short of the Husky goal line. With 3:39 left to play and the ball on their own 32, they marched 67 yards upfield, the key plays coming on Humphries completions to Williams for 11 yards and to Stewart for 19. With only seconds remaining and the ball on the Washington one, a mixup on the center snap from Bill Laveroni resulted in a Humphries fumble, which Washington recovered. The Bears dropped to 11th in the rankings.

Next, alas, the Trojans. Led by their all-world tailback, O.J. Simpson, who gained 164 yards and scored twice, they walloped the Bears, 35–17. Southern Cal quarterback Steve Sogge, an all but forgotten figure in all the O.J. hoopla, tossed three TD passes. The Bears didn't score at all until late in the game, on Humphries passes of six yards to Williams and 15 to Stewart. Miller kicked a 28-yard field goal, his eighth of the year, thereby surpassing by one the old Cal record set by Bill Blewett in 1923.

The Bears recovered from the S.C. pummeling with a 36–8 win over Oregon, a team that had won four of its previous five games. Long-gainers were the feature, Williams scampering 56 yards on the flanker reverse for one score and Humphries passing 53 yards to Stewart for another. Miller chipped in with his second 50-yard field goal of the season. Penhall got his first extended action and tossed his first touchdown pass, a seven-yarder to tight end George Harris. The defense held the Ducks to just 17 yards rushing and intercepted four passes, two by Wiedemann, who was on his way to a new Cal record in that statistical category. White made 14 solo tackles and was named Northern California Lineman of the Week.

Cal entered the big Game with unusually impressive credentials. The Oregon game had clinched the team's first winning season in a decade and Willsey's first as head coach. The 226 points scored were the most by a Cal team before a Big Game since the 1951 Bears racked up 287, and the defense had given up a mere 82, the least since Pappy's 1950 Rose Bowl team allowed 69. But the Indians also had a winning record for a change, and in the passing combination of sophomore quarterback Jim Plunkett to receiver Gene Washington, they had one of the deadliest weapons in all of college football. Washington, himself a converted quarterback, would become Stanford's first 1000-yard receiver that year. And Plunkett was only two seasons away from the Heisman Trophy.

The stars were as advertised, but the Bears hadn't reckoned on an obstinate Stanford defense that held them to 51 yards rushing, 75 passing and no points. Washington scored on a 17-yard flanker reverse and Plunkett completed 17 of 32 passes for 241 yards and a touchdown of three dinky yards to tight end Bob Moore. Indian kicker Bill Shoemaker booted field goals of 20 and 33 yards to complete the 20–0 shellacking. It was Cal alum John Ralston's fourth win in five Big Games against Cal alum Ray Willsey.

The Bears played one more game after the Big one, beating Hawaii, 17–12, in Honolulu. The Stanford loss aside, their 7-3-1 finish was even better than the '58 team's (counting that season's Rose Bowl loss). It was, in fact, the best record by a Bear team since 1952. There were also some fine individual performances. Stewart caught 50 passes for 679 yards and four touchdowns. His 95 catches over just two seasons on offense surpassed Schraub's 82 as the Cal career record. Fowler was the leader in both rushing—665 yards in 162 carries—and scoring, his 60 points on 10 touchdowns exceeding Miller's 55 on 25 PATs and then Cal record 10 field goals (on 22 tries). Williams justified the position switch, rushing 20 times for 141 yards and two scores and catching 26 passes for 418 and two more. All told, the flanker had long gains of 56 yards running, 47 receiving and 49 on a kick return. Humphries completed 98 of 207 pass attempts for six touchdowns. But he also suffered 15 interceptions. Safety Weidemann had seven interceptions, giving him a Cal record 13. And he had another season remaining to improve on that.

But the real star of the '68 team was nose guard White, who made four All America teams, the most by a Cal lineman since Les Richter was voted onto five in 1951. White was joined on the All Conference team by Stewart, Wiedemann and McCaffrey.

It had been quite a year. No matter how you looked at it.

CHAPTER TWENTY-FOUR

# THE WAY THE BALL BOUNCES

The most violent and emotionally charged of all the many clashes between campus demonstrators and police came in the spring of 1969.
The battleground was a scrubby three-acre lot on Telegraph Avenue
a few blocks from campus that the university owned and had cleared
for future development either for student housing or as an intramural playing field. But when the property stood vacant for more than a
year, students and street people began planting grass and flowers there
in April of 1969 with the intention of transforming it into a so-called
"People's Park."

University officials did not take kindly to this seemingly benign
neighborhood project. After all, the lot, vacant or not, was theirs. And
the last thing they needed in these unsettling times was a conveniently
situated campground for revolutionaries bent on turning them out.
And so, in the early morning of May 15, workmen were dispatched to
construct an eight-foot-high chain link fence around the lot to ward
off "trespassers."

The reaction among People's Park advocates was entirely predictable. At a noon rally at Sproul Plaza, student body president-elect Don
Siegel urged the crowd of three hundred or more to "take back the

park." Siegel was not exactly your traditional student body officer—the earnest, glad-handing activities major (slang for an undergrad who's involved in extracurricular activities) looking eagerly forward to a lifetime career in the corporate world. But he was a perfect fit for the times. In a *Blue and Gold* essay on the plight of his contemporaries, he wrote, "students are drafted by the Army, exploited by landlords and merchants, programmed and bored by required courses, and manipulated by politicians."

The Sproul crowd responded enthusiastically to Siegel's entreaties and marched, like so many latter day Marseillais, down Telegraph Avenue to vanquish the fence builders. They were met by police and Alameda county Sheriff's deputies armed with shotguns and tear gas dispensers. The ensuing battle raged over parts of ten days involving as many as five hundred law enforcement officers and two thousand or more rock-throwing People's Parkers. Finally, Governor Reagan, not the most popular man on campus, called in the National Guard to quell the rioting and enforce a citywide curfew. The Governor told reporters he considered Park territorial rights a "phony issue" fomented by radicals intent on overthrowing the establishment.

But the People's Park conflict led to nearly a thousand arrests, more than a hundred serious injuries and one death. Struck by shotgun pellets in the liver and heart on the first day of battle, twenty-five-year-old James Rector of San Jose died four days later in Berkeley's Herrick Memorial Hospital. Apart from those hospitalized with injuries, there were countless others left gasping for air from tear gas spraying, at least one such from a National Guard helicopter. Wiedemann recalls playing in a varsity baseball game at Edwards Field that was delayed not by any of the usual causes, like rain or darkness, but by tear gas.

And for all of that, People's Park remains to this day a scrubby park for people, some of them homeless or otherwise on the fringe.

Meanwhile, new movements were popping up on campus with almost desperate frequency in what would finally prove to be the waning days of rampant radicalism on the Berkeley campus. Women and gays by now both had their "Liberation Fronts." In a publication accurately named "The Militant," the lot of women was fervently bemoaned: "We are economically exploited, psychologically oppressed and socially 'kept in our place' by men and by a capitalist system that has institutionalized male supremacy—in a more subtle way than the caveman but just as destructively."

And then there appeared on campus a twenty-seven-year-old academic named Jack Scott, who in a course entitled Education 191D called for what amounted to an Athletes' Liberation Front. His message, not entirely original but certainly in tune with "liberation" rhetoric, charged that "athletic programs as constituted have no place in the academic community." College sports are "coached by pros and played by semi-pros," wrote Scott, himself a former college track athlete. "And both are on campus to do a job." While in the classroom "athletes are asked to open their minds to new ideas, they are asked to close them to supreme authority on the athletic field."

Athletic Director Brechler was no fan of Scott's class. "I don't think Jack Scott is any more qualified to teach that course," he grumbled, "than I am to teach Russian languages." Chances are, though, that if the A.D. had actually been given the opportunity to lecture undergraduates on the complexities of the Ukrainian subjunctive, his course would have attracted nowhere near the coverage on television and in the press that Scott was getting for Education 191D's castigation of college athletics.

Among Scott's celebrity guest lecturers were such disaffected sports luminaries as women's Olympic discus champion Olga Connolly, former 49er star receiver Bernie Casey and Harry Edwards, the black educator (soon to teach sociology at Cal) who influenced the "Black Power" protest at the 1968 Olympic Games. Scott's class was among the more popular on campus with an enrollment of nearly five hundred, not including those who simply "audited" it for the pleasure of hearing big-time sports placed on the hot seat. And Scott, though professorial in manner, rarely disappointed his fans. "Athletes," he'd say, "get the rap of being dumb jocks, mainly because they live in isolation...Coaches don't want a critical intelligence...A man who behaves himself only when under the control of someone else is not a mature person."

All things considered, this was not an especially congenial time to be head football coach at the University of California. But Ray Willsey, with guns to the right of him and guns to the left of him, charged bravely ahead. The 1969 schedule did him no favors: half of the opposing teams were nationally ranked and four were in the Top Ten when the Bears played them. The opener was with Texas, coached by Willsey's old mentor, Darrell Royal. The Longhorns were ranked fourth in the pre-season polls, but after winning 11 straight games, the last against Notre Dame in the Cotton Bowl, they finished the '69 season as number one in the country. Their first victim, Cal, did well to hold them to 17–0, although Royal's wishbone offense piled up 311 yards rushing.

Indiana was ranked 10th when the Bears pulled off a 17–14 upset in Bloomington. The game's unexpected hero was Steve Curtis, a transfer from Glendale (junior) College who, though a better runner than passer, had won the quarterback job in spring practice over an increasingly erratic Humphries, of whom it was said, "when he's good there's no one better, but when he's bad there's no one worse." But Humphries was the starter in those first two games of '69 while Curtis nursed a hand broken at the end of spring workouts. Against Indiana, though, Humphries was having one of his bad days, and the Bears were behind, 14–0, when Curtis came on to lead a late rally that began with Wiedemann's 18-yard touchdown on an interception return. Randy Wersching kicked a 29-yard field goal in the fourth quarter to reduce Indiana's lead to 14–10, And then, on a rollout, Curtis passed to Kenny Adams for 61 yards and the winning touchdown.

Curtis was the starter in a 31–21 win over Rice and was at the throttle in a 44–13 win over Washington until a dislocated shoulder truncated his season. When Curtis went down, Penhall, who had been watching the game in street clothes from the stands, was summoned to the field by the coaching staff and instructed to suit up in case a similarly untoward fate should await Humphries. It was a scene straight from the 1930s screen oeuvre of Jack Oakie, except that Penhall wasn't needed.. But after a particularly embarrassing 32–0 loss to UCLA in the next game, he became the starter for the rest of the season.

As if Willsey didn't have enough to worry about, injuries such as the one to Curtis became the norm that season. Before its merciful conclusion, disabilities of varying severity would afflict center Laveroni, running back Darby, and defensive backs Keeles, Jim Sheridan and, most lamentably, Wiedemann. Well on his way to All America recognition, the star defender suffered a season-ending knee injury in the UCLA loss. His three interceptions in the four-and-a-half games he played that season gave him 16 for his career, a record that, as of this writing, still stands after forty years. Of all the 1969 casualties, Fowler was the most intrepid. Switched to fullback to make room for the flashier Darby at tailback, he again led the team in rushing (741 yards on 157 carries) while playing through a broken wrist, cracked ribs and a shoulder separation.

Behind Penhall, the Bears best Washington State, 17–0, then lost two in a row, to USC (14–9) and Oregon State (35–3) before overwhelming San Jose State (31–7). The Bears were 2-2 under their new quarterback and 5-4 before meeting heavily favored Stanford (6-2-1) in the 72nd Big Game. An easy win was contemplated for the Plunkett-led Indians. The Stanford quarterback had already shattered Pacific-8 single season records for passing yards, total offense and touchdown passes. Gene Washington was no longer around to plague the Cal secondary, but in little (5-10, 181 pounds) Randy Vataha the Indians had a receiver who had averaged 19.3 yards for 31 catches before the Big

Game. For shorter distances, Plunkett threw to tight end Bob Moore, who actually had more receptions (35) than Vataha, and split end Jack Lasater, who had 30. And on the ground, backs Bubba Brown and Howie Williams had both gained better than 450 yards before playing Cal. The Indians were then ranked 14th in the country and had scored an average of 36 points per game. On paper, this didn't figure to be one of the better Big Games. In fact, it would be one of the best.

It didn't start out that way, though. Five minutes after the opening kickoff, the Indians had a 17–0 lead, built on Plunkett pass plays of 47 yards to Williams and 72 to Lasater and a 24-yard field goal by Steve Horowitz. Then, amazingly, the Bears recovered. Still in the first quarter, Sherman White intercepted a deflected Plunkett pass and returned it to the Stanford 21. Four plays later, Penhall sneaked in from the one. Late in the second quarter, the Bears drove 72 yards in just six plays, Fowler, the valetudinarian, scoring from the four. But with only seconds left in the half, Horowitz booted a 34-yarder to give Stanford a 20–14 lead.

A scoreless third quarter preceded a thrill-packed fourth. Horowitz led off with his third field goal of the game, a 25-yarder which expanded Stanford's lead to 23–14. Penhall put the Bears back in the game, hitting Kenny Adams with a 55-yard pass to the Indians' 14 and Geoff DeLapp for 11 more to the three. He scored himself from there after first bobbling the snap. Wersching's extra point reduced Stanford's lead to 23–21.

Two minutes later, Youngblood intercepted Plunkett at the Stanford 44. Darby gained seven on first down and then Penhall found wingback Jim Fraser for a 37-yard touchdown that gave the comeback Bears a 28–23 lead with 9:23 left to play. Stanford Stadium was strangely silent, save for the joyful clamor on the Cal side.

After the kickoff, Plunkett engineered a time-consuming 80-yard drive. He passed only twice, for a meager 19 yards, relying instead on the ball-packing prowess of Brown and Williams. From the Cal 11,

Brown powered seven to the four and Williams scored from there. Coach Ralston faced a now familiar dilemma. His lead was just 29 to 28, which even with a Horowitz point-after would leave his team vulnerable to a game-winning field goal by the left-footed Wersching. He decided to try for two points, which, barring a Cal touchdown, would assure him of at least a tie. The theory made sense, but it didn't work. Plunkett's pass for the two fell incomplete.

There were four minutes left, ample time for Penhall and company to put together a march long enough for a Wersching game-winner. But the Bears couldn't move at all on their possession after the kickoff. Neither could Stanford after they regained control of the ball. And, with 55 seconds remaining, the Indians were forced to punt from their own end zone. Cal had time. Wersching was busy warming up for the decisive boot. Stanford's punter was Bob Reinhard, who, as coincidence often has it in this rivalry, was the namesake son of the Cal All America tackle who had led Cal to a Big Game upset 28 years earlier with his punting and defense. The shoe, as it were, was on the other foot this time, and Reinhard knocked Cal back on its heels with a booming, unreturnable 51-yarder. Starting now on its own side of the 50, Cal stalled, and the 29-28 score held until the final gun.

Plunkett finished the day with 381 yards on 22 for 41 passing, but he was intercepted three times. Penhall was 23 for 36 for 321 yards and a touchdown. He also scored twice on QB sneaks, and in the view of many observers actually outplayed his more celebrated counterpart. Fowler led the ground-gainers with 106 yards on 15 carries and DeLapp the receivers with 12 catches for 115 yards. In total offense, the two teams gained the staggering total of 1027 yards, 563 by Stanford, 464 by Cal. It was Ralston's sixth win in seven Big Games, Willsey's fifth loss in six. Though Stanford now led in the series, 33 wins to 29, the two teams were tied with 893 points apiece, a statistical oddity indicative of the rivalry's extraordinary competitive balance.

And yet, because of extenuating circumstances—the increased

popularity of the professional game, the paucity of winning seasons and the riotous demonstrations on both campuses (Stanford, though late to the front, now had its own anti-war protests)—Big Game attendance markedly declined in the 1960s, from an average of 86,244 in the 1950s to 75,576. The Bears, for that matter, weren't much of a draw for any of their home games that last year of the decade. Only thirty-one thousand turned out for the opener against top-rated Texas, thirty-seven thousand for Rice, thirty-five thousand for Washington, twenty-two thousand for Oregon State, eighteen thousand for San Jose State and a comparatively small crowd of fifty-two thousand for archrival USC.

But the new decade seemed somehow more promising. Willsey had now gone three seasons without a losing record, and the 1970 team had a winning look to it. Penhall, who finished '69 with 76 for 145 passing, would be back and so would Curtis, this time as a backup. The left-footed soccer-style kicker, Wersching, had been 1969's leading scorer with 58 points, and he, too, would return for his senior season. Big Game hero DeLapp would head a receiving corps improved by the addition of Steve Sweeney, a sure-handed junior-college transfer from Yakima, Washington. The defense would be led by Sherman White in the line and Youngblood in the secondary.

But the most exciting player on the roster was a running back with sprinter's speed from the '69 freshman team named Isaac Curtis. He had been one of the most heavily recruited prospects in the nation out of Santa Ana High School, where he scored 40 touchdowns despite missing much of his senior season with injuries. He set a new Cal freshman rushing record by gaining 478 yards in just four games. And in the 1970 NCAA track meet, he led the Bears to the team championship by scoring 22 of their 40 points with a second in the 100-yard dash, a fourth in the 220 and as a member of the winning quarter-mile relay team. Curtis had a best time of 9.3 seconds for the 100-yard dash, and at 6-1 and 195 pounds, he ran with power. The Cal football coaching staff thought so much of him that they gave him the sacred number 36 jersey, previously worn by the two most revered running backs in school history, Jackie Jensen and Johnny Olszewski. Curtis would indeed make a name for himself at Cal, but not necessarily in the manner predicted for him.

Willsey decided to change his offense in 1970 from the conventional pro-set to a variation of Royal's Texas wishbone, featuring rollout passing and quarterback option plays better suited to Penhall's talents. In another unusual development, the team would play two night games, the opener against Oregon in Portland and the fourth game against Rice in Houston. And shades of modern day television-dictated scheduling, the kickoff in Austin against Texas was for four o'clock, a twilight game.

In a subsequent 28–0 loss to Rice, the Bears fumbled four times. But they beat Washington, 31–28, then lost to UCLA, 24–21. The Bruin loss was especially hard to take since the deciding score appeared to have been the result of an official's mistake, as photographs showed convincingly that UCLA quarterback Dennis Dummitt's knee had touched the turf at least two yards short of the goal line.

This was a classic up-and-down season for the Bears. They overwhelmed Washington State, 45–0, and squeaked by USC, 13–10, in a game highlighted by a pair of goal line stands supported by the twin pillars of the defensive line, the Whites, Sherman and O.Z. The game was finally won on Wersching's 46-yard field goal. After this upper came a downer, a 16–10 loss to Oregon State. The Bears then won a 35–28 close one over San Jose State, a disappointing win at that since the Spartans had won only two games all season and had been trounced by Stanford, 34–3.

Cal was a topsy-turvy 5-5 entering the Big Game, having scored 215 points and surrendered 207. Stanford had already clinched a Rose Bowl invitation and was, as customary in the Plunkett era, a heavy favorite to demolish the Bears. But Cal took an early lead on a 25-yard

Wersching field goal and a Penhall-to-Darby 15-yard touchdown connection that concluded a crisp 61-yard drive. Then after a surprise onside kick and recovery, Wersching booted a 33-yarder to give his team a 13–0 lead only minutes before the half. Stanford finally scored with seconds left on a 39-yard Plunkett pass to Vataha that caught the Cal defense unawares, the Indians having lined up, with third and one, in a two-tight-end running formation.

Stanford took the lead with 4:55 left in the third quarter when a scrambling Plunkett found a safety valve receiver in Jackie Brown, who sped 74 yards for the TD. Horowitz's extra point brought the score to 14 –13. The Bears then got a rare, for them, lucky break. With the ball on the Stanford 23 after a short drive, Penhall tossed up a jump-ball pass in the end zone intended, he hoped, for either Fraser or 6-3 tight end Jim Brady. In the ensuing melee with defenders. Stanford was called for pass interference. Cal was given the ball on the one. Still, it took three plays to push it across against the Indians' vaunted "Thunder Chicken" front four, Penhall finally sneaking in. A two-point conversion attempt failed, but with 52 seconds left to play, Wersching's 26-yard field made the final score, Cal 22, Stanford 14. Just another Big Game upset.

Once again the lightly regarded Penhall had held his own with the famous Plunkett. The Stanford quarterback completed 20 of 37 passes for 280 yards and two touchdowns, but he was sacked four times and intercepted twice, and his fumble in the last minute set up Wersching's clinching field goal. Penhall completed 18 of 26 for 231 yards and one touchdown, and he ran for another. The Big Game loss, humbling though it may have been, scarcely distracted the Indians from the job at hand in the Rose Bowl, where they upset the undefeated Ohio State Buckeyes, 27–17, behind Plunkett's 20 for 30 passing.

Back at Cal, Willsey savored both his second winning season and the extension of his non-losing-season streak to four. His 1970 Bears had gained more yards (3924) and scored more points (272) than any Cal team since 1951 and had gained more yards passing (2126) than any since 1964, Morton's senior season. Wersching's last field goal increased his Pac-8 record to 25 and his school record for points scored kicking to 124. Sweeney in his first varsity season had tied Wayne Stewart's Cal record for receiving yards at 679.

Prize recruit Isaac Curtis had not quite measured up to his lofty promise, although he did have decent numbers—427 yards rushing, 217 receiving and a team-leading 237 yards on 11 kickoff returns. He scored four touchdowns. Unfortunately, his real celebrity came off the field. On entering Cal as a freshman, he had failed, inadvertently, it appeared, to take a test required by the NCAA—but not by the university or the Pacific-8 conference—designed to determine if he was capable of achieving a 1.6 (C-minus) grade point average in his class work. Curtis was actually a much better student than that, averaging about a B-minus as a freshman and sophomore.

He also insisted that he was unaware of the 1.6 test requirement. "Nobody ever told me about it," he said when the inquiry began. "And they haven't told me yet." The university maintained that a letter had been mailed informing him of the test, but officials conceded that, considering the bulk of correspondence a hot football prospect might receive from competing schools, the letter could easily have been lost in the shuffle or accidentally discarded. And what in the final analysis did it matter since Curtis had established in his actual class work that he was better than a C-minus student?

Cal itself informed the NCAA of what it considered a forgivable oversight. "If we were trying to pull the wool over anyone's eyes," said an unapologetic Willsey, "we sure wouldn't have gone out and turned ourselves in."

"But rules are rules," declared the NCAA governing body. And violators must be punished. Curtis's points in the 1970 NCAA track meet were subtracted from the Cal total, thus depriving the Bears of their championship. The university was also placed on indefinite probation that would be extended further if Curtis should compete in football during the 1971 season. Willsey was outraged by the severity of the penalty. "You don't get the electric chair for stealing apples," he argued.

Actually, there was already a movement underway to have the 1.6 rule abolished. At its forefront, were the Ivy League schools, all properly offended that their scholar-athletes should be subjected to an examination determining whether they were capable of lowly C-minus work. But the NCAA held firm in what became known infamously as the "Curtis case," a designation Willsey considered unfair since what was involved was administrative oversight, not the intentional wrong-doing of a young athlete.

Curtis was declared ineligible for the 1971 NCAA track championship, a penalty of little consequence, since with tendinitis in his ankle he couldn't compete under any circumstances. But he was healthy enough for football, and his coach was determined that he should not be deprived of what some experts envisioned as his shot at gridiron immortality. Willsey elected to defy the NCAA and, if necessary, take it to court. The Bears would therefore remain on probation, which meant they would be denied television coverage of their games and be ineligible for the Rose Bowl, apparently a game played then only by Stanford, anyway. With tepid approval from the administration, Curtis would play. As far as the university was concerned, he was a student in good standing.

And he contributed generously to a second straight 6-5 record, finishing among the nation's Top 20 in all-purpose yardage with 799 yards on 30 kickoff returns, 475 rushing on 110 carries and 175 on 15 pass receptions. He scored five touchdowns and was the team's second leading rusher behind Steve Kemnitzer, who gained 686 yards on 157 carries.

The Bears had played through another arduous schedule, much of it contested in hostile territory against teams coached by football royalty. They opened against Arkansas, coached by Frank Broyles, and lost, 50–21, in Little Rock. After consecutive wins at home over West

Virginia and San Jose State, they were beaten, 35–3, in Columbus by Woody Hayes's Ohio State Buckeyes. Newcomers Jay Cruze and Reed Chastang had competed in the spring for the starting quarterback spot, but Chastang bowed out early with a shoulder separation suffered in the opener. Cruze was the starter thereafter, and he had a decent season, completing 119 of 242 passes for 1,284 yards and six touchdowns. And he threw last-ditch game-winners over Oregon State (30–27) with no time left and UCLA (31–24) with just a minute on the clock.

The Bears had already assured themselves of a winning season by the time they met Stanford, the defending Rose Bowl champion. But they were hardly the flashy point-makers of the year before. Only one of their six wins, a 34–10 breather against San Jose State, was by more than ten points and four were by seven or fewer. During a mid-season three-game winning streak, the margins were three points over Oregon State, one over Washington State and a lopsided seven over UCLA, the result of Cruze's last-minute touchdown toss to Sweeney. And some of the losses: 28–0 to USC, 30–7 to Washington, exposed defensive vulnerability. Stanford was made a 13½-point favorite.

This time the odds were not out of line. Led by Plunkett's able successor, Don Bunce, the Indians won handily by 14–0. Bunce passed 58 yards to running back Jackie Brown in the second quarter for the first TD, and Reggie Sanderson ran for the second at the conclusion of a 76-yard, 10-play drive. Stanford went on to win its second straight Rose Bowl game, a 14–13 thriller over previously unbeaten Michigan.

Despite his sixth loss in eight Big Games, Willsey had strung together consecutive winning seasons, the first time that had happened since he was a player nearly twenty years before. And yet, he would lose his job.

To begin with, he lost a friend and ardent supporter when Chancellor Heyns resigned in November of 1970 to return to the relative serenity of teaching psychology at his old school, Michigan. Heyns insisted he was not leaving because of the continuing acrimony on the

Cal campus that had placed him uncomfortably "In an adversary position in relation to the students" or because of "hostility" to the university from the outside, most particularly from the governor's office. On the contrary, he wrote in the *Blue and Gold*, "the more difficult the situation was the more disinclined I was to resign." His goal, at least partially achieved, had been to create "a state of equilibrium before leaving." His real reason for returning to the classroom, he admitted, was that he had simply lost the energy to work the sixteen-hour days the chancellorship required. Now, "I'll have time to reflect and to spend time with students." Instead of being pressured to call the cops on them.

Willsey was devastated. "We'd been such good friends. We spent a lot of enjoyable time together," enough time, he now suspected, to arouse the jealous ire of ambitious Heyns subordinates. With this chancellor gone, the coach realized he stood alone.

The new Cal chancellor, hired in April of 1971, was Albert Bowker, chancellor for eight years of the multi-campus City University of New York. A graduate of MIT with a doctorate in statistics from Columbia, Bowker was actually no stranger to northern California, having taught at Stanford from 1947 to '63. He came west again, he said, because "Berkeley is still the best single campus in the United States—and one of the greatest academic institutions in the world."

Although he dutifully attended home games in '71, "Bowker," said Willsey, "didn't care for football. I could hardly get into his office." It was not a good situation for a coach now estranged from the power structure and under criticism both for the Curtis affair and, more recently, for what was deemed unnecessarily aggressive recruiting tactics by some of his assistant coaches.

And then, in a further piece of irony, there was the Stanford factor, After his repeat Rose Bowl victory, Ralston left the Farm to become the new head coach of the NFL Denver Broncos, He wanted to take with him his offensive coordinator and fellow Cal grad, Mike White.

At the same time, Stanford wanted White to become Ralston's replacement. And, finally, Cal, too, was interested in him. Paul Brechler had resigned as A.D. in 1971, joining what was fast becoming an administrative diaspora. With his departure, Willsey took on the added duties of Acting Athletic Director, all the while harboring aspirations to win the job full-time. Instead, Dave Maggard, Cal's thirty-two-year-old track coach, was promoted. When he was passed over for A.D., Willsey had the uncomfortable feeling his days at Cal were numbered.

"I was called back from a convention in Florida," Willsey recalled. "I met first with Arleigh (Williams) and then with a small group before being called into Bowker's office. I'd already fired the coach they accused of recruiting violations. But they told me I'd have to get rid of my entire staff. I told them that if that's what they wanted, they'd better start with me. And they did."

Willsey was fired as head football coach and Acting Athletic Director on January 18, 1972. Mike White replaced him as coach and Maggard assumed his A.D. duties less than a month later. Willsey's 40-42-1 record was the best by a Cal coach since Waldorf's, and it was achieved under circumstances that might at a minimum be described as onerous. Willsey coached through a student revolution that condemned football as nothing more than a tool of the despised capitalist establishment. He coached through a succession of campus riots that culminated in a lethal conflict over a vacant lot. He coached at a time when a campus radical was more famous than his All America quarterback. And how many of his colleagues could say that their star safety had been tear gassed while playing baseball?

Through it all, Willsey retained his sense of humor and his perspective, which are really the same thing. After he was fired, he took some needed time off, traveling in Europe with his wife Barbara and children, before resuming a career that carried him to success both as a coach and an administrator in professional football.

Isaac Curtis, the root cause of at least some of his coach's problems, also left Cal after the 1971 season. He transferred to San Diego State and, declared eligible for '72, was moved by Aztec coach Don Coryell to wide receiver. It was a good move. Curtis led his new team with 44 catches for 832 yards and seven touchdowns. He was drafted by the Cincinnati Bengals and enjoyed a highly successful twelve-year NFL career.

Footballs do bounce in funny ways.

## CHAPTER TWENTY-FIVE

# STAR-SPANGLED

White, the new coach, was, at thirty-six, youthful in both appearance and demeanor, a lean, floppy-haired bundle of energy. While he, too, was a Pappy's Boy, he inherited little of the great man's impenetrable calm. Nor did he possess that protective shield of irony that kept Willsey functioning in bizarre times. White's strength was his exuberance, his Panglossian conviction that this was the best of all possible worlds. But he needed no more than one season as Cal head coach to recognize the folly of this discredited philosophy.

White had been a multi-sport athlete at Cal, a varsity letter winner in football, rugby and track and a junior varsity basketball player. He played end on the football team at a time when the forward pass was not exactly a key part of the offense. Still, as a senior, he was one of the three captains of Pete Elliott's first team in 1957. Track, though, may have been his best sport, for he'd been an accomplished hurdler and high jumper. After graduation, he joined Elliott's staff as a graduate assistant on the '58 Rose Bowl team. He became a full-time assistant the next season and remained with the Bears under Levy before joining Ralston at Stanford in '64. He was the quick-thinking offensive coordinator on the Cardinal Rose Bowl teams of 1970 and '71.

White was not without some reservations about accepting the Cal job. "It was a completely spontaneous decision," he recalled nearly forty years later. "I'm afraid I didn't even discuss it with my family. There were two determining factors. First, I was flattered to be asked to be the head coach at my own school. In that sense, it was a dream come true. Secondly, I did not want to follow John Ralston at Stanford. What he accomplished there was a miracle. That would have been a really tough act to follow. And yet, in making my decision, I gave up the continuity and the stability I had at Stanford. And I remembered that Pappy always told us never to accept a head coaching job at your own school."

Like Ralston, White was a devotee of the passing game, a preference not uncommon among coaches who once had at their behest quarterbacks on the Heisman level of Jim Plunkett and receivers as speedy and sure-handed as Gene Washington and Randy Vataha. White's return to Cal was in this sense timely, since he was seemingly blessed with not one but three excellent quarterbacks and in senior Steve Sweeney a record-breaking receiver.

The new coach had several other factors working in his favor in 1972. The NCAA had ruled that for the first time since the immediate post-World War II years, freshmen would be eligible for varsity play, thus clearing the way for, among other promising fledglings, quarterback Vince Ferragamo, receiver Steve Rivera and a defensive back from Monterey named Herman Edwards, who would somewhat later make a name for himself in coaching.

White was additionally rewarded with an observable decline in campus radicalism, the result no doubt of the withdrawal in August of '72 of U.S. troops from Vietnam and the imminent termination of the military draft. "There's a lot more people talking football than when I first came here," commented cornerback Scott Stringer. "And when winning comes there will be a lot more interest and more people at games." An anonymous student was quoted in the *Blue and*

*Gold* suggesting that while there were still speakers on campus urging revolution, "few stop to listen—the issues and the interest are no longer there." "We're more aware now," undergrad David Sanchez told a *Chronicle* reporter investigating the phenomenon. "If you were a radical before, you accepted everything the radical leaders said. Now, we want more facts."

Willsey should have been so lucky. "My heart went out to Ray," recalled White. "He had an unbelievably hard time with all that was going on then."

There were other developments of a less positive nature. The Bears were still on probation because of the Isaac Curtis matter, so they were deprived of Rose Bowl eligibility and their games could not be televised. Then, on June 23, 1972, President Nixon signed into law the so-called Title IX federal statute which rules that, at risk of losing federal funding, public schools and colleges must provide "equal opportunity" in athletics for women. Among other provisions, the statute requires that the percentage of female athletes at a school should be roughly the same as the percentage of female students enrolled. So if the student body happens to be 60 percent female, somewhere near 60 percent of the school's athletes should also be female. On the other hand, a school may be considered in compliance with Title IX if it demonstrated a history of improving gender equity or has instituted a program that successfully accommodates all the athletic interests and needs of the general student population.

In other words, college athletics, once virtually the exclusive province of male students, must now include women in fresh numbers and in a variety of sports. Even though Title IX's provisions were sufficiently vague to leave ample room for interpretation, the NCAA was outraged. "This may well signal the end of intercollegiate athletic programs as we have known them in recent decades," declared a spokesman for that perpetually agitated ruling body, apparently envisioning college football giving way to women's field hockey.

But Cal's new A.D. Maggard expressed a different view. "It's our feeling that this needed to be done," he told the *Chronicle*. "I have no hang-ups about women's athletics." That very year, he hired the first woman, Jane Kirksey, ever to serve as the business manager of a major co-educational college athletic department. And to oversee Cal's ten women's varsity sports, the university employed Barbara Hoepner, who wrote in the *Blue and Gold*, "The law was changed because it was wrong." But Ms. Hoepner could scarcely be characterized as a fierce women's libber. In fact, she opposed granting scholarships to women athletes, a policy that seemed implicit in Title IX's gender equality message. "The girls come here for the education Berkeley has to offer," she insisted. "Athletics are secondary."

Over the long haul, Title IX seems to have exercised a more profound effect on the minor, non-income-producing male sports. Many schools felt obliged, for example, to discontinue or seriously reduce their programs in wrestling, boxing, gymnastics and even, in some instances, baseball and track and field. As for football, it was pretty much business as usual.

Mike White's talent pool was certainly full—too full, actually, at one position. The last thing a new coach needed was the distraction of a quarterback controversy, and White had a beauty. The incumbent and front runner to open the season was senior Jay Cruze, who had started nine games in '71. But he had formidable competition from sophomore Steve Bartkowski, who had broken passing yardage records on what appeared to be Cal's last freshman team in 1971. Add to this surplus, the precocious freshman Ferragamo, newly eligible for the varsity. Although a latecomer to the competition—he didn't turn out until one week into the fall practice—he arrived with impressive credentials from Banning High School in Carson, where, conveniently, his older brother Chris was the head coach. At the North-South Shrine California high school all star game, Vince passed for 364 yards and four touchdowns.

Actually, Ferragamo was originally recruited by White for Stanford in the months before the coach accepted the Cal job. In fact, Ferragamo had signed a letter of intent to enroll at Stanford that was intercepted at the post office by brother Chris when he learned of White's move to Berkeley. Ferragamo's only interest in Cal, as it developed, was in the coaching staff, five of whose members, including quarterback coach Roger Theder, had joined White in his new job. "Vince never really wanted to go to Cal," White admitted many years later. "He just wanted to play for us."

Absent freshman ball, the eighteen-year-old would get his initial seasoning on the Bear junior varsity, once known as the Ramblers. But after he'd passed for 535 yards and four touchdowns in three J.V. games, he was abruptly promoted to the varsity and to what would become a traffic jam at his position.

As John Sullivan wrote in his history of the Big Game, "No school in the country had three such fine quarterbacks." Three, however, is a crowd.

Bartowski, who completed 13 of 20 for 244 yards and three touchdowns in the final spring scrimmage, was White's choice to start the season. And he passed for 261 yards in the opener, a 20–10 loss to Colorado. The Bears beat Washington State, 37–23, in their second game, then lost six in a row, including one by 17–10 to former whipping boy San Jose State, and three straight to conference foes USC (42–14), UCLA (49–13) and Washington (35–21). Bartowski, troubled by an elbow injury, had given way during this appalling collapse to Cruze, and the senior established a new Cal record by passing for 354 yards in the fourth game, a 34–27 road loss to Missouri.

But as the losses continued unabated, Ferragamo advanced through the ranks, finally replacing Cruze in the ninth game and leading the Bears in his very first start to a 31–12 streak-ending win at home. "You wouldn't know he was only a freshman watching him play," said running back Kemnitzer of the youth's unusual poise. In a disappointing

25–23 loss to Oregon State in Portland, Ferragamo rang up 300 yards in total offense, 285 of them passing. He was White's choice to start the Big Game—the quarterback's first, the coach's first as a head coach and his first, after an eight-year stay at Stanford, on the Cal side of the field.

The 2-8 record he would take into the game had further eroded White's natural buoyancy. "I felt that we could and would enjoy immediate success," he wrote of that season in the *Blue and Gold*. "I believed this because I had been a part of great success at Stanford during the past few years…As coaches we had forgotten the long years it took to get Stanford to the Rose Bowl." A place, he might have added, the Bears hadn't seen in fourteen years.

There had been some changes that year on the Stanford farm as well. The school had dropped the "Indians" nickname it had used since 1930, deeming it racially insensitive at a time of profound social and cultural change. Many conservative old grads deplored this break from tradition, damning it as a meek surrender to what was becoming known as "political correctness." Now, they would be deprived of such pre-game and halftime attractions as the "authentic" Indian war dances of Geronimo look-alike Prince Lightfoot and the prancing of pom pom maidens with feathers in their hair. Instead, Stanford would resurrect a nickname that pre-dated the redskin years and was actually more of a reference to the school color. Stanford's teams would thenceforward be "The Cardinal," or, to the ill informed, "Cardinals."

Like the Bears, the Cardinal had a new coach who, like White, had been part of Ralston's Rose Bowl staff. He was Jack Christensen, a former All-Pro defensive back and kick-returner on the very fine Detroit Lions teams of the 1950s. And he'd had a better debut coaching season than his onetime colleague, entering the big Game with a 6-4 record. Stanford was, as usual in those years, a heavy favorite to wallop the Bears.

It had rained all week before the November 18 game in Berkeley, and though the clouds had cleared before the kickoff, the Memorial Stadium turf was a turbid stew. Fearing another downpour or just plain dispirited by the lousy season, a less-than-capacity crowd of sixty-eight thousand showed up for the playing of the 75th Big Game. Those who stayed home missed a classic.

Stanford scored first on a 24-yard pass from Mike Boryla to Eric Cross after a Cal turnover. Boryla was another in a long line of exceptional Cardinal quarterbacks dating to Frankie Albert and continuing with Bob Garrett, John Brodie, Dick Norman and Plunkett. Boryla would complete 183 of 350 passes for 2284 yards and 14 touchdowns in this, his first season on the job. But Cal recovered from his opening shot and put together a ponderous 18-play, 78-yard drive through the quicksand that was capped off by a 29-yard field goal from Ray Wersching, the right-footed successor to his left-footed brother Randy. And a future 49er star.

Then with just eight seconds left in the half, Stanford linebacker Gordon Riegel intercepted a Ferragamo pass and returned it 71 yards for a touchdown that gave the Cardinal a comfortable 14–3 lead at the intermission. But there was life yet in the Bears. On the second play after the second half kickoff, Cal defensive end Dave Gleason recovered a botched Cardinal handoff on the Stanford 32. Five plays later, Sylvester Youngblood scored from the four. A successful two-point pass play from Ferragamo to Kemnitzer reduced the enemy lead to 14–11.

On the Bears' next possession, White gambled on fourth down, but the fake punt fooled no one and Stanford took over on the Cal 38. The Cardinal then marched to the eight and what appeared to be a certain score of one sort or another. But two Boryla pass attempts fell incomplete and on third down the quarterback was sacked for a 15-yard loss by Gleason and star linebacker Loren Toews. The Bears were further emboldened when Cardinal kicker Rod Garcia, who had booted the last-second game-winner in January's Rose Bowl, missed from 40 yards.

In what would prove to be another socko finish, the Bears opened the fourth quarter confidently. Stringer returned a punt 34 yards to the Cardinal 17. On the fifth play from there, Youngblood powered in from the six. Wersching's extra point gave Cal the lead, 18–14. But not for long. Boryla completed passes of 25 yards to Cross and 21 to Don Alverado on a drive that led to Reggie Sanderson's touchdown from the three. The Cardinal had regained the lead, 21–18, with but 3:42 left to play. And when Ferragamo was intercepted again, this time by Stanford safety Steve Murray, Bear rooters began chanting, "Bart! Bart!" in the hope that White would replace poor Vince with Bartkowski.

Ferragamo was indisputably having a bad day. He'd completed up to this point just four of 18 passes and been intercepted four times. Could this have been, even for one celebrated for his élan, a case of freshman jitters? And yet, when the next Stanford possession stalled on the Cal 38, White stubbornly sent Ferragamo in for one last try. With 1:13 to play and 62 yards to go, the situation looked grim. But the freshman suddenly found his range. He passed 18 yards to little (165 pounds) Dave Bateman and 20 more to Sweeney, playing his last Big Game. Then the Bears were awarded consecutive interference calls, the second placing the ball on the Stanford five. But in these waning seconds, Youngblood lost three on an ill-advised running play and Kemnister picked up just a yard on a swing pass. And on third down, Ferragamo misfired on a desperation throw.

It was fourth down on the Stanford seven with all of three seconds remaining. White audaciously passed up a chance for a tie by declining a field goal try. As an old Big Game hand, he considered anything short of victory unacceptable. "I never even thought of going for the tie," he said afterward. "This game means too much." On this last play of the game, though, he was not above a touch of deception, having wide receiver Sweeney line up at tight end, a position the lanky (6-4, 205) star had played with little distinction in an early season experiment.

And true to that form, he got off the line clumsily on the most important play of his fine college career, colliding after only a few steps with Stanford defensive back Jim Ferguson. He was lurching through the slime, struggling to regain his equilibrium, when Ferragamo lofted a pass to the corner of the end zone. Sweeney dived awkwardly for the ball and caught it just before a three-point landing in-bounds. As hysterical fans streamed onto the field, there was no try for the extra point. Cal had won, 24–21, and an otherwise abysmal season ended gloriously.

White's record would improve by one win in '73. Cruze was gone from the quarterback squeeze, but Bartkowski and Ferragamo were still trapped there. As an illustration of the closeness of the competition in '72, consider these final passing statistics:

| | ATTEMPTS | COMPLETIONS | COMP% | YARDS | TDs | INTERCEPTIONS |
|---|---|---|---|---|---|---|
| Bartkowski: | 165 | 70 | .424 | 944 | 4 | 13 |
| Cruze: | 109 | 67 | .615 | 829 | 8 | 10 |
| Ferragamo: | 83 | 43 | .518 | 640 | 6 | 8 |

So now there were two. They were, in fact, differently talented. Although he was a year behind Bartkowski at Cal, Ferragamo was the more polished of the two. "He had great command of the game," White recalled. "Vince was a great play-action quarterback. He had a fine touch on his passes and great anticipation. Steve was raw. He was a flamethrower, one of those guys who could stand on the goal line and throw the ball 80 yards. Hell, in those days, a lot of people thought that was the way you did it. But he had no touch on the ball when we got him. We knew, though, that with all that talent he would blossom with time. They were both such good guys and both NFL prospects. It was a juggling act for us over two seasons. Frankly, I don't know how we got through it."

Ferragamo would win the starting job at the beginning of the '73 season, partly because of his Big Game tour de force but mostly because Bartkowski passed up spring practice to play baseball for the Bears. It was a game at which he was almost equally adept, and he had quite a season that year playing first base and catcher. He led the team in hitting with a .329 average and also in runs, hits and RBIs. He hit 12 homers in 51 games, erasing Jackie Jensen's twenty-six-year-old record of eight in a season. In the old Golden Boy's defense, though, it must be said that he played in ten fewer games, was a pitcher in twenty-one of those and batting right-handed, like Bartkowski, played his home games in a ballpark with a left field fence 538 feet away down the line, 200 feet longer than it was in the younger man's day. Coincidentally, Jensen would become Cal's baseball coach in 1974. By then, though, football was Bartkowski's game.

But he was Ferragamo's backup for most of the '73 season, starting only three games. And yet, he played almost as often as his rival. The two quarterbacks, good as they were, hardly represented all of Cal's offense that year.

In sophomore Chuck Muncie, for example, White had a running back who before his college career was complete would establish himself as one of the great players in the game. He was also, in keeping with the times, a sometimes exasperating free spirit.

Originally from the western Pennsylvania mining town of Uniontown, Muncie had an otherwise idyllic childhood marred by a bewildering succession of life-threatening mishaps. At age six, riding his tricycle, he was run over by a dump truck, leaving him with bones broken nearly the length of his small body. He spent months afterward in a full-body cast. At eight, he tore a foot apart while running barefoot over a broken bottle. At thirteen, standing too close to an open fire, his clothes were ignited, causing serious burns to his back and legs. The way things were going, he was lucky to make it as far as high school, where, inexplicably, his feet went flat.

But in an athletic family that had already spawned three older brothers who played professional football, Chuck emerged as the champion of them all. At Uniontown High, he was a high scoring guard who led his team to the state basketball championship. He was a 9.7 100-yard dashman on the track team and, amazingly enough for one of his considerable size, a 6-9 high-jumper. In football, he was virtually unstoppable, despite the fact that he suffered from an astigmatism that rendered him nearly blind without his glasses. And with, as he put it, "flat eyeballs," he could not keep contact lenses in place for more than a few seconds so he played football, high school, college and pro, wearing the same black horn rims he sported in the real world. He merely taped them on, protecting them not always adequately with helmet face bars running horizontally and perpendicularly. "The lenses would cloud up on misty days and defensive players were constantly trying to tear them off," he recalled. "I think I broke my nose in every game."

In the second game of his senior year in high school, football's only bespectacled star suffered more than cloudy lenses and a broken nose, dropping from a head-to-head concussion. His season was over, as well as, Muncie thought, his football career. Basketball, he decided, would now be his game. On the recommendation of a friend and with the belief that he would be residing in a desert oasis, he enrolled at Arizona Western Junior College in Yuma, a top school in basketball, football and baseball. It was in the desert, for certain, but not exactly an oasis. "The palms shown in the brochure," said Muncie, "were midgets. Everything else was sand." One look at the newcomer's 6-4, 220-pound physique and his 4.3 speed in the 40 convinced the school's football coach, Ray Butcher, that the lad should give the gridiron one last try. He did, running 90 yards for a touchdown in his first carry for the nationally ranked J.C. team.

Like Ferragamo, Muncie was initially recruited by White and Theder for Stanford. And he, too, had signed a Cardinal letter of intent, only to receive that now familiar urgent phone call instructing him to tear it up and apply for Cal. Muncie was the fourth Cal player, behind Rick Bennett, Morton and Ferragamo, to be rescued from life on the Farm. But he sat out the 1972 season making up grades at Laney College before entering Cal.

"I went to Cal strictly on faith," he said many years later. "Faith in Mike and Roger as coaches. I don't think I'd even had an official campus visit. But I loved the place on sight. It was the best thing ever to happen to me. I'd come from a little "Leave-It-To-Beaver" kind of town. I'd never even seen an Asian person before. And Cal had every nationality, every culture, every level of society. I hadn't been on campus long before I spotted another friendly looking black man. He was dressed weirdly, though, in some kind of ceremonial robes. 'Hi there, brother,' I called out to him. 'I am not your brother,' he answered in a very thick British accent."

Joining Muncie in the '73 backfield was another junior college (San Bernardino Valley) transfer with sprinters' speed, Howard Strickland. And though Sweeney had moved on, White had in sophomore Rivera and freshman Wesley Walker two future record-breaking receivers. Rivera had been Ferragamo's primary receiver at Banning High and Walker, a 9.6 sprinter on the track team, was a deep threat the likes of which the Bears had never before been blessed.

The 1973 team's weakness was defense, as made plain in the season-opening 66–0 loss to coach Bear Bryant's Crimson Tide in the scorching heat of Birmingham. "We brought something like fifty players back there," Muncie recalled. "They had at least ninety, and they just platooned us to exhaustion in all that heat and humidity." A 27–7 loss to Illinois at home the next week was a minor improvement. Then the Bears went on an offensive tear, beating Army at West Point, 51–6, while racking up 622 total yards. Back in Berkeley, they gained 625 yards in "edging" Washington, 54–49. In their first four games, they had scored 112 points, 105 of them on consecutive weekends, and had 148 scored against them. It would be that way all season. Twice more teams would pierce that diaphanous defense for 50 points or more, UCLA winning 61–21, and USC, 50–14. Oregon came close finally settling for a 41–10 win in Eugene.

The Bears themselves could move the ball; they just couldn't stop the other team from moving it farther. By Big Game time, both Muncie and Strickland had gained more than 600 yards rushing, Muncie scoring ten touchdowns in the first ten games, Strickland eight. Those restless bedfellows, Ferragamo and Bartkowski, had each passed for more than 800 yards and together accounted for nine touchdowns. Walker had three TDs while averaging 25.4 yards per catch. Rivera had averaged 14.3 for his 25 receptions. The Bears were 4-6 before the game, Stanford 6-4. The Cardinal until then had scored only four rushing touchdowns, three by leading ground gainer Scott Laidlaw. But Boryla had thrown for 17 scores.

With all that firepower, the halftime score was a feeble, 3–3, Stanford's Garcia and Cal's Ron VanderMeer having traded field goals. The Cardinal attack was distinctly slowed by the loss of Boryla to injury in the first half. His sub, Dave Ottmar, the team's punter, took charge in the second half. Bartowski had started for Cal, but both he and Ferragamo were not up to snuff, Bart finishing the game five for 21 for 95 yards and Vince four for 11 for 23. But the Bears did have a ground game, albeit a fumbling one. Early in the third quarter, they marched 70 yards. Muncie gained 31 yards on one play to the Stanford 15 and then scored from there on his next carry to give Cal a 10–3 lead.

The Cardinal tied the score when, after recovering a Strickland fumble, Doug Jena ran in from the Cal eight. On the Bears' next possession, a Muncie fumble was recovered by the Cardinal's John Snider on the Cal 25. Garcia's 37-yard field goal gave Stanford a 13–10 lead. But Cal regained it when Bartkowski passed for 56 yards to Walker to set up a Ferragamo sneak from the one.

By this time, Bartkowski had also become the team's punter, replacing the injured Scott Overton. He'd done a creditable job until early in the fourth quarter when a low pass from center caused him to shank the ball only 21 yards to the Cal 30. Ron Inge scored for the Cardinal four plays afterward, returning the lead to his team, 20–17, after Garcia's extra point. After a pallid beginning, this was turning into another Big Game thriller.

But no. With five minutes remaining, the Cardinal increased its lead on an 81-yard drive which featured runs of 38 yards by Laidlaw and 23 by Jena. Laidlaw finally scored from the ten for the 26–17 final score.

Muncie's 129 yards on 22 carries in the Big Game gave him 801 for his rookie season. It was the highest rushing total for a Cal back since the glory days of Jensen and Olszewski a generation earlier. Muncie also led the team in receiving with 27 catches for 283 yards and in scoring with 12 touchdowns, the first Cal "triple crown" winner since Jack Hart in 1957. Actually, this was but a warmup for better things to come for the big back. Walker, meanwhile, had been sensational in his debut season, averaging 27.8 yards for his 13 receptions, rushing ten times for an average gain of 6.4 and returning 21 kickoffs for a 20.2 average.

The competition between the two quarterbacks revealed no obvious winner. Ferragamo hit on 82 of 170 passes for 1,014 yards, five touchdowns and 12 interceptions; Bartkowski was 61 of 129 for 910, four and seven. The prospect of sharing the position for a third season was, in the minds of both, unthinkable. Bartkowski had even considered abandoning football to pursue what was demonstrably a promising career in baseball. It was only after White painted a glowing and, as it were, entirely accurate picture of his gridiron future that he agreed to play one more season. Ferragamo chose otherwise, transferring to the University of Nebraska. It seemed a curious move at the time since the Cornhuskers' second-year coach, Tom Osborne, was no fan of the passing game.

"It's funny," said White, "but I actually think the Nebraska offense was a better fit for him. Vince was, after all, a great play-action guy. We appreciated him coming to Cal. He won that Big Game for us. But he was never really happy here. I think he was always looking for a way out the door."

So Bartkowski had the job all to himself for '74, and with Muncie, Strickland, Walker and Rivera, he had the ingredients for a bang-up season. Add to this bunch a runty (5-7, 155 pounds) soccer-style place-kicker named Jim Breech, and it was clear the Bears could score points. The question remained whether they could prevent opponents from scoring more. In '73, the Bears had scored 245, averaging three touchdowns a game, despite scoring only one in their first two games. Ah, but they'd had 380 scored against them, an average of nearly seven TDs per. White's answer was to shift to a 3-4 pro-style defense (three down linemen, four linebackers) that would give his players increased flexibility, particularly against option offenses. While this scheme did yield yardage, it cut back on rampant scoring. Because it easily bent but only occasionally broke, it was dubbed, the "Rubber Band Defense."

Alas, the Rubber Band lost some elasticity in a 21–17 opening loss to Florida in Gainesville. Muncie scored both Cal touchdowns—on a 17-yard pass from Bartkowski in the second quarter and on a three-yard run in the fourth. The Bears then ran up five straight wins, starting with a 17–16 squeaker with San Jose State and finishing similarly with a 17–14 close one over Oregon State. Along the way, there were convincing victories over Illinois (31–14), featuring two Bartkowski-Rivera touchdowns, and over Oregon (40–10), in which Bart connected with Walker for a 70-yard TD and Muncie scored twice.

After this winning streak, Cal's longest in twenty-two years, the team was whipped, 28–3, by UCLA. In defeat, Bartkowski passed for the first of four late-season 300-yard games, denting the Bruins for 300-even on 26 of 44 completions. The Bears tied sixth-ranked and undefeated USC, 15–15, the next week in Los Angeles, a possible victory denied by a controversial interception call on a Bartkowski pass that Rivera and Trojan defender Marvin Cobb both seemed to catch. In a 52–26 win over Washington, Bartkowski passed for 316 yards, including touchdowns to Walker of 56 and 43 yards. He was good for 304 the next week in a 37–33 win over Washington State. And he would connect for a third straight 300-yarder in what would become another Big Game for the ages.

With a 7-2-1 record against Stanford's 4-4-2, the Bears were made the betting favorite for the first time in this series since 1960 when Levy's one-win team was picked over Stanford's winless one. And they marched an impressive 89 yards in ten first quarter plays for a Muncie touchdown from the one. Rivera made two spectacular catches en route, snatching a 42-yarder away from two Cardinal defenders and plucking a 23-yarder one-handed. Stanford made it, 7–3, in the second quarter on a 29-yard field goal by Mike Langford, an anachronistic straight-ahead, toe-first booter at a time when the soccer-style approach was de rigueur. That was all the scoring in the first half.

It was Stanford's turn that season to have a quarterback controversy, Mike Cordova and Guy Benjamin unhappily alternating as starter and reliever. Cordova started this game without much success. And his first pass of the third quarter was picked off by Cal's undersized (185 pounds) linebacker, Rick Booth, on the Stanford 38. Bartkowski passed to Bateman for 22 yards to the Stanford 16. But the Bears could progress no farther, and Breech kicked a 34-yard field goal for 10–3.

Coach Christiansen went to his bullpen at the start of the third quarter, replacing the ineffective Cordova with Benjamin. When the new quarterback's first drive sputtered to a stop barely past midfield, the coach kept it alive with a fake punt on fourth and four from the Cal 47, punter Tom Lynn scampering 20 yards for the revivifying first down. Benjamin then passed 18 yards to tight end Brad Williams. But the Rubber Band Defense did not break, and Langford was obliged to kick a 31-yard field goal to close the scoring gap to four points. The Cardinal were back in business when defensive back Jeff Siemens recovered a loose ball on the Cal nine after a misdirected snap to the punter. Laidlow carried it in from the one four plays afterward, and Stanford had its first lead of the day, 13–10.

Siemens was at it again on Cal's next possession, intercepting Bartkowski on the Stanford 18 and returning the ball 21 yards to the 39.

Benjamin quickly found the swift Tony Hill for a spectacular pass-run touchdown of 61 yards. The extra point was blocked, but the Cardinal now held a solid 19–10 lead. The Bears threatened once more, mainly on a 35-yard Bartkowski-to-Rivera third down pass, before the Cardinal defense aborted the advance. Cal got on the board, though, with a 40-yard Breech field goal. The score was now a tantalizingly close and touchdown-vulnerable, 19–13. But time and opportunity were running short for the home team.

The Bears would get one more chance. With 2:27 remaining, they began a desperation drive from the Stanford 48. The yards came hard for them and they were stuck with a fourth-and-ten dilemma on the 37. From there, Bartkowski found Rivera for 24 yards to the 13, a game-saving completion if ever there was one. Then, after two running plays gained nothing, Bartkowski again hit Rivera, this time in the corner of the end zone for what certainly seemed the game-breaker. Hysterical Cal fans spilled onto the field in a premature victory celebration. But the score was only tied. The crowd fell nervously silent as Breech tried the extra point. And amid renewed bedlam, he made it. Cal had apparently pulled off a heart-stopping 20–19 win in the last few seconds.

There were, in fact, twenty-six seconds left when Cal kicked off and 19 after the Cardinal returned the ball out of bounds on the 19. Benjamin then passed to Ted Pappas at the 38. After two quick incompletions, the Cardinal QB hit Williams on a crossing pattern, and the tight end somehow bulled his way out of bounds near the Cal 40 to stop the clock with all of two seconds left. There was time only for a 50-yard field goal try.

Langford had booted a 52-yarder earlier in the season against Michigan. But this, after all, was the Big Game with all of its built-in tension. It was also Langford's first as a player, and by his own admission, "my knees were shaking." These, of course, are body parts a kicker ordinarily wants intact under such exacting circumstances. Shaky or not, and with his then unorthodox form, Langford kicked that ball straight and true. Final score: Stanford 22, Cal 20.

Despite its frustrating finish, it had been a banner season for White and his Bears. Cal hadn't won seven games in a year since 1968, and the '74 stars set records galore. Rivera, who caught nine passes for 205 yards in the Big Game, established new season records with 56 receptions for 938 yards. Walker averaged 27.2 yards for his 14 catches. Muncie picked up another 791 yards rushing and 410 receiving. He scored 11 touchdowns, one more than Strickland, who gained 724 on the ground. Muncie and Rivera were All-Conference and offensive guard Chris Mackie received All America mention.

Bartkowski was a consensus All American, the nation's leading passer. With his 318-yard day against Stanford, he shattered Morton's Cal record for passing yardage in a season with 2,580 and for attempts with 325. His 182 completions fell three short of Morton's mark. Bartkowski was the Most Valuable Player in the College All-Star game in Chicago against the Pittsburgh Steelers and was the first player selected (by Atlanta) in the NFL draft. In a game he had seriously considered quitting, he became, in 1974, the best college player in the country.

Muncie, Rivera and Walker would all return for 1975, but Bartkowski was off to become the NFL's Rookie of the Year. After two years with a surplus at quarterback and one year with the best in the land playing there, the Bears found themselves without an established player at the position.

But the right man would emerge soon enough, and he would become, in too short a time, one of the most compelling figures in all of Cal's football history.

CHAPTER TWENTY-SIX

# UNINVITED

The world did not stop turning during Mike White's surprising march to the winners' circle. Events in those years moved with their usual bewildering rapidity. A U.S. president resigned in disgrace, his successor survived two assassination attempts in the same month, and a newspaper heiress—and Cal student—was kidnaped by a radical group whose ranks she later inexplicably joined. Those were the days.

White, meanwhile, firmly believed he'd found his quarterback for 1975. Junior Fred Besana decided to sit out the '74 season as a redshirt sophomore rather than watch Bartkowski's record-setting season from a seat on the Andy Smith bench. But he was fully prepared to take over in '75. Indeed, he knew the system and he was an accurate passer, a player skilled enough to be drafted eventually by the pros. But fate, as it will, intervened, and Besana would spend much of the next two seasons on the Andy Smith Bench watching another brilliant quarterback set records.

Besana was, however, the starter when the Bears opened the new season on the road against Colorado, and he played well enough in a 34–27 loss, passing 53 yards to Walker for one touchdown and scoring himself on a one-yard sneak set up by Muncie's 62-yard run. Muncie scored twice in that game and gained 112 yards rushing, but Colorado bruised the Bears for 545 yards, 437 on the ground. Besana was 12 for 25 passing for 177 yards. But he threw an interception in the dying seconds that snuffed out Cal's remaining hopes.

The Bears lost again with Besana at the controls, and by the less encouraging score of 28–10, to West Virginia. The Bears only touchdown was scored in the second quarter while Besana was taking a breather for one series of downs. The replacement QB was a 1974 junior college All American out of Grossmont College in El Cajon near San Diego. And Joe Roth, taking his first snaps for the Bears, led a 67-yard drive to the enemy end zone, keeping progress alive on a critical third-and-15 situation with a 22-yard pass to tight end George Freitas. Three players later he hit Rivera for 12. Tom Newton then plunged in from the one. It was an impressive debut.

And yet Besana remained the starter, at least for one more quarter of one more game. Roth replaced him against Washington State at the start of the second quarter. And in Cal's first win of the season, by 33–21, he completed 13 of 23, including a 41-yard touchdown to long-gainer specialist Walker. Besana was now the backup.

The Washington State win was the first of four straight with Roth at the controls. He salvaged a narrow victory over San Jose State when, trailing 24–20 in the final two minutes and stuck deep in his own territory, he passed 25 yards to Muncie, found Rivera at midfield for 23 more and then, with 1:98 on the clock, connected with Walker on third down for 46 yards and the winning T.D. He missed the first half against Oregon in Eugene with a shoulder injury, but in the second half hit tight end Roy Fiebiger for a 32-yard score. This, though, was Muncie's game, the star back gaining 207 yards and scoring thrice in a 34–7 win.

Muncie had 149 yards and three more scores in a 51–24 romp over Oregon State. He also completed a 47-yard option pass to Walker for another touchdown. And Walker scored again on a 25-yard run from the antiquated end-around play. The streak ended with what would ultimately prove a disastrous 28–14 loss to UCLA in the Coliseum. Roth was 17 for 31 for 236 yards and a 10-yard touchdown to Rivera, who caught 10 in the game for 154 yards. Muncie gained 126 on 23 carries and in the process broke Olszewski's twenty-three-year-old Cal career rushing record of 2,504 yards. But the Bears were undone by five fumbles.

Though his play didn't show it, Muncie disclosed later in life that "I just hated playing in the L.A. Coliseum. I don't know whether it was the smog or what, but I had this mental block. I didn't feel we could ever win there. The funny thing is, though, it made me play all that much harder."

The Bears bounced back in a big way the next week, downing USC, 28–14, before 51,871 in Berkeley. White called it his "finest victory." It might have been achieved, however, through an emotional letdown by the Trojans. Their coach, John McKay announced the night before the game that he would be leaving—after sixteen years and four National Championships—at the end of the season to coach the new Tampa Bay team in the NFL. His last S.C. team was ranked fourth in the country before playing Cal, and in tailback Ricky Bell, he had a legitimate Heisman Trophy contender. But these Trojans were no match for the emotionally charged Bears. Roth was 19 for 31 for 244 yards with touchdown tosses to Walker and Freitas. Rivera had nine catches for 131 yards and Muncie gained 143 on 18 carries, plus another 62 yards on five receptions. It was Cal's first win over USC in Berkeley since 1957 and only the second anywhere since '58.

Then in a narrow 27–24 win over Washington, Roth completed 24 of 36 for all four touchdowns (a PAT was blocked) and a new Cal record of 380 yards passing. Rivera caught two of his touchdown passes, Walker and Muncie the other two. Roth added another 248 yards and two touchdowns in a 31–14 win over Air Force in Colorado Springs. Walker caught both TD passes, a 34-yarder in the first quarter and a more typical, for him, 65-yarder just before the half. Muncie ran 32 yards for a score and Breech booted a 51-yard field goal. The Bears had so many quick-strike weapons, they looked unstoppable.

And for the first time in seventeen years, they had a decent shot at a Rose Bowl invitation. For that matter, both teams in the '75 Big Game were in the running, each with a 5-1 record in conference play, their only losses to UCLA, which was also 5-1, having lost to Washington the very day Cal upset the Trojans. All of which meant that, depending on the outcome of the USC-UCLA matchup down south, the winner of the Big Game could go to the Rose Bowl. There hadn't been a Cal-Stanford game this meaningful in forty years. Cal was finally free of the "indefinite" probation it had labored under since 1972 and was at long last bowl-eligible. A quirk in the scheduling, however, did neither Big Game competitor a favor. Because of a television commitment, UCLA and USC would be playing the following Friday night, a full six days after Cal-Stanford, thus imposing an agonizing waiting period before the Rose Bowl choice could be made.

There was yet another foggy element in this unclear situation. The Pac-8 had decided before the season that other teams in the conference besides the Rose-Bowl-bound champion could now play in bowl games. This hadn't happened since 1948 when the old Pacific Coast Conference permitted co-champion Oregon to play in the Cotton Bowl after Cal was picked for the Rose. USC, out of the running by now for the '75 conference title, took advantage of the Pac-8's bowl generosity by accepting on November 14 an invitation to the Liberty Bowl in Memphis. Cal decided to wait out the Rose Bowl bid, which it would surely get if it beat Stanford and USC beat the Bruins.

The immediate task at hand was eliminating the Cardinal. And that might be a problem. Stanford was 6-3-1 in all games and had another crack offensive unit, featuring the dual quarterbacks and receiver Tony Hill, who was at least comparable in terms of productivity (55 catches that season) to Rivera and in yardage (916) to Walker. But there was no Muncie on the Farm. And he would be the difference.

Despite his ever-accumulating statistics, the great Bear running back's season had not been exactly free of turmoil. Stories had circulated all year on campus and beyond of his apparently dogged resistance to being educated. Muncie was certainly bright enough—he had a keen wit and even a touch of the poet—but he developed an aversion to attending class. "We'd take him right to the front door of his classrooms," White recalled, "then he'd walk out the back way as soon as we weren't looking."

Muncie protested that, as he put it years later, "I went to enough classes. I once carried eighteen (course) units. But there were some professors I couldn't take. I never did get along with Harry Edwards when he was teaching sports sociology. That's because I think he hated athletes. I know he'd get really pissed off at me."

The cerebral Edwards, himself a former college athlete, was, in fact, quoted in the *Blue and Gold* suggesting that sports represented a "sickness" for blacks, removing them from other, more worthy endeavors. Professional sports, he said, remain "the only institution in the dominant society in which blacks participate in numbers."

Rumors also spread of Muncie's drug use, which he never refuted. "It was a crazy time in Berkeley then," he recalled. "There was partying and drugs. Everybody was doing it, even the campus leaders. Athletes probably the least." Muncie used drugs during his successful but oft-suspended professional career, finally stopping after serving a prison sentence in the late 1980s for attempting to sell two ounces of cocaine. He has been a model citizen since, working with boys and girls clubs and operating a nationwide college scouting service. Asked if he might have been an even better player had he not used drugs, he said, "Probably. The thing was, I was such a natural athlete that I could get by. I never even worked out in the offseason. I could get off a beach and still run a 4.3 40."

But his foibles had come to public notice before the 1975 Big Game, and he recalls "feeling down. I'd had some bad publicity that week and I was pretty low. And then, just before we took the field, Roger (assistant coach Theder) told me someone was here to see me. It was my mom. Now, that changed everything."

Revified by maternal ministration, Muncie turned in one of the greatest of all Big Game individual performances. He rushed for 169 yards on 30 carries, scored three touchdowns on the ground, caught a seven-yard pass from Roth for another and threw a 46-yard touchdown pass of his own to Walker. That's five touchdowns altogether! As more than one astonished spectator observed, watching Muncie that day was like watching a man play against boys. Freshman fullback Paul Jones got another Cal score on a six-yard run and Breech kicked two field goals for a final score of 48–15. After a whipping of this magnitude, it was clear Stanford would not be headed for any post-season games, but as Cardinal coach Christiansen said of the Bears, "They certainly deserve to be in some bowl."

They certainly did. This was not only a winning team (8-3) but one with some of the game's most exciting players. The Bears in '75 led the nation in total offense, averaging 458.5 yards per game. And never before or since has there been a team with a more perfectly balanced attack. In what can only be seen as a statistical improbability, the Bears accumulated exactly 2,522 yards rushing and 2,522 passing that season.

Muncie ran for a new Cal record 1,460 yards, breaking Jensen's twenty-seven-year-old single season standard. He carried for another record 228 times, averaged 6.4 yards per and scored 13 rushing touchdowns. He also caught 39 passes for another 392 yards and two more TDs. He was a consensus All American, finished second to Ohio State's Archie Griffin in the Heisman voting and was a first-round draft choice of the New Orleans Saints.

Though he didn't start until the fourth game, Roth completed 126 of 226 passes (55.8 percent) for 1,880 yards and a record-equaling 14 touchdowns. And at a time when interceptions were far more common, he was picked off only seven times. Rivera's 57 catches that season made him Cal's new career leader with 138 receptions. He, too, was a consensus All American. Walker, meanwhile, caught 39 in '75 for 839 yards and an eye-popping average of 23.3 per catch.

But there would be no bowl game. UCLA, under coach Dick Vermeil, edged the Trojans, 25–22, and then defeated Ohio State, 23–10, in the Rose Bowl. And USC, which finished well behind the conference co-champion Bears in the standings, shut out Texas A&M, 20–0, in the Liberty. The Bears stayed home. The week's interlude between the Big Game and that other one down south had cost them dearly, since most of the top bowls had locked in their teams by then.

It is also true that Cal was still not all that popular within the conference and, for that matter, with the NCAA, whose authority it had vainly and perhaps foolishly challenged over the Curtis affair. Muncie's capers were not looked upon favorably by either governing body. And White's increasingly aggressive recruiting methods had aroused further suspicion. The coach, for his part, was furious over the oversight—and remained so thirty-three years later.

"Someone should have gotten us in a bowl," he yet protests. "We had talent everywhere. There's no sin in having a great football team. The university didn't seize the moment for us."

John McCasey, who was Cal's Sports Information Director at the time, blames in part the Pac-8's inexperience with post-season politics for the slight. "We had a chance at the Fiesta or the Sun Bowl, but the conference basically screwed up. Nobody there knew anything about bowls other than the Rose. Until that season, they'd only had one to think about. They just couldn't find a place for us."

The disappointment was keen on campus. It had been nearly twenty years since the Bears had been to a bowl, and who knew when they'd get another chance? The 1976 team would lose Muncie and Rivera, and injuries would restrict Walker. The outlook for another winning season was in doubt.

There was, however, one great saving grace: the Bears still had Joe Roth at quarterback. His rise from nowhere had captivated the entire student body, as well as the local and national media. Raised as a good Catholic boy with few vices beyond a typically collegiate taste for beer, he was actually the quintessential campus football hero of a time long gone, a figure vaguely reminiscent of Jensen in his Golden Boy persona. Tall and blond, with good looks and an engaging manner, he scarcely fit the mold of the bearded, pot-puffing undergraduate of the rock 'n roll 1970s. Roth, in fact, had told his parents that his only reservation about entering Cal was that he didn't consider himself sophisticated enough. And yet, in the space of a single season, this innocent abroad had become enormously popular, a latter-day Big Man on Campus. Somehow, there remained in a hippie world a yearning for Frank Merriwell.

A telling moment occurred after Roth's triumphant performance against USC. He walked from the stadium down Piedmont Avenue to the apartment he shared with non-player John Matlock only a few blocks away. In her 1984 biography of her son, Lena Roth, described the scene: "As he made his way down the hill past fraternity and sorority houses—lawns and porches teeming with students and alumni—they all basked in the glory of Joe's success. Shouts of congratulation, words of praise and looks of awe followed Joe all the way home."

"It took him two hours to walk those few blocks," Matlock recalled. "There was so much cheering, so many people anxious to see and talk to him. Joe was a humble guy, but he was loving every minute of it."

Matlock and Roth moved in together in August of 1975 after Matlock, who had tried out for placekicker, retired from the game after one practice in the face of competition from Breech. "I had the apartment, though, and coach White told me Joe was looking for a place to live. He didn't like living in a dorm, and neither of us was much for fraternity life. We became friends forever. Joe had a great sense of humor, but he would go out of his way not to hurt anyone's feelings. Off the field, he was very concerned about other people. He was an innocent, sort of, but he was eager to learn. He was a beer drinker, but I taught him about fine wine. The girls loved him. They crowded around him. I had to field his calls, he got so many. Well, what is there to say—everybody loved Joe."

And that would include Besana, whose job he'd taken. In an interview twenty-five years later with the Contra Costa *Times*, Besana said, "It was pretty hard not to root for Joe. He was a great guy, and he never had a bad word for anyone."

"Joe was not perfect," his mother wrote. He was often late, it seems. And his musical taste was in question. "He couldn't stand Lawrence Welk," she said. "Still he had fewer faults than most."

Muncie, whose idea of a good time back then was not necessarily Joe's, was another "really good friend" and one of the quarterback's most ardent boosters, envisioning for him a brilliant career in the NFL, maybe even with the cross-Bay 49ers. "Just think," he reminisced, "if the Niners had signed Joe, they probably never would have drafted Montana."

And the 49ers, along with many other NFL teams, were interested. Jack White, then the team's vice president for personnel, told Cal coaches before the '76 season, "We have him rated as the top quarterback in the country. We expect him to be a first-round pick."

For his part, Roth was frankly bewildered by his sudden celebrity. After starring in football and baseball—and graduating in the top eight percent of his class—at Granite Hills High in El Cajon, he received exactly zero scholarship offers from major colleges. He was brutally disappointed. At the same time, he acknowledged that college recruiters may well have looked askance at his then slight build and his not yet fully developed throwing arm. But instead of sulking, he worked hard in the summer to add muscle and increase his arm strength. He ran constantly. He enrolled at Grossmont near his suburban home to add playing experience to his resumé. Under coach Dave Jordan, he started every game in his first season and led the Griffins to a 7-2-1 record. The next year, 1974, he completed 211 of 370 passes for 2,663 yards and 28 touchdowns while steering his team to, first, the Mission Conference Championship and then to the Orange Coast title. He was a junior college All American.

He'd also gained weight, carrying 205 pounds on his 6-4 frame. And he could throw along with the best of college quarterbacks. He continued to do B-plus classwork. Scholarships offers flooded in from Oregon, San Diego State, Brigham Young, Stanford, San Jose State, Oregon State, Washington, Utah, Colorado State and Cal. And Brown of the Ivy League recruited him.

On a visit to the Berkeley campus, he became fascinated with the wildly diverse scene on Telelgraph avenue. He liked Mike White's enthusiasm and his pro-style offense. He developed an instant friendship with quarterback coach Paul Hackett. But the "deciding factor," he told his parents "was the advantage Cal had academically. The main reason for going to college, after all, is to get a degree, and Cal is one of the best colleges in the country."

Now, approaching the 1976 season, his second and last in Berkeley, he found himself, to his amazement, a front-runner for the Heisman Trophy. As his mother recalled, Joe said, "Things are happening so fast, I don't know where I am. A few years ago, I was a nobody. Now I'm supposed to knock buildings down with my passes. I'm just going to go out and do the best I can. All this publicity is fine, but I can only do what my abilities allow me to do. I'm only as good as the players around me."

## CHAPTER TWENTY-SEVEN

# OUT, OUT, BRIEF CANDLE

In the spring of 1974, before his last football season at Grossmont, Joe Roth was bothered by a mole directly in front of his left ear. It was no more than a small dot at first, at worst a minor irritant. But it continued to grow and it bled when Joe nicked it while shaving and when his baseball batting helmet scraped against it. He had it removed by a dermatologist.

But it reappeared. This time he was told to have it examined for possible malignancy. Doctors told him it was a black mole or melanoma, a possibly lethal form of skin cancer. He had emergency surgery the very day he was examined. The tumor was removed, along with lymph nodes, skin tissue and some salivary glands, five ounces of tissue altogether. The cancer had not spread, he was told. And apart from some difficulty in swallowing because of the loss of salivary glands, he should be fine. He was pronounced cancer-free.

His performance on the football field for Grossmont only a few months later seemed to substantiate that diagnosis. Joe was bigger, stronger and more resilient than ever. He had triumphed not only on the gridiron but in a larger battle against a deadly disease. He was good newspaper copy, although he was so reluctant to discuss his medical history that the press finally left the story alone. Cal coaches were certainly aware of his bout with melanoma, but they were convinced, along with Joe himself, that it was all in the past, merely a case of a southern California beach boy spending too much time in the sun. Looking at him, no one could imagine Joe Roth ever being seriously ill. He easily passed all of his football physical examinations, as well as periodic checkups with his surgeons and Cal's team doctor, Jerome Patmont. And in his debut season with the Bears, he definitely hadn't played like a sick man. Joe felt confident and ready for the new season. He had always benefitted from a strong family support group, which included two brothers eleven and fourteen years older. As his mother wrote, "We four hovered over him like ants around a cookie crumb." So in May of 1976, he celebrated both his twenty-first birthday and the second anniversary of his operation, an event he jauntily called "Big O Day."

The '76 schedule was a wicked one, with more games away than at home. The first three were, in fact, all on the road, two against highly ranked Georgia and Oklahoma. Despite debilitating heat and humidity, the Bears took a 24–12 lead over Georgia into the third quarter, mainly on Roth-to-Walker bombs of 69 and 88 yards, the 88-yarder standing still as the longest pass play in Cal football history. But Walker, nursing a rib injury incurred in pre-game drills—the result of a playful bumping match with a teammate—played little in the second half, depriving Joe of his deep threat. And the Bears finally wilted in the Georgia heat and lost, 36–24. Joe was terrific in defeat, completing 21 of 36 for 379 yards, then the second highest single game passing yardage total in Cal history, exceeded only by his 380 yards against Washington the year before. But, as White told his players after the game, "Joe can't be expected to do it all for us."

He was 27 of 46 for 284 yards against Oklahoma in Norman, but the Bears lost again, 28–17. Then, on the flight to Phoenix for the Arizona State game, he was told that in his most recent checkup the x-rays seemed to show a spot on his lungs. Had the cancer returned? The next day, Dr. Patmont assured him this was a false alarm; the spot was nothing more than a flaw on the screen. Four doctors examined those X-rays, he said, and they all agreed there was no cause for concern. Joe was not fully convinced. "From that day forward," wrote his mother, "he was never the same."

At the time, he was leading the nation in pass attempts and completions, and he was regularly besieged by reporters and television interviewers. His Heisman candidacy, even at this early stage of the season, was on track. But almost as a harbinger of gloom, a violent electrical storm drenched Phoenix the day before the game. It was warm and dry again by the 7:30 p.m. kickoff Saturday night, but the field was still mushy from the heavy rain. Joe was no stranger to these conditions, but he was well off the mark that night. His first four passes fell incomplete and the fifth was intercepted and returned for a touchdown.

Cal was playing without star sophomore fullback Paul Jones, who was injured in the Oklahoma game, but Tom Newton, Oliver Hillmon and former San Francisco High School flash Markey Crane sparked a compensating ground game that piled up 276 yards. The Bears upset the Sun Devils, 31–22, even though Joe completed just ten of 27 passes for 104 yards with two interceptions. He missed so many open receivers that at one point quarterbacks coach Al Saunders turned in confusion to backup Besana and asked, "What's wrong with Joe out there?"

Joe recovered somewhat the next week in a 43–16 win over San Jose State, completing 16 of 30 for 229 yards. Walker set a new Cal record with 289 yards receiving, which included a 57-yard touchdown pass from Roth and 73-and-48-yard TDs from Besana. Once again, despite the improving numbers, Joe was off target much of the day. Again, he threw two interceptions. The "zip" seemed to be missing from his passes, many of which fell short of their intended receivers.

By then Joe suspected something his coaches, teammates and doctors did not: the cancer was back. He told no one of his fears, "living the nightmare," as White later said, "by himself." He would eat meals at the team training table, then lose them secretly in the bushes on his way back to the apartment he shared with Matlock, who urged him to seek medical help. He was losing weight, but he continued to play, sometimes surprisingly well under the conditions. He was 18 of 28 for 208 yards and a touchdown in Cal's third straight win, by 27–10, over Oregon.

Then the team dropped four in a row. The absence of such heroes from the season before as Muncie and Rivera was one reason, observers said. And Jones, the burgeoning star, missed all but the first two games with a knee injury. Walker played in only five before spraining his foot against Oregon State. Joe himself suffered a knee injury against the Beavers with just a minute left in that 10–9 loss. He missed the 35–19 loss to UCLA, a game in which Besana, playing in his stead, completed 24 of 42 for 175 yards.

Besana's playing time was increasing incrementally, a circumstance the fiercely competitive Joe accepted without complaint. "Fred's a great quarterback," he told the press. "If I got hurt tomorrow, he could go in and play the rest of the season and nobody would be able to tell the difference." White was baffled by such magnanimity. "When we take Joe out, he actually seems relieved. You'd think it would make him mad. I can't figure him out." The coach much later acknowledged he "didn't have a clue" about his quarterback's declining health at the time.

Joe's brother Tom, who had played quarterback at Washington State and later coached, told their mother that Joe seemed to be playing in a daze. Joe's best friend on the team, nose guard Bob Warner, told the family of Joe's disturbing inability to keep food down. And yet, to the casual observer, the player seemed relaxed and untroubled. Asked about his unusual lapses on the field, he told a reporter, "I knew in the beginning I wasn't Superman."

The Bears finally did break their losing streak, shutting out Washington, 7–0, in the eighth game and then surviving, 23–22, against

Washington State, a game decided in the final thirteen seconds when Cal defensive end Burl Toler, Jr., sacked Cougar quarterback Jack Thompson on a try for a two-point conversion. Joe was 15 of 29 for 147 yards, but with three more interceptions.

Entering the Big Game, both teams had 5-5 records. Joe remained philosophical about the downturn from '75. "We could have had an easier schedule and finished with a better record," he said, "but we played some of the great teams in the country, and I cherish that."

The Big Game started badly for the Bears even before it began. The day before, Stanford Athletic Director Joe Ruetz announced that he had fired coach Christiansen, effective after the game. The by now wearisome quarterback controversy had aroused alumni ire and though Christiansen had yet to have a losing season in his five years on the job, his teams were hardly the offensive juggernauts of Ralston's last three seasons. Christiansen was, however, popular with his players, and in an emotional demonstration of their affection for him, they carried him *onto* the field before the kickoff. Watching this extraordinary spectacle, White said he knew the Bears were in for a long afternoon.

Sticking to his guns, the Cardinal coach continued alternating his signal callers in his final game. Benjamin started and late in a scoreless first quarter, he began what would finally become an 80-yard scoring drive. But he wouldn't finish it. On cue, Cordova came off the bench at the start of the second quarter and connected on passes to Bill Kellar for 29 yards and then 28 to Hill for the game's first touchdown. On the ensuing kickoff, the Bears were plagued by another one of those eerie plays that have characterized their gridiron history. Ken McAllister, an excellent return man, fielded the ball on his one-yard line, but a slight collision with teammate Wade Johnson bumped him back into the end zone. Believing incorrectly that this was where he'd been all the time, McAllister touched the ball down...for a safety. Stanford now led 9–0.

But Cal fought back to a 10–9 halftime lead on a 51-yard Breech field goal and an eight-yard touchdown pass from Roth to Jesse

Thompson. Stanford scored twice in the third quarter, on a Mike Michel field goal and a 13-yard Benjamin pass to Don Stevenson, to take a 19–10 lead. Besana came off the bench at the start of the fourth quarter and led a 16-play, 66-yard drive finished off by a Newton plunge from the one. With the score at 19–17 late in the action, this was shaping up as yet another of the decade's famous Big Game cliffhangers.

Cal finally reassumed the lead when Mike O'Brien intercepted Cordova on the Cardinal 42 and returned the ball to the 13. Markey Crane scored from there on the next play, a fine run of tackle-breaking decisiveness. Only 5:08 remained. Cal led, 24–19.

Stanford was stopped cold on its next possession. Although there were barely two and a half minutes left to play, Christiansen elected to punt on fourth down and gamble on somehow getting the ball back. Michel's kick was downed by James Lofton on the Cal two.

Despite the unfavorable field position, the Bears only needed to retain possession to win. A first down would pretty much cinch the outcome, but even if they were forced to punt, Stanford would need at least 40 yards to travel and with little time to do it. And the Cardinal would have to score a touchdown to win. Cal fans were already celebrating as the seconds ticked away.

On first down, Roth pitched back to Crane, who had been until that moment the game's hero. He fielded the ball cleanly but unaccountably lost it at the line of scrimmage and it squirted into the hands of Stanford defensive end Duncan McColl, an All American like his father Bill before him. The happy circumstances of seconds before had been reversed...just like that! Stanford, not Cal, had the ball on the Cal two with time running out. Three plays later, Ron Inge plunged into the end zone for the winning T.D. A two-point conversion run by Cordova made the final score, 27–24. Just another one of those games.

Christiansen was now carried *off* the field by his jubilant and tearful players. "We all respect coach Christiansen more than any man we've been around," said a weeping Cordova in the locker room afterward. "It is a difficult thing to see a man who cares so much for us having to be fired...I'll never get over it."

Crane was also crying, but for entirely different reasons. "I wanted to win," he said several times in an interview with the *Examiner's* Glenn Schwarz. "If I hadn't dropped it, they wouldn't have gotten that touchdown."

In defeat, Roth was 11 of 27 for 100 yards and a touchdown. He finished his final season at Cal 154 of 295 for 1,789 yards and seven touchdowns. But unlike the year before, when his passes were consistently on the money, he threw 18 interceptions. The Heisman Trophy speculation stopped by mid-season. He did make at least one All America team (the Sporting News) along with Bear tackle Ted Albrecht (Associated Press) and he was invited to play in three post-season all-star games—the Shrine East-West at Stanford Stadium, the Hula Bowl in Honolulu and the Japan Bowl in Tokyo, the west team in each providentially coached by Mike White.

Two weeks after the Big Game, Joe's terrible secret was revealed, but only to family, coaches and close friends like Matlock and Warner. Joe wanted to keep his cancer out of the newspapers and off television. He sought out Dr. Patmont in early December and showed him the emerging lumps – numbering at least twenty—on his chest that began appearing around Thanksgiving. The doctor telephoned his parents, who had moved earlier that year from El Cajon to Jerome, Idaho. Joe had only a short time to live, he told them, maybe months at the most. But their son hadn't given up. He was sent to the care of Dr. Michael Friedman, then director of cancer research at the University of California Medical Center in San Francisco. He underwent extensive chemotherapy treatments there, but to little avail. The disease had spread to his lungs and liver. He was given only a 20 percent chance of recovery. "Joe," said Matlock, "was handed a death sentence."

Still, he insisted on showing up for those all-star games. White arranged for Matlock to accompany him to each game—to lend emotional support, offer protection from media interviewers and to act as his roommate instead of another player. Together, coach and good friend would look after him. But Joe missed the East-West Game on January 2, 1977, with what White described to reporters as "muscle spasms" in the back. Actually, the pain was caused by a tumor on his spine. His only appearance on the field as one of the West team captains was for the coin toss. Although, miraculously enough, he looked healthy enough to play, Joe's absence on the field aroused suspicion among the watchful sports writers. Something was definitely amiss.

At the Hula Bowl in Honolulu, the public found out what that was. Some reporters knew beforehand, but they acceded to Joe's wishes to bury the story for the time being. Skip Bayless, then writing for the Los Angeles *Times*, was not among them. Joe finally gave in to the writer's frequent requests for an interview. And it was with a final sense of relief that he acknowledged having cancer. "At least I know what my problem is and how to cope with it," he said, in a manner Bayless found surprisingly matter-of-fact. "Right now, I'm thinking positively. But if everyone starts coming up and feeling sorry for me, I'm afraid it will start making me feel the same way. I mean, I fear I won't be the same Joe Roth anymore. Instead I'll be Joe Roth, (Underdog), the guy everyone feels sorry for. I don't want that."

Joe played briefly and inconsequentially in the Hula Bowl. At the Japan Bowl, though, he seemed reinvigorated. The Japanese saw him not as a cancer victim but as an All American boy, tall, good-looking and highly skilled in a game with which they were not all that familiar. Joe responded to their interest by appearing often in public, agreeably signing autographs and posing in a camera-crazed country for photographs. A heartbroken White described him as the perfect good will ambassador. While other players avoided these fan attentions, Joe, the condemned man, seemed to revel in them. "And," said the coach, "he had a heckuva game."

In fact, he completed five of his six passes for more than a hundred yards and was named the Japan Bowl's Most Valuable Player. He finished a star.

That game was played on January 18, 1977. On February 19, attended by family, friends, teammates and coaches, Joe Roth, age twenty-one, died in his Berkeley apartment. The #12 he wore is the only football jersey number ever retired by the University of California.

CHAPTER TWENTY-EIGHT

# PHILOSOPHICAL DIFFERENCES

The 1977 season was played under overcast conditions unrelated to meteorological phenomena. Roth's unexpected death had left his former teammates under a cloud of emotional confusion, grieving and yet all the more determined to memorialize him with a winning performance. They wore black number 12s on their uniform sleeves.

Away from the field, there was a major storm brewing in the athletic offices, the consequence of what apologists described as "philosophical differences" between White and Athletic Director Maggard. Philosophically speaking, these might be the same sort of "differences" one might expect to find in the unlikely event of, say, Freiderich Nietzchke and Louisa May Alcott sharing the same office. Or as Chuck Muncie bluntly put it, "Those two hated each other from Day One." "Hate" is a strong word, but it's safe to say coach and A.D. did not see eye-to-eye on matters of policy.

White, the pragmatist, wanted to win at any cost; Maggard, the idealist, wanted to win without plunging the university back into the limbo of NCAA sanctions. In fact, since taking office in February of 1972—and, in his first act, persuading White to return to Cal—Maggard had run an effective department. Cal teams had won national championships in water polo, gymnastics and crew and had achieved top ten rankings in swimming and tennis. He had been instrumental in organizing the Bear Backers, the department's principal fund-raising arm. At the same time, he had restored much of the school's standing with the NCAA and Pac-8 Conference. Maggard's mentor had been the saintly Brutus Hamilton and, like Brutus, he was dedicated to running a clean ship.

White was all for that. With some reservations. But he was also eager to make amends for the sadness and disappointments of '76. He was emotionally spent caring for and protecting Roth. Now he wanted to get back to coaching winning football. His '77 team surprisingly won its first four games, getting off to the best start by a Cal team in a quarter-of-a-century. The 27–17 win over Tennessee in Knoxville, played before a then record local crowd of 84,421, was the first opening day triumph of White's six seasons at Cal. And it spoiled the coaching debut of former Tennessee tailback legend Johnny Majors. White's starting quarterback was Charlie Young, a lightweight at 180 pounds. As the season progressed, though, Young would share time with the even smaller Gary Graumann, a walk-on who would be the first recipient of the new Joe Roth Scholarship for unheralded players. Like so many of White's enlistees, both Young and Graumann were junior college transfers.

The Bears returned home for a 24–14 win over Air Force. Young was 17 of 29 passing for 182 yards and two touchdowns. Missouri was next, back there, and with sophomore fullback Paul Jones rushing for 200 yards and Graumann completing all five of his passes, one for a TD, the Bears won, 28–21. San Jose State was demolished, 52–3, Young hitting on 12 of 15 passes for 199 yards and three scores. And in Pullman, the Bears squeezed out a 17–10 win over Washington State, holding star Cougar quarterback Jack Thompson to just 84 yards passing, while Graumann had 220, including the 22-yard game-winner with 1:07 left to Floyd Eddings. On the very first play from scrimmage in a 41–17 rout of Oregon State, Young found Eddings, Wesley Walker's long-ball heir apparent, on an 83-yard scoring play. For the day, Young completed 17 of 25 for 375 yards. The Bears finished with 596 yards gained, 436 passing. It didn't seem all that long ago when 436 passing yards represented the Cal total for an entire season.

But all good things must end, and they usually did back then against UCLA, a team White had yet to beat. The Bruins' winning points came this time on a blocked punt returned for a touchdown in the fourth quarter. Cal managed only a Young yard-long sneak and four Breech field goals in the 21–19 loss. White said afterward, "I have a life-size picture of us not making the critical plays."

The Bears rebounded with a 17–14 win over USC before the largest non-Big-Game crowd—76,780—at Memorial Stadium since 1953. It was the first of the now traditional Joe Roth Memorial games, and proceeds from a dollar surcharge on game tickets went to the Scholarship Fund named in honor of the late quarterback. It was only White's second win over the Trojans, and because of the Roth tribute a memorable one. It was also a rough-housing affair reminiscent of long-ago bouts with the S.C. bad boys. Only this time, the team complaining about dirty play was USC's. Cal defensive end Ralph DeLoach, who starred in the game, rejoiced that the Bears refused to be intimidated by the Trojans, and then in a comment that did his coach no favors in the halls of academe, told reporters, "That's the way we're coached—to apply physical and mental pressure." Did he mean, excessive pressure?

The team was flat and overmatched the next week in a 50–31 loss to Rose-Bowl-bound Washington. With Jones on the sidelines with a sprained knee, the Bears gained only 66 yards rushing. The time-sharing QBs had respectable showings, Graumann passing for 172 yards and a touchdown, Young for 149 and two.

After their opening burst, the Bears devolved into an up-and-down sort of team. They were up in Eugene, where, with Graumann starting his first game, they walloped Oregon, 48–16. But they were way down the next week—and against the worst possible foe. Indeed, Cal's only points in a 21–3 loss to Stanford came on Breech's Cal record 50th career field goal. The remainder of the long afternoon was occupied watching Benjamin, the nation's leading passer that season, throw to future NFL star Lofton while Cardinal freshman Darrin Nelson scooted for 116 yards rushing and 50 receiving. Nelson would become after this game Stanford's first 1,000-yard rusher and only the sixth freshman then in college football history to achieve that distinction, the last before him being Pitt's Tony Dorsett.

The dazzling, multi-faceted Stanford offense that season was the creation of a football veteran, already in his mid-forties, who, as Christiansen's replacement, was enjoying his first season, college or pro, as a head coach. He and White had been assistants together in years past at both Cal and Stanford. It just took Bill Walsh a little longer to get to the top.

As for White, he had put together his third winning season (7-4) of the last four, despite the roller coaster ride at the end. And with a record of 34-31-1 for his six years, he'd become the first Cal coach since Waldorf to win more games than he lost in his Cal career. Nevertheless, not quite two weeks after the Big Game, Maggard fired him.

"Cal Shocker," headlined the *Chronicle* of December 1. "Suddenly and surprisingly," wrote Bruce Jenkins in the lead sports story, "Mike White was fired as California's head coach yesterday." Jenkins quoted Graumann as saying, "I'm still sitting here in disbelief over this." Said defensive lineman Duke Leffler, "He's a damn good man, and I feel for him. I don't think he deserves this…it's such a shock."

And since Maggard offered no explanation for his decision beyond describing it as "best for the future of Cal football," there was plenty of room for newspaper speculation. *Chronicle* sports editor Art Rosenbaum thought that accusations of dirty play in the USC game might have been White's undoing. Particularly damaging, he wrote, was DeLoach's remark to writers hinting that White coached them to play

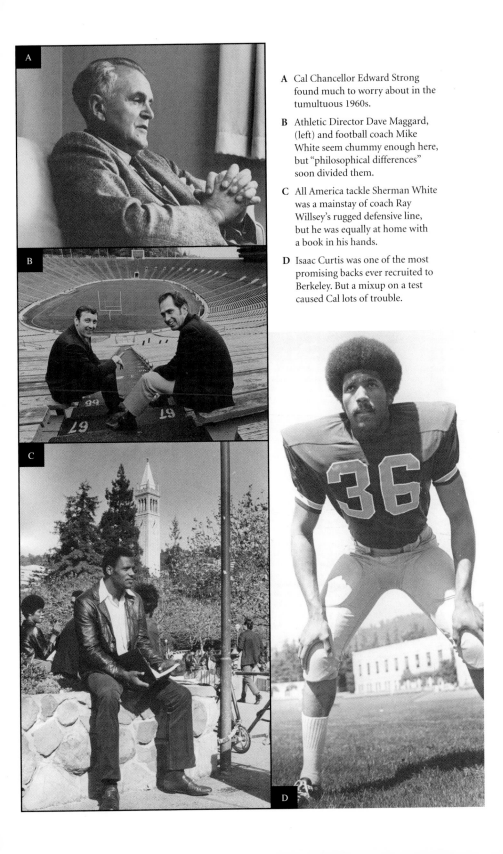

A Cal Chancellor Edward Strong found much to worry about in the tumultuous 1960s.

B Athletic Director Dave Maggard, (left) and football coach Mike White seem chummy enough here, but "philosophical differences" soon divided them.

C All America tackle Sherman White was a mainstay of coach Ray Willsey's rugged defensive line, but he was equally at home with a book in his hands.

D Isaac Curtis was one of the most promising backs ever recruited to Berkeley. But a mixup on a test caused Cal lots of trouble.

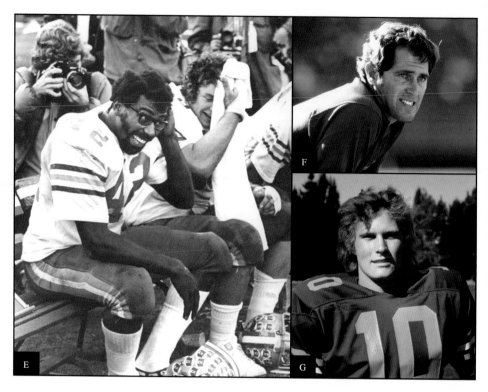

E  Bespectacled Chuck Muncie saw enough openings to set ground-gaining records for the Bears in the mid-1970s. And he had a wonderful time doing it.

F  Controversial coach Mike White combined intensity with raw enthusiasm.

G  Rifle-armed Steve Bartkowski became the nation's leading passer in 1974.

H  Steve Sweeney's diving catch in a treacherously muddy end zone gave the Bears a last-second win in the thrilling 1972 Big Game.

I

J

I  Kevin Moen completed the famous Play of 1982 by bounding through the Stanford band into the end zone.

J  Coach Joe Kapp studies the action.

K  Joe Roth had a smile for everyone except opposing pass rushers.

L  Ted Albrecht was a dominating defensive tackle for coach Mike White in the mid-1970s.

K

L

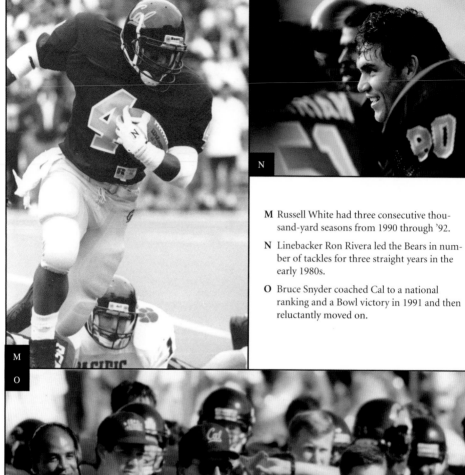

M Russell White had three consecutive thousand-yard seasons from 1990 through '92.

N Linebacker Ron Rivera led the Bears in number of tackles for three straight years in the early 1980s.

O Bruce Snyder coached Cal to a national ranking and a Bowl victory in 1991 and then reluctantly moved on.

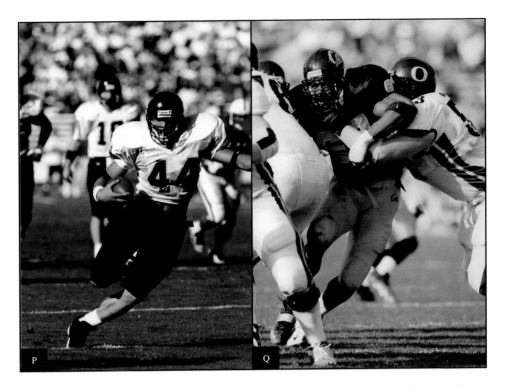

P  Tony Gonzalez started a career at Cal that would eventually make him one of the greatest tight ends in the history of the game.

Q  All America defensive end Andre Carter was a force to be reckoned with at the turn of the last century.

R  Deltha O'Neal led the 1999 Bears in scoring while playing defense.

S  Todd Steussie ushered in the era of massive interior linemen in the 1990s.

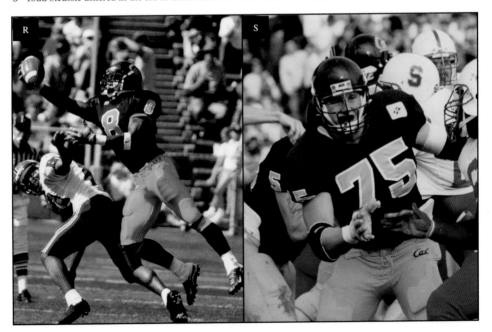

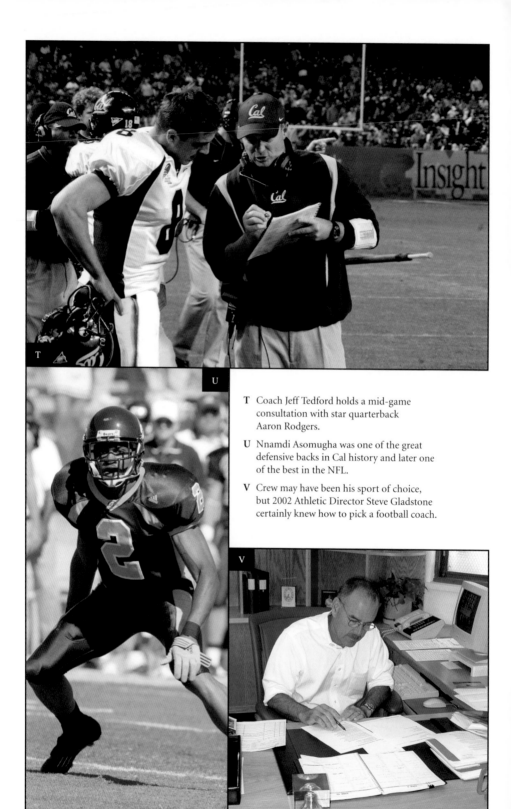

**T** Coach Jeff Tedford holds a mid-game consultation with star quarterback Aaron Rodgers.

**U** Nnamdi Asomugha was one of the great defensive backs in Cal history and later one of the best in the NFL.

**V** Crew may have been his sport of choice, but 2002 Athletic Director Steve Gladstone certainly knew how to pick a football coach.

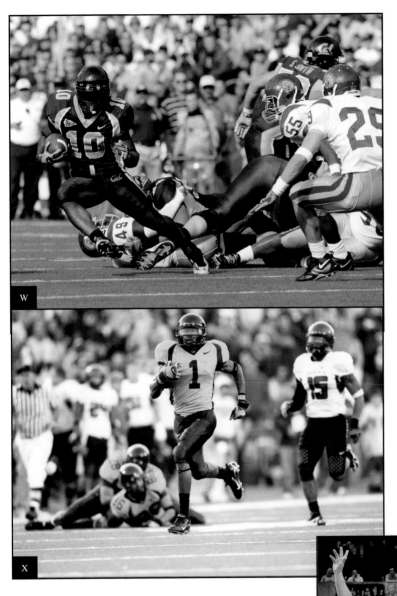

W Among Marshawn Lynch's many attributes as a
running back was his uncanny ability to break free
when seemingly stopped cold.

X DeShawn Jackson, an All America selection in both
2006 and '07, was a threat as a receiver, kick returner
and runner on reverses.

Y All America center Alex Mack gave new credence
to the term scholar-athlete.

**Z** Lightning swift Jahvid Best overcame a succession of injuries to lead the Pac-10 in rushing in 2008, averaging an astonishing 8.1 yards per carry.

**AA** Athletic Director Sandy Barbour plans to take Cal football into a new era of excellence.

**BB** Jeff Tedford revived a once dormant Cal football program and transformed it into one of the nation's best.

that way. Columnist Glenn Dickey, meanwhile, argued in favor of the "philosophical differences" postulate. "The way he (White) built his teams often brought him into direct conflict with Maggard's ideal... It seems likely that he (Maggard) looked and hoped for a change in White's philosophy. That change didn't come."

White finally called his own press conference nearly a week after his dismissal, saying he was "shocked beyond belief" and believed he'd been the victim of "an injustice." He still felt pretty much that way thirty-one years afterward.

"Dave basically just let me go," he said many coaching jobs later. "I didn't want to leave Cal then. Maybe we were moving faster than Dave wanted. I just know the thing was not handled professionally. There might even have been some jealousy involved."

"We had some NCAA issues and some within the university," Maggard said, also three decades after the fact. This was in reference to White's recruiting, although he didn't specify any flagrant violations. "It (firing the coach) was a very hard thing for me to do. We lived in the same town (Lafayette) and our kids played on the same basketball team. I hold no ill will toward Mike. He's an ingratiating guy, a likable guy. But he's also very ambitious, and he'll do anything he can to get an edge. Mike never felt he could play it straight and win. And we were just coming off probation. I said back then I was not going to make my reasons for doing what I did public. I didn't want to besmirch anyone's reputation. But I can tell you that by then, everybody at Cal was pretty sick of Mike, from the chancellor on down."

"Mike was always critical of Dave, but Dave never said a word publicly," recalled McCasey, then the sports information director. "Dave always held his temper inside, but one day he came in and plopped an 18-inch high stack of papers on my desk. They were warnings and reprimands he'd issued to the football coaches and correspondence from others about their actions. I could tell Dave was really angry. Mike was a lovable rogue kind of guy, and I suspect he was breaking a lot of rules.

He got involved in some fund-raising. Dave said not to do that, but I don't think he stopped. There wasn't just one thing, though. It was more of an accumulation of things."

Roger Theder, thirty-nine, was picked as White's replacement. A longtime associate of White's at both Stanford and Cal and his top assistant in '77, his name was not listed among the early potential candidates for the job, a roster that included among others Ralston and Jim Sochor, the highly successful coach at U.C. Davis. But Theder had an excellent reputation. He was popular with the players and considered among coaching colleagues an offensive savant who had helped shape the careers of quarterback aces Plunkett, Bartkowski and Roth. Bartkowski, then an established NFL star, was especially enthusiastic about Maggard's choice, calling Theder "one of the most brilliant offensive minds I have ever worked with. His coaching techniques are the best I have ever come in contact with, including the three years I've spent in the pros. It didn't take me long to realize that it was his coaching that helped me in my rookie season." Bartkowski was 1975's NFL Rookie of the Year.

Like so many others, Theder was "shocked" by White's abrupt dismissal. "I was busy recruiting in Fresno at the time," he recalled. "Then I received a phone call from Mike telling me I'd better come home, because he'd been fired. Mike and I had been together a long time and were very close. I had no idea I was under consideration to replace him. And when I was offered the job, Mike was very supportive. Naturally, I was excited about being a head coach."

After fourteen years as an assistant, Theder was convinced his time had come at long last. And he must have warmed Maggard's frosty heart when he announced on taking the job that he planned "changes in philosophy," specifically by recruiting more high school kids than older junior college players. He also said he thought the 7-4 record of '77 could easily have been 9-2 "with a little more effort," adding that "when people are genuinely disappointed in 7-4 marks, your football program is on the right foot."

Theder's immediate task was to reconstruct an offensive line that save for Leffler was sorely lacking in experience. He would have Paul Jones back at fullback, who had been an 805-yard rusher in '77 despite missing the last two games with a sprained knee. He had potentially star distance receivers in Eddings and newcomers Matt Bouza and Holden Smith, both of whom had redshirted in '77. Ever the quarterback seer, Theder looked past the relatively experienced Graumann to a sophomore named Rich Campbell, the launcher of three passes in '77, one of which was caught for a gain of two yards.

What the new coach could not foresee in that first season was an epidemic of injuries that would deprive him of at least 11 starters and a better record than White's last one.

The 1978 season would induct the two Arizona schools into the conference, transforming it into the Pac-10. Theder's Bears would play them both on the road, defeating Arizona in Tucson, 33–20, and losing to Arizona State in Tempe, 35–21.

The recurring casualties in his ranks made Theder's debut season a curious sort of enterprise. After an opening loss to top-ten Nebraska by the respectable score of 36–26, the Bears won their next five games. And save for a fourth quarter 22-point rally by the Cornhuskers, they might have started with a Pappyish six-in-a-row. The winning streak opened with a 34–22 win over Georgia Tech in Atlanta and continued past the University of the Pacific (24–6), West Virginia (23–21), Oregon (21–18) and Arizona. No runaways there, but solid play throughout. Along the way, though, stretcher-bearers were as busy as noseguards.

Star linebacker Greg Bracelin didn't make it past the Nebraska opener. Eddings first sprained an ankle against West Virginia, missed the Oregon game, then when tackled after his 50-yard return of the opening kickoff against Arizona was lost for the rest of the season with a knee injury. Guard David Heck was out for the year after the Georgia Tech win. Running back Allen Blackmon and linebacker John Harris didn't play after the UOP game. Bouza, who had averaged 18.3 yards for his eight receptions, was out after West Virginia except for a cameo appearance in the Big Game. And Graumann was finished off by a knee injury in a decisive streak-busting 45–0 loss to UCLA.

With their wounded filling hospital beds, the Bears lost four of their last five games. USC embarrassed them, 42–17, in Los Angeles and Arizona State gained 421 yards rushing in its two-touchdown win before 70,876 rabid home fans welcoming their team into the "big time." The suddenly vulnerable Cal defense was further impaired in that game when injuries claimed safety Ron Coccimiglio, who'd had 17 tackles against Nebraska; linebacker David Shaw, who'd had 16 tackles against Oregon, and All-Conference defensive end DeLoach.

The three-game losing streak was interrupted by a 22–14 win over Washington State, a game in which the mercifully intact Jones gained 232 yards on a Cal record 46 carries. It was the fullback's second career 200-yard game, another school record for the time.

But that was the season's last blast. In the Big Game, Walsh's second straight bowl-bound team undid the Bears, 30–10, before 77,880 in Memorial Stadium. The Cardinal offense insulted Theder's tattered defenders by accumulating 538 total yards. For the second year in a row, a Stanford quarterback led the nation in passing. In '77, it was Benjamin, freed of Cordova's competition, who turned the trick. In '78, it was Steve Dils, and he completed 19 of 33 against the Bears for 297 painful yards. And then there was scatback Darrin Nelson. He picked up 177 yards rushing in the game on only 17 carries and another 36 yards on four receptions. Cal defensive tackle Rich Miller best described Nelson's maddening elusiveness: "It's embarrassing to try to tackle him…When I get there, I hit everything where he used to be. I was like a runaway train going through an empty tunnel."

Despite the plague of injuries, Theder finished with a 6-5 record, the first winning season by a new Cal coach since Pappy bolted out of the blue more than thirty years before. And his few healthy players put together some impressive statistics. Campbell, Theder's newest quarterback prospect, completed 164 of 239 passes for 2,287 yards, 14 touchdowns and 19 interceptions. Newcomer Holden Smith caught 26 for 641 yards and a Walker-like 24.7 yards per catch. His five touchdowns included a 72-yarder against Nebraska and an 80-yard beauty against Arizona. In the Oregon game he had eight receptions for 174 yards and two touchdowns. Jones had a second consecutive 800-yard rushing season, gaining 801 on 212 carries. He scored seven touchdowns running and another receiving, finishing second to Smith in receiving, with 25 catches. There were no Olszewskis or Bartkowskis on this roster, but how can a team led by a Smith and a Jones go wrong?

Barring further talk of tendons, cartilage and ligaments, 1979 looked to be a good year for Cal football. Say what you will about White's philosophy, he restored excitement and interest in the game at a time when the Berkeley campus was still more renowned for rioting than rooting. By the time Theder took charge, campus publications were, in fact, deploring the "mellowing out" of the student body. The school yearbook even suggested some "political causes" that a diminishing number of activists might embrace in the next decade—the Cambodian boat people, for example; the "preservation of People's Park" (always a good one) and, of course, the burgeoning Iranian hostage crisis. And finally there was serious talk about campus nemesis Ronald Reagan running for president. Now, if that couldn't rouse dormant radicals into riot mode, what could?

Or was it too late to bring back the good old days?

## CHAPTER TWENTY-NINE

# THE MOUSE TRAP

Theder's preference for high school recruits turned his second season at Cal into a sort of youth pageant. There were forty-two freshmen on the 1979 varsity roster, a callow cohort that included such developing stars as tackle Harvey Salem and running back John Tuggle, as well as a walk-on named, at his own insistence, J Torchio. J was the son of Lloyd Torchio, a Cal Linebacker and Big Game hero of the Waldorf era, and his given names were actually Lloyd John. But J it would be, and, if not initially, he would finally have his moments in the Berkeley sun. Almost lost in the crowd of youngsters was defensive back Kevin Moen, who would in due time become the pivotal figure in what remains the most famously bizarre finish to a game in all of football history.

The Bears also had some seasoned talent on the roster. Campbell was back at quarterback and Jones at fullback, and an injury-free Bouza was ready for a breakout season at wide receiver. Holden Smith would miss the season with a bone spur, but Michael Buggs would prove a fine replacement as the deep threat. Still, by any measure, certainly Theder's, this was a rebuilding year. It was also one in which the Bears, through a quirk in scheduling, would play all nine conference opponents.

Defying expectations, they won their first three games, if by unimpressive margins. Heavily favored Arizona State fell, 17–9, in the opener. Campbell, who was 22 of 30 for 271 yards, and Buggs, who caught six passes for 131 yards, led the way. The Bears made a clean sweep of the desert schools by beating Arizona, 10–7, thanks to a 31-yard field goal by Joe Cooper with two seconds on the clock. Despite such deeds, Cooper would lose his kicking job that season to the English-born rugby star Mick Luckhurst. In their first home game, the Bears nipped San Jose State, 13–10, though behind, 7–6, with two minutes left to play. Then, from their own 48 they advanced on six straight Campbell completions, the last to Bouza for ten yards and the game-winner. Campbell finished the day with 27 completions in 42 attempts for 316 yards and Jones rushed for 132 on 26 carries. The fullback would finish his career that year with a Cal record 715 carries.

Although the Bears led 10–0 at the half, Michigan rallied for two third-quarter touchdowns to give them their first loss, 14–10. Oregon gave them their second a week later in Eugene. Again, the Bears blew a halftime lead as the Ducks scored 16 in the second half for a 19–14 final. Cal rebounded handsomely with a 45–0 trouncing of Oregon State. Then came another loss to UCLA, a frustratingly close one by 28–27. Once more, the Bears led at the half, this time by a seemingly secure 27–7. Theder even interjected some trickery into the attack when, on the team's first score, Allen Blackmon took a handoff from Campbell and appeared to be sweeping left end from the OSU eight. But he stopped and passed the ball back to his quarterback, who ran in for the TD. The Bears were still leading, 27–21, well into the fourth quarter when Bruin star Freeman McNeil scored the third of his three touchdowns with 5:09 remaining. In defeat, Luckhurst kicked two field goals and Jones ran for two touchdowns, one for a season-long 43 yards in the first quarter.

"This was a game," mused Theder afterward, "in which nothing went right."

His team lost again the following week, 24–14, to that other southern California school, Southern California, in the third annual Joe Roth Memorial Game before 76,780 at Memorial Stadium. On one successful Trojan drive, Heisman Trophy winner Charles White gained all of the 68 yards either running or receiving. Cal's first touchdown came when Bracelin blocked a punt and safety Darnell Chapman retrieved the ball in mid-air and ran 74 yards with it.

Washington made it three losses in a row, winning 28–24 in Berkeley under what were, for the Huskies, favorable weather conditions—a driving rainstorm. Campbell had touchdown passes of 58 yards to Buggs and ten to Bouza. He completed 21 of 35 for 322 yards, 11 of which were caught by Bouza for 175 yards. The deciding touchdown for Washington came on a 64-yard punt return late in the last quarter by Mark Lee.

A 45–13 throttling of Washington State eased some of the pain this reversal of fortune had inflicted, so the Bears entered the Big Game with another 5-5 record that might have been considered disappointing had it not been for the team's extreme youth. Bill Walsh had blessedly moved out of the Farm to begin his Hall of Fame career with the 49ers, leaving Cardinal coaching responsibilities to one of his former assistants, thirty-six-year-old Rod Dowhower. The new coach was, like his Cal counterpart, considered an offensive expert, but his had not been a happy season. Despite a winning 5-4-1 record before the Big one, he'd been assailed regularly by Walsh-spoiled alums.

"You're dealing with two frustrated teams," he said, including the Bears in this assessment. "Both had the chance to distinguish themselves…but both came up short." Theder generously refrained from telling him to speak for himself.

Dowhower had been criticized for losing to mediocre teams like Army and Tulane and for not offering more playing time to freshman quarterback John Elway, who had the all-round goods—mighty arm, shifty feet—to erase the records of such revered predecessors as

Brodie, Garrett, Norman and Plunkett. Instead Dowhower stayed with the more experienced Turk Schonert as his starter, thereby delaying Elway's race toward immortality. And to make matters worse, the Cardinal coach lost the Big Game.

The Bears scored first, driving 91 yards in just five plays on their first possession, the big ground-gainers coming on a 53-yard Campbell strike to freshman Greg Woodard and a 23-yarder to tight end Joe Rose for the touchdown. This was the first of two Rose TD catches in Cal's 21–14 win, although the second, coming midway through the fourth quarter, was at first called incomplete. Rose had caught the 17-yard pass from Campbell at least two yards inside the end line, but back judge John Barger incomprehensibly ruled he was out of the end zone. There followed such a commotion on the field and in the stands that Barger felt impelled to discuss the issue with his fellow officials. As it turned out, when Barger made the call he was astride a chalk line other than the one defining the parameters of the end zone. He was like a meter maid ticketing a legally parked car. So touchdown after all. And Bear victory.

Rose commended the embarrassed man for correcting his mistake. "He had the guts to change his call," the receiver said. "I've seen many bad calls that were let stand. You have to admire what he did."

Stanford played the game without the dangerous Nelson, who missed the entire season with a torn hamstring. But Vincent White, a stubby little back approximating Nelson's modest dimensions, played well in his place, catching one of two Schonert touchdown passes. And his team came within a yard of either tying or winning the game. Starting from its own 20, the Cardinal ground out 18 plays to reach the Cal one before finally stalling. With forty seconds left and on fourth down, Schonert, survivor in the drive of two sacks and two third-and-long crises, tried a pass. Although clobbered as he released the ball, he appeared to have running back Mike Dotterer open in the end zone. The pass was true, but with a mighty leap Coccimiglio batted the ball away at the last possible instant, preserving Cal's first Big Game win in three years and precipitating Dowhower's departure for an assistant's job with the Denver Broncos of the NFL.

Theder had pieced together a second straight 6-5 regular season record, the first coach to begin his Cal career with back-to-back winners since...who else?...Pappy.

This achievement led to, of all things, a post-season bowl invitation, the Bears first in twenty years. Theder, for the moment, was the man of the hour. And so on December 15, his team played Temple in the Garden State Bowl at the 79,466-seat Giants' Stadium in East Rutherford, New Jersey. Cal hadn't actually won a bowl game in forty years, and this one would be no exception. Temple, with a 9-2 regular season record, scored 21 points in the first quarter and coasted to a 28–17 win. Campbell threw TD passes to Bouza and Rose in the second quarter and Luckhurst booted a 34-yard field goal in the fourth to account for Cal's scoring. But the Bears gained only 23 yards rushing to Temple's 300.

So the 6-5 record became 6-6. Not at all bad, considering the team's lack of seasoning. Campbell, in fact, had a tremendous season, completing—bowl totals included—241 of 360 passes for 2859 yards and 15 touchdowns. His .699 completion percentage shattered Paul Larson's previous Cal high of .641. Until then, only Larson and Morton had completed better than 60 percent of their passes. Bouza led the receivers in '79 with 59 catches for 831 yards, while both Rose and Jones caught 49. Buggs caught 37 for 575 yards and topped the regulars with an average of 15.5 yards per reception. But freshman Woodard averaged an astronomical 29.8 for his 12 catches. Luckhurst scored a team-high 60 points and hit on 10 of 17 field goal tries.

On now to a new decade. In the beginning at least, the '80s looked like the new '60s. The election of Ronald Reagan revived some of those otherwise suppressed revolutionary impulses within the Cal student body. Their old antagonist was burned in effigy at People's Park, to which years earlier he had dispatched National Guardsmen to quash the insurgency. Some three thousand students marched through the streets of Berkeley on election night, demanding the impeachment of the president-elect and hoisting placards gloomily declaring, "The End is Near." The demonstrators gathered for old times' sake, at Sproul Plaza for an invigorating round of inflammatory rants.

It was a nostalgic occasion, but in a decade notable for conservative politics and a "greed-is-good" philosophy, the mood could not be sustained.

On June 30, 1980, Chancellor Bowker retired and was succeeded by longtime law professor and Vice Chancellor Ira Michael "Mike" Heyman. Although the new chancellor was fully as innocent of football's charms as Bowker had been, he nevertheless included among his administration's fondest aspirations, "to see Cal go to the Rose Bowl."

The passage of the state initiative, Proposition 13, which froze property taxes at 1975 levels, imposed further reductions in the university's sources of revenue, a process that had begun with Reagan. University president David Saxon told the Regents, "The impact on the university's fiscal and academic vitality could be devastating" and that "an era of reallocation and consolidation" would begin. He encouraged the individual campuses to compensate for the loss of public money with vigorous fund-raising efforts within the private sector.

The Cal Athletic Department under Maggard took that counsel to heart, launching in 1980 a $5 million drive to renovate and upgrade the campus's sports facilities, most of which, he said, had "dropped behind other universities with which we compete." In a complaint which would become achingly familiar over ensuing decades, Maggard said that "when student-athletes come to Berkeley for the first time, particularly those without a family tradition to fire their enthusiasm, few are impressed with what they see of our athletic accommodations in comparison with other Pac-10 schools."

Former chancellor Roger Heyns and businessman and loyal alum

Walter A. Haas, Jr., co-chaired the fund-raising drive, which would, among other projects, finance the expansion of locker and weight room facilities at Memorial Stadium, add a Hall of Fame room there and, at the risk of inducing Andy Smith's ashes to scatter themselves elsewhere in despair, replace the grass field with artificial turf in time for the 1981 season.

The 1980 Bears looked for much of the season as if they were playing on fields of broken glass. They lost their first four games, won a couple, then lost four more, some by preposterous scores. In the opener, a 41–13 shellacking by Florida, Campbell set or tied pages of records by completing 43 passes in 53 attempts for 421 yards. But only one of those myriad heaves, a 24-yarder to tight end David Lewis, went for a touchdown. Two Luckhurst field goals accounted for Cal's only other points.

The Bears were nevertheless two-touchdown favorites over an Army team that would finish with just three wins. This game would be one of them. Three lost fumbles, two drives that stalled on the one and an insecure defense contributed to Cal's 26–19 loss. Campbell was 19 of 31 for 246 yards, including a 57-yard TD to Holden Smith, who had returned to the battle after a year on the sidelines.

In losing to Arizona, 31–24, the Bears blew 21–3 halftime and 24–10 fourth quarter leads. It was not a good day for the otherwise capable punter, Mike Ahr. Early in the second quarter, he fumbled the snap from center, and Arizona recovered the ball on the Bear 17. The Wildcats scored from there. In the last quarter, Ahr's punt was blocked by Arizona's Bill Redman and returned for a 15-yard touchdown by Gary Gibson. It was one of three Wildcat scores in the fourth quarter. Campbell was again heroic in defeat, completing 30 of 43 for 350 yards and a touchdown to Tuggle. Then, before 104,621 in Michigan's "Big House," the Bears were trounced, 38–13, the Wolverines grinding out 388 yards rushing.

It was not a promising start, even for another rebuilding season.

"I'm numb right now," said Bouza, who was lively enough to gain 94 receiving yards against Michigan. "When you lose week after week, you get numb. You don't have any answers, just questions."

The Oregon schools provided an answer to the question Cal alumni were now raising on the prospect of a winless season. Oregon gave the Bears their first victory, 31–6, and Oregon State their second, 27–6, before smallish thirty thousand crowds at the Memorial Stadium construction site. Campbell passed for 293 yards against the Ducks and 230 against the Beavers.

Then it was back to losing. UCLA won its ninth straight from the Bears, by 31–9 before fifty-three thousand in Berkeley. The next week in Los Angeles, USC, led by the nifty running of Marcus Allen, handed Cal its worst defeat, 60–7, since the Trojans of 1930 terminated Nibs Price's career as a head coach with that infamous 74-zip whopping. This time, the Bears not only lost the game, they lost their star quarterback. Late in the opening quarter, Campbell went down with a torn ligament in his left knee. The injury ended his season and, as a senior, his Cal career. In '80, Campbell had an amazing .707 completion percentage, accomplished while throwing into overloaded secondaries contemptuous of the Bears' inconsequential running game. All told, Campbell had set nine Cal passing records in his career. He, too, would move on to the NFL.

In the USC debacle, Torchio replaced him and instantly led the 58-yard drive that would provide Cal's only score, on his 8-yard completion to Bouza. Torchio sprained a knee late in the game, bringing on as his substitute a promising freshman euphoniously named Gale Gilbert.

Gilbert started the next week while Torchio recovered. He completed 11 of 24 for 161 yards in the 34–6 loss to Arizona State. Torchio was back in time to play in a 31–17 loss to Washington State. For a team situated so far up north, the Cougars seemed to have a special attraction in those years for South Sea island quarterbacks. First there was Jack Thompson, the "Throwin' Samoan." In 1980, they had a signal-caller who required no nickname to signify his ethnicity. He was Samoa Samoa, and he hit the Bears like a typhoon, scoring two touchdowns, throwing for another of 69 yards to Bill Keller and adding, for good measure, a two-point conversion. Torchio was 18 of 30 for 241 yards, but the Bear hero in defeat was Tuggle, who gained 80 yards rushing, 47 receiving and scored twice.

Stanford seemingly had all the advantages before the Big Game—John Elway at quarterback, a host of able runners and receivers and, with a 6-4 record, an invitation to the Peach Bowl all but pocketed if they could win one more game. The Cardinal was favored by 15 points over the 2-8 Bears. Stanford also had a new head coach in Paul Wiggin, an All America tackle in his playing days on the Farm in the 1950s, an All Pro player in the NFL and a former head coach of the Kansas City Chiefs.

Darrin Nelson, who had gained 888 yards rushing and caught 49 passes before the game, was listed as questionable against the Bears since he had sprained an ankle the week before in a 34–9 loss to the Trojans. He carried just once in the Big Game, gaining a yard, and then limped to the sidelines. In his absence, Vincent White once more afflicted the Bears with his all-round game, scoring all three Cardinal touchdowns while gaining 83 yards rushing and 109 on nine pass receptions. But his team lost, a stupefying blow to Wiggin and Stanford supporters that was to be surpassed only by the unlikely events of a couple of years hence.

The Bears rambled 80 yards on their first series of plays, the big one a 56-yard pass from Torchio to tight end Don Sprague out of a third-and-13 situation. Tuggle scored from the 15 on the play afterward. Stanford came right back, though, traveling 97 yards in 13 plays, White diving in for the score. The Bears resumed the lead early in the second quarter on a 24-yard touchdown pass from Torchio to Tyrone Portee. And on Stanford's following series, Elway was sacked by Richard Rodgers (another name to contend with in the near future) and stripped of the ball on his way turfward by noseguard Kirk Karacozoff.

Reggie Camp recovered for Cal on the Cardinal four. Two plays later, Tuggle, who gained 127 yards for the day, scored from the two, giving his team a surprising—to put it mildly—21–7 halftime lead.

The third quarter was scoreless. But on the third play of the fourth quarter, Elway connected with White on a 32-yard screen pass to reduce the Bear lead to 21–14. Midway through the quarter the Cardinal moved into a tie with a 74-yard drive that ended with White's plunge from the four. Then, with a little more than four minutes remaining, White fumbled on his own five and Cal guard Dupre Marshall recovered the ball on the three. Torchio bootlegged in for the score on the next play. Cal now led, 28–21.

The Cardinal had lots of life left, though. Starting from the 26 after the kickoff, the Elway-led troops marched resolutely up field until they reached the Cal four, where with two minutes remaining they had a first-and-goal prospect. They could tie with a touchdown and point-after or win it all and secure that bowl bid with a TD and two-point conversion. Of such possibilities are Big Games made. Two plays later, however, they had advanced the ball no farther than the one. On third down, Elway handed off to the diminutive White who tried ramming the middle of Cal's unforgiving line. Linebacker Steve Cacciari met him head-on and sent him spinning backward. But White regained his equilibrium and tried running wide for the goal line. Cornerback Fred Williams was in his way and dropped him for a five-yard loss. It was now fourth and goal from the six. Elway dropped back to pass, but, pressured by a blitzing Moen, he threw the ball harmlessly awry. With only twenty seconds left, Theder, fearing either a blocked punt or a long return, ordered the ball centered out of the end zone for a safety. Final score: 28–23.

The Big Game win, Cal's second straight and first at home since 1972, was credited with saving Theder's job. Recognizing the peril he was still in after a 3-8 season, the coach decided desperate measures were indicated if he intended to remain part of the work force. So he took them.

Like teenagers, filmmakers, book publishers and practitioners of haute couture, football coaches are slaves to fashion. Whenever something new comes along in the game—be it Pop Warner's double wing, Clark Shaughnessy's T, Red Hickey's shotgun, Bud Wilkinson's wishbone or Bill Walsh's "West Coast offense"—it is certain that coaches everywhere will quickly fall under its spell. The trendiest formation of the late 1970s was something called the "Run and Shoot." It was largely the creation of the head coach at then Division II Portland State, Darrel Davis, who went by the nickname "Mouse," which was given him by an older brother amused by his small stature as a child.

With four wide receivers, no tight end and only one set back, the Run and Shoot was, to the virtual exclusion of the running game, a passing offense. Implemented well by a mobile quarterback with an accurate throwing arm, it did gobble up yardage. In his six winning seasons at the helm of Portland State, Mouse's teams gained at least 5,000 yards every year. And in that relatively brief span, he graduated two of his QBs, June Jones and Neil Lomax, to the NFL. Mouse had by the end of the '70s become all the rage in coaching circles. As the 1981 Cal media guide described his sudden popularity, "His office at Portland State became a virtual hotel lobby over the past few years, with coaches from college and pro teams all over the country constantly visiting to learn Davis's offensive philosophy."

Among these supplicants was Roger Theder. But the Cal coach wanted more than advice. In an attempt to "shake things up a little," he wanted Mouse to be his new offensive coordinator. And Davis, a native Oregonian whose entire coaching career—fifteen years of it at high schools—had been in that state, accepted his offer.

Theder was confident that in 6-3½ sophomore Gilbert, who had thrown all of 31 passes the season before, he had a quarterback with the arm and legs to run the wide-open new offense. And in the final intrasquad scrimmage that spring, Gilbert rewarded that confidence by completing 28 of 43 passes for 441 yards. Skeptics were quick to observe that this otherwise sterling performance was executed against a less than impregnable Cal defense, but Theder felt he had his run-and-shooter. Torchio, as usual, was loyally in the wings, suspicious though he was of the new system.

"I just didn't think we had the personnel to make it work," he said many years later. "Taking me out of the equation, Gilbert was basically a dropback passer. We had a true tight end (Lewis) who didn't fit the system. And we didn't have those little scatback receivers the run-and-shoot likes."

But Torchio would be the one running it that year, since in the opening 29–28 loss to Texas A&M, Gilbert suffered a severe knee injury that ended his season. So for all of his doubts, Torchio took over. "I was no speed-burner back there," he admitted, and he soon learned that the formation's "everybody out" approach left him vulnerable to a strong pass rush.

Georgia, behind the spectacular running of Herschel Walker, downed the Bears, 27–13, in the second game. They somehow got past Arizona, 14–13, then dropped four in a row, starting with a 27–24 loss to San Jose State, then coached by John Elway's father, Jack. Also included in the skid was a tenth straight loss to UCLA, a 34–6 breather for the Bruins.

Theder, meanwhile, reached the conclusion that hiring Mouse and using his offense was "not a great decision on my part."

Actually, said Torchio, "It was a huge mistake. We had no audible system and though I made a lot of physical mistakes, Mouse blamed everybody but himself when things went wrong. At one team meeting, I even told Roger that this guy has slipped a rope around your neck. We had a good offense before. And good people coaching it. This was too drastic a change. I think it hurt our program."

Theder, ruminating on the Mouse problem years later, acknowledged that the R&S was "not right for us. Our fine tight end was wasted (Lewis, in fact, redshirted). I don't know, maybe we would have been better if Gale had been able to play. We'll never know."

Theder resumed command of the offense with four games left and the Bears sunk in a 1-6 hole in their new carpet. Though he was offered other duties, Mouse Davis packed up his playbook and headed back to Oregon.

"The guy just quit," said Torchio, clearly no Mouseketeer. "That's everything you need to know about Mouse Davis."

The Bears did defeat Oregon, 45–3, with Theder calling the shots. But the season ended with losses to USC (21–3), Washington State (9 –0) and finally to Stanford by the un-Big-Game-like score of 42–21. Elway threw for 245 yards and three touchdowns in what would be the only Big Game win of his college career. Torchio played well in defeat, completing 19 of 43 for 312 yards and two touchdowns. But one of his two interceptions was returned by the Cardinal's Charles Hutchings for a 14-yard score.

Torchio threw more passes (363) in this unusual season than anyone at Cal—including Morton, Bartkowski and Campbell—ever had before. But he was harried throughout by defenders taking advantage of the run-and-shoot's inherent deficiencies in pass protection, and he completed just 42.7 percent of those attempts for 2,112 yards, nine touchdowns and 12 interceptions.

Theder's 2-9 record was the worst since Levy's 1-9 in 1962. And even though a few players, led by Salem, expressed their support of the likable coach before the Big Game, Maggard fired him the day after it. Theder had made a daring move that hadn't worked out. Maggard would soon make one himself that would cause hiring Mouse to seem no more adventurous than taking a walk across the avocado-green rug that passed for a playing field back then at Memorial Stadium.

PART V

1982-2008

CHAPTER THIRTY

# THE PLAY

On December 5, 1981, just two weeks after the Theder-skewering
loss in the Big Game, Maggard hired Joe Kapp as his latest football
coach. Joe, of course, had been a campus legend, the dynamic leader of
Cal's last Rose Bowl team more than two decades earlier. He had also
become a legend of sorts in the professional game. Despite his superlative senior season at Cal in 1958 operating Pete Elliott's option attack,
he was not drafted by an NFL team until the eighteenth round, when
the Washington Redskins claimed him. The prevailing explanation
for this oversight had it that pro scouts, unimpressed by Joe's oscillat-
ing passes, dismissed him as just another running option QB. Kapp
attributed the wobble in his deliveries to his habit of "grabbing the old
seed" anywhere convenient without regard to such niceties as finger-
ing the laces. More often than not, though, the ball got to where he'd
aimed it.

Offended by the NFL snub, Kapp went to Canada, where in eight
seasons he passed for 22,725 yards and 136 touchdowns and led the
British Columbia Lions to the Canadian Football League championship in 1964. By now, the NFL scouts were impressed, and in 1967 Joe
signed with the Minnesota Vikings. Two seasons later, he had them

in the Super Bowl. During that 1969 season, he also tied a league record by throwing seven of his imperfect spirals for touchdowns in a game against the then defending NFL champion Baltimore Colts. He'd also achieved by then a reputation as a swashbuckler on and off the field who, occasionally fortified by generous dollops of tequila, was no stranger to barroom altercations.

Kapp's stay in the NFL was, however, brief. At least as a player. After a contractural disagreement with his new team, the Patriots, he elected to challenge in court the legality of the league's Standard Player Contract, football's equivalent to baseball's finally banished "reserve clause" limiting player movement. This battle consumed eight long and wearying years, and though Kapp at first won a summary judgement declaring the contract illegal, he and his lawyers ultimately "got our tails kicked." While all this was going on, Joe pursued an alternative career in movies, both before the camera as an actor and behind it as a producer.

What earned Maggard derision for hiring such a person was not Kapp's adventures as a litigator or free spirit but the salient fact that he'd never coached before at any level, high school, college or pro. The Cal Athletic Director was fairly besieged with complaints from the coaching community that Kapp had not properly "paid his dues." Bill Walsh may have been football's resident genius at the time, having taken the formerly woebegone 49ers to a Super Bowl championship, but, so the argument went, he'd started as a high school coach more than twenty years earlier and had paid his dues as an assistant in college and the NFL before earning his first head coaching job—at Stanford—when he was in his mid-forties.

Maggard acknowledged that signing a relative novice to run his faltering football program was, in the eyes of coaching veterans, "simply heresy. One coach called me," he recalled at the time, "and gave me a lengthy recitation of his personal credentials—graduate assistant, assistant coach, high school coach, college head coach and so on. 'And you,' he finally shouted at me, 'you go out and hire a guy who hasn't coached a down!'"

Kapp defended himself against such accusations by saying that in Canada he not only called the plays but pretty much coached himself. And he brought to his new job an impressive library of playbooks accumulated during his peripatetic career. Besides, if he needed more information, he had friends in the business—though not necessarily in front offices—more than ready to help.

Maggard, who had not only known Kapp at Cal in the late 1950s, but had been recruited by him, was convinced his choice could add much needed enthusiasm and feel for tradition to a program that had drifted off track. "Certainly Joe doesn't fit the image of the big-time coach," he agreed, "but Joe doesn't even fit his own image. People who think of him as a wild man don't know the compassionate, intelligent, sensitive person he is. Sometimes it takes an unusual guy to get something done."

Kapp returned to his alma mater with the full support of old colleagues and teammates. His basketball coach, the highly respected Pete Newell, spoke of "the magnitude of his leadership." Former Sports Information Director Bob Steiner said, "I think what we have here is the best of the university returning to the university." And teammate and good friend Jack Hart said, "His enormous love for Cal is genuine...If I were to have brain surgery, I would hope that the surgeon would have the same sort of dedication to his job that Joe has to his."

At a glance, the new coach's prospects for a winning season did not seem favorable. His quarterback, sophomore Gale Gilbert, had played only one quarter of one game in 1981 before injuring his left knee and red-shirting the rest of the way. Then, during the off-season, he slipped and fell down a flight of stairs in his apartment building and injured his right knee. In two prior abbreviated seasons, he had thrown a total of just 41 passes and completed 19 for 308 yards and one touchdown. There was no denying his potential, however. And in tight end David

Lewis—back in action after the Mouse extermination—and wide receivers Mariet Ford and Wes Howell he had outstanding playmakers as targets for his throws.

Tuggle would return for a final season at running back, backed by the capable Ron Story and a multi-talented (runner-receiver-returner) freshman named Dwight Garner, of whom we shall learn more later. All Coast tackle Salem would anchor an offensive line that, lamented the media guide, "spent most of the 1981 season in a pass offense and without the benefit of a tight end." The strength of the defense lay in linebackers Ron Rivera and Rich Dixon, the latter returning after a serious knee injury, and noseguard Gary Plummer. Richard Rodgers, John Sullivan and Fred Williams were proven defensive backs. Still, Kapp's Bears were picked to finish near the bottom of the conference standings, barely above the two ineffectual Oregon teams.

But they won their first two games, 31–17, over Colorado and, 28–0, over San Diego. Gilbert was 16 for 25 for 234 yards and two touchdowns against San Diego and Lewis caught five passes for 129 yards and the two scores, one for 73 yards in the third quarter. Fourteenth-ranked Arizona State interrupted the mini-streak with a 15–0 shutout in Memorial Stadium limiting Gilbert to 113 aerial yards while intercepting him three times. The Bears then beat San Jose State, 26–7, with Gilbert connecting on 25-yard touchdown passes to Howell in the second quarter and Lewis in the fourth. After four games, they were a confident 3-1.

Then they traveled to Seattle to play the nation's number-one-ranked team, Washington. A 50–7 stomping put the season into cold perspective. After throwing two interceptions in the first half, Gilbert was replaced in the second by the ever-ready Torchio, who accounted for Cal's lone score with a 15-yard pass to Andy Bark with 54 seconds left in the game. Not much, for sure, but better than 50–0.

The Bears beat Oregon, 10–7, on the strength of a 26-yard Gilbert-Lewis touchdown pass with 53 seconds remaining. Then UCLA,

11th ranked at the time, beat the Bears 47–31, mainly on the passing of quarterbacks Tom Ramsey and Rick Neuheisel. Gilbert left the game in the third quarter with an injury, passing the torch again to Torchio. All told, the Bear quarterbacks completed 25 of 46 for 323 yards, but the Bruin pair was good for 397 yards.

Behind Torchio, Oregon State was beaten, 28–14. The industrious sub completed 17 of 32 for 232 yards, while Tuggle gained 102 more on 27 carries and scored twice. But USC trounced the Bears, 42–0, in Los Angeles, a game in which Gilbert was intercepted six times and Torchio two. They recovered in time to beat Washington State, 34–14, back home. Gilbert displayed laudable resilience after the Trojan debacle, completing 24 of 35 for 266 yards, three touchdowns and zero interceptions.

The Bears were already assured of a winning season before the Big Game, but it was Stanford, at 5-5, which attracted interest from the post-season bowl people. Four of the Cardinal losses had been by close scores, two by four points or fewer. But the main attraction for the bowl selectors was Elway, who had established himself in this, his senior season, as, beyond argument, the best college quarterback in the game, maybe even, as some experts were proclaiming, the best ever. That year, he would pass for 3,242 yards and 24 touchdowns on 262 completions in 405 attempts. And he had that élan and dash that characterized all the great ones. He was an adept scrambler and with his powerful arm, he could connect with receivers while throwing off balance and on the run. Coach Wiggin enjoyed standing behind him in practice listening to the whistling sound those bullet passes made on their way to denting receivers' breastbones.

Despite a porous defense, Elway and his teammates were a joy to watch. They had scored upset wins on national television over Ohio State, 23–20, and Washington, 43–31—the same Washington team that whipped the Bears by 43 points. Their coach, with nine years as an NFL assistant and two-and-a-half as head coach of the Chiefs, had definitely paid his dues. But in three years at Stanford, he'd had only one winning season, his first, and had lately heard complaints from alums to the effect that "if this guy can't win with the best quarterback in the history of college football, what happens after that quarterback leaves?"

Indeed, unless his team beat the Bears and moved on, as expected, to the Hall of Fame Classic—later the All America Bowl—in Birmingham, Alabama, Wiggin's stay at his alma mater could well be terminated.

The Cardinal was, however, a solid seven-point favorite over Kapp's unpredictable Bears. This 85th Big Game would be the first played on an artificial surface, a crime against nature that would be somewhat mitigated by deeds performed on that ersatz gridiron that day.

The game started innocently enough with a scoreless first quarter. Joe Cooper put Cal on the scoreboard with a 30-yard field goal early in the second quarter. Then with 2:42 left in the half, Mariet Ford made an astonishing one-handed catch in the end zone of a 29-yard Gilbert pass that gave the Bears a surprising 10–0 halftime advantage. It was a catch so sublime that under ordinary circumstances it surely would have been the play of the game. But not in this game.

Stanford pulled ahead in the third quarter on two Elway TD passes to the always troublesome Vincent White, one for two yards, the other a short swing toss that White transformed into a 43-yard dazzler. A Cooper field goal early in the fourth quarter closed the scoring gap to 14–13. And then with 11:24 left to play, Howell made a diving catch of Gilbert's 32-yard throw in the end zone that rivaled Ford's. Gilbert's pass for the two-point conversion was broken up by Stanford safety Charles Hutchings. The Bears led by a precarious 19–14, and the 75,662 at Memorial Stadium were by now acutely aware they were aboard for another Big Game barnburner. Actually, they didn't know the half of it.

After an exchange of punts, Elway led a drive to the Cal five, where on third down, Sullivan batted away his pass for Emile Harry in the end zone. Mark Harmon's field goal reduced the Cal lead to 19–17 with 5:32 remaining.

After both teams failed to advance, Stanford took over on its own 20, following a Cal punt, with 1:27 left and one timeout unused. The sun was sinking over the stadium's west rim, and the crowd, realizing that this already great game hung now in the balance, rose as one in the deepening shadows to experience whatever excitement it could still generate in these dying seconds.

Elway's first pass, another swing to White, lost seven yards when the elusive back slipped on a carpet dampened by weeklong rains. The quarterback's next two attempts fell incomplete, one slapped out of Harry's groping fingers by Rodgers. Elway now found himself in a 4th-and-17 quandary with the ball on his own 13 and 53 seconds left to play. Seemingly unfazed, he rifled a bullet to Harry amidst a swarm of Cal defenders for 29 yards and an amazing first down.

"He did it!" bellowed broadcaster Joe Starkey over radio station KGO.

Elway then hit flanker Mike Tolliver for 19 more yards to the Cal 39. With 31 seconds left, the Bears were caught off guard by a running play, Mike Dotterer scampering 21 yards to the 18. Dotterer carried again for no gain, but he moved the line of scrimmage near the right hash mark, a favorite spot for kicker Harmon. Elway, standing along-side referee Charles Moffett, allowed the game clock to run down to eight seconds before calling the time out that would bring Harmon into the game. As subsequent events would prove, he should have waited even longer. Harmon kicked the field goal that presumably gave his team a glorious 20–19 victory as the crowd and the Stanford bench went wild. Jubilant Cardinal players rushed onto the field to celebrate. That would also be a mistake. Moffett penalized Stanford 15 yards for the on-field party, the yardage to be assessed on the kickoff.

Since teams then kicked off from the 40, Harmon was now obliged to work from the 25. The celebration had given Cal a shorter path to the goal line, but, after all, there were only four seconds left, not enough time after the return for even one play from scrimmage. Almost everyone in the stadium—excluding Kapp and his return team—was convinced the game was over, decided by a masterly 80-yard drive with only seconds to play.

"What a finish for John Elway, to pull this one out!" an exhausted Starkey hollered in praise of the quarterback. "This is one of the great finishes. Only a miracle can save the Bears."

"There are no miracles, except maybe the one at Guadalupe (where the Virgin Mary was allegedly spotted )," said Kapp more than a quarter-century after the game. What happened next on that Saturday in November of 1982 was merely the product of Sunday noon warmup sessions, he insisted, during which players, linemen included, were encouraged to toss the ball back and forth on the dead run, just for the fun of it. No miracle, just good coaching.

Never mind that after the kickoff return, Cal's Tuggle described what he saw as "an act of God."

Here from the *Sports Illustrated* college football issue of September 1, 1983, is my account of what would be known forever after as "The Play:"

When the two teams lined up for the kick, there was, as Cal Special Teams Coach Charlie West said, "pandemonium everywhere." Stanford was busily clearing the field of players who weren't supposed to be on it. Cal didn't have enough. In expectation of a squib kick West had called for his onsides-return team, composed exclusively of players accustomed to handling the ball. In the chaos, two members of the unit, defensive backs Gregg Beagle and Jimmy Stewart, did not hear West call this return formation and did not take the field. So Cal lined up with only nine men, until West, responding to frantic gestures from his players, sent in Running Back Scott Smith to take Beagle's place in the center of the front line. Still more waves and shouts from the field. West was reluctant to act because, as he and Kapp agreed, in such situations "twelve men is a whole lot worse than ten." A skinny 170-pound defensive back named Steve Dunn was standing next to the perplexed coach.

"Let me go in," pleaded Dunn, who seldom played, even on special teams. West hastily counted his forces—Kapp calls his special teams "special forces"—and sent Dunn in just as Harmon approached the ball.

Smith reached the field in time to fill the gap left by Beagle's absence, but Stewart's position, second from the left on the front line, was unoccupied. This left Cal with only four players in the restraining area between the Stanford 35 and 40, not five, as the rules stipulate. But this violation calls for only a correction by the officials before the kick, not a penalty that would nullify the return. In the confusion—players shuttling on and off the field, fans crowding the sidelines—none of the six officials noticed the oversight. Rodgers, captain of the special forces, was on the front line at the far left. Stewart's disappearance left a gap between him and Smith. Linebacker Tim Lucas and Cornerback Garey Williams were on the right side of this line. The second line should have consisted of Tight End David Lewis, Moen, Running Back Ron Story and Wide Receiver Howell, but Moen, for reasons unclear to West, was playing five yards deeper.

"I noticed we were a man short," says Moen, "so I decided to protect us farther back." It was one of those inspired decisions by which history is altered and football games are won. Garner was the intermediate return man and Ford the deep man—deeper at first than necessary, for he was not immediately aware that Stanford was kicking from the 25. Dunn had gotten no more than five yards onto the field when the ball was kicked, so in effect he was playing no position at all. He would play it well.

The return formation may have been a hodgepodge, but the Bears did have a vague idea of what they wanted to do, although at least two of the principals, Moen and Ford, didn't know what it was. Recalls Rodgers, "I saw our onsides team coming on, so as Mariet ran past me, I called out to him, 'If you're tackled, lateral the ball.' Then I thought that's what we should do—just keep the ball alive. Stanford might be expecting one or even two laterals, but they wouldn't be looking for us to go crazy. I walked into the huddle and said, 'Look, if you're gonna get tackled, lateral the ball.' Everybody just looked at me. I mean, don't fall with that ball.' That seemed to do it. Don't fall with the ball."

It seemed a terrific idea to young Garner. "I didn't know what we were going to do," he says. "But Richard came into that huddle with a very positive attitude. 'Don't fall with the ball.' I liked that. Why not? If they're gonna beat us, we'll go out fighting. Coach Kapp instilled that in us—100 percent for sixty minutes; never give in until the last second has ticked off. We all held hands after Richard told us what to do. I knew then it wasn't hopeless."

Moen wasn't so sure. "I wasn't in the huddle," he said. "I was just walking around in the middle of the field. I was mad and frustrated. I thought we'd played a good game, good enough to win. I didn't have a lot of hope. I didn't know about the lateraling. But I did have a weird feeling. I just wanted to see what was going to happen."

Ford had heard Rodgers yelling at him, "But I really couldn't hear what he was saying. There was too much noise." And he was having troubles of his own. "My legs started cramping up in the third quarter," he says. "I'd expected it to be cold for the game, so I'd worn tights under my uniform to keep my legs warm. Then it turned up warm [57 at the kickoff], and it was too late to take them off. I did a lot of running in that game, and it finally caught up with me. At the start of the fourth quarter I took off the tights. That seemed to help, but I could still feel the knots in my legs as I stood standing there waiting for the kick."

Stanford went for the squib kick because, according to Wiggin, "That takes away the timing of the return." But not of this one. The ball found the gap between Rodgers and Smith. Then it took a big hop directly into Moen's hands. Had he been playing in position, the ball would most likely have bounced over his head into a virtual no man's land, where Garner, the nearest player, would have had to track it down under pressure. Instead, Moen fielded the ball cleanly at about the Cal 44. He started running to his right "until I saw white shirts"—primarily Stanford Strong Safety Barry Cromer's. On the Cal 48, Moen wheeled in front of Cromer, spotted Rodgers perhaps 12 yards away near the left sideline, stopped and threw an overhand pass back to him on the Cal 46. "I did it instinctively," says Moen. "I thought Richard might have a seam on the left side. I was a quarterback in high school, so I knew I could get the ball to him. Then I ducked past the Stanford tackler and started running toward Richard, circling so that I was behind him, just to be there if he needed me."

Rodgers was startled to get the ball. "I saw Kevin looking around, then the ball was in the air and I had it," says Rodgers. "I started to run, but a Stanford man was in the way." This was Cornerback Darrell Grissum, who would surely have tackled Rodgers the moment he received the ball had not Dunn, trying somehow to get into the action from his nowhere spot, rushed up and delivered a perfect block on Grissum near the sideline. Dunn's block enabled Rodgers to lateral to Garner on the Cal 43.

"When Richard pitched it back to me, I made one fake and

then attracted a crowd," says Garner, understating the case. Stanford Linebacker David Wyman was the first to hit him, on the Cal 49. Then Linebacker Mark Andrew joined in, and, finally, what seemed to be the entire Stanford team. Harmon, the kicker, leaped for joy when he saw Garner stopped. "I thought he was down," says Harmon. "Half of our guys were going to the sidelines to celebrate." But there was no whistle, and Garner was resourceful. "My knee never touched the ground," he says. "They had my legs, but they were parallel to the ground. My upper body was free. I could hear Richard calling to me, 'Dwight, the ball!' I shovel-passed it back to him, then I hit the ground. I popped right back up to see if I could get another lateral."

At least nine players from the Stanford bench charged onto the field at that point in the mistaken belief that Garner had been stopped and the game was over. Line Judge Gordon Riese tossed his flag, charging Stanford with unsportsmanlike conduct. However, with the ball changing hands so rapidly, in the eyes of fans and players from both teams the flag could just as well have been against the Bears for something or other. From the south end zone the Stanford band also rushed onto the field, some members reaching as far as the 20-yard line.

But Rodgers, running now with the second lateral he'd received, started upfield from the Cal 48, not quite knowing whom to dodge, because so many illegal players were on the field. Two of them, in fact, were Cal men, Quarterback Gale Gilbert and Cornerback John Sullivan, both of whom took one step onto the gridiron from opposite ends of the Bears' bench when Garner was hit. They stepped back undetected as soon as they realized the ball was still in play. The most obvious of the trespassers was Stanford's Tolliver, who had run perhaps 15 yards from the bench before he realized the game wasn't over.

Rodgers reached the Stanford 46, where he was confronted by Cardinal Defensive Back Kevin Baird. "The second Dwight got the ball to me," says Rodgers, "I thought, 'Hey, we've got a chance.' I could see that Kevin and Mariet were running alongside me and that the Stanford man was in front of me. I acted like an option quarterback, drawing that man to me. Then I lateraled into an area, hoping that Kevin and Mariet wouldn't fight each other for the ball."

Ford took this fourth lateral on the Stanford 47 and swung swiftly to his right, speeding by players—legal and illegal— toward the startled Stanford band. Tolliver, meanwhile, had slipped and fallen on his backside trying to get off the field. He was lying helplessly on the Stanford 34 when Ford ran by him. "His entourage ran right over me," says Tolliver. "Sometimes I wonder why I didn't just turn around and tackle that guy." Moen was directly behind Ford. "I knew Kevin was close," says Ford, "but I didn't know how close. I figured if I looked back, one of the Stanford players would go for him."

Ford was also grimly aware that at any moment his legs might again cramp. At the Stanford 27, Ford was trapped by three Cardinal defenders—Outside Linebacker Tom Briehl, Safety Steve Lemon and Harmon. "I just threw my body into all three of them," says Ford. As his feet left the ground, he made a remarkable over-the-shoulder toss—without looking back. "I didn't have much on it," he says. "I wanted it to stay in the air as long as possible so Kevin could get to it."

Ford's dive carried him to the Stanford 24. It also flattened the three Cardinal players and altered the course of three others. Moen, racing under Ford's blind toss, actually overran it. He reached back for it at the 25, at approximately the point from which it had been released. Embittered Stanfordites later protested that this pass, though thrown back over the shoulder, was still somehow forward. The films clearly show that the ball was thrown backward and that if Moen hadn't reached back for it, it would have hit the turf at about the 27.

Ford's climactic play removed virtually the entire Stanford team from the pursuit except Outside Linebacker Mike Noble, who was behind Moen, and Grissum, who was in front of Moen as he received the lateral. Howell took Grissum out with a block that was more of a shove. No flag was dropped. The Stanford band, 144 strong, was on the field by now. One bandsman, unaware that the game was being lost behind him, stood facing the Cal rooting section, waving his cap and dancing in victory. The Axe committeemen were similarly rejoicing with the victory trophy on the Stanford 17-yard line. Another member of the band frolicked near the goal line in a conehead. Most of the musicians, along with two cheerleaders, were congregated between the goal line and the 15. Then, suddenly, Moen, in determined full flight, bore down upon them. Like a Red Sea they parted for the miracle worker. "It was a bizarre feeling," says Moen. "There were so many people on the field, and I could see flags all over the place. And here I was running right through the band."

"I was following the play," says Referee Moffett, "and then I saw the band running toward me. It was the damnedest thing. Now I know how Custer felt."

Moffett admits he didn't see Moen cross the goal line because the band was in the way. Kapp didn't see the touchdown. Wiggin probably didn't, either. The only player with a reasonably unobstructed view of the proceedings was Noble, running in futile pursuit of Moen through his own school band. "I didn't know what was going on," says Noble. "At one point I may have had a shot at him, but it was a madhouse out there. Once I hit the band I slowed down. I didn't know where the end zone was, but I figured the band must be in it."

As Moen passed the goal line, he brushed past saxophonist Scott DeBarger, a former high school football player who later acknowledged he toyed with the notion of trying to tackle the runner, a deed that would have thrown what was already football's most improbable play into even greater chaos. Moffett shudders to this day at the awful prospect. "Imagine the confusion if Moen had run into or tripped over or been tackled by a band member," says Moffett. "Then we would have had to make a decision on whether to award a touchdown." Fortunately, DeBarger's better instincts prevailed. As it was, Moen bumped the sax from DeBarger's grasp as he soared in jubilation in the end zone. Gary Tyrrell, leader of the band's trombone section, was standing in the end zone playing the Stanford band's fight song, "All Right Now" (the school's fight song is Come Join the Band), when he looked up to see Moen descending on him. "I had no idea why a Cal football player should be in our end zone with the game over," says Tyrrell. "I was apparently at the spot where he was going to spike the ball. I barely had time to brace myself."

Moen landed on Tyrrell and sent him and his trombone flying. Robert Stinnett, a photographer for the Oakland *Tribune*, was standing next to the musician at the time of the collision. His on-the-spot photos of the occasion have been made into two posters that have taken their place among countless other artifacts of The Play. Stinnett's pictures made Tyrrell as famous as Moen.

Moen said he never saw the trombone player, so eager was he to celebrate the first touchdown of his college career. Disengaging himself from Tyrrell, he pranced about the end zone with the ball held aloft. Then he had a sobering thought: There were flags on the field. Perhaps the highlight of his athletic career would be wiped out by a penalty. "I finally just sat down to await the verdict," says Moen. The officials had not confirmed the touchdown, and the spectators, thoroughly drained, held their reaction in check. The silence after so many minutes of wild cheering was startlingly abrupt. The crowd had been transformed into a mute, befuddled giant.

Starkey was now virtually speechless, his baritone voice reduced to a grating falsetto whisper. "The ball is still loose," he had shouted incredulously as The Play took form. "He's going into the end zone! There are flags on the field! The band's on the field...." Starkey once worked for Moen's father, Donne, in the banking business in Southern California, and he had been concerned that he had scarcely mentioned the boy's name throughout the game. Now he was maniacally screaming it into the microphone.

But something had to be wrong with a play that had four players throwing a total of five laterals, had illegal players from both teams on the field and had the Stanford band forming a corridor for the conclusion of a touchdown run. Moffett, a Pac-10 official for twenty-two years, was indubitably the man on the spot. As soon as Moen crossed the goal line, several Stanford assistant coaches confronted Moffett. Wiggin, who had been taunted by a finger-waving Cal nose guard, Bruce Parker, was fuming on the sidelines. Moffett extended a restraining hand toward the coaches, players, rooters and band members who were crowding around him. He called his fellow officials into an on-field conference.

"I assumed the man had scored," says Moffett, "but I had to admit I lost him in the band. I asked the other officials if he had crossed the goal line. They said he had. I asked if anyone had blown a whistle during the return. No one had. I asked if every one of those laterals was clearly backward. They said they were. And the penalty flag? On Stanford for extra players and band on the field. Well then, I said, we have a touchdown. I threw my hands in the air to signify as much. And it was like starting World War III."

Upstairs in the broadcast booth, Starkey rallied for one final paroxysm: "The Bears have won. Oh my God, this is the most amazing, sensational, heartrending, exciting, thrilling finish in the history of college football. I've never seen any game like it in my life.... The Stanford band just lost their team that ballgame.... This place is like it's never been before. It's indescribable here.... I guarantee you, if you watch college football for the rest of your life, you'll never see one like this...."

With thousands of people now on the field, Moffett and the other officials broke into a perilous sprint for their dressing quarters at the opposite end of the stadium. "Everyone was yelling at us—players, coaches, fans, both bands," Moffett recalls. "It was an alltime experience. Never in my wildest dreams had I imagined that a game could end that way. This one will be down in my memory book forever."

The officials' locker room was scarcely a sanctuary. Within minutes, Wiggin, his offensive coordinator, Ray Handley, and Stanford Athletic Director Andy Geiger were bursting through the door demanding an explanation, insisting that they had photographic proof that an official had waved the play dead when Garner was tackled. "They were in a state of shock," says Cal Sports Information Director John McCasey, who acted as a pool reporter in the officials' room. "Paul was saying how people's livelihoods depended on the officials' decisions." Moffett held his ground under the barrage. No whistle had been blown. Head Linesman Jack Langley had been in perfect position to call the play dead when Garner was tackled. "He was looking right at it," says Moffett. "All through that play I was saying to myself, 'Keep cool.' It was a weird situation, but we're trained to keep our cool." The Stanford team, meanwhile, sat fully dressed for twenty minutes after the game, waiting, as one member, Lemon, recalls, "for something else to happen. We thought we would probably have to do this play all over again. We sat there in total disbelief."

The Pac-10 has no provisions for an official protest, so none was filed. The best Stanford could do was persuade conference Executive Director Wiles Hallock to issue a public statement acknowledging that Cal had only four men in the restraining area on the fateful kickoff. Hallock added, however, that it was a violation that required no penalty. And, he said later, "I'm pleased that in all the confusion, the officials never stopped officiating." As for the play? "Well, it was just one of those marvelous things that happen in football."

The Play remains, these three decades later, the most played of all football videotapes, usually with Starkey's hysterical broadcast as narration and the William Tell Overature as musical accompaniment. An ESPN poll taken twenty years after the event ranked The Play as "the most fantastic finish" to any game ever, college or pro. In the weeks and months following the game, the four Play-makers—and the trombone player—became national television celebrities. T-shirts, tapes, replica trombones and other Play arcana sold briskly for months afterward. The Play appears regularly on the Memorial Stadium electronic message board and draws cheers nearly as rousing as those raised when it was seen live. At The Play's 25th anniversary, the Cal band dedicated its halftime show to it. In fact, as late as 2008 the band recreated the madcap lateraling, some of its members dressed in Stanford band uniforms.

Of the four Players, only Rodgers opted to stay in the game as a coach. Moen and Garner pursued careers in business. And Ford, whose blind lateral made the whole thing work, was tragically removed by an act of violence from any semblance of a normal life. In April of 1998, he was found guilty by a Sacramento jury of the second-degree murders of his eight-months pregnant wife and their three-year-old son a year earlier. He was sentenced to serve forty-five-years-to-life in State prison. All appeals of the verdict have been denied, though Ford has long protested his innocence.

The murders were described by prosecutors as the consequence of an "angry, unpremeditated explosion of violence." Friends and old teammates remain baffled by the case. "I grew up with Mariet Ford (in Contra Costa County)," says Torchio. "And everything I ever knew about him was positive."

"As an athlete, as a student, Mariet was everything a coach could ask for," says Kapp. "He was a leader by example on our team. He was wired, though. He had that intensity, which is considered a good thing in football. And yet that intensity is the only clue I can see for such a terrible thing."

In a 2002 interview from prison with the *Chronicle*'s Ron Kroichick, Ford recalled The Play. "When I get very depressed I think back to that game...I have a place there I can always go to. That one moment of time keeps me going."

## CHAPTER THIRTY-ONE

# KAPP'S LAST JAPE

"The ship is launched," Kapp proclaimed on the eve of the 1983 season. "The players know what is expected of them."

Could the coach conceivably have had The Play in mind when he said that about expectations? If so, his team staged a similarly preposterous finish in the very first game of the new season—the next one after The Play itself—against Texas A&M in far off College Station.

As in the Big Game, the Bears assumed a commanding lead in the first half, scoring almost immediately after they recovered the Aggies' surprise onside kick attempt on the opening kickoff. Two plays later and just a minute into the game, Garner sped 43 yards for a touchdown. The Bears also scored on their next two possessions—on a 28-yard field goal by new kicker Randy Pratt and a one-yard plunge by Story, set up by a fumble recovery on the Aggie 25. They led at the half, 17–0. But not for much longer.

The Aggies moved from their own 20 to the Bear 19 after receiving the second half kickoff, finally connecting on a 36-yard field goal by their Alan Smith. Two minutes later, A&M quarterback Scot Mazur passed 44 yards to Rich Siler for a touchdown. The same two connected again for 18 yards and the tying score with 3:07 left in the third quarter. The Bears had gained just 19 yards the entire quarter.

Until its closing seconds, the fourth quarter unfolded as a series of missed opportunities for both teams. After intercepting Gilbert on the Cal 27, the Aggies couldn't gain and botched a field goal try. The Bears in turn drove from their own 21 to the Aggie one, Gilbert completing four of six passes en route, two to freshman tight end Don Noble. But the Aggies held, stopping Garner inches from the goal line on a fourth down plunge. There were six minutes left to play.

The Bears drove goalward on their next possession and again were held short of a touchdown. This time on fourth down, Kapp ordered a field goal, and Pratt made it from 22 yards out. The Bears had seemingly taken a 20–17 lead with 1:20 left. But no. Pratt had been roughed after the kick, raising the possibility of a penalty that would give Cal the ball on the A&M 2 ½-yard-line.

A dilemma? In conventional thinking a team doesn't take points, particularly possible game-winning points, off the board. But these were the Bears, Joe Kapp's Bears. Torchio, who had been the holder, looked to the sidelines for instructions.

"But I got no response," he recalled twenty-five years later. "The coach was nowhere to be seen. Now the officials were telling me I had to make a call. 'What do you want do do?' they kept asking me. We were down so close, I figured we should be able to score from the two. So I said we'll take the penalty."

Of course, they had to make that touchdown. And only a few minutes earlier, they'd been stopped cold on the Aggie one. Still, they had four downs to make a measly two-and-a-half yards. Actually, they didn't. On first down, Gilbert fumbled the snap and the Aggies recovered. Time was running out and those three points were gone. How foolish can you look?

The scenario had not yet run its course, though. On second and nine from the four, A&M fullback Jimmie Hawkins tried to sweep his right end. He never made it out of the end zone, the Bears' All America linebacker Ron Rivera downing him there for a safety with 57 seconds remaining. The Bears had won, anyway, if by 19–17 instead of 20–17. Torchio said no one on the coaching staff said a word to him afterward about his ultimately sound decision.

That game was the start of a so-so 5-5-1 season. Kapp's metaphorical ship didn't sink, but she barely made it to port. And if Gilbert hadn't been such an exceptional presence at the helm, she would have been sadly adrift. But enough of these nautical images; the Bears played on a carpet, not a pond. Gilbert in '83 established new single season school records with 2,769 yards passing and 365 attempts. His 216 completions tied him with Campbell for that record and his four 300-plus-yard games tied Bartkowski for another. All that aerial productivity was sorely needed because the Bears gained only 620 net yards on the ground, a record low accounted for in no small part by the 332 yards Gilbert lost on sacks.

After the Texas A&M weirdness, the Bears were humiliated by San Diego State, 28–14. Gilbert passed for both scores, 68 yards to Lewis and 23 to Rance McDougald, but he was intercepted four times and the Bears netted just 23 yards rushing. Gilbert was sacked six times against San Jose State, contributing measurably to the puny 49 yards his team gained on 44 rushes. But they beat the Spartans by the convincing score of 30–9. Then, in another wild one, they tied Arizona, 33 apiece, after falling in arrears by 23 points (26–3) midway through the third quarter. In the comeback launched that quarter, Gilbert found Lewis for an 80-yard score and Garner returned a punt 67 yards for another. In the fourth quarter, Gilbert passed to Andy Bark for a 61-yard TD and Scott Smith scored from the three after Gilbert set up the touchdown with a 28-yard completion to Bark. After freshman linebacker Hardy Nickerson recovered a Sun Devil fumble on the Arizona State 21, Pratt kicked the tying field goal with 48 seconds left. Pratt attempted another from 62 yards out with no time at all left, but the kick fell short.

The Bears then lost to Oregon, 24–17, in a game that wouldn't have been nearly that close had it not been for the larcenous play of Rivera. The All-American recovered an Oregon fumble on the Cal one, saving an almost certain score, stripped the ball from Duck quarterback Mike Jorgensen, which led to a 47-yard Pratt field goal at the very end of the first half, and stole the ball from Oregon back Todd Bland and carried it 36 yards for his own touchdown with five seconds left in the game.

Rivera's talent for thievery was scarcely needed in a 44–19 romp over Oregon State that with a 3:45 p.m. starting time became by the second half the first night game played in Memorial Stadium, lights courtesy of CBS television. Gilbert was 23 for 27 for 342 yards and three touchdowns, two caught by McDougald. His 85.2 completion percentage broke Campbell's previous single-game record of 84.6 set in 1979.

The Bears next dropped a pair to the southern schools. UCLA overcame a 341-yard passing game by Gilbert with two fourth-quarter scores, the first on a pass from one future Bruin head coach, Neuheisel, to another, Karl Dorrell. The following week, an uncharacteristically mediocre USC team (2-4-1 before the game) held Gilbert to 145 yards and churned out a 19–9 win before 65,867 rain-soaked fans at Memorial Stadium.

Gilbert passed 73 yards to McDougald for a touchdown only 48 seconds into the game and Pratt kicked a field goal 48 seconds from its end to preserve a 26–24 win over Arizona State. In between, Gilbert passed for 57 yards to McDougald for another touchdown and Pratt kicked three more field goals. The light-fingered Rivera had another busy day, recovering two fumbles, intercepting a pass and making 12 tackles.

With Gilbert gone after the second quarter with an injured shoulder, neither Torchio nor freshman Kevin Brown could generate much offense in a 16–6 loss to Washington State. Together the sub quarterbacks were just 7 for 19 passing with three interceptions and a fumble.

Gilbert was back for the not-so-big Big Game. The Bears were 4-5-1 going in and Stanford, in Wiggins's last season, was a miserable 1-9. And in the 27–18 Cal win, the Cardinal coughed up seven turnovers, four on interceptions of John Paye passes and three on lost fumbles. Gilbert threw touchdown passes to Lewis for 37 yards and 10 to Bark. Pratt kicked two more field goals, giving him a new Cal record 22 for the season, and Garner scored on a one-yard run. But the victory belonged to the defense. David Carter had two interceptions and Rodgers and Nickerson one each. The fumbles were recovered by linebackers Eddie Walsh and Chris Hampton and tackle Don James.

In the larger scheme of things, 1983 had been a good year for the U.C. system. The state's new governor, Republican George Deukmejian, became the first since Edmund G. "Pat" Brown twenty years earlier, wrote Cal historian Patricia Pelfrey, "to make higher education a priority." And in new U.C. president David Gardner, the university had a demon fund-raiser who convinced the Governor and the State Legislature to approve a 30 percent increase in U.C.'s operating budget. The fresh funding allowed Cal to remain competitive in faculty salaries with the nation's leading universities. By then, fourteen Cal professors had won Nobel Prizes in fields ranging from physics and chemistry to literature and economics. And a survey by the Associated Research Council rated the Berkeley campus in the top ten in thirty of thirty-two academic fields, well ahead of such competitors as Harvard and Stanford. President Gardner had also promoted the university's status as an educational arm of the Pacific Rim and had promised to increase substantially minority enrollment. The school's future looked encouraging.

Not necessarily the football team's, though. In 1984, the first of three straight losing seasons for Kapp, the Bears finished with just two wins and nine losses. The wins came over Pacific, 28–12, in the second game and over Arizona State, 19–14, in the fifth. The season ended with six straight losses, the most in a row since White's first season in

1972. Among those defeats were some serious clobberings: 44–14 to Washington, 33–7 by Washington State, 31–7 by USC and 33–18 by San Jose State. The Bears made it close against Oregon State, but the 9–6 loss was the first to the Beavers in eight years. They stayed with Arizona until the Wildcats scored 16 points in the second half to pull away to a 23–13 win. They nearly brought UCLA's 13-game winning streak against them to a merciful end before losing, 17–14, on a fourth-quarter field goal. It was a game in which Gilbert, hobbled by a sprained ankle, was sacked ten times.

The only noticeable Cal improvement was in the running game which, with 1,287 yards gained, more than doubled the 1983 output. City College of San Francisco transfer Ed Barbero was the leading rusher with 554 yards. Gilbert, in his senior season, was not the pass master he'd been the year before, finishing with 166 completions of 306 attempts for 1,693 yards and just six touchdowns against 14 interceptions. But he finished second only to Campbell with 6,566 career passing yards to his predecessor's 7,174. Gilbert was backed in '84 by sophomore Brown and freshman Brian Bedford who together completed 31 of 71 for 357 yards, two touchdowns and three interceptions.

Kapp had won two of three Big Games as a player and was famously 2-0 as a coach before the 1984 matchup. The new Stanford coach was John Elway's amiable father, Jack, and he had some fine young players at his command in freshman running back Brad Muster and sophomore quarterback Paye. Muster powered past the Bears in '84 for 204 yards and Paye passed for one touchdown and ran for another in a comfortable 27–10 Cardinal win. The Bears had actually taken a 10–0 lead early in the second quarter, on Gilbert's 12-yard pass to Keith Crockett and a 43-yard field goal by placekicker-punter Tom Gandsey. But the Cardinal held the home team scoreless from then on. Gilbert finished just 10 of 21 passing for 110 yards and was intercepted twice.

"The strength of our football team is character," Kapp declared before the 1985 season. "Going through the adversity of last season will help us develop the mental toughness it takes to win." Well, sort of. The Bears did win a couple more games, but with Gilbert and Rivera gone, they'd lost much of their offensive and defensive panache.

Brown and Bedford shared the quarterbacking, but, save for the occasional flash of competence, neither could provide a winning touch. Together, they tossed up 19 interceptions, 12 by Brown, seven by Bedford, as opposed to eight touchdowns, six by Brown, two by Bedford. On defense, though, the 230-pound Nickerson stepped smartly into Rivera's linebacking shoes, setting an impressive new school record with 167 tackles, to surpass the record of 141 that he had set the season before.

Barbero was back as the power runner and Garner as the shifty one. And in freshman Marc Hicks, Kapp had a back of single-wing versatility, a runner, passer, punter and receiver. Hicks gained 13 yards the first time he carried the ball in the opener that season, a 48–21 win over San Jose State. And in a mid-season 39–32 win over Missouri, he became the first Cal freshman since Jackie Jensen to gain more than 100 yards in a game. For the season he gained 538 yards, second on the team to Barbero's 586, and averaged 5.1 yards per carry.

The Bears had a balanced attack in '85 that approximated the perfect one of ten years earlier. Despite their frequent misfires, the Brown-Bedford combo gained 2,119 yards in the air and the runners added 2,011 more. But the team was incapable of maintaining the remotest semblance of consistency and finished just 4-7. And there was some bad luck along the way. Three of those losses—against Washington State (20–19), Oregon State (23–20) and Arizona (23–17)—were dealt them within the last three minutes of play. In fact, only late-season defeats by UCLA (34–7) and Arizona State (30–8) qualified as old-fashioned thumpings. As the bromide goes, the 1985 Bears were just good enough to lose.

After the opening win over San Jose, they lost those three heartbreakers in succession, enough suffering right there to douse the spirit of the truest of Old Blues. Against Washington State, they led by 19 –0 as late as eight minutes into the final quarter. But the Cougars scored three quick touchdowns, the last a pass from Mark Rypien to Rick Chase, with 41 seconds on the clock. Against Oregon State, the winning field goal by the Beavers' Jim Nielson was kicked with no time left. It came after the Bears had tied the score earlier in the quarter on Todd Powers' one-yard plunge. Lee Rix kicked two field goals for the Bears and, after his holder, Brown, fumbled the snap on a third try, alertly picked up the ball and shoveled a touchdown pass to Don Noble. Against Arizona in the third of these cruel losses, the winning three-pointer was kicked by Max Zendahas with 2:43 left. There remained enough time, however, for the Bears to win with a touchdown, and they did drive as close as the Arizona 19 before, with 1:10 left, Brown was intercepted. Vince Delgado had scored twice for the Bears earlier, on a nine-yard pass from Brown and 37-yard run from the flanker reverse.

In the Missouri win, the two teams combined for 969 yards and 59 first downs. Both Cal quarterbacks had industrious afternoons, Brown passing for 176 yards and Bedford for 84 on just four completions. Washington scored 14 points in both the first and last quarters in a 28–12 win over a Cal team that never could catch up despite outgaining the Huskies, 392 yards to 268. The Bears did catch up with Oregon, though, after falling behind 21–0 in the first quarter. Bedford entered the game late in that quarter and over the remaining distance passed for 197 yards, rushed for 52 and scored twice in a gratifying 27–24 victory. Then came the UCLA and Arizona State pummelings. Against the Sun Devils, Bear passers gained a season-high 289 yards but were intercepted seven times. The loss to the Bruins was Cal's fourteenth straight in the sibling rivalry—a streak that wouldn't end until it had reached eighteen.

The Bears did halt USC's seven-year domination with a 14–6 win before sixty-three thousand five hundred at Memorial Stadium.

Hicks scored both Cal touchdowns and gained 113 yards on 22 carries while Nickerson on defense had 17 tackles, three behind the line, and caused two fumbles. The once fearsome Trojans were held without a touchdown, the first time in twenty-eight years a Cal defense had so deprived them.

Stanford piled up a 24–0 lead as late as the middle of the third quarter in what appeared to be a runaway victory in the Big Game. Suddenly, the Bears awakened and before the quarter ended scored three touchdowns on runs by Bedford, Garner and Delgado and a safety when linebacker Miles Turpin pressured Paye into grounding a pass in the end zone. This looked for all the world like another one of those down-to-the-wire Big Game specials. But neither team could score in an anti-climactic fourth quarter. Even so, Stanford's 24–22 win was the forty-second of these games decided by fewer than seven points.

Much of the excitement and alumni bonhomie Kapp's arrival had occasioned was now conspicuously waning. The coach had won only six games against sixteen losses the last two years and, worse yet, his team had lost two straight Big Games. His assistant coaches seemed to come and go talking of Michelangelo and the player talent pool was turning out to be not as deep as touted. The 1986 Cal media guide perhaps inadvertently put Joe on the spot, reporting that "there is little doubt that this is a Joe Kapp football team—one fully recruited by the dynamic coach and one which seems to understand and accept the fact that it takes hard work to achieve success." Joe was then quoted as saying, "We're doing things the right way at Cal…We are going to start seeing some good results."

But those results were all but invisible in '86, After beating Washington State, 31–21, in the second game—following a 21–15 loss to Boston College in the opener—Kapp's Bears lost eight in a row, a Cal record of futility matched then only by Levy's team in 1962 and Elliott's in 1959. The losing streak got off to a particularly odious start with consecutive thrashings by San Jose State, 35–14, and Washington,

50–18. The California Bowl-bound Spartans chalked up 565 total yards, 348 on the passing of Quarterback Mike Perez. And nine turnovers contributed to the Huskies' overwhelming victory. Cal's lone bright spot in that defeat was the debut of running back Chris Richards, a transfer from Oklahoma. He ran 67 yards for Cal's first score in the second quarter and gained 101 for the day on 15 carries.

By now, Bedford had been shifted, willingly, to wide receiver clearing the way at quarterback for a highly regarded freshman, Troy Taylor. The neophyte completed his first six passes and nine of his first 11, but the Bears still lost to Oregon State, 14–12, the closest game of a sorry lot. Cal's lone touchdown came early in the third quarter when Hicks hit the right side of his line, shed a few tacklers and continued for 80 yards. It was the longest run by a Cal back since Hicks's coach ran for 92 against Oregon in 1958.

After that near miss came the deluge. UCLA made it 15 in a row with a 36–10 win; Arizona triumphed, 33–16; Oregon, 27–9; Arizona State, 49–0; USC, 28–3. The Bears' only points in the Trojan game came as a result of another one of those freakish plays that veteran Cal observers now accepted as the norm. In the second quarter, facing a 4th-and-12 situation on the USC 43 and behind 7–0, Bear punter Scott Tabor faked a kick and lofted a sky-high spiral downfield toward receiver James Devers. Trojan defenders, believing the pass was a punt and that Devers was covering it, blocked the Bear out of the play. USC was called for pass interference and penalized 15 yards. The Bears, who hadn't scored a touchdown in three games, finally settled for a 35-yard Rix field goal.

Kapp knew he'd been fired three games before the end of the season. "Maggard told me he couldn't get any support for me," he recalled with lingering sadness more than twenty years later. "Losing that job was not at all like living happily ever after. In fact, it still hurts. Maggard was a bureaucrat. But for me Cal football was more than a business. Pro-football, yes. But I didn't think of the Cal experience in those terms. All you have to do is visit the campus and you fall in love with the place."

Kapp at heart was forever a Pappy's Boy, a true disciple. Unlike so many of his wonkish contemporaries in the coaching trade with playbooks the length of a Tolstoy novel, Kapp espoused the old do-or-die-for-alma-mater approach. He denounced coaches who, in his opinion, used the Cal job as a stepping stone to the NFL or to more aggressive football schools. For him, Cal was the last stop, the realization of his fondest hopes. "I've lived my movie," he liked to say. He peppered his conversation with inspirational catch-phrases. "The Bear will not quit, the Bear will not die," he preached to increasingly sophisticated players, some of whom must have regarded his sermons as the residue of old Pat O'Brien movies. As the game steadily fell under the influence not only of bureaucrats but technocrats, Joe Kapp became something of an anachronism, Pericles exhorting delegates to a Google convention.

But he did have one more game to coach. And for this one, the Big Game, he had no difficulty rousing his charges to old school fervor. The sad fact of his own leaving was more than enough. That and the overwhelming odds against the team. In 1986, Jack Elway had the best of all his Stanford squads, one that with post-season play would finish with an 8-4 record. The Cardinal was 6-3 coming into the Big Game, the Bears a measly 1-9. Elway's stalwarts had beaten at least three teams—San Jose State, UCLA and Oregon—that had trounced the Bears.

But emotion does count for something, and after a scoreless first quarter, Rix nailed a 34-yard field goal barely a minute into the second. Then Brown, starting in place of Taylor, whose jaw had been broken in the USC game, led a 93-yard march, the standout play a 61-yard pass to freshman Mike Ford, subbing for the injured Delgado. Brown next connected with Devers for 18 yards and Wendell Peoples for the final five. Stanford's David Sweeney kicked a 48-yard field goal with 48 seconds left in the half to reduce Cal's lead at intermission to 10–3.

The third quarter, like the first, was scoreless. But with 7:36 left in the game, Ford ran 47 yards on the reverse play Delgado had used so effectively and upped the Cal lead to 17–3. Two minutes later, Paye hit receiver Jeff Jones for a 69-yard touchdown that, with Paye's pass to Jim Price for the two-point conversion, brought the Cardinal within a touchdown. The once porous Cal defense held on, though, aided by Tabor's intimidating punts, one good for 58 yards inside the Stanford 20. Paye was sacked seven times in the game. And in their coach's last stand, the Bears had pulled off a memorable 17–11 victory.

In a scene reminiscent of Pappy's last game thirty years earlier, Kapp's players hoisted him to their shoulders and carried him off the field in triumph and sorrow. It goes without saying that, held aloft by his loyal "young men," the coach wept copiously. So, for that matter, did many of his players.

It would be years, though, before this good man would find it in him to return to the campus he loved.

## CHAPTER THIRTY-TWO

# STRANGER IN A STRANGE LAND

Barely two weeks after Kapp's theatrical exit, Maggard hired as his replacement a coach, Bruce Snyder, who, unlike his four immediate predecessors, was completely outside the Cal family circle. Snyder had been neither a student nor a coach there. He had no friends among influential alumni or within the university hierarchy. In fact, he came to Berkeley straight from the NFL, where for the previous four seasons he'd been the backfield coach for the Los Angeles Rams under former USC headman John Robinson.

But his experience was largely in the college game, and he'd built an impressive resumé there. After graduation from Oregon in 1963 with a degree in mathematics, he'd taught and coached for a couple of years at Sheldon High School in Eugene before returning to the university as an assistant for eight years. He was the offensive coordinator at New Mexico State in 1972 and at Utah State in '73. He coached the running backs—"student body right, student body left"—under John McKay at USC in 1974 and '75. And from 1976 through '82, he was the head coach at Utah State, where his '78 and '79 teams had been conference co-champions. With nearly twenty-five years of coaching experience the forty-seven-year-old Snyder was in many important respects Kapp's polar opposite. As one might expect of a math major, he was a demon for details, and his practices were crisply orchestrated. These were qualities that often led to perhaps unfair comparisons by some players with the more free-wheeling Joe.

"We needed direction, someone who had a plan," said James Devers. "We needed to be told step by step how to win instead of being told just to go out and win."

"It's really exciting," said Bedford, "being around a coach who is so knowledgeable."

When you look at Coach Snyder's background," said linebacker David Ortega, "and the players he's been associated with and the way he's running this program, it's obvious he knows exactly what he's doing and it breeds a lot of confidence and respect."

The Cal Media Guide, boosting the new coach—somewhat at the expense of the old—chimed in: "Things such as the attitude of his football team, the work ethic of both his staff and team members and the genuine rapport between players and coaches all have undergone dramatic turnarounds under his (Snyder's) leadership."

There was also praise from on high. "Bruce has one of the keenest minds in football today," said Bill Walsh. "He's extremely gifted in motivating players, and he's a very assertive and demanding coach."

The question remained: Why would such an accomplished craftsman leave the then glamorous Rams and the NFL for a football program that was, from all the pertinent evidence, on another one of its periodic downslides, a winner of just eight games, total, in the past three years? And for a school with which he'd had no previous association and certainly no sentimental attachment?

Good questions, agreed Snyder more than twenty years later.

"The over-riding factor," he forthrightly explained, "was that I wanted to be a head coach. And I'd been a college coach all my professional life except for those four years with the Rams. Also, I'm a Pac-10 guy. I'd played and coached at Oregon. I told John Robinson about applying for the Cal job. I liked working for the Rams. In fact, we were still playing when the job in Berkeley opened up. John told me to go ahead and submit my application, but to keep quiet about it with the Rams ownership. Then he joked that with my lack of connections at Cal I would probably rate on a list of forty-five applicants somewhere around forty-sixth. As it turned out that list got down to about five, and then Dave Maggard made his choice. So for awhile I was working two jobs, putting together a staff for Cal and coaching the Rams in the playoffs."

When he finally reached Berkeley that December, he was in for a double shock. "My first impression coming in from the NFL was that these players were a lot smaller and certainly not as fast as the pros. When I met my quarterback, Troy Taylor, I was amazed at how thin (6-4, 185) he was. I soon learned, though, how tremendously courageous and tough he also was."

But size and speed were not this team's biggest handicaps. "That first season," Snyder recalled, "we were playing Minnesota in their dome (Cal's first indoor game) and we were ahead, 14–3, at the half. I'd had a brief interview on the field, and when I returned to the locker room, I expected it to be lively in there. But it was dead quiet. Then it dawned on me that these players were thinking something would go wrong in the second half. They were good kids, but they were saddled with an anticipation of losing."

And so they did lose. After an easy, 42–0 win over Pacific in the 1987 opener, they dropped four in a row, predictably including that Minnesota game when the Gophers outscored them, 29–9, in the second half. San Jose State beat them, 27–25, on a field goal with one second left to play. USC won easily, 31–14, despite the power punting of Scott Tabor, who set school records with an 89-yard boot in the second quarter and a 55.6 average for nine punts. Tennessee beat them, 38–12, before 91,688 in Knoxville. They tied Arizona, 23–23, and then took the usual clobbering—the sixteenth straight—from UCLA, 42–18, on the strength of future NFL Hall of Famer Troy Aikman's three second-half touchdown passes. Except for that late burst, Taylor had a better day than the famous Bruin, completing 21 of 35 for 312 yards.

After this 1-5-1 start, Snyder's debut team finished relatively strong, beating Oregon, 20–6, and Arizona State, 38–20, before losing to Stanford, 31–7. The Bears played the Big Game without Taylor, who had broken the index finger on his throwing hand against Arizona State. The sophomore quarterback would also miss a season-ending 17–17 tie with Washington State that was played in Tokyo and was the Bears' first football game in a foreign land. Although he played only nine games that season, Taylor broke the school record with 18 touchdown passes. Ortega set another Cal season record with his 142 tackles, 21 of which came against USC. He also established a new season record for linebackers with six interceptions.

After his first Cal team finished an inauspicious 3-6-2, Snyder set as his top priority the expulsion of what he now came to believe was a culture of losing that extended even beyond the locker room. He was visited in his office one day during the season by an administrator who, commenting forlornly on a botched punt return in a recent game, told him, "When that happened, I just knew we were going to lose." Snyder clapped hand to forehead. "I suddenly realized it was not just the players who felt that way, it was the entire system. The team was always waiting for something to go wrong and so was the administration. I knew then we had to start playing in the present. We had to get rid of all that baggage from past seasons. So we on the coaching staff came up with what was admittedly a corny slogan: 'One at a time.' Now, that didn't mean playing one game at a time. That meant one snap at a time. One block at a time. In fact, everything in life one at a time. We put that simple slogan everywhere—on the lockers, the players' notebooks, even their pencils."

Snyder was also looking for recruits who had a zest for playing the game. Coming to Cal as he had from the outside, he made no pretense of observing the usual academic pieties in interviewing candidates for football scholarships. In one of these sessions with a promising young player, he asked him why he wanted to come to Cal. The boy, obviously well-versed on the proper response, quickly said, "for the education." Now, that's pretty much what Cal scholarship applicants had been saying, to approving nods, since the days of Andy Smith. But it didn't work with Snyder.

"That's not what you want to hear when you're building a football program," he candidly recalled. "With all due respect, you want to hear a boy say, 'because I love playing football.' That's not to say I didn't want good students. I did. And we had plenty of them on our team. I wanted people who could do the academic work and still have that love for the game."

The kid who innocently said he wanted an education had to look elsewhere to get it. Snyder did not offer him a scholarship.

The coach's 1988 team was well stocked with football lovers. And it finished a much-improved 5-5-1. In four of those five wins, the Bears had breathlessly come from behind. At the same time, in three of the five losses they blew leads in the closing minutes. One of those defeats came against Oregon State in a game that because of a timekeeper's error lasted a full minute beyond the conventional sixty. The extra time allowed the Beavers to kick the game-winning field goal with sixteen seconds left on the malfunctioning clock, this after the Bears had built a 16–3 lead in the third quarter on a Taylor TD pass and three field goals by sophomore punter-placekicker Robbie Keen. The final score of Oregon State 17, Cal 16 may have revived many of those supposedly banished bad expectations.

But the Bears bounced back from that literally ill-timed defeat to overwhelm Kansas, 52–21, racking up the most points by a Cal team in 14 years. And they stayed on track the following week, coming from behind to beat San Jose State, 21–14, thanks to Taylor's 370 passing yards.

The quarterback was shaken up in a 44–13 loss to Washington State and replaced by redshirt freshman Mike Pawlawski, who immediately led a drive to the Cougar 15, principally on his 52-yard completion to Darryl Ingram. But the Bears could move no farther and Keen kicked his second field goal of the day. UCLA made it 17 in a row with a 38–21 beating, Aikman passing for 322 yards. Again the Bears bounced back, defeating Temple, 31–14, and then Arizona, 10–7, before losing to USC, 35–3, and then, dishearteningly, to Washington in a close one that was at least achieved without benefit of a faulty clock.

The Bears actually led the Huskies, 24–3, at the half, Keen booting a school record 55-yarder as time ran out in the second quarter. He nailed a 47-yarder in the third quarter, but the Huskies scored three touchdowns after that and made the final score, 28–27, with a field goal in the last two seconds of play.

If nothing else, that frustrating finish served as preparation for another extraordinary Big Game. Snyder's team needed just one more victory to give Cal its first winning season since 1982; Stanford, in Coach Jack Elway's last season there, was only 3-6-1 going in. And when neither team could manufacture much in the way of an offensive threat, the game devolved into a kicking duel between Keen and the Cardinal's John Hopkins, each of whom booted four field goals. Stanford's only touchdown came on a 95-yard kickoff return by Kevin Scott in the second quarter. Cal matched that early in the fourth when, at the conclusion of an 80-yard drive, Taylor completed a 19-yard end zone pass to Mike Ford. Though he was then playing in his third varsity season, that was Taylor's first Big Game scoring pass. For that matter, it was the Cal quarterback's first Big Game, injuries having kept him out of the two before.

With the score tied at 19, the Bears finally got what appeared to be the break they needed when, with not quite four minutes to play, noseguard Majett Whiteside hit Cardinal QB Jason Palumbis as he was throwing and the resultant butterfly of a pass was picked off by Ortega on the Cardinal 39. The Bears advanced to the eight before the Stanford defense stiffened. With time expiring, Keen was sent in to win the game with a fifth field goal, this one a veritable chip shot for a kicker who had already made good on 21 of his 25 attempts that season, including 11 of 12 for 40 or more yards. Though by now they should have known better, some Cal fans were already celebrating as Keen trotted onto the field. The more knowledgeable among them remained silent.

And sure enough, an until then obscure Stanford safety named Twan Van Le raced in from approximately nowhere to block that kick as time ran out. It was the first Big Game tie in thirty-five years. Cal would have to wait at least another year or two for a winning season.

There was little question, however, that Snyder had his team heading in a positive direction. Taylor had another fine season, hitting on 202 of 330 passes (61.2) for 2,416 yards and 16 touchdowns. Chris Richards led the rushers with 729 yards on 162 carries, and a freshman of considerable promise, Brian Treggs, averaged 14.9 yards on his 19 receptions. But Keen was the numbers czar, finishing among the NCAA's top twelve in both placekicking (86 points) and punting (42.6 average). All but Richards would return in 1989.

More positively, the players seemed to have rid themselves of low expectations. "He won't let us look at ourselves as losers," Ortega said of the head coach. "He just won't permit it…Everybody believes that if we do as Coach Snyder and his coaches tell us, we're going to win.

"He'd given us confidence," recalled Taylor twenty years later. "He'd brought with him a great staff—Terry Shea, Steve Mariucci, Kent Baer, Rod Marinelli…all of them head coaching material. I was fortunate in many ways. Joe (Kapp) recruited me and gave me some of that real love for Cal he had. And Bruce impressed me with his sense of detail. Everything with Bruce was well thought out. Nothing was ever left to chance."

By 1989 Taylor's slender physique had ballooned up to 190 pounds, and Snyder, possibly carried away, found himself comparing his quarterback to the incomparable Joe Montana—at least in terms of "his ability to make things happen and his leadership qualities." Taylor would be backed up by sophomore Pawlawski, who had appeared in only four games in '88, mainly because of a bleeding ulcer caused, he was told, by the anti-inflammatory medication he'd been taking for a sprained ankle. The team seemed particularly deep at receiver with Treggs, Junior Tagaloa, Ford, freshman Mike Caldwell and Brent Woodall, a 230-pounder shifted from running back to tight end. Anthony Wallace, a smooth-striding transfer from Pasadena Junior College, was expected to be the primary ball-carrier, at least until high school sensation Russell White could become academically eligible after meeting the conditions of the Proposition 48 special admissions program under which he'd been accepted. Some dropoff in kicker Keen's productivity was anticipated since the NCAA had banished the kicking tee in 1989.

In truth, the season was not a great success. The Bears dropped their first two games to Oregon (35–19) and Miami (31–3) on the road, both played in enervating heat—90 degrees (yes!) in Eugene and 93 in Miami. They beat Wisconsin, 20–4, back in balmy Berkeley and absorbed the usual punishment from UCLA, 24–6. Then, after edging San Jose State, 26–21, they lost three in a row to USC (31–15), Washington (29–16) and Oregon State (25–14). The Washington and Oregon State games in late October were played before Memorial Stadium crowds in the underwhelming range of twenty thousand because of the devastating Loma Prieta earthquake of October 17 that shut down the Bay Bridge, caused widespread damage on both sides of the Bay and even delayed the resumption of the so-called Bay Bridge World Series between the Oakland Athletics and the San Francisco Giants.

The Bears upset 15th-ranked Arizona, 29–28, on November 4 before another small crowd of twenty-nine thousand in Berkeley. They had trailed the Wildcats, 21–0, in the second quarter and 28–10 as late as the third quarter before reeling off three straight touchdowns behind Wallace's slippery running (96 yards on 15 carries) and Taylor's consistently accurate passing. For the day, the Cal QB hit on 28 of 44 attempts for 372 yards.

The mini-streak carried over through the following week with a 38–26 win over Washington State. Taylor had another big day, connecting on 25 or 33 for 368 yards and two scores. Ford caught five for 90 yards, Michael Smith five for 87 and Treggs six for 70. This game was the last played on the artificial turf first installed in 1981. Alas, a new carpet, equally appalling, was laid for the 1990 season.

Taylor had his third straight 300-plus-yard passing game against Stanford before 86,019 there, completing 29 of a then record 57 attempts for 377 yards. As illustration of how unbalanced the Bear offense had become, Taylor was also the team's leading rusher with 21 yards. Stanford gained 299 yards rushing, with J.J. Lasley, Scott Eschelman and sophomore Tommy Vardell doing the ground work. The 24–14 loss convinced Snyder he needed to improve his running game if he intended to win more games than the paltry four he had in '89. Although his passing offense was ranked fifth in the nation, the Bears had averaged only 2.8 yards per rush, the lowest in 16 years, and they'd averaged 18.2 points per game, not nearly enough, the coach reasoned, to compete in the high-scoring Pac-10.

Snyder's 1990 starting offensive front five averaged 279 pounds, big enough for a time just before the influx of 300 pounders, and he'd have 1989's leading ground-gainer (560 yards) Wallace back for the new season, along with the reliable if unspectacular Greg Zomalt. But the lad he would look to for the big play in the new season was the thus-far sequestered Russell White. At Crespi High in Van Nuys, White had rushed for two yards shy of 6,000 and been named to the state's All-Decade Team. He weighed 210 pounds and had been timed in the 40, football's sprint distance, in a speedy 4.38 seconds. And running with a football was in his genes, since his uncle Charles had been the 1979 Heisman Trophy winner carrying the ball for USC.

Taylor would be gone for the 1990 season, replaced by the relatively inexperienced Pawlawski. Snyder was quoted in the 1990 Cal Media Guide musing on his team's dependence the past three years on Taylor's passing: "We had a great quarterback, and we tried to take advantage of his intelligence and passing skills. What ended up happening is that by choosing to emphasize our strengths, other parts of our game suffered, and you can't win in this league without balance."

In fact, Taylor departed as Cal's all-time leader in passing yardage with 8,126, a record that survived into the twenty-first century. Pawlawski was a quarterback in the rough-hewn mold of Kapp in the 1950s. Not for him the gingerly two-step out of bounds when threatened by behemoths. Mostly idle during his time as Taylor's sub, he'd volunteered for service on the kick-return teams, heedlessly charging downfield in the suicidal manner of such players. But, like Taylor, he could both throw the ball and, when necessary, run with it.

The Bears, however, were picked to finish near the bottom of the conference at the start of the new decade. They would play four teams ranked in the top twenty-five nationally in a schedule that *USA Today* called the second toughest in the country. But the Bears muddled through handsomely, finishing 7-4-1. It was a landmark season in several important respects. It was a winner, for starters. It also brought to a blessed close the UCLA hex and it would include Cal's first win in a post-season bowl game since January 1, 1938. And it would be an understatement to say the formerly anemic running game improved. Not only did these Bears have their first 1,000-yard runner since Muncie, they had two—Wallace with 1,002 and White with 1,000. Not even in the ground-gobbling days of Jensen and Swaner or of Olszewski, Monachino and Schabarum had the team ever produced two thousand-yard men.

White's debut was as spectacular as Snyder had hoped. In addition to the yardage amassed from scrimmage, he added 629 more on kick-off returns and 127 receiving for a total of 1,756 in the relatively new

— 438 —

"all-purpose yardage" statistical category. He scored 14 touchdowns, 11 rushing, two receiving and one on a serpentine 99-yard kickoff return the very first time he handled the ball in Memorial Stadium, in the season's second game, against Miami.

Pawlawski in what was basically his debut season completed nearly 60 percent of his 299 passes for 2,069 yards and 17 touchdowns. Treggs caught a team-leading 45 for 564 yards and six scores.

But the Bears didn't exactly roll unimpeded over the opposition. After an opening 28–12 win over Wisconsin, they lost to defending national champion Miami by the considerable score of 52–24, and to Washington State by 41–31. They then won four in a row, none by more than seven points, one by one (35–34 over San Jose) and another by five (30–25 over Arizona). Against San Jose state, White gained 162 yards and Wallace 143.

The big event in this series of squeakers was the 38–31 win over UCLA at Memorial Stadium that at long last ended the younger sibling's mortifying eighteen-year win streak. In a departure from the norm, the Cal team entered the field not from the stadium's north tunnel as usual but from out of the rooting section, rousing the partisan crowd of fifty thousand to an early burst of anticipation. And with the new running game in high gear, the Bears took a 17–0 lead in the first quarter and increased it to 27–10 at the half. The Bruins, behind the passing of Tommy Maddox, rallied in the second half, but they were too late. Wallace gained 134 yards on 28 carries, White 125 on 25.

The banishment of Bruin hoo-doo may have taken too much out of the Bears, though, and they were drubbed, 46–7, by seventh-ranked Washington in Seattle. But they had tied 21st-ranked USC in Los Angeles, 31–31, and after downing Oregon, 28–3, they accepted an invitation to play in the Copper Bowl, their first bowl bid in eleven years.

Ah yes, but they still had to play the then 4-6 Cardinal in the Big Game. And in what would become known in Peninsula precincts as the "Revenge-for-The Play" game, they were victimized by a bewildering succession of last-second catastrophes. Trailing 25–18, Stanford scored with just twelve seconds remaining on a 19-yard pass from Palumbis to future NFL star receiver Ed McCaffrey, who made a fine catch in the corner of the end zone. With victory in sight, the Cardinal went for the two-point conversion. But Palumbis' pass was intercepted by Cal's John Hardy, preserving what now appeared to be the home team's insurmountable 25–24 lead. Cal players and fans, relieved of the terrible tension McCaffrey's catch had initiated, stormed onto the playing field in a celebration reminiscent of Stanford's pre-Play party eight years earlier.

The Bears were duly penalized 15 yards on the kickoff. And the Cardinal recovered the ensuing onside kick on the Cal 37, too close for comfort although just outside normal field goal range. There were nine seconds left. On the next play Palumbis's pass fell incomplete, and the Cal celebration began anew. But Bear noseguard John Belli was called for roughing the passer, placing the ball on the Bear 22. There were five seconds left. The packed stadium was as silent as a study hall. Cardinal coach Denny Green summoned kicker Hopkins. And with no time showing on the clock, his 39-yard try was good. Final score: Stanford, 27, Cal, 25.

The last-second loss ruined another big day for White, who gained 177 yards on 18 carries. He was no match, however, for the Cardinal's Glyn Milburn, who set a Pac-10 record with 379 all-purpose yards, 196 of them rushing.

The Copper Bowl was played in Tucson on December 31, 1990—and not without controversy. Protesters, curiously absent from Cal affairs in these years, began demonstrating on campus as soon as the Bowl invitation was issued, arguing that since Arizona voters had rejected accepting Martin Luther King's birthday as a holiday, the university should not send a team to such a racist state. The players themselves met to discuss the issue and finally voted to go. As their own form of silent protest, they wore "MLK" emblems on their uniform sleeves.

Snyder himself wore one on his game jacket.

It had been a season clouded over by tragic circumstances around the campus. The day of the opening game at Wisconsin, a fire destroyed the Phi Kappa Sigma fraternity house on Warring Street barely a block from Memorial Stadium, causing three deaths. There had been a bomb scare on campus the week of the Washington State game. And two days before the Arizona game, a crazed gunman held some forty customers at Henry's Publick House on Durant Avenue hostage for seven hours, killing one, before he was shot dead by police.

The protested Copper Bowl game against Wyoming scarcely matched these sad events for drama. In fact, it was mostly a dull affair, Cal carrying a seemingly safe, 17–3 lead well into the fourth quarter before the Cowboys scored twice in the last six minutes. Failed two-point conversion attempts after both touchdowns left the final score a deceptively close 17–15. Pawlawski, who completed 15 of 26 passes for 172 yards and a touchdown, was selected the game's Most Valuable Player.

It had been, to put it mildly, a tough year, but Snyder was by now convinced that his players, once so wary of the unforeseen, were now confident, if not outright cocky about winning. As the next traumatic season would show, he was absolutely right about that.

## CHAPTER THIRTY-THREE

# THE FOREST AND THE TREES

Snyder began what would become his crowning season with two new bosses. Maggard, who had hired him, departed in the winter to become the new Athletic Director at the University of Miami. Before he left, though, he had offered his coach a new long-term agreement, with the approval of new Chancellor Chang-Lin Tien. It was, Snyder recalled, a "handshake agreement," between friends, the details to be worked out by Maggard's as yet unnamed successor. "Dave wanted to see me secure in the job before he left." Snyder's already extended contract ran through the 1993 season. The new one, when written and signed, would presumably give the coach another five years at Cal.

And in Tien, who became chancellor in July of 1990, Snyder knew he had an unusually committed football fan. Born in China, the chancellor had graduate degrees from the University of Louisville and Princeton. He began teaching in the engineering department at Cal in 1959 and after chairing several departments, had become a vice chancellor under Heyman. He then served for two years in the late 1980s as executive vice chancellor at U.C. Irvine before returning to Berkeley in the head job. As gregarious as Heyman was reserved, Tien enjoyed strolling the campus and chatting with students for at least an hour each day, somewhat in emulation, save for the horse, of Benjamin Ide Wheeler. He was a visible presence at home football games, pacing the sidelines, leading the occasional cheer and sometimes situating himself behind the goal posts to signal Cal touchdowns and field goals.

The new athletic director he hired, Robert L. "Bob" Bockrath, was described accurately enough as favoring "substance over style." And certainly business over pleasure. He had come to Cal after eleven years in athletic administration at the University of Arizona, the last three as associate director of athletics under A.D. Cedric Dempsey. The Cal job, for which he was hired in August of 1991, was his first as an A.D. At Cal he would assume the additional responsibility of merging the previously separate men's and women's departments. Bockrath was known as an effective fund-raiser as well as a boss dear with a dollar. He and Snyder were not destined to become bosom buddies.

It was an eventful year away from the gridiron. The Soviet Union had disintegrated into a collection of individual states, thus bringing to a close—at least for the moment—the forty-five-year-old Cold War. The U.S.-led Persian Gulf War had expelled Iraqi dictator Sadam Hussein's invading army from neighboring Kuwait. And on the Berkeley front, the war over People's Park erupted once more after a tenuous twenty-two-year cease fire.

In May of 1991, the university, anxious to rid itself of that burdensome acreage, agreed to lease the park to the city of Berkeley for one dollar a year. But first, the administration intended to erect some volleyball courts there. Noble gesture, bad move. When the bulldozers arrived under police escort on the morning of July 31, protesters armed with rotten apricot missiles opened fire on workmen and police alike. Within two hours, thirty-six of the fruit-flingers were arrested. Nine more were jailed that night as, shades of the 1960s, crowds demonstrated along Telegraph Avenue, shattering store windows and creating general havoc. The resumption of Park hostilities lasted six days and resulted in eighty-three arrests. But this time the political ideology that sustained the original war was absent, even the most radical of latter-day students finding it difficult to rise in defense of turf now occupied primarily by homeless drifters, dopers and drug dealers. So no ringing oratory accompanied this particular conflict.

By the following spring, the university succeeded in installing rest rooms and basketball courts on the leased property, wisely hiring many Park-dwellers to do the labor. Like the Cold War, the People's Park War, which seemed to last almost as long, had reached—for the moment—a peaceful resolution.

So, on to football. The '91 Cal football team would reach heights previously achieved only by Wonder Teamers and Pappy's Boys. Snyder had assembled an all-star cast which featured Pawlawski's passing, White's broken-field running, Doug Brien's kicking, the receiving of Treggs and Dawkins and the blocking of an offensive line powered by the 6-7, 285-pound Troy Auzenne and the 6-6, 290-pound Todd Steussie. Add to this a tenacious defense sparked by a precocious freshman linebacker, Jerott Willard, and the Bears had the makings of a winner.

In fact, they won their first five games, the first time that had happened since 1952. In the opener, an 86–24 mismatch with UOP, six of Pawlawski's 11 pass completions went for a Cal record six touchdowns. After a 42–18 pummeling of Purdue in the second game, they eked out a 23–21 win over Arizona on a Brien field goal with no time remaining. White, though battling an upper respiratory infection finally diagnosed as "walking pneumonia," gained 150 yards on 35 carries and sophomore Lindsey Chapman had 108 on 17. It was Cal's fourth straight win over Arizona, all by five points or fewer.

The Bears had another close call before beating the once unbeatable UCLA Bruins, 27–24, thanks to another last-second Brien field goal, this one a heroic 47-yarder. Though the still-ailing White missed most of the second quarter, he gained 121 yards on 25 carries, six of those carries in a row on the final scoring drive. After a relatively comfortable 45–7 win over Oregon, the then seventh-ranked Bears took on third-ranked Washington before seventy-four thousand five hundred at Memorial Stadium on the sunny afternoon of October 19.

The two unbeaten teams traded long scoring plays from the beginning of this thriller. Cal scored first on a 59-yard pass from Pawlawski to Dawkins, but the Huskies came right back with a 35-yard touchdown pass from Billy Joe Hobert to Mario Bailey. In the third quarter, with Washington leading, 17–10, Chapman, on a draw play against a Husky blitz, sped 68 yards to tie the score. Three plays later, Washington recaptured the lead on a 64-yard run by Beno Bryant. The game came down to the final eight seconds when, with the ball on the Washington 23, Pawlawski tried to hit Treggs on the goal line. But the pass was batted away at the last second by the Huskies' Walter Bailey. Despite the disappointing 24–17 loss, the Cal players were accorded a prolonged standing ovation by the huge crowd as they left the field. Football was back in Berkeley.

The next day, a massive brush fire broke out in the nearby Oakland hills and, propelled by unusually strong winds, cut a two-mile swath through expensive neighborhoods there. Towering pillars of black smoke were visible throughout the Bay Area. When the flames were finally doused, twenty-five people had lost their lives, and damage estimates ranged as high as $1.5 billion. Among those who lost homes in the conflagration were seventy U.C. faculty members and sixty-two administrative employees. Some three hundred sixty students residing in the vicinity were displaced. Cal had lost more than a football game.

The team at least recovered, winning its next four, including a 52–30 thrashing of USC before another seventy thousand-plus crowd at the stadium. The points were the most yet scored against the Trojans and White's 229 yards rushing were then the most ever gained on them. White scored three touchdowns, one on a 72-yard dazzler, and Dawkins caught all three of Pawlawski's touchdown passes.

After that signal victory, the Bears scored relatively lackluster wins over Oregon State (27–14) and Arizona (25–6) before a Big Game showdown with the 7–3 Cardinal. There they played a stinker, allowing Stanford three touchdowns in the last twelve minutes and being assessed 11 penalties, five of them for personal fouls. The 38–21 loss was attributable to a series of botched opportunities, many of them because of the penalties. A taunting penalty against the Cal bench after a Stanford incompletion kept one Cardinal scoring drive intact. And there were other mistakes. The impeccable Brien, then the nation's leading field goal kicker, missed all three of his ordinarily makeable attempts. And the defense could not contain the Cardinal's "Touchdown Tommy" Vardell, who gained 182 yards and scored three times. The Bears had few shining moments in this ragged Big Game. Pawlawski completed 21 of 35 for 312 yards and all three of his team's touchdowns. Dawkins had two TD catches among his six for 139 yards.

The otherwise sterling 9-2 record earned the Bears an invitation to play 13th-ranked Clemson in the Citrus Bowl at Orlando, Florida. It was Snyder's second straight bowl bid and second straight winning season. He had converted a perennial loser into a consistent winner within five years, an achievement scarcely overlooked by other schools in search of coaching talent. Strangely enough, Snyder had not reached an agreement with Bockrath on a new contract, the signing of which had previously been considered a mere formality. The stumbling block, said Snyder, was the athletic director's insistence on what Snyder called a "penalty" clause but was more genuinely known as a "buyout" provision requiring anyone hiring the coach before his contract expired to pay Cal a substantial sum in return.

Snyder said that in his discussions with Bockrath he had emphasized that in the "handshake agreement" with Maggard no such buyout was included. "I felt it was improper to add one," Snyder recalled years later. "I told Bockrath that, but he was insistent. 'That's the way I do business,' he told me. Now, I wanted to stay at Cal, but this was something new, something added to the original agreement. After all, I'd taken something of a career gamble just coming to Berkeley."

In the weeks before the January 1 Citrus Bowl, rumors of Snyder's departure for supposedly greener fields were widely circulated. One had him rejoining Maggard in Miami if Hurricanes coach Dennis Erickson should take a job, as also rumored, in the NFL (that didn't happen until four years later). But the most substantial of these rumors involved Arizona State, which had just fired head coach Larry Marmie and was anxious to get its once successful program back on track. The school was prepared, sources said, to put together a pay package that, with peripheral income, amounted to $500,000 or more, at least twice what Snyder was earning at Cal.

The coach steadfastly refused to discuss such speculation, saying that his focus in these weeks was wholly on finding ways to beat Clemson. When it was suggested he might use the supposed Arizona State offer as a bargaining tool in his negotiations with Bockrath, Snyder replied, "I'm not interested in holding a gun to anyone's head. And I don't want this nine-win season to be an aberration at Cal."

But as *Chronicle* college football reporter Jake Curtis wrote, "Bockrath brings his own agenda to the contract talks." And when it came to money, Bockrath was quoted as saying that any new contract would pay Snyder "slightly more, but not substantially more" than he was already making. And that new contract would not only have a buyout clause but a provision forbidding the coach to take a job elsewhere in the Pac-10. Furthermore, he added, Cal would not engage in a bidding war with Arizona State, should it come to that. The distance separating the experienced coach from an athletic director four months into his job was by then galactic.

And there was still a game to play. Despite all the distractions, the Bears played it superbly, soundly beating the Atlantic Coast Conference champions, 37–13. They built an overwhelming 12–0 lead in the first quarter and fairly coasted home. Clemson had not allowed any runner to gain 100 yards against its defense in three seasons; White ran for 103 on 22 carries. Brien kicked three field goals, Pawlawski completed 21 of 32 for 230 yards and Treggs returned a punt 72 yards for a touchdown. The Bears also pulled off a flea-flicker pass play and a fumblerooski in which guard Eric Mahlum gained 16 yards to set up Brien's last field goal.

An exuberant Snyder led the Cal Band afterward in the playing of the "Big C"—"We are sons of California/Fighting for the Gold and Blue..." The Bears were ranked eighth in the final Associated Press national poll and seventh in the coaches' poll conducted by *USA Today* and CNN. These were the highest season-ending positions any Cal team had reached in forty years. And not since 1949 had the Bears won ten games in a season. In his five years, Snyder had achieved the best winning percentage—.544—of any Bear coach since Waldorf. And yet his time was at an end.

Pawlawski, having played his last game for Cal, joined his coach for a beer in an airport bar before the flight home from the Citrus Bowl. "Bruce was on top. I think at that point everybody loved him. Even the alumni. His consistency, his focus on the job at hand, were by now legendary. And we were drawing sixty thousand on Saturdays." But Pawlawski sensed a certain pensiveness, even melancholy, in his coach's ordinarily upbeat demeanor.

On the plane ride back to Berkeley from Orlando, Snyder said he told Bockrath he'd received a phone call after the game from Arizona State representatives. Their offer was firm, and they needed an answer. He told the A.D. he wanted to stay at Cal if the two of them could iron out their differences on a new contract. "But," he recalled, "Bockrath never budged from his position on the buyout clause."

Bockrath's recollection some years later of these events is somewhat at odds with the coach's. "Yes," he acknowledged, "I did feel strongly about the buyout. It represents a commitment on both sides. All contracts have that in there now. And the cost of the buyout was hardly insurmountable, hinged as it was to Bruce's salary. As to the prior agreement with Dave Maggard, I pointed out to him that he was no longer working for Dave Maggard. Anyway, as I recall, money was the issue. At the time it was said that Terry Donahue (the football coach at UCLA) was the state of California's highest paid employee. There was admittedly a disparity between what he was making and Bruce's salary at Cal. Using that as a measurement, Dan Boggin (Cal's vice chancellor for business) and I worked hard to develop a formula that would reduce that disparity. We didn't know then what the Arizona State offer was because Bruce didn't talk about it. He consistently told me he'd had no contact with Arizona State until just after the Citrus Bowl. We were committed to do what we could at Cal in terms of a pay raise. Apparently, it was not good enough."

And yet the Cal A.D. could not have been entirely unaware of reports in both Bay Area and Arizona media of the supposedly lucrative offer.

Before the week was out, Bruce Snyder became the new head football coach at Arizona State.

"Everyone on the team was shocked that Bockrath hadn't found a way to keep him," said Pawlawski sixteen years later. "We all understood why Bruce was leaving. Not one guy faulted him. Bockrath was an egomaniac, a head-roller. He just wanted his own people. The man was clearly a bad athletic director. And on top of that, he was an arrogant jerk. I had no use for him."

The press reaction to Snyder's defection suggested, as Bockrath had, that the coach only had dollar signs in his eyes. C.W. Nevius, writing in the *Chronicle*, viewed the episode as just another sign of the greedy times.

"Remember the days when the football coach was a fixture on the campus? When he was offered another job, he'd laugh. He'd have to change all his ties—they were all in the school colors…Isn't loyalty to the old school worth anything any more? Sure, it's worth about half-a-million bucks. Let's put it this way. Suppose someone came to you and said the following: 'You're terrific, do you know that? We love the way you do your job. In fact, why don't you come to our company, do the same job, and we'll double your salary? Not only that, we're going to give you better facilities and a nicer office. We're just going to make it easier in every way for you to do your job, and we're going to pay you more for it.' What's your answer?...The days of settling into a job and becoming a part of the university are gone."

Bockrath acknowledged that coaching at Cal was not then the easiest job in sports and that life in the desert had, as it still had for him, its attractions. "Cal at the time had minimal facilities," he recalled. "The stadium needed work. Because of the academic standards, it was hard to recruit. It's an expensive place to live. And over there at Stanford, Bill Walsh was back." Bockrath himself moved back to Arizona years later.

Snyder regretted for years afterward that he had been portrayed so often as a "money-grubber...The money was better, yes, but that hadn't been the biggest issue." Details of the Arizona State contract, as reported in the *Chronicle*, revealed in fact that the coach's guaranteed income actually amounted to $315,000, not $500,000. Only if he fulfilled certain incentives—bowl invitations, top ten ranking, increased season ticket sales—would his package exceed $400,000.

Snyder's former quarterback, Troy Taylor, was among those who bemoaned his departure. "Bruce had things really rolling at Cal. When you win, recruits are there for you. It's not easy getting to that point, but he got there. The program was definitely set back when he left. I think Bockrath was someone who couldn't see the forest for the trees."

Bockrath would agree with the part about Snyder raising Cal's football image. As he told the *Chronicle* at the time, "Bruce has brought us to a level where we can be attractive to a lot of coaches."

Well, that certainly was one way of looking at it.

# CHAPTER THIRTY-FOUR

# GILBY

Bockrath found his man soon enough. In the process, thirty-six-year-old Steve Mariucci, Snyder's offensive coordinator and a strong favorite among the players, was passed over, some said almost cavalierly. Pawlawski recalled making an impassioned plea on his behalf that was apparently ignored. Taylor also expressed support for Mariucci to no avail. "There are a lot of good coaches," he said, "but not that many who are both good coaches and really good people. Steve Mariucci was one of them. I was told that Bockrath advised him right off that he wouldn't be the new coach at Cal."

Bockrath insists the decision was not his alone. "At Cal you had to work with a search committee, and the members preferred someone with head coaching experience." Mariucci took a job instead as quarterback coach of the Green Bay Packers where he was instrumental in developing a young and inexperienced signal caller named Brett Favre.

Bockrath's choice—and presumably the search committee's—to lead the Bears in 1992 was Keith Gilbertson, a former head coach at Idaho in the late 1980s and for the previous three years an assistant and, in 1991, the offensive coordinator of the undefeated Rose Bowl champion Washington Huskies. Called "Gilby" by friends, colleagues and even casual acquaintances, Gilbertson was raised in Snohomish, Washington, where his father had been a high school coach. And except for a short stay as a student at the University of Hawaii and two seasons as an assistant with the Los Angeles Express of the short-lived United States Football League, he had spent most of his 44 years in the Pacific Northwest. As a head coach at Idaho from 1986 through '88, he had built a 28-9 record, his last team finishing 11-2.

Whereas Snyder had been intense and seldom off-message, Gilbertson had a folksy and droll manner. As the 1992 Cal media guide observed, "When most programs around the country reflect the fact that college football has become big business and in the vanguard of the computer age, 'Gilby' is a people person." After first extolling Gilby's coaching acumen, his childhood friend and former boss at Idaho, Dennis Erickson, said of him, "He's got a great sense of humor, he works very hard at what he does, and he's an awful lot of fun to be around."

But that first season at Cal, a 4-7 loser, wasn't much fun for him, supplying as it did critical fodder for Snyder loyalists and ex-players, Pawlawski and Taylor prominently among them, who considered amusing fellows like Gilby career assistant coaches. Indeed, if Andy Smith had his Wonder Teams and Stub Allison his Thunder Teams, Gilby seemed stuck with what, with one notable exception, might be called "Blunder Teams."

The '92 Bears were guilty of 34 turnovers—18 interceptions and 16 lost fumbles, five of which came on kick returns. In fact, there was nothing at all special about Gilby's special teams that inaugural season. Although punter Chris Noonan averaged an impressive 42.6 yards per punt, the Bears were dead last in the Pac-10 in net punting because too many of those kicks were returned vast distances, two for touchdowns.

Most inconveniently, in a 35–16 loss to Gilby's old team, the Huskies, the Bears had five turnovers and allowed five quarterback sacks. They had a 3-1 winning record before that giveaway game, but they lost three straight afterward, all to ranked teams. They would beat UCLA convincingly, 48–12, then lose their final three, including a 42–21 pasting from Stanford, coached once more by Walsh after a fourteen-year absence doing something or other.

After a ten-win season the year before he arrived, Gilby's Cal debut could not have been more humiliating, particularly since so many of the same players were still on hand. He did have some injuries to key players, though. Star defenders Mack Travis and Mike Barsala missed six games between them and White was disabled with a groin pull in the 27–24 loss to USC and played sparingly the next week in a 24–17 loss to Arizona. Still, he gained more than a thousand yards (1,069) for the third consecutive season and finished his Cal career with a new school record 3,367 yards. But he was merely second-team All Pac-10 along with kicker Brien and linebacker Willard. Cal's first-teamers were Dawkins (also an All-American), who caught 65 passes for 1,070 yards and 14 touchdowns; defensive end Chidi Ahanotu and Steussie, then a 305-pound terror at offensive tackle. Dawkins, who thereupon entered the NFL draft, eschewing his senior season, was a first-round pick of the Indianapolis Colts, along with Ahanotu by Tampa Bay.

White, whose career seemed mysteriously to decline after his first burst of fame, was a third-round pick of the Rams. He played just one year with them.

Gilby still had on his roster the ingredients for improvement in '93. Dave Barr's 2,343 passing yards and 19 touchdown passes in '92—on 199 completions in 344 attempts—were the most ever by a Cal sophomore. Chapman and Reynard Rutherford, a freshman in '92, both had their moments subbing for White. There were dependable receivers in Caldwell, Damien Semien and a Nigerian-born sophomore with, as the media guide slyly observed, "a name worth remembering"—Iheanyi Uwaezuoke. Brien, who succeeded on 16 of 18 field goal attempts and didn't miss an extra point try, had joined a long line of Cal kicking stars. The offensive line, with Steussie and Mahlum at its core, was solid. And the defense, with the hyperactive Willard at its middle, looked much better after a season in which it gave up exactly as many points—284—as the offense scored.

The 1993 results, considering the backward strides of the previous season, were gratifying, even astonishing. The Bears won their first five and, after a 42–41 squeaker against Oregon in the last of these, were ranked 15th in the national polls. The Oregon win was a certified confidence-booster, since Gilby's stalwarts were down 30–0 in the second quarter. But in the first play from scrimmage of the second half, Chapman took a lateral pass from Barr in the far flat and raced 61 yards to a revivifying touchdown. From then on, it was pretty much all Bears, Barr passing for three scores, including a 72-yard gem to Semien. The winning points came with 1:17 to play when Barr, who completed 21 of 31 for 368 yards that day, passed 26 yards to Uwaezuoke for the touchdown that brought the Bears within a point, 41–40, of the Ducks. Gilby, bless him, went for the win, and he got it on a Barr-Caldwell two-point conversion.

The winning streak included another close one, 27–25, over UCLA, the fourth straight over the Bruins after nearly two decades of despair, and a 45–25 romp over San Diego State. In the San Diego game the Cal defense held Aztec star Marshall Faulk to a measly 64 yards on 22 carries, the least yardage he had gained when given the ball 20 times or more that season. There were also high-scoring wins over San Jose State (46–13) and Temple (58–0), a game played before a sparse 12,138 spectators in Philadelphia's 62,418-seat Veterans Stadium.

After this surge there followed four straight losses, all to conference foes. The decline began with a 24–23 heartbreaker against Washington, just a week after the happier one-point finish with Oregon. In this one, the Bears led by 20 points as late as midway into the third quarter. And this time, it was the foe who scored the winning touchdown in the final minute—on a seven-yard Damon Huard to Mark Bruener pass.

The other losses were more decisive: 34–7 to Washington State,

42–14 to USC and, oh woe, 41–0 to Snyder's Arizona State, Gilby's second straight to his deified predecessor. But his team rallied to win its last four games, a skein that included a 46–17 defeat of Walsh's suddenly ineffective Stanfordites and a 42–18 lark over Hawaii. The win in Honolulu earned the Bears an invitation to play Iowa on December 31 in the Alamo Bowl at San Antonio. And they responded with a 37–3 vengeful stomping of Cal's old Rose Bowl nemesis. Barr, who completed 21 of 28 for 266 yards, was the Bowl's offensive MVP and Willard, who made four tackles behind the line and returned an interception 61 yards for a touchdown, was the defensive MVP. Brien's three field goals added to his new Cal record of 56.

"I still think we were the best team in the conference in '93," said Gilbertson sixteen years later. "But we lost some really good players to injuries in the middle of the season." True enough. Barr strained his shoulder in the loss to Washington, missed the Washington State game the next week and played hurt through much of the rest of the season. Injuries also slowed Chapman for several weeks and felled star safety Eric Zomalt during that mid-season slump. When the Bears were healthy, they were unbeatable. And charming Gilby was a great coach.

There were other splendid performances in this protracted thirteen-game season, the longest since Jimmie Schaeffer's 1915 team brought football back at Cal. Barr tied Pawlawski's record of 21 touchdown passes, and three receivers—Caldwell (55 for 962 yards), Semien (32-515) and Uwaezuoke (25-422)—averaged better than 16 yards per catch. Chapman gained 1,037 yards on 207 carries and scored 17 touchdowns, 14 rushing, three receiving.

That very December, in a delicious piece of irony enjoyed by unreformed Snyderites, Bockrath resigned after just two years at Cal to become the Athletic Director at Texas Tech University. His reason for passing up the rich cultural life of Berkeley for Lubbock, Texas: Money. "It was a financial issue," Bockrath recalled years later. "I was offered a big raise. I have the greatest memories of the Cal lifestyle. It's a unique place. But I couldn't afford it."

"He came to Cal," said Taylor, "created as much damage as he could, and then he left."

The university wasted little time finding a replacement, hiring, still in December of 1993, John Kasser, who had been the A.D. at U.C. Santa Barbara for three years. He was an executive with considerable experience in the business world outside college athletics, principally in the auto industry. A basketball and baseball letterman as an undergraduate at Pepperdine, Kasser cut an imposing figure, tall, good-looking and silver-haired. And he had a salesman's gift of gab. In his first few months on the job, the new A.D., then fifty-five, averaged at least three speaking engagements per week, and he was readily accessible to the media. While at Santa Barbara, he organized fund-raising campaigns that financed much improved athletic facilities on campus, a talent much in demand in Berkeley at a time when the university was contemplating extensive additions to and reconstruction of its own antiquated facilities. The septuagenarian Memorial Stadium, once considered an architectural wonder, was by then crumbling into a state of ruin approaching that of the very building after which it was modeled—the Roman Colosseum. The quake of 1989, though on a different fault line from the stadium's, had also raised new concern about its capacity to survive the apocalyptic "Big One" regularly forecast by seismologists.

As it developed, Bockrath's timing in leaving was much better than Kasser's in arriving, since Gilby's 1994 team reverted to the losing ways of his first season, finishing with the same 4-7 record.

"Our '93 team was senior-dominated," recalled Gilby. "We lost that in '94. But that's the way it goes." In fact, the coach lost many of his finest players that year, including Chapman, Caldwell, Steussie, Semien, Mahlum and Zomalt. As a result….deja vu. Once again, the few wins and many losses came in streaks, beginning with opening upsets by two supposedly inferior Western Athletic Conference opponents, San Diego State (23–21) and Hawaii (21–7). The Hawaii defeat was sadly emblematic of the entire season. Two of the Rainbows' scores came as a result of blocked punts, and the Bears effectively stopped their own progress dead by accumulating seven penalties for 84 yards lost.

Among the six turnovers in a late season 31–19 loss to Washington were two—returns of 79 yards of an interception and 38 of a fumble recovery—that went for touchdowns. In a 26–23 loss to Washington State, the Bears lost five of six fumbles and had a blocked conversion kick returned 75 yards for two Cougar points.

Then there was the 61–0 loss to USC. On the opening kickoff Longwell slipped as he kicked, nudging the ball all of 16 yards. The Trojans scored shortly afterward. Still in the first quarter, a Longwell field goal attempt was blocked and returned 60 yards for another touchdown. In the second quarter, Longwell had another field goal try blocked and a punt returned 75 yards to the Cal five, leading, it goes without saying, to a Trojan touchdown. This was no game in which to kick and wait for the breaks, since the breaks were all bad.

All told, the Bears committed 29 turnovers in '94, prompting Gilby to conclude, "We have to stop giving the ball to other teams." To add to the coach's miseries that forgettable season, his starting quarterback, Barr, was lost for the rest of the year in the fifth game with a broken collarbone, and second-stringer Kerry McGonical went down with a separated shoulder against Washington State in the eighth game. And since third-stringer Pat Barnes was unable to play in the Cougar game because of a nerve injury to his non-throwing shoulder, fourth-stringer Ziv Gottlieb, who had been a wide receiver until five days earlier, became the quarterback. And straight from the pages of an old movie script, he sparked a drive in the third quarter that led to a miraculously non-blocked Longwell field goal, giving the Bears a momentary 23–15 lead. But the Cougars scored a touchdown, a two-point conversion and a field goal in the final quarter, to hand the Bears the third of five straight losses, 26–23.

In the fourth of the filthy five, against Arizona, sophomore Barnes made the first start of his college career. And he showed the talent expected of him, completing 16 of 27 passes for 197 yards. His 50-yard completion in the second quarter to fellow soph Na'il Benjamin was the Bears' longest of the season, and it propelled a drive that carried from the Cal ten to the Arizona two. On third down from there, Gilby chose to bamboozle the Wildcats with a trick play. Barnes handed off to tailback Tyrone Edwards and then drifted unobserved into the end zone where Edwards, instead of bucking the line, was to throw him a touchdown pass. But Edwards was hit as he released the ball and his fluttering delivery was picked off by the Wildcats' Mike Shurlock and returned 97 yards for the winning touchdown in a 13–6 game. The turnover ruined the Bears' chance for an upset over a team favored to beat them by 18 points. And it obscured some fine individual performances. Longwell kicked field goals of 39 and 42 yards for Cal's only scores and averaged 48.8 yards on six punts. Willard had ten unassisted tackles, and the Cal defense sacked Arizona quarterback Danny White four times.

Barnes, meanwhile, had established himself as the quarterback of the immediate future. Against Washington, he completed 33 of 44 for 389 yards and the first two touchdowns of his Cal career. He threw for another TD in the season-ending, 24–23 win over Walsh's last and worst (3-7-1) team at Stanford. It was also the last game played on Memorial Stadium's execrable artificial turf. Mother Nature's good green grass would be planted there for the '95 season at a cost of $1.5 million.

The Big Game was the sort of messy affair one might expect of two teams with three wins apiece. For once, the Bears were outfumbled, eight to three, but Stanford only lost two of them, the same as the home team. Barnes had an interception returned 69 yards for a touchdown, and the Cardinal's Scott Frost had one picked by Cal's Matt Clizbe less than a minute into the game that set up a nifty 41-yard touchdown run by Tyrone Edwards on the very next play. The score was tied, 17–17, at the half. Then, after a scoreless third quarter, the Bears moved 92 yards early in the fourth, Edwards scoring again, this time from the eight.

But with less than four minutes to play, Stanford recovered a fumble (naturally) on Cal's 22 and scored on a pass from Frost to Justin Armour. Walsh decided to try for two, but Frost's pass was knocked down by the omnipresent Clizbe. The Cardinal would have one last chance with forty-nine seconds left, but it was thwarted when Cal safety Dante DePaola intercepted Frost at the Stanford 41.

Edwards, a onetime defensive back, closed out his Cal playing days with the game of his life, gaining 205 yards on 24 carries and scoring twice. Rutherford added 96 yards on 18 carries as the Bears cut their rug for 270 yards rushing, minus sacks. Neither quarterback had a great day. Barnes was 13 of 21 for 127 yards and Frost 11 of 29 for 148. Despite the loss, Walsh finished his bifurcated career on the Farm with a positive 34-24-1 record.

The next season would be Gilby's last. He entered it cautiously optimistic, citing the advantages of six home games on the new grass, the return of fifteen starters, among them defensive All America candidates Regan Upshaw and Duane Clemons. He would have a more experienced Barnes back at quarterback as well as receivers Benjamin and Uwaezuoke, who combined for 101 catches in '94.

"We have the best balance of returning starters on both sides of the football since I've been here," the coach exulted. "However, we have to prove what we're all about on the field."

Ay, there's the rub.

The '95 Bears were unable to win as many as two games in a row, their three wins that season isolated among a series of baleful losing streaks. Once again, they dropped their first two to lesser known teams. And with the usual want of dexterity. In a 33–9 loss at San Diego State in the opener, a blocked punt and two interceptions either led to Aztec scores or terminated Cal drives. Then, against Fresno State, the Bears fumbled five times in a 25–24 defeat. They actually led, 24–12, early in the fourth quarter, one touchdown coming spectacularly on an 84-yard screen pass from Barnes to Benjamin. But the Bulldogs scored twice in the last eleven minutes to squeeze out a win. It was Gilby's fourth straight loss to WAC teams.

There followed a comforting 40–7 win over San Jose State, Barnes connecting on 16 of 20 for 305 yards and three touchdowns. Sophomore wide receiver Bobby Shaw caught three for 134 yards and soph tight end Tony Gonzalez caught five for 72. Both were on the threshold of stardom.

In a philanthropic loss to Arizona, Gilby's Bears gave away 14 points in as many seconds. After the Wildcats scored their first touchdown following an 80-yard drive seven seconds into the second quarter, their try for the extra point was blocked. But on the ensuing kickoff, Cal's Jason Sharp fumbled and Arizona recovered on the Bear 13. The Wildcats scored on the next play. Again, their try for the extra point was blocked. No matter. On this kickoff, the Bears' Je'Rod Cherry committed the classic gaffe of first stepping out of the end zone under the misapprehension that he was still in it and then stepping back in to touch the ball down. Safety! Arizona led, 14–3, on the way to a 20–15 triumph. The Bears did have one bright moment, though, when, after a third Wildcat blocked conversion try, Marquis Smith recovered the ball and ran 100 yards for two points, admittedly a long way to travel for such a modest reward.

The Bears lost the next two, to USC by only 26–16, a vast improvement over the year before, and to Oregon by a degrading 52–30, a game in which they netted minus-one-yard rushing. They did beat Oregon State, a one-game winner in '95, but only by 13–12. And they were lucky to get that winning point. Barnes scored the tying touchdown with 6:40 left at the end of a 74-yard drive in seven plays. Unfortunately, in his exuberance, his end zone celebration drew the ire of the officials. His team was penalized 15 yards for unsportsmanlike conduct, to be assessed on the conversion try, and he was ejected for taunting. Instead of the usual "gimme" point-after, Longwell, with the game on the line, was obliged to try a 36-yard kick. It was good. The defensive star of this defensive struggle was Clemons, who had been transferred from defensive end to linebacker. It was a brilliant move. Against the Beavers, Clemons made nine tackles, caused two fumbles, knocked down two passes and blocked the conversion kick that, with Longwell's long PAT, gave Cal the win.

Then the Bears fell back into their old bumbling ways, surrendering four turnovers in a 33–16 loss to UCLA. The boo-boos ended Cal's four-game win streak over the Bruins and tainted a day in which Barnes passed for 343 yards, Uwaezuoke caught seven for 150 and Shaw eight for 100. They beat Washington State, 27–11, by scoring 24 points in the last quarter and then lost to Arizona State 38–29, raising Snyder's record over his old team to 3-1.

Stanford, under new coach Tyrone Willingham, finished off the Gilby Era with a 29–24 win. The two teams combined for 917 total yards, Barnes leading the way with 334 on 29-for-43 passing. Rutherford, playing his last game for Cal, gained 114 yards on 28 carries and 51 more on six receptions. But Stanford's two scores in the fourth quarter won the day.

The 3-8 record was the Bears' worst since Kapp's last season in 1986. There were some redeeming individual efforts, though. Barnes, playing his first full season, completed 197 of 362 passes for 2,685 yards and 17 touchdowns. Four Cal receivers—Benjamin, Shaw, Gonzalez and Uwaezuoke—caught 30 or more for at least 500 yards apiece. Rutherford led the rushers with 868 yards on 191 carries. Longwell hit on 12 of 17 field goal attempts, two of the misses being blocks, and on 21 of 23 extra points. Doing double duty again, he punted 67 times for a 40.4 average. Clemons and Upshaw won defensive All America honors. But the Bears lost 14 of 27 fumbles, many of them setting up enemy scores, and Barnes was intercepted 11 times. They gained only 1,236 net yards rushing, losing 255 on sacks.

Under Gilby, they had suffered three losing seasons out of four. It was time for A.D. Kasser to step away from the speaker's rostrum and go find a new coach. Fortunately, there was a familiar name handy.

## CHAPTER THIRTY-FIVE

# THE NADIR

On December 14, 1995, Kasser hired the "People's Choice" of four years before, Steve Mariucci, as Cal's new head coach. Mariucci returned with an even gaudier reputation as an offensive football mastermind after his interlude with the Green Bay Packers. The Pack was just 4-12 the season before the former Bear offensive coordinator arrived as the quarterback coach. His star pupil was Brett Favre, until then a highly touted but as yet unproven talent. Under Mariucci's tutelage, Favre led Green Bay to three straight playoff seasons, and in 1995 was named the league's Player of the Year. The future Hall of Famer was lavish in praise of his mentor:

"There's no doubt that the bulk of my success in the NFL has been due to Steve Mariucci. I wouldn't be where I am today without his coaching and just as importantly his friendship. He can do the X's and O's and knows the offense as well as anybody, but the thing that makes the biggest difference is his ability to motivate players and his personality."

Mariucci's Cal team in 1996 was hardly the ten-game winner he'd worked for in 1991, but it was not without some star power. Barnes, Benjamin, Shaw, Gonzalez and Longwell were still there. And in freshman Deltha O'Neal, he had a speedy back of such rare versatility he could play offense and defense and return kicks with undiminished flair. He also had an offensive line coached by Tom Cable that, averaging 303 pounds, was the heaviest yet in school history. The anchors of that pachydermic front five were the 6-6, 350-pound Tarik Glenn and the 6-5, 300-pound Jeremy Newberry, both considered top pro prospects. Gonzalez, also a starter on the basketball team, was, at 6-6 and 240, not exactly a shrimp at tight end.

At the tailback position the new coach had speed but slight experience with Tarik Smith (how many teams could boast then of two Tariks in the starting lineup?) and newcomer Brandon Willis. And Barnes not only had Shaw, Benjamin and Gonzalez to field his throws but a swift and sure-handed sophomore named Dameane Douglas. There was no question Mariucci had the tools for a high-scoring offense. The defense, on the other hand, was suspect, and its vulnerability, along with the customary assortment of injuries, would finally lead to this team's collapse.

Still, the Bears won their first five games, encouraging those who still insisted that the university had made a grievous error not hiring Mariucci when it first had the chance. Tailback Smith got off to a blistering start, rushing for 163 yards in an opening 45–25 win over San Jose State at Spartan Stadium and 174 in the home opener against San Diego State, a defense-free 42–37 affair. But after gaining 43 yards in little more than a quarter in a 33–15 win over Nevada, a knee injury ended for him what could have been a 1,000-yard season. Willis stepped into the breach, however, and strung together three straight 100-yard-plus games, one of them a historic-of-sorts 48–42 win over Oregon State. As the score would suggest, this win did not come readily. In fact the game was tied, 35–35, at the end of regulation play. But under a new rule introduced that year, teams could avoid a deadlock by playing overtime periods during which each team was allowed an offensive series beginning on the 25-yard line.

This was the Bears' first overtime game ever, and they made the most of it, continuing on for three extra periods until Barnes finally brought things to a merciful conclusion with a three-yard run that followed a blocked Beaver field goal try. The length of the game produced some inflated statistics. Barnes, for example, completed 20 of 27 passes for 323 yards, four touchdowns and four interceptions. Willis rushed for 129 yards on 37 carries. The teams gained a combined 912 yards and scored 90 points.

It was downhill for the Bears after that uphill victory, though.

Mariucci's undefeated season ended with a 21–18 loss to Washington State in Pullman, a desultory affair in which the Bears gained just 44 yards rushing, Willis gaining 26 of them. Barnes compensated by attempting 52 passes, 33 of which were completed for 371 yards. There were no interceptions despite the prolificacy, and just one touchdown, a 23-yard strike to Gonzalez. But the Bears were never able to overcome a 21–0 lead the Cougars had built as early as the second quarter.

That was the first of six losses against one win that would wind down this seesaw season. But that win, over Arizona, was something to behold—if, that is, you had the stamina for it. It went to four overtimes before the Bears pulled it out—or had it pulled out for them— by a score of 56–55. It was the longest Division 1A game yet played, longer by one overtime and more absurdly high-scoring than the whopper played a month earlier. Once again, the teams were tied at 35 points at the end of four quarters, but there was plenty of scoring after that. Actually, the game could well have gone to a fifth overtime had not Arizona coach Dick Tomey, motivated either by exhaustion or impatience, decided to try for two points and a win instead of kicking the point-after to tie the score at 56 each. (A later rule made it mandatory at such junctures to go for two as a means of avoiding marathons such as this one) But the coach's fake-kick trickery was foiled when after holder Ryan Hesson pitched the ball back to kicker Matt Peyton, Cal's Andre Rhodes jumped in to stop the ball carrier five yards shy of the end zone.

As one might expect, the stats for this one were Macy's parade balloons. Barnes completed 35 of 46 for a Cal record 503 yards and a school and Pac-10 record eight touchdowns. And with Arizona's Keith Smith passing for 418 yards and five scores, the opposing quarterbacks combined for 921 yards and 13 touchdowns. And with Smith's 109 yards rushing and Barnes's 25 they were good for well over a thousand yards. Shaw had 132 yards receiving, Benjamin 107, Gonzalez 96 and Douglas 83. With all that overhead activity, O'Neal led the runners with 95 yards on only 15 carries. Two weeks later, the future All America defensive back gained 126 yards on 14 carries in a 40–23 loss to Oregon.

As the late-season defeats piled up, including a nasty 35–7 loss at Arizona State, Mariucci declared that in "the long run" the experience "will be good for our players...We're just in the first year of our rebuilding program, and I think this gives us a gauge of where we need to go."

Long run? Rebuilding program? Gauge of where to go? Actually, in the short run, Mariucci himself would be the only one doing the going. Although not very far away.

A 42–21 loss to Stanford in the 99th Big Game still left the Bears with a 6-5 winning record. Barnes had three more touchdown passes—to Benjamin, Shaw and Gonzalez—against the Cardinal and finished the regular season with a Cal single season record of 31. His 3,499 yards set another record, as did his 503 in one game. For his career at Cal, Barnes had ten 300-yard passing games, surpassing Campbell and Taylor, who both held the previous record at six.

Two hours after the Big Game, the Bears, despite their el-foldo at the end, were invited to play Navy on Christmas Day in Honolulu's Aloha Bowl. It was not an especially Merry Christmas as the Midshipmen overcame a 10-point Cal lead after three quarters to score twice in the fourth and win, 42–38. In doing so, they perforated Cal's deteriorating defense for 646 yards.

The Bears were first in the Pac-10 that year in passing offense and second only to conference champion Arizona State in total offense, averaging 457.6 yards per game. But they were dead last in total defense, allowing opponents a generous 6.1 yards per play. Only last-place Oregon State gave up more than Cal's 33.2 points per game. And those numbers do not include the Aloha Bowl's extravagant stats. But the 6-6 record was an improvement and hopes were tremulously raised by the new coach's opening season. And then, just like that, he was gone.

"Steve and I were on a recruiting trip in southern California," recalled Tom Holmoe, Mariucci's defensive coordinator. "He made a phone call, and afterward he looked really nervous. I could see he was in a state of shock, so I asked him what was wrong, and he said Carmen Policy of the 49ers had just asked him to be their new head coach."

As Policy, then the 49ers president and CEO, recalled the event, he had originally suggested to Mariucci at an otherwise social occasion that he take the job as the team's offensive coordinator for one year or a maximum of two until George Seifert retired as head coach. Then the top job would be his. Policy said he had a feeling Mariucci wouldn't go for the idea, having had just that one season at Cal. Then, fortuitously, Seifert decided, on a suggestion from Policy, to retire earlier than anticipated. "George and I agreed it was time to move on," Policy said years later. "In the NFL, everybody has a shelf life. It's just the way it works."

"Tom and I were at the Ontario airport ready to take a flight home," Mariucci remembers. "I always call my wife before I get on an airplane. When I did, she told me that Carmen had called and wanted me to call him back. She said it sounded important. I thought he knew I wouldn't leave Cal for a coordinator's job. It just wasn't the right thing to do. Cal was the only job I would have left the Packers for, because I was very happy in Green Bay, near where I grew up as a kid. But I loved Cal and the Bay Area and had wanted to be their coach before. My intentions were to stay there a long time. Then Carmen told me things had changed."

Policy says that at first Mariucci didn't grasp what he was getting at: "Steve was so busy on the phone giving me reasons why he couldn't take the coordinator's job with us—can't walk away from Cal and so on—that I couldn't get in a word. Finally, I interrupted to tell him the situation was different now, that George was leaving, and we wanted him to be the new head coach of the 49ers. There was dead silence on his end of the line. Then he said, 'You're kidding, aren't you?' I said I wasn't. Steve went home and talked to his wife and agreed to take the job. I told him he'd be in for the ride of his life. The next day, we met with the chancellor and John Kasser, who was really upset. In the end, the 49ers made a substantial contribution to the athletic department—$500,000."

"I had a buyout in my contract," Mariucci said, "but (49er owner) Eddie DeBartolo added a lot more. I think Chancellor Tien and John (Kasser) understood this was an opportunity I couldn't pass up."

"I was unhappy about it, to say the least," said Kasser more than ten years after the parting. "I felt Steve had been the right person for the job at Cal, that he would bring new energy to the program. He seemed to me to have some of what Pete Carroll would bring to USC. I thought we had found the solution to our problems. Not having Steve stay tarnished my football experience at Cal."

Thus ended Mariucci's checkered history at the university. Passed over in his first try for the head coach's job, he then became the first in fifty years to leave after one season, and the first to do so voluntarily since Buck Shaw. And in another twist of fate, Holmoe, a former 49er player and assistant coach, was named, somewhat to his surprise, his replacement.

"I suppose I could've gone with Steve back to the 49ers," he said on reflection years later. "I'd enjoyed my time with them, but I'd wanted to get back into college football. At first, I'd wanted to be in administration, then I got hooked on coaching. Steve wanted me to take the Cal coaching job. And I did love the school with all its spirit and tradition. It's an awesome place. What was I at the time? Thirty-seven. And they were asking me to be the head coach of a Pac-10 team. How could I pass that up?"

Holmoe was asked...nay, told...by Kasser to keep as many of the assistant coaches new to the job as possible, a concern as well of the departing Mariucci. He did hold onto at least five. "But that became a difficult situation because some of them had wanted the head coaching job," Holmoe recalls. "Some just left. Still, we'd turned the program around a little in '96, and I really believed we could win. I soon learned there was a lot I didn't know."

Holmoe may have seemed an odd choice, since the defense he had coached under Mariucci was easily the worst part of Cal's game. But it was also the least experienced, with only four seniors among the thirty defensive players. And Holmoe had in his favor what he now recalls as an almost naive enthusiasm, a keen appreciation of Cal tradition and, as a former 49er player and assistant, a firm grasp of the fundamentals and myriad nuances of the by then hallowed West Coast Offense.

He was also one of the nicest guys in the game, liked and respected by coaching colleagues and administrators. Not that niceness is a qualification for coaching football. But it sometimes helps. Holmoe didn't look much like a coach, more closely resembling your high school geometry teacher. But Kasser hoped he would bring some stability to what was beginning to seem like a stopover position. So he signed him to a five-year contract on January 12, 1997.

"Tom seemed like a natural for the job," said Kasser years later. "I talked to Bill Walsh and LaVell Edwards (Holmoe's coach at BYU) and they both described him as one of the brightest young coaches in the business. And I'd also seen how Mariucci tended to lean on him for advice. He remains to this day one of my favorite people. The trouble was, Tom is such an upright, dedicated person that he couldn't understand why everybody else was not that way."

Tien, too, would retire as chancellor in 1997, explaining in the jock-speak he'd so eagerly assimilated that he "wanted to spend more time with my family." He would be succeeded by Dr. Robert M. Berdahl, a renowned historian who had been president of the University of Texas for the previous three-and-a-half years. Although he'd come to Cal from a school famous for its football prowess, Berdahl scarcely distinguished himself as a gridiron scholar when, speaking at a Pappy's Boys banquet early in his administration, he severely botched the names of two of that organization's iconic members, Pete Schabarum and Jim Monachino.

In Berdahl's defense, he had other chores in mind, not the least of which was dealing with the regents' rejection two years earlier of the university's Affirmative Action admissions policy. It was a distinctly unpopular ruling among academics, students and certainly African-Americans at a time when the university was striving to have its campuses more closely reflect the demographics of the nation's most diversely populated state. And, shades of the old days, a massive protest rally was held at Sproul Plaza, featuring black leader Jesse Jackson as principal speaker. If Affirmative Action—a term supposedly first used by President John F. Kennedy—survived at Cal it was in the form of the Special Students policy which now allowed admission to as many as six percent of academically unqualified applicants if they were able to demonstrate unusual talent in other fields, athletics included. Interestingly enough, at least one ethnic group ceased to be a minority of the student body in the 1990s. As early as '94, Asian enrollment had surpassed Caucasian, 39.4 percent to 32.4.

Holmoe, typically, promised that his ethnically mixed roster would be peopled by true student-athletes of whom "everybody at the university can be proud. I absolutely believe we can build a consistent winner and do it with student-athletes who want to excel not just on the football field but also in the classroom."

Chances are those student-athletes did better in the classroom. The 1997 team finished 3-8, losing five in a row after winning the first two, over Houston (35–3) and Oklahoma (40–36). With Barnes gone, Holmoe had as his starting quarterback a junior college All American named Justin Vedder. And Vedder got off to a quick start, passing for 321 yards in his first game, the Houston win, on 24 completions in 31 attempts. Eleven of those completions for 204 yards and two touchdowns were to Shaw. The defense seemed much improved under Lyle Setencich, the coordinator Holmoe hired to take his own place. Houston was held to just 165 yards in total offense.

Vedder was 24 for 39 for 253 yards and three scores in the Oklahoma win, and Shaw caught 11 more for 158 yards and two more touchdowns. Then came the five losses, some close—41–34 to Louisiana Tech—some reasonably close—27–17 to USC—and some not at all close—30–3 to Washington, 63–37 to Washington State, 35–17 to UCLA. The Bears were revived in time to win one more game, 33–14, over Oregon State. Vedder threw four touchdown passes in that one and Tarik Smith, healthy again, gained 125 yards.

But the season ended with three more losses, all of them heartbreakingly close. The Bears bounced back from a 17–0 Arizona State lead at halftime to score twice in the final quarter to bring the final score to 28–21. Two overtimes were needed to decide Arizona's 41–38 win at Tuscon, a loss in which emerging star Douglas caught 11 passes for 143 yards. He caught 12 more for exactly the same yardage in the ballyhooed 100th Big Game, but Stanford still won, 21–20. Vedder connected with Shaw for a 12-yard touchdown with 4:44 to play to clear the path for another one of those classic Big Game home stretch finishes. And the Bears did get the ball back in the closing moments when Big Games are won. But with 1:22 on the clock, Vedder lost his footing as he threw from the Cardinal 33 and linebacker Chris Draft intercepted on the 14 to stymie this might-have-been spellbinder.

A disappointing first season, yes, but Holmoe was encouraged by the efforts of his newer players. Vedder had a statistically productive first season, completing 221 of 390 passes for 2,718 yards and 20 touchdowns. He had three 300-yard-plus games. Douglas finished with 53 catches for 610 yards, second to Shaw's school record 75 for 1093 yards. New punter Nick Harris, a husky former high-school linebacker, averaged 42.2 yards on 77 boots, and, no stranger to contact, ran twice on fake punts for 28 yards. O'Neal, who began the season as a running back and finished it playing some cornerback, led the team in all-purpose yardage with 172 rushing, 223 receiving, 256 on punt returns and 646 on kickoff returns. In his final season, Smith led the rushers with 636 yards on 162 carries.

The team did improve in 1998, finishing 5-6, but with a tailspin finish so depressingly characteristic of Cal football in the decade. Holmoe's Bears won four of their first five games, then lost five of the last six, the lone win by a single point. Actually, three of the Bears' five wins that year were by that minuscule margin. In the early season euphoria, they trounced Oklahoma, 13–12, behind Marcus Fields' 140 yards rushing and Tim Wolleck's two field goals, and then crushed USC, 32–31, as Douglas, en route to a fabulous season, caught 13 passes for 151 yards, and O'Neal set up a field goal with a 57-yard kickoff return and, for good measure, tossed a touchdown pass. During the downturn, the Bears stampeded Oregon State, 20–19, with Douglas catching a school record 15 passes for 140 yards.

In a heroic loss, the Bears held Conference champion UCLA to 28 points, the Bruins' lowest-scoring game that far into the season. Cal's All Pac-10 linebacker Sekou Sanyika contributed his second safety of the year to his team's 16 points. The Bears also made a game of it in a 27–23 loss to ninth-ranked Arizona. Fields scored twice on a 41-yard run and a 25-yard pass from Vedder. The quarterback was on the rebound from a 55–22 defeat at Arizona State where he was intercepted five times and lost a fumble. That was not as painful, at least physically, as the 13 sacks he fell victim to in a 21–13 loss to Washington in Seattle.

Stanford again won the Big Game—Holmoe would never beat the Cardinal—by the inconsequential score of 10–3. It was the lowest-scoring game in the series since the Bears won, 7–6, in 1948, but not the lowest-scoring ever, a distinction belonging to the scoreless tie of 1932. Cal's only score in '98 was from a 34-yard field goal in the first quarter by Ignacio Brache. Stanford scored twice in the second half on a seven-yard pass from Todd Husak to Troy Walters and an 18-yard field goal by Kevin Miller. Nick Harris kept the Cardinal backed up most of the day with seven punts averaging 44.4 yards.

For the season, Harris averaged 40.8 yards on 87 punts, 27 of which came to rest inside the 20. Fields, a bruising 220-pound back, led Bear runners with 734 yards on 166 carries. Vedder's last season was not as productive as his first, his completion percentage dropping a few points to 54.4, his yardage to 2322 and his touchdowns to 11. The statistical stars were Douglas, who surpassed Shaw's reception record of the year before with 100 catches for another school record of 1,150 yards, and O'Neal, who had a 76-yard interception return for a touchdown and 57-yard punt and kickoff returns.

Holmoe believed his third season would prove a turning point. He had recruited players with considerable potential, including quarterback Kyle Boller, safety Nhamdi Asoumugha, defensive end Tully Banta-Cain, kicker Mark Jensen and running backs Joe Igber and Joe Echema. And he still had Fields, Harris, Langston Walker and Andre Carter in the fold. But the coach's "bridge to the 21st century," proved no more substantial than the one on the River Kwai.

The '99 team finished a sorry 4-7. For the third year in a row, though, the Holmoes won the opener, by 21–7 over Rutgers. O'Neal returned an interception 75 yards for a touchdown and freshman Boller made his first appearance in the second quarter, finishing with eight completions in 15 attempts for 89 yards and a touchdown.

Then reality set in. Nebraska beat the Bears, 45–0, and, after another one of those one-point victories, 24–23, over Arizona State, first Washington State (31–7) and then Brigham Young (38–28) brought the Bears to heel. They did beat UCLA, 17–0, in Pasadena despite a 7.0

earthquake in the Los Angeles area that morning. Then Washington beat them, 31–27, despite Igber's 182 yards rushing in a game he did not finish because of a shoulder injury. The Bears ended the season in customary style by losing four of the last five, the only win by 17–7 over USC. In that game, O'Neal returned an interception 67 yards for one TD and his 60-yard punt return set up a Jensen field goal. Igber played, but sparingly.

O'Neal's 100-yard kickoff and 58-yard punt returns were Cal's only touchdowns in a 31–13 loss to Stanford. Strictly a defender and kick-returner in this, his last season, he led the team in scoring with six touchdowns, four coming on an NCAA record for interception returns and one each on punt and kickoff runbacks. At this writing, he is still Cal's career leader in all-purpose yardage. He was a consensus All America choice in '99 and joined Carter, Harris (a 44.6 average on 85 punts), Sanyika and defensive tackle Jacob Waasdorp on the All Pac-10 team. Despite his injury problems, Igber gained a team-leading 694 yards rushing on 148 carries. He had a peculiar jittery stop-and-go running style that relied more on lateral quickness than on straight-ahead speed, but it worked. Freshman Boller, who before coming to Cal had played only one season in high school at quarterback, completed just 38.6 percent of his 259 passes for 1,303 yards, nine touchdowns and 15 interceptions, but there was little question about his potential because of his tremendous arm strength. He lacked only the finesse and the judgement he would presumably acquire with experience.

Boller did improve in his second season. But his team didn't, dropping to an ignominious 3-8 at a time when the rest of the nation was welcoming the Millennium. The 2000 Bears did do their part, however, in furthering the cause of ethnic diversity on campus by including in their ranks six players—Igber, Echema, Asoumugha, Chidi Iwuoma and the brothers Daniel and David Nwangwu—who were either born in Nigeria or who had family roots there. On the whole, though, the Bears played as if they hailed from Narnia. They won the opener, of course, by 24–21 over Utah, then lost four in a row, though by a mere 17–15 in their second game, at Illinois, and just 21–17 to Washington State in their fourth. The Bears played atrociously in a 17–3 loss at Fresno State and were clobbered 30–10 by Arizona State, their sixth loss to the Sun Devils in their last eight meetings. They upset 13th -ranked UCLA, 46–38, in three overtimes, the winning TD scored by Igber on a three-yard run. By then, sixty-minute games seemed the exception, not the rule at Cal.

They did beat USC, 28–16, in regulation, a game in which Boller outpitched Trojan limelighter Carson Palmer two touchdowns to one. They came perilously close in a 38–32 loss to 14th-ranked Oregon State, thanks to Boller's 249 yards and three touchdowns, one of them for 81 yards to Derek Swafford, a twenty-five-year-old sophomore who had spent five years playing minor league baseball. They held their own in a 25–17 loss to sixth-ranked Oregon, the Ducks scoring twice in the fourth quarter. Boller threw a 63-yard touchdown to another promising freshman, Geoff McArthur.

The Big Game was the first in that long series to be played in...what else?...overtime. But it took Stanford only one extra period to win, 36 –30, on a 25-yard pass from Randy Fasani to back Casey Moore. The Bears were guilty of four interceptions, two blocked punts and two lost fumbles. It was the Cardinal's sixth straight Big Game victory.

There were some statistical highlights in this otherwise exasperating season. Boller completed 163 of 349 passes for a much improved 46.7 percent completion average and 15 touchdowns. He was intercepted 13 times. The stutter-stepping Igber gained 901 yards on 195 carries and caught 23 passes for another 229. Newcomer McArthur averaged nearly 17 yards on his 20 receptions. Harris, in his final season, punted 73 times for an average of 41.5 yards. But his most astonishing achievement was dropping better than a third of those kicks, 26 of them, inside the 20-yard line.

Harris would not be around for 2001, a season in which the Bears lost their first ten games before winning their last. No crowd at Memorial Stadium that year exceeded forty thousand, the biggest, 38,160, witnessing a 44–17 loss to Illinois in the opener. The low attendance was not, however, entirely attributable to the team's travails, for on September 11, three days after Cal's 44–16 loss to Brigham Young, terrorists hijacked commercial airliners and crashed them into the twin towers of New York's World Trade Center and the Pentagon in Washington, D. C. A fourth hijacked plane crashed in a field eighty miles outside of Pittsburgh. The Trade Center towers were brought down by the flaming impact of the two planes, causing nearly three thousand deaths. It was the most devastating attack on U.S. soil since Pearl Harbor and it left the entire nation in a state of acute anxiety.

The Berkeley campus remained in shock for months afterward. On the morning of the attack, Chancellor Berdahl issued a statement urging distressed students to "turn to faculty, administrators and campus staff" for emotional support. There was a candlelight vigil that night outside Sproul Hall attended by more than two thousand. As the student body soon learned, two former Cal athletes were among the "9-11" dead. Brent Woodall, a tight end in the late '80s and early '90s, was at work as a stock trader on the eighty-ninth floor of the Trade Center's south tower when the planes hit. And '90s rugby player Mark Bingham was aboard United Airlines flight 93 when it crashed short of its intended target in Pennsylvania farm land. Bingham died a hero as one of a few passengers on that doomed flight who reportedly resisted the terrorists and thereby brought the plane down before it could reach its target, possibly the White House or the Capitol Building in Washington.

At noon on Friday, September 14, a moment of silence for the victims was held on campus. "The only sound was that of the wind in the trees," reported the *Blue and Gold*. "Even the people who streamed out of class for the noon hour did so in utter silence."

Cal's game at Rutgers, originally scheduled for Saturday, the fifteenth, was postponed until after the Big Game. And on Monday, the seventeenth, an estimated crowd of twelve thousand—the largest on campus since the 1960s—assembled in Memorial Glade for non-denominational services. Among the speakers was ASUC president Wally Adeyemo, who cautioned, "We cannot let the spirit of terrorism blow out our lights of hope, compassion and love. If we allow our lights to be smothered by those that promote terrorism, we will have allowed them to take more than our buildings."

The football season resumed on September 22 with a 51–20 loss at Washington State. The Bears played at home for the first time in three weeks, on September 29, against Washington in a half-filled Memorial Stadium. It may have been their best game of the year. Boller threw a then career-high four touchdown passes, but the Huskies rallied with 21 points in the second half to win, 31–28.

Actually, 21 points in a half represented a defensive triumph for the Bears in 2001, since in seven of their losses opposing teams scored 21 or more in just one quarter. It was a season of lava spills. In three of the ten defeats foes scored more than 50 points. In the first six games alone, the winning team averaged 45.7 points. The Bears finished last in 11 Pac-10 statistical categories and allowed a school record 431 points. There were, to be sure, injuries. Boller missed a couple of games with a sore back and Igber's season ended with a broken clavicle in the seventh game, a relatively hairbreadth loss to Oregon State by 19–10. His replacement, freshman Terrell Williams, finished as the team's rushing leader with 688 yards, all but 62 picked up after Igber's exit.

Holmoe announced his resignation, effective at season's end, on November 4, the day after his team's eighth straight loss, by 38–24 to Arizona, and the week of a 55–14 whipping by Pete Carroll's first team at USC.

Years later, he admitted on candid reflection that he may have taken the job before he was ready for it. "I had learned football from some of the best—LaVell Edwards at BYU and Bill Walsh and George

Seifert with the 49ers. But some of that just didn't work at Cal. I tried too hard to force what I knew on the team when a more seasoned coach would have made some changes. There were problems that a stronger leader might have resolved."

The Bears stayed with Stanford, a 9-3 team that year in coach Tyrone Willingham's last season, before losing again, 35–28. The ten losses that year were the most ever for a Cal football team, and discounting three no-win seasons in the nineteenth century, in which the teams played one, three and five games, this was the worst record ever for a Cal football team. The Bears did finish on a positive note, though, with a 20–10 win over an almost equally feckless (3-8 record) Rutgers team before a sparse crowd of 18,111 back in New Jersey.

Holmoe returned to BYU, his alma mater, to begin a career he had long aspired to in athletic administration. As first an assistant athletic director and then as the athletic director, he presided over winning teams there and the construction of millions of dollars in improved facilities.

"I put to work what I'd learned at Cal," he said eight years after leaving Berkeley. "I finally got back to what I'd always intended to do. But I still love Cal. I may have some regrets about the way I ran things there, but I always loved the place. In fact, I still find myself humming those Cal fight songs. And the day they go to the Rose Bowl, I'll be there."

Kasser also left Cal in 2001, wisely enough before the football season. Like Holmoe, he still loves the place, despite similar regrets. Kasser's time in office had been active and productive. He oversaw the reconstruction of the Harmon Gym into the $60 million Walter A. Haas, Jr., Pavilion that somehow preserved much of the old joint's intimacy while nearly doubling its seating capacity. And he also presided over the $3 million renovation of Edwards Stadium/ Goldman Field. Major achievements but, "I just wish I could've got that football program going."

Kasser was replaced as athletic director by Steve Gladstone, the highly successful crew coach. It fell to him to find a coach willing to take on a football operation that hadn't produced a winning team in eight years and had just completed a 1-10 season.

He did find one, though. Did he ever!

CHAPTER THIRTY-SIX

# THE PHOENIX

The search for a new coach lasted six weeks from the time of Holmoe's resignation. Gladstone and his confederates—Vice Chancellor Horace Mitchell, Associate A.D.'s Dan Coonan and Mark Stephens and championship rugby coach Jack Clark—wanted to be absolutely certain this time that they hired the right man. The final decision would be Gladstone's, and in making it the then sixty-two-year-old coach of five National Champion Cal crews would rely, in large part, on his instincts.

"I remember at a Grid Club luncheon some people asking how a rowing coach could be in charge of hiring a football coach," Gladstone recalled. "But, you see, I was a coach, and coaches know other coaches. It would have been grossly immodest of me to have said that at the time, but it served me well in the process. Your radar, your senses are heightened when you see the right man. I was not merely looking for someone who had a _desire_ to win, I was after someone who _needed_ to win. Need is much deeper."

After interviewing a number of candidates, some flashier, more articulate and a few carrying "large books extolling their attributes," he hired on December 12, 2002, a career assistant coach named Jeff

Tedford, who was then the offensive coordinator at the University of Oregon.

"I could feel Jeff's overwhelming passion for coaching. It was at the very core of his being," said Gladstone. "Although he was quiet and not at all demonstrative, he came across loud and clear as someone who could make sure our athletes were maximally prepared. Also, he'd had great success at Oregon and he knew the west coast territory inside out. I had a pretty doggone sure sense that this was our man."

Even though, like his immediate predecessors, Tedford had never been a head coach, he, significantly, had been an offensive coordinator for nine of his thirteen years in the business, first at Fresno State, his alma mater, and then at Oregon for a team that whomped the Bears, 48–7, in '01 and had fashioned a six-game winning streak over them. He had also coached and played in the Canadian Football League. A former quarterback himself in college and the pros, he was widely regarded as a premier developer of talent at that all-important position. Already, four of his pupils—Trent Dilfer, David Carr, Akili Smith and Joey Harrington—had become first-round NFL draft choices. At Cal, he would have as a major project bringing to fruition the as yet untapped gifts of Kyle Boller, who in three seasons had completed only 45.1 percent of his 880 passes and thrown more interceptions (38) than touchdowns (36). But Tedford would prove to be a good deal more than just a QB guru.

"I really didn't know a lot about Cal when I took the job," Tedford recalled. "When someone asked me if I was bleeding blue and gold, I said, no, not yet. After not hearing from the Cal people for awhile after they asked me if I was interested in the job, the deal was done so quickly I didn't really have time to think about it."

And like Snyder fifteen years before him, he found his first look at the situation not exactly reassuring. "My first observation of the players was that their self-esteem was low. Their body language alone showed that. It affected them not only on the field but in the classroom.

It was as if they were ashamed to be seen."

And the stadium, beautiful though it may once have been, was a mess. "When I got there, trash from the last game played there in November hadn't been removed. There was no attention to detail. There seemed to be a lack of pride in the environment, a satisfaction with mediocrity. I was told, 'Oh, that's just the way it is here.' Well, in those first weeks, I was probably the most unpopular guy on campus, because I was rocking the boat. There was some head-butting."

Tedford conducted personal interviews with all the players, listening to their complaints, their feelings of inadequacy. He began formulating rules, imposing discipline, creating order out of the existing chaos. For starters, he insisted that players begin finding seats in the first several rows in classrooms, not in the back as if ready to flee. Nearness to the professors might encourage them to ask more questions, to listen more intently. "Besides, what happens when you sit in the back? If you do ask a question, everyone turns to look at you. Up front, they're still looking at the professor."

As for the athletic environment, Gladstone assured him he would remove the obstacles, or as he put it, "get all the brush out of the road." One obstacle he couldn't remove was the NCAA probation Cal teams endured in 2002, the result mainly of offenses committed in 1999, specifically for allowing wide receivers Ronnie Davenport and Mike Ainsworth to play when both were academically ineligible after receiving credit for a course in ethnic studies they did not complete. The involved professor, Alex Saragoza, admitted, "I allowed my heart to prevail in the accommodation which I made to the two students in question." He was suspended from teaching in the fall of 2001. Tedford's first team would not be able, under the terms of probation, to play in a bowl game. Not that anyone expected them to, anyway.

But the coach and his young staff conducted a brisk, efficient and hopeful spring practice. And they took the field in the opener at Memorial Stadium in garish new uniforms, looking not at all woebegone but ready for business.

The first play from scrimmage was an eye-opener. Boller passed cross-field behind the line to Terrell Williams who, a quarterback himself in high school, then threw downfield to a wide open David Gray, who made an off-balance catch and scooted into the end zone for a 71-yard touchdown. Tedford had not only begun his career at Cal with a trick play, his players made it work for a score. That qualified as a fresh start.

The Bears won that game, over Baylor, by the astonishing score of 70–22. Boller, the low-percentage-high-interception-rate passer, was 18 for 26 for 213 yards, three touchdowns and no interceptions, while playing only three quarters. His teammates intercepted four passes, one of which was returned the length of the field by linebacker Matt Nixon.

The Bears won their first three under their new coach, running their point total to 150, a figure it required the '01 team nine games to reach. Boller had seven TD passes in that brief span. New Mexico State fell 34–13 and 15th-ranked Michigan State, 46–22. The win over the Big Ten Spartans was Cal's first over a top 15 team on the road in twenty-eight years. Tedford enlivened this stunning upset with yet another touch of trickery, having wide receiver LaShaun Ward first take a pitchout from Boller, then wheel and pass to him for a 14-yard touchdown.

"That Michigan State win was a pivotal game for us," Tedford recalled. "The players were excited. They'd traveled all the way back there and got the win. We coaches could see they had trust in us."

As if all this were just too good to be true, the Bears dropped the next two, to Air Force on a last minute field goal, 23–21, and to Washington State by a more substantial, 48–38. The fans were not yet believers, since in the first four home games, only one crowd exceeded thirty thousand, and then just barely, Air Force attracting 31,816. After years of staring into the abyss, it was not that easy looking up.

But Tedford's revived team was big box office outside Berkeley, drawing seventy thousand-plus at Michigan State and for a 34–27 win over Washington in Seattle, a game in which Boller threw for five touchdowns and no interceptions. One of those TD tosses went for 55 yards to a walk-on wide receiver, Vincent Strang, who at 137 pounds was a throwback to the days of Kangaroo Kaarsberg.

Before 63,113 in Los Angeles, the Bears lost a 30–28 thriller to USC after leading, 21–17, at the half. The Trojans rallied late behind quarterback Carson Palmer and tailback Sultan McCullough. Defense made the difference in the team's 17–12 win over UCLA before an encouraging audience of 46,697 back home. Two fourth-quarter goal line stands frustrated a last gasp Bruin rally. Cal defenders held a UCLA offense that had been averaging 437 yards per game to just 226. Boller's 24-yard TD pass to tight end Tom Swoboda was his Cal career record fifty-fifth. He would add nine more by season's end.

After a 24–13 loss to Oregon State in Corvallis, due largely to Steven Jackson's 239 rushing yards and three TDs, the Bears walloped 25th-ranked Arizona State, 55–38. Boller enjoyed his second five-touchdown day of the season and Asomugha returned an interception 85 yards for another score. Then Arizona beat them, 52–41, despite Ward's 94-yard kickoff return and 25-yard TD reception.

The Bears whipped Stanford, 30–7, breaking a seven-game losing streak to the Cardinal, the longest by either team in Big Game history. Joe Igber, who had quietly been putting together a thousand-yard season (1,139) pounded out 226 yards on 26 carries, scoring on a 42-yarder up the middle in the second quarter. Jemeel Powell had an 84-yard punt return in the third. With eleven seconds remaining, spectators—there were 71,224 believers in the stadium that day—rushed onto the field and hoisted the rejuvenated Boller off his feet in triumph. The quarterback had thrown for 2,813 yards that season and 28 touchdowns. He had completed 53.4 percent of his 421 passes and had thrown only 11 interceptions.

But if anyone deserved to be carried off the field that day, it was the head coach. He had transformed a 1-10 team into a 7-5 winner, pulling off the biggest turnaround in Cal football history since Pappy made of a 2-7 loser a 9-1 winner fifty-five years before. Tedford's Bears had averaged 35.6 points per game, nearly double the 18.3 of the year before. They'd forced twice as many turnovers (36) as they'd made in 2001. And they'd beaten three top 20 teams. Had they been eligible, it stands to reason they would have been invited to a bowl game. Tedford, though, was named the Pac-10's Coach of the Year.

So how do you follow an act like that? By doing pretty much the same thing, only more so, it turned out. The '03 Bears won one more game and lost one more for an 8-6 finish, the fourteen games the most ever played by a Cal team in American football. The protracted slate also introduced at least three new stars to the Bear constellation, one a missing person returned, repaired and re-named, the other two arriving, as it were, from out of the blue.

Consider, first of all, the curious case of Adimchinobe Echemandu. He first appeared in a Cal football uniform as Joe Echema, an Anglicized rendition of the name he was born with in Lagos, Nigeria. He'd been just plain Joe since his school days in southern California. In 1999 and 2000 as a running back and part-time receiver, he carried the ball a total of only 68 times and averaged just 3.5 yards per. He missed the entire 2001 season because of academic ineligibility. The next spring, eligible again, he appeared to have won the starting tailback job from Igber when he tore up his knee and missed yet another full season. In the meantime, he hit the books industriously and earned a degree in sociology. And in '03 he'd begun work on a Master's in education. He'd also gained 25 pounds above the 200 he'd packed in his previous incarnation as Joe Echema. And, to the grief of broadcasters and headline writers, he'd returned to his original tongue-twisting moniker. As the '03 season opened, Adimchinobe Echemandu was ready to make a name for himself.

In pre-season forecasts, Aaron Rodgers, a transfer from Butte College in Oroville, was mentioned mostly *en passant* as a backup to scheduled '03 starter Reggie Robertson. As Boller's sub in '02, Robertson had thrown fewer passes than running back Terrell Williams' three. In '01, he'd completed 43.1 percent of 65 attempts, hardly the numbers expected of a successor to first-round NFL draft choice Boller. But Robertson was well thought of because he could run a little and was a natural leader. Sophomore Rodgers had those same qualities and more, but he'd had just the one year of junior college experience. That was a good year at any level though: 28 touchdown passes with just four interceptions. Tedford correctly saw him as a star in the making.

The media guide wrote of J.J. Arrington, another junior college transfer (College of the Canyons in Santa Clarita) that, considering the uncertainties at the position, he was "expected to challenge for playing time at tailback." Arrington played his high school ball in faraway Rocky Mount, North Carolina. He too was thought of as a work in progress.

The Bears lost fifteen starters from '02, including not only Boller but Igber, Ward, Swoboda, Powell, Banta-Cain, Asomugha and kicker Mark Jensen. Only two starters returned on defense, roving safety Donnie McCleskey and star tackle Lorenzo Alexander.

The team lost the opener to Kansas State, 42–28, in Kansas City's Arrowhead Stadium, the Wildcats' tiny Darren Sproles exploiting that inexperienced defense for 175 yards. The game was played on August 23, the earliest start for a Cal team since the 19th century. In a 34–2 win over Southern Mississippi at home before 35,880, both starter Echemandu (17-127) and backup Arrington (16-114) surpassed a hundred yards rushing. They did it on the stadium's brand new Momentum Turf, an artificial surface Tedford had campaigned for because of its durability and resilience. Unlike the previous carpeting, this stuff looked like real grass, with tufts and all.

A field goal within the last two minutes gave Colorado State a

23–21 win before another smallish home crowd of 34,096. Robertson passed for all three Bear touchdowns. But Rodgers was pressing him, and in a 31–24 loss to Utah in Salt Lake City, the new kid took over on Cal's fourth possession, completing 15 of 25 for 224 yards and two touchdowns to another injury returnee, Geoff McArthur. Rodgers got his first start the following week, and the Bears won, 31–24, in an old fashioned humdinger. The Illini had the ball on the Cal eight with four seconds to play after recovering an onsides kick and driving downfield. Then, on the last play of the game, Cal linebacker Wendell Hunter sacked QB Jon Beutijer to preserve the win. Strang, now up to a massive 150 pounds, returned a punt 68 yards for one Bear touchdown and Rodgers, 20 of 37 for 263 yards, connected with McArthur for another. The agile Cal receiver had a busy day, catching 10 for 155 yards. On defense, Hunter had 15 tackles, including three sacks, and McCleskey 12 and one.

The 2-3 Bears then pulled off the upset of the year, beating third-ranked USC in three overtimes before a Memorial Stadium crowd of 51,208. This was a Trojan team with two future Heisman winners in Reggie Bush and Matt Leinart, as well as future NFL star LenDale White. The distinguished visitors tied the game at 24 apiece with sixteen seconds left in regulation on a 33-yard field goal by Ryan Killeen. The first overtime period was scoreless. The teams traded touchdowns in the second. Then after the Trojans were blanked in the third, Cal kicker Tyler Fredrickson won the day with a 33-yard field goal. Echemandu had 147 yards on 37 carries and another 25 receiving. Rodgers was 18 for 25 for 217 yards and two scores.

The Bears were beaten, 35–21, by Oregon State the following week, Steven Jackson once again the troublemaker with 227 yards and three touchdowns. And they lost in overtime to UCLA, 23–20, spoiling Rodgers' 322-yard day on 28 of 41 passing with no interceptions. McArthur caught nine for 128 and Burl Toler III of Cal's and USF's famous football family had seven for 104. Toler's grandfather starred on USF's undefeated 1951 team and later became a top NFL official. His father was a starting linebacker on Bear teams in the mid-1970s.

The team rebounded from this mini-dip to blow past the desert schools, beating Arizona, 42–14, and Arizona State, 51–23. Echemandu gained 201 yards against Arizona and scored three times, one on a 49-yard ramble. Arrington was 11 for 92 and two scores, one a 45-yarder. All six Bear scores came on the ground as Rodgers threw only six passes in the rout. But he passed for 207 yards and three touchdowns against Arizona State, and for the third week in a row had no interceptions. Echemandu's 128 yards in the game pushed him past a thousand for the season.

Oregon beat the Bears, 21–17, in Eugene in a game delayed twenty-three minutes in the last quarter when the lights went out at Autzen Stadium. The close loss darkened Tedford's return to his former home grounds. By the same token, his Bears spoiled Gilbertson's return to Berkeley as Washington's head coach with a 54–17 trouncing. Rodgers completed 20 of 33 for three touchdowns and, routinely by now, zero interceptions. McArthur caught six for 180 yards, including a dazzling 79-yard TD reception. Echemandu missed the game with a sprained ankle, but Arrington in his stead picked up 185 yards on only 14 carries and third-stringer Marcus O'Keith had 103 on 12. All told, the Bears gained 729 yards, 381 rushing, 348 passing. It was the most lopsided win in the Washington series since Smith's Wonder Team walloped the Huskies, 72–3, in 1921. To Gilby's merciless detractors it seemed like old home week.

The yardage continued to roll in Cal's 28–16 win in the Big Game. Rodgers passed for 359 yards and three scores, two of them to McArthur, who set a Cal record with his 16 receptions, good for 245 yards. By gaining another 55 yards rushing, Rodgers also established a Big Game standard for total offense with 414 yards, five more than Plunkett accumulated for Stanford thirty-four years earlier.

With a 7-6 regular season record, the Bears were invited to play nationally ranked Virginia Tech in the Insight Bowl at Phoenix. Playing before 42,364 at BankOne Ballpark, home of the baseball Diamondbacks, the two teams staged a memorable offensive show, the Bears finally breaking a 49–49 tie on the game's last play, a 35-yard field goal by Fredrickson. Rodgers completed 27 of 34 for 394 yards and two TDs. He also ran for two more scores. His Virginia Tech counterpart, Bryan Randall, did even better, passing for four more yards and two more touchdowns. Between them, the two QBs accounted for 792 passing yards on 68 attempts, and neither of them threw an interception. Chase Lyman, playing in place of McArthur, who suffered a broken right forearm in practice five days earlier, didn't have a bad day either. Oft-injured himself—shoulder, ankle, groin, hamstring, hip, even appendix—Lyman caught five passes for 149 yards, one a 33-yard touchdown.

The Bears in '03 set a school record with 6,061 total yards gained. With leaders Echemandu gaining 1195 and Arrington 607, the team led the conference in rushing for the first time in forty-five years, averaging 168.2 yards per game. Rodgers in his first collegiate season, a starter in just 10 of the 14 games, had a year comparable with the very best of Cal quarterback stars. He connected on 215 of 349 attempts for a 61.6 completion percentage, 2,903 yards and 19 touchdowns. And of those many passes, only five were intercepted, the lowest percentage per attempt in school history. And unlike his illustrious predecessors at QB, Rodgers finished with positive yardage rushing, 210, despite sacks. McArthur caught 85 passes for a Cal record 1,504 yards. His average of 115.7 per game was second nationally to Pitt's Larry Fitzgerald, of whom much more would be heard in the NFL. The '03 Bears were 'in," as they say, almost every one of their games. Of the six losses, four were either decided in the last two minutes of regulation or in overtime. All of them, said Tedford, "were games we could have won."

So how do you follow an act like that? Well, with something even better.

The incoming freshman class included, for example, such names as Marshawn Lynch, Justin Forsett, Alex Mack, Bernard Hicks, Robert Jordan and Worrell Williams. Most would immediately figure in Tedford's plans, some prominently. And he still had Rodgers, Arrington, McArthur, Lyman, stellar offensive tackle Ryan O'Callaghan and Marvin Philip, a fine center who returned to school in '03 after completing a two-year Mormon mission. On defense, he had McCleskey, who performed the rare feat for a defensive back of leading the team in tackles, 100, in '03. Also returning were nifty cornerback and kick-returner Tim Mixon, cornerback Daymeion Hughes, defensive end Ryan Riddle, linebacker Hunter and tackles Alexander and Brandon Mebane. For good measure, Tedford had added a 6-6 Australian, David Lonie, as his punter.

It was a formidable team, Tedford's best yet, with a 10-2 record. And the fans, long absent from Strawberry Canyon, returned in glorious abundance. The average attendance of 64,019 for the five home games would recall Waldorf's golden seasons.

The Bears won their first three with consummate ease, over the Air Force (56–14), New Mexico State (41–14) and Oregon State (49– 7). In these three Arrington racked up, respectively, 181, 177 and 108 yards on his path to a season in which he gained at least 100 in every game and became Cal's first 2,000-yard rusher and only the third in conference history. Rodgers, meanwhile, was his usual unerring self. He teamed with the temporarily healthy Lyman for a 78-yard touchdown against the Air Force and a 79-yarder against the Beavers. In the three games, Lyman had 12 receptions for 386 yards, an eye-popping average if 32.2 per catch.

The only loss of the regular season came in the fourth game against number-one-ranked USC before 90,008 in the L.A. Coliseum. The Trojans led all the way in winning, 23–17, despite a mind-boggling performance by Rodgers who completed his first 23 passes before tossing one out of bounds in the fourth quarter when all of his receivers were covered. He was a cool 29 for 31 for 267 yards with less than two minutes to play. But the stout Trojan defense sacked him and then hurried him into three straight incompletions, the last barely beyond the grasp of Jon Makonnen in the S.C. end zone. He did all of this without much help from Lyman, whose season ended after two catches with a serious injury to his knee, virtually the only part of his anatomy that had until then escaped harm in his valetudinary career. Not since the days of Hank Schaldach and Jim Jurkovich had there been such an exceptional player so cursed by injury.

There was no stopping the Bears after the USC setback. Arrington gained 205 yards and Rodgers passed for 260 in a 45–28 dismantling of UCLA before 69,898 in Berkeley. In an unusual turn of events, this was the first home game in five weeks, from September 11 to October 16. The team's scheduled third game with Southern Mississippi was postponed until December because of hurricane weather on the Gulf Coast, creating a second bye week, and the next two games were on the road. Then, for the first time ever, the Bears blanked the two Arizona schools, and on successive weekends, Arizona falling, 38–0, and Arizona State, 27–0. Rodgers was 20–27 and three first half touchdowns against Arizona. Arrington added 188 yards to his mounting totals in the Arizona State shutout. And Robert Jordan, who was expected to be redshirted, was obliged to play in that game because of injury depletions in the receiving corps. He did just fine, catching seven passes for 116 yards and a touchdown in his first start.

The Bears had a close call against Oregon before 65,615 in Memorial Stadium, but a missed Duck point-after gave them a 28–27 win. A Rodgers-McArthur 19-yard touchdown in the last quarter won it for the home team. Arrington again ran for 188 yards and a touchdown. The win broke a seven-game losing streak against Oregon.

In a 42–12 win over Washington in Seattle, both Arrington and freshman Lynch gained exactly 121 yards, Lynch on just nine carries. He scored three touchdowns on runs of 32 and 70 yards and on a

29-yard pass from Rodgers.

Stanford was clobbered, 41–6, the two tailbacks again topping a hundred yards, Arrington running for 169, Lynch for 122,. The freshman sensation demonstrated as well his all-round game, scoring on a 55-yard run and passing to Toler for a 29-yard TD. Then came the rescheduled Southern Miss. match, a 26–16 Cal win on December 4 in Hattiesburg. Arrington enjoyed his most productive day, gaining 261 yards on 31 carries and setting up Lynch's clinching 12-yard TD with a 56-yard ramble late in the fourth quarter.

The big season earned the Bears a second straight bowl bid, this time to the Holiday in San Diego. There, sadly they fell victim to both hubris and a Texas Tech spread offense they couldn't successfully resolve. Tech won, 45–31, with its quarterback, Sonny Cumbie, completing 39 of 60 passes for 520 yards and three scores. Arrington recorded his 12th straight 100-yard game, picking up 173 on 25 carries.

Despite the loss, the Bears were ranked ninth nationally, their highest spot since 1952. Their undefeated and untied record at home was the first since 1949. They set a Cal record in averaging 492.4 yards per game and their 6.05 yards per rush led the NCAA. The defense held nine of the twelve opponents under a hundred yards rushing. A Cal team hadn't had three consecutive winning seasons since the Waldorf era, and Tedford was again voted the Pac-10's Coach of the Year.

Individually, Arrington's 2,018 yards led the nation, and in conference history only USC's Marcus Allen with 2,427 in 1981 and Charles White with 2,050 in 1979 had ever gained more. By catching 57 passes for 862 yards, McArthur became Cal's career leader with 202 receptions for 3,188 yards. Freshman Lynch averaged a conference leading 8.8 yards on his 71 carries and classmate Jordan caught 29 passes for 332 yards after his late start. Riddle's 14.5 sacks broke Andre Carter's single season Cal record of 13.5. Rodgers had another brilliant season, completing 66.1 percent of 316 passes for 2,566 yards and 24 touchdowns. He had just eight interceptions, a tad high for him but unspeakably low for most other quarterbacks. Rodgers two-year totals were 43 touchdowns and a measly 13 picks. They would stand as his career stats since he chose to pass up his senior season and enter the NFL draft. Not surprisingly for a Tedford-trained QB, he was selected in the first round, by the Green Bay Packers.

Unfortunately, these joyful seasons were played in wartime, if not exactly in wartime conditions. On March 19, 2003, the war in Iraq began. And yet, because this war, the so-called "War on Terror," did not involve a military draft, the protests on U.S. college campuses were, in the beginning at least, relatively mild, particularly when compared with the explosive reaction to the Vietnam conflict.

Not necessarily, though, at Cal. The first anti-war demonstration on the Berkeley campus was held as early as September 20, 2001, a full eighteen months before the war actually started. And the day after Iraq was invaded and subjected to "shock and awe" bombing, a sit-in was held at Sproul Hall, involving an estimated fifteen hundred demonstrators. Police arrested one hundred seventeen, ninety-eight of them Cal students. In an effort to forestall further disruption, Chancellor Berdahl organized on April 1 a "Faculty Forum" on campus to discuss from various points of view the controversial and increasingly unpopular conflict.

Law and history professor Thomas O. Barnes stood with President George W. Bush: "I think most Americans are prepared to take casualties in a just war. And I think that the judgement of this country is that the war is just. It may not seem so in Berkeley, but it is elsewhere."

Laura Nader, a professor of social cultural anthropology, argued otherwise: "Today we face the consequences of unilateral invasion of a sovereign country, which at the time of the invasion posed no threat to the United States. It is, as my neighbor said, like taking a baseball bat to a bees' nest, playing free and easy with American lives."

## CHAPTER THIRTY-SEVEN

# PLANNING FOR THE FUTURE

In January of 2004, Chancellor Berdahl endorsed a multi-million dollar plan to improve the university's athletic training facilities and to begin the necessary restructuring and earthquake retrofitting of 81-year-old Memorial Stadium so that Cal sports might be "on equal footing with other schools in the Pac-10."

It was certainly not the first time a project approximating this magnitude had been proposed. Kasser had a plan on paper before he retired as A.D. in 2001 which he said would have upgraded the stadium and placed new offices and training quarters beneath the stands. And Holmoe recalls reviewing a similar plan one day in his office when someone dropped off another dated a decade earlier. Berdahl left later in 2004 before significant progress had been made. The new chancellor, Robert J. Birgenau, a renowned physicist, longtime MIT faculty member and more recently president of the University of Toronto, got cracking on it almost before he settled behind his desk. His first act on taking office on September 22, 2004 was hiring a new athletic director, Sandy Barbour, to replace Gladstone, who stepped down to return to coaching full-time. It was an inspired if somewhat controversial choice, since Barbour, given name, Anne, was a woman, the first of her sex, needless to say, to hold the position at Cal.

But her credentials were impeccable. She'd come to Berkeley from Notre Dame, where, as deputy director of athletics, she developed and implemented the school's $127 million athletic facilities master plan. Before that, she served as Tulane's athletic director where, considering Southern attitudes toward women and football, she encountered in the beginning some snarky opposition. But within her first few months there, she hired a football coach, the estimable Tommy Bowden, who in his first season, 1997, gave the school its first winning record in 16 years. In his second season, he was 12-0.

"People at Tulane were asking, what can a woman know about football? She's obviously never coached it," Barbour recalled. "Will she dump the sport for field hockey? But once you prove that what you want is what the school wants, that sort of talk goes away. Down there, if I did what I did and we weren't winning, I'd have been driven out of town on a rail."

Barbour was keenly aware of the challenges she faced at Cal. She needed first of all, to raise lots and lots of money to do the necessary work on the stadium and put up a new training facility. Phase one of the overall project would be construction of a $124 million "Student-Athlete High Performance Center," a building virtually adjacent to the west side of the stadium that would house offices and training, meeting and locker rooms. The center would be a boon to the football team, but it would also accommodate as many as fourteen other sports. Next would come important improvements to the stadium.

Barbour also had to find a way to keep the coach who had resurrected a moribund football program under contract and in doing so had become a hot property ardently pursued by other major colleges and NFL franchises. Actually, the projects were intertwined, since Tedford had vigorously championed the improvements now on the drawing board. He had insisted on the installation of the high-tech playing field so that it might be used both for practice and games without undue wear and tear.

Meanwhile, the coach had to be paid a salary commensurate with his success on the field. Barbour had resources available from donations and football ticket proceeds, both of which had increased dramatically during Tedford's time, so his wages would not cost the university a dime. Average attendance for Cal games had climbed from thirty-seven thousand in his first season to a school record 64,318 in 2006 and season ticket sales had gone from sixteen thousand in 2002 to nearly forty-two thousand. There was no question the coach was good for business. So after three contract extensions, Tedford was earning $1.8 million by 2008, in addition to incentives, and was signed through 2015. If he fulfills that contract, as expected, he will become Cal's longest serving football coach, exceeding the ten-year terms of Smith, Allison and Waldorf. Remarking on the athletic department's commitment to him, Tedford told the *Chronicle*, "When other opportunities come along, it makes it easy to say no."

The coach certainly proved his worth in the "rebuilding" season of 2005. With Rodgers gone to Green Bay, he was left with zero experience among his quarterback candidates. Neither of the front-runners, redshirt freshman Nate Longshore and City College of San Francisco transfer Joe Ayoob, had yet thrown a pass in major college competition. And the projected third-stringer, Steve Levy, had played fullback in '04, carrying the ball twice for a net gain of three yards. The receiving corps, though similarly deprived of experience, looked promising. Sophomore Jordan was the veteran, while freshman DeShawn Jackson and Lavelle Hawkins, Ayoob's big play target at CCSF, added dazzling speed and mobility, if not much size, to the position. Hawkins, at 175 pounds, was the big guy among them. Sophomore Craig Stevens, a 255-pound expert blocker and competent receiver, would be the tight end.

There was far more experience on the defensive side, particularly in a secondary staffed by stalwarts such as Hughes, Mixon, DeCoud,

McCleskey and Harrison Smith. Brandon Mebane and Matt Malele were fixtures in the defensive line and another CCSF transfer, Desmond Bishop, along with freshman Anthony Felder were expected to step forward as linebackers.

But the strength of the team was at tailback where the '04 freshman sensation, Marshawn Lynch, was the heir apparent. Stockily structured at 5-11 and 215 pounds, Lynch was a runner of whom the encomium, "hard to bring down," was a gross understatement, because there were instances when he was impossible to bring down. When trapped in heavy traffic, Lynch shed would-be tacklers with the apparent ease of Labrador retriever shaking itself dry after a swim. He represented something entirely new in Cal power running. Whereas Olszewski bowled over defenders in his day and Muncie ran straight through them in his, Lynch found ways to wriggle free when he appeared hopelessly ensnared; he was more Houdini than Nagurski. Lynch would have as his backup that season a sophomore dash-and-darter from Texas named Justin Forsett. Together, they would more than compensate for the absence of Arrington.

The Bears won their first five in '05 on the way to an 8-4 season. But they lost their starting quarterback, Longshore, to a broken ankle in the opener that would finish him for the year. Ayoob replaced him and, scarily, failed to complete any of his ten pass attempts. But the Bears won anyway, humbling overmatched Sacramento State, 41–3. Lynch gained 147 yards on 24 carries. Then in game two, a 56–17 throttling of Washington in Seattle, he broke a finger and missed the next two wins, 35–20 over Illinois and 41–13 over New Mexico State. In his stead, Forsett went 16 for 187 yards and two touchdowns against the Illini and 31 for 235 and a score against the Aggies in Las Cruces. Ayoob seemed to get a handle on quarterbacking, too, throwing for seven touchdowns in three games, four against the Huskies alone. Lynch returned and gained 107 yards in a 28–0 whitewashing of Arizona and Jackson caught nine passes for 130 yards.

Both teams were undefeated and ranked in the Top 20 when Cal played UCLA before 84,811 in Pasadena. There, alas, the Bear streak ended as the Bruins won, 47–40, on the strength of a 19-point fourth quarter, their Maurice Drew (later Maurice Jones-Drew) scoring twice in that stretch, the last TD on a 28-yard swing pass from quarterback Drew Olson. Lynch was 22 for 135, Forsett 10 for 153. Jackson caught ten passes for 128 yards and a touchdown.

The team lost another close one the next week to Oregon State, 23–20, as the Beavers' sophomore tailback Yvenson Bernard gained 194 yards and scored the winning touchdown with 6:41 left to play. Blessed with two top tailbacks, the Bears seemed incapable of stopping the other teams' during this run of bad luck. But they reversed these two narrow losses with a narrow win of their own, 42–38 over Washington State, the deciding TD a nine-yard pass from Ayoob to Hawkins with 1:50 remaining. Ayoob enjoyed another four-score day and Lynch gained 160 yards. Forsett had 111 on 12 carries and another new receiver, LaReylle Cunningham, caught five passes for 112 yards.

Thirteenth-ranked Oregon beat the Bears, 27–20, in overtime on--need it be said?—a cold, rainy day in Eugene. Lynch nearly saved the day, carrying 25 times for 189 yards and two touchdowns. But the loss dropped the team out of the Top 25. And then, number one USC beat them, 35–10, before a capacity crowd of 72,981 in Berkeley. No embarrassment there since the Trojan lineup contained two Heisman trophy winners—Matt Leinart (2004) and Reggie Bush (2005)—and the Pac-10's leading scorer (26 touchdowns) in LenDale White. But Ayoob, his fortunes declining as the season progressed, was intercepted four times, giving him seven in the last two games. Tedford replaced him with Levy in the fourth quarter and the onetime line-plunger had a perfect four-for-four passing day.

The regular season ended, as it always should, with a convincing 27–3 win in the Big Game. Levy got his first start and went a decent 10 for 18 and 125 yards, his longest a 56-yard touchdown in the first quarter to Jackson. The Cal defense sacked Stanford QBs Trent Edwards and T.C. Ostrander nine times for minus 70 yards. Linebacker Mickey Pimentel, another J.C. transfer, had 3.5 tackles behind the line, 2.5 sacks and one forced fumble.

The win earned the Bears an invitation to the Las Vegas Bowl, where they beat Brigham Young, 35–28, in a game not as close as the score would suggest, the Bears having led 35–14 after three quarters. Levy started again and finished 16 of 23 for 228 yards and two touchdowns, both to Jackson. Lynch gained 194 yards on 24 carries and scored thrice, the yards and the TDs both Cal bowl game records.

It had been a breakthrough season for the Bear tackle-breaker. Despite missing two games and playing only half of another, he gained 1,246 yards on 196 carries for an average of 6.4 per. He scored ten touchdowns. Forsett wasn't far behind with 999 yards on 132 carries, an average of 7.6. He scored six touchdowns. The Bears came within thirty-six inches of having two thousand-yard rushers on the same team for the second time in their history. Jackson was the leading receiver in his first season with 38 catches for 601 yards and a 15.8-yard average per catch. He scored seven touchdowns receiving and another on a 49-yard punt return. Jordan had 34 receptions and Hawkins 18. Speculation abounded over what these three might accomplish with a more settled situation.

The answer was near at hand. With a healthy Longshore at quarterback throwing to them in '06, Jackson had 1,060 yards and averaged 18 yards on 59 receptions. Hawkins had 705 on 46 and Jordan 571 on 46. They accounted for 18 touchdowns. Jackson had nine of them plus another four on punt returns, a Pac-10 record. Only Lynch with 11 rushing scores and four receiving topped his 13 touchdowns, and the tailback led the conference in rushing with 1,356 yards. He, Jackson and cornerback Hughes, who had eight interceptions, received All America honors. They, along with Bishop, center Alex Mack and tackle Mebane were All Pac-10. Longshore was worth the wait; he completed

227 of 377 passes for 3,021 yards, a 60.2 percentage and 24 touchdowns. He became only the second passer in Cal history to throw for more than 3,000 yards, trailing only Pat Barnes, who had 3,499 ten years before him.

The 10-3 record in '06 gave Tedford five straight winning seasons at the start of his Cal career, a figure surpassed only by Pappy's six. It was his second ten-win season, tying Pappy, although the Bears of the late 1940s and early '50s played fewer games in a year.

And yet, 2006 started poorly with a 35–18 loss to Tennessee in Knoxville before the largest crowd—106,009—ever to see a Cal team play. The Bears were never a factor in this game, trailing 35–0 as late as the third quarter before a Tom Schneider field goal put them on the board. Worse yet, the Volunteers beat them at their own game by scoring four of their five touchdowns on plays of 42 yards or longer. The loss was a tough one for Tedford to take. But there would be a chance for retribution since the Vols would again open the Cal season in '07, this time in Berkeley.

Losing the opener hardly plunged the Bears into despair. In fact, they won their next eight in a row, the longest Cal winning streak in fifty-six years. Longshore pitched seven touchdown passes in the first two of those, over Minnesota and Portland State, and Lynch scored five times, once on a 71-yard ramble in and out of the futile embraces of Portland State defenders. In each of the first five wins, the Bears scored more than 40 points—42 against both Minnesota and Portland State, 49 over Arizona State, 41 over Oregon State and 45 over 10th-ranked Oregon. Lynch gained more than 100 yards in four of the five and Forsett picked up 163 against the Ducks. Longshore had two 300-yard games, an even 300 against Minnesota and 341 against Oregon State.

The scoring mechanism sputtered a bit in wins by 21–3 over Washington State and 31–24 in overtime over Washington. Lynch was 25 for 152 and two touchdowns against the Cougars and 21 for 150 and two more scores, including the game-winning 22-yarder in overtime, against the Huskies. Bishop was the defensive hero in that long game, making 16 tackles and intercepting a pass in Washington's overtime series and returning it 80 yards before being felled, mostly by exhaustion. Actually, the linebacker could have saved himself the effort. All he needed to do at that point was drop to one knee, and the game would have ended.

The Bears were ranked tenth in the country when they played UCLA before yet another capacity crowd at Memorial Stadium. A 38–24 win, their eighth of the season, moved them up another notch. Jordan caught two of Longshore's three touchdown passes and Lynch snared the other. But it was Jackson who electrified the crowd with a 72-yard punt return, propelled at the start by a fine block from Thomas DeCoud and finished off with a dazzling juke of Bruin punter Aaron Perez.

Arizona ended the streak with a 24–20 upset in Tucson. The Bears had one apparent touchdown called back by a penalty and another cancelled by replay. The loss spoiled a vintage game for Jackson, who returned a punt 94 yards for one TD and caught a 62-yard pass from Longshore for another. The Bears actually led, 17–3, at the half, but were held to a 20-yard Schneider field goal in the last two quarters.

They were then beaten by number one USC, 23–9. Again, they had two would-be scores called back, an 80-yard fumble return by Pimentel that was ruled an incomplete pass and a 70-yard run by Lynch nullified when the replay showed that in one of his wriggling escapes his knee had touched the turf after just nine yards. Cal's only official touchdown was scored by Hawkins on a six-yard pass from Longshore. And yet the Bears were leading, 9–6, (Mebane forced a safety) with twenty minutes left to play. A pair of touchdown passes within five minutes of each other from John David Booty, to Dwayne Jarrett and Steve Smith, dashed Cal hopes for a Rose Bowl invitation.

The Bears were ranked 21st when they beat Stanford, 26–17, before the third home sellout of the season. Schneider kicked four field goals, his 55-yarder in the first quarter equaling the Cal record for distance. The victory was largely a defensive effort, though, with Bishop and sophomore cohort Zack Follett applying the crunchers. In his first start at outside linebacker, Follett had ten tackles, three for losses. Freshman cornerback Syd'Quan Thompson, who started every game that year after Tim Mixon was injured in pre-season practice, scored on a 15-yard fumble recovery return despite losing a shoe en route.

The Bears then scored their most convincing of all bowl victories, 45–10, over Texas A&M in the Holiday. The 35-point margin was the widest yet for Cal in post-season play. In his last game before being drafted in the first round by the Buffalo Bills, Lynch gained 111 yards and scored twice. Forsett was even better, gaining 124 on just eight carries. Bishop had 12 tackles and Pimentel seven. Bishop finished as the Pac-10's leading tackler with 114.

The Bears tied USC for the conference title, the first time since 1975 they'd had at least a share of the crown. Only their loss to the Trojans kept them out of the Rose Bowl, but they went to a bowl, anyway, for a Cal record fourth straight time. And they'd won their fifth straight Big Game, a feat unequalled since Wonder Team days. Tedford and his players were riding high.

In the meantime, the big building project was stalled by litigation. The city of Berkeley opposed construction of the High Performance Center, citing it is an earthquake hazard and source of unwanted traffic problems. An environmental organization, the California Oak Foundation, and a neighborhood group, the Panoramic Hill Association, wanted work stopped for various reasons, most specifically the planned removal of some forty-four trees, including at least one redwood, on the eighty-seven-tree, 1.2 acre grove opposite the stadium. University seismic experts countered that the Performance Center would not sit, as the stadium did, on the Hayward Fault and it would benefit from the latest earthquake protection engineering. And administrators assured the environmentalists that for every tree cut down a mature new one would be planted in its place. Besides, according to arborists, the redwood slated for removal was sick and would have been axed anyway, High Performance Center or no.

Nevertheless, lawsuits were filed in December of 2006 to stop the project. At the same time, a band of tree-sitters, inspired by arboreal demonstrations elsewhere, arrived, ascended and established households of Tarzan-ish ingenuity among the branches of the threatened grove. There, in one form or another, they would remain for 649 days and almost two football seasons, the longest urban tree-sit-in on record. From their nests above, the tree people became either a source of outrage or amusement for fans filing into the stadium on gamedays. At their peak, the sitters numbered as many as twenty, cheerfully identifying themselves to authorities or inquiring passersby by such pseudonyms as Millipede, Huckleberry, Dumpster Muffin, Mando and Cricket. No Cheetas or Janes, though, a consequence, one suspects, of the generation gap.

In February of 2007, work on the Center was blocked by a court injunction which was not lifted until July of 2008 when Alameda County Superior Court Judge Barbara Miller ruled that since the university was in compliance with the law, work could begin anew. Two months later, a State appeals court upheld her decision, rejecting pleas by the environmentalists and neighborhood activists (the city by then had dropped out of the litigation). In September, the trees started coming down, as did, safely, the last four of the tree-dwellers.

The 2007 season may well have reflected the instability of these proceedings. One can only imagine the reaction of the many hundreds of orange-clad fans from Tennessee in town for the '07 opener as they made their way to the stadium past tree houses occupied by presumably adult human beings. It was, by all odds, a scene somewhat alien to southern football culture. Then their team was trounced, 45–31, by vengeful Bears. The points were the most scored against the Volunteers in a dozen years. Some came in unexpected ways. Cal's first TD, early in the first quarter, came when linebacker Worrell Williams rumbled 44 yards with a recovered fumble. A few minutes later, Jackson fielded a punt, nonchalantly sidestepped the first wave of tacklers and sped 77 yards, the record sixth punt return touchdown of his Cal career.

This was the start of a five-game winning streak that featured among other nuggets a 73-yard TD by Jackson on a reverse in a 34–28 win over Colorado State, a 64-yard TD dash in the same game by freshman flash Jahvid Best and three consecutive 100-plus-yard games by Forsett in wins over Louisiana Tech (42–14), Arizona (45–27) and Oregon (31–24).

The Bears were ranked second in the nation before playing Oregon State at the stadium. Longshore missed the game with an ankle injury, so Kevin Riley, a highly regarded redshirt freshman from, coincidentally, Oregon, got the start. And he played exceedingly well until what shouldn't have been but was the last play of the game. The Bears were unaccountably trailing, 31–28, with 1:27 left to play, no time outs remaining and the ball on their own five. Out of this unpromising situation, Riley led an almost flawless drive, firing superbly executed sideline passes—19 to Hawkins (on fourth and 18) and 37 to Jordan. Finally, a pass interference call moved the ball to the Beavers 12 with fourteen seconds left. Riley dropped back to pass again, but this time his receivers were blanketed. Then, instead of throwing the ball away and giving his team a chance to tie the game with a field goal and send it into overtime, he made the foolhardy decision to run for the winning touchdown himself. He was stopped after only two yards. The clock ran out before the field goal team could leave the sidelines. The Bears lost not only their first game of the season but, because top-ranked Louisiana State had been beaten by Kentucky earlier in the day, their chance to achieve the school's first number one ranking since mid-season of 1951.

That frustrating finish seemed to cause an abrupt descent into near oblivion. The Bears lost five of their next six regular season games, the lone win by 20–17 over Washington State. During this precipitous slide, Longshore, still hobbled by his ankle injury, developed an unnerving propensity for throwing rally-stopping late-game interceptions. In a 30–21 loss to UCLA, his pass with 1:33 left to play and the Bears behind by only two points, was picked off by the Bruins' Alterraun Verner and returned 76 yards for the clinching touchdown. In a 24–17 loss to USC, a Bear drive in the final three minutes was stopped when Longshore's pass intended for Jordan was intercepted by the Trojans' Terrell Thomas. And in the 20–13 loss to Stanford in its new and smaller Stanford Stadium, the Bears had advanced to the Cardinal 19 in the final minute, thanks to a Longshore connection with Hawkins. But on third down, after a drop and an incompletion, the Cal QB was intercepted in the end zone. It was Tedford's first Big Game defeat.

Of course, Longshore was not wholly at fault for the sorry end to a season that began with such promise. Even with six losses, the Bears did receive another post-season invitation—to the Armed Services Bowl in Fort Worth against the Air Force. And they finished on a positive note, winning 42–36, behind a redeemed Riley—16 for 19, 269 yards and three touchdowns—who replaced an apparently unredeemed Longshore after the Bears fell behind 21–0. Riley hit all three of Cal's receiving stars for scores—40 to Jackson, 18 to Jordan, five to Hawkins—and ran himself for another. Forsett, playing in his home town, rushed for 140 yards and two TDs, giving him 1,546 yards and 15 touchdowns for the season. Tedford had tied Pappy with six straight winning seasons at the start of a Cal career. Andy Smith still held the overall school record with eight winners, from 1918 through 1925.

The quarterback rivalry continued unabated through the 2008 season, helped not at all by the departure of the receiving triumvirate to the NFL. Forsett, third at that point behind White and Lynch on Cal's career yardage list with 3,220, was also gone. And so was the fine tight end, Craig Stevens. Forsett's designated successor, the speedy Best, had off-season hip surgery after missing the last three games in

'07. Redshirt freshman Shane Vereen had impressed in Best's place in spring drills, but he had yet to play a down. Even the place-kicking spot was up for grabs. The incumbent, Jordan Kay, had two bad knees, his backup, David Seawright, was a true freshman, and walk-on Giorgio Tavecchio wasn't even listed in the media guide. The punter, redshirt freshman Bryan Anger, had yet to take a long snap.

On the positive side, All-Conference center Mack was back. A true scholar-athlete, he'd already graduated with a degree in legal studies, but he chose to enter graduate school and play his final season of eligibility rather than enter the NFL draft. And the defense, featuring star linebackers Follett, Felder and Williams, along with cornerbacks Thompson and Darian Hagan, was impressive. Under Defensive Coordinator Bob Gregory, the Bears would play a 3-4 defense this season, sophomore Michael Mohamed joining the veteran backers. Still, there seemed to be more questions than answers about the quality of Tedford's seventh team.

The answers came quickly enough. The Bears defeated Michigan State, 38–31, in the opening game, limiting the Spartans' touted tailback, Javon Ringer, to a comparatively paltry 81 yards on 27 carries, while both Best and Vereen topped 100. Vereen's total was enhanced by an 81-yard sprint down the sidelines for a last quarter score. Riley, given the nod as starter, at least temporarily, hit on 17 of 24 for 202 yards and two second half TDs.

The Bears demolished Washington State, 66–3, in the second game. Best had the sort of game Cal fans had hoped for from such an accomplished back, running for 200 yards on 14 carries, including an 80-yarder on the game's first play from scrimmage. Vereen scored from 39 yards out and Follett returned a blocked punt 68 yards for a touchdown. Thompson set up another with a 90-yard interception return.

Maryland ended the mini-streak with a 35–27 win back there, Cal's first trip to the east coast in seven years. Riley threw a school record 58 passes, completing 33 for 423 yards and three scores. Then, following a bye week, Colorado State fell, 42–7, a win sparked by Thompson's 73 yard punt-return touchdown but tarnished by a new injury to Best, a dislocated left elbow. He missed his team's 24–14 win over Arizona State, a game in which Longshore started and passed for three touchdowns. Best returned to run for a 67-yard score against Arizona, but the Bears lost, 42–27. They beat UCLA, 41–20, embarrassing the Bruins with four interceptions, two of which were returned for touchdowns by safety Marcus Ezeff and linebacker Michael Mohamed. Oregon was beaten, 26–16, in a Biblical downpour that left Memorial Stadium's water-resistant new turf with puddles deep enough for a Jacques Cousteau expedition. Best, now bothered by a bum left foot, gained only 30 yards in a 17–3 loss to USC before 88,523 in the L.A. Coliseum.

It was at this juncture that the sophomore tailback decided that, injuries be damned, he was going to step up the pace. A state champion sprinter in high school, Best was possibly the fastest back Cal had ever had. At the same time, he had the deft moves of a Forsett if not, at 193 pounds, the tackle-proof power of a Lynch or Muncie. His runs were not so much artful as startling, since they were over so quickly. And as the season moved toward a close, he shifted into high gear. He began modestly enough with a 65-yard TD and 116 yards gained in a 34–21 loss to Oregon State in Corvallis. Then, home again, he put on an unforgettable show.

In a 37–16 win in the Big Game, he sped for 201 yards on 19 carries and scored three touchdowns, outshining and certainly outgaining Stanford star Toby Gerhart, who picked up 103. Then, against winless Washington, he outdid himself and every other back who'd ever carried the ball for the Bears by rushing for 311 yards on 19 carries and scoring on runs of 60, 84, 20 and one in a 48–7 victory. His yardage easily surpassed the old Cal record of 283 gained by Jerry Drew against Oregon State in 1954. Best graciously credited the lead and downfield blocking of Mack, fullback Will Ta'ufo'ou and guard Noris Malele for his success. But there was more to come.

The Bears accepted an invitation to cross the Bay and play Miami on December 27 in the Emerald Bowl game at AT&T Park, home of the San Francisco Giants. Best sprained a thumb in this game, but still sped for 186 yards on 20 carries, including an Emerald Bowl record 42-yard TD. The defense set up the winning score, though, in the Bears' 24–17 win. With 4:24 left to play and the score still tied after Tavecchio, the late-season kicker, missed a 34-yard field goal, Follett jarred the ball loose from Hurricane's quarterback Jacory Harris with one of his cannonball hits. Defensive end Cameron Jordan scooped it up on the nine and carried it to the two. From there, Longshore, making only the third start of his senior season, found freshman tight end Anthony Miller for the score. It was the fifty-first and last touchdown of the quarterback's teeter-totter career and the first of Miller's short one.

The Bears finished with a 9-4 record, Tedford's seventh straight winning season and fourth straight bowl victory. But it was Best who captured the public's fancy with his closing surge. Despite his assortment of injuries, he gained 698 yards in the final three games and scored nine touchdowns. He finished the season with 1,580 yards rushing, second only in Cal history to Arrington's 2,018. More remarkably, he averaged 8.1 yards for his 194 carries, the best ever for a Cal back with more than 100 rushes, bettering Forsett's 7.6 in 2005 and Jensen's 7.3 in 1948. Best had seven runs in that '08 season longer than 60 yards, three of them longer than 80. And he still hadn't played a full season.

Not since Locomotive Smith has a Cal player had a name more consonant with his deeds.

# EPILOGUE

The legal issues caused a two-year delay in work on the High Performance Center and, therefore, on the stadium's rehabilitation. But Barbour remained hopeful in January of 2009 that the entire project would be completed by 2013—the High Performance Center by 2011, the stadium two years later. Latest plans for the stadium went well beyond replacing splintered seats, building a new press box and finishing the necessary retrofitting. In fact, the beloved old saucer would take on a twenty-first-century state-of-the-art look when completed. There would be several luxury-box-type preferred seating levels with lounges and restaurants. The installation of three thousand chair seats would reduce the seating capacity by nearly ten thousand. But none of these extensive changes would affect the building's classic exterior beauty.

Financing would chiefly be done through an innovative Endowment Seating Program in which investors would not only be assured of primary seating but would also, according to Barbour, help "sustain our institution's unparalleled tradition of academic and athletic excellence for years to come." Despite the economic downturn of 2008-09, the athletic director expressed confidence that the cannotenough

endowment program would do the job. She based this on the unwavering support of longtime season ticket holders and the many financial contributors to Cal athletics. In fact, she said, "I have never been involved in anything where there's been such passion. We've made huge progress." In the meantime, at least as of this writing, she has to find a place for the football team to play while Memorial Stadium is under construction.

Tedford's office in early 2009 was in the very bowels of the stadium. There were comfortable leather couches and chairs in the waiting room outside his doors. The inner office was a model of neatness and order, a reflection of the preoccupations of its occupant. But Tedford's passion for precision does not make him prim and proper. On the contrary, he has an easy manner free of pretense. He is taller than he appears standing on the sidelines next to one of his mammoth linemen and, despite the occupational malady of imminent baldness, can be described as ruggedly handsome.

He speaks candidly about the success of his teams: "After our first year, it didn't take long to change the mind-set of our players." And honestly about the late-season failures of his promising '07 team: "I couldn't see it coming, and it's my job to keep my finger on the pulse beat of the team. I probably should have dealt with it a little differently. But I've discovered that each year brings a new challenge. The challenge we accepted in 2008 was to redeem ourselves."

Before every season, Tedford and his assistants hold what he calls a "Unity Meeting," which every member of the team is required to attend. There is assigned seating arranged so that each table of seven has a mix of veterans and newcomers, of players from different backgrounds and with different interests outside of football. "It's a way for them to get to know each other," the coach says. They are asked questions. "We might start just asking them what their favorite movie is. Or their most embarrassing moment. Then we'll get more serious. Whom do you trust, and why? What are the characteristics of a good teammate? What's your definition of common courtesy? What does Cal football mean to you? In the end, they learn a lot about each other."

Tedford seems at least as interested in the academic progress of his charges as in the athletic. There is not a coach alive, of course, who does not give at least lip service to these concerns, but Tedford is not one for idle chatter, sincerity being his strong suit. His players are given what he calls an "Academic Game Planner," a playbook in which they monitor their own classroom progress. "It's about discipline," he says. "Discipline adhered to in all aspects of life. With the Game Planner, we get immediate feedback. If a player is having trouble in a class, we ask him what we can do to help. I tell them that this is like a job in that they're being paid (through scholarships) to go to school. If they miss a class, it's a strike against them in the game planner. If they miss as many as four, they meet with me or I'll call their home. A suspension for a game under our system can as well be for academic reasons as any other."

As linebacker Worrell Williams told the *Chronicle*'s Tom Fitzgerald during the 2008 season, academic achievement for athletes at Cal "is a serious thing. Our football success has overshadowed it a little bit, but this is definitely an academic school. If you miss a class or you're late to a tutoring session, you'll have to do a lot more than you already have to do for homework." Worrell had reference to the tutoring services available to them through the university's invaluable Athletic Study Center with sixty staff members.

Despite the number who leave school early for the NFL, the graduation rate for football players has increased in Tedford's time. Out of his first recruiting class in 2002, 83 percent earned degrees. "We promise our kids here that they'll graduate," he says, "We want them to leave here as fully developed, well-rounded young men." When center Alex Mack received in 2008 the Draddy Trophy as College football's number one scholar-athlete, Tedford was so proud he treated it as if it were the Heisman. Mack, after all, had proved to skeptics that, even with the demands on time that football imposes, a player can give real meaning to the euphemism "student-athlete."

Head coaches at Cal have historically carried the extra burden of trying to win games while making certain their players are worthy of the school's standing as—according to a 2007 survey by *U.S. News and World Report*—the nation's top public university. As many of them learned painfully, coaching the Golden Bears is not the easiest job on the planet.

Tedford is keenly aware of this responsibility. When asked if he'd ever felt inclined to leave Cal for a college more congenial to football's demands or for the pros, he admits to frustration over the various institutional challenges he's encountered. "But you build a passion for and a love of something you've invested so much time and effort into. It's a huge investment, this bleeding blue and gold. But Cal feels like home to me. I have great faith in and respect for the people I work for, especially Sandy Barbour." He swivels forward in his chair, the better to catch the view from his office window. "And the quality of life becomes an important factor. The Bay Area is a special place. This university is a special place." He says no more, but gestures toward the window. Below lies the hilly and forested wintergreen campus sloping toward the Bay.

As I left the coach's office, I wondered if, like Andy Smith and Pappy Waldorf before him, this busy man takes the time to stroll in meditation among the trees alongside Strawberry Creek? Does he pause before Pappy's bronze statue in Faculty Glade, reflecting on that great man's glory years? Is he familiar with the inscription on the Andy Smith Bench—"It is far better to play the game squarely and lose than to win at the sacrifice of an ideal?" Does he stand beneath the Campanile and look out, from about where Frederick Billings once stood, at the shimmering Golden Gate? Has he seen the Tilden statue commemorating Garrett Cochran's winning teams of the 1890s?

He must know that there are ghosts on that campus of football past. And that they keep a watchful eye on football present. He should take comfort as he stands on the sidelines of a cool, bright Saturday afternoon in autumn that they, too, are there with him. In spirit.

# ALL-TIME CAL TEAMS BY ERAS

## PURPOSE AND PROCEDURES

In recording California football history and the players who have given their all for the Golden Bears over 127 years, we felt the need to recognize "the best of the best" by honoring the greatest players of their own eras. Thus, the selection of five All-Time Cal teams for each of the eras detailed in the book. We recognize that the selection of the five All-Time Cal Teams covering the years from 1882 through the 2008 season is an entirely subjective exercise and that any reader of this book will have candidates worthy of inclusion on these teams. However, while the process we used to select the teams was disciplined and rigorous, as detailed below, we expect and welcome hearty debate on these selections as we look forward to the continuation of Cal's colorful football history.

The process of selection on the teams started with listing more than 250 candidates on a ballot that was sent to donors, Cal fans, and the press. In listing the nominees, we wanted to avoid influencing voters in any way. So we left space for write-in candidates, listed players at several positions when appropriate, and did not give guidance whether a player should, or should not, receive votes at more than one position. Several players were the popular choice at more than one position. But in the final selection process, no player occupied more than one spot on a team. This meant that for several positions the leading vote getter was not selected because he had also been the leader somewhere else. We were delighted at the number of write-in candidates who received votes and that nearly two hundred Cal fans voted with their selections for the teams.

After the votes were tabulated we realized that several popular selections were based on factors outside of on-field performance. These included contributions to Cal athletics after graduation, success in professional football, long time association with the University or participation in an isolated event on the field. We discounted these and based our initial selections only on performance while playing for the Golden Bears. The factors considered were:

- *The length of a candidate's career at Cal.*
- *All America, All-Conference or All-Opponent selections.*
- *Respect shown by teammates as evidenced by nominee's selection as team captain, Most Valuable Player, etc.*
- *Setting school records.*
- *Finally, we reviewed the NFL draft status of players in the modern era as another significant measure of talent.*

We then passed the preliminary selections on to a small group of Cal coaches-past and present, Memorial Stadium press box veterans, and long-time supporters of Cal football for their comments and evaluation. Their responses enabled us to further refine the initial selections. The final review group was weighted heavily to insiders who had long-term contact with Cal football. Their input was most welcome and valuable.

The results follow. Congratulations to the Bears named to the five All-Time Cal teams. The players named to the All-Time teams and those that received Honorable Mention are certainly a remarkable group, and any Cal fan can only dream of having all these greats playing for the Bears at one time.

1892-1925

# THE EARLY DAYS

E- Harold "Brick" Muller, 1920-22

E- Bob Berkey, 1920-22

L- Stan Barnes, 1918-21

L- Cort Majors, 1918, 1920

L- Walter Gordon, 1916-18

L- Orval Overall, 1900-03

C- Edwin "Babe" Horrell, 1923-24

QB- Charles Erb, 1920-22

B- Jesse "Duke" Morrison, 1920-22

B- Warren "Locomotive" Smith, 1898-99, 1901

B- Arthur "Wolf" Ransome, 1893-96

*Honorable Mention:* E-Howard "Brodie" Stephens, 1920-21; L-Dan McMillan, 1920-21; C-George "Fat" Latham, 1919-21; B-Archie Nisbet, 1920-22, Albert "Pesky" Sprott, 1918-20, Irving "Crip" Toomey, 1920-21, Talma "Tut" Imlay, 1924-25.

*Comments:* Brick Muller was the leading vote getter in this era. The closest call was at center between Horrell and Latham. Both were team captains on undefeated Bear teams but Babe's first team selection as a Walter Camp All-American gave him the edge.

1926-1946

# AFTER SMITH TO WALDORF

E- Perry Schwartz, 1935-37

E- Irv Phillips, 1926-28

T- Larry Lutz, 1933-35

T- Bob Reinhard, 1939-41

G- Vard Stockton, 1935-37

G- Ted Beckett, 1928-30

C- Bob Herwig, 1935-37

BB- John Meek, 1935-37

TB- Vic Bottari, 1936-38

WB- Sam Chapman, 1935-37

FB- Ralston "Rusty" Gill, 1929-31

*Honorable Mention:* T-Dave DeVarona, 1936-38, Lee Artoe, 1939; G-Bert Schwarz; 1926-29; C-Roy Riegels 1927-29; TB-Benny Lom, 1927-29, Arleigh Williams, 1933-35, Floyd Blower, 1933-36; FB-Dave Anderson, 1936-38.

*Comments:* Vic Bottari led the popular vote during these years. Again, the hardest selection was at center with both Herwig and Riegels getting All-American calls. The choice went to Herwig based on his size and all-around athleticism (he lettered three years in basketball). Picking two guards from Stockton, Beckett and Schwarz, first-team All-America selections all, was also difficult.

1947-1956

# THE WALDORF YEARS

| OFFENSE | DEFENSE |
|---|---|
| E- Jim Hanifan, 1952-54 | E- Bob Minahen, 1948-50 |
| E- Bud Van Deren, 1947-48 | E- Ed Bartlett, 1949-51 |
| T- Bob Karpe, 1950-51 | T- Jim Turner, 1946-49 |
| T- Ralph Krueger, 1950-52 | T- Dick Day, 1951, 1953 |
| G- Rod Franz, 1946-49 | G- Don Gilkey, 1954-56 |
| G- Jon Baker, 1944, 1946-48 | LB- Les Richter, 1949-51 |
| C- Charles "Ozzie" Harris, 1950-51 | LB- Matt Hazeltine, 1951-54 |
| QB- Paul Larson, 1952-54 | LB- Forrest Klein, 1948-49 |
| RB- Jackie Jensen, 1946-48 | DB- Carl Van Heuit, 1949-50 |
| RB- John Olszewski, 1950-52 | DB- Bob Celeri, 1944, 1947-49 |
| RB- [tie] Jim Monachino, 1948-50, | DB- Dick LemMon, 1949-51 |
| Pete Schabarum, 1948-50, | Punter- Tom Keogh, 1951-52 |
| Jack Swaner, 1946-49 | Kick Returner- Frank Brunk, |
| Punter- Tom Keogh, 1951-52 | 1947-49 |
| Kicker- Jim Cullom, 1947-49 | |
| Punt Returner- Paul Keckley, 1946-48 | |

*Honorable Mention:* E-John Cunningham, 1946-48; T-Don Curran, 1950-52; Glen Gulvin, 1950-52; G-Tom Dutton; 1950-53; C-Doug Duncan, 1946-48; B-Jerry Drew, 1953-54, 1956; Don Johnson, 1952; Don Robison, 1949-51; John Graves, 1941-42, 1947; LB-Hal Norris, 1951-54.

*Comments:* Jackie Jensen, Rod Franz, Les Richter, John Olszewski, and Matt Hazeltine led the voting for the All-Time team during the Waldorf years. Several of these standouts were listed and received votes at several positions. Rapid changes in the substitution rules, our decision to list a player at only one position on the All-Time teams, and the opening up of the Cal offense (in the 1950 Rose Bowl season Cal only attempted 108 passes while four years later QB Larson completed 125 passes and was the NCAA passing yardage leader) made the selection of this team and particularly what position to place such all-around players as Jensen, Richter, Bud VanDeren, Franz, Jim Cullom, Turner, and Hazeltine extremely difficult. Jensen was the top choice at four different positions and since even this remarkable athlete needed an occasional rest we selected five, rather than three, running backs. Jim Monachino, Pete Schabarum, and Jack Swaner joined Jensen and John Olszewski as RBs on the team. To leave any one of them off the team would have been an injustice.

1957-1981

# THE CHANGING GAME

## OFFENSE

WR- Wesley Walker, 1973-76
WR- Steve Rivera, 1973-75
TE- Joe Rose, 1977-79
OT- Ted Albrecht, 1974-76
OT- Harvey Salem, 1979-82
OG- John Garamendi, 1963-65
OG- Chris Mackie, 1973-74
C- Bill Laveroni, 1967-69
QB- Craig Morton, 1962-64
RB- Chuck Muncie, 1973-75
RB- Joe Kapp, 1956-58
K- Jim Breech, 1974-77

## DEFENSE

DE- Mike McCaffrey, 1966-68
DE- Irby Augustine, 1967-69
DT- Ed White, 1966-68
DT- Sherman White, 1969-71
DT- Ralph DeLoach, 1976-78
LB- Rich Dixon, 1978-80, 1982
LB- Loren Toews, 1971-72
LB- Jeff Barnes, 1975-76
DB- Ray Youngblood, 1969-71
DB- Jack Hart, 1956-58
DB- Ron Coccimiglio, 1978-80
DB- Ken Wiedemann, 1967-69
KR- Isaac Curtis, 1970-71
KO- Randy Wersching, 1969-70
P- Dan Melville, 1977-78
PR- Jerry Bradley, 1964-66

*Honorable Mention:* WR-Wayne Stewart, 1966-68; Steve Sweeney, 1970-72; Matt Bouza, 1979-80; TE-John Beasley, 1964-66; OT-Frank Sally, 1957-59; OG-Pat Newell, 1957-59; C-Duane Wiliams 1975-76;

QB-Steve Bartkowski, 1972-74; Joe Roth, 1975-76; Rich Campbell, 1978-80; DE-Dallas Hickman, 1973-74; DT-Proverb Jacobs, 1957; LB-Rob Swenson, 1972-74; DB-Tom Blanchfield, 1962-64; K-KO-Mick Luckhurst, 1979-80.

*Comments:* While Chuck Muncie was the leading vote getter for this era's All-Time team the vote at quarterback was split among four remarkable athletes, all of whom achieved first team All-America recognition while playing for the Bears. Craig Morton was our final choice. Craig set a Pac-8 passing record as a three-year starter on undermanned Bear teams. He was selected as the most valuable senior on the West Coast and the fifth pick in the 1965 NFL draft. Joe Kapp, one of the greatest leaders in Cal football history, was named to the All-Time team as a running back. Joe led the '58 team to the Rose Bowl and as a split T quarterback was the top Bear rusher for the season. Kapp was a three-year starter at QB and also doubled at defensive back. Steve Bartkowski and Joe Roth both had shorter time as starters for the Bears. Bartkowski split QB duties with Vince Ferragamo during his junior season, and Roth came to Cal as a JC transfer and really played only one completely healthy Cal season. Joe led the '75 Bears to a PCC co-championship. His All America status in 1976 was achieved while he battled cancer. He died only a few months later in February of 1977.

Other highly competitive selections were at defensive end between Mike McCaffrey, Irby Augustine, and Frank Sally, and among kickers Jim Breech, Randy Wersching, and Mick Luckhurst.

1982-2008

# THE MODERN ERA

## OFFENSE

WR- Sean Dawkins, 1990-92
WR- DeSean Jackson, 2005-07
WR- Geoff McArthur, 2000, 02-04
TE- Tony Gonzales,1994-96
OT- Todd Steussie, 1990-93
OT- Troy Auzenne, 1988-91
OG- Ryan O'Callaghan, 2002-05
OG- Jeremy Newberry, 1995-97
C- Alex Mack, 2005-08
QB- Aaron Rodgers, 2003-04
RB- Marshawn Lynch, 2004-06
RB- Russell White, 1990-92
K- Ryan Longwell, 1993-96

## DEFENSE

DE- Andre Carter, 1997-2000
DE- Regan Upshaw, 1993-95
DT- Brandon Mebane, 2003-06
DT- Chidi Ahanotu, 1989-92
DT- Brandon Whiting, 1994-97
LB- Ron Rivera, 1980-83
LB- Hardy Nickerson, 1983-86
LB- Zack Follett, 2005-08
DB- Deltha O'Neal, 1996-99
DB- Nnamdi Asomugha, 1999-02
DB- Daymeion Hughes, 2003-06
DB- Thomas DeCoud, 2004-07
KO- Robbie Keen, 1987-89
P- Nick Harris, 1997-2000

*Honorable Mention:* WR-Bobby Shaw, 1994-97; LaVelle Hawkins, 2005-07; TE-David Lewis, 1979-83; OT-Tarik Glenn, 1993-96; C-Marvin Philip, 2000, 2003-2005; QB-Gale Gilbert, 1980, 1982-84; Mike Pawlawski, 1988-91; Kyle Boller, 1999-2002; RB- J.J. Arrington, 2003-04; Justin Forsett, 2004-07; K- Doug Brien, 1991-93; DE- Tully Banta-Cain, 1999-2002; LB- Jerrott Willard, 1991-94; David Ortega, 1986-89; Ken Harvey, 1986-87; Duane Clemons, 1992-93, 1995; Desmond Bishop, 2005-2006; DB-Jerod Cherry, 1992-95; Erik Zomalt, 1990-93; Jemeel Powell, 1999-2002; P-Scott Tabor, 1986-87.

*Comments:* Tight End Tony Gonzales was the top vote getter among the Modern Era players. Sean Dawkins and DeSean Jackson were easy choices for two of the wide receiver spots while Geoff McArthur edged Bobby Shaw and LaVelle Hawkins for the third position. With Todd Steussie, a strong selection at offensive tackle, Troy Auzenne was a close pick over Tarik Glenn, based on Auzenne's play as a Bear, for the second OT. Center Alex Mack and Linebacker Zack Follett were the only players selected from the 2008 Bear team and along with Jeremy Newberry and Ryan O'Callaghan were strong choices at the three offensive line inside positions. Returning punts and kickoffs would be well handled by Jackson, Lynch, White, and O'Neal.

Two members of the 2009 Bear team, running back Jahvid Best and defensive back Syd'Quan Thompson, would certainly deserve consideration for this team upon the completion of their Cal careers.

# BIBLIOGRAPHY

Adams, Ansel and Newhall, Nancy: Fiat Lux, McGraw-Hill, 1967.

Andrada, Randy: *They Did it Everytime*, self-published, 1987.

Bernstein, Mark F. *Football: The Ivy League Origins of an American Obsession*, University of Pennsylvania Press, 2001.

Brands, H.W.: *TR, The Last Romantic*, BasicBooks, 1997.

Brechin, Gray: *Imperial San Francisco*, University of California Press, 1999.

Brodie, S. Dan: *66 Years on the California Gridiron*, The Olympic Publishing Company, 1949.

Cameron, Steve and Greenburg, John: *Pappy, the Gentle Bear*, Adday Publishing Group, 2000.

Clark, Kristine: *Undefeated, Untied and Uninvited*, Griffin Publishing Group, 2002.

Clary, Jack: *Army vs. Navy (the First 100 Games)*, Signature Publications, Inc., 2000.

Cohen, Robert and Zelnik, Reginald: *The Free Speech Movement (Reflections of Berkeley in the 1960s)*, University of California Press, 2002.

Congdon, Don (editor): *The '30s, A Time to Remember*, Simon and Schuster, 1962.

Fimrite, Ron (editor): *Pappy's Boys*, Pappy's Boys, Publishers, 1996.

Florence, Mal: *The Trojan Heritage*, Jordan & Company, Publishers, Inc., 1980.

Goines, David Lange: *The Free Speech Movement* (Coming of Age in the 1960s), Ten Speed Press, 1993.

Goldstein, Richard: *Ivy League Autumns*, St. Martin's Press, 1996.

Goulden, Joseph G.: *The Best Years—1945-1950*, Atheneum, 1976.

Herzog, Brad: *The Sports 100*, MacMillan, 1995.

Klingaman, William K.: 1941—*Our Lives in a World on Edge*, Harper & Row, 1988.

Lee, Eugene C.: *The Origins of the Chancellorship*, Regents of the University of California, 1995.

Levy, Marv: *Where Else Would You Rather Be*, Sports Publishing LLC, 2004.

Liebendorfer, Don E.: *The Color of Life is Red*, Stanford University Board of Trustees, 1972.

LoCasale, Al and Newhouse, Dave (editors): *Legend—The 50 Most Significant Bay Area Sports Figures of the 20th Century*, CWC Sports, Inc., 2001.

Mades, Bruce: *Michigan, Champions of the West*, Sports Publishing, Inc., 1997.

Martin, George: *The Golden boy*, Peter E. Randall, Publisher, 2000.

May, Henry: *Three Faces of Berkeley*, U.C. Institute of Governmental Studies, 1993.

Michelson, Herb and Newhouse, Dave: *Rose Bowl Football*, Stein and Day Publishers, 1977.

Migdol, Gary: *Stanford, Home of Champions*, Sports Publishing, 1997.

Mirrielees, Edith: *Stanford: The Story of a University*, G.P. Putman's Sons, 1959.

Neft, David and Cohen, Richard: *The Football Encyclopedia*, St. Martin's Press, 1991.

Oriard, Michael: *Reading Football*, University of North Carolina Press, 1993.

Pelfrey, Patricia: *A Brief History of the University of California*, University of California Press, 2004.

Peters, Nick: *100 Years of Blue and Gold*, JCP Corp. of Virginia, 1982.

Samuelson, Rube: *The Rose Bowl Game*, Doubleday & Company, Inc., 1951.

Seaborg, Glenn with Colvig, Ray: *Roses from the Ashes*, Institute of Governmental Studies Press, University of California, Berkeley, 2000.

Springer, Steve and Arkush, Michael: *60 Years of USC-UCLA Football*, Longmeadow Press, 1991.

Stiles, Maxwell: *Football's Finest Hour*, Nashunal Publishing Company, 1951.

Sullivan, John: *The Big Game*, Leisure Press, 1983.

The Sporting News: *Saturday's Shrines*, The Sporting News, 2005.

Time-Life Editors: *This Fabulous Century (1920 through 1960 editions)*,: Time-Life Books, 1970.

Vecchione, Joseph (editor): *The New York Times Book of Sports Legends*, Random House, 1991.

Wilson, Garff: *The Unidentified Man on the Right*, Garff B. Wilson, 1986.

PLUS

University of California *Blue and Gold* yearbooks, published by the Associated Students of the University of California, 1890-2008.

*University of California Athletic Department Media Guides, 1947-2008.*